M000317089

HANDBOOK OF ARCHAEOLOGICAL METHODS

HANDBOOK OF ARCHAEOLOGICAL METHODS

Volume I

Edited by Herbert D. G. Maschner
Christopher Chippindale

ALTAMIRA
P R E S S

A Division of Rowman & Littlefield Publishers, Inc.
Lanham • New York • Toronto • Oxford

ALTAMIRA PRESS
A division of Rowman & Littlefield Publishers, Inc.
A wholly owned subsidiary of The Rowman & Littlefield Publishing Group, Inc.
4501 Forbes Boulevard, Suite 200
Lanham, MD 20706
www.altamirapress.com

PO Box 317
Oxford
OX2 9RU, UK

British Library Cataloguing in Publication Information Available

Library of Congress Cataloging-in-Publication Data

Handbook of archaeological methods / edited by Herbert D. G. Maschner
and Christopher Chippindale.
    p. cm.
  Includes bibliographical references and index.
  ISBN 0-7591-0078-0 (alk. paper)
  1. Archaeology—Methodology—Handbooks, manuals, etc. I. Maschner,
Herbert D. G. II. Chippindale, Christopher, 1951-

  CC75.H337 2005
  930.1'028—dc22   2004026317

Printed in the United States of America

♾™ The paper used in this publication meets the minimum requirements of
American National Standard for Information Sciences—Permanence of Paper
for Printed Library Materials, ANSI/NISO Z39.48-1992.

Contents

Volume II
Part 3
APPLYING ANALYTIC METHODS

Part 4
FRAMEWORKS FOR METHODS

1

Introduction

Herbert D. G. Maschner

When Augustus Lane-Fox Pitt-Rivers was developing field methods to better understand the archaeology of his inherited estate in southern England in the late nineteenth century (Pitt-Rivers 1887–1898) or when William Matthew Flinders Petrie was formulating the skills and techniques in Egypt that led to the publication of *Methods and Aims in Archaeology* in 1904, neither could have imagined the range and complexity of archaeological methods available today. Most of the methods developed, elaborated, or codified up to World War II were built on the shoulders of some of our nineteenth-century founding fathers and emphasized skills to *discover* the past. These were refinements to already tested methods in excavation, site mapping, stratigraphy, architectural analysis, and of course, relative dating.

Postwar, the character of archaeology radically changed. Archaeologists were not so concerned with building better methods to discover the past but rather with methods to *organize* the past in time and space. Dating techniques, taxonomies and classifications, taphonomy and faunal analysis, multivariate analyses, regional surveys, and detailed regional chronologies dominated archaeology. The literary arguments of the time were not built on field methods per se nor were they yet fully concerned with interpretations; rather the methods for organizing the past, as typified in the great debate between Albert Spaulding (1953) and Richard Ford (1954) about the best methods for ceramic classification, dominated the archaeological dialogue. This period in the history of archaeology is perhaps best summarized in one of the most important archaeological works ever done: Gordon Willey and Philip Phillip's *Method and Theory in American Archaeology* (1958), where they laid out what they considered the methods of organizing the past.

In the 1960s this changed. What began as an effort to find a means to better excavate the past as the bridge to building more robust interpretations, which became methods to better organize the past, now was focused on developing methods to better *interpret* the past to build stronger theoretical statements about people and society. I was in grade school when Lewis Binford published his three most provocative works of the 1960s: "Archaeology as Anthropology" (1962), "A Consideration of Archaeological Research Design" (1964), and "Archaeological Systematics and the Study of Cultural Processes" (1965). Although he was considered by most to be the founding father of the new archaeology, and further considered by nearly all to have been primarily concerned with archaeological theory, the bulk of these critically important contributions were substantially about archaeological method. For Binford, theory building was really about the construction of robust methods that allowed us to link the statics, or material remains, of the archaeological record with the dynamic behaviors of the people who created it. Here theory was in most instances about the methods of interpretations.

Binford was my undergraduate advisor when some of his most enduring works were published. Again, papers such as the "Dimensional Analysis of Behavior and Site Structure" (1978a), "Willow smoke and dogs' tails" (1980), and "The Archaeology of Place" (1982) were not articles about theory; they were papers about methods of analysis and methods of interpretation. Even more so, his monographs such as *Nunamiut Ethnoarchaeology* (1978b) and *Bones: Ancient Men and Modern Myths* (1981) were methods landmarks, not new developments in archaeological theory per se. It was at about this time that Michael Schiffer created his classic work on the cultural and natural processes that affect the archaeological record (1976) and that Kent Flannery put together *The Early Mesoamerican Village* (1976), in my mind perhaps the greatest volume on method ever written. In fact, many of the most classic works on the method of interpreting archaeological data were created at this time, such as Renfrew's work on polities (1978), Brains's important taphonomic studies (1981), and Coles's research into the archaeology of wetlands (1984). Although some archaeologists were truly concerned with theory (e.g., Salmon 1982; Watson et al. 1971), even Flannery's classic parody on the culture of archaeology in the late 1970s, published as "The Golden Marshalltown" (1982), was really a statement about the method of archaeology, not about the theoretical developments of the time.

In the 1980s archaeology split in two directions. One was truly theoretical and involved the development of symbolic, structural, interpretive, contextual, and other archaeologies that became known as postprocessualism (Hodder 1982a, 1982b, 1986; Leone 1982; Wylie 1982). These are discussed little in this volume because there were few methods available to pursue any form of analysis under these headings, and in fact, many forms of analysis already in place were considered inappropriate, imperialistic, gender biased, or simply irrelevant to the subject. Thus, for the first time, theory and method became disarticulated. It took nearly 20 years for Ian Hodder to develop reflexive methods that could be formulated in terms that were usable in the field and laboratory (1999, this volume) and move these theoretical perspectives beyond critique and into the realm of applicability.

The other developments of the 1980s split are directly relevant to this volume. With the rise of the personal computer, the demographic diversification of the field, and the increasing sophistication of many analytic techniques, new methods changed the face of archaeology. A suite of elaborate methods were created that changed everything, from our surveys and excavations to how we organized the data to how we ultimately interpreted those data. Regional analyses coupled with geographic information systems (GIS) or the use of a GIS to organize spatial data at the site level, satellite- and ground-based remote-sensing techniques, and the development of computer programs for statistical calculations opened up entirely new areas of research for all archaeologists (Ebert 1980; Kvamme 1985, 1989), which were further elaborated in the 1990s (Aldenderfer and Maschner 1996; Allen et al. 1990; Kvamme 1999; Maschner 1996a).

Methods to investigate many of the more pressing theoretical debates of the new archaeology, such as the origins of agriculture, trade and exchange, craft specialization, urbanism, and inequality, proliferated as an entirely new set of graduate students descended on Mesoamerica, the U.S. Southwest, the Mississippi, the Andes, and prehistoric Europe (see Renfrew and Bahn 2004 for a review; chapters in this volume and in the forthcoming *Handbook of Archaeology Theory* [Bentley, Maschner, and Chippendale 2005]). Building on the writings of Binford, hunter-gatherer studies evolved (Bettinger 1991) with highly sophisticated methods for investigating sedentism, subsistence, inequalities, and social organization, which occurred largely through the recognition of complex hunter-gatherers (Ames 1981, 1995; Hayden et al. 1985; Yesner 1980).

Throughout the last 25 years, as many of our more technical skills in archaeology have become more refined, analytic techniques developed in other fields have also made greater contributions to archaeology, especially in the laboratory. Chemistry, physics, mathematics, ecology, and even literary methods have made significant contributions to the field, even if the methods were originally developed for nonarchaeological applications. Much like the case of reflexive theory now having a method, as previously discussed (Hodder 1999), method has become again integrated with theory in other areas as well, especially in the realms of Darwinian approaches (Maschner 1996b; O'Brien and Lyman 2000, 2003; Shennan 2002), complex systems (Bintliff 1999; Bentley and Maschner 2003), gender (Nelson 1997; Nelson and Rosen-Ayalon 2002; Walde and Willows 1989; Wylie 1991) art and symbolism (Chippindale and Taçon 1998; Whitley 2001), and a suite of mixed processual and postprocessual approaches that began with Stephen Mithen's important paper that demonstrated the common goals of postprocessual approaches and modern Darwinian approaches (1989).

Finally, and much to the betterment of the discipline, archaeological method has become more plural with a greater emphasis on historical representation and power (Arnold 1987; Gero and Root 1996) and alternative voices and interpretations (Anawak 1996; Anyon et al. 1997; Preucel and Hodder 1996; Trigger 1996). Traditional knowledge is becoming important to how methods are applied and in which contexts. Cultural sensitivity and spirituality must be considered when applying certain methods to sacred places and landscapes. Indigenous groups are now taking an active role in creating research designs that ultimately must affect the kinds of methods used (Ferguson and Watson this volume; Swidler et al. 1997). With the rise of applied archaeology, where the past is investigated at least in part to specifically address problems faced by disenfranchised groups today (Maschner and Reedy-Maschner 2005), the methods one employs must stand up to legal scrutiny across many jurisdictional boundaries.

Thus, archaeological methods have diversified, been elaborated, become specialized, and in some cases, have become an independent field of study. On the other hand, many of the methods developed in the nineteenth century survive in the twenty-first century with little alteration. It is the goal of this volume to put these methods in context.

This Volume

In some areas of archaeology today, theory for the sake of theory is an appropriate end product. But for most of us, theory structures the questions that we eventually want to ask of the past, and this requires a set of rigorous methods. This companion volume to the *Handbook of Archaeological Theory* (Bentley, Maschner, and Chippendale 2005) is an overview of the methods necessary to put theory into practice. What exactly is method? If your research question is what you want to know and your theoretical stance is why you want to know it, then your method is how you intend to know it. This is critical to the research process, because your method will not only determine your results, but will tie everything back together when you finally get to the point of organizing your research.

Introductions to archaeology tend to be dominated by methods whereas more advanced undergraduate courses and graduate courses tend more toward theory—why? Because a detailed understanding of the methods of archaeology, and their limitations, is much more difficult and time-consuming to master.

They are at the same time much more practical in that they are used more often and under a greater range of conditions than any particular theoretical stance. These are material methods. They are the means by which one deals with the remains of the past in the context of a research design.

In the past, we developed methods for method's sake. Scientific technique was equated with method. It is not seen this way today. Techniques are not methods. Early developments of techniques were a way of exploring the range of things that could be measured. Some of them turned out to be useless because they do not tell you anything about what you are interested in. Some, like the taphonomic ones, are not interesting for their own sake but are interesting because it is important to know how they work. Some turned out to be just good ways of doing archaeology. Many have been improved over the years because of a self-conscious desire to improve our abilities. Any object contains an indefinite amount of information, and an indefinite number of observations can be made on it.

No matter how well planned or developed, and regardless of skills, background knowledge, or previous investigations, the methods initially formulated in one's well-thought-out research design seldom survive contact with the field. One must have a suite of options available at any one time and must be prepared to implement them on the spot. Some methods are highly specialized and require training unavailable to every archaeologist. What is important is to have enough knowledge to recognize when a certain method should be employed, to find the requisite skills among colleagues, and to understand and evaluate the results when finished. I hope that this book will provide the necessary knowledge, skills, and background for archaeologists to work comfortably in their research pursuits.

This book is certainly not exhaustive in coverage, although an attempt was made to cover most of the bigger topics in the field. Some of the topics might be considered classic methods, such as lithic analysis or pottery analysis. Others were generated because of major theoretical developments in the field such as craft production or even postprocessualism. These chapters are both about how the methods work and the appropriate contexts where they should be used. The student should find here the links between what is questioned, hypothesized, or theorized and the means by which those things can be investigated.

This *Handbook of Archaeological Methods* is organized into five parts: "In the Field," "Analytic Methods," "Applying Analytic Methods," "Frameworks for Methods," and "Managing Archaeology." One could divide a work such as this in many ways, and in all, any individual chapter might find reason to be in one of several parts. So this organization should be seen as one of convenience, not as the definitive structure for organizing the methods of archaeology.

Regardless of structure, headings, and organization, there is no better way to begin a work such as this than with a chapter on the history of archaeological method, and there is certainly no better person to write that history than Brian Fagan. Taking us on a highlighted tour of methods and the archaeologists who created them, Fagan reviews the growth of archaeology from the 1860s to the 1960s—the period when all of our most fundamental skills were developed. Following developments in both Europe and the United States, we are left with the clear recognition that archaeological methods have traditionally been considered a means to an end, not a separate field of study as they are pursued in some instances today.

In part 1, "In the Field," we begin with the logistics of fieldwork. The management of archaeological field projects, whether small-scale with just one professional and a number of students or a massive interdisciplinary project that might have 6–10 PhDs and many students, is one of the most time-consuming and frustrating aspects of archeological field research. I have had projects where travel logistics in the remote islands of the western Gulf of Alaska took more of my time than the actual logistics of field research. In this volume logistics transcends simply working out details of travel and scheduling to include the actual implementation of a data collection effort in the field. At that point where it looks impossible to collect the data you originally described in your research proposal, John Steinberg tells us that "proper logistics will allow you to triumph at that juncture when things look bad." This is where flexibility, experience, and an eye for opportunity are your best skills.

Building from such classic projects as Gordon Willey's Viru Valley survey (1953) and Charles Reher's lesser-known Lower Chaco River project (1977), and forming the foundation of nearly all field research projects, archaeological survey is still one of the most important and enduring legacies of the development of archaeological methods, and it is certainly a needed first step if one wants to use many of the other methods discussed in this volume. Brian Molyneaux reports that "the results of a survey are mediated by one fundamental, irresolvable problem: a survey is an indeterminate, culturally relative activity designed to seek traces of many other indeterminate, culturally relative activities." In this sense, the archaeological survey provides the ultimate source of discovery that is bounded by cultural practices of both the surveys and the producers of the archaeological record.

With years of field experience in a variety of contexts in the Santa Barbara Channel region, Michael Glassow takes us on a tour of excavation methods. These are not the methods of Schliemann at Troy (1880) or even Wheeler at Mohenjo Daro (1966), these are the methods of everyday modern archaeology. In the United States, the greatest number of excavations consist of a 1 × 1 m square, or some small combination of them. Glassow discusses this critical form of excavation and demonstrates the complexities of an excavation project, from site grids to sampling, one's choice of tools, recording, cleaning, and ultimately the curation of finds.

Sequence and stratigraphy are the foundations of all archaeological excavations, and Barbara Mills and Rafael Vega-Centeno, specialists in the prehistory of the southwest United States, the region where Kidder excavated Pecos Pueblo and spent so much effort on its stratigraphy (1924), are uniquely qualified to review this important foundation to archaeological inquiry. The authors state that "the concepts of sequence and stratigraphy are so fundamental to the excavation and interpretation of archaeological sites that they are often assumed, rather than explicitly discussed." But here the authors provide a detailed and enlightening study of the concept and its practical applications.

The reader might wonder at the inclusion of ethnoarchaeology in this early section of the volume. But building on the pioneering studies of, among many, Lewis Binford (1978b), William Longacre (1970), Carol Cramer (1979), Richard Gould (1980), and

John Yellen (1977) we find that ethnoarchaeology, founded in early studies of analogy and the direct-historical method, has become a key field method for interpreting and organizing the archaeological record. Here young scholars John Arthur and Kathryn Weedman demonstrate that the role of ethnoarchaeology is not only important but critical to understanding the dynamics of social interactions and their effects on archaeological patterning. Writing from firsthand experience in Africa, the authors review not only the methods and assumptions inherent in ethnoarchaeology but also the ethical and political consequences of doing studies with living peoples.

There is perhaps no more romanticized area of field research than maritime archaeology. Visions of crystal clear blue waters, sunken ships, and priceless treasures dominate both the imagination and public perception. Yet Mark Feulner and J. Barto Arnold III demonstrate that in reality this is a highly sophisticated area of archaeological field research providing data that are not available in any other research context. Maritime archaeology is being used today in many contexts, from Phoenician trading ships in the Mediterranean to the sea battles of World War II (Delgado 2001) and is providing important data, if not individual time slices, on the role of the sea in the structure of many societies.

Part 2, "Analytic Methods," begins with radiocarbon dating. As Paul Pettitt points out, no other method or skill has had a greater impact on the field than Libby's initial development of radiocarbon dating. Now refined and highly accurate with detailed calibration curves from a number of contexts, radiocarbon dating is the primary means by which archaeologists organize their data in many areas of the world. When radiocarbon dating is combined with a suite of alternative dating techniques ranging from dendrochronology to uranium isotopes, Alistair Pike and Paul Pettitt suggest that the fundamental question of when something occurred is of less debate today so that scholars can spend more of their time on explanations for past events.

Perhaps no method developed largely since 1980 has had a more profound effect on archaeological research than the proliferation of geographic information systems (GIS). As Mark Gillings and David Wheatley point out, the use of GIS is now widespread and integrated into almost every area of research.

They also state that "virtually everything archaeologists are interested in was found somewhere, and through their location in space, archaeological features and artifacts are related to other features of the natural or cultural environment." GIS techniques are being used for a suite of archaeological problems and have recently entered the analytic areas of spatial perception, cognition, symbolism, and landscape (Lock and Harris 1996; Maschner 1996c, 1996d; Ruggles and Medyckyj-Scott 1996; Wheatley 1996). When combined with a suite of remote-sensing and geophysical methods, we are now able to organize, analyze, and visualize large amounts of spatial data, which has revolutionized both site-specific and regional analyses. Ken Kvamme, perhaps best known for the early development of GIS techniques in archaeology, takes us on an in-depth tour of the available remote-sensing techniques of today and reviews the appropriateness of each for today's archaeological research. As he states, "archaeological remote sensing allows large regions to be rapidly investigated for archaeological features, at relatively low cost; it can detect features unseen on the surface, precisely map them, and offer interpretations based on their form, distribution, and context. In short, archaeological remote sensing may offer the only pragmatic means to locate, map, and inventory much of the world's archaeological resources." Reviewing both ground- and satellite-based techniques (e.g., Pasquinucci and Trément 2000), Kvamme argues that these technologies form the foundation of twenty-first-century archaeological survey.

For many of us, archaeological chemistry is an arcane method that seeks to identify trace elements or the molecular structures of things and then use those data to investigate everything from manufacturing techniques to craft specialization to trade and exchange. Although a few archaeologists such as Alexander Bentley and colleagues use bone chemistry to investigate migrations and marriage patterns (Bentley, Price, and Chikhi 2003; Bentley, Krause, Price, and Kaufmann 2003), most archaeological chemistry is done by chemists with an interest in the past. Joseph Lambert is one such scholar, and his initial book on the subject (1997) made an impact on the field. Here Lambert argues that "chemistry is concerned with matter and its changes. All of the materials of archaeology, from stone tools to human skeletal remains, have compositions that may be analyzed by modern chemical techniques." Chemistry can be used for everything from diet to manufacturing techniques to artifact origins. It can be applied to a suite of other critical discoveries and is important to many archaeological investigations.

Quantification has played an important role in archaeology for nearly a century, yet the development of statistical methods in archaeology is a product of the last 50 years, first in the taxonomic debates of the 1950s and later as multivariate methods of association and clustering that closely mirrored the development of modern computing power (Aldenderfer 1987; Shennan 1997; Thomas 1976). As Mark Aldenderfer makes clear, there is little one can do in archaeology today without a basic understanding of statistical methods. The computing revolution of the 1980s not only changed our approaches to statistics, putting analytic power in the hands of all archaeologists, but further changed the way we use mathematical techniques in general. This is clear in the discussion of computer modeling and simulation, which form the basis for many studies in physics, ecology, and mathematics and also, as James McGlade shows, are critical both to the archaeology of the 1970s (Doran 1970; Hodder 1978a) and to modern archaeology (van der Leeuw and McGlade 1997). McGlade points out that modeling should not be seen as an end product to research, but it also should not be dismissed as simply a game of computer aficionados. Rather, it is a simple technique for investigating the relationships between very complex phenomena.

Experimental archaeology has been important for many years, and it was one of the critical areas of research with the development of the new archaeology in the 1960s and 1970s, especially with the debates regarding analogy, ethnoarchaeology, and the use of middle range theory (Coles 1979), and is still important today (Mathieu 2002). Izumi Shimada has done much to continue and propagate experimental studies over the last 20 years, especially with his work on metallurgy on the Andean coast (Shimada and Merkel 1991; Shimada and Wagner 2001). He argues that "experimental archaeology is a method of testing our ideas about and discovering the past through experiments." He then outlines a history of experimental research in archaeology and reviews many of its most common and modern applications.

This part concludes with a review of reflexive methods. When Ian Hodder first started to discuss the importance of structural, contextual, and reflexive archaeologies nearly 25 years ago (1982a, 1982b), they were difficult to apply because no one had laid out the methods to put them into action. His recent work along these lines (1999) provides a framework for a post-processual research program. He argues that there is a real need for a reflexive research effort in response to the overly codified methods of most archaeologists but that these need to be situated in the contexts of interpretation with an emphasis on the ethics of archaeology, especially with regard to alternative voices of interpretation.

Part 3 is titled "Applying Analytic Methods." There is no doubt that the two most important areas of investigation conducted at some point by nearly all archaeologists concern technology and subsistence. The topics discussed here include the primary methods that archaeologists employ to investigate the material record of the past—the methods by which material things are counted, measured, described, and compared. These are also the chapters that cover the basic questions of the subsistence economy—what people hunted, gathered, fished, or farmed. Technology and subsistence form the foundations of archaeological inquiry. Bioarchaeological studies take us far beyond these more basic questions, and we will see that so much can be learned from human remains that nearly all aspects of the material record are weak in comparison. Finally, few categories of remains allow us to make inferences about the cognitive, spiritual, and symbolic realms of the past, but rock art is a great place to begin such investigations.

The famous Paleolithic archaeologist C. B. M. McBurney wrote in his classic volume on the site of Hauh Fateah that stone tools were man's extracorporeal limbs (1967). I think many of us see most aspects of technology in this light, and this is certainly the case for ceramics and lithics. Throughout much of the world ceramics are the most important material remains in the archaeological record of the last 10,000 years (Rice 1987). So many regional chronologies have been constructed based on fragments of pottery that it would be difficult to imagine many sequences without them. Using examples from the eastern Mediterranean,

Carl Knappett shows that ceramics can inform us on an entire suite of activities that go far beyond typology and chronology. Lithic studies solve many of the same problems as ceramic analysis, but with less stylistic interference. In many areas of the world, especially when investigating the past lives of hunter-gatherers, stone tools are often the only remains, leading many archaeologists to base all of their interpretations on this highly durable material item. As William Andrefsky (1998, 2001; see also Odell 2004) points out, "lithic artifact variability is extremely complex and is linked not only to technological, cultural, and functional requirements but also to aberrations in raw-material availability and other situational constraints," which makes it suitable for a suite of detailed and replicable analyses.

Understanding what people ate at different times in the past under different social, demographic, and environmental conditions provided archaeologists with their first views of the socioeconomic past. Although archaeologists have been concerned with these topics for a century, these investigations became paramount with the advent of the new archaeology and its preoccupation with human-landscape interactions and cultural adaptations to the environment—continuing today as one of our most critical areas of investigation. The two means by which archaeologists do this are paleobotany and zooarchaeology. As Gayle Fritz points out, paleobotany is concerned with the analysis of plant remains in all of their forms, from pollen to charred plants, and is still one of our most important methods for understanding foraging and domestication (e.g., Piperno and Stothert 2003). She states that "paleoethnobotanists study past interrelationships between people and plants using various kinds of archaeological evidence" and that the numerous scenarios of human-plant interactions require a suite of both macroscopic and microscopic methods. Perhaps more widespread because of the commonality of the remains, zooarchaeology is now considered one of our most important and basic methods of investigation (Grayson 1984). In this volume Lee Lyman tells us that the analysis of faunal remains, and the parallel study of taphonomy (Lyman 1994), provide the bulk of the data on major mammalian, avian, and fish species used by the prehistoric inhabitants for food, tools, and the greater economy. Faunal remains can also be used to reconstruct past ecosystems and their study contributes to the solution of modern environmental problems (Lyman and Cannon 2004).

There is no method available to an archaeologist that provides a greater breadth of data than bioarchaeology (Larsen 1997). As Buzon, Eng, Lambert, and Walker point out in this volume, demography, social relations, inequality, gender roles, violence, warfare, disease, diet, genealogies, economic activities, migration, technology, and many other topics can be investigated from human skeletal remains. There is little surprise that, in nearly every region where the archaeological record has been studied for decades, when a detailed bioarchaeological analysis of an area becomes available, our understanding of the past grows exponentially (Lambert 2002; Walker 1997). Most recently and with spectacular results, bioarchaeological studies of health, violence and warfare, diet, and genetics are changing our basic perceptions of the past in many ways (Billman et al. 2000) and are contributing to the rewriting of history (Novak and Kopp 2003).

The last chapter in this part concerns the analysis of rock art. The reader might wonder why the analysis of rock art around the world has become so important over the last 20 years and why it is now considered one of our most important methods of investigation. I believe rock art studies are now important because they are one of the few means by which archaeologists go beyond investigations of the economy, politics, and social worlds of a prehistoric people (Chippindale and Taçon 1998; Holl 2004; Keyser 2004; Whitley 2001). Following some dissatisfaction with the economic emphasis of the 1960s and 1970s, archaeologists sought ways to investigate more cognitive aspects of past human lives, and rock art was the obvious choice. As David Whitley and Lawrence Loendorf make so clear through their careful discussion of the means by which archaeologists investigate the symbolic and spiritual past, these techniques can be applied to many forms of art and architecture, not only rock art, and provide clues to areas of the past unavailable in any other form of analysis.

Part 4 in this volume is titled "Frameworks for Methods." Studies of demography and geoarchaeology have had a long history in archaeology and have evolved through a suite of theoretical changes and technological achievements into important methods in their own right. Studies of craft specializations, historical archaeology, trade and exchange, and regional analysis are methods that were originally developed or elaborated to further the agendas of the new archaeology, but now have been turned toward many of the modern theoretical developments in the field. All are critical to our explanations of both cultural processes and individual events. They are methods that have been used in the context of heavily empirical and environmentally based studies and in the context of poststructuralist, neo-Marxist, and feminist theoretical approaches.

Population size, growth, and demography have played such an important part in archaeological explanation over the last 40 years that it is difficult to imagine a scenario where an archaeologist hasn't spent time attempting to reconstruct past populations and their regional distributions. From the population pressure arguments of the 1960s (Binford 1969; Boserup 1965) to the population growth and scale arguments of the 1970s (Johnson 1982) to the paleodemographic studies of the 1990s (Paine 1997), demography has been a central theme in all these studies. Richard Paine lays out the method and theory of investigating prehistoric demography. Building on regional analysis, cemeteries, genetics, and other data, Paine states that "studies of prehistoric demography rely on three main courses of data: archaeology, archaeologically recovered human skeletons, and the genetic structure of living human populations. Each of these has great potential but presents obstacles that have yet to be surmounted."

Geoarchaeology in a general sense might be considered one of the classic methods of archaeology and many of us still remember some of the classic works that integrated geology and environmental archaeology, such as Butzer's *Environment and Archaeology* (1964). But today geoarchaeology is much more sophisticated and provides the methods to build many of our most important behavioral and even postprocessual interpretations. Christopher Hill provides this overview and makes obvious that, although basic studies of landscape evolution, site geography, climate, and geomorphic context are still the most important contributions of geoarchaeology, studies of everything from microstratigraphy and site formation processes to global change events (Bradley 1999) are now within the realm of the field.

Craft production and specialization has become one of the primary methods for investigating the rise, development, organization, and structure of more complex societies (Costin and Wright 1998; Wailes 1996). Craft specialists are some of the first individuals in a society with economic goals transcending traditional food-related production. Part-time craft specialists are common in many village-based societies, even hunter-gatherer villages such as those along the north Pacific Rim and California (Ames 1995; Arnold 1987). But full-time craft specialists, which require an economic system with enough surplus food to support these individuals, are usually found in much more complex societies (Brumfiel and Earle 1987). As Cathy Costin points out, "crafting is best viewed as any transformational process involving skill (knowledge, talent or proficiency, effort), aesthetics, and cultural meaning and consider the results of that crafting (verb) to be crafts (noun)." This broad but succinct definition allows craft production to be used to address topics in nearly every theoretical perspective in a wide variety of contexts.

Whether investigating slavery, colonial expansion, military heritage, or the legacy of the Cold War, historical archaeology has come into its own in the last 40 years (South 1977a, 1977b). In Europe, historical archaeology takes many forms, from the Romans to medieval times to the Industrial Revolution, whereas in the Americas it deals specifically with the time since European colonization. Kenneth Kelly tells us that historical archaeology is defined from "the broad and literal (archaeology with a documentary component) to the chronological (archaeology of the post-fifteenth-century period), from the cultural (the archaeology of European expansion and its impact on the rest of the world) to a concern with the theoretical (the archaeology of the origins and spread of capitalism)." In this light, historical archaeology is applicable in an array of theoretical, temporal, and spatial contexts, resulting in one of the fastest-growing areas of archaeological method and theory.

When archaeologists in the 1970s were searching for methods to better understand cultural processes through regional interaction, studies of trade and exchange were important (Earle and Ericson 1977). Today, when studies of processes have changed to include agency, power, gender roles, and historical contingency, studies of trade and exchange provide a powerful means of investigating the past. Closely related to craft production, trade and exchange is certainly integrated into many other methodological arenas and is really a methodology of studying interaction. Marilyn Masson states in this volume that production and trade are intertwined, and we find that many of the processes already discussed in the chapter on craft production are again presented here but in an entirely different methodological context.

Perhaps no area of research has been more historically romanticized than regional analysis. From the Viru Valley in Peru (Willey 1953) to the basin of Mexico (Sanders et al. 1979) to the rolling chalk hills of Wessex in southern England (Renfrew 1978), regional analysis has been one of the critical areas of investigation for studying social evolution, interaction, political complexity, and economy. With the addition of quantitative approaches in the 1970s (Clark 1977; Hodder 1978b) and the rise of GIS technologies in the 1980s and 1990s for regional studies (Aldenderfer and Maschner 1996; Maschner 1996a; Wheatley and Gillings 2002), regional analysis has continued as a major theme in archaeological analysis. John Kantner, building on his own research in the American Southwest, argues that "although the goals, methods, and theory vary in all . . . examples of regional analysis, what is shared is an interest in how humans interact with, use, and modify space on a broad spatial scale."

If one surveys the many introductory textbooks on archaeological methods, it is difficult to find even a mention of the management or politics of archaeology until quite recently (e.g., Renfrew and Bahn 1996). In part 5, "Managing Archaeology," we look in detail at some of the critical topics faced by archaeologists in the research process. The chapters survey how one curates and manages archaeological sites once they have been found and the methods for curating the immense amount of data generated in most archaeological investigations. The methods for funding research and ultimately writing and publishing the results of research are equally important because the article, book, or chapter is a critical end product of any investigation. But perhaps most important today, the archaeologist must also be a good steward, and working with indigenous peoples has become critical to being a good manager and investigator of the past.

The biggest danger to archaeology today is the destruction of our archaeological heritage by looting and development (Fagan 1990; papers in Green 1984). Although most countries have laws protecting heritage resources, the management of those resources goes far beyond legal protections (King 1998). Francis McManamon states that "managing archaeological resources involves a set of activities intended to ensure the preservation, protection, proper treatment, and appropriate use of these resources." Appropriate use may mean research, heritage, tourism, protection, or some combination of these factors. This is similarly true for the curation of archaeological data. With the proliferation of computers and software, the management of archaeological data has grown from simply data storage and retrieval to data analysis and redistribution. Fred Limp and the staff of the Center for Advanced Spatial Technologies have been at the forefront of archaeological data management. In this volume Limp argues that "all archaeologists know that the archaeological resources that they study are nonrenewable. But data that they recover *can* be kept safe for the future. It does no good to rescue a site and then lose the data."

One of the biggest barriers to archaeological research is securing adequate funding for the project in mind. Funding can come from a number of sources, but as Michael Love points out, "in archaeology, what counts is not the project that you want to do but the one that you can get funded." This means that sometimes the funding one receives for a particular project that must be done, such as a cultural resources management project or a contract with an agency, can be turned into the research effort that you want to do by merging both goals. But there are opportunities for funding pure research that are highly competitive, and the process of creating a quality proposal is sometimes as time-consuming as the proposed research. Regardless of the approach one takes, adequate funding is the single most important barrier to conducting research.

Perhaps the most important facet of being a professional archaeologist is writing and publishing. One can be the greatest archaeologist with the greatest research in the world, but if no one can read about your work, then everything else is meaningless. Chris Chippindale argues that "knowledge is not public knowledge until other people know it; while it remains locked inside the head of the individual who found it out, perhaps it is not knowledge at all." He then takes the student through the process of getting research recognized, participating in conferences, and getting published. He believes that the ability to write about your research is intimately tied to the ability to talk about your research, and therefore public presentations and written presentations are equally important.

Last but certainly not least, and a chapter that perhaps should have been the first chapter because it is so centrally important, is one's ability to work with local and indigenous peoples. This requires finding research themes that are important to archaeology, on the one hand, but that create data and provide information that is important to local and indigenous peoples as well (Dongoske et al. 2000; Layton 1989; Swidler et al. 1997). It also requires the ability to adjust research plans to satisfy local cultural sensitivities. This can be a difficult but highly rewarding endeavor. As T. J. Ferguson and Joe Watkins emphasize, "as a discipline, we need to develop symbiotic, rather than parasitic, relationships and we need to integrate the values and needs of the indigenous peoples into the scientific agenda of archaeological research." But this should be the essence of any ethical and humanistic approach to good archaeology and makes us not only better stewards of the past but better conveyors of prehistory to the larger world.

The methods of archaeology are clearly diverse, situational, and unlimited in scope. The methods one employs must be chosen from those that most interesting or important for the research at hand. There are few cases where all of these methods are warranted, but in certain cases of long-term research efforts with a multidisciplinary cast of scholars, all of these methods are used at some point in the research effort.

Methods in Action

The student might wonder how all these different methods can be used and how they might be incorporated into research projects. I am writing this introduction while preparing to lead an archaeological project on the Sanak Islands, a small archipelago on the edge of the continental shelf about 40 miles south of the Alaska Peninsula in the western Gulf of Alaska. Nearly 20 archaeologists, geologists, ecologists, and others will spend 2 months conducting a research project that may change the way we do studies of long-term human and landscape interactions. The theory is quite simple. The Aleuts have inhabited the north Pacific for at least 10,000 years. This means that there has not been a north Pacific ecosystem without human harvesting since deglaciation, and thus there is no "natural" ecosystem without humans as primary predators. Conversely, this is one of the most dynamic landscapes on the north Pacific, with evidence of 25-m tsunamis, hundreds of volcanic eruptions, rapid sea level change, dramatic climatic fluctuations, transpacific cultural contacts, intertribal warfare, and other factors that also structured the relationship that the Aleuts had with the marine ecosystem. Our basic research question thus becomes: First, what have been the roles of prehistoric, historical, and modern Aleuts in the structure and functioning of the north Pacific ecosystem and is it possible for the modern role to sustain the communities that live in this ecosystem today? Second, how have major changes in the environment, such as sea level, climate, tsunamis, and volcanic eruptions, conditioned human social behavior in the context of humanity's role as a key condition in the engineering of the north Pacific ecosystem?

The theory is easy, but how does one now turn that theory into something practicable? This book is in essence the nuts and bolts of turning theory into practice. By describing a few of the details of how my research incorporates every chapter in this book, the student of archaeology will better appreciate the complexities of creating a research project and incorporating a diverse array of research methods.

The Aleutian Islands are a fascinating place to work, as much for the environment and people today, as for the archaeology and history and the *history of archaeological methods* (chapter 2) in the area. It was here that William Healy Dall (1877) made some of the first observations that North American archaeological sites had stratigraphies that could tell us about the histories of the people who made them. It was the Aleutians that produced the first true mummies in North America that fascinated early naturalists (Weyer 1929). It was here in the 1930s that Hrdlicka pillaged site after site on his collecting expeditions (1945) but defined a long history of Aleut occupations. It was at the site of Anangula in the 1950s that William Laughlin (1951) and his colleagues found an early core and blade site that initially played a key role in our understanding of the peopling of the New World and now, perhaps more importantly, is considered one of the earliest villages in the Americas at more than 9,000 years old (Aigner and Del Bene 1982). This history has contributed directly to the history of American archaeology in general.

The first part of any project in the Aleutian Islands is creating a dialogue with one or more of the local tribal councils. *Working with indigenous peoples* (chapter 34) has been an important part of Alaska archaeology for many years. The Aleuts are fascinated by their history and heritage and very supportive of archaeological research. But one must also be aware of the research problems they are interested in, which is why, in the context of this project, we are creating an applied archaeology, one that creates data that are also usable to the local people in fisheries negotiations, fights with environmental groups, and land claims—what Hodder considers part of the goal of *reflexive methods* (chapter 17). This includes spending a few weeks each year teaching in the village schools, creating local displays of findings, giving public lectures in the communities, and if asked, acting as an expert witness at state and federal board meetings.

Working with the local people of the eastern Aleutians is a pleasure, but mounting an expedition to the Aleutians is difficult. Many islands are completely inaccessible except by boat on a reasonably calm day. Therefore, *field logistics* (chapter 3) plays a critical role in the success of the project. Although field logistics should be about collecting data and answering questions as Steinberg suggests in this volume, it is sometimes simply about getting into the field and staying alive there. On a barge somewhere in the eastern Pacific is 5,000 pounds of food and field gear heading to the Aleut community of King Cove, Alaska. Already in King Cove, stored in a building where indigenous commercial fishermen keep their nets, I have another 5,000 pounds of field gear. This includes not only the standard excavation equipment of buckets, shovels, screens, trowels, and line levels but also the more important equipment for work in the north. Three 20-foot shelters that can withstand 120-mph winds, solar powered electric fences to keep out brown bears, shotguns and rifles, stoves, coolers, survival suits, life jackets, inflatable boats, outboard motors, fuel cans, soil corers, and solar panels. Carried with me on the plane will be digital cameras, computers, differential global positioning system (GPS) units, shortwave radios, VHF radios, satellite telephones, and walkie-talkies. Each student must have a four-season tent and the best rain gear available. We must be completely prepared for 2 months without resupply. Then all this is loaded on a 50-foot fishing boat and, many hours later, we shuttle all of this equipment to shore in skiffs to set up camp and begin the research.

Once on the islands, *field survey* (chapter 4) is our first priority. Sites are easy to identify as the Aleuts lived in pit houses for thousands of years, and because there are no trees, these pits are often the only surface features. In fact, we have found that the species of vegetation on these sites is a signature of prehistoric occupation. Many years ago Ted Bank (1953) noticed that the vegetation on ancient Aleut sites is more dense, more lush, and of different species than the surrounding maritime tundra. Our research has shown that this is indeed the case but also that the majority of the edible plants are found on the sites, not off. The unique vegetation communities on these ancient sites, whether the site is 5,000 or 1,000 years old, are the same regardless of time, meaning that these are artificially constructed climax ecosystems. Because some of the villages cover 140,000 m^2, they play an important role in the modern ecosystem. The vegetation is so different that I have been able to use *remote sensing* (chapter 12) to identify the locations of villages long before the field project begins. Using palynology and other aspects of *paleobotany* (chapter 20), we have shown that these new ecosystems arise shortly after the initial occupation and provide an important summer food source for Aleuts. In fact, these sites might be considered Aleut gardens because they are artificially created by Aleuts bringing edible plants back to village sites and then passively (or actively) dispersing the seeds.

The survey is organized around the modern landscape and our *geoarchaeological* investigations (chapter 25) play an important part because beach ridges, sand dunes, tides, and other factors determine the location and preservation of sites. Here lies the importance of a quality *geographic information system* (GIS; chapter 11), one that is constructed before the field research but can be updated in the field using GPS to document new finds, landforms, and construct maps at will. The GIS helps us determine which sites will be tested, the first step to determining where to invest our time in full-scale *excavation* (chapter 5). The goals of the excavations are focused on recovering faunal remains, because *zooarchaeology* (chapter 21) is the primary means by which we can reconstruct the ecosystem history of the islands and also provides the data that local peoples are most interested in at this time. These middens are very complex, often with thousands of years of house constructions, storage-pit excavations, and other features that require detailed observations of *sequence and stratigraphy* (chapter 6). All further investigations and interpretations are founded in our ability to tease out the intricacies of these shell middens.

But also critical to these interpretations is *radiocarbon dating* (chapter 9), which is not as straightforward here as one might expect. First, most all wood used by the Aleuts is driftwood. This means that any wood dated in these sites might have been dead for hundreds of years. We have tried to use burned grass and small willows instead, but these are often hard to find. Second, all of the house floors are permeated with sea mammal oils, and because sea mammals live in the ocean, they notoriously have old carbon in their bodies, contaminating the charcoal and also making sea mammal bone useless for dating. This requires extensive laboratory pretreatment before the sample is analyzed. When on one of the few islands that had caribou, antler makes a great source for dating, and we have been very successful using it. But to make the story even more complicated, the Aleut used coal as a fuel source, and small fragments of it are often mixed with wood charcoal. This is the reason why we occasionally get dates older than 50,000 years in the region! *Other dating methods* (chapter 10) are less used in the region, but beach ridge stratigraphy and tephrachronology (the dating of sites based on volcanic ash falls) have played important roles in our research.

We have an important advantage in explaining the archaeological record because many of these islands were occupied until recently, and the Sanak Islands are no exception. Many residents of the modern communities grew up on Sanak and have a detailed knowledge of life there. After our research project passed its human-subjects review by our institutional review board, interviews were conducted with many peoples from the area. Although not *ethnoarchaeology* per se (chapter 7), the result was much the same because it created a means of linking the historical archaeological record of the islands with the dynamics of the history and people who created it. Unexpectedly, stories of shipwrecks and beach finds led us into *maritime archaeology* (chapter 8). The Sanak Islands and adjacent reef systems are notorious for their shipwrecks, and ships have been foundering here for a long time. It looks as if Asian iron was entering the region on these ships up to 1,000 years ago, providing the inhabitants with novel sources of wood and rare materials. The abandoned villages are still there, dilapidated houses, the old school, remnants of an Orthodox church, storage pits and smokehouses for salmon and cod, all representing the interface between the indigenous peoples and European colonial expansion. This requires that *historical archaeology* (chapter 27) also be central to our investigations of changing dynamics in the region.

The villages we excavate were inhabited by what archaeologists term *complex hunter-gatherers*. Complex hunter-gatherers generally have curated lithic technologies that are functionally specific. In very limited excavations we find thousands of tools and sometimes 10,000 or more fragments of debitage per cubic meter. Thus *lithic studies* (chapter 19) have a central place in our research even though they are not necessarily central to the theoretical questions we are interested in. The stone tools are made primarily of fine-grain andesitic basalt; some are of obsidian. Our *experimental archaeology* (chapter 16) studies have shown that this raw material is extremely hard, leaving little or no use wear on tool edges. Because there is little visible difference between basalt sources, we have used *archaeological chemistry* (chapter 13) to identify the stone tools' source locations, allowing us a first look at regional *trade and exchange* (chapter 28). Equally interesting, the Aleuts did not make pottery, but the Yupik and Koniag Eskimo peoples to the east did, and this pottery occasionally was traded down to the islands. We have used *ceramic analysis* (chapter 18) to monitor trade relations across the region over the last 2,000 years and have found that pottery, because it is so rare, is a good indicator of changing political dynamics. We have no *rock art* (chapter 23), but the art of the Aleuts is analyzed in much the same way. Ivory figurines, designs on harpoons, masks of whalebone or wood, and elaborate items of body ornamentation all provide a small glimpse into the symbolic and spiritual world of the Aleut. Many Aleuts participated in part-time *craft specialization* (chapter 26), especially in art, basketry, stone tools, and kayak construction—a characteristic that is still manifested today in modern Aleut society. Overall, artifact analyses provide the foundation for interpreting the daily lives of Aleuts, and zooarchaeology and geoarchaeology provide the ability to place the Aleuts in a regional context.

We generally do not excavate burials, partly in deference to the wishes of the local people, but also because they have not been central to our analysis. But we have excavated burials that the Aleuts asked us to excavate, and we have rescued burials being eroded by the sea to return them to the local people. But Aleuts are very interested in what can be learned from burials, and *bioarchaeology* (chapter 22) is critical here. The findings from investigations of health, diet, and genealogy using skeletal remains are important to many local peoples in the Aleutians because they can be used to support modern political goals. Thus, in the context of *Native American Graves Protection and Repatriation Act* (NAGPRA) investigations, the Aleuts have had us and others conduct analyses to create bioarchaeological data useful to solving their modern problems.

One of the primary means by which we have analyzed the landscape and social histories of the western Alaska Peninsula and eastern Aleutian Islands is through *regional analysis* (chapter 29). Regional analysis requires an investment in a GIS and a good understanding of the role of *statistics in archaeology* (chapter 14). Although statistics are critical in many areas of investigation already described, I find them most important in teasing out patterns of long-term change or stability, in comparing the archaeology with the ecological records, and in solving multidimensional problems. Statistics are also important in investigating *demography* (chapter 24). Because we have such a detailed chronological record, because houses can be measured on the surface, and because population size determines to some extent how the Aleuts engineered their ecosystem through harvesting, we have spent an inordinate amount of research energy on reconstructing ancient population levels.

Our research has generated an enormous amount of data: more than 200,000 lithics, 500,000 faunal elements, 250 village sites plus pollen cores, soil samples, plant samples, rock samples, interview tapes, field notebooks, photographs, drawings, and many gigabytes of digital data that must be managed, stored, and archived. When considering the long-term needs in *curating sites* (chapter 30) and *curating data* (chapter 31), a number of problems must be addressed. Much of our work is on lands owned by Native corporations, which ultimately own everything we find. But a large portion of our data is from lands managed by the U.S. Fish and Wildlife Service (USFWS), which has its own goals and regulations in managing archaeological data. Thus, we have had to create both laboratory and digital-data curatorship strategies that meet the needs of multiple entities, all while meeting our research goals as well.

As principal investigator on a project now in its tenth year, I have been responsible for getting the majority of the *research funding* (chapter 32) by writing proposals. This project costs between $150,000 and $300,000 per year, and over the last 10 years I have had five National Science Foundation (NSF) grants plus grants from the National Oceanic and Atmospheric Administration (NOAA), the USFWS, and local sources totaling more than $2 million. Archaeologists often claim that laboratory analysis is the most time-consuming aspect of archaeological research, but if this is so, then grant writing comes a very close second. It is certainly the most important because, unless you can drive to your research area in a few hours, the level of funding determines the quality, breadth, and intensity of the research effort. But getting funding from NSF or other agencies requires another major investment—*writing and publishing* (chapter 33). All of the students on this project, graduate and undergraduate alike, give one or two conference papers every year. All are included in the analysis and reporting. Most are full participants on future publications. Writing and publishing must be done for three audiences: the scientific community, the funding agencies, and the local communities. Each of the three requires very different approaches.

Through this discussion of my own work it should be clear that regardless of one's theoretical questions, or even the particular theory one wishes to investigate, all of the methods of archaeological analysis can be critical to the success of the research project. Gone are the days when one could be proud to know the differences between methods and methodology; today they are tightly integrated. Some of the chapters in this volume are indeed methodological, being an investigation of the method itself and an evaluation of the underpinnings of the method. Others are purely methods chapters, describing the appropriate use and implementation of the method in question. The relationship between method and theory? Today they generally cannot be separated in a research context, but they certainly can be discussed apart. But as the reader will clearly see in this volume, few today can discuss an archaeological method without some review of the theoretical repercussions or implications.

Final Thoughts

I remember so well the last quantitative methods course taught by Albert Spaulding, in which there were only three graduate students, myself included. Spaulding felt that all archaeological data, whether a measurement, an observation, a count, or a classificatory system, could be reduced to categories and thus analyzed as a series of nested or hierarchical chi-squares. Now, nearly 20 years later, this notion still invades nearly everything I do in archaeology. Yet perhaps subliminal in this message, and even unrecognized by Spaulding, is that the methods of hierarchical categorization are a metaphor for everything that archaeologists do in modern archaeology. Hierarchies of theory require hierarchies of methods that lead to hierarchies of things where hierarchies of interpretations are created. Smart methods are those with a good coherence between the technique and the method, and the method and the theory. The chapters in this volume provide the foundation for making these linkages and go far to show the range of expertise currently situated in our field.

I am fully aware that this volume is not inclusive, but Chris Chippindale and I tried to make it so. In hindsight, we wish that we had continued to search for a writer of a chapter on ancient DNA, but after the sixth or seventh specialist was completely uninterested, we let it drop, and this important topic is only briefly surveyed in this volume. On the more technical side, certain areas of analysis, such as neutron activation or the developing area of photon activation for elemental analysis of artifacts (Glascock 2000; Segebade et al. 1988; Tonchev et al. 1999) and a suite of new imaging techniques (Mantler and Schreiner 2001; Pillay 2001), should have had their own part or chapter, but again, this was not pursued after initial contacts. Among more practical subjects, there is little discussion of digital imaging, video, and other developing techniques for recording the archaeological record (although Glassow provides some good observations on this topic), and there is no chapter on the teaching of archaeology—perhaps both of these should also have been discussed in detail, either in an existing chapter or separately. I would have also liked a chapter on architecture, sculpture, and art, perhaps as a companion to Whitley's chapter, as well as a separate chapter on oral history, ethnohistory, and traditional knowledge use (Berkes 1999), discussed nicely in this volume by Ferguson and Watkins and to some extent by Hodder, but chapters on these topics were eventually left out because of space constraints. Some topics are covered more than once in this volume, and rightly so. None of these methods stand alone, so it should come as no surprise that GIS are discussed in a number of chapters, or that the craft-production and trade-and-exchange chapters have some overlap, or that references are made throughout to some of the greats of archaeology while being covered in detail in the history-of-methods chapter. Any major gaps in coverage that the reader might note as also missing in this volume, such as methods for investigating complex systems, social inequality, cultural resource management, or the origins of agriculture are instead included in the forthcoming *Handbook of Archaeological Theory*.

Ultimately, I hope that advanced undergraduates and beginning graduate students find this an important and necessary reference work as they seek to improve their knowledge and skills in archaeology. This volume, composed of chapters written by both leaders in their fields and young scholars just beginning their careers, should provide the background and foundation for the range of methods currently employed in the field and the contexts in which they should be used.

References

Aigner, Jean S., and Terrance Del Bene
    1982   Early Holocene Maritime Adaptations in the Aleutian Islands. In *Peopling of the New World*, edited by J. E. Ericson, R. E. Taylor, and R. Berger, pp. 35–67. Ballena Press, Los Altos, California.

Aldenderfer, Mark S. (editor)
    1987   *Quantitative research in archaeology: Progress and prospects.* Sage Publications, Newbury Park, California.

Aldenderfer, Mark, and Herbert D. G. Maschner (editors)
    1996   *Anthropology, Space, and Geographic Information Systems.* Oxford University Press, New York.

Allen, Kathleen M. S., Stanton W. Green, and Ezra B. W. Zubrow (editors)
    1990   *Interpreting space: GIS and archaeology.* Taylor and Francis, London

Ames, Kenneth M.
    1981   The Evolution of Social Ranking on the Northwest Coast of North America. *American Antiquity* 46:789–805.
    1995   Chiefly power and household production on the Northwest Coast. In *Foundations of Social Inequality*, edited by T. Douglas Price and Gary M. Feinman, pp. 155–187. Plenum Press, New York.

Anawak, Jack
    1996   Inuit Perceptions of the Past. In *Contemporary Archaeology in Theory: A Reader*, edited by Robert Preucel and Ian Hodder, pp. 646–651. Blackwell Press, Oxford.

Andrefsky, William, Jr.
    2001   *Lithic debitage: Context, form, meaning.* University of Utah Press, Salt Lake City.

1998 *Lithics: Macroscopic approaches to analysis.* Cambridge University Press, Cambridge.

Anyon, Roger, T. J. Ferguson, Loretta Jackson, Lillie Lane, and Phillip Vicente
1997 Native American oral tradition and archaeology: Issues of structure, relevance, and respect. In *Native Americans and archaeologists, stepping stones to common ground,* edited by Nina Swidler, Kurt E. Dongoske, Roger Anyon, and Alan S. Downer, pp. 77–87. AltaMira, Walnut Creek, California.

Arnold, Bettina.
1990 The Past as Propaganda: Totalitarian Archaeology in Nazi Germany. *Antiquity* 64:464–478.

Arnold, Jeanne
1987 *Craft specialization in the prehistoric Channel Islands, California.* University of California Publications in Anthropology Vol. 18. University of California Press, Berkeley.

Bank, Theodore P.
1953 Ecology of Prehistoric Aleutian Village Sites. *Ecology* 34:246–264.

Bentley, R. Alexander, R. Krause, T. D. Price, and B. Kaufmann
2003 Human mobility at the early Neolithic settlement of Vaihingen, Germany: Evidence from strontium isotope analysis. *Archaeometry* 45:481–96.

Bentley, R. Alexander, and Herbert D. G. Maschner (editors)
2003 *Complex systems and archaeology: Empirical and theoretical approaches.* University of Utah Press, Salt Lake City.

Bentley, R. Alexander, T. D. Price, and L. Chikhi
2003 Comparing broad scale genetic and local scale isotopic evidence for the spread of agriculture into Europe. *Antiquity* 77:63–65.

Berkes, Fikret
1999 *Sacred ecology: Traditional ecological knowledge and resource management.* Taylor and Francis, Philadelphia.

Bettinger, Robert L.
1991 *Hunter-gatherers: Archaeological and evolutionary theory.* Plenum Press, New York.

Billman, Brian, Patricia Lambert, and Banks Leonard
2000 Cannibalism, warfare, and drought in the Mesa Verde region during the twelfth century A.D. *American Antiquity* 65:145–178.

Binford, Lewis R.
1962 Archaeology as anthropology. *American Antiquity* 28:217–225.
1964 A consideration of archaeological research design. *American Antiquity* 29:425–441.

1965 Archaeological Systematics and the Study of Cultural Processes. *American Antiquity* 31:203–210.
1969 Post Pleistocene Adaptations. In *New Perspectives in Archaeology*, edited by S. R. Binford and L. R. Binford, pp. 313–341. Aldine, Chicago.
1978a Dimensional Analysis of Behavior and Site Structure: Learning from an Eskimo Hunting Stand. *American Antiquity* 43:330–361.
1978b *Nunamiut Ethnoarchaeology*. Academic Press, New York.
1980 Willow smoke and dogs' tails: Hunter-gatherer settlement systems and archaeological site formation. *American Antiquity* 45:4–20.
1981 *Bones: Ancient men and modern myths*. Academic Press, New York.
1982 The Archaeology of Place. *Journal of Anthropological Anthropology* 1:5–31.

Bintliff, John (editor)
1999 *Structure and contingency: Evolutionary processes in life and human society*. Leicester University Press, London, New York.

Boserup, Esther
1965 *The conditions of agricultural growth: The economics of agrarian change under population pressure*. Aldine, Chicago.

Bradley, R. S.
1999 *Paleoclimatology: Reconstructing climates of the Quaternary*. 2nd ed. International Geophysics Series, v. 64. Harcourt/Academic Press, San Diego.

Brain, C. K.
1981 *The Hunters or the Hunted? An Introduction to African Cave Taphonomy*. University of Chicago Press, Chicago.

Brumfiel, Elizabeth, and Timothy Earle (editors)
1987 *Specialization, exchange, and complex societies*. Cambridge University Press, Cambridge.

Butzer, K. W.
1964 *Environment and archaeology: An introduction to Pleistocene geography*. Aldine, Chicago.

Chippindale, Christopher, and Paul S. C. Taçon (editors)
1998 *The archaeology of rock-art*. Cambridge University Press, Cambridge.

Clark, David L. (editor)
1977 *Spatial archaeology*. Academic Press, New York.

Coles, John M.
1979 *Experimental archaeology*. Academic Press, New York.
1984 *The Archaeology of Wetlands*. Edinburgh University Press, Edinburgh.

Costin, Cathy Lynne, and Rita P. Wright (editors)
1998 *Craft and social identity*. Archaeological Papers of the American Anthropological Association No. 8. Washington, D.C.

Dall, William Healy
  1877   On Succession in the shell-heaps of the Aleutian Islands. In *Tribes of the Extreme Northwest*, pp. 41–91. *Contributions to North American Ethnology 1*. U.S. Government Printing Office, Washington, D.C.

Delgado, James P.
  2001   *Lost warships: An archeological tour of war at sea*. Douglas and McIntyre, Vancouver, Canada.

Dongoske, Kurt E., Mark Aldenderfer, and Karen Doehner (editors)
  2000   *Working together: Native Americans and archaeologists*. Society for American Archaeology, Washington, D.C.

Doran, J. E.
  1970   Systems theory, computer simulations, and archaeology. *World Archaeology* 1:289–298.

Earle, Timothy K., and Jonathon E. Ericson (editors)
  1977   *Exchange systems in prehistory*. Academic Press, New York.

Ebert, James I.
  1980   Remote Sensing in Large-Scale Cultural Resources Survey: A Case Study from the Arctic. In *Cultural Resources Remote Sensing*, edited by T. R. Lyons and F. J. Mathien, pp. 7–54. Remote Sensing Division, Southwest Cultural Resources Center, National Park Service and the University of New Mexico. National Park Service, Washington, D.C.

Fagan, Brian
  1990   The Rose Affair. *Archaeology* 43(2):12–14, 76.

Flannery, Kent V.
  1982   The Golden Marshalltown. *American Anthropologist* 84:265–278.

Flannery, Kent V. (editor)
  1976   *The Early Mesoamerican Village*. Academic Press, New York.

Ford, James A.
  1954   On the Concept of Types. *American Anthropologist* 56:42–53.

Gero, Joan, and Doloris Root
  1996   Public Presentations and Private Concerns: Archaeology in the Pages of *National Geographic*. In *Contemporary Archaeology in Theory: A Reader*, edited by Robert Preucel and Ian Hodder, pp. 531–548. Blackwell Press, Oxford.

Glascock, M. D.
  2000   The status of activations analysis in archaeology and geochemistry. *Journal of Radioanalytical and Nuclear Chemistry* 244(3):537–541.

Gould, Richard A.
  1980   *Living Archaeology.* Cambridge University Press, Cambridge.

Grayson, Donald K.
  1984   *Quantitative zooarchaeology: Topics in the analysis of archaeological faunas.* Academic Press, Orlando.

Green, E. L. (editor)
  1984   *Ethics and Values in Archaeology.* Free Press, New York.

Hayden, Brian., M. Eldridge, A. Eldridge, and Aubrey Cannon
  1985   Complex Hunter-Gatherers in Interior British Columbia. In *Prehistoric Hunter-Gatherers: The Emergence of Cultural Complexity,* edited by T. D. Price and J. A. Brown, pp. 181–200. Academic Press, Orlando.

Hodder, Ian (editor)
  1978a *Simulation studies in archaeology.* Cambridge University Press, Cambridge.
  1978b *The spatial organisation of culture.* University of Pittsburgh Press, Pittsburgh.

Hodder, Ian
  1982a Theoretical Archaeology: A Reactionary View. In *Symbolic and Structural Archaeology,* edited by I. Hodder, pp. 162–177. Cambridge University Press, Cambridge.
  1982b *Symbols in action: Ethnoarchaeological studies of material culture.* Cambridge University Press, Cambridge.
  1986   *Reading the past: Current approaches to interpretation in archaeology.* Cambridge University Press, Cambridge.
  1999   *The archaeological process: An introduction.* Blackwell, Malden, Massachusetts.

Holl, Augustin
  2004   *Saharan rock art: Archaeology of Tassilian pastoralist iconography.* AltaMira, Walnut Creek, California.

Hrdlicka, Ales
  1945   *The Aleutian and Commander Islands and Their Inhabitants.* Wistar Institute of Anatomy and Biology Press, Philadelphia.

Johnson, Gregory
  1982   Organizational Structure and Scalar Stress. In *Theory and Explanation in Archaeology,* edited by C. A. Renfrew, pp. 389–421. Academic Press, New York.

Keyser, James D.
  2004   *Art of the warriors: Rock art of the American Plains.* University of Utah Press, Salt Lake City.

Kidder, Alfred V.
1924 *An Introduction to the Study of Southwestern Archaeology.* Rev. ed. 1962. Yale University Press, New Haven, Connecticut.

King, Thomas F.
1998 *Cultural resource laws and practice: An introductory guide.* AltaMira, Walnut Creek, California.

Kvamme, Kenneth L.
1985 Determining Empirical Relationships between the Natural Environment and Prehistoric Site locations: A Hunter-Gatherer Example. In *For Concordance in Archaeological Analysis: Bridging Data Structure, Quantitative Technique, and Theory,* edited by C. Carr, pp. 208–238. Westport, Kansas City, Missouri.
1989 Geographic Information Systems in Regional Archaeological Research and Data Management. In *Archaeological Method and Theory:* Vol. 1., edited by Michael Schiffer, pp. 139–204. University of Arizona Press, Tucson
1999 Recent Directions and Developments in Geographical Information Systems. *Journal of Archaeological Research* 7(2):153–201.

Lambert, Joseph B.
1997 *Traces of the Past: Unraveling the Secrets of Archaeology through Chemistry.* Helix Books/Perseus Books, Reading, Massachusetts.

Lambert, Patricia M.
2002 The archaeology of war: A North American perspective. *Journal of Archaeological Research* 10:207–241.

Larsen, Clark S.
1997 *Bioarchaeology: Interpreting Behavior from the Human Skeleton.* Cambridge University Press, Cambridge.

Laughlin, William S.
1951 Notes on an Aleutian core and blade industry. *American Antiquity* 17(1):52–55.

Layton, Robert (editor)
1989 *Who needs the past? Indigenous values and archaeology.* Routledge, London.

Leone, Mark P.
1982 Some Opinions about Recovering Mind. *American Antiquity* 47:742–760.

Lock, G. R., and T. M. Harris
1996 Danebury revisited: An English Iron Age hillfort in a digital landscape. In *Anthropology, space and geographic information systems,* edited by M. Aldenderfer and H. D. G. Maschner, pp. 214–240. Oxford University Press, New York.

Longacre, William A.
1970   *Archaeology as anthropology: a case study.* University of Arizona Press, Tucson.

Lyman, R. Lee
1994   *Vertebrate taphonomy.* Cambridge University Press, Cambridge.

Lyman, R. Lee, and Kenneth P. Cannon (editors)
2004   *Zooarchaeology and conservation biology.* University of Utah Press, Salt Lake City.

McBurney, Charles Brian Montagu
1967   *The Haua Fteah (Cyrenaica) and the Stone Age of the South-East Mediterranean.* Cambridge University Press, London.

Mantler, M., and M. Schreiner
2001   X-ray Analysis of objects in art and archaeology. *Journal of Radioanalytical and Nuclear Chemistry* 247(3):635–644.

Maschner, Herbert D. G. (editor)
1996a *New methods, old problems: Geographic information systems in modern archaeological research.* Occasional Paper, 23. Southern Illinois University, Carbondale.
1996b *Darwinian Archaeologies.* Plenum, New York.
1996c Theory, Technology, and the Future of Geographic Information Systems in Archaeology. In *New Methods, Old Problems: Geographic Information Systems in Modern Archaeological Research,* edited by H. Maschner, pp. 301–308. Center for Archaeological Investigations Press.
1996d The Politics of Settlement Choice on the Prehistoric Northwest Coast. In *Anthropology, Space, and Geographic Information Systems,* edited by M. Aldenderfer and H. Maschner, pp. 175–189. Oxford University Press.

Maschner, Herbert D. G., and R. Alexander Bentley (editors)
2005   *Handbook of Archaeological Theory.* AltaMira, Walnut Creek, California, in press.

Maschner, Herbert D. G. and Katherine L. Reedy-Maschner.
2005   Letter from Alaska: Aleuts and the Sea. *Archaeology* March–April, pp. 63–70.

Mathieu, James R. (editor)
2002   *Experimental archaeology: Replicating past objects, behaviors, and processes.* Archaeopress, Oxford, England.

Mithen, Stephen
1989   Evolutionary Theory and Post-Processual Archaeology. *Antiquity* 63:483–494.

Nelson, Sarah Milledge
1997   *Gender in archaeology: Analyzing power and prestige.* AltaMira, Walnut Creek, California.

Nelson, Sarah Milledge, and Myriam Rosen-Ayalon (editors)
2002   *In pursuit of gender: Worldwide archaeological approaches.* AltaMira, Walnut Creek, California.

Novak, Shannon A., and Derinna Kopp
2003   To feed a tree in Zion: Osteological analysis of the 1857 Mountain Meadows massacre. *Historical Archaeology* 37(2):85–108.

O'Brien, Michael J., and R. Lee Lyman
2000   *Applying evolutionary archaeology: A systematic approach.* New York: Kluwer Academic/Plenum.
2003   *Cladistics and archaeology.* University of Utah Press, Salt Lake City

Odell, George H.
2004   *Lithic analysis.* Kluwer Academic/Plenum Publishers, New York.

O'Rourke, Dennis H., M. Geoffrey Hayes, Shawn W. Carlyle
2000   Ancient DNA Studies in Physical Anthropology. *Annual Review of Anthropology* 29:217–242.

Paine, Richard R.
1997   *Integrating archaeological demography: Multidisciplinary approaches to prehistoric population.* Occasional Papers 24, pp. 191–204. Center for Archaeological Investigations, Carbondale, Illinois.

Pasquinucci, Marinella, and Frédéric Trément (editors)
2000   *Non-destructive techniques applied to landscape archaeology.* Oxbow Books, Oxford.

Pitt-Rivers, Augustus Henry Lane-Fox
1887–1898   *Excavations in Cranborne Chase, near Rushmore, on the borders of Dorset and Wilts.* 4 volumes. Harrison and Sons, Printers, printed privately, London.

Petrie, Sir William Matthew Flinders
1904   *Methods and aims in archaeology.* Macmillan, New York.

Pillay, A. E.
2001   Analysis of Archaeological Artifacts: PIXE, XRF or ICP-MS? *Journal of Radioanalytical and Nuclear Chemistry.* 247(3):593–595.

Piperno, Dolores R., and Karen E. Stothert
2003   Phytolith evidence for early Holocene *Cucurbita* domestication in southwest Ecuador. *Science* 299:1054–1057.

Preucel, Robert, and Ian Hodder
1996   Representations and Antirepresentations. In *Contemporary Archaeology in Theory: A Reader,* edited by Robert Preucel and Ian Hodder, pp. 519–530. Blackwell Press, Oxford.

Reher, Charles A. (editor)
1977   *Settlement and subsistence along the lower Chaco River.* University of New Mexico Press, Albuquerque.

Renfrew, Colin
1978   Space, Time, and Polity. In *The Evolution of Social Systems,* edited by J. Friedman and M. J. Rowlands, pp. 89–112.

Renfrew, Colin, and Paul Bahn
1996   *Archaeology: Theories Method and Practice,* 2nd ed. Thames and Hudson, London.
2004   *Archaeology: Theories, Methods, and Practice.* 4th ed. Thames and Hudson, London.

Rice, Prudence M.
1987   *Pottery analysis: A sourcebook.* University of Chicago Press, Chicago.

Ruggles, C., and D. J. Medyckyj-Scott
1996   Site location, landscape visibility and symbolic astronomy: A Scottish case study. In *New methods, old problems: Geographic information systems in modern archaeological research,* edited by H. D. G. Maschner, pp. 127–146. Southern Illinois University, Carbondale, Illinois.

Salmon, Merrilee H.
1982   *Philosophy and archaeology.* Academic Press, New York.

Sanders, William T., Jeffrey R. Parsons, and Robert S. Santley
1979   *The basin of Mexico: Ecological processes in the evolution of a civilization.* Academic Press, New York.

Schiffer, Michael B.
1976   *Behavioral archaeology.* Academic Press, New York.

Schliemann, Heinrich
1880   *Ilios: The city and country of the Trojans.* Harper and Brothers, New York.

Segebade, C., H. P. Weise, and G. J. Lutz
1988   *Photon Activation Analysis.* deGruyter, New York.

Shennan, Stephen
1997   *Quantifying archaeology.* 2nd ed. Iowa City: University of Iowa Press.
2002   *Genes, memes, and human history: Darwinian archaeology and cultural evolution.* Thames and Hudson, London.

Shimada, Izumi, and John F. Merkel
1991   Copper alloy metallurgy in ancient Peru. *Scientific American* 265:80–86.

Shimada, Izumi, and Ursel Wagner
2001   Peruvian black pottery production and metal working: A Middle Sicán craft workshop at Huaca Sialupe. *Materials Research Society Bulletin* 26:25–30.

South, Stanley
    1977a *Method and theory in historical archaeology*. Academic Press, New York.
    1977b (editor) *Research strategies in historical archeology*. Academic Press, New York.

Spaulding, Albert C.
    1953 Statistical Techniques for the Study of Artifact Types. *American Antiquity* 18:305–313.

Swidler, Nina, Kurt E. Dongoske, Roger Anyon, and Alan S. Downer (editors)
    1997 *Native Americans and archaeologists: Stepping stones to common ground*. AltaMira, Walnut Creek, California.

Thomas, David Hurst
    1976 *Figuring anthropology: First principles of probability and statistics*. Holt, Rinehart and Winston, New York.

Tonchev, A. P., J. F. Harmon, and B. D. King
    1999 Application of Low Energy Photon Spectroscopy in Isomer Production of Hf, W, Ir, Pt, Au and Hg Using (gamma, gamma') Reactions. *Nuclear Instruments and Methods in Physics Research A*:422–510.

Trigger, Bruce
    1996 Alternative Archaeologies: Nationalist, Colonialist, Imperialist. In *Contemporary Archaeology in Theory: A Reader*, edited by Robert Preucel and Ian Hodder, pp. 616–631. Blackwell Press, Oxford.

van der Leeuw, Sander, and James McGlade (editors)
    1997 *Time, process, and structured transformation in archaeology*. Routledge, London, New York.

Wailes, Bernard (editor)
    1996 *Craft specialization and social evolution: In memory of V. Gordon Childe*. University of Pennsylvania Museum, Philadelphia.

Walde, Dale, and Noreen D. Willows (editors)
    1989 *The archaeology of gender: Proceedings of the Twenty-second Annual Conference of the Archaeological Association of the University of Calgary*. University of Calgary, Calgary.

Walker, Phillip L.
    1997 Wife beating, boxing, and broken noses: Skeletal evidence for the cultural patterning of violence. In *Troubled Times: Violence and Warfare in the Past*, edited by D. Martin and D. Frayer, pp. 145–175. Gordon and Breach, Amsterdam.

Watson, Patty Jo, Steven A. LeBlanc, and Charles L. Redman
    1971 *Explanation in archeology; an explicitly scientific approach*. Columbia University Press, New York.

Weyer, Enrst M., Jr.
  1929 *An Aleutian burial.* Anthropological Papers, Vol. 31, Pt. 3. American Museum of Natural History, New York.

Wheatley, David
  1996 The use of GIS to understand regional variation in Neolithic Wessex. In *New methods, old problems: Geographic information systems in modern archaeological research,* edited by H. D. G. Maschner, pp. 75–103. Southern Illinois University at Carbondale, Carbondale, Illinois.

Wheatley, David, and Mark Gillings
  2002 *Spatial technology and archaeology: The archaeological applications of GIS.* Taylor and Francis, New York.

Wheeler, Robert Eric Mortimer, Sir
  1966 *Civilizations of the Indus Valley and beyond.* Thames and Hudson, London.

Whitley, David S. (editor)
  2001 *Handbook of rock art research.* AltaMira, Walnut Creek, California.

Willey, Gordon R.
  1953 *Prehistoric Settlements in the Virú Valley, Peru.* Smithsonian Institution, Washington D.C.

Willey, Gordon R., and Philip Phillips
  1958 *Method and Theory in American Archaeology.* University of Chicago Press, Chicago.

Wylie, Alison
  1982 Epistemological issues raised by a structuralist archaeology. In *Symbolic and Structural Archaeology,* edited by I. Hodder, pp. 39–46. Cambridge University Press, Cambridge.
  1991 Gender Theory and the Archaeological Record: Why is There No Archaeology of Gender? In *Engendering Archeology: Women and Prehistory,* edited by Joan M. Gero and Margaret W. Conkey, pp. 31–54.

Yellen, John E.
  1977 *Archaeological approaches to the present: Models for reconstructing the past.* Academic Press, New York.

Yesner, David R.
  1980 Maritime Hunter-Gatherers: Ecology and Prehistory. *Current Anthropology* 21:727–750.

2

Short History of Archaeological Methods, 1870 to 1960

Brian Fagan

When the German businessman-turned-archaeologist Heinrich Schliemann dug into the Hissarlik mound in search of Homeric Troy in 1871, he enlisted the assistance of engineers who had worked on the Suez Canal. Schliemann had an eye for the big picture and thought on a grand scale. His trenches were enormous, his labor force in the hundreds. In a time of frenzied archaeological discovery, no one thought twice about having engineers do the excavating or the damage that such excavation—and it really was industrial-scale excavation—would do to the priceless archaeological record in Hissarlik's layers. Schliemann's excavations were one of the last whimpers of the heroic age, when one could find an ancient civilization in a week and dazzle the world with exhibitions of truly spectacular finds. His excavations resembled a construction site rather than a scientific investigation.

To attempt a survey of the early history of archaeological methods requires navigating an enormous literature of excavations and other innovations. I have chosen to be selective, to identify a few major individuals who made important contributions and those methodological milestones, such as radiocarbon dating, that truly changed the course of archaeology. Inevitably, most of these come from the Old World, where most early discoveries were made, but I also describe some major innovations in American archaeology. Wherever possible, I have cross-referenced the text to the original publications written by the pioneers. Some are beautifully written. Others are remarkable for their turgid prose. But they all give a unique impression of the world in which our archaeological predecessors worked. The cadences and balances in their publications, the illustrations, the very appearance and feel of the books carry meaning beyond what one reads in a general history of the subject—and I list a few such synthetic works in the references at the end of this chapter.

Conze, Curtius, and Pitt-Rivers

Even as Schliemann's discoveries hit the headlines, the first stirrings of more scientific methods were apparent, notably in the hands of German classical archaeologists. Working on the Aegean Islands and Greek mainland under the sponsorship of the king of Prussia, Alexander Conze (1831–1914) excavated the shrine of the Cabiri on the island of Samothrace in the northern Aegean with meticulous care in 1871 (Conze 1875–1880). An architect was on site at all times, a photographer recorded the excavations, and a warship anchored offshore provided logistical support. This work, it can reasonably be said, marks the beginning of systematic excavation, of archaeological methods as we know them today. Hence, in this chapter, I begin at 1870.

The Germans under Conze's student Ernst Curtius (1814–1896) then moved to Olympia, site of the Olympic Games, where between 1875 and 1880 they excavated the stadium, surrounding temples, and other buildings, again with an architect present at all times (Curtius 1882). The archaeologists also renounced all claims to the finds, which were housed in a specially constructed museum on the site. Both the Olympia and Samothrace excavations were published in full in sumptuous detail, complete with architectural drawings and photographs.

Conze and Curtius set new standards for archaeological excavation and recording, paying careful attention to even small finds, a far cry from the unbridled treasure hunters of yesteryear. They had the advantage of almost unlimited resources and all the time in the world, so the impact of their research on the wider world of archaeology was regrettably small.

In southern England, General Augustus Henry Lane-Fox Pitt-Rivers (1827–1900) excavated with rigor equal to, if not greater than, the Germans, but on much smaller and more compact sites located on his vast country estates of Cranborne Chase (Bowden 1991). Pitt-Rivers was of aristocratic birth but modest means. He pursued a successful career as an artillery officer and became an expert on firearms of all kinds. His professional specialty kindled an interest in antique guns and in the evolution of weapons of all kinds. While still in the army, he was strongly influenced by Charles Darwin's *On the Origin of Species by Means of Natural Selection* (1859), arguing that natural selection also applied to artifacts. He carried out some minor excavations, where he applied his exact military mind to the observation of stratigraphic trenches cut across Roman and Iron Age earthworks.

In 1880 a series of unexpected family deaths made him the sole heir of his uncle's immense fortune and master of the 10,900 ha of Cranborne Chase in the chalk country of southern England, a huge estate exceptionally rich in archaeological sites of all kinds. Cranborne Chase was a rural landscape, a great tract of medieval hunting country that had never been plowed. Pitt-Rivers realized that he had a unique chance to investigate ancient burial mounds, earthworks, and Roman villas on his property. He started with Bronze Age barrows (burial mounds), then moved on to Winklebury Camp, an Iron Age fort. There he cross-sectioned ramparts to date the earthworks from artifacts found in the strata.

In 1884 he turned from earthworks to a Roman military camp at Woodcutts Common, several acres of low banks, humps, and hollows. Pitt-Rivers had workers clear off the top soil, then dig out the dark irregularities in the white chalk subsoil and trace the outlines of ditches, hearths, pits, and postholes. This was revolutionary archaeology in the 1880s. In 1893 he shifted his attention to Wor Barrow, a Stone Age earthwork used for communal burials. His predecessors had simply trenched into burial mounds and removed the human remains and grave furniture. Pitt-Rivers excavated the entire mound, including 16 skeletons, leaving a row of earthen pillars down the center, which recorded the layering. At one end of the mound he found a rectangular outline of trenches in the chalk, where the uprights of a large building protected six bodies. In a final exercise in archaeological science, he left the ditches that surrounded the mound open for 4 years, then re-excavated them to see how chalk ditches broke down and filled with sediment after abandonment as a way to better interpret his excavations.

Pitt-Rivers was gifted with superb organizational skills. He compiled four privately printed volumes, *Excavations on Cranborne Chase* (1887–1898), heavily illustrated large-format books describing every detail of his excavations. He ran his excavations on disciplined, military lines, working with small teams of trained workers under site supervisors, who had two assistants, one a draftsman, the other a model maker. From the very beginning, Pitt-Rivers recorded the position of every find, including animal bones and seeds, however small. Throughout his excavations, he thought of his sites in three dimensions, a legacy from his surveying days and a cornerstone of modern excavation methods. Each site was excavated completely down to bedrock, each layer recorded, and human disturbances of the soil noted. Pitt-Rivers pioneered the use of photography to record his sites and insisted on prompt publication of the results. Unlike his contemporaries, he was interested in how earthworks were formed and weathered by the elements.

Pitt-Rivers had no patience for archaeologists who just searched for objects. He considered science "organized common sense," a principle he followed throughout his excavations. His contemporaries considered him eccentric, but he was unrepentant. In the museum housing his collections, firearms, tribal artifacts, and archaeological finds were displayed in evolutionary sequences, from the simple to the more complex. Pitt-Rivers believed that archaeology should be part of everyone's education, so that the public could learn the links between past and present. He provided free Sunday concerts for visitors to the museum.

General Augustus Lane-Fox Pitt-Rivers was years ahead of his time, but his methods are the cornerstone of all modern archaeological excavation. It was not until the 1920s that other European researchers took proper note of his pioneering excavation methods.

Flinders Petrie, Potsherds, and Cross-Dating

Both the Germans and Pitt-Rivers had stressed the importance of the small object in the study of the past. Another Englishman, William Matthew Flinders Petrie (1853–1942), first went out to Egypt in 1880, just as Pitt-Rivers was starting work on Cranborne Chase (Drower 1995). A surveyor's son, Petrie had little formal schooling but picked up an excellent knowledge of surveying and geometry from his father. In 1872 the two of them made the first accurate survey of Stonehenge in southern England. Eight years later, Petrie went out to Egypt, where he spent 2 years making the first scientific survey of the Pyramids of Giza (Petrie 1883). He had plenty of time to collect potsherds and other small objects, which made him realize that many of archaeology's most significant clues came from the small and seemingly unimportant. At the same time, he was disgusted with what passed for excavation along the Nile. "It is sickening to see the rate at which everything is being destroyed, and the little regard paid to preservation," he wrote in *Methods and Aims in Archaeology* (1904).

Petrie's monograph on the Giza survey (1883) established his reputation. He now turned from survey work to excavation, digging on behalf of the Egypt Exploration Fund from 1883 to 1887. Then he branched out on his own as a freelance excavator, digging in Egypt each winter and writing up his finds in England the following summer. Petrie's methods, rough by today's standards, were a vast improvement on those of many of his contemporaries. Living under very primitive conditions and working with minimal funds, Petrie supervised large gangs of laborers, whom he paid for reporting small finds such as beads and papyri. Year after year, he excavated pyramids and tombs, towns and cemeteries, paying careful attention to small objects. Several generations of archaeologists learned excavation under him, a demanding experience. Receiving little formal instruction, they were sent out to work without close supervision for many hours in the hot sun and spent hours each evening sorting and classifying pot fragments. There were few creature comforts. Petrie was notorious for the austere regimen in his camp, where the food was appalling. But those who survived several seasons with him became tough, competent excavators, among them the artist Howard Carter, who was to discover the undisturbed tomb of the pharaoh Tutankhamun in 1922.

Petrie was one of the first to realize that ancient Egyptian civilization did not flourish in isolation but traded with much of the eastern Mediterranean world. He used the precisely dated and highly distinctive pottery at the New Kingdom community at Ghurab to date Schliemann's Mycenaean civilization to approximately 1500 to 1000 B.C. (Petrie 1891). This innovative method, known today as cross-dating, used closely dated sites in Egypt to date distant prehistoric sites as far afield as temperate Europe: when the same pot fragments known at Ghurab were found at a site on the Greek mainland, they provided a date for that otherwise undatable occupation level far from the Nile. Petrie's cross-dating method, still widely used by archaeologists today, proved a vital dating tool for establishing the chronology of the Minoan civilization in Crete (see later description).

In 1892 Petrie was appointed the first professor of Egyptology at the University of London, a remarkable appointment for a man who never earned a university degree. Two years later, Petrie made one of his most important discoveries, a series of enormous desert cemeteries near the town of Naqada in Upper Egypt that dated to centuries before the beginning of pharaonic Egypt in about 3100 B.C. He cleared more than 2,000 graves in 1894 alone, each containing a skeleton and decorated clay pots. Petrie studied them grave by grave, each as a separate sealed unit, and found there were gradual changes in the shapes of vessels and their decoration over time. What were once practical handles for lifting pots eventually degenerated over time into mere painted squiggles. So many graves were found that Petrie was able to arrange them in chronological stages of development, working back from a royal grave that linked his stages to older and otherwise undated graves. This bold and revolutionary attempt to date cultures much earlier than Egyptian civilization was used for years and became known as *sequence dating* (Petrie 1889, 1896). The same principles of artifact ordering are still used in the elaborate seriations of potsherds and other objects commonplace today.

Max Uhle and Stratigraphic Observation

By the closing decade of the nineteenth century, the small archaeological world was still largely made up of amateurs, many of them people of independent means. Most excavators worked in Europe or the eastern Mediterranean. Everyone knew everyone else, which meant that there was a constant interchange of information. Training was at best rudimentary, aspiring archaeologists learning excavation on someone else's dig before commencing their own. Many people started major excavations with virtually no experience at all, among them Arthur Evans (1851–1941), who discovered the Minoan civilization of Crete at Knossos in the first major excavation of the twentieth century (J. Evans 1943). Fortunately for science, he employed an experienced archaeologist, Douglas Mackenzie, as his field assistant.

Excavation was still a crude science, but stratigraphic observation was assuming increasing importance in the field. The inspiration for such observations came from many sources—geology, excavations in the Cro-Magnon caves of southwestern France, and pioneering studies in European culture history by the Swedish archaeologist Oscar Montelius (1885) and others. Stratigraphic excavation also took hold in the Americas during the middle to late nineteenth century in the hands of Ephraim Squier and Edwin Davis, who excavated earthworks in the Ohio Valley during the 1840s, and with the Mound Builder researches of Cyrus Thomas during the 1880s and 1890s (Squier and Davis 1848; Thomas 1894). These were crude observations at best compared with the more careful investigations by the German-born archaeologist Max Uhle (1856–1944), a gifted excavator who carried out some of the first stratigraphic excavations on the Peruvian coast, notably at Pachamachac (Uhle 1903).

Uhle was a careful and perceptive observer, above all a stratigraphy man. He also knew that the artifacts in each level were valuable markers—evidence of possible cultural change through time. In 1902 Uhle was retained by the University of California, Berkeley, to excavate a huge shell mound at Emeryville, on the east shore of San Francisco Bay. Trenching into the mound "stratum by stratum," Uhle boldly identified no less than 10 principal layers. He took his excavation down to the water table and below, until he reached sterile alluvial clay. His carefully drawn cross section delineates his levels and even counts the number of artifacts found in each one. He pointed out that the artifacts in the upper strata were entirely different from the implements found in the lower levels. At the same time, he recognized much cultural continuity from one layer to the next (Uhle 1907).

In the end, Uhle segregated two major components in the mound, each comprising 5 of his 10 strata. The people of the lower component had subsisted mainly on oysters rather than bent-nose clams; they buried their dead in a flexed position and made their simple stone tools almost entirely from local chert, a finely crystallized quartz. The later inhabitants cremated their dead, consumed enormous numbers of clams rather than oysters, and used imported obsidian for many of their stone tools. The young German's excavation methods—nothing to write home about by modern standards—were better than those of most of his contemporaries. He used picks and shovels to uncover stratified layers but took the trouble to record the occupation levels with drawings and photographs. Unlike most others, he also took the trouble to publish his finds in a carefully prepared monograph in 1907.

Direct-Historical Method

Uhle worked in California at a time of rapid change in archaeological methods. The researches of Adolph Bandelier and Frank Cushing and others in the Southwest and those of Cyrus Thomas on eastern earthworks had shown the close links between living and ancient Native American groups and the potential for working back from the present into the past, the direct-historical method (Fowler 2000).

By the dawn of the twentieth century, that notion of working from the present into the past was well understood by many American archaeologists, but it was rarely applied on a large scale until the Harvard archaeologist Alfred Kidder excavated the great middens at Pecos, New Mexico, in 1915–1921.

Alfred Kidder (1885–1963) attended a field school in the Southwest run by the pioneer archaeologist Edgar Hewitt in

1907 (Givens 1992). As a doctoral student, he received training in field methods from the Egyptologist George Reisner, whose methods were far superior to those of Petrie. Art historian George Chase gave him a sound grounding in the analysis of ceramics (clay vessels) of all kinds. It was no coincidence that Kidder's doctoral dissertation was on the style and decorative motifs of Pueblo pottery. He also learned from Franz Boas, who gave Kidder a sense of the importance of detailed analysis of any human society, a point he took to heart. Kidder also traveled in the Near East, where he had a chance to visit excavations by George Reisner and others on the Nile. There he absorbed excavation methods unknown in the United States, such as systematic burial excavation and careful observation of sequences of human occupation through time. Such techniques were still in their infancy. He also realized just how important the humble pot fragment and other tiny artifacts were for the study of the past.

In 1915 Alfred Kidder embarked on the most important work of his career, excavating into the deep, stratified layers of Pecos Pueblo, New Mexico, a settlement close by a Spanish mission and known to have been occupied far back into ancient times. Up until then, most southwestern excavation had been little concerned with recording different periods of occupation, more concerned with recovering fragile artifacts such as baskets, clearing ruins, and beautifully decorated Pueblo pots. In 1914 archaeologist Nels C. Nelson had dug into San Cristobal Pueblo, New Mexico, in 0.3-m levels, from which he recovered different pottery types. But it was left to Kidder to explain what these differences meant.

Kidder excavated into the deep layers of Pecos on a massive scale. During the early seasons, he refined Nelson's San Cristobal approach by abandoning arbitrary levels and making detailed sketches of the way the refuse discarded by the inhabitants had accumulated. He traced the natural strata of the middens and carefully recorded the pot fragments found in them. Kidder (1924) followed Reisner's example in Egypt. He used pegs and strings to record the precise rise and fall of even the smallest ash layers. His potsherd catalogs were also modeled on those used by Reisner, employed along the Nile to develop a meticulous analysis of the profound changes in pottery forms and, above all, in surface decoration over many centuries. For example, Kidder found that the first occupants of the pueblo made a distinctive black-on-white style of pottery. At the same time, he recovered hundreds of human skeletons.

While waiting for induction into the U.S. Army in 1917, Kidder visited modern-day Hopi and other pueblos in the Southwest and learned much about southwestern ethnography and modern Pueblo culture. In all his subsequent researches, he melded anthropology and archaeology, the living culture and the ancient, into definitive summaries of ancient Pueblo society.

Excavations at Pecos resumed in 1920, with the discovery of still more human burials. Kidder called on the expert services of biological anthropologist Ernest Albert Hooton. He insisted that Hooton visit the excavations, so he could study the human remains as they emerged in the trenches and witness the actual field conditions of their discovery. This was one of the first cases where a skeletal expert worked in the field alongside a North American archaeologist. Soon Kidder had data on the sex and age of the skeletons, as well as some interesting information on life expectancy and ancient pathology. Hooton (1930) showed, for example, that most of the Pecos people died in their twenties.

By 1922 Kidder had turned his attention to the architecture and expansion of the pueblo and excavated some of the earliest occupation levels. By 1924, when he published his classic *An Introduction to Southwestern Archaeology,* he was confident enough to develop a detailed sequence of ancient Pueblo and pre-Pueblo cultures for the Southwest, using his stratigraphic excavations and pottery studies from Pecos. This was the first culture-historical sequence of any region in North America. Kidder's sequence began with Basket Maker cultures, at least 2,000 years old, which eventually evolved into the Pueblo societies.

Alfred Kidder established many of the basic principles of North American archaeology. The artifact classification systems he developed at Pecos arranged potsherds by such categories as method of manufacture, decoration, and form, in much the same kind of taxonomy that Carolus Linnaeus had used for plants. His influence is felt in Southwest archaeology to this day.

Field Archaeology and Aerial Photography

Archaeology was a gentleman's pursuit and often a country gentleman's calling in the first half of the twentieth century. Thus was born a long and vibrant tradition of European archaeology—walking the countryside in search of earthworks, burial mounds, artifacts, and less-conspicuous archaeological sites. The tradition went back to medieval times in Britain and Scandinavia, involving a wide spectrum of amateur and professional archaeologists. They came to what they called "field archaeology" with a keen eye for country and landscape and strong instincts for archaeological discovery. The sophisticated settlement archaeology of today was born in such researches in the hands of countrymen such as O. G. S. Crawford (1886–1957), a trained geographer who spent the early years of his career surveying earthworks and ancient landscapes. Crawford became the first archaeology officer of Britain's Ordnance Survey and was responsible for the first archaeological maps produced by the government (Daniel 1991).

Crawford served as an observer in Britain's Royal Flying Corps in World War I. He flew over the western front, spotted ancient earthworks from the air, and realized at once the potential of aerial photography for studying archaeological sites in the context of a wider landscape. Both French and German aviators working in military intelligence also studied archaeological sites from the air, especially in Mesopotamia. Crawford and marmalade heir Alexander Keiller hired an aircraft in 1927 to photograph more than 200 archaeological sites in southern Britain over 2 months. Their joint volume, *Wessex from the Air* (1928), was the first archaeological monograph devoted entirely to aerial photography of archaeological sites.

Meanwhile, landscape geographers exercised a strong influence on British archaeology. Cambridge-trained archaeologist Cyril Fox came under the influence of human geographers and applied geographic interpretations of the past to a region within a 40-km radius of the city of Cambridge, studying the distributions of archaeological sites against a background of natural environment and ancient vegetational cover (Fox 1923). He then applied his approach to all of England, Scotland, and Wales, where he distinguished between the highland and lowland areas of Britain, describing his research in a landmark book, *The Personality of Britain* (1932), which caused a major stir.

Both Crawford's and Fox's work, like that of human geographers, was based on simple notions of environmental change and ecology, combined with aerial photography and long hours of surveying archaeological sites on the ground. They were not alone in this approach, which some French human geographers and a few German scholars also adopted.

At the time, most British and European archaeologists were enmeshed in artifacts and artifact classification, just as their nineteenth-century predecessors had been. They were preoccupied with artifact classification, chronology, and cultural groups, work stemming directly from the researches of Jens Worsaae, Montelius, and other Scandinavian scholars. In a sense, archeology of this genre was a little like stamp collecting, an activity more concerned with artifacts than with the people who made them. A few voices were raised to express a contrary view, many pointing to the remarkable organic finds that came from Swiss lake dwellings and from Mesolithic sites in Denmark. The Cambridge University archaeologist Miles Burkitt, a Stone Age specialist, argued that "the prime objective of prehistoric archaeology was not only to classify and date artifacts so much as to throw light on the life of the communities that made and used them" (Burkitt 1921). A few years later, his student Grahame Clark, later to become a world-famous prehistorian, rebelled even more strongly. "I was concerned to attack . . . the kind of archaeology promoted by museum curators" (Clark 1939a).

Leonard Woolley and Ur:
The Last of the Classic Excavations

Leonard Woolley (1880–1960) learned his excavation techniques on a brief and very casual dig in a Roman fort on Hadrian's Wall in northern England (Winstone 1990). He was appointed assistant director of the Ashmolean Museum under Arthur Evans in 1905 and then spent five seasons, 1907–1911, working in the Sudan on large cemeteries. This gave him hard experience with handling local people, at which Woolley became exceptionally skilled. At the time, hands-on experience in the Nile Valley was the best archaeological training in the world.

In 1912 Woolley became field director of the British Museum excavations into the Hittite city at Carchemish, by a strategic crossing on the Euphrates in Syria. His assistant was T. E. Lawrence, later to achieve immortality as Lawrence of Arabia. The Carchemish excavation was a classic example of large-scale excavation at the height of the imperial era. From the beginning, Woolley took a firm hand with local officials and with his workers, who adored him. When a local official refused to issue an excavation permit, Woolley drew a revolver and held it to the official's head until he signed. He could get away with it, because British power and prestige in the area was at its height (Woolley 1920).

The Carchemish excavations began with the removal of much of the Roman city (Woolley 1912–1952). Woolley was able to dispose of the stone to the German engineers who were building a railroad line to Baghdad nearby. At the same time, he and Lawrence spied on German activities for the Foreign Office. Once the lower, Hittite levels were exposed, Woolley divided his workers into teams of pickmen, supported by shovelers and basketmen, a method he used for a half century at all his excavations. There was nothing new in this approach, which had been established practice since Austen Henry Layard's excavations at Nineveh a century earlier. Woolley introduced one new wrinkle. Important finds were rewarded with a cash payment and a volley of rifle fire. A silly practice to the outside observer, perhaps, but Woolley knew that his men prized this noisy symbol of success. He worked closely with his assistant, Sheikh Hamoudi, a man who admitted to two passions in his life: archaeology and violence.

Woolley could never relax in the volatile political situation. The archaeologists carried firearms for protection. Woolley found that the best strategy was to behave like the surrounding desert chieftains, so that he was treated as one of their equals. As a result, he was trusted on all sides and uncovered a magnificent Hittite city at the same time.

Carchemish was the final stage in Woolley's apprenticeship. During World War I, Woolley served as an intelligence officer in the Mesopotamian theater and became a prisoner of war of the Turks for 2 years. When World War I ended, the British Museum and the University of Pennsylvania received an excavation permit to conduct a major excavation at the biblical city of Ur, celebrated in the Old Testament as Abraham's home. For 13 seasons, 1922–1934, Woolley uncovered the Sumerian city of Ur with a ferocious energy that exhausted those around him (Winstone 1990).

Woolley was an exacting taskmaster who ran the excavations with the smallest of European staffs, relying heavily on his foreman Hamoudi and his three sons to handle the laborers. He was the ideal archaeologist for the job, capable of unraveling layers of long-abandoned buildings from jumbles of mud brick with uncanny skill. He could dissect a temple or recover the remains of a fragile wooden harp from the ground with equal deftness. He also had a genius for knowing when to wait. One of his 1922 trial trenches uncovered gold objects, perhaps from a royal cemetery. Woolley waited 4 years to excavate it fully, gaining the required expertise in the meantime. "Our object was to get history, not to fill museum cases with miscellaneous curiosities" (Woolley 1929:1).

To Woolley (1929), Ur was not a dead city, but a crowded settlement with busy streets. His huge excavations uncovered entire urban precincts. The excavations studied the architecture of the great ziggurat (pyramid) at Ur and probed to the depths of the city mound, to the earliest settlement of all—a tiny hamlet of reed huts, now known to date to before 5500 B.C.

The climax of the Ur excavations came in the late 1920s, when Woolley finally exposed the Royal Cemetery, with its spectacular burial pits. The scale of the excavation beggars the imagination. Woolley cleared more than 2,000 commoners' burials and 16 royal graves, using teams of specially trained workers. A series of death pits chronicled elaborate funeral ceremonies, where dozens of courtiers dressed in their finest regalia took poison, then lay down in the great pit to die with their master or mistress. Unfortunately, Woolley's notes are inadequate for modern archaeologists to establish from them whether his vivid reconstructions were, in fact, accurate. The spectacular finds rivaled those of Tutankhamun's tomb but were overshadowed by the golden pharaoh.

Leonard Woolley was one of the last archaeologists to work on a grand scale. Today's excavator moves less dirt in 3 months than Woolley's teams would move in a few days. The loss of significant information at Ur is incalculable.

Mortimer Wheeler and Scientific Excavation

Leonard Woolley's archaeological achievements were remarkable, but his methods were already outdated by 1930. One cannot blame him for using destructive methods, because he worked in the context of generally accepted standards for Mesopotamian archaeology at the time. His late-twentieth-century successors learned about excavation from a very different tradition, whose roots went back to the Victorian excavator General Pitt-Rivers.

The development of scientific excavation after World War I was, to a considerable extent, in the hands of one archaeologist, the British archaeologist Mortimer Wheeler (1890–1976; see Hawkes 1982). Wheeler's colorful life spanned the decades when archaeology was transformed into a scientific discipline. He studied classics at London University and then Roman pottery in the Rhineland before serving with distinction as an artillery officer in World War I.

By 1918 Wheeler had acquired the background and experience that were to guide his career. He had a fluent writing style inherited from his journalist father, a background in classics and archaeology from university, and a gift for logistics and organization, acquired in the army. In 1920 he was appointed keeper of archaeology at the newly founded National Museum of Wales. Four years later, he became director.

Between 1920 and 1926, Wheeler and his wife Tessa revolutionized Welsh archaeology with a series of major excavations on Roman frontier forts (Wheeler 1925, 1955). At the time, most archaeological excavation was little more than an uncontrolled search for spectacular artifacts. The Wheelers adopted and refined the almost forgotten excavation methods of General Pitt-Rivers. They fastidiously observed even minute layers in the soil, recovered the smallest of potsherds and other artifacts, and published technical reports promptly, illustrated with Wheeler's own fine drawings.

Every summer between 1926 and 1939, Wheeler excavated Roman and, later, Iron Age sites. In 1928 and 1929 he worked at a Roman sanctuary at Lydney in Gloucestershire (Wheeler 1932). Then he turned his attention to the late Iron Age and Roman city of Verulamium (modern-day Saint Albans) just north of London, where he spent 4 years, 1930–1933. Verulamium lay in open country, unlike many Roman towns that are buried under modern cities. He and Tessa exposed 4.45 ha of the city and traced the complicated history of its outlying earthworks and the smaller forts and settlements that had preceded it (Wheeler 1936).

The culmination of Wheeler's British excavations came when he turned his attention to the enormous Iron Age hill fort at Maiden Castle in southern England. During the summers of 1934 to 1937, he and Tessa developed the art of archaeological excavation to heights never achieved before, using a combination of vertical and horizontal excavation. They excavated deep trenches through Maiden Castle's serried earthen ramparts. They investigated broad areas of the interior with area trenches. An entire generation of young archaeologists worked at Maiden Castle, many of whom made major contributions to the field after World War II. Despite the tragic early death of Tessa and his return to the Royal Artillery with the outbreak of World War II in 1939, Wheeler published the final report on Maiden Castle in 1943.

Wheeler was appointed director general of the Archaeological Survey of India in 1943. During his 5 years' service, he taught an entire generation of Indian archaeologists his scientific excavation methods while excavating the Harappan cities of Harappa and Mohenjodaro and the frontier city of Charsada (Wheeler 1959, 1962).

Mortimer Wheeler dominates the history of excavation like a colossus. He was a formidable personality with bristling mustache and flowing hair, who tolerated little criticism and did not suffer fools. No one denied his talents as an organizer and leader, as the archaeologist who brought British and much European excavation and fieldwork into the modern world. His methods rubbed off on many archaeologists of the 1930s, among them Alexander Keiller and Stuart Piggott, who carried out a combination of limited excavation and restoration at the Avebury stone circles. German and Dutch archaeologists also developed sophisticated excavation methods, epitomized by the German excavator Gerhard Bersu, who exposed the plan of an Iron Age village at Little Woodbury in southern Britain with meticulous area excavation and innovative approaches to three-dimensional recording of stratigraphy (Bersu 1940).

The Wheeler tradition of excavation continued into the 1950s and 1960s, albeit refined, notably in the hands of such skilled excavators as Philip Barker, Martin Biddle, and Barry Cunliffe, working on Iron Age and later sites. All scientific excavation today is based on the principles that Wheeler enumerated in his classic manual, *Archaeology from the Earth* (Wheeler 1954).

Dating and Artifacts

Archaeology came of age during the first half of the twentieth century, not only in field survey and excavation but also in the study of artifacts in time and space. Culture history achieved a high degree of refinement during the 1920s and 1930s.

Gordon Childe and European Prehistory

There is not the space to discuss the development of typological approaches in the Old World and New, but the research of Oscar Montelius and many others resulted in the first culture-historical sequences for Europe, which were refined between the 1930s and 1950s by Vere Gordon Childe (1892–1957; see Trigger 1980). Childe, a brilliant linguist, wrote a series of syntheses of European prehistory based on wide travels and intensive research in the Danube basin. This research—a kind of narrative culture history in which artifacts and ancient societies take the place of kings, statesmen, and people—resulted in Childe's concepts of a "Neolithic" and "Urban Revolution" (Childe 1942). In this preradiocarbon era, Childe's revolutions and his typological methods dominated European thinking for a generation. The latter were based on a maze of stylistic connections and limited numbers of cross-dates from the eastern Mediterranean. Childe's European chronologies were based, very largely, on inspired guesswork, on which in turn he based his hypotheses that all ideas and innovations in prehistoric Europe derived from southwestern Asia: what he called *ex oriente lux* (from the east came inspiration).

When radiocarbon dates threw out Childe's timescales, he became so depressed at the failure of his life's work that he committed suicide in 1957.

North American Archaeology

The pace of archaeological research in North America accelerated in the early twentieth century, at a time when there was an increasing realization that ancient native American cultures had changed quite profoundly through time and space. Cultural distributions, in particular, drew early attention, notably in the definition of several Mound Builder societies, among them the Fort Ancient and Hopewell cultures by William C. Mills in Ohio as early as 1902—the first to use the word *culture* in an archaeological context in North America (Willey and Sabloff 1993). These and other cultures were predominantly geographic entities, defined by site distributions rather than chronologies, an approach that stemmed in part from Franz Boas's use of the ethnographic culture as a basic unit of study. Boas favored diffusionism and cultural relativism. He was himself little interested in North American archaeology, but his approaches strongly encouraged the assumption that Indian cultures had changed in the past.

As in Europe, the greatest problem facing American archaeology was that of reliable dating. In 1916 anthropologist Alfred Kroeber (1916) made surface collections of painted potsherds in the Zuni region and then used simple ordering methods, working back from the present, to place them in rough chronological order. Alfred Kidder (1924) applied Kroeber's ordering approach at Pecos, also stratigraphic observations and pottery from sealed graves, to work back from the present into the past.

Kidder's scheme offered a long chronological sequence and raised considerable interest, but it lacked an accurate timescale.

A University of Arizona astronomer, A. E. Douglass, developed tree-ring dating (dendrochronology) in 1901; it proved to be the key to southwestern chronology. Douglass developed a borer for sampling ancient beams without removing them, then used tree-ring sequences from them to work out a relative chronology for pueblos. For years he looked for a beam that would link his master curve, which was anchored to historical trees, to an earlier "floating" chronology for ancient pueblos. In 1929 Douglass finally recovered a beam from a ruin at Show Low, Arizona, that linked the ancient with the historical tree-ring sequences. Within a few weeks, he produced an accurate chronological framework for southwestern archaeology and the major pueblos. This, in turn, enabled him to date Pecos and its sequence of changing pottery styles (Douglass 1929).

The chronology of the rest of North American archaeology was a matter of informed (and usually inaccurate) guesswork until the 1960s. Not that many archaeologists of the time were that concerned, for they believed that North American prehistory had a relatively short timescale, no more than a few thousand years.

The Pecos sequence soon came under close scrutiny. A husband-and-wife team, Harold and Winifred Gladwin (1934), pointed out that Kidder's scheme referred more to the northern Southwest than the south. They proposed a hierarchical classification of cultural units for the entire Southwest, with three general roots—Basket Maker (later called Anasazi [now Ancestral Pueblo]), Hohokam, and Caddoan (later to become Mogollon). The Gladwins proposed a treelike classification stemming from these roots, with different regional branches and twigs, based on an implicitly chronological assumption—that southwestern cultures diversified through time.

In 1932 W. C. McKern and a group of Midwestern archaeologists developed the Midwestern taxonomic method to classify enormous amounts of data collected by both amateur and professional fieldworkers in a region where stratified sites were relatively uncommon (McKern 1939). In this purely taxonomic system, based on artifact forms, there was once again an implicit assumption that cultural differences at a single location occurred over time, so that the widespread distribution of cultures over wide areas was a sign of contemporaneity.

McKern and his colleagues developed a hierarchy of archaeological entities, starting with artifact *assemblages*, the sum of all the artifacts found in a site (McKern 1939). Then he moved on to *components*, assemblages representing a single period of occupation at a site. A *focus* comprised several components with almost identical artifact types. Then there were *aspects*, made up of foci with "a preponderating majority of traits," and finally *patterns*, cultural reflections of the "primary adjustments of peoples to environment, as defined by tradition." McKern identified three patterns: *Archaic*, which lacked pottery but included ground slate artifacts; *Woodland* with semisedentary sites, cord-marked pottery, and stemmed or side-notched projectile points, and finally *Mississippian*, a sedentary pattern with incised pottery and small triangular stone points.

The Midwestern taxonomic method owed much to Franz Boas's historical particularism, to his assumption that cultures were collections of individual traits that came together as a result of historical accidents. Whereas Gordon Childe paid much attention to human behavior and the uses of artifacts, the Midwestern taxonomic method made no inferences about human behavior; it just recorded the presence or absence of artifacts. Any form of quantification, such as percentages of artifacts, was considered suspect, because the archaeological record was incomplete and such counts were inaccurate. But it was conceded that quantitative similarity in percentages of shared artifact types had significance as a way of fitting individual occupation levels and sites into a broader framework.

Both the Gladwin system and the Midwestern taxonomic method with their treelike organizations came into widespread use between the 1930s and 1950s (Willey and Sabloff 1993). They stimulated a great deal of local research, where stratigraphic observation and careful artifact ordering (seriation) produced convincing local chronologies. Much of this work came from extensive Army Corps of Engineers canal and dam-building projects in the South and Southeast during the 1930s, the famous River Basin Surveys, when many young archaeologists, among them James A. Ford and Gordon R. Willey (1941), developed culture histories of entire river drainages from extensive field surveys and selective excavations. They and others moved away from the treelike assumptions of a few years earlier, to a view that cultures formed elaborate mosaics of different units, each with their own chronology and local distribution. Some of these cultures and artifact types diffused over larger areas to form cultural traditions, very much along the lines proposed by Gordon Childe in Europe, who derived much European prehistoric culture from southwestern Asia.

The River Basin work culminated in a major article by James Ford and Gordon Willey in the *American Anthropologist* for 1941, "An Interpretation of the Prehistory of the Eastern United States." It used the River Basin Survey data and a mass of other publications to group eastern cultures into five stages of development, ranging from Archaic through two stages of "Burial Mound" (Woodland) and to two of "Temple Mound" (Mississippian). Each stage was thought to come from the south, from Mesoamerica, before spreading north through the Mississippi Valley.

With the notable exception of Ford and Willey's work, almost all interpretations in American archaeology were at this era largely descriptive, with little effort made to explain the meaning of the archaeological record. Cultural change and development had indeed taken place, but only in limited ways—"a continuous process of adaptation to local environments, of specialization, and of independent invention" that led to a series of regional cultures, as three authors of a major synthesis of North American archaeology put it in 1947 (Martin et al. 1947:520).

As the preoccupation with artifact typologies and jigsaw puzzles of cultures intensified, North American archaeology rapidly became decoupled from ethnology and from any concern with living Native Americans. Acceptance of change in ancient times was minimal, methodologies of culture history dominated all archaeological thinking, and there was still a patronizing, even colonial attitude to native people that permeated archaeology. It was as if Indians were museum specimens. American archaeology became intensely conservative, often a mindless collecting and ordering of artifacts without any theoretical or even historical context. Inevitably, many younger scholars became disillusioned. Gordon Willey and Philip Phillips developed the concepts of North American culture history to their most refined in *Method and Theory in American Archaeology*, a short book published in 1958 that remains on the reading list of any prospective professional archaeologist.

The culture-historical approach encouraged American archaeologists to excavate and define ancient cultures. Excavation with this mind-set focused on middens, where artifacts tended to be most abundant, an approach that was to persist in many parts of North America into the 1960s and even later. This was cheap, easy excavation, focused on artifacts and their classification, a basis for increasingly elaborate artifact seriations to create sequences of sites based on artifact percentages, what Alfred Kroeber (1916) had once called "frequency seriation." In Europe, artifact classification made use of much earlier evolutionary typologies developed by nineteenth-century archaeologists, much of the work being devoted to splitting or refining existing types established by Oscar Montelius and other luminaries. American archaeologists did not have this evolutionary perspective or background, so they spent enormous amounts of time debating the theoretical significance of artifact classification, a debate that began in the 1920s and continues to this day (Willey and Sabloff 1993).

Initially the debates surrounded the issues of objectivity. James Ford and others argued that types should be recognized only when they were useful chronological or spatial markers (1954). Types were tools for historical analysis. The debate then shifted: Did archaeological types coincide with those created by their original makers? What were the relationships between the type and the various attributes (or features) used to define them? By the 1950s, archeologists like Albert Spaulding (1953), a pioneer of statistical methods, proposed "natural types," defined by statistically grouped clusters of attributes that would reveal more about human behavior. Spaulding's approach is still commonplace today. These prolonged, and often dreary, debates about types represented the first attempts to make the analytic basis of American archaeology more explicit.

Grahame Clark and
the Birth of Ecological Archaeology

Even as excavation focused on artifacts and single sites, a new precision in archaeological methods was developing, notably in Europe, where there was a new concern with wider questions than merely tool classifications. How had people lived in the past? What had they worn? What were their domestic arrangements? Answering such questions required much better standards of excavation, also the recovery of far more comprehensive data.

In 1931 the trawler *Colinda*, working in the southern North Sea, dredged up a lump of peat from the shallow seabed that had once been moorland, until it was covered by rising sea levels after the Ice Age. As the lump split open on the deck, a bone spearhead fell out. Fortunately for science, the trawlermen kept their find, which was soon identified as a classic example of a Mesolithic bone point (Burkitt 1932).

One of those who examined this chance find was a young Cambridge archaeologist, Grahame Clark, who was just completing a study of Mesolithic cultures in England for his doctoral dissertation (Fagan 2001). The discovery was a turning point in Clark's career. Discussions with his friend Harry Godwin, a pioneer of pollen analysis in Britain, helped Clark realize that such finds offered great potential for studying major environmental change and the ways prehistoric people adapted to changing climatic conditions. For the rest of his long life, Clark argued for the importance of wet sites, where organic and environmental data might be found in close association. He also advocated multidisciplinary archaeological research, a novel idea at the time.

In 1932 Clark was one of a small group of scientists who founded the Fenland Research Committee, a loose association of scientists who worked on the fens, the wetlands and lowlands close to Cambridge. In the years that followed, Clark carried out small-scale excavations at a series of locations, among them a site at Peacock's Farm, where he found stratified peat deposits, clays, and sands associated with a scatter of Mesolithic stone tools, and in a higher level, some Neolithic pottery (Clark et al. 1935). Peacock's Farm, for all its few archaeological finds, was very important at the time, because it placed the Mesolithic and

Neolithic within an environmental context of changing vegetation and provided an entirely new direction for research that was radically different from merely studying stone tools.

Grahame Clark now widened his intellectual horizons. He wrote a memorable book, *The Mesolithic Settlement of Northern Europe*, published in 1938, in which he placed changing human societies after the Ice Age in their environmental context, an important innovation at the time. During World War II, in the intervals of military service, he wrote a series of important essays on economic archaeology, which looked at major topics like bee-keeping and honey, seals, sheep-farming, and whaling—to mention only a few. He had set out his views on archaeology in *Archaeology and Society*, a textbook published in 1939, in which he stated that archaeology's primary concern was to find out how people lived. He published a famous diagram in this book that showed the relationships between habitat, economy, and biome. This drawing, albeit much elaborated, was the foundation of much of Clark's archaeological thinking.

Clark's interest in simple forms of ecological systems and ancient economic life culminated in his classic series of essays, *Prehistoric Europe: The Economic Basis* (1952). Based on archaeology, ethnographic analogy, and folk culture from European peasant societies, this important book broke firmly away from culture history and looked at general economic practices. The book was based on the assumption that all human societies operated in a state of equilibrium within ecological systems and changed constantly, often in response to climatic change. *Prehistoric Europe* was, as Clark wrote, "essentially an act of propaganda." The more conservative of his colleagues criticized him for eschewing culture history but many welcomed its sophisticated insights into a realm of archaeology that had been little explored. In many respects, this book foreshadowed much of archaeology's concern in the 1960s with ecological systems and ancient subsistence, but few of the proponents of the new archaeology of that era read it.

Study of Archaeology

By the 1950s, increasing numbers of archaeologists were uncomfortable with the narrow culture-historical perspective that dominated most archaeological thinking. This discomfort was reflected in the new interest in ecological archaeology and cultural ecology, the emergence of the functionalist perspective, and Gordon Willey's pioneering settlement research (Willey 1953). Changes in the archaeology of the 1950s were triggered both by dissatisfaction among a younger generation of archaeologists and by the development of radiocarbon dating. This new chronological method made it possible to think of a truly global archaeology, world prehistory.

Inevitably, the widespread concern over the narrow perspectives prevalent in archaeology produced a defining study. In 1948 a young scholar, Walter W. Taylor, published a scathing review of American archaeology. *A Study of Archaeology* was an extended polemic, written to provoke discussion, and it did. Taylor pointed out that most American archaeologists were culture historians who said that they sought to reconstruct the past. Instead, they preoccupied themselves with what he called "mere chronicle"—culture history in space and time. As for culture change, that was attributed to diffusion and migration.

Taylor wrote a searing critique of an archaeology with limited goals, where fieldwork methods were careless, analysis incomplete. Stone tools and potsherds received meticulous attention; other categories of evidence such as animal bones, plant remains, and even basketry were virtually ignored and sometimes not even collected. The excavators compiled long lists of culture traits, quantified them, and then compared them, mainly on the basis of the absence or presence of different artifact types. An obsession with chronology had put blinkers on many archaeologists' perspectives. They ignored provenience, also data on relationships between houses and hearths, much valuable information that would tell one a great deal about the way people behaved, lived, and interacted with one another—to say nothing of what they ate.

Walter Taylor balanced his devastating critique with a proposal for what he called a "conjunctive approach," which added studies of the interrelationships between artifacts and features to the traditional culture history. Taylor urged careful consideration of quantitative aspects of artifacts, of the spatial distribution of all finds, as well as evidence as to how they were used and made. Like Grahame Clark's thinking, Taylor's conjunctive approach defined cultures as mental constructs, their material remains as products of culture rather than culture itself. Many aspects of culture, which was, in the final analysis, ideational, survived in the archaeological record, not just material objects.

Above all, Taylor argued, the archaeologist should strive to recover just as much information from a site as possible. Taylor stressed the importance of environmental reconstruction, of ethnographic analogy. His conjunctive approach aimed to understand how people lived at a site as a "functionally integrated pattern." Ultimately, the archaeologist should aim at a functional understanding that was the equivalent of the ethnologist's insight into living cultures. Under this rubric, archaeologists should work alongside anthropologists in the study of culture.

A Study of Archaeology caused a considerable stir. Not surprisingly, ardent culture historians and many in the archaeological establishment of the day savaged the book. It is said to have wrought permanent damage to Taylor's career. But a decade later many people hailed the volume as a major break with the past, as a precursor of the major theoretical advances of the 1960s. In fact, *A Study* resembles in many respects the by-then-familiar approach of Grahame Clark, who also advocated the study of how people lived in the past, as well as close use of ethnographic sources and the need to pay attention to social, political, and other institutions of the past. But Taylor was no ecologist and had no interest in human cultures as adaptive systems as Clark did, so he lacked a perspective that was to become one of the foundations of archaeological theory in the 1960s. Taylor's ideas about culture coincided more closely with the Boasian notion that cultures were made up of shared concepts and traits.

A Study of Archaeology was, however, a powerful call for improved standards of archaeological research and more detailed analysis of artifacts. Taylor reinforced the functionalist approach and, with his polemic, foreshadowed the theoretical furores of the 1960s. But he did not initiate the major revolution in archaeological thinking that came a decade later.

Radiocarbon Dating

The 1940s and 1950s saw the beginnings of a shift in emphasis toward a greater concern with ecology, to the first settlement surveys, notably by Gordon Willey in Peru's Viru Valley (Willey 1953), and toward multidisciplinary projects like Robert Braidwood's research on agricultural origins in the Zagros Mountains of southwestern Asia (Braidwood and Braidwood 1983). But the great sea change in archaeological methods came from radiocarbon dating.

Willard Libby and J. R. Arnold of the University of Chicago announced this new way of dating organic materials from archaeological sites in 1949, a direct offshoot of Libby's work on the atomic bomb during World War II. Libby and Arnold tested their new dating method on objects of known historical age, such as wooden Egyptian mummy cases. When these dates agreed well with known chronologies from written sources, they extended the method to prehistoric sites. Soon charcoal samples poured in to the University of Chicago laboratory by the dozen, sent by archaeologists from all over the world, because everyone realized that this was the first dating method that promised accurate dates for sites dating back as much as 40,000 years (Libby 1955).

Radiocarbon dating revolutionized many well-established chronologies for such events as the origins of agriculture in southwestern Asia, which until then was thought to date to somewhat before 4000 B.C. (Childe 1942). At one swoop, the chronology of early food production from early farming sites at Jarmo in the Zagros and Jericho in the Jordan Valley jumped back in time more than 3,000 years. The surprises were not confined to the origins of agriculture. The chronology of the European Neolithic and Bronze Age was pushed back at least 1,000 years, overthrowing years of carefully reasoned but erroneous guesswork based on artifact typologies by Oscar Montelius, Gordon Childe, and others.

Within a few years, it became apparent that radiocarbon dates offered the first opportunity to reconstruct a truly global chronology for the last 40,000 years of human prehistory, from the late Ice Age to as recently as A.D. 1500. It also allowed the comparison of cultural sequences in widely separated parts of the world and the first measurements of the *rates* of cultural change, a critically important consideration. For the first time, prehistorians could think in terms of a world prehistory, the first book on the subject being published by Grahame Clark in 1961.

This chapter ends in 1960, an arbitrarily chosen date when archaeology was about to change dramatically. By 1960 the major elements of scientific archaeology were in place—ecological approaches, multidisciplinary field research, radiocarbon dating, and sophisticated excavation methods. The stage was set for an explosion in archaeological activity throughout the world, which coincided with the expansion of higher education and dramatic increases in the number of archaeologists working in every corner of the globe. In the nearly half century since then, archaeology has become dramatically more sophisticated and science based, but much of the new methodology still depends on applications from other sciences, such as the physics of dating methods of all kinds. The most dramatic changes have come in the information society—Web-based research and publications, geographic information systems, satellite imagery, and so on. Above all, in a more globalized world, archaeologists from what were once entirely different research traditions are in communication with one another, often over vast differences. As a result, we are seeing the emergence of more consistent methodologies and higher, state-of-the-art standards of field and laboratory research being adopted more widely.

The past five decades have seen major advances that I suspect will be even more important in the near and distant future. The inexorable tide of destruction of archaeological sites will see increasing emphasis being placed on conservation of the record. The formerly destructive methods we have used in the past will be replaced increasingly by nonintrusive field methods and remote sensing. A revolution in paleoclimatology will give us fine-grain insights into how environmental changes affected ancient societies, indeed the course of civilization itself. And, above all, the explosion of sophisticated methodology will allow us to peer into the dim mirror of the intangible, to achieve a better understanding of our forebears as thinking, fallible human beings. The future of archaeology is bright, thanks to our ingenuity and because what the Elizabethan antiquarian William Camden called our "Backward Looking Curiosity" is alive and well.

References

Notes on Further Reading

General histories of archaeology include

Bahn, Paul (editor)
    1996   The *Cambridge Illustrated History of Archaeology.* Cambridge University Press, Cambridge.
        A comprehensive and lavishly illustrated history, with global coverage.

Daniel, Glyn
    1991   *A Short History of Archaeology.* Thames and Hudson, London.
        Daniel's quick once-over focuses mainly on the Old World. Readable, but somewhat dated.

Fagan, Brian
    1985   *The Adventure of Archaeology.* National Geographic Society, Washington, D.C.
        A typical National Geographic coffee-table book with many illustrations. Emphasis on adventure and discovery.
    2004   *A Brief History of Archaeology.* Prentice Hall, Upper Saddle River, New Jersey.
        A short textbook that surveys major developments in the history of archaeology.

Trigger, Bruce G
    1989   *A History of Archaeological Interpretation.* Cambridge University Press, Cambridge.
        Trigger's analysis of the subject is definitive.

Willey, Gordon R., and Jeremy A. Sabloff
    1993   *A History of American Archaeology.* 3rd ed. W. H. Freeman, New York.
        The standard history of American archaeology.

References Cited

Bersu, Gerhard
    1940   Excavations at Little Woodbury, Wiltshire. *Proceedings of the Prehistoric Society* 6:42–111.

Bowden, Mark
    1991   *Pitt Rivers: The Life and Work of Lieutenant-General Augustus Henry Lane Fox Pitt Rivers.* Cambridge University Press, Cambridge.

Braidwood, Robert J., and Linda S. Braidwood (editors)
    1983   *Prehistoric Archaeology along the Zagros Flanks.* Oriental Institute of the University of Chicago, Chicago.

Burkitt, Miles
1921   *Prehistory.* Cambridge University Press, Cambridge.
1932   A Maglemose Harpoon Dredged Up from the North Sea. *Man* 238:99.

Childe, V. Gordon
1942   *What Happened in History.* Pelican Books, Baltimore.

Clark, J. G. D., H. Godwin, and M. E. Godwin
1935   Report on Recent Excavations at Peacock's Farm, Shippea Hill, Cambridgeshire. *Antiquaries Journal* 16:29–50.

Clark, J. G. D.
1938   *The Mesolithic Settlement of Northern Europe.* Cambridge University Press, Cambridge.
1939a   Editorial Comment. *Proceedings of the Prehistoric Society* (2):260.
1939b   *Archaeology and Society.* Methuen, London.
1952   *Prehistoric Europe: The Economic Basis.* Stanford University Press, Palo Alto, California.

Clark, J. G. D., H. Godwin, and M. E. Godwin
1935   Report on Recent Excavations at Peacock's Farm, Shippea Hill, Cambridgeshire. *Antiquaries Journal* 16:29–50.

Conze, Alexander
1875–1880.   *Archaeologische untersuchungen auf Samothrake.* C. Gerold's sohn, Vienna.

Crawford, O. G. S., and Alexander Keiller
1928   *Wessex from the Air.* Clarendon Press, Oxford.

Curtius, Ernst
1882   *Olympia und Umgegend.* Weidmannsche Buchhandlung, Berlin.

Daniel, Glyn
1991   *A Short History of Archaeology.* Thames and Hudson, London and New York.

Douglass, A. E.
1929   The Secret of the Southwest Solved by Talkative Tree rings. *National Geographic Magazine* 56(6):736–770.

Drower, Margaret
1995   *Flinders Petrie: A Life in Archaeology.* 2nd ed. University of Wisconsin Press, Madison.

Evans, Joan
1943   *Time and Chance.* Longmans, London.

Fagan, Brian
2001   *Grahame Clark: An Intellectual Biography of an Archaeologist.* Westview Press, Boulder, Colorado.

Ford, James A., and Gordon R. Willey
    1941   An Interpretation of the Prehistory of the eastern United States. *American Anthropologist* 43(3):325–363.

Ford, James A.
    1954   On the Concept of Types. *American Anthropologist* 56:42–53.

Fowler, Don D.
    2000   *A Laboratory for Anthropology.* University of New Mexico Press, Albuquerque, New Mexico.

Fox, Cyril
    1923   *The Archaeology of the Cambridge Region.* Cambridge University Press, Cambridge.
    1932   *The Personality of Britain.* Cambridge University Press, Cambridge.

Givens, Douglas R.
    1992   *Alfred Vincent Kidder and the Development of Americanist Archaeology.* University of New Mexico Press, Albuquerque, New Mexico.

Gladwin, Winifred, and Harold S. Gladwin
    1934   *A Method for Designation of Cultures and Their Variations.* Gila Pueblo Medallion Papers 15. Globe, Arizona.

Hawkes, Jacquetta
    1982   *Mortimer Wheeler: Adventurer in Archaeology.* Wiedenfeld and Nicholson, London.

Hooton, Earnest A.
    1930   *The Indians of Pecos Pueblo.* Department of Archaeology, New Haven, Yale University, Connecticut.

Kidder, Alfred V.
    1924   *An Introduction to the Study of Southwestern Archaeology.* Yale University Press, New Haven, Connecticut.

Kroeber, Alfred L.
    1916   Zuñi Potsherds. *American Museum of Natural History Anthropological Papers* 18(1):1–37.

Libby, Willard F.
    1955   *Radiocarbon Dating.* University of Chicago Press, Chicago.

Libby and Arnold
    1949   Age Determination by Radiocarben Content: checks with samples of known age. *Science* 110: 678–680.

Martin, Paul S., George I. Qimby, and Donald Collier
    1947   *Indians Before Columbus.* University of Chicago Press, Chicago.

McKern, W. C.
    1939   The Midwestern Taxonomic System As an Aid to Archaeological Culture Study. *American Antiquity* 4:301–313.

Montelius, Oscar
    1885   *On the Dating of the Bronze Age, particularly in relation to Scandinavia.* Macmillan, London.

Petrie, Flinders
    1883   *The Pyramids and Temples of Gizeh.* Macmillan, London.
    1889   Sequences in Prehistoric Remains. *Journal of the Royal Anthropological Institute* 29:199–226.
    1891   *Illahun, Kahun, and Gurob.* Egypt Exploration Fund, London.
    1896   *Naqada and Ballas.* Egypt Exploration Society, London.
    1904   *Methods and Aims in Archaeology.* Macmillan, London.

Pitt-Rivers, Augustus Henry Lane-Fox
    1887–1898.   *Excavations on Cranborne Chase.* Privately Printed.

Spaulding, Albert C.
    1953   Statistical Techniques for the Study of Artifact Types. *American Antiquity* 18:305–313.

Squier, Ephraim G., and Edwin H. Davis
    1848   *Ancient Monuments of the Mississippi Valley.* Smithsonian Institution, Washington, D.C.

Taylor, W. W.
    1948   *A Study of Archaeology.* American Anthropological Association, Menasha, Wisconsin.

Thomas, Cyrus
    1894   *Report on the Mound Explorations of the Bureau of Ethnology.* Twelfth Annual Report of the Bureau of American Ethnology, Washington, D.C.

Trigger, Bruce G.
    1980   *Gordon Childe: Revolutions in Archaeology.* Thames and Hudson, London.

Uhle, Max
    1903   *Pachamacac: Report of the William Pepper, MD, LLD Peruvian expedition of 1896.* Department of Archaeology, University of Pennsylvania, Philadelphia.
    1907   The Emeryville Mound. *University of California Publications in American Archaeology and Ethnology* 7(1).

Wheeler, Mortimer
    1925   *Prehistoric and Roman Wales.* Clarendon Press, Oxford.
    1932   *Report on the Excavation of the Prehistoric, Roman and Post-Roman Site in Lydney Park, Gloucestershire.* Society of Antiquaries, London.
    1936   *Verulamium: A Belgic and Two Roman Cities.* Society of Antiquaries, London.
    1943   *Maiden Castle.* Society of Antiquaries, London.

1954   *Archaeology from the Earth.* Clarendon Press, Oxford.
1955   *Still Digging.* Michael Joseph, London.
1959   *Early India and Pakistan.* Thames and Hudson
1962   *Charsada: A Metropolis of the North-West Frontier.* British Academy and the Government of Pakistan, London.

Willey, Gordon R.
1953   *Prehistoric Settlements in the Virú Valley,* Peru. Smithsonian Institution, Washington, D.C.

Willey, Gordon R., and Philip Phillips
1958   *Method and Theory in American Archaeology.* University of Chicago Press, Chicago.

Willey, Gordon R., and Jeremy A. Sabloff
1993   *A History of American Archaeology.* 2nd ed. Thames & Hudons, London.

Winstone, H. V. F.
1990   *Woolley of Ur.* Secker and Warburg, London.

Woolley, Leonard
1912–1952   *Carchemish: Report on the excavations at Djerabis on behalf of the British Museum.* British Museum, London.
1920   *Dead Cities and Living Men.* Oxford University Press, New York.
1929   *Ur of the Chaldees.* Edward Benn, London.

PART 1

IN THE FIELD

3

Logistics of Fieldwork and Collecting Field Data

John M. Steinberg

In almost every archaeological research project, there comes a defining moment when the project either becomes a success or a failure. The moment seems to come about two-thirds of the way into the first field season with the realization that the data you have been collecting do not address the issue you set out to explore. To make matters worse, the little data that you have collected (which looks like it is going to be only a small portion of what you planned to collect) do not seem to say anything at all. Unfortunately, there is no way to avoid that moment.

We have all been there.

But you can prepare for that moment. If you are prepared, you are on the verge of something wonderful. For at that moment of realization—when it seems all hope of doing some original research is lost—archaeology advances.

You are in good company. Kent Flannery, in the introduction to *Early Mesoamerican Village* (1976), begins with that critical moment. He quotes from a review article of R. E. W. Adams (1969), in which Adams laments that "an archaeologist cannot even predict the question that most of the data recovered will bear on." Yet, as you will see, archaeologists must come up with questions before going into the field. You should formulate those questions so that they can be changed. Not only will your questions change but, in most cases, so will your data collection strategy.

Logistics is the key. Logistics in archaeology is the proper co-ordination of the questions and the approach to data collection. Every archaeologist has to work out logistics in the field, at the time that data is recorded. That means that you must keep in mind the goals of the research while implementing the methods of collecting the data. Most importantly, you must be able to change both the questions and the data collection strategy to make sure that they are harmonious. Change the questions so that they can be answered by the data that are being collected and then change the data collection strategy to better answer those questions. Proper logistics will allow you to triumph at that juncture when things look bad. It will allow you to figure out what questions you can answer and how you can answer them. To do this you do not need to know *the* answer to *the* question, just what questions and answers look like.

This chapter will help you understand what questions and answers look like. The chapter is written for students starting their own research (e.g., for a senior honors thesis, master's thesis, or Ph.D. dissertation). The goal of problem-oriented research projects is to collect field data that will help solve some regional, methodological, or theoretical problem in archaeology or anthropology. That is, you are going to try to link some question about the past (e.g., why did people do X) with some data that you plan to collect (e.g., how many Y artifacts are at Z sites). The specific goal is to describe how to solve the most common problem of a young researcher: what to do when your data do not seem to answer the question you set out to address. There are no universal answers to what coordinate system to use, which truck to buy, how to get a permit, or what field forms to use. The approaches to these issues and others like them are all regionally mandated or project specific. What is universal is that you will find things that are unexpected. As strange as it may sound, you can be prepared for the unexpected.

Questions to Answer

Why are you supposed to start out with a question? Why not go out, see what is there in the archaeological record, and then figure out what it tells you about the past? Having the archaeological record determine what you should study would solve the problem of collecting the wrong data as previously described. The reasons that archaeologists ask research questions are both simple and complex.

The simple reason is that most archaeology is destructive. There are two justifications for doing destructive archaeological work. First, the site is going to be destroyed anyway so it is better that some information is salvaged by archaeologists under cultural resource management (CRM) programs. Second, getting answers to questions about the past is important enough to warrant the partial destruction of the past. Either way, the destruction means that, in many cases, the data that you collect will be all that is ever collected. Therefore, the instinct is usually to collect every piece of data from a survey or excavation. So much data can be recorded from the simplest test pit that an archaeologist might never get to a second test pit. Research archaeologists have found that the way to address the plethora of data that could be collected is to ask very specific questions. Then, beyond the standard information described in the following chapters, one has only to collect the information that will answer the question at hand. Research questions both guide us to the *right* information and, at the same time, free us from collecting every shred of information that could be collected during survey or excavation. It also means that the inherent bias of the researcher, who will decide what data are to be collected, is made explicit.

The complex reason for asking research questions is that archaeology advances when discoveries are made. A discovery is really just finding out something that nobody knew before. Discoveries are made at a variety of levels and in innumerable ways. Many discoveries are just luck (stumbling across that site, bone, or burial), but in general, archaeology is uncomfortable with luck. Rarely do archaeologists personally make great discoveries; our luck is not that good. In fact, in most accounts of great discoveries, archaeologists are shown a site, cave, location, or temple by local farmers. The archaeologist simply realizes the significance (e.g., Fagan 1994). Rather than depending on fickle luck, research archaeologists have found that by proposing, and then answering, specific questions about the past they will almost guarantee interesting results, without depending on chance.

This sounds at least odd and at most contradictory: archaeologists ask questions and collect data to answer those questions, but in fact, we don't really know what questions our data will help us answer.

The difficulty with academic, problem-oriented archaeology is that it takes a lot of fieldwork to collect enough data to be able to even see if you could answer the question you proposed. By the time you realize you are on the wrong track, you have collected a substantial amount of information. This scenario describes most academic projects, whether a senior honors thesis or a multiyear interdisciplinary international project—any project where the goal is to do original research. The wonderful news is that the wrong track is not really wrong; you are just answering a different question—a question that could be more important than the one you proposed.

Archaeological research consists of three areas of investigation: method, region, and theory. A methodological advance, in its extreme form, is the invention of a new data-gathering technique or laboratory analysis that yields information about the function or the age of objects or sites. However, most methodological advances consist of using already employed methods in new areas or in new ways or improving the reliability of those methods. Contributing to the understanding of a region consists of finding, dating, quantifying, or describing one or more activity areas that help explain how areas or sites interact. Contributing to the theoretical understanding of the development of human societies is probably the most difficult archaeological endeavor. This involves discovering something about the past that addresses the whole suite of issues described in volume 1. A good honors thesis will investigate one of these areas, a master's thesis will explore two of these areas, and a PhD dissertation will have to make contributions to all three areas of investigation.

The questions that you ask about each of the three areas will be quite different but should be sequential. For example, the questions, Does the variation in a particular artifact or feature category tell us about social structure over time in a particular place? and Can those changes be understood given current ideas about human social change? contain all three aspects.

The first step in any research project is to discover whether there is variation in an attribute, artifact, site type, or class and, if so, what it varies with. For example, is variation associated with time, economic wherewithal, or environment? These types of questions are not about the past per se but about the archaeological record and its contents, preservation, and quality. These types of questions are the first that a researcher will ask, and they will be followed up by questions about method, region, and human behavior.

Old Answers

Why is it that in academic problem-oriented research the one who proposes the question is the same one who will lead the team into the field to survey and excavate and is also the one who will write up the results and comment on the significance of the work? Gavin Lucas (2001:9) answers that "the credibility and reliability of any material generated through fieldwork takes its validity directly from the command of self/personnel on site."

This might seem odd, because one would think that the person posing the questions would have a vested interest in one answer or the other, and it should be an unbiased archaeologist who actually investigates the question. Furthermore, this is odd because archaeology is a destructive science and the results can sometimes be difficult, if not impossible, to replicate. In most cases an excavation can only be done once and therefore the objectivity of the archaeologist is critical. But Lucas's (2001) answer is correct, because archaeology has taken the opposite approach. We have assumed that all archaeologists are biased toward one view or another, and therefore it is best when the biases are made manifest.

The advantages of a having a manifest bias go back to the beginnings of scientific archaeology. In the early 1840s, Jens J. Worsaae (1849) began to excavate burial mounds in Denmark to show the validity of Carl J. Thomsen's (1962 [1837]) division of the archaeological record into three technical stages (stone, bronze, and iron). Thomsen had proposed this division in his ordering of the national collection, which contained mostly artifacts of unknown provenience. Worsaae asked a relatively simple question that can be paraphrased as, could the Three Age System ordering be found in primary contexts? If it could not, then differences in the technology of the artifacts could not be attributed to the passing of time. Worsaae's question may seem so basic and fundamental as to be irrelevant to students. But on closer examination, his question was absolutely modern, and in some ways students can still ask similar questions. In essence, he asked, What is the cause of the variation in the archaeological record? Are the different materials a result of chronology or, as previously proposed, a function of different social classes (i.e., the rich have bronze and iron, whereas the poor have only stone)?

Jens Worsaae believed that if he could find and excavate burials in which the upper and most recent burials contained iron artifacts and the lower and oldest graves contained only stone, with the middle containing copper and bronze, it would confirm Thomsen's theory that time was the critical variable. Worsaae would have to excavate and report on the position of these archaeological finds.

Thomsen demonstrated his ideas about the causes of variation in the past in the organization of his museum. If you did not believe him, he would show you around his museum. You could analyze the artifacts, look at the various styles, and study the designs, and then you would begin to see how they changed over time (Trigger 1989). That is, for Carl J. Thomsen, the Three Age System could be demonstrated almost by the artifacts themselves. Thomsen published his ideas about the organization of the past only as a museum guide, to be used to help one understand his large national collection (Graslund 1987).

But the proof for the chronological variation in artifact material had to come from the ground. Not only was it impractical for anyone who was skeptical to come out and actually observe the excavation as it progressed, but if there were chronological variation, the excavation would destroy most of the evidence. This forced Jens J. Worsaae to extensively document his excavation, possibly more so than had he simply been excavating for artifacts to be housed in the National Museum. Worsaae's explicit bias, combined with the relatively careful excavations, set the stage for a scientific archaeology in which the careful documentation of basic archaeological data was the product of a researcher with a specific theoretical bias.

Following Worsaae, the contrasting styles of Heinrich Schliemann (1976 [1881]) and Augustus Henry Lane-Fox Pitt-Rivers (1887) galvanized researchers to ask the questions and direct the actual excavation or data collection. Both men are called founding fathers of archaeology, in part because they asked specific research questions. Schliemann asked relatively narrow questions, whereas Pitt-Rivers asked broad sweeping questions. In both cases the questions determined the logistics of their excavations.

Heinrich Schliemann was obsessed with proving the validity of the Homeric epics. His obsession can be viewed as a research question: Were the Homeric stories true? The obsession led to spectacular publicity because Schliemann sent letters back to the *Times* in London describing the excavations as they progressed. The obsession also led to fundamental mistakes in correctly identifying critical stratigraphic breaks. Schliemann's question (was Troy real?) dictated his approach and allowed him to ignore upper layers and go straight to the bottom to what he believed would be the Troy he sought (Stiebing 1994). It was only later, with the help of the careful hand and observant eye of Wilhelm Dörpfeld, that Schliemann was able to understand the stratigraphic sequence at Troy and connect various levels with other parts of Greece. In his zeal to get to the lowest layers, Schliemann probably dug right through the Troy he was looking for. It was only during a reassessment of the site, with the help of Dörpfeld, that Schliemann was able to begin to answer his questions about the relationship between the site and the Homeric epics.

General Augustus Henry Lane-Fox Pitt-Rivers believed that the evolutionary changes in human society could be understood through the changes in material culture. Pitt-Rivers (1906) drew an analogy between genes (the stuff of biological evolution, although he did not use the term *gene*) and technology (the stuff of cultural development) that ushered in the era of scientific archaeology. His general research question concerned the shape of the evolutionary tree of material culture. To paraphrase, Pitt-Rivers asked (1906:49), what are the leading shoots and what are the inner branches? The answer was to be found by studying artifacts, particularly ones used daily by ordinary people. Pitt-Rivers arranged these artifacts on an evolutionary scale throughout the world. These sweeping ideas about the connection of everyday life with human social evolution necessitated that archaeologists act like ethnographers and record every bit of information and collect every artifact. In his seminal excavation of his inherited estate of Cranborne Chase, Pitt-Rivers took personal responsibility for all aspects of the planning, crew training, excavation, analysis, and write-up. We have Pitt-Rivers to thank for bringing the geologic tradition of field work to archaeology. Pitt-Rivers believed that archaeology is so specialized that only the excavators can truly control the data that they recover. Pitt-Rivers died with his work unfinished, and it was left to the organized and efficient Henry Balfour to carry out Pitt-Rivers's ideas and to create the museum that makes manifest the connection between archaeology and anthropology. Pitt-Rivers collected too much, and the aspects that were important for understanding the evolution of human society are almost lost in his voluminous report (1887) if they are there at all.

Archaeologists as diverse as Flinders Petrie (1904) and Ian Hodder (1999) agree that the questions that archaeologists bring to fieldwork not only dictate their approach but also directly impact the kind of data they recover and prescribe what they will ignore. The enduring legacies of Schliemann and Pitt-Rivers center on the reevaluation of the questions they were asking and the methods that they were using to answer them. Schliemann, with the help of Dörpfeld, realized that his questions were too narrow and that he was collecting too little data, and Pitt-Rivers, with the posthumous help of Balfour, outlined the collection of rather specific categories of artifacts that showed change over time and space, rather than collecting everything. Ever since these two men, archaeology has been struggling with the connection of logistics with questions and method with theory.

That these two fathers of archaeology did not immediately hit on the right connection between method and theory is not surprising. What is clear is that they hit on the right questions and proper logistics only after a profound reevaluation.

Answering Questions

Logistics is the branch of military science that deals with housing, transport, and equipment of soldiers. It is therefore no coincidence that our notion of archaeological field logistics can be traced directly back to General Pitt-Rivers and his military organization. Even with his rigid excavation style (he dug in squares so that every artifact's provenience could be properly assigned), combined with unlimited time and money, Pitt-Rivers was never able to successfully answer his questions about the relationship of technology and the evolution of complex society.

Today, running an archaeological project, or an aspect of a larger project, is just as complicated as it was in Pitt-Rivers's day. Several guides specifically deal with archaeological logistics. For instance, in *A Guide to Basic Archaeological Field Procedures* (1978) Fladmark describes how to choose a campsite, what to do when you get lost, and even how to cook on a wood stove, in addition to site surveying, mapping, and equipment. In *Practical Archaeology*, Dillon (1993a) writes on how to choose a field vehicle. Although these may seem rather mundane, camp living and field vehicles are every bit as important to the successful project as the right research question. The problem is that every situation is so idiosyncratic that it is difficult to offer any useful advice on these real logistical issues that is not common sense. What dictates field logistics is the interplay between research questions and data collection.

Most archaeology is done as CRM or salvage archaeology. In these surveys and excavations, although there is a problem to be solved—a site or region is impacted—the solution is to find out as much as possible before it is destroyed forever. Although much of the data collected during CRM work is directly relevant for basic research, the connection need not be made explicit. For more information about CRM see Cooper et al. (1995), King (1998), and McManamon and Hatton (1999).

Whereas some students learn field logistics in the process of doing CRM, most start in field school. Field schools are specifically designed to teach basic skills such as excavation or survey. For a list of archaeological field schools, see http://www.cincpac

.com/afos/testpit.html. In both CRM and field-school situations, beginning archaeologists learn about much of the content of the archaeological toolbox and when to properly apply those tools. There are several excellent fieldwork guides to help you determine the proper techniques and tools for any given situation. In addition to this book, there is, for example, Ellis (2000), Hester et al. (1997), Joukowsky (1980), McMillon (1991), and Purdy (1996) in the United States and Drewett (1999), Renfrew and Bahn (2000), and Webster (1974) in the United Kingdom.

The organization of archaeological projects, whether salvage or research, is usually at odds with the goals of the project and the goals of archaeology in general. Archaeology is an inherently destructive science and as such, the goal of learning about the past is contra the preservation of the past. That being said, over the years the logistics of a project has become so specific to the project's methods, region, and goals that specific advice is almost impossible. Logistics is born, not out of excavations, but out of excavations that are aimed at answering a series of questions. Logistics is an outcome of the desire to excavate at the appropriate scale and employ the recording techniques to answer specific questions.

Are there any universal principles of project design? In 1974 Gordon Willey put together retrospectives by leading figures in archaeology and anthropology who had managed significant multinational, interdisciplinary projects. In that book people such as Braidwood, Sanders, Movius, Clark, MacNeish, and Willey himself reflect on their big digs. There are two common themes in these retrospectives. First, it appears that these directors were very lucky. However, on closer inspection, their own attribution of their success to luck is superficial. Their luck is really an outcome of putting themselves in the right place, sometimes being directed there but mostly following hunches—in other words, research design. Second, the directors describe how they constantly reevaluated their research strategy on the basis of data they recovered. Not only did they change their research strategy but they began to tailor their methods and techniques to their new questions. The idea of the feedback between questions, methods, and results has been formalized by Charles Redman (1973) in his description of a multistage research design (see also

Binford 1964; Daniels 1978; Redman 1987; Redman and Rathje 1973; and Struever 1971).

Multistage research designs are now almost universal in large academic projects. Most projects operate in the same way, although they may have different labels for the stages of work. In most cases, the work progresses in definite steps that are a part of a never-ending cycle of research. In general, research proposals are put forth and—if funded—the logistical problems are worked out, the data is acquired during a fieldwork phase, the information is processed and reviewed, and in most cases further collection is done. Following these steps, there is a more formal stage of analysis and interpretation of the results, which can lead to a new research proposal being put forth (Drewett 1999; Sharer and Ashmore 1993). Publication (chapter 33) usually fits in after several of these cycles. One of the best descriptions of how cycles work is English Heritage's MAP 2 (which can be seen at http://www.eng-h.gov.uk/guidance/map2/index.htm; Andrews 1991).

There is a very tight feedback in archaeological work in which research design, fieldwork, analysis, and interpretation loop back into research design and so on. The tight loop is necessary for a slew of reasons. The most important, as mentioned earlier, is because archaeology is a destructive science, and therefore most fieldwork can be done only once. The destruction combined with limited field time and tight budgets mean that collecting the relevant data—determined by the research questions—is paramount for a successful research project. However, archaeological data almost never directly address the big issues. Rather, what we collect is a proxy that must be interpreted to address the big issues (see volume 2). That interpretation is done through the research design—the questions.

In archaeology it is sometimes easier to change the questions to better fit the data. Nonetheless, archaeology is a process where both questions and data come together, and making them come together is the logistics of the project. Planning an archaeological investigation is serious work and attention must be paid to the logistics of fieldwork. However, the importance of the best possible solution may be overrated. Dillon (1993b) proposed that efficient field techniques should produce a surplus of field time, which can be used for collecting more data. Although this sounds wonderful, archaeologists at all levels start their projects already so pressed for time that simply getting enough data to address any questions that are at all archaeologically relevant is difficult.

A much more practical note is sounded by John Alexander (1970) in *The Directing of Archaeological Excavations*. According to Alexander, directing an archaeological excavation is really solving a series of problems, the paramount one being the research question. His premise is that sites and regions that are easy to assess (i.e., well preserved with straightforward stratigraphy), are the exception. At ideal sites the craft of archaeology would consist of the application of the proper technique. However, almost every site presents problems. Nothing is ever straightforward in archaeology—if it were, your original research design would work. Archaeology is really overcoming a series of problems caused by the unpredictability of the archaeological record.

The problems that a beginning researcher must overcome are quite different from those of a more advanced one. When working on a senior honors thesis, master's thesis, or even PhD dissertation, the long-term, multistage research approaches are not easily applicable. For student-driven research, the moment of realization that the data and research questions do not connect could come after the fieldwork—when it is too late to change methods. To avoid this disconnect, you should present your preliminary data and your interpretations to either the project team or to archaeologists from outside while you are still in the field.

I have been following this practice for the last 10 years on the projects that I work on and run. I take a day or two off, usually about two-thirds of the way through the field season. On that day, we present preliminary results. If the moment of realization—that your data do not answer your questions—has not yet come, the presentation of preliminary results and interpretations will force that moment. Presenting preliminary results, long before you are ready, compels you to reevaluate your data collection strategy and your research questions. To my mind, this is the single most important logistical aspect of an archaeological project.

What Questions Look Like

Like Alexander (1970) it seems most archaeologists approach the logistics of fieldwork as a series of problems. For the beginning student, most of the problems that you will encounter will be particular. However, three problems you will encounter I see as almost universal: your sample size is too small to say anything meaningful, your database is too complex and full of notes to get anything meaningful out of it, and finally, not only can you not answer the question you set out to study, you cannot find anything meaningful in your data.

If you encounter these problems, you are doing everything right. Nonetheless, these problems can and must be solved. The best way to solve them is to prepare for them in advance. Oddly, the problems are solved in the reverse order that you encounter them. You must first figure out what question you can answer. This section will help you define or redefine a question using examples of questions of other researchers

Defining a good question is difficult. If you could define a really good question, you would, in all likelihood, already have a very good idea of the answer. Defining a question actually comes from having a hunch about what the answer should be. Thus, rather than trying to define the question right off the bat, some researchers find it helpful to begin with a possible answer. Not necessarily *the* answer, but rather, what *an* answer might look like. That is, you must identify the key aspects of variability. Interestingly, most answers do not contain more than three dimensions, and many of them have two. The four figures that follow show what some answers look like and the units the questions are phrased in.

Ammerman and Cavalli-Sforza's (1973) graph (Figure 3.1) addressed the key question, How did agriculture spread? By demonstrating that variation in time is related to variation in space, Ammerman and Cavalli-Sforza argue that people moving out from a center (Jericho), in a relatively even wave of advance spurred by population growth, are responsible for the spread of agriculture. At first glance, Figure 3.1 is straightforward: It plots time against space and shows a distinct relationship. The units of

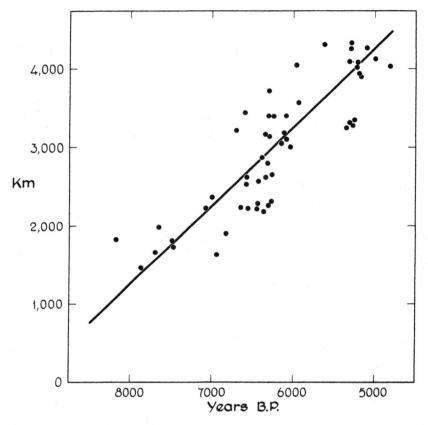

Figure 3.1.   Plot of radiocarbon dates for early Neolithic sites vs. distance from Jericho. From Ammerman and Cavalli-Sforza (1973).

variability appear to be kilometers and years, but further study reveals a more complex graph.

Each dot is an early Neolithic site in Europe and each site has two variables associated with it. On the *x* axis (abscissa) is the earliest radiocarbon date associated with domestication. On the *y* axis (ordinate) is the distance, in any direction, from Jericho. That is, the two-dimensional map location has been converted to a one-dimensional distance. A dot represents a site's time of domestication in space relative to Jericho. Ammerman and Cavalli-Sforza have also drawn the principal axis (a regression line) that highlights the general trend. Many of the sites deviate substantially from the general trend. Nonetheless, the trend is quite apparent, showing the distinct relationship between date of domestication and distance from Jericho. Almost all answers to questions about the geographic spread of any trait are a relationship between time and space. In Ammerman and Cavalli-Sforza's study the date of domestication at sites and their distance from Jericho are proxy measures of the spread of agriculture; the actual spread has to be interpreted from these two variables.

Kristiansen's (1987) bar graph forcefully makes its point (Figure 3.2). The graph has also just two dimensions: sword-hilt type

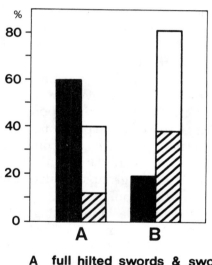

A   full hilted swords & swords with pommel
B   flange hilted sword

■ 1 NO SHARPENING

□ 2 MODERATE SHARPENING

▨ 3 HEAVY SHARPENING

Figure 3.2. Amount of sharpening on Danish Early Bronze Age Period 2 sword blades according to hilt type. From Kristiansen (1987).

and amount of blade sharpening. Kristiansen finds that full-hilt swords are unlikely to be sharpened, whereas flange-hilt swords have substantial sharpening. Kristiansen uses this covariation to argue that there were two kinds of swords that differ in both their manufacture and use. He argues that the full-hilt sword was a chiefly sword and the flange-hilt sword was used by warriors.

The visual impact of the graph is substantial. The different sizes of the black bars that represent the percentage of swords that have not been sharpened highlight the differences in the two types of hilts. Furthermore, sharpened swords have been divided into two subcategories: moderate and heavy sharpening. Although assessing moderate or heavy sharpening is more subjective than its presence or absence, the subdivision reinforces the depiction of basic presence or absence on the graph.

The easiest way to add a third axis of variation is to contrast a two-dimensional graph from one time or place with a similar graph from another time or place. For example, Stein's (1999) graphs are in fact three-dimensional, even though they look only two-dimensional. The graphs show animal bone percentages by site (Figure 3.3). To be more exact, the percentages of bones from goats (caprines), cows (*Bos*), pigs (*Sus*), and other fauna at eight sites are presented as a bar chart. The third dimension is the subdivision of the sites into two groups, Uruk colonies (top) and local late Chalcolithic sites (bottom).

The graph makes clear that, as a percentage of the diet, late Chalcolithic sites (bottom) consume much more cow and pig than late Uruk colonies (top), which tend to consume goats. Using percentages reduces the effects of preservation and recovery biases but may hide variables such as site size, length of time occupied, and rate of consumption. This graph is part of a complex argument concerning the differences in preferences at two types of sites from the same time period during the fourth millennium B.C. in Mesopotamia.

Brumfiel's (1976) graphs, although apparently simple, stretch the amount of information presented in a single work (as Tufte [1983] would have us always do). These graphs (Figure 3.4) contrast site size against productive potential (which is the multiplicative product of the area of agricultural land around the site and the relative present-day fertility of that land). To make the

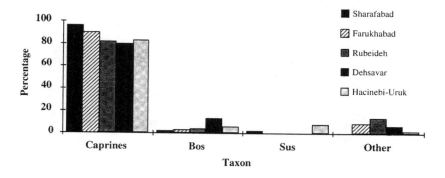

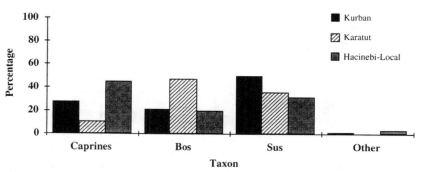

Figure 3.3. Contact phase C fauna. The top series are sites associated with Mesopotamian Uruk colonies, and the bottom series are sites associated with Southeast Anatolian local late Chalcolithic. From Stein (1999).

graph of the variation of these two variables a diagonal line, it uses the logarithm of the site size, which compresses large values more than small values. The third dimension (time) is added in the form of the second, similar graph. Brumfiel argues that the sites on the upper part of the graphs are receiving tribute from the sites on the lower part. Comparing the Late Formative with the Terminal Formative, she argues that it shows an increase in the amount of tribute in the latter pottery phase.

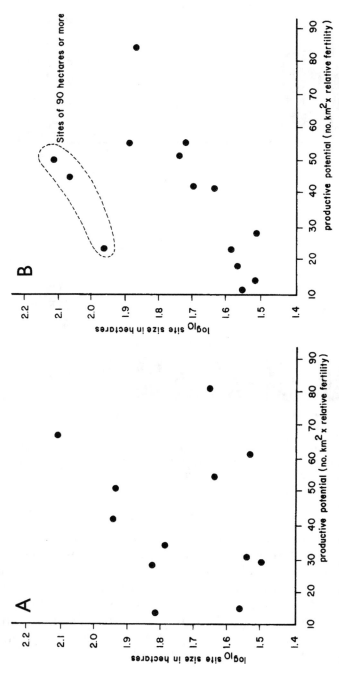

Figure 3.4. Plots of productive potential vs. site size. A is of Late Formative sites (550–250 B.C.); B is of Terminal Formative sites (250 B.C.–A.D. 100). From Brumfiel (1976).

These two graphs display a number of interesting features. First, two sites of the same size, one surrounded by a large area of poor land and one surrounded by a smaller area of good land, can have the same location on the graph. This is because Brumfiel has determined that neither absolute catchment area nor absolute productivity is the key variable. By taking a measure of productivity per unit land and multiplying it by land area, she is able to estimate productivity. Steponaitis (1981) takes Brumfiel's graphs a step further and argues for a three-tier settlement hierarchy. Nonetheless, Brumfiel exploits the lack of an expected linear relationship between site size and total productivity (i.e., the bigger the site, the greater the productivity of the surrounding area) to argue for tribute relationship.

All four figures in the preceding examples use apparently simple data to answer complex questions. In all the cases, the variation itself is quite obvious, once the proper dimensions are identified. The problem is identifying the right variables. These graphs' simplicity and elegance belie their complexity. None of these sprung from raw data; they are heavily compressed and thought out. These graphs are not presented data; rather they are part of the interpretation. The location of the dots, the bar heights, and the frequency distributions are the answers; the axes of variation are the questions.

In most of these graphs the role of negative evidence is profound. The lack of sites or artifacts with specific characteristics is as important to the interpretation as the positive evidence. In Figure 3.1, there are no Neolithic sites with very early dates far from Jericho. In Figure 3.2, there are few sharpened flange-hilt swords. In Figure 3.3, there are few cattle or swine at Hacinebi Tepe. In Figure 3.4, there are no medium-size sites with corresponding productive potentials. The evidence sought and not found is as important as the positive evidence and therefore plays a critical role in any research design. In many cases, your refined questions will focus on the gathering of negative evidence, which is usually a much more rapid process.

The graphs also juxtapose variables that are accessible in the archaeological record and easily measured with variables that are much more difficult to measure and that are the outcome of complex cultural processes. This juxtaposition allows the researcher to argue for divisions and differences that are difficult to detect but critical for interpreting and understanding cultural, economic, and political differences. The distance from Jericho in Figure 3.1 is easily measured, but determining the radiocarbon date for earliest Neolithic domestication is a little more difficult. The juxtaposition indicates that distance from Jericho, which on its face is somewhat arbitrary, is correlated with the complex appearance of the early Neolithic over a wide area of Europe. Ammerman and Cavalli-Sforza use the simplicity of a distance measure to understand the complexities of the Neolithic. The sword-hilt type, displayed in Figure 3.2, is straightforward to assess, whereas the amount of sharpening on a sword blade is more subjective and may be the outcome of preferences that could change over areas or time periods. Showing that hilt type is related to amount of sharpening indicates that the hilt, although not strictly functional, correlates with the function of the sword. This allows Kristiansen to argue for two entirely different types of swords, based on both style and function. The bone percentage in Figure 3.3 is determined archaeologically, whereas the attribution of a given site to one cultural tradition or another is more subjective. The consistency of bone percentages within Stein's division of sites (along with a whole suite of other data) allows Stein to argue that these differences are not due to environment or other local factors but cultural preference. The productive potential in Figure 3.4 is determined from modern maps, and site size is determined from archaeological survey: both straightforward measures. On the other hand, the division of Late Formative (A) and Terminal Formative (B) in Figure 3.4 is made on the basis of pottery style. Although not strictly subjective, there is no inherent reason that tastes in pottery should change with political organization. Brumfiel is not arguing that pottery and social organization are related, rather that it is possible to use changes in pottery as an accurate temporal marker to assess changes in the political structure. The greater division between sites on the upper tier in the Terminal Formative, as compared with the previous period, allows Brumfiel to argue for increased social complexity over time.

The creators of these graphs all use simple archaeological variables juxtaposed against more subjective divisions to create proxies to help them argue for the causes and consequences of social, political, economic, environmental, and cultural differences. The basic idea behind all of these graphs is to juxtapose straightforward archaeological variables against more subjective divisions and measures to bring out complex cultural processes. In the end, the questions are usually a combination of one more or less objective variable and one more-subjective variable—usually the important one for making archaeologically relevant interpretations.

What Answers Look Like

Archaeologists go into the field with shovels, screens, and field forms. They come out of the field with maps, profiles, zip-lock bags of samples, and artifacts. The point is to turn those things into a description, map, graph, chart, or table. To turn holes into samples and samples into tables, charts, and graphs is only the beginning. The graphs and tables are then used as the basis of interpretation of causes of cultural change and stasis. A database is, in most cases, where the questions and answers are formulated. A proper research design and appropriate logistics will allow you to create a database where the categories are the questions and the input data are the answers. Creating a workable database is one of the most difficult tasks for the beginning researcher.

Attributes form the basis of any classification or typology, which is the grouping of artifacts with similar characteristics. The brilliant insight of C. J. Thomsen (previously discussed) was his grouping of artifacts of similar material (an attribute) and looking at how the material changed over time to form the Three Age System. The most basic catalog is that of the attribute (Table 3.1). There can be no more fitting concept for archaeology than the attribute. On the whole, archaeologists use the concept in the grammatical sense (a word or phrase that is subordinate to another and limits or identifies the other's meaning). Attribute is also connected with notions of cause and origin; the word comes from the Latin *tribus*, to assign to a tribe (*tri* being associated with a division of the Roman peoples). Attribute conjures notions of characteristics that can be ascribed to social and political groups. In the example given in Table 3.1, the attribute being studied is the quality of the retouch, not nearly such a telling attribute as some others but still helpful.

Databases are not a substitute for artifact or site catalogs. Databases may be produced out of those catalogs, but they are not inherently the same thing nor are they motivated by the same goals. The database is the foundation for the creation of critical parts of the analysis and interpretation. The research design (including a sampling strategy) is the blueprint for creating that database. Here we will look at only the construction of the tables and very basic statistics that allow you to formulate questions that go with answers.

Although you might think of your data as going into a single database, in fact, if you are doing things right, there will be several databases, each with its own level of analysis. The most common method for constructing databases today is to use computer programs like Excel, FileMaker, FoxPro, and Access. There are more complex statistical programs that use databases, such as SPSS and Systat. These all work on similar principles. The most basic is Excel. Each line, or row, is an instance (attribute, artifact, excavation level, site, region, time period), and each column is a variable (length of retouch, number of flakes, percentage of retouch flakes). This organization is generally necessary for a database, and tables for publication are constructed in a similar manner. The leftmost variable defines the particular instance covered in the rest of the row. This basic organization means that for most projects, a whole series of databases are required, which can be combined in various ways by using a relational database such as FileMaker.

The tables that follow are hypothetical examples of a series of databases. They start at the smallest attribute and the level of analysis becomes larger with each successive example. As we move up the progression, attributes are summarized and some of the details are lost. In Table 3.1, each line displays information about a retouched segment (a small bit of serrated edge that helps in cutting through meat and such; see chapter 19 for more on stone tools). The artifact numbers refer to particular flakes,

Table 3.1.   Artifact Attributes from Single Hypothetical Excavation Unit

Artifact No.	Retouch Segment No.	Length (cm)	Quality	Total for Each Artifact
1	1	0.5	High	
1	2	0.2	Medium	0.7
2	1	0.3	Low	
2	2	0.4	Medium	
2	3	0.3	Low	
3	1	0.6	High	0.6
4	1	0.4	Medium	0.4
Total		**2.7**		

Quality	Total Length (cm)	No. of Segments	Avg. Segment Length (cm)
Low	0.6	2	0.3
Medium	1.0	3	0.3
High	1.1	2	0.6
Total	**2.7**		

small stone chips struck off a larger block. Flakes can be waste products of stone tools, but they can also be used as tools themselves. In these examples, we will study only retouched flakes. Two of the flakes (artifact numbers 1 and 2) have more than one retouch segment. The retouch segment numbers refer to a particular segment of a flake. Listed next to the retouch segment are its length and quality, a more subjective category.

An analysis of the listed variables of the retouch segments indicates that high-quality segments tend to be longer. Although comparing variables from two segments on two artifacts yields far from statistically significant results, the comparison shows that this is the kind of graph, chart, or table that might be helpful to guide further analysis. Many other attributes can be taken: measurements can be made of the height of the retouch, the location of the retouch, and so on. Many of those variables will always covary with each other, because they are inherently related (either because of physical properties or the nature of stone tools). Taking redundant variables is a waste of time, unless subtle variations within the redundancy have other implications.

In Table 3.2, 10 artifacts are listed, each on its own line. The four flakes from Table 3.1 are artifacts 1–4. At this level there is no place in the table for retouch segment. Instead we have opted to list the sum of all the retouch (no matter how many different segments) found on each flake. We could also look at the number of retouched segments or the average length of those segments at the artifact level. That is, all of these are artifact attributes. At the artifact level, the weight of the artifact and whether it has cortex are common variables (a cortex is the outer rind, or original surface, of the stone before it is chipped away). Many other attri-butes can be tracked at this level, possibly thousands. The problem is to pick the ones that yield interesting results—variables that either change with other factors or vary unexpectedly.

An analysis of artifacts by whether they possess a cortex in-dicates that flakes with cortex seem to be slightly heavier and have slightly more retouch. Notice that in this example we can no longer look at the quality of the retouch, at least in a simple way, although it is probably something to explore because, ac-cording to Table 3.1, high-quality retouch seems to come in longer segments.

Table 3.2. Hypothetical Artifact with Retouch and Cortex

Artifact No.	Total Retouch (cm)	Weight (g)	Cortex
1	0.7	4	Yes
2	1	3	No
3	0.6	4	No
4	0.4	4	Yes
5	0.6	5	Yes
6	0.4	3	Yes
7	0.3	2	No
8	6	6	Yes
9	0.1	3	Yes
10	0.3	4	Yes
Total	**10.4**	**38**	
Avg.	**1.04**	**3.8**	

Cortex	n	Total Weight (g)	Avg. Weight (g)	Total Retouch	Avg. Retouch
Yes	7	29	4.1	3.1	0.4
No	3	9	3.0	1.9	0.6

We can now look at retouch flakes by level of an excavation. If the total number of artifacts excavated in each level is the same, the number of flakes with retouch can inform us as to the importance of that activity. If levels have different volumes of excavation, then a count of retouch flakes per volume of soil excavated (e.g., per cubic meter) must be used. Percentages are also a good way to skirt the problem of different densities. In Table 3.3, level 1 with 10 flakes summarizes all of the information presented in Table 3.2.

A cursory glance at the data by levels indicates that level 1 and 2 are quite similar. The retouched flakes from those levels both average about 1 cm of retouch, both weigh an average 3.6 g, and about 70 percent of the flakes have cortex. Retouched flakes from levels 3–5 also share similarities. Retouched flakes from these contexts have much shorter retouch segments, higher average weights, and a lower percentage of cortex. The sample size from level 6 is too small to be meaningful.

It would appear that retouch, weight, and cortex are correlated with depth. The change is not regular with depth but rather seen when comparing levels 1 and 2 with levels 3 through 5. The first question is why. Is there some depositional or post-depositional process that causes this (e.g., plow damage in the first two levels), or is this correlation a function of a change in flake use or flake manufacture? If so, is this difference due to change over time, change in use, change in material, or change in cultural taste? These are the new questions that need to be asked, and field and laboratory work should be reorganized to

Table 3.3. Hypothetical Retouched Flakes by Level

Level	No. Flakes w/retouch	Total Retouch (cm)	Avg. Retouch (cm)	Total Weight (g)	Avg. Weight (g)	No. w/ Cortex	% with Cortex
1	10	10.0	1.00	38	3.8	7	70
2	22	20.0	0.91	78	3.5	15	68
3	30	18.0	0.60	140	4.7	10	33
4	15	9.1	0.61	80	5.3	6	40
5	10	6.0	0.60	55	5.5	4	40
6	1	0.2	0.20	4	4.0	1	100

answer them. These new questions are, in many ways, more important than the answers. The real trick is to figure out what those answers look like. What does the graph or chart or map look like that will allow you to make an argument that explains the variation?

New Questions

Are the questions really as important as the answers? They probably are. Certainly the secret to doing successful original research has more to do with asking the right questions than getting the right answers. The secret to leaving the field with something interesting that contributes to anthropology and archaeology is figuring out what the answer looks like. The logistics of your research should be driven by an attempt to fill in a graph. Once you know what the answer looks like, you can ask the appropriate question of your archaeological data.

One of the most famous graphs in archaeology (Figure 3.5) is a mosaic of European archaeological cultures arranged in space and time by V. Gordon Childe (1957 [1929]). This type of chart is now universally used to depict regional chronologies in all parts of the world (Trigger 1989). Childe created the chart to show the diffusion of traits from the Near East and across Europe. The specifics of the graph are wrong (Renfrew 1973), but the question, What is the relationship between cultures across space and time? is critical and the answer looks like Figure 3.5. Childe's answer may have been wrong, but the question, How do traits spread? and the shape of the answer—a graph of time against space where archaeological cultures are outlined in blocks—seem to have been spot on. The questions may be just as important as the answers.

The logistics of archaeology is about making the questions and answers go together. The archaeological research process is really a wonderful logistical dance, and sometimes it is hard to tell whether the questions or the answers are leading. To take the analogy even further, the question that you bring to the dance may not go home with you. You may have to find a new question. In archaeology that seems to happen a lot, so it is best to

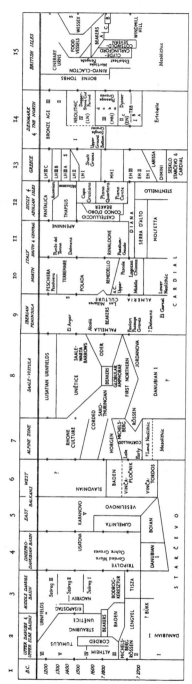

Figure 3.5.   Outdated chronological and geographic distribution of archaeological cultures in Europe. From Childe (1957).

start looking around for your questions before the dance and then be prepared to change questions. Archaeology is fickle, and it is best not to get too attached to a question. After all, if you dance well, you may go home with an even better question.

Acknowledgments

This paper is a result of teaching regional analysis at both the California State University, Northridge, and the University of California, Los Angeles. Tim Earle, my dissertation chair, always organized a conference two-thirds of the way through every field season. I am indebted to him for making that moment of realization come early and often. The computer programs mentioned are not endorsements, just examples. Remember, garbage in, garbage out (unless you are dealing with midden deposits).

References

Adams, R. E. W.
  1969 Maya archaeology 1958–1968, a review. *Latin American Research Review* 4:3–45.

Alexander, John
  1970 *The directing of archaeological excavations.* John Baker, London.

Ammerman, Albert J., and L. L. Cavalli-Sforza
  1973 A population model for the diffusion of early farming in Europe. In *The explanation of culture change*, edited by C. Renfrew, pp. 343–357. Duckworth, London.

Andrews, Gil
  1991 *Management of archaeological projects (MAP2).* English Heritage, London and the Historic Buildings and Monuments Commission for England.

Binford, Lewis R.
  1964 A consideration of archaeological research design. *American Antiquity* 29:425–441.

Brumfiel, Elizabeth M.
  1976 Regional growth in the Eastern Valley of Mexico: A test of the "population pressure" hypothesis. In *The Early Mesoamerican village*, edited by K. Flannery, pp. 234–247. Academic Press, New York.

Childe, V. Gordon
1957 [1929] *The Dawn of European Civilization.* 6th ed. Vintage, New York.

Cooper, Malcom A., Antony Firth, John Carman, and David Wheatley (editors)
1995 *Managing Archaeology.* Routledge, London.

Daniels, S. G. H.
1978 Implications of error: Research design and the structure of archaeology. *World Archaeology* 10:29–35.

Dillion, Brian D.
1993a The archaeological field vehicle. In *Practical Archaeology: Field and laboratory techniques and archaeological logistics*, 3rd ed., edited by Brian D. Dillon, pp. 39–62. Institute of Archaeology, University of California, Los Angeles.
1993b (editor) *Practical Archaeology: Field and laboratory techniques and archaeological logistics.* 3rd ed. Institute of Archaeology, University of California, Los Angeles.

Drewett, Peter L.
1999 *Field archaeology: An introduction.* UCL Press, London.

Ellis, Linda (editor)
2000 *Archaeological method and theory: An encyclopedia.* Garland Publishing, New York.

Fagan, Brian M.
1994 *Quest for the past: Great discoveries in archaeology.* Waveland Press, New York.

Fladmark, Knut R.
1978 *A guide to basic archaeological field procedures.* Department of Anthropology Publication #4. Simon Fraser University, Burnaby, Bristish Columbia

Flannery, Kent V.
1976 Research strategy and formative Mesoamerica. In *The Early Mesoamerican village,* edited by Kent V. Flannery, pp. 1–11. Academic Press, New York.

Graslund, Bo
1987 *The birth of prehistoric chronology: Dating methods and dating systems in nineteenth-century Scandinavian archaeology.* New studies in archaeology. Cambridge University Press, Cambridge.

Hester, Thomas R., Harry J. Shafer, and Kenneth L. Feder
1997 *Field methods in archaeology.* 7th ed. Mayfield, Mountain View, California.

Hodder, Ian
1999 *The archaeological process: An introduction.* Blackwell, Oxford.

Joukowsky, Martha
1980   *A complete manual of field archaeology: Tools and techniques of field work for archaeologists*. Prentice-Hall, Englewood Cliffs, New Jersey.

King, Thomas
1998   *Cultural resource law and practice: An introductory Guide*. AltaMira, Walnut Creek, California.

Kristiansen, Kristian
1987   From stone to bronze—the evolution of social complexity in Northern Europe, 2300–1200 BC. In *Specialization, exchange and complex societies*, edited by E. Brumfiel and T. Earle, pp. 30–51. Cambridge University Press, Cambridge.

Lucas, Gavin
2001   *Critical approaches to fieldwork: Contemporary and historical archaeological practice*. Routledge, London.

McManamon, Francis P., and Alf Hatton
1999   *Cultural resource management in contemporary society*. Routledge, New York.

McMillon, Bill
1991   *The archaeology handbook: A field manual and resource guide*. New York: John Willey and Sons.

Petrie, W. M. Flinders
1904   *Methods and aims in archaeology*. Macmillan, New York.

Pitt-Rivers, A. H. L. F.
1887   *Excavations in Cranborne Chase*. Printed Privately.
1906   *The evolution of culture*. Clarendon Press, Oxford.

Purdy, Barbara A.
1996   *How to do archaeology the right way*. University Press of Florida, Gainesville.

Redman, Charles L.
1973   Multistage fieldwork and analytical techniques. *American Antiquity* 38:61–79.
1987   Surface collection, sampling and research design: A retrospective. *American Antiquity* 52:249–265.

Redman, Charles L., and William L. Rathje (editors)
1973   *Research and theory in current archaeology*. Wiley, New York.

Renfrew, Colin
1973   *Before Civilization*. Knopf, New York.

Renfrew, Colin, and Paul Bahn
2000   *Archaeology*. 3rd ed. Thames and Hudson, New York.

Schliemann, Heinrich
　　1976　[1881] *Ilios: The city and country of the Trojans; the results of researches and discoveries on the site of Troy and throughout the Troad in the years 1871, 72, 73, 78, 79; including an autobiography of the author.* Arno Press, New York.

Sharer, Robert J., and Wendy Ashmore
　　1993　*Archaeology: Discovering our past.* Mayfield, Mountain View, California.

Stein, Gil
　　1999　*Rethinking world-systems: Diasporas, colonies, and interaction in Uruk Mesopotamia.* University of Arizona Press, Tucson.

Steponaitis, Vincas P.
　　1981　Settlement hierarchies and political complexity in nonmarket societies: The Formative Period in the Valley of Mexico. *American Anthropologist* 83:320–363.

Stiebing, William H., Jr.
　　1994　*Uncovering the Past: A History of Archaeology.* Oxford University Press, Oxford.

Struever, Stuart
　　1971　Comments on archaeological data requirements and research strategy. *American Antiquity* 36:9–19.

Thomsen, Carl J.
　　1962　[1837]. The various periods to which heathen relics can be assigned. In *Man's discovery of his past,* edited by Robert F. Heizer, pp. 21–26. Prentice-Hall, Englewood Cliffs, New Jersey.

Trigger, Bruce Graham
　　1989　*A history of archaeological thought.* Cambridge University Press, Cambridge.

Tufte, Edward R.
　　1983　*The visual display of quantitative information.* Graphics Press, Chelshire.

Webster, Graham
　　1974　*Practical Archaeology: An introduction to archaeological field-work and excavation.* St. Martins Press, New York.

Willey, Gordon (editor)
　　1974　*Archaeological researches in retrospect.* Winthrop, Cambridge.

Worsaae, J. J. A.
　　1849　*The primeval antiquities of Denmark.* John Henry Parker, London.

4

Archaeological Survey

Brian Leigh Molyneaux

The essence of an archaeological survey, or prospection, is the search for material traces of past cultural activity. The landscape offers the promise of artifacts, and surveyors try to find them so they can begin the process of analyzing and interpreting what the past was like.

Survey and Design

Archaeologists thrive on the search for the unknown, but rarely are surveys random explorations. Although intuition always plays an important role in creative thought, prospection requires careful planning, because the recognition, recording, and recovery of material culture are specific to individual surveyors and to the circumstances they face in the field. It makes sense, therefore, to develop a research design outlining background theories, analytic and interpretive methods, information categories, and research expectations before the first step in the field—even if the goal is to locate as many cultural resources in a survey area as possible. This plan is not only a guide to the fieldwork but also may help inform subsequent analysis and interpretation by establishing the parameters of the investigation: what surveyors attended to and what they ignored.

The routine application of a systematic research design may also lead to intellectual complacency and the decline of the sort of critical thinking that moves archaeology forward (as Thomas Kuhn [1962] captured in his notion of intellectual paradigms). Historiographic studies show that despite the doggedness of archaeological practice—surveying, digging, classifying, and interpreting as faithfully as possible within the constraints of empirical methods—archaeology undergoes epistemological change, variation in the validity and limits of data, in step with fundamental changes in science and culture. This is evident in the history of archaeological theory, which at a fundamental level varies between formalism (an emphasis on objects and their relationships) and contextualism (an emphasis on environments). At times of intense interest in the data potential of objects, surveys tend to focus on artifact collection—for example, in the late nineteenth century when Sir Flinders Petrie developed the concept of seriation deep in his excavation trenches in Egypt and during the earlier twentieth century in North America when archaeologists began to define cultures by ceramic and projectile point styles. With the post–World War II development of cybernetics and systems theory, which gave theoretical support to studies of culture and environment that had begun in the 1930s, an increasing number of archaeologists explored the relationships between humans and their surroundings. Scientists involved in other land-based research, especially biologists and geomorphologists, eventually joined archaeologists in comprehensive studies of past ecological systems, and routine data collection expanded to include animal and botanical remains, soil and landform development, and other evidence associated with cultural-environmental interactions. The need to characterize complex multidimensional environments using cartography and the growth of computer use in research led in the 1960s to what is now known as geographic information systems (GIS): in 1963 Canada established the Canada Geographic Information System (CGIS), designed to inventory its vast landmass, and the following year Harvard University established its Computer Graphics and Spatial Analysis laboratory for the development of software to handle spatial data. By the late 1980s, when GIS and other computer-related research in archaeology began to flourish, artifacts and even sites had become very small indeed. At the same time, the translation from Russian of Sergei A. Semenov's study of wear on stone tools (Semenov 1964) opened up an equally vast landscape. For the first time, once could conceive of surveys devoted to cultural activity at multiple scales, from geographic regions to the surfaces of individual tools.

Given the complexity of these various intellectual and material landscapes, it is clear that surveys are not merely data collection or routine preludes to the more rewarding task of interpretation. By providing evidence appropriate to prevailing theories of culture and understandings of the past, they inspire and shape the work that follows.

Sample of Epistemological Issues

The results of a survey are mediated by one fundamental, irresolvable problem: a survey is an indeterminate, culturally relative activity designed to seek traces of many other indeterminate, culturally relative activities. Field archaeologists are therefore reduced to gathering objects and recording material relationships among physical and environmental variables as a prelude to analysis and interpretation. Although it may be tempting to avoid thinking through the survey process to expose other practical and conceptual problems in knowledge acquisition and representation, the way that individual archaeologists approach such problems, implicitly or explicitly, helps to determine the character of their surveys—and, from a broad historical perspective, the approach of entire generations of archaeologists. Below are a few typical issues that may be worth pondering while designing a survey because they relate to different aspects of the process: the visualization of the landscape to be explored, the nature and goals of the search, and the creation of knowledge through discovery and recordation.

The landscape that shaped the cultural material may be substantially different from the landscape that shaped the original activity.

A profound difficulty with surveys is that the environment explored may not resemble the environment of previous occupations. The perceptual cues a surveyor uses for navigation and the interpretation of spatial relationships may be either misleading or wrong. For example, the modern setting of Stonehenge and other Neolithic monuments in southern England and in France enhances their emotional impact, because they stand gray and mysterious in treeless landscapes. The effect, and perhaps the trend of interpretations, may have been very different if the landscape had not lost its forests and, eventually, its soil mantle thousands of years ago to agriculture.

Because erosion, deposition, and other physical processes slowly and endlessly transform landscapes, the ground may bear little or no relation to original land surfaces, consisting instead of mixed or poorly separated soils and other geologic materials, flora and fauna, and traces of human activity of different ages. We humans rarely notice these formation processes at work or the palimpsests that result; geomorphological changes, along with bioturbation and cryoturbation and other ground disturbances, tend to take place too slowly to catch our attention. Hence the spatial relationships among artifacts and landforms may reflect the deformation of the environment, rather than any specific intact landscape with all its relationships.

Even if old landforms are buried and preserved as paleosols, sheer visibility is a problem. In the Great Plains of North America, for example, the shifting of vast loads of sediment into river valleys over millennia sometimes buries all evidence of human occupation meters below the surface. How can we survey these regions and explore the nature of ancient cultural adaptations when the only traces appear in stream cutbanks? In many other places, the opposite is true. It is common to find scatters of artifacts, separated in origin by hundreds or thousands of years, in a single deposit, produced as their soil matrices eroded. Resolving these endlessly refashioned landscapes is equally complex, because the present situation may be nothing like earlier times (see Wandsnider 2003 for a recent discussion of problems in the interpretation of complex archaeological surfaces).

At each moment, places, people, and material culture have a world of connections, and each change that severs a connection increases the obscurity of the past, its history and nature, meaning, function, and significance. The continuous action of natural and cultural forces on the environment ensures that there can never be a pristine landscape, a discrete culture, or a simple tool. Every material thing has links beyond the horizon and dissolved in time. The traces we find are selectively preserved and randomly presented, subject to the vicissitudes of land formation processes and site taphonomy.

A survey may seem like a search for the past, but the past is already gone.

It may be difficult to think that artifacts and features are really phenomena of the present, especially when they emerge, fresh with mystery, from long-buried soils. They certainly originated in the past—earlier presents—but once an archaeologist recognizes and retrieves them in a survey, they take on a different function, becoming tools that serve the institution of archaeology and the contemporary narratives about the past it constructs and promotes. Understanding this intellectual conceit is crucial to interpretation. Archaeology may provide empirically valid information about past phenomena, but no comprehensive vision of history and culture that results is sacrosanct. Nonarchaeologists may view these traces differently, even creating interpretations that ignore or deny material evidence in conflict with their own historical understandings. That these alternative stories are equally valid in a cultural sense should not be troubling. The clues to what happened in history may be evident in its traces, but there are different ways of teasing out interpretations, using different rules of evidence that respond to different needs. Archaeology's unstinting focus on the material evidence that systematic surveys and excavations retrieve is its greatest asset. Although epistemological change affects even the most palpably scientific interpretations, the network of relationships between artifacts, places, and regions provides a good foundation for the critical reinterpretation that follows.

Discovery and recording create objects, boundaries, and relationships that may not have existed in the past.

The recognition of material culture in surveys is a matter of training and experience, knowledge of the categories of objects, features, and relations that archaeology deems important. Given that the discovery process involves two highly subjective steps—the perception of a specific material object or formation within the available visual array and its recognition as a phenomenon worthy of further study—all surveys are highly selective in their results. A surveyor might not even perceive information outside the familiar, which shows that truly comprehensive surveys are impossible.

Once an entity gets a name, it effectively stands out from the undifferentiated background, with form, substance, and boundaries that give it independent existence. This process is, of course, inevitable, because data are not retrievable otherwise, but it reinforces the fact that the information in artifacts is not immanent: archaeologists create it through their interpretations.

Such necessity sometimes confers an artificial significance on an object or accumulation of cultural material. Artifacts have long traveled in the guise of social groups or cultures, because the Beaker Folk in western Europe, the Oneota in the late prehistoric of the central Great Plains in North America, and other hypothetical groups were afforded cultural status by virtue of stylistic patterns in material culture. The collection of artifacts and features known as the "site" is similarly problematic, because human activity is continual at different densities across the landscape, forming loci of activity, rather than series of bounded entities. This condition is so even if a culture occupies walled settlements; in such instances, the boundaries between high- and low-activity areas may simply be more abrupt. Yet, despite the introduction of the global positioning system (GPS) and GIS mapping technologies, which are precise enough to make non-site approaches more viable, archaeologists still have to be able to differentiate things and places. Under the circumstances, it is wise to remember the nature of site distinctions when they appear on a map, whether they reflect the vagaries of a survey or evidence of variations in activity within a past environment.

Such objectification may also distract attention from nonmaterial aspects of a cultural phenomenon—particularly the culturally mediated behavior that produced it. It should not be difficult in a field that attempts to derive information on past culture from material things to argue that artifacts are merely the traces of more significant actions, but objects have the advantage of sheer existence—and hence a direct means of engagement.

This is especially so with visual representations. Generations of art historians and archaeologists have pored over the Paleolithic artwork in the caves of France and Spain and other rock paintings and carvings across the world, seeking their elusive meanings and functions. However, what if the *act* of painting or carving was sometimes the goal and the completed image was merely a residue of these significant actions, as is a votive offering or, in other domains, lithic debitage or performance art? Exploring this aspect directs attention to the *situation of production* and to studies as diverse as the analysis of image construction or the detailed analysis of a rock art site as a theater of human action, using insights from approaches to behavior as various as proxemics, ergonomics, and agency (Molyneaux 1997). Given this alternative potential, art theorists and surveyors might spend more time considering images as artifacts of behavior than as windows to the imagination.

The crucial effect of this epistemological problem on archaeology cannot be minimized. The accumulation of artifacts, sites, and interpretations, and the institutionalized patterns and habits of thought and action that result, create an enormous burden on the shoulders of every archaeologist who sets off into the field. Historiography is useful in that it records how archaeology changes over time, as data are focused on or ignored, methods are supported or abandoned, and theories are championed or rejected. With this in mind, a surveyor may walk across previously surveyed ground knowing that each survey is unique and always full of potential.

Although it is now easier to justify resurveys or reinvestigations of excavated sites, it is not as easy to change fundamental directions; this awaits the sort of revolutionary change embodied in paradigm shifts. The routinely derided Mound Builder theory, a belief popular in the eighteenth and nineteenth centuries that a culture unrelated to North American Indians constructed the massive earthworks scattered along major river valleys in the eastern United States, was reasonable for the time, given the prevailing concepts of prehistory and the nature of investigative techniques. So are theories of catastrophic social change, such as those applied to the culture known as the Anasazi of the southwestern United States, the Maya of Mexico and Central America, or Late Bronze Age cultures around the Mediterranean. The visibility of such abrupt declines is literal, marked in each instance by the collapse of monumental architecture. It is possible, however, that this salience obscures a subtle denouement that simply lacks the sort of markers that we have learned to interpret as civilization, making these continuously developing cultures invisible for a time to ordinary archaeological survey.

The nature, significance, and success of survey results vary with the scale of interpretation.

Large-scale views of the archaeological record tend to resolve the unknown better than site-level studies do. This is not surprising, because the larger the scale, the less visible are the problematic relationships among artifacts, features, and places. It is certainly easier to suppose that a hunting and gathering culture adapted to the resources a drainage basin had to offer than it is to elucidate daily life at a particular place along the river. And it is simpler to imagine that a tool is a projectile point or a scraper than a surface containing features of its manufacture and evidence of its use to penetrate, cut, or scrape specific types of material.

These examples suggest that, as the scale of perception changes, the information we derive also changes. The effect is especially problematic today, with the increasing use of GIS technology as a mapping and data visualization tool. The problem is what has been termed the *ecological fallacy*. To put it simply, the relationships observed at a large scale do not necessarily hold at smaller scales, because the larger-scale view eliminates potential variation.

The effect of scale also underlines a practical problem in ground-level surveys: if a feature resolves at a scale sufficiently larger (or smaller) than a viewer's field of perception, it will be invisible. It was this effect that made O. G. S. Crawford's introduction of aerial photography in Britain after World War I so revolutionary.

When even the most mundane human action—say, making a cup of coffee—is profoundly difficult to describe and analyze as a physical and cultural act, the efforts of archaeologists to survey landscapes with perhaps tens of thousands of years of human occupation and interpret the results seem absurd. It is, however, a matter of scale. The challenge is to work at a scale appropriate to the information at hand and to the desired outcome!

Survey in Practice

A survey is mediated by a host of variables, including the goal of the archaeological study articulated within theoretical and methodological paradigms, the nature and extent of background knowledge of the regional archaeology, the type of survey, the size and boundaries of the survey area, the scale of observation, the sampling strategy, and the subjective perceptions and actions of the surveyors within the actual circumstances of the search.

Current State of Theory and Method

The selection of epistemological issues outlined above shows that a survey is not simply a set of procedures that will yield appropriate results if applied with suitable rigor. Every project has an implicit conceptual orientation. In formalist approaches, the landscape is typically a source of scarce cultural resources that are waiting to be discovered, analyzed, and interpreted. In contextualist approaches, cultural resources are conceived within the totality of cultural and natural phenomena in the landscape. The battling theoretical paradigms of the late twentieth century, which persist in less-contentious forms in ordinary archaeology, show these tendencies. The culture process approach, which tends toward formalism, has a pragmatic materialism, dogged attention to logical structure and formal detail, and an interest in systemic interactions for the purpose of creating general theory. Postmodernist approaches (commonly known as postprocessualism) exhibit a concern with social configurations and the role of the archaeologist as participant in the process, with the goal of extending archaeological analysis beyond behavioral ecology.

Theorizing aside, survey routines are essentially unchanged since the regional studies in the 1930s and 1940s that established methodologies oriented toward cultural life in local and regional environments. The fundamental epistemological problems remain, as they would be, unresolved, and new ones have emerged, as intellectual and practical control over survey shifts increasingly from academic institutions to government bureaucracies. The new archaeology of the 1980s, cultural resources management, has also increased its hold over the profession, feeding off the growth in government regulations associated with the protection of cultural resources and becoming the chief employer for archaeologists outside government agencies. Although academic archaeology continues to play an influential role, its traditional theoretical agenda suffers from these external political and economic forces, as well as from increasingly strong pressures, in some countries, from indigenous peoples who question the rights of archaeologists to explore their pasts.

The most significant influence on archaeological survey today relates to the implementation in the past two decades of computerized detection and mapping technologies that have dramatically enhanced the utility of GIS: laser survey equipment (electronic total stations) and satellite-based terrestrial locational systems (i.e., GPS). The spatial precision of total-station coordinate data for artifact piece plotting has reached subcentimeter scale, and the geographic precision of artifact and feature coordinate data with real-time error correction is now routinely submeter.

With the overlay of increasingly precise locational data, derived from total station and GPS recording, on digital versions of topographic base maps and aerial photographs, GIS now provides exciting new possibilities for analysis and interpretation. Topographic variables such as absolute distance, elevation, slope, aspect, and viewshed, which are almost impossible to characterize by hand, can be quickly enabled over entire regions in a digital elevation model, correlated, and compared to other data. GIS technology does not resolve the fundamental problems that all archaeologists face when attempting to derive cultural information from material data captured in coordinate space, but the improvement over traditional mechanical and paper-mapping technologies is so substantial that laser recording, GPS, and GIS are quickly replacing traditional methods.

Because GIS relates to any coordinate system, it has no bias toward strictly environmental variables, just as geography itself ranges from psychological concepts of place to chorography. As Maschner (1996) and others show, GIS is a system for organizing and representing information having a spatial aspect, whether it is essentially material or ideological in nature.

Survey Types

A typical survey is a ground-level search, increasingly guided by an explicit research design, that samples the required terrain at a predetermined density, aided by topographic maps and aerial photographs. Archaeologists in some environments, particularly those with a past that included structured settlement (e.g., house and village sites, field systems, and formal transportation routes), may work with remote-sensing imagery before engaging in field walking. Surveyors may also attempt to increase the probability of discovery by using site-potential models developed with a GIS. The subsurface remains generally opaque, even as geophysical exploration techniques become more precise, because most surveyors still eschew these methods (often because of cost) in favor of probing the subsurface mostly to little effect, given the absurd disproportion between the scale of any subsurface matrix and the difficulties exploring it. Working under such limitations with highly fragmented data in generally impoverished contexts will always be archaeology's lot and the source of its creativity and strength of purpose.

The most basic survey is the simple inventory, concerned with locating all past cultural resources in an area. This approach is required in cultural resource management surveys, where governmental regulations may specify a cutoff date for recent cultural material (e.g., it must be more than 50 years old to warrant attention), necessary in regions where little archaeological work has been done, and wise in areas where the archaeological record derives mainly from historical, rather than current, research.

Large regional inventories emerged during the broad shift in epistemology from objects to environments that began in the late 1930s, as archaeologists tried to make sense out of the traditional patchwork of excavated sites. Gordon Willey devised a methodology for his survey of settlement in the Viru Valley, Peru, in the late 1940s that influenced all large-scale surveys to come. It featured extensive background research, including terrain analysis through maps and the relatively new technology of aerial photography, on-the-ground survey, location and mapping of sites, surface collection, selective excavation, chronological analysis of the artifacts, and the preparation of distribution maps showing settlement patterns over time and space (Willey 1953).

Surveys may also focus on specific cultures, time periods, or activities: for example, Roman colonization, pre-Clovis occupation in the New World, or lithic procurement and distribution. Although the approach may seem simpler than an inventory because it limits the range of potential data, surveys of this kind usually require extensive background research to enable the field walker to discriminate relevant cultural material within the normal clutter of a lived-in landscape. Geologic and geomorphological research may also be necessary to trace appropriate formations if there have been extensive changes in topography. For example, archaeologists searching for late Pleistocene occupations in the Great Lakes region must identify terrace remnants of glacial Lakes Agassiz and Algonquin, now in woodlands and agricultural uplands far from the modern lakes (e.g., Storck 2004), whereas surveyors seeing their evidence along the world's coastlines may have to locate sites either submerged or uplifted after the glacial retreats.

Some selective surveys target specific artifacts over large regions, such as obsidian or other lithic material with an identified source, precious metals, or manufactured goods, to identify wider social interactions through the evidence of trade and exchange networks. One classic example, established by regional surveys and excavations, charts the influence of complex agriculturist societies, centered in the Mississippi and Ohio river valleys during the Middle Woodland period (ca. 1950–1550 B.P.), across central and southern North America east of the Rocky Mountains. Caldwell (1964) first identified this distribution of stylistic traits and preferences in material culture, architecture, art, and ritual as the Hopewell Interaction Sphere; subsequent researchers regard the phenomenon as the action of discrete, widely shared social and symbolic systems, as opposed to a more systematically interrelated culture. Another selective survey

traces Roman influence across the Mediterranean and throughout Europe by the distribution of amphorae used in the oil and
wine trade. Such studies have the advantage that they can use
existing artifact inventories to establish the area of dispersion before directing surveys and excavations to explore cultural connections in more detail—a crucial aspect, because it takes more
than the presence or absence of a product to indicate a direct cultural relationship. McCann et al. (1987), for example, used the
distribution in western Europe of amphorae produced by the
Roman mercantile family Sestii to define the trading network of
the Roman town of Cosa; with a region of influence defined,
they were able to explore Cosa's significance against the background of Rome's transition from a provincially focused agricultural society to an aggressive mercantile nation.

A new kind of selectivity relates to issues of cultural sensitivity. In Australia and North America especially, surveyors may
avoid working in areas significant to contemporary native peoples unless they can gain their consent. Although such avoid-
ance may be legally mandated, archaeologists are increasingly
aware that their work may have a considerable social impact beyond the discipline. By its very nature as a material discipline,
archaeology objectifies the past, so it tends to conflict with indigenous beliefs. Indeed, native people may view surveys as in-
trusions and excavations as desecrations, even if the work is
outside current tribal areas. To ease this problem, archaeologists
may design surveys in cooperation with tribal groups who own,
or have a traditional claim over, the lands in question.

Scale of Approach

There is a traditional dichotomy in archaeology between
large-scale regional surveys, which attempt to provide an
overview of patterns of intercultural activity, adaptation, and
change, and small-scale site-level surveys, bent on understanding specific behaviors in a particular place over time. The scale
an archaeologist chooses is not simply a matter of perspective.
The cost of large surveys has tended to confine these studies to
larger institutions with easier access to research funds. With the
onset of GIS, however, large-scale surveys are no longer outside

the reach of other archaeologists. It is now possible to gather existing data sets relating to the archaeology, ecology, and geomorphology of a region, process them within a GIS environment, and develop a practicable survey strategy using selective surveys and excavations. In addition, because a GIS is by nature variable in scale, archaeologists may ignore the old dichotomy altogether, moving seamlessly (with due regard for the ecological fallacy) from particular to general perspectives—that is, as long as they remember that regional studies constructed from smaller surveys and excavations are only as good as their component parts. The democratization of survey archaeology in this way may eventually bring a greater diversity of archaeologists into the mainstream and infuse method and theory with new energy.

Survey Boundaries

Site concepts have also changed little since their nineteenth-century beginnings: a site is a locus of cultural activity that an archaeologist encloses within a boundary, cultural resources are inside sites, and cultural relationships are between and among sites. Drawing boundaries around activity areas makes sense in a world where all land is property, and it makes even more sense when land is managed and cultural resources must be explicitly defined and located, but it is also obvious that people occupy environments rather than places and that cultural material is actually distributed in varying densities across the land. With this in mind, some archaeologists conduct surveys that record all visible evidence of human activity across a survey area without imposing artificial boundaries (e.g., Ebert 1992). Unsurprisingly, this technique works best in areas with mass wasting, such as deserts and cultivated lands, where artifacts are readily exposed, but it suffers from the problem of horizontal stratigraphy: variations in landscape morphology through erosion may result in a skewed distribution of surface artifacts from different times.

Conventional site surveys that extend outside the euclidean boundaries of grids or property lines into the unstructured landscape may gain a more comprehensive picture of land use and settlement. If they are focused on drainages and other naturally bounded ecological zones, they tend to minimize the significance of individual sites by simply adopting a larger scale of view. Ideally, the search area should be large enough to encompass the primary activities of a cultural group, especially with respect to the actions that yield the most material evidence: settlement and resource exploitation. Otherwise, it may be impossible to identify the network of relations that help to characterize them. Although cultural landscapes with specific boundaries, such as walled settlements or field systems, may appear to be already delimited, activity spills over these artificial divides in response to other cultural and environmental factors.

The separable elements in a landscape survey are measurable environmental variables such as climate, terrain, soils, slope, elevation, ecology, distance to water, and efficiency of access to the surrounding territory. These physical features tend to shape cultural activity, mediated by the fact that humans may respond to cultural preferences and imperatives that bear little relation to what archaeologists think are optimal. The relative significance, or weight, of each variable depends on the nature of the cultural adaptation: the land-use patterns of mobile hunters and gatherers who range in a seasonal cycle along a river drainage system or coastline may be profoundly different from those of a sedentary horticultural group settled in a fertile valley.

Research designs that incorporate human factors in a landscape survey may benefit from a strategy based on the work of James J. Gibson, the perceptual and environmental psychologist, that defines boundaries according to the *affordance* potentials in a given environment (Gibson 1979). Affordances are possibilities for action; different cultural and natural environments *afford* various options for behavior (see Costall 1995). Because humans usually prefer to live on fairly level ground (or they make it so) and close to water and other resources, terraces along river valleys and coastlines tend to have a high affordance value for human habitation. However, there are exceptions—for example, one affordance (protection from enemies) might sometimes take precedence over others (level ground, distance to water and food). In addition, an environment may present different affordances at different times. The winter environment in northern climates, for example, is drastically different from the summer environment. People may aggregate in the winter and disperse in the summer, as the Inuit do; they may choose different land-scapes for habitation and travel. And a specific group may select, or avoid, a certain locality for ideological reasons, rather than for its landscape attributes. If a survey attempts to be comprehensive, it is therefore important to consider all forms of behavior (social, technological, economic, ideological) and attempt to model the environmental features or aspects that might afford these behaviors in the lands under study.

Unless the goal of a survey is to add data to an inventory rather than explore cultural and environmental relationships, it will never encompass all the cultural relationships it may seek. In the archaeology of Palestine, for example, several scenarios have been touted over the years to account for the rise of Israelis in the land of Canaan. At first, archaeologists sought simply to affirm the biblical story of Joshua, which tells of his military con-quest of the Promised Land. Their excavations at some cities mentioned in the Bible seemed to bear out these accounts—but some others did not. Eventually, the mass of contrary data from regional surveys and excavations provoked alternative interpre-tations, including peaceful infiltration, internal revolt, and com-binations of the two. Although debates continue over which model is best, Stiebing (1989) points out that, because the eastern Mediterranean world at the end of the Late Bronze Age saw the collapse of cities across the region and dramatic changes in set-tlement patterns, the events in Palestine can hardly be isolated from these larger-scale disturbances. Clearly, wider regional studies, incorporating specifically designed survey and excava-tion results, need to replace smaller-scale glosses here and else-where.

Sampling Strategies

All archaeological surveys are selective in their retrieval of information, varying with the proportion of an area examined and the nature and circumstances of detection. Although intu-itive and unstructured exploration may be highly effective, for-mal sampling strategies, which rely on statistical probability to mitigate the effects of substantially reduced coverage across an area, reduce the effects of bias in the coverage and provide a record of the actual ground surveyed. Success in both ultimately depends on the skill of the surveyor, of course, rather than on the thoroughness of the approach or the putative logic of the sampling.

The most common form of intentional sampling is the transect survey: coverage along predetermined lines set a predetermined distance apart. This is especially useful where there is little or no exposed ground. The simplest statistical technique is random sampling. Surveyors divide the area under study into transects or grid blocks and sample a percentage of them, the choice usually made by a random-number generator. Although these techniques are the stock-in-trade of the archaeologist conducting small area surveys, large-scale transect surveys also provide efficient, if coarse, pictures of site distributions across a region, as at the Greek island of Melos, where an island-wide, 20 percent sampling of 5-km survey blocks almost tripled the number of recorded sites (Cherry 1982; see description in Renfrew and Bahn 1996).

The problem with purely logical sampling strategies is that they are planned on a theoretical plane surface, making no reference to environmental variability. If the survey area is an arid plain, this may be a suitable way to make sense of widely scattered artifacts and sites. For most areas, however, it may be better to take account of environmental differences that might influence cultural activity and bias results. In a survey that crosses various terrains, for example, a stratified sampling design requires random sampling on each terrain separately before the concatenation of results.

A distinct form of sampling derives from GIS-based predictive models of site potential. These constructs create probability surfaces—maps of the landscape that show the relative probability for the discovery of an archaeological site in any given place. Within the vast literature on this subject, the notion that the probability of site discovery relates to an interplay of variables associated with the surveyor, the knowledge resources behind the survey, land-use preferences, and the survey environment has inspired a variety of computational approaches that take human factors into account in search strategies. They derive essentially from Bayes's theorem, formulated in the eighteenth century by the English mathematician Thomas Bayes to account for the fact that probability changes with experience: searching is not conducted mindlessly, but rather is continuously informed by prior results—as in the intuitive method of an experienced surveyor. By adopting a Bayesian approach, which in essence quantifies subjective knowledge, a survey strategy may become a process of continuously updating probabilities of discovery rather than a sterile exercise appealing to mathematical logic alone (for a general reference to archaeological applications, see Buck et al. 1996).

Mapping the distribution of probability that a survey will locate prehistoric sites across a landscape requires the identification of features or variables associated with their locations. Because a GIS can characterize environmental variables at any scale and process them selectively in relation to cultural-resource data for any locality, a survey incorporating Bayesian inference may be advantageous. One could take the following steps to create a simple predictive model of this kind for archaeological sites in a GIS. First, compile a database of existing cultural resources, their locations, and cultural and temporal affiliation. Then, in the GIS project, create a background of digital base maps, elevation models, and remote-sensing imagery; add layers that record environmental attributes, such as soils; add the existing cultural resources database as a layer or theme; and finally, see if the distribution of resources that appears as an overlay on the maps favors specific environments. To further inform the process, one could take advantage of this prior knowledge by calculating the degree of correlation of landscape variables with sites (or other resources), weight the environmental variables numerically (e.g., at its simplest, 0 is low site probability, 1 is moderate or high probability), and reprocess the data so that the selected environmental attributes reflect a higher or lower probability for sites.

In practice, the most serious problems in the development of such predictive environmental models, outside issues related to specific cultural preferences, are the quality of the locational data for objects and places recorded before the introduction of GPS and the resolution of GIS base maps and imagery. For example, as part of a Bayesian study of prehistoric site distributions along the American River and Cosumnes River in the Central Valley of

California, contributing to the enhancement of a predictive model for the region, Hansen et al. (2002) explored the problem of spatial uncertainty in site locations. After identifying several environmental aspects of recorded sites in the region—landform type, proximity to stream channels, elevation range, and slope range—they attempted to correlate specific attributes and the recorded site locations. They used the weights of evidence technique, giving each landform variable a different numeric weight to reflect the relative strength of its association with archaeological site locations. Of the 170 sites they examined, only 47 had locations on the probability surface (at a scale of 1:24,000) that correlated strongly with landform position, proximity to a stream channel, and location above the active floodplain. To account for the remainder, most recorded before 1960, they compared the verbal descriptions of the settings in the original reports with the mapped site locations and concluded that the locations were simply incorrect. Although these and other researchers have developed GIS-based predictive models using a variety of computational methods, going beyond what traditional archaeologists would predict intuitively, the creation of three-dimensional probability surfaces in a GIS continues to suffer from problems of resolution. Most readily available digital elevation models (DEMs) are far too coarse (e.g., 30 m of elevation for U.S. Geological Survey DEMs), but with digitized aerial photographs now available at 1 m resolution in color or false-color infrared and high resolution LIDAR (light detection and ranging) elevation models at a vertical precision of 15 cm now coming on line, the potential is great for refining sampling strategies informed by probability surfaces and other predictive models.

Emerging Approaches

For detailed ground surface exploration, there is yet no substitute for the traditional visual survey. Subsurface detection by magnetometry, resistivity, electromagnetic conductivity, ground-penetrating radar, and side-scanning sonar continue to improve in resolution and practicability. Three-dimensional subsurface modeling is now a reality: in a recent project, for example,

Molyneaux (Molyneaux and Copsey 2005) used a Syscal 3D soil resistivity system to locate a buried paleochannel and explore the subsurface structure of an amphitheater at the Marcham-Frilford Romano-British ceremonial center, currently being excavated by the University of Oxford (Lock et al. 2001). These models resolve depth more accurately than conventional two-dimensional pseudosections and they can be explored dynamically within three-dimensional GIS or other virtual-reality-modeling software. Remote visualization via satellite is increasingly precise and more readily available, further improving the facility of GIS to reveal patterns of cultural activity in the landscape. In particular, the production of submeter DEMs will provide a tremendous impetus to the study of human spatial behavior in the landscape. When remote-sensing imagery and elevation models are detailed enough that they can characterize environmental features at a scale commensurate with human behaviors, a wide variety of large-scale studies associated with charting the movements of peoples through topography, from natural pathways to navigation to migration and recolonization studies (see, for example, papers in Rockman and Steele 2003), will undoubtedly benefit.

Real-time data recording and transmission technologies are also beginning to have an impact in field studies. The traditional field book record, usually written in retrospect with the benefits of reflection, will always be a valuable document. However, short-range wireless computer systems using radio wave broadcasters (for example, the 802.11 standard and Bluetooth technology), installed on handheld computers (PDAs, or personal data assistants) that are designed as data collectors, enable archaeologists to make site observations and record other survey and excavation data in familiar text, spreadsheet, and database formats as work progresses.

Computational approaches that account for uncertainty, using, for example, fuzzy logic and neural networks, may be valuable in survey planning. Fuzzy logic accommodates partial, rather than absolute, truths and is therefore more tolerant of the vicissitudes of human behavior and the relatively coarse nature of archaeological evidence. A neural-network analysis is a type of expert system that extends the Bayesian strategy by adding a training period, during which it processes evidence with known causes and effects and learns to generate the appropriate outputs —learning through experience to recognize patterns in data. Once a neural network is educated, it takes on the task of detecting and interpreting new trends and patterns, classifying them through the experience it has gained in the analytic process, and it can theoretically create new rules for future analysis from the results. Reeler (1999), for example, experimented with the use of fuzzy variables in a neural network in a study of Maori *pa* (fortified hilltop settlements), exploring the interplay of 20 variables derived from excavations and the surrounding topography and assessing their fit with existing interpretive models of the development of this settlement type. Although such statistical methods are still relatively novel in archaeology and difficult to apply, as Barcelo et al. (1996) attest in their pioneering application of neural networks in an image-processing survey of use wear on stone tools, a combination of advancing technology and further experimentation will undoubtedly improve results.

Because such approaches allow for prior knowledge and experience, they can at least theoretically accommodate some of the indeterminacies of cultural behavior. Surveyors may eventually be able to analyze highly complex sets of multidimensional land-focused information that incorporate material, behavioral, and ideological elements, rather than be limited to superficial associations of material culture and environment. The probability surfaces that result may therefore increase the effectiveness of conventional surveys by providing more-informed evidence of selectivity in land-use and other spatial behavior.

Quite apart from technology is another recent change in archaeological survey, influenced by the recognition that as there are other, nonarchaeological, ways to interrogate the past, there are also other ways to study the landscape. Indeed, the landscape is not neutral, and the first theater of confrontation between archaeologists and the outside world is often the survey. In parts of North America, some archaeological crews include monitors appointed by the aboriginal tribe or nation with traditional rights to the land; these monitors are essentially the eyes and ears of the elders and other tribal authorities, informing nontribal archaeologists when they encounter sacred places and other parts of the landscape with tribal significance. Although such monitoring may not appear to be advantageous with respect to the traditional goals of archaeology, surveyors in fact may benefit significantly from the radically different ways of seeing offered by these or other inhabitants of an area under study. A GIS-driven environmental approach, which tends to be rather sterile, may take on a new life if it includes visualizations and other configurations of the landscape as encoded in oral traditions and other localized knowledge resources (e.g., Maschner 1996); this information may capture ways of using and interpreting the landscape that have developed over many generations, providing a better background for site-potential models and studies of local and regional cultural activity.

Compromising the aims of a survey to address the concerns of indigenous people or others with claims to the land and its resources may appear controversial to some, but in practice, archaeology adjusts its methods and theories according to the situation on the ground. Because so much of archaeological exploration is perception, openness to radically different points of view—and worldviews—may increase the potential for unanticipated knowledge, lying outside carefully constructed research designs and interpretive paradigms. This has always been the way forward for archaeology.

Selected Readings

Alcock, S. E., J. F. Cherry, and J. L. Davis
   1994   Intensive survey, agricultural practice and the classical landscape of Greece. In *Classical Greece: Ancient Histories and Modern Archaeologies*, edited by Ian Morris, pp. 137–170. Cambridge University Press, Cambridge.

Aston, Michael
   1997   *Interpreting the Landscape—Landscape Archaeology and Local History.* Routledge, London.

Banning, E. B.
   2002   *Archaeological Survey.* Kluwer Academic/Plenum Publishing, New York.

Bintliff, J., and A. Snodgrass
1988   Off-site pottery distributions: A regional and interregional perspective. *Current Anthropology* 29(3):506–513.

Bowden, Mark
1999   *Unravelling the Landscape.* Tempus Publishing, London.

Cherry, J. F.
1983   Frogs round the pond: Perspectives on current archaeological survey projects in the Mediterranean region. *Archaeological Survey in the Mediterranean Area*, pp. 375–416. British Archaeological Reports International Series 155. Oxbow Books, Oxford.

Cherry, J. F., J. L. Davis, and E. Mantzourani (editors)
1991   *Landscape Archaeology as Long-Term History: Northern Keos in the Cycladic Islands from Earliest Settlement until Modern Times.* UCLA Institute of Archaeology, Los Angeles.

Collins, James M., and B. L. Molyneaux
2003   *Archaeological Survey. Archaeologist's Toolkit Volume 2.* AltaMira, New York.

Dunnell, Robert C., & W. S. Dancey
1983   The siteless survey: A regional scale data collection strategy. In *Advances in Archaeological Method and Theory*, edited by M. B. Schiffer 6:267–287. Academic Press, New York.

Ebert, James I.
1992   *Distributional Archaeology.* University of New Mexico Press, Albuquerque.

English Heritage
1995   *Geophysical Survey in Archaeological Field Evaluation.* Research and Professional Services Guideline No. 1.

Fish, Suzanne K., and S. A. Kowalewski (editors)
1990   *The Archaeology of Regions: A Case for Full-Coverage Survey.* Smithsonian Institution Press, Washington, D.C.

Haselgrove, C., M. Millett, and I. Smith (editors)
1985   *Archaeology from the Ploughsoil: Studies in the Collection and Interpretation of Field Survey Data.* Department of Archaeology and Prehistory, University of Sheffield, Sheffield.

Hope-Simpson, Richard
1983   The limitations of surface surveys. In *Archaeological Survey in the Mediterranean Area*, edited by D. R. Keller and D. W. Ruppe, pp. 45–48. British Archaeological Reports International Series 155. Oxbow Books, Oxford.

King, Thomas F.
1978   *The Archaeological Survey: Methods and Uses.* Heritage Conservation and Recreation Service, U.S. Department of the Interior, Washington, D.C.

Lightfoot, Kent G.
1986   Regional surveys in the eastern United States: The strengths and weakness of implementing subsurface testing programs. *American Antiquity* 51:484–504.

Mattingly, D. J., and S. Coccia
1995   Survey methodology and the site: A Roman villa from the Rieti survey. In *Settlement and Economy in Italy 1500 BC–AD 1500*, edited by Neil Christie, pp. 31–43. Papers of the Fifth Conference of Italian Archaeology. Oxbow Monograph 41. Oxbow Books, Oxford.

McManamon, F. P.
1994   Discovering and estimating the frequencies and distribution of archaeological sites in the Northeast. In *Cultural Resources Management*, edited by J. E. Kerber, pp. 99–114. Bergin and Garvey, Westport, Connecticut.

Muir, Richard
2000   *The New Reading the Landscape: Fieldwork in Landscape History.* University of Exeter Press, Exeter.

Nance, Jack D., and B. F. Ball
1986   No surprises? The reliability and validity of test pit sampling. *American Antiquity* 51:457–483.

Palmer, R., and C. Cox
1993   *Uses of aerial photography in archaeological evaluations.* IFA Technical Paper 12. IFA (Institute of Field Archaeologists), Birmingham.

Plog, S., F. Plog, and W. Wait
1978   Decision making in modern surveys. In *Advances in Archaeological Method and Theory*, edited by M. B. Schiffer, 1:383–421. Academic Press, New York.

Rossignol, J., and L. Wandsnider
1992   *Space, Time and Archaeological Landscapes.* Plenum, New York and London.

Schiffer, M. B., A. P. Sullivan, and T. C. Klinger
1978   The design of archaeological surveys. *World Archaeology* 10:1–28.

Schofield, John (editor)
1997   *Interpreting Artefact Scatters: Contributions to Ploughzone Archaeology.* Oxbow Monograph 4, 1991 (reprinted). Oxbow Books, Oxford.

Shott, Michael J.
  1985   Shovel-test sampling as a site discovery technique: A case study from Michigan. *Journal of Field Archaeology* 12:458–469.

Stafford, C. R.
  1995   Geoarchaeological perspectives on paleolandscapes and regional subsurface archaeology. *Journal of Archaeological Method and Theory* 2:69–104.

Sullivan, A. P., III (editor)
  1998   *Surface Archaeology*. University of New Mexico Press, Albuquerque.

Talmage, Valerie, and Olga Chesler
  1977   *The Importance of Small, Surface, and Disturbed Sites as Sources of Significant Archaeological Data*. Interagency Archeological Service, National Park Service, Washington, D.C.

Wandsnider, L.
  1998   Regional scale processes and archaeological landscape units. In *Unit Issues in Archaeology*, edited by A. F. Ramenofsky and A. Steffen, pp. 87–102. University of Utah Press, Salt Lake City.

Wandsnider, L., and E. L. Camilli
  1992   The character of surface archaeological deposits and its influence on survey accuracy. *Journal of Field Archaeology* 9:169–188.

Waters, M. R., and D. D. Kuehn
  1996   The geoarchaeology of place: The effect of geological processes on the preservation and interpretation of the archaeological record. *American Antiquity* 61(3):483–497.

Wobst, H. M.
  1983   We can't see the forest for the trees: Sampling and the shapes of archaeological distributions. In *Archaeological Hammers and Theories*, edited by J. A. Moore and A. S. Keene, pp. 32–80. Academic Press, New York.

References

Barcelo, J. A., A. Vila, and J. Gibaja
  1996   An application of Neural Networks to use-wear analysis. Some preliminary results. In *Computer Applications and Quantitative Methods in Archaeology*, edited by K. Lockyear, T. J. T. Sly, and V. M. Birliba, pp. 63–70. British Archaeological Reports S845. Archaeopress, Oxford.

Buck, C. E., W. G. Cavanagh, and C. D. Litton
  1996   *Bayesian Approach to Interpreting Archaeological Data*. John Wiley, London.

Caldwell, J. R.
  1964   Interaction spheres in prehistory. In *Hopewellian Studies*, edited by
          J. R. Caldwell and R. L. Hall, pp. 133–143. Scientific Papers Vol. 12.
          Illinois State Museum, Springfield.

Cherry, John F.
  1982   Preliminary Definition of Site Distribution on Melos. In *An Island
          Polity: The Archaeology of Exploitation in Melos*, edited by C. Renfrew
          and M. Wagstaff, pp. 10–23. Cambridge University Press, Cambridge.

Costall, Alan P.
  1995   Socialising affordances. *Theory and Psychology* 5:467–482.

Ebert, James I.
  1992   *Distributional Archaeology*. University of New Mexico Press, Albu-
          querque.

Gibson, James J.
  1979   *The Ecological Approach to Visual Perception*. Houghton Mifflin,
          Boston.

Hansen, D. T., G. J. West, B. Simpson, and P. Welch
  2002   *Modeling Spatial Uncertainty in Analysis of Archeological Site Distribu-
          tion*. Proceedings of the 22nd Annual ESRI International User Con-
          ference, San Diego, California.

Kuhn, Thomas
  1962   *The Structure of Scientific Revolutions*. University of Chicago Press,
          Chicago.

Lock, G., C. Gosden, D. Griffiths, P. Daly, V. Trifkovic, and T. Marston
  2001   *The Hillforts of the Ridgeway Project: Excavations at Marcham/Frilford,
          Oxfordshire*. Electronic document, http://www.arch.ox.ac.uk/
          schoolarch/institute/projects/ridgeway/frilford.html.

Maschner, Herbert D. G.
  1996   The Politics of Settlement Choice on the Northwest Coast: Cogni-
          tion, GIS, and Coastal Landscapes. In *Anthropology, Space, and Geo-
          graphic Information Systems*, edited by M. Aldenderfer and H. D. G.
          Maschner, pp. 175–189. Oxford University Press, Oxford and New
          York.

Molyneaux, Brian L.
  1997   Representation and reality in private tombs of the late eighteenth
          dynasty, Egypt: An approach to the study of the shape of meaning.
          In *The Cultural Life of Images*, edited by Brian L. Molyneaux, pp.
          108–129. Routledge, London and New York.

Molyneaux, Brian L., and Reed D. Copsey
  2005   *Animated 3D soil resistivity model of a section of a Romano-British am-
          phitheatre at the Frilford/Marcham Romano-British Ceremonial Site, Ox-*

fordshire, England. CTech Development Corporation, Huntington Beach, California.

McCann, Anna M., and J. Bourgeois, with E. K. Gazda and J. P. Oleson
1987   *The Roman Port and Fishery of Cosa: A Center of Ancient Trade.* Princeton University Press, Princeton, New Jersey.

Reeler, C.
1999   Neural Networks and Fuzzy Logic Analysis in Archaeology. In *Computer Applications and Quantitative Methods in Archaeology 1998.* BAR International Series 750 (supplementary), Oxford.

Renfrew, Colin, and Paul Bahn
1996   *Archaeology: Theories Method and Practice.* 2nd ed. Thames and Hudson, London.

Rockman, Marcy, and James Steele (editors)
2003   *The Colonization of Unfamiliar Landscapes: The Archaeology of Adaptation.* Routledge, London and New York.

Semenov, Sergei, A.
1964   *Prehistoric Technology.* Translated by M. W. Thompson. Adams and Dart, Bath.

Stiebing, William H.
1989   *Out of the Desert? Archaeology and the Exodus/Conquest Narratives.* Prometheus Books, Buffalo, New York.

Storck, Peter L.
2004   *Journey to the Ice Age: Discovering an Ancient World.* University of British Columbia, Vancouver.

Wandsnider, L.
2003   Solving the Puzzle of the Archaeological Labyrinth: Time Perspectivism in Mediterranean Surface Archaeology. In *Side-by-side Survey: Comparative Regional Studies in the Mediterranean World,* edited by S. Alcock and J. Cherry, pp. 49–62. Oxbow Press, Oxford.

Willey, G. R.
1953   *Prehistoric Settlement Patterns in the Viru Valley, Peru.* U.S. Bureau of American Ethnology Bulletin 155. U.S. Government Printing Office, Washington, D.C.

5

Excavation

Michael A. Glassow

Over the last 70 years quite a number of texts on methods and techniques of archaeological fieldwork have been published, most being several hundred pages in length and some more specific in scope than others (e.g., Wheeler 1954; Kenyon 1961; Fladmark 1978; Dancey 1981; Barker 1993; Hester et al. 1997; Bowkett et al. 2001; Stewart 2002). The more recently published of these will provide the reader with detailed discussion of topics necessarily given cursory treatment in this brief overview. I place emphasis here on the range of excavation techniques and approaches available to the archaeologist and the research contexts in which these are appropriately used. I am also concerned with excavations at sites with either no preserved architecture or structures no more complex than simple domestic architecture and relatively small, discrete monuments such as cairns and simple tombs.

Considering that a typical archaeologist's firsthand experience with excavation is limited to a few regions of the world, it is not surprising that any exposition on excavation method and technique, this one included, inevitably will be incomplete and will display some degree of naïveté. Consequently, although texts and other published treatments of excavation method and technique have their place in training and furthering the development of the discipline, they can only supplement the knowledge gained from working with mentors and acquiring field experience as a means of building competence.

Fundamental to selection of particular approaches to excavation are of course the data requirements of a project research design (Binford 1964). Data requirements imply that specific collections be made and that specific information about immovable archaeological phenomena be recorded. The greater the care given to the links between data requirements and the products of excavation (and other kinds of archaeological fieldwork), the more successful will be the project in reaching research objectives. In making these links, it is worth considering the basic nature of archaeological phenomena and how an archaeologist identifies and treats them in order that they may yield useful data. Three types of archaeological phenomena are defined in Table 5.1: *objects*, *surfaces*, and *deposits*, each of which can yield particular sorts of measurements that may be related to data requirements. In developing a research design, a table such as this may be reversed; that is, data requirements specified in a project

Table 5.1.   Archaeological Phenomena Encountered during Excavation

Type	Examples	Field Identification	Field Treatment	Basic Measurements
Objects	Manufactured artifacts, bones, waste flakes, charcoal chunks, building stones	Discrete objects recognized in soil matrix or in sifting screens	Collect; if very large, draw profiles and photograph; if to be discarded, record attributes and frequency	Frequency and density according to categories of size, shape, and composition
Surfaces	Divisions between strata, floors, wall faces, holes, pits, underground cysts	Contrast between adjacent deposits, peel lines, thin zones of rootlet concentration	Draw profiles and plan views, photograph, make topographic map	Dimensions, frequency according to categories of shape, area, capacity (volume)
Deposits	Midden strata, soil strata, fill of concave surfaces, walls, rubble from fallen walls	Relative homogeneity of contents, consistent color and texture of matrix	Draw profiles and plan views, collect samples, record color, describe texture or constituents	Thickness, area of extent, volume

research design may be matched with the kinds of archaeological phenomena that are necessary to investigate, each of the basic phenomena being divided into particular types expectable at a specific site. However, an archaeologist also makes collections and records information relevant to long-term regional research, largely because these collections and information otherwise would be lost because of the destructive nature of any excavation.

Most often, a specific site excavation is a segment of a larger research project or program that is divided into a series of sequential stages (Redman 1973). The stages may entail different kinds of fieldwork both within a region surrounding the site and within a single site. An example is site survey leading to the discovery of series of sites, one or more of which becomes the subject of excavation. Fieldwork at a site typically involves initial stages designed to provide information relevant to designing the most effective and economical approach to an excavation undertaken in a later stage. Any relatively large-scale excavation surely would benefit from preceding stages of fieldwork that allow the specific goals of the fieldwork to be refined.

Control and Documentation of Provenience

Of course, the three-dimensional context of archaeological phenomena within a site is fundamental to constructing chronologies of cultural change and inferring past behavior. Ultimately, three-dimensional measurements (in meters or centimeters) are tied to a master datum that may be located either on or off the site. The master datum ideally is some kind of permanent marker, such as a brass cap implanted in concrete filling a posthole. Regardless, the master datum should be linked by azimuth and distance measurements to at least one permanent landmark such as a geodetic benchmark or a discrete topographic feature not likely to be moved or modified by natural or human forces. This would allow the datum to be relocated or reestablished at some time in the future when another archaeologist may wish to investigate a site. In most excavations subsidiary datums are also defined, whether these be for particular areas of a large site or for specific excavation units.

Two means of defining area context may be used: area segments where excavation takes place and points. Area segments are usually called units; normally they are of constant dimensions such as 1 × 1 m, but dimensions may vary from one unit to the next. Points typically are where relatively small samples are taken, such as an auger hole that may be as small as 3 cm in diameter.

To facilitate placement and designation of units or points, an archaeologist may overlay on a map of the site a Cartesian coordinate system, consisting of two baselines at right angles to each other. When convenient, one of the baselines runs north–south and the other runs east–west, but the baselines may instead be oriented with respect to topography or other geographic features. The two baselines may originate at a point beyond the site boundary so that the baselines too are beyond the site boundaries or they may cross each other at a point near the middle of the site. The baselines are divided into intervals equal to the length of a unit side or the minimum interval between sample points, and each interval is given a number starting at the origin point. If baselines cross each other within the site, the number assigned to an interval must be supplemented with a letter indicating direction from the intersection of the baselines (e.g., N, S, E, W). Thus, each unit may receive a designation referring to the intersection of two lines or intervals extended perpendicularly outward from each baseline. In some cases, however, unit locations are dictated by distinctive surface phenomena of interest and may not necessarily be referenced to a Cartesian coordinate system. In these instances unit locations are defined by the azimuth of the unit location (specifically a unit corner) and distance from a datum. Units located in this manner may simply be designated with consecutive numbers.

Within an excavation the dimension of depth usually also is of concern. Depth may be defined in three basic ways: the position of a particular stratum of deposits with respect to strata above or below, an arbitrary depth interval (i.e., an arbitrary level), and an exact measurement below a datum plane, that is, the vertical depth below a datum point. Verticality in archaeology, of course, is along the direction of gravity, and a datum plane is an imaginary horizontal plane perpendicular to the direction of gravity that passes through a datum point.

The degree of resolution of three-dimensional context— that is, provenience—depends on particular research needs. In some situations reference to a particular stratum or arbitrary level within an excavation unit is sufficient. For instance, in unstratified site deposits disturbed by burrowing rodents, an archaeologist may conclude that the original positions of arti- facts have been disturbed to a point that provenience informa- tion more precise than the excavation unit location and a relatively thick arbitrary level is meaningless. In other situa- tions, point-provenience documentation may be required. For example, the position of artifacts on the intact floor of a struc- ture, measured to the nearest centimeter, may be important in demonstrating spatial relationship between specific artifact types.

In addition to the various means of keeping track of prove- nience in the course of excavation, archaeologists place consid- erable emphasis on the precision of excavation itself. The edges of a unit are delineated by strings stretched tautly between stakes or spikes, and these serve as guides to excavation in that the unit sidewalls ideally should extend vertically directly below the strings. The base of an arbitrary level is measured with ref- erence to a datum plane. However, in the case of a significantly sloping ground surface, arbitrary levels may slope in accord with the surface and therefore be defined with reference to a sloping plane. If deposits are stratified, excavation of a stratum within a unit must stop at the base of the stratum. Archaeologists are concerned with straight sidewalls and precisely defined and recorded levels to calculate volume of excavated deposits, whether a stratum or an arbitrary level within a unit. Volumetric data of this sort are important in studying variation in densities of objects.

Layout of an Excavation

Numerous factors may affect decisions regarding where to excavate within the area of a site. The overarching factor, of course, is the data requirements of the project research design. For instance, if research is concerned with household activities, the focus of excavation needs to be within houses. Alternatively, research may be concerned with changes in dependence on large-game hunting, implying that food-refuse deposits be the focus. Before excavation pertaining directly to the research design begins, however, information may need to be collected to know where to place excavation units so as to maximize their effectiveness in acquiring needed information. Given that sites often contain different kinds of deposits, surfaces, and objects in different areas, initial-stage investigation may be focused on ascertaining this variation through careful scrutiny of the site surface to discern topographic irregularities indicative of building locations or through systematic collection of objects on the surface. Small-scale subsurface testing and geophysical survey are other approaches.

A geophysical survey may entail use of a ground-penetrating radar device, a cesium vapor magnetometer, an electromagnetic conductivity meter, or other such devices (Dalan 1991; Dalan et al. 1992; Heimmer 1992; Conyers and Goodman 1997). Often two or three of these devices are used to produce complementary data. Although the equipment is expensive and requires special expertise in its operation, geophysical survey is becoming increasingly popular. A geophysical survey is especially useful in discerning buried remains of structures such as house floors and walls, baking pits, and concentrations of fire-affected rocks.

Whenever an archaeologist must choose to excavate between locations that have equal potential to yield information of value to the research, whether these be all the potential test-pit locations within the area of a site or all identified features of a particular type, some sort of sampling design must be developed. Careful attention to sampling designs is justified because different kinds of human activity and the distinctive refuse that each generates may not be evenly distributed throughout the area of a site. Consequently, an archaeologist cannot assume that findings from any one location within a site are representative of the site as a whole. Some sites indeed may be characterized by relative homogeneity in the distribution of different kinds of refuse, but an archaeologist must have prior knowledge before assuming or arguing that this is the case.

To argue that a sample is representative of the whole, archaeologists use some form of probability sampling (Binford

1964:427–428; see also Asch 1975; Redman 1975; Reid et al. 1975). The most common form is systematic sampling, which involves equal intervals between sample units. If the sampling is of an area, whether all or a portion of a site, excavation units are placed at equal intervals along both dimensions of area; if the sampling is a transect or transects through the area, the units are placed at equal intervals along a transect line. In the case of such features as houses, the interval would be a count—for instance, every fourth house in a row of houses if the selected sampling proportion is 25 percent. In situations where strong patterning exists in the areal distribution of what is being sought in the excavation, systematic sampling is likely to produce erratic results. Consequently, some form of random sampling, particularly stratified random sampling, is often employed.

Stratified random sampling entails dividing the area of a site, or a series of identified features, into groups of potential sample units, each group being a sampling stratum. With regard to a site area, the sampling strata generally are based on differences in archaeological phenomena defined in an initial stage of investigation, although the stratum divisions may simply be arbitrary; that is, strata may be equal-size groupings of sample units. Within each stratum, one or more sample units may be selected by reference to some sort of random-number generator or table. Sampling designs for a site may be quite complex, entailing sampling strata of different sizes defined in different ways, as well as different approaches to sampling within each stratum. In general, sampling designs that entail a relatively even (albeit still random) distribution of units within the area being sampled yield statistically more accurate estimates of site characteristics than do sampling designs in which distributions are rather irregular, as would be the case if simple random sampling with a relatively small sampling proportion were used over a relatively large area of a site. Indeed, within a sampling stratum it often makes sense to employ arbitrary stratification to increase evenness in the distribution of sample units.

In many situations sampling is not an issue. For example, if research focuses only on structures present at a site and all structures are excavated, then sampling is not involved. Yet it would be inappropriate to generalize from the structure excavations to the nature of the site as a whole because other kinds or proportions of archaeological phenomena may characterize other parts of the site where structures are not located. In other situations, only one portion of a large site may be investigated; it may be the only portion containing materials relevant to the research design, the only one accessible, or site deposits may be so deep that the only feasible approach is to concentrate excavation in one large pit (Brown 1975). Again, in such cases generalization from the area tested to the site as a whole is not justified in a statistical sense. In extreme situations the number of possible locations where excavation can take place may be so severely constrained that all such locations become the subject of excavation. A fairly common example is a site located in an urban setting where buildings, landscaping, and roads cannot be disturbed. When significant proportions of a site are arbitrarily excluded from consideration, the sample of excavated deposits cannot be assumed to be representative of the whole site. Indeed, the lack of a justifiable argument of representativeness of a sample is a major consideration in efforts to generalize from it.

Common Tools and Supplies for Excavation

As a rule of thumb, an archaeologist selects the tool that will allow achieving a specific excavation task efficiently with respect to time and energy expenditure. A shovel is preferred over a trowel so long as there is no danger of damaging objects of interest; if there is danger, however, then the excavation task may require a trowel or perhaps a smaller tool. An archaeologist may also use different tools to excavate intact deposits as opposed to deposits disturbed by recent activities such as plowing or building construction, intact deposits typically calling for smaller tools more carefully used.

In hand excavation, most dirt typically is excavated with a shovel, and two types of shovels are most commonly used: pointed (also known as round-end) and square-end shovels, both with long handles. The pointed shovel is most effective when soils are firm, but if soils are relatively soft, a square-end shovel allows the excavator to create a flatter exposure surface and more even sidewalls. Excavation with shovels usually entails peeling off relatively thin layers of soil, often no more than 5 cm thick, and with some experience an excavator learns to avoid dislodging objects of interest.

Trowels are used when more careful exposure is necessary. In the United States and many other countries, a mason's pointing trowel is the most popular type, typically with a blade between four and six inches long. Some archaeologists also use margin trowels (having a square rather than pointed end) or garden trowels. Trowels are effective in exposing surfaces of floors and walls as well as relatively durable objects, and they also are used in scraping a soil surface to see stratification or other kinds of soil variation. (Sometimes a square-end shovel may serve this latter purpose more efficiently.) To facilitate scraping and cutting of rootlets, many archaeologists sharpen the trowel edges. Smaller tools such as an ice pick or dental pick are used to expose delicate objects once most of the surrounding soil is removed with larger tools. An ice pick or a carpenter's awl also may be used as a probe to determine whether objects lie within several centimeters below the level of exposure.

Firm soils may require loosening with a pick, either a small hand pick or a large pick such as a railroad pick or a mattock. Because picks of any size can easily damage unexposed objects, they must be used with restraint in situations where objects of interest may be present.

Soil that cannot be removed directly from an excavation unit with a shovel, dustpan, or scoop is placed in a container such as a bucket or, in the case of large excavations, a wheelbarrow. Brooms or brushes may be used to clean loose soil from an exposure such as the base of a stratum or arbitrary level within a unit. However, if the soil is damp, a broom or brush tends to smear variation in soil color or texture. Consequently, the surface instead has to be carefully scraped with the edge of a square-end shovel or trowel.

A plumb line (a plumb bob attached to a string) is used to maintain straight, vertical sidewalls of units. Similarly, constant depth is maintained by use of a line level that is attached to a string tied to a datum stake. Measurement down from the leveled line to an object or surface is done with a pocket or folding tape.

Archaeologists also use a variety of heavy equipment, including bulldozers, road graders, backhoes, and front-end loaders (Van Horn 1988). Although an archeologist may rent and personally operate such heavy equipment, having learned to remove soil with considerable precision, typically he or she contracts for the services of a heavy equipment operator. Heavy equipment may be used to remove overburden covering a buried archaeological site; to dig trenches for locating site boundaries, discovering site features, or determining stratification of deposits; or to backfill units. In some circumstances, heavy equipment may be used in lieu of hand tools to excavate large volumes before a site is to be destroyed by land development or it may be used after some amount of hand excavation to scrape off the plow-zone soils for discovery of features, particularly pits with fill of a different color than the surrounding soil.

A variety of containers are used for transport of artifacts from a site excavation to a field laboratory and eventually to the locus of more intensive collections processing and analysis. If all residues caught by sifting screens are retained for laboratory processing, 5-gallon plastic buckets with tops are convenient containers. These also work for collection of matrix samples. Four-mil plastic bags also may be used for this purpose. Many of the objects encountered during excavation may be relatively fragile and therefore require special packaging as a conservation measure (see later discussion). Paper bags, although not as sturdy as 4-mil plastic, may be appropriate in some circumstances, especially because they do not hold moisture.

Screening of Deposits

Most archaeological excavations entail use of sifting screens, at least in certain circumstances. The objective of sifting, that is, screening, is to remove the soil matrix of excavated deposits to obtain objects too small or too obscure within the deposits to see until most of the soil matrix is removed. The mesh of sifting screens may be as fine as 1.5 mm (1/16 in; window screen) or as coarse as 25 mm (1 in). (In the lab even finer meshes may be used in specialized sifting of matrix samples.) Some screens have large areas of mesh, especially those used in large-scale excavation, whereas others are small and portable so that they can be backpacked into remote locations. Some screens are suspended from a tripod or tetrapod, others are supported by legs, still others are handheld, and finally some are mechanized in that some sort of motor is the source of power for shaking the screen.

The decision to screen deposits, and the mesh size to use, must take into consideration the nature of the deposits and the presence of objects most appropriately recovered with screens of a particular mesh size. Some archaeological deposits may contain no objects at all, whereas others contain only large and easily seen objects; in such cases screening makes no sense. However, if small objects are present and if the archaeologist wishes to obtain a numerically large and systematic sample of them, screening is necessary, and consideration must be given to which mesh size would result in systematic recovery (see, for example, Schaffer and Sanchez 1994). Because screening consumes time and effort, an archaeologist often must weigh the benefits of screening against cost. Commonly a sampling design must be devised for screening to obtain a representative sample of objects in numbers sufficient for analysis.

The effort devoted to screening and to sorting the objects caught by screens is quite variable. Dry, clayey soils are most difficult to screen because the excavated soil remains in relatively large clods. To obtain objects systematically if this is the case, water sprayed onto the screen full of excavated deposits may be necessary to remove the adhering soil, and the deposits may have to be pretreated by soaking in buckets, perhaps with the addition of a defalocculant to disperse the soil (Ross and Duffy 2000). Dark humic soils often prevent systematic recognition of small objects, making problematic any attempt at sorting from the screens while excavation is in progress. Using water to aid screening is often called water screening, and this technique has the advantage, even when soils are not clayey, of cleaning much of the soil from objects of interest so that they are more easily recognized. In fact, in some regions archaeologists regularly use water screening to enhance the representativeness of samples of very small objects such as fish bones or shell beads. In these situations, sorting through objects caught by screens may take place only after water screening is completed and the material has dried, often in a laboratory rather than in the field.

Screening may be destructive. Fragile objects, particularly fish and bird bone and many species of shell, are likely to break as they bounce against rocks when a screen is shaken. Water-screening reduces the prospect of breakage, as does removal of larger rocks before any sort of screening takes place. Flotation is the gentlest process for separating items of interest from soil matrix (Wagner 1988:18–19), but the complexity and labor intensity of flotation prevent it from being used to process all excavated deposits produced in the course of a large field project.

Test Excavation Techniques

The objectives of test excavation are quite variable. At the most elementary level, an archaeologist may test to discover a site, especially if archaeological deposits are buried under a mantle of alluvial or eolian deposits or organic duff. Testing may also be done to establish site boundaries or to obtain basic information about the nature of a site—the depth of deposits, density of midden constituents, or the presence of distinct, relatively large-scale features such as house pits, prepared structure floors, and baking pits. Finally, testing may be done to obtain representative samples of objects that are in relatively high density and ubiquitous, and the samples obtained may be sufficient to address research problems without any future larger-scale excavation. Indeed, even very limited testing may yield collections sufficient for research objectives. For instance, the objective may be to obtain small samples of organic material to assess the age of a site by radiocarbon dating.

Although the variety of approaches to testing a site are almost infinite, they may be conveniently, albeit somewhat arbitrarily, classified as large-unit and small-unit testing. In large-unit testing, a person can enter and work within a test unit; in small-unit testing a person cannot. Small-unit testing often but not always is relatively casual and is aimed at obtaining a basic idea of the nature—or presence—of archaeological deposits (McManamon 1984:253–276), whereas large-unit testing almost always is more formal, with the objective of obtaining quantitative samples of objects. This distinction is not perfect.

Different kinds of small-unit testing usually are named by reference to the tool used: shovel test pitting, auger sampling, coring, or probing. A shovel test pit (abbreviated STP and often simply called a shovel test) is a roundish (sometimes squarish) pit up to about 50 cm in diameter, usually excavated with little concern for keeping vertical walls or recording the volume excavated. Shovel testing that simply exposes soil below a vegetation or duff layer is called *divoting* (McManamon 1984:259; see also Lovis 1976:369). Generally a shovel test pit cannot be excavated much deeper than about 75 cm, and the choice of diameter and depth is based on the anticipated nature of the deposits being investigated. If the objects being sought are small and obscured by the soil, the contents of the pit may be sifted through a screen. Shovel testing typically is used to determine with minimal expenditure of time and effort a site's presence or its boundaries, but it may also be used to assess roughly the types and densities of objects present. In the latter case, volume of soil excavated from the pit may be measured by placing the soil before screening in a container such as a bucket with liter increments marked on its side. Often the objects obtained in the test are returned to the pit when it is backfilled, after tabulating the type and frequency of objects seen or simply noting their presence.

Other kinds of small-scale testing require the use of more specialized tools (Stein 1986). A popular small-scale excavating tool is the bucket auger, which collects a sample from a hole with a constant diameter of 5 to 10 cm. Bucket augers are twisted into the ground and bring up soil in increments roughly equal to the capacity of the tubular bucket. The bucket auger works best in soils containing few rocks or dispersed rocks less than about 5 cm in diameter, and it may have difficulty penetrating dry, compact, clayey soil. If obstructions are not encountered, a bucket auger can dig a hole 3 to 4 m deep if extension rods are added between the handle and the bucket. Because the hole diameter is constant and increments of depth may be measured, a bucket auger may be used to collect volumetric samples from regular depth intervals. However, the raising and lowering of the bucket nearly always dislodges soil and objects from the pit walls, thus contaminating to some extent deeper increments with material from shallower ones. Nonetheless, a bucket auger can be effective in determining the depth of deep sites, the depth of obvious soil color or texture changes, and variation in density of objects abundant enough to be in relatively high frequency in each depth increment (e.g., Cannon 2000). A posthole digger may be substituted for a bucket auger, particularly if soil is rocky. A posthole digger is about 20 cm in diameter, and the manner in which the tool works limits depth to about 75 cm. Some types of screw augers also can yield samples of deposits down to about 3 m, but the diameter of the sample generally is smaller than a bucket-auger sample.

A probe is another commonly used soil-sampling tool, consisting of a sharp-edged tube that is pushed into the ground. Its use is limited to relatively soft soils free of rocks. A probe produces a core of soil accessible from an elongate slot on the side of the tube. The inside diameter of the tube usually is less than 3 cm, so the primary use is to ascertain obvious differences in soil color and texture. With extensions, a probe may penetrate to depths of a few meters. A solid-core sampler is similar to a probe in that it consists of a tube that is pushed into the ground. However, its diameter is much larger, and it must be driven into the ground using a hammering device or more complex technology. Because inside diameters of tubes typically are 5 to 7.5 cm, overcoming friction in extracting the tube if soils are compact may be a problem. A great advantage of a core sampler is that it yields an undisturbed sample of soil (except for some compaction), whereas a bucket auger churns the soil as it is twisted into the ground. Solid cores also may be obtained by using a truck-mounted rig in which larger-diameter tubes are driven into the ground and extracted hydraulically.

Small-unit testing also may entail excavation of square or rectangular units. Those less than 30 cm square require the use of small hand tools rather than shovels to excavate if relatively precise dimensions are to be maintained. Generally, the advantage of such units is greater control over volume of excavated soil and larger sample sizes, but they cannot be excavated to depths more than about 50 cm. Such units are especially appropriate for obtaining representative samples of objects when variation in density within site deposits is of concern. Such testing may take advantage of vertical exposures of archaeological deposits along banks created by erosion or human earthmoving activities. In these situations column samples through the whole thickness of deposits may be obtained. As the term implies, a column sample is a column of deposits excavated from a vertical profile of site deposits, its area typically ranging from 10 × 10 cm to 30 × 30 cm. The face of the bank may first have to be trimmed to make it plumb. The column is divided into depth segments based on stratification or arbitrary divisions. A great advantage of column sampling (and large-unit sampling) along a bank is that the stratification of deposits, if present, may be seen before excavation begins, not only in the restricted area of the column or larger unit but also on either side. Therefore, a better appreciation of the significance of stratigraphic differences is gained (Flannery 1976). Column samples also are frequently used to obtain samples of deposits (i.e., matrix samples) from the sidewalls of completed units.

As mentioned, large-unit testing entails units in which an excavator can work. The smallest practical size of conventional dimensions is 0.5 × 1.0 m. Even this size may be too small for a large person, and an average-size person would find the dimensions cramped when the unit depth reaches more than about 50 cm. Viewing stratification of deposits also diminishes below this depth. The advantage of units this small is that for a given total volume that can be excavated during a project, a maximum number of units may be dispersed throughout the area of a site, thus maximizing the spatial evenness of the sample collected.

Selection of the size and dimensions of a test unit depends on the kind of information being sought. If a sample of relatively dense objects is sought, larger numbers of smaller units are generally optimal. However, if the density of objects is low and the objective is to obtain frequencies per unit meaningful in quantitative analysis, then units of a size sufficient to yield the critical minimum frequency must be used (Workman and Workman 1998). Furthermore, if phenomena such as structure floors or relatively thin soil strata are being sought, the unit size may have to be relatively large to recognize these (e.g., Winter 1976:63), especially if the surface or deposit is disturbed or identifiable only by relatively subtle changes in soil color and compactness. Similarly, relatively long trenches may be best for discerning stratification of deposits.

In summary, test excavation may be undertaken as a means of site discovery, site boundary definition, initial characterization of site deposits, acquisition of data for addressing major research issues, or some combination of these. The size of test units varies greatly, as does the nature of excavation tools used. Test excavation is probably the most common approach for investigating a site in the United States because it produces information relevant to compliance with federal and state laws protecting cultural resources and is an efficient approach to acquiring data relevant to a wide variety of research problems of concern. Nonetheless, a test excavation may not be able to yield information sufficient for or appropriate to some kinds of research objectives, particularly those that require information about the spatial distribution of objects across large, continuous areas or the nature of architectural features.

Area Excavation Techniques

An area excavation, sometimes called a block excavation, entails exposing a large area more or less at the same time. The most common purpose of an area excavation is to expose a continuous series of features, which may include a variety of surfaces such as structure floors, granary foundations, storage pits, burials within a cemetery, and concentrations of refuse. Although some area excavations are relatively small, such as one limited to the area of a small structure's floor, others are truly huge, some in Japan covering several hectares. Some area excavations have the purpose of documenting the areal distribution of different classes of objects, particularly of flaked stone, so that sequences of discrete activities may be documented at a high level of specificity. These most often take place at relatively small sites that were occupied for perhaps only a few weeks or months. Finally, some area excavations are undertaken for logistical and safety reasons, because deposits are several meters deep, too deep for practical and safe excavation of small, discrete units.

Sample representativeness may be an issue when only one or very few area exposures are excavated at a site substantially larger than the total area excavated. In such a situation, large areas would be left out of the sample; if a site has a complex areal structure, the sample produced from an area excavation may result in significant biases in the resulting data. The prospect of bias, however, may be relatively low where previously obtained data about a site—or experience at other sites of the same class—indicate relative homogeneity in the distribution of objects and features of interest. Furthermore, some area excavations may be purposefully located in areas of a site known to contain particular kinds of archaeological phenomena of interest, structure remains being an obvious example. If research objectives are met through investigation of such functionally specific portions of a site, then generalizations derived from data analysis pertain only to those portions.

An area excavation is often undertaken in a contiguous series of units, the units usually being defined by a grid superimposed over the area. Dividing an area excavation into grid units allows control of provenience. This is especially important if some of the objects of interest are small enough that they can be recovered systematically only through screening of excavated deposits. In addition, grid units provide convenient divisions of area for recording features with plan-view drawings and photography, and if an initial series of grids are excavated before the rest, the exposed stratigraphic profiles in these grids may serve as a guide to excavation by individual strata in the remaining grids (often called the vertical-face approach).

When a grid of units is used in an area excavation, maintaining the unit divisions as excavation proceeds becomes an issue. A variety of techniques have been conceived to ensure that divisions are maintained. Perhaps the most common is a grid of string, cord, or even pipes stretched across the excavation area from which excavators can drop a plumb line to check a unit boundary or corner. Because this approach creates a good deal of inconvenience to movement of excavators if the depth of excavation makes the grid too high to step over but too low to easily pass underneath, the grid guides may be designed to be removed and replaced relatively quickly. In deep excavations, grid strings may have to be occasionally lowered to maintain their effective use or, rather than using grid strings, measurements may have to be made from the perimeter walls of the area excavation. If the maximum depth of the area excavation is relatively shallow, columns of unexcavated soil may be left in place at some or all grid intersections, with a large nail or pin on each marking a grid intersection. Alternatively, balks (or keys; unexcavated ridges of soil) may be left along some of the grid lines. Of course, balks may run along all grid lines in both directions so that each unit in the grid in essence is a separate pit.

Balks serve another important purpose: they retain a record of soil stratification that may be difficult to discern if excavation proceeds without them. Although stratification may be evident on the perimeter walls of the area excavation, this may not be sufficient if stratification varies significantly within the area. For this reason, balks may be left in place at critical intervals within an area excavation even if they are not needed for maintaining the location of grid units.

Keeping track of the depth of excavation also presents challenges in area excavations. If excavation is proceeding downward in arbitrary levels, the excavator needs some means of knowing that the bottom of a level is reached. Similarly, if excavation is proceeding by stratigraphic levels, the depth of the base of each stratum in each grid must be measured and recorded. One way to make depth measurements is simply to measure down from a level line tied to a datum at the edge of the excavation. This approach works if the area of excavation is relatively small and depths are not beyond the reach of an excavator. However, in larger, deeper excavations, one or more temporary datums, tied into a datum on the surface beyond the excavation, may have to be established within the excavation. For instance, one or more grids may be left partly excavated on which a temporary datum may be placed. Of course, the location of the temporary datum or datums would have to be changed now and then so that the overall depth of excavation can remain relatively even. The presence of balks also can facilitate depth measurements in that level lines may be attached to temporary datums on balk surfaces, or points or lines of known depth on the face of the balk may serve for convenient depth measureme...

Some area excavations do not require the use of a grid for maintaining and recording provenience. If objects of interest are relatively large and easy to discern during excavation, their three-dimensional position, or point provenience, may be recorded once they are exposed. The horizontal position may be recorded as Cartesian coordinates measured from two adjacent boundaries of the area excavation or along an azimuth emanating from a datum. Depth may be measured from a level line or by means of an optical instrument such as a level or theodolite. In fact, a total station (an electronic theodolite with electronic distance-measuring capability) allows the three-dimensional position of an object to be recorded in one quick operation. Recording the variation in depth of a surface on which objects occur also may entail the use of a depth-measuring instrument. As is true of any kind of excavation, both grid and point-provenience approaches for documenting the position of archaeological phenomena may be used in a complementary fashion. For example, the location of very abundant objects such as small chert flakes may be recorded with reference to grid and level, whereas the location of each flaked stone tool may be recorded as a point provenience.

In summary, although area excavation is undertaken for a variety of purposes, its greatest value is in its potential to provide data on the areal distribution of objects and features at a high level of resolution. However, area excavation requires a good deal of careful planning so that means of recording provenience are maintained.

Exposure of Architectural Features

Architectural features within the scope of this chapter include houses and other kinds of structures on a buried ground surface as well as pithouses and other types of recessed structures. Structures may be associated with standing portions of walls of masonry or soil and with prepared surfaces such as a platform on which a structure is constructed. Floors of structures are surfaces of relatively compact soil, imported mud or lime plaster, fired clay tiles, or flagstones. Walls typically are constructed of wood or other plant material, stone, mud plastered over a wickerwork of saplings or cane (wattle and daub), coursed adobe mud, adobe bricks, fired clay bricks, or some combination of these. Wall surfaces may be unplastered or plastered.

Discovery of architectural features of all sorts generally entails recognition of horizontal or vertical surfaces. As Table 5.1 indicates, surfaces of architectural features may be discerned as a sharp, even division between different kinds of deposits, a peel line along which one deposit easily breaks free of another, or a thin zone of rootlets that have grown along the surface. Because surfaces of architectural features sometimes are difficult to discern, excavation units often must be large enough to expose a large portion of a feature's surface. Nonetheless, it is often possible to discover the surface of architectural features in 1-×-1 m or smaller test units, even if the exposure is too small to be certain that the surface pertains to architecture. In such situations a larger exposure must be made to ascertain whether the surface indeed is of an architectural feature. Given the variety of materials used to construct architecture and the great diversity of deposits in which architectural features occur, an archaeologist often must acquire special expertise to identify architectural features in contexts peculiar to a particular region. Architectural features may be difficult to recognize if the deposits of the feature itself (e.g., a mud brick or coursed adobe wall) are very similar to deposits surrounding it. Such features may be identified only when they are bisected by excavation so that differences in deposits may be seen in profile.

If a suspected floor surface is discovered in a test unit, the next task is to determine where its perimeter lies. Sometimes the curvature of the exposed portion of the floor is a clue, given that the floor of many prehistoric houses curves slightly upward toward its margin. If no such clues exist, the archaeologist might resort to auger sampling if there is a strong contrast between the deposits above and below the floor surface. Alternatively, one may simply excavate a sequence of units in one direction from the discovery unit until the floor margin is reached. In the case of a pithouse, the margin will be the vertical bank; in the case of houses constructed on a buried ground surface, which may lack any vestige of the wall that enclosed the structure, other clues must be used. The curvature of the floor's margin encountered within a test unit may serve as a basis for inferring its approximate extent. If the walls of the structure were supported by perimeter posts, then discovering one or more postholes may indicate the floor edge. Pithouses often are discovered by encountering a portion of the pit edge rather than the floor because the deposits filling the pithouse frequently are different in color and texture than soil into which the pit was dug. If the pithouse burned, the walls of the pit may be fire reddened. Consequently, when the pit edge is bisected during archaeological excavation, the fire-reddened side may be seen as a distinct line of reddish orange soil. Similarly, structures with wall vestiges still intact may be discovered by encountering a wall stub. If the wall was constructed of some sort of hard material such as rock or fired brick, then the wall stub will be very obvious when encountered. Walls of adobe mud, whether unfired bricks or coursed adobe, may be more difficult to discern; subtle differences between color and texture of deposits may be the only clue.

Exposure of floor surfaces often involves some very careful and complex excavation to obtain information regarding activities that took place within the structure, especially if the structure was a house. Ideally, the floor should not be exposed until the perimeter of the structure is defined, but this may not always be possible. If possible, however, a grid may be superimposed over the floor area for purposes of collecting items in high density on the floor surface and recording floor features. The size of grid squares may need to be much smaller than the those used for the general site excavation. Often the deposits resting directly on a floor are the collapsed remains of the structure's walls and roof, and if the structure burned, considerable quantities of charcoal may be included. On top of the wall and roof rubble may be alluvial or wind-blown deposits or refuse from occupation of the site after the house was destroyed or abandoned. If the collapsed remains of walls and roof are clearly identifiable, their careful exposure and detailed documentation may provide information about the construction and architectural details of the structure. Perhaps the most important dictum of floor excavation, however, is that the objects actually resting on the floor should be distinguished from those that are beneath the floor surface or within the roof and wall rubble, because inferences about activities that took place within the house must be based on objects—and sometimes deposits—confidently known to have been resting on the floor, or possibly incorporated into the soil or plaster immediately below the floor surface.

A variety of architectural features may be part of a floor. Dwelling floors found in many prehistoric sites have a central hearth or fire pit, which may have a margin or collar of stone or soil. Because a hearth often is filled with ash and charcoal that may yield information about the kind of firewood used and food prepared, hearth deposits typically are collected as a matrix sample for flotation. Excavation of hearth deposits may entail removal of half to create a profile for recording stratification of these deposits. Sometimes the pit itself is profiled through excavation into the floor so that the profile of the pit may be recorded. Aside from hearths, postholes may be encountered either around the margin of the floor or at other floor locations, and these may also be sectioned to record their profiles. The number, position, and size of postholes are evidence of the framework supporting the walls and roof of the structure. Instead of perimeter postholes, however, the base of an exterior wall may have been placed in a narrow wall trench. Another floor feature often encountered in prehistoric houses is a sub-floor storage cist, sometimes lined with rock slabs. Its contents also may be collected and processed as a matrix sample in an effort to determine the cist's function. All of these various pit or hole features typically are identified by the presence of a spot of soil that is softer and of a different color in comparison with the surrounding floor. In addition, postholes may contain the actual remains of posts. Floors also may have evidence of partitions in the form of rows of postholes or the remains of a wall of mud or masonry, and such features as raised surfaces or benches also may be present. In short, whereas the floors of some structures may be flat, uniform surfaces, others may be quite complex surfaces requiring a good deal of care in exposure.

The extant lower portions of structure walls can provide a great deal of information about construction techniques such as the manner in which masonry is laid and the nature of plaster on masonry surfaces. Patterns of wall abutments may also indicate the sequence of room addition and remodeling. If present, wall stubs also allow the archaeologist to define the perimeter of a structure. With regard to a multiroom structure, individual rooms may be identified, allowing the archaeologist the basis for selecting a sample of rooms to excavate. In fact, room identification may require exposure only of diagonally opposite wall corners. The fallen portions of walls also may be important to expose in an effort to determine construction techniques and perhaps to estimate the original height of the walls.

Of course, this brief treatment of architectural exposures does not do justice to the great variety of forms and depositional contexts in which they occur. Emphasis is placed on the simpler forms of architecture found in North American archaeological sites or in rural areas of ancient civilizations. To become competent in architectural exposure, an archaeologist must obtain training and experience in exposing architecture of particular time periods within a particular region of interest. Nonetheless, the most basic procedures mentioned here do apply to most instances of architectural exposure.

Specialized Exposures

Aside from various kinds of structures used for shelter, human populations have created many other kinds of phenomena that are of interest to archaeologists. Among these are various kinds of open-air surfaces, concentrations of objects, various kinds of monuments, and interments of human remains. Surfaces include what have been called "living surfaces" or "living floors," these being the surfaces beyond structures where site inhabitants carried out a variety of outdoor activities and left on the surface various kinds of refuse. A plaza or courtyard surrounded by buildings is a more specialized type. Techniques for exposing such surfaces, if they are preserved, are similar to those for exposing structure floors. An archaeologist often is concerned with the distribution of objects confidently associated with the surface, and the location of these objects may be identified by point provenience or collected from relatively small grid squares. Various kinds of pits may occur on these living floors, including outdoor hearths, baking pits, storage cists, and postholes of relatively ephemeral structures providing shade. As is the case with pit features inside a structure, profiles of the fill of these pit features, and sometimes of the pits themselves, may be created by excavating a trench through the feature or by initially excavating one half. Concentrations of objects may or may not be associated with a recognizable surface. For instance, the pit in which a cache of objects was placed may or may not be recognizable, given soil conditions and extent of postdepositional disturbances. Where objects are suspected to have been deposited within a pit that no longer is visible, a profile through the artifact concentration may reveal the likely contour of the pit by the positions of objects that presumably rested against its sides.

Monuments are of a variety of sizes, shapes, and composition, and only the smaller and simpler are given attention here. Included are small constructions associated with ritual, including mortuary practices, but some monuments simply may be unusually large aggregates of refuse. The monuments considered here generally are no more than a few meters tall, perhaps the most common being earth mounds and rock cairns. Excavation of mounds or cairns may be limited to a trench entering from the perimeter to the center, or from one side to the opposite, to document stratification and to seek a central cache or burial. At the other extreme, the complete monument may be excavated, as may be the case if caches or burials are scattered throughout the total volume of deposits. Excavation may entail creating two bisecting profiles through the monument by excavating diagonally opposite quarters. The remaining quarters may be excavated after recording stratification. Alternatively, balks may be left in place by excavating those portions of the remaining quarters set back from the profiles at the desired thickness of the balks (e.g., Wheeler 1954:Plate 14). Documenting the stratification of a mound or cairn may be very important if the construction was intermittent over years, decades, or centuries.

Raised platforms are another commonly occurring monument. These also may be constructed of soil or rock or a combination of the two, and excavation entails an approach similar to that used for earth mounds and cairns. However, the shape of the platform, including its faces, may be of special concern, requiring greater attention to the margins than may be the case with earth mounds and cairns. Platforms are also likely to have had structures of some sort on their surfaces, so excavation may have the purpose of identifying this surface and remains of construction on it. If the surface is not preserved, evidence of structures may still be present in the form of postholes and other construction features that penetrated the surface. In either case, the excavation of a platform surface may entail use of a grid, much as would be the case with any horizontal surface on which different sorts of activities may have taken place.

Excavation of burials, whether in a tomb, cemetery, or isolated pit, requires special procedures, not only because of the nature of the human remains but also because of strictures imposed by modern society (Ubelaker 1989). Generally, an archaeologist is interested in documenting the mortuary practices associated with a burial as well as acquiring information from the human remains themselves and any associated objects. As a consequence, excavation must be concerned with the context of the human remains as well as exposure of the burial. Strictures imposed by contemporary society may limit the amount of exposure of a burial and specify disposition of the human remains and associated objects. A tomb, an enclosure in which human remains are placed, in many instances has collapsed or disintegrated; if remains of the enclosure are identifiable, they would require exposure and documentation before attention turns to the burial or burials within.

A burial may be of a complete skeleton, cremated and sometimes highly fragmented bones either in a cache or some sort of container, disarticulated bones buried after flesh and connective tissue have deteriorated or been removed, or an isolated skeletal element or a group of elements. Once a burial is encountered, an attempt should be made to identify its context in some sort of pit if there is any prospect that a pit surface is preserved. Exposure of a burial requires knowledge of human osteology, so a bioarchaeologist ideally should be on hand to direct the exposure and recording, especially if the bones cannot be removed because of contemporary social strictures. In this instance, the bioarchaeologist must document, as much as is possible or allowable, the condition and nature of the bones before they are reburied. In general, the exposure of a burial proceeds in the same manner as exposure of any object or cluster of objects, but knowledge of the human skeleton often guides the strategy of exposure. Furthermore, if the bones are in fragile condition, relatively small excavation tools may be required. Associated grave goods also require careful attention, because the position of these with respect to the burial provides information about mortuary practices and perhaps the attire in which the individual was buried. Some items of attire may be very small, such as the beads in a necklace; exposure of these, if their original positions have not been disturbed, may require extremely careful work with tools such as a dental pick and a small paintbrush.

Excavation of a cemetery adds another dimension because the location of individual burials with respect to others can be very important not only to investigation of mortuary practices but also to determining duration of cemetery use and isolating one individual burial from another in instances where a later burial disturbed an earlier one. Sometimes all the burials in a cemetery are exposed before any bones are removed or reburied, but this is often not feasible. Instead, exposure of burials within a unit or set of contiguous units is the more common practice, especially if bones are in fragile condition and cannot be left exposed to air and sunlight for very long.

Documentation of a Site's Depositional History

The soils in which an archaeologist digs come from a variety of sources and have been affected by any of a large number of post-depositional processes (Limbrey 1975; Waters 1992). Consequently, analysis of data derived from the findings of an excavation must take into consideration how archaeological site deposits were formed. Sources of deposits include importation of organic and inorganic materials left behind by site occupants, alluvial action of streams and rivers, runoff from higher elevation lands adjacent to a site, and wind transportation of sand and silt. These deposits are modified by groundwater and the chemicals it contains, by the plants and animals residing on the site and within its deposits, by the activities of the people who used the site, and by various modern land-use activities such as plowing and modification of topography with heavy equipment. Objects may be of an age completely different from the deposits containing them. For instance, soil-disturbing processes such as tree throw and rodent burrowing may introduce surface objects into a soil that may be many thousands of years older than the objects (Johnson 1989).

Because few archaeologists have the training and experience in soil science and geomorphology necessary for full-scale analysis of soil formation processes, most depend on the skills and expertise of a soil scientist or geoarchaeologist when information on the characteristics and origins of soils is necessary. Nonetheless, an archaeologist should have a basic knowledge of soil science sufficient for identifying the soil formation processes commonly occurring in the region where the site under investigation is located.

Archaeologists also are concerned with documenting the stratification of archaeological deposits so as to understand the sequence of site occupation and the various deposits and surfaces created by site occupants. In sites with complex stratification caused by a long sequence of building construction and destruction or accumulation of discrete trash deposits, documentation may be an involved procedure requiring a good deal of time and effort. In the ideal situation, documentation of stratification entails scrutiny of a vertical profile of deposits, typically in the form of a carefully smoothed and cleaned sidewall. It should be emphasized, however, that recording differences in deposits visible on horizontal surface exposures often is just as important as the stratification seen on a vertical profile. In both instances, care must be taken to ensure that the excavated surface is prepared in such a way that differences between deposits are discernible. Depending on the nature of the deposits, preparation may entail careful scraping and perhaps also brushing. In some instances, spraying with a fine mist of water will enhance stratigraphic differences, but in others allowing the exposure to air-dry will produce the desired effect.

A popular approach to documentation, once the stratification of the profile has been drawn and photographed, is the production of a Harris matrix (Harris 1989). This entails first assigning a number to each deposit (and possibly also surface) on a stratigraphic drawing and then producing a branching diagram (the matrix) that shows the temporal arrangement of the deposits and surfaces to the extent that temporal relationships can be inferred.

Conservation of Objects

Conservation during fieldwork may be as simple as placing an object in a protective container for transport to the archaeological laboratory or as complex as consolidating an object with fixatives before it is moved. Carbonized objects, objects of wood or plant fiber, and objects of fur and leather often require conservation treatment by a trained conservator; when such perishable objects are expected, a conservator generally would be one of the field staff (Sease 1992). Regardless of whether preservation of such objects is required, a number of relatively simple conservation measures commonly are practiced. The most obvious is carefully exposing fragile items with small tools and placing them safely in a type of container that will ensure that they will not break during transport to the laboratory. For instance, fragile objects such as delicate bones and chunks of carbonized wood often are wrapped in bathroom tissue and placed in a rigid container with enough padding to prevent abrupt movement. Flaked-stone objects with the prospect of preserved microwear should be collected directly after exposure and wrapped in bathroom tissue before being placed in an individual bag. Ground-stone artifacts used for milling may be treated in a similar fashion so as to preserve the scum of soil clinging to the working surfaces, which may contain particles of milled seeds or pollen. Segments of carbonized timbers from a burned structure, retained for wood identification and chronometric dating, may be wrapped in string and placed in a padded container for transport. Even more simple than these procedures is collecting fragile objects from a deposit before it is screened, as they are likely to break when the screen is shaken. Reference to an up-to-date conservation manual during project planning will provide the basis for developing a project-specific conservation plan.

An archaeologist often faces a dilemma in reconciling time and resources against the greater amount of information that may be derived from objects if they are given optimal conservation treatment. Relatively fragile objects such as delicate animal bones or artifacts with easily destroyed use wear ideally receive special handling and packaging to ensure they are not damaged, but the quantities coming from an excavation may be too large to give the optimal conservation to every one. Consequently, the archaeologist may be forced to conserve only a sample of such objects or to conclude that the information value is too low to justify conservation. Nonetheless, such decisions should be made with knowledge of conservation measures that could be employed.

Record Keeping

A typical excavation project generates a substantial compendium of various kinds of records that document findings and the course of excavation. Many of the records are forms filled out by fieldworkers. Project directors often design their own forms to accommodate particular excavation situations and obtain information relevant to research objectives. Forms may also elicit information useful in designing subsequent stages of site investigation, such as the amount of time required to excavate a given volume of deposits. Probably the most common type of form elicits information about excavation in a particular unit or a particular level within a unit—a unit record form or a level record form. In designing a form, one should consider what kind of information it makes sense to collect. For example, if unstratified site deposits are being excavated in arbitrary levels, it would be reasonable to use a form pertaining to the excavation that takes place in a unit during the course of a day rather than a form for each separate level of a unit.

Another commonly used form elicits information about a feature, that is, any phenomenon encountered during an excavation for which an archaeologist wishes to collect more specific information than is routine. Generally it is something out of the ordinary—an object, a cluster of objects, a discrete deposit or surface, or some combination of these. More specific provenience information and more detailed description are elicited on a feature record form than would be entered onto a unit or level record form. Specialized feature record forms may be used for a burial, a particular kind of structure, a pit of a particular sort, and the like. All kinds of feature forms often are associated with drawings made on graph paper, as well as photographs.

Other record forms keep track of work activity and crew assignments, photographs, and collections. Forms pertaining to work activity and crew assignments may document where work took place at a site on a given day and who was assigned to particular units. A photographic record is basically an inventory of photographs taken during the course of a project; it generally includes information about the subject of each photograph and type of camera and film used. Records documenting collections may take the form of an inventory of artifacts encountered or the containers in which collections are placed for transport. If an object's point provenience is identified, the object usually is assigned its own field number that is recorded on its container and on the record forms.

Labels are an especially critical aspect of record keeping. These may be slips of paper enclosed within a container or tags attached by wire or string to a container, or they may be writing on the container itself. Often a label is a kind of form with standard categories of information. Any container of collected material must have a label having all pertinent provenience information. It may also have the date of collection and the names of excavators. If an inventory of containers is being kept, the label may also include a container number. Double labeling may be done as a precautionary measure, with one label inside the container and another on the outside.

Various kinds of drawings typically are made in the course of an excavation. These include site maps, sketch maps showing unit layouts, profile drawings, and plan-view drawings. Site maps include topographic information, generally in the form of contour lines, location of natural features such as drainage channels, trees and other discrete vegetation, modern land development features such as roads and buildings, location of excavation units, and site datums. They are produced with one or another, or a combination, of mapping instruments. A plane table setup has the advantage of producing the map as topographic and other data are collected, whereas a theodolite or level entails some delay between data acquisition and map production. Profile drawings of unit sidewalls or other kinds of vertical exposure show stratification of deposits and their relationship with distinct surfaces, areas of disturbance such as *krotovina* (filled-in rodent burrows), and natural and archaeological objects protruding from the sidewall or bank. Plan-view drawings show the distribution of objects and the extent of deposits or surfaces exposed at a particular depth of excavation. Both profile and plan-view drawings may accompany a feature record, but they may be made for other purposes too.

A field director may elect to keep a journal during the course of a project. This is a day-by-day narrative presenting a description of the different activities taking place at the site, the various factors or events that affected the course of fieldwork such as weather or crew sickness, and a description and initial interpretation of patterning in the archaeological record. The journal may serve as a means of cross-checking the accuracy of other records, and it typically presents information important in evaluating the quality of certain data for analysis. Perhaps most important, however, are observations of patterning in the site's archaeological record as the excavation proceeds and possible interpretations, because these may be the basis for revising aspects of the research design, especially during the data processing and analysis phases of the research.

Even on relatively small excavation projects, it often makes sense to assign a crew member to manage the record keeping. This person's task is to ensure that records are produced when they need to be, that they are neat and accurate, and that they are organized for reference. A crew member may also be assigned to check all container labeling and to account for all containers when they arrive at the laboratory. Checking of records should be done very soon after they are produced, when the prospect of correcting errors is greatest.

Most field records are eventually archived, usually in a collections repository of a museum or university. Consequently, their paper should be of archival quality (i.e., acid free); any handwriting ideally should be in pencil, the only writing medium stable over the very long term. Information filled out on labels often is an exception, as these may be exposed to water as the collections are processed. Indelible markers therefore are used; because field labels usually are discarded after the collections have been processed and cataloged, the long-term stability of the marker ink is not an issue.

Photography is another important recording medium. Most field photography is done with 35-mm or medium-format single-lens reflex cameras, and often one camera is used as a backup of another to ensure that at least one of them acquired a usable photograph. Both black-and-white and color film are used. Black-and-white film has the advantage of recording a greater range of light intensity than color film, but of course much of interest to an archaeologist is color variation, so color film nearly always is required. Digital photography has become very popular in archaeological fieldwork because of the advantage of knowing almost immediately whether an acceptable image has been acquired. However, the range of light intensity recorded in a digital camera image is less than is typical of color film, and if enlargements beyond 8 × 10 inches are desired, the resolution of an image produced by a digital camera may not be sufficient. Subjects of photography include the site and its environs, excavation activities, profiles of deposits and plan views of horizontal exposures, and any phenomena recorded as features.

A common difficulty in photography is coping with adverse lighting conditions, especially contrast between sunlit and shaded portions of a subject being photographed. Judicious use of such devices as sheets to block light, reflectors, and flash units usually can mitigate high contrast; if time permits, the photography may be done at a time of day when lighting is optimal. Another common difficulty is gaining enough height to encompass everything in a horizontal exposure. Archaeologists have used a variety of means for gaining camera height such as ladders and various devices from which a remotely operated camera is suspended or attached, including large tripods or booms, balloons, and miniature radio-controlled airplanes. Taking good photographs requires training and experience, and as a consequence, photography during excavation often is assigned to a person who has had more than an average background in photography.

As archaeology enters the digital age, many archaeologists have started using computers in the field as well as various electronic devices that collect data in digital form. Instead of paper records, each excavation crew records data into a laptop computer, and images from a digital camera may be collected directly by a computer and then annotated. In fact, digital photography may take the place of various kinds of drawings, especially plan-view drawings, and may entail the use of geographic information system (GIS) software to produce a graphical record of excavation (e.g., Aldenderfer 2001). However, readily available computers are not adapted to all the different weather conditions encountered in fieldwork, and protecting them from the copious amounts of dust created during excavation is often difficult. It seems, therefore, that paper records will continue to be used for some time to come.

Field Laboratory

Long-term excavation projects, lasting weeks or months, usually have a field laboratory that operates in conjunction with the excavation. Depending on the nature of collections being generated by an excavation and various logistical constraints, a field laboratory operation varies considerably in complexity. In its most elaborate form, a field laboratory carries out all the collections processing and cataloging and may also perform some specialized analyses. In its most minimal form, a field laboratory simply prepares collections for transport. If an excavation takes place near the home base of an archaeological consulting firm or a university or museum, the field laboratory has the best opportunity to be a complex operation. Conversely, if an excavation is in a remote location away from sources of water and electricity, a field laboratory necessarily will be a limited operation.

In general, it makes sense for a laboratory to be active during an excavation because it can provide information to the excavation staff useful for refining the approach to excavation. This information may be as simple as tabulation of relatively raw data or as complex as statistical analysis, especially that referred to as exploratory data analysis. Also the field laboratory staff should be in the best position to correct errors in field records soon after they are made, given that the staff usually takes care of checking many of the records produced during excavation. Other tasks that a field laboratory may perform are washing, drying, and cataloging collections; flotation; taxonomic identification of floral and faunal remains; preparing samples for specialist laboratories (e.g., radiocarbon samples); producing maps and refining various kinds of field drawings; conservation of objects; and packaging for transport and curation.

Safety and Health Issues

Safety and health during an excavation are partly the responsibility of each individual participant and partly the responsibility of the project director and administrative staff. Common sense goes a long way in ensuring health and safety, but knowledge acquired through training and experience also is fundamental. Novices to archaeological excavation are particularly at risk, especially because they may never have worked with the tools of archaeology and may also be unfamiliar with working outdoors.

Over the last three decades archaeologists working in the United States have become increasingly aware of responsibilities to ensure a healthy and safe working environment during excavation because of the passage of the Occupational Safety and Health Act of 1970 (Niquette 1997). Many states in the United States have their own regulations comparable to the federal regulations and approved by the Occupational Safety and Health Administration (OSHA). Of course, other nations also have comparably explicit laws and regulations meant to ensure safety and health of workers and to provide guidance to both workers and employers.

Safety and health issues encountered during an excavation may be caused by extreme weather conditions, contact with certain plants and animals native to the region, dust inhalation, overexertion, loss of agility while moving around an excavation, misuse of excavation equipment, collapse of sidewalls in deep excavations, and poor sanitation. A wide variety of actions may be taken to avoid or minimize safety and health problems. Some of the more obvious actions include the following:

- Become familiar with environmental threats to safety and health characteristic of the region and the specific location where the excavation is planned and take appropriate measures.
- Know where the nearest medical facilities are and how to transport a person with a serious medical condition to the nearest appropriate facility. Have some means of quickly contacting medical or rescue services when they are needed.
- Wear proper clothing, including appropriate work shoes or boots and a hat, as well as protective gear appropriate to particular activities or situations (and perhaps mandated by law).
- Obtain tetanus shots and take other medical measures to prevent infections or diseases endemic to the region where the excavation is to take place.
- Ensure that the project has a general first-aid kit with supplies appropriate for the environmental conditions and type of excavation. Included in the first-aid kit should be a first-aid manual such as *The American Red Cross First Aid and Safety Handbook* (Handal 1992). If an excavation project is located where medical services are several hours or more away using the most rapid form of transportation available, a useful manual is *Where There Is No Doctor: A Village Health Care Handbook* (Werner et al. 1992). Individual first-aid kits with limited supplies also may be appropriate.
- Become familiar with safety and health regulations pertaining to the workplace and comply with them.
- Write or obtain a safety and health manual or manuals for field technicians and project directors and devise ways to ensure that excavation participants are familiar with them.
- If units are more than 1.5 m deep, institute measures such as shoring of sidewalls to assure safety of workers. OSHA regulations deal specifically with shoring.

Another realm of safety and health not often recognized (but see Stewart 2002:94) is the mental health or well-being of an excavation crew. Of course, ensuring that a crew's physical safety and health needs are met is the foundation for mental well-being. Other important factors are clear lines of communication so that fieldworkers understand responsibilities and tasks at hand, effective management and efficient management structure, appropriate response to complaints of fieldworkers, and compatibility of excavators who work as a team. Many members of an excavation crew may never have worked together before and may have much different backgrounds in fieldwork training and experience; consequently, many problems in interpersonal relations could arise that could endanger the morale of the field crew as well as the objectives of the excavation.

Directing an Excavation

Acquiring the abilities necessary to be an excavation project director is largely a matter of accumulating experience, first as a field-crew member, then as a crew chief, and later in higher supervisory posts. As one acquires field experience, the observant novice archaeologist will come to realize that some projects are well run and others are not, and from this gamut of experience the thoughtful novice may learn much about project direction. However, there is no one best way to direct an excavation. The approach must be adjusted to such factors as the nature of the site; the data requirements; the scope of the excavation; the size, organization, and experience of the excavation team; and the environmental conditions under which the work is undertaken. Individual personality traits also must be taken into account, because they can affect the smooth running of a project, especially among the supervisory staff. Care taken in recognizing all of these factors during excavation project planning and the course of the project will ensure that goals are reached without undue difficulties.

The project director also must consider how collaborators, if any, will be involved in the excavation. Collaborators may be members of a project direction team, whereas others may undertake such specialized aspects of fieldwork as documenting the skeletal remains of human burials or collecting pollen samples. Collaborators who will undertake analyses of parts of the collections may be more peripherally involved in the excavation. Collaborators may also include experienced archaeologists who could serve as consultants during project planning and execution if the project director has comparatively little experience in project direction.

Planning an excavation project requires careful attention to the constraints of funding and time, both of which determine how much excavation can be accomplished. Calculation of what can be accomplished within a specified amount of time and with a particular level of funding generally is based on experience of the project director and colleagues. Generally, the field records and budgets of comparable projects at sites with characteristics similar to those at which the proposed excavation is to take place will provide the most definitive information. Of course, the greater attention to detail in planning and the more definitive the data used in making projections, the more likely the project will not encounter serious problems in its execution. Nonetheless, there is always some amount of uncertainty associated with any project from such factors as unpredictable characteristics of sites, anomalous adverse weather conditions, or accidents of one sort or another. Sophisticated planning usually is able to minimize the effects of such factors.

In the end, a successful excavation director must have effective leadership skills, including self-confidence balanced with humility, the ability to admit ignorance and the enterprise to compensate for it, the sense to know when to delegate authority, and above all, a concern for the well-being of project personnel.

Conclusion

I have emphasized that excavation project planning, including selection of particular excavation techniques, must take into consideration two principal factors. The first is the kinds and quantities of data to be derived from objects, surfaces, and deposits for addressing research objectives—in short, data requirements.

Of course, data requirements are derived from the various hypotheses being addressed in the course of a specific project as well as the long-term research interests of the group of archaeologists working in a particular region. The second factor is the nature of the site: its area extent, its depth, the density and distribution of objects, surfaces and deposits of interest, soil characteristics, and many other site characteristics.

The techniques of excavation that have become conventional in a region always should be evaluated to determine whether they make sense with respect to the factors just mentioned. Excavation techniques sometimes are slavishly followed without careful evaluation, under the assumption that they must be the most appropriate ones because they always have been used. In some cases traditional techniques do make sense, even if the rationale for them has not undergone much scrutiny, but in other cases they may actually be hindering the development of knowledge about a region's prehistory because they preclude generation of data important to regional research.

Becoming proficient in excavation techniques requires accumulation of hands-on experience within a particular region. Formal training and a familiarity with descriptions of excavation techniques in the regional literature are necessary adjuncts, but the distinctive aspects of a region's archaeological record have to be experienced directly to have a basis for making informed decisions about which excavation techniques would be most appropriate to use. This is not to say that each region's archaeological record is so individual that experience in one region is not applicable to another. Nonetheless, there is so much variability among the world's regions, let alone among sites within a region, that any experienced archaeologist beginning work in a new region has to become familiar with new characteristics and how to deal with them effectively.

To ensure that all data obtained during an excavation project are comparable, techniques should be systematically applied. All members of an excavation crew must have an appropriate level of experience, and they must be aware of project goals and procedures being used to reach these goals. The project director and other project staff members have the responsibility of ensuring that the field crew is sufficiently oriented and trained. Furthermore, the project staff must monitor all aspects of excavation to ensure that each crew member indeed is carrying out excavation in the intended manner.

The concern for comparability of data derived from excavation extends beyond the end of the project. An archaeologist interested in using previously obtained corpora of data for comparative analysis must have some basis for knowing that all data included in the analysis are comparable, and the ultimate basis for comparability is that they were derived from excavation using the same excavation techniques. To determine this, an archaeologist must review documentation of excavation techniques; the more thorough this documentation, the more confidence one may have in comparability of data (or lack of comparability as the case may be). Even if a review of documentation reveals that different techniques were used that would make data not directly comparable, knowing the kinds of data biases that different techniques create may allow at least limited comparison. The documentation needed generally would not be the descriptions of excavation techniques one finds in publications. Instead, it would be the field records, maps, drawings, and photographs produced in the course of a project. These, of course, would be archived at an appropriate repository and would be accessible for research.

In conclusion, it is worth pointing out that surprisingly little formal dialogue takes place in the archaeological literature about excavation (and more generally, field) techniques and their relationship to the generation of data. Texts that are compendia of excavation (and other field) techniques are continually published, but these are aimed mainly at students. Although a number of article-length publications concern the utility of a particular excavation technique, they represent only a small portion of the broad range of techniques in use. It seems that acquiring the skills of fieldwork has been left almost entirely to student-mentor relationships, both formal and informal, and to the creativity of individual archaeologists. Considering how important excavation techniques are to ensuring the quality and appropriateness of data, they should be the subject of dialogue and critique.

References

Aldenderfer, Mark
    2001   Project Chamak Pacha: Real time GIS of archaeological excavation. Electronic document, http://titicaca.ucsb.edu/chamak_pacha/.

Asch, David L.
    1975   On sample size problems and the uses of nonprobabilistic sampling. In *Sampling in archaeology*, edited by James W. Mueller, pp. 170–191. University of Arizona Press, Tucson.

Barker, Philip
    1993   *Techniques of Archaeological Excavation.* 3rd ed. Routledge, London.

Binford, Lewis R.
    1964   A consideration of archaeological research design. *American Antiquity* 29:425–441.

Bowkett, Laurence, Stephen Hill, Diana Wardle, and K. A. Wardle
    2001   *Classical archaeology in the field: Approaches.* Bristol Classical Press, London.

Brown, James A.
    1975   Deep-site excavation strategy as a sampling problem. In *Sampling in archaeology*, edited by James W. Mueller, pp. 155–169. University of Arizona Press, Tucson.

Cannon, Aubrey
    2000   Assessing variability in Northwest Coast salmon and herring fisheries: Bucket-auger sampling of shell midden sites on the central coast of British Columbia. *Journal of Archaeological Science* 27:725–737.

Conyers, Lawrence B., and Dean Goodman
    1997   *Ground-penetrating radar: An introduction for archaeologists.* AltaMira, Walnut Creek, California.

Dalan, Rinita A.
    1991   Defining archaeological features with electromagnetic surveys at the Cahokia Mounds State Historic Park. *Geophysics* 56:1280–1287.

Dalan, Rinita A., John M. Musser, Jr., and Julie K. Stein
    1992   Geophysical exploration of the shell midden. In *Deciphering a shell midden*, edited by Julie K. Stein, pp. 43–59. Academic Press, San Diego.

Dancey, William S.
    1981   *Archaeological field methods: An introduction.* Burgess, Minneapolis, Minnesota.

Fladmark, Knut R.
1978   *A guide to basic archaeological field procedure.* Department of Archaeology, Simon Fraser University, Burnaby, British Columbia.

Flannery, Kent V.
1976   Excavating deep communities by transect samples. In *The Early Mesoamerican Village,* edited by Kent V. Flannery, pp. 68–72. Academic Press, New York.

Handal, Kathleen A.
1992   *The American Red Cross first aid and safety handbook.* Little, Brown, Boston, Massachusetts.

Harris, Edward
1989   *Principles of archaeological stratigraphy.* 2nd ed. Academic Press, London.

Heimmer, Don H.
1992   *Near-surface, high resolution geophysical methods for cultural resource management and archaeological investigations.* Geo-Recovery Systems, Golden, Colorado.

Hester, Thomas R., Harry J. Shafer, and Kenneth L. Feder
1997   *Field methods in archaeology.* Mayfield, Mountain View, California.

Johnson, Donald L.
1989   Subsurface stone lines, stone zones, artifact-manuport layers, and biomantles produced by bioturbation via pocket gophers (*Thomomys bottae*). *American Antiquity* 54:370–389.

Kenyon, Kathleen M.
1961   *Beginning in archaeology.* Phoenix House, London.

Limbrey, Susan
1975   *Soil science and archaeology.* Academic Press, London.

Lovis, William A., Jr.
1976   Quarter sections and forests: An example of probability sampling in the northeastern Woodlands. *American Antiquity* 41:364–372.

McManamon, Francis P.
1984   Discovering sites unseen. *Advances in archaeological method and theory,* Vol. 7, edited by Michael B. Schiffer, pp. 223–292. Academic Press, Orlando, Florida.

Niquette, Charles M.
1997   Hard hat archaeology, *SAA bulletin* 15:15–17. Electronic document, http://www.saa.org/publications/saabulletin/15–3/SAA12.html.

Redman, Charles L.
1973   Multistage fieldwork and analytical techniques. *American Antiquity* 38:61–79.

1975   Productive sampling strategies for archaeological sites. In *Sampling in archaeology*, edited by James W. Mueller, pp. 147–154. University of Arizona Press, Tucson.

Reid, J. Jefferson, Michael B. Schiffer, and Jeffrey M. Neff
1975   Archaeological considerations of intrasite sampling. In *Sampling in archaeology*, edited by James W. Mueller, pp. 209–224. University of Arizona Press, Tucson.

Ross, Anne, and Ryan Duffy
2000   Fine mesh screening of midden material and the recovery of fish bone: The development of flotation and deflocculation techniques for an efficient and effective procedure. *Geoarchaeology* 15:21–41.

Sease, Catherine
1992   *A conservation manual for the field archaeologist*. 2nd ed. Institute of Archaeology, University of California, Los Angeles.

Schaffer, Brian S., and Julia L. J. Sanchez
1994   Comparison of 1/8-inch and 1/4-inch mesh recovery of controlled samples of small-to-medium-sized mammals. *American Antiquity* 59:525–530.

Stein, Julie K.
1986   Coring archaeological sites. *American Antiquity* 51:505–527.

Stewart, R. Michael
2002   *Archaeology, basic field methods*. Kendall/Hunt, Dubuque, Iowa.

Ubelaker, Douglas H.
1989   *Human skeletal remains: Excavation, analysis, and interpretation*. 2nd ed. Taraxacum, Washington, D.C.

Van Horn, David
1988   *Mechanized archaeology*. Wormwood Press, Calabasas, California.

Wagner, Gail E.
1988   Comparability among recovery techniques. In *Current Paleoethnobotany*, edited by Christine A. Hastorf and Virginia S. Popper, pp. 17–35. University of Chicago Press, Chicago.

Waters, Michael R.
1992   *Principles of geoarchaeology*. University of Arizona Press, Tucson.

Werner, David et al.
1992   *Where there is no doctor*. Rev. ed. Hesperian Foundation, Palo Alto, California.

Wheeler, Mortimer
1954   *Archaeology from the earth*. Clarendon Press, Oxford.

Winter, Marcus C.
1976   Excavating a shallow community by random sampling quadrants. In *The early Mesoamerican village*, edited by Kent V. Flannery, pp. 62–67. Academic Press, New York.

Workman, Karen Wood, and William B. Workman
1998   Sampling vs. block excavation at two recent archaeological sites on the southern Kenai Peninsula, Alaska. *Arctic Anthropology* 35:99–112.

6

Sequence and Stratigraphy

Barbara J. Mills
Rafael Vega-Centeno

The concepts of sequence and stratigraphy are so fundamental to the excavation and interpretation of archaeological sites that they are often assumed, rather than explicitly discussed. However, new field and laboratory methods have been developed over the past few decades that provide important new ways of recording, analyzing, and interpreting stratigraphy. In addition, several important issues surrounding the use of these concepts have ramifications for how stratigraphic data are collected and interpreted. These issues range from the philosophical to the pragmatic. In this chapter, we review the historical development of the concepts of sequence and stratigraphy, contemporary methods, and current issues of a more theoretical nature.

Like Stein (2000), we see a divergence between practitioners of geological stratigraphy versus archaeological stratigraphy in contemporary archaeological practice. We argue that both approaches are necessary to the interpretation of archaeological sites and their deposits. We review the history of archaeological stratigraphy in this chapter and point out that different archaeological contexts and different questions may emphasize one suite of techniques over another—or indeed, the use of both. We then discuss different methods that have been used in the organization and interpretation of stratigraphic information.

Definitions

In archaeology, *sequence* is used both as a verb (as in "to sequence") and a noun (as in "to create a sequence"). Both usages refer to the passage of time, usually in a limited geographical area, in a historical linear manner. Sequences are created and verified through the use of *stratigraphy*, the description and interpretation of stratification or the layering of deposits. Along with seriation and cross-dating, stratigraphy is one of the major methods of relative dating used by archaeologists (see O'Brien and Lyman 1999 for extended discussions of all three methods).

The interpretation of stratigraphy depends on several general principles, discussed in more detail below. The very use of these principles in interpreting stratigraphy is, however, founded on a different way of thinking about time than is the interpretation of sequence. Accurate stratigraphic interpretation depends on knowledge about general cultural and natural processes and then the construction of inferences about their action in a particular setting. Thus, although sequence and stratigraphy are often discussed in tandem, they represent distinctly different ways of thinking about time—the former more particular and the latter more general. These two conceptions of time are discussed metaphorically by Stephen Jay Gould (1987:15–16) as time's arrow and time's cycle: "Time's arrow is the intelligibility of distinct and irreversible events, while time's cycle is the intelligibility of timeless order and law like structure." His comment that both concepts are necessary to appreciate and understand time is as true for the geologists who are the subject of his book as it is for archaeologists (Harris 1989:41–42).

In addition to the above terms, several others are used when recording and interpreting stratigraphic units. A *stratum* is a distinctive three-dimensional unit or layer. It is often used synonymously with the term *deposit* (Lyman and O'Brien 1999:58). Although O'Brien and Lyman (1999:144) suggest that the term *level* is often used by archaeologists as a synonym to stratum, we prefer to use the former term to refer to the three-dimensional unit of archaeological excavation. Thus, a stratum may include more than one level, and levels may bisect multiple strata. Ideally, each stratum should be excavated in separate levels and subdivided into multiple levels if it is of any great depth.

Some archaeological stratigraphers differentiate between natural and cultural strata. Natural strata are those formed through noncultural formation processes, whereas cultural strata are those produced through human agency (Schiffer 1987:7). Examples in which wholly natural formation processes are responsible for layers in archaeological sites include episodes of alluvation and volcanism. Many strata in archaeological sites are, however, the result of the interaction of both natural and cultural formation processes. An accurate understanding of the difference between these two different sources of archaeological deposits depends on the observation of artifactual (including architectural) materials as well as the use of geological techniques. This underscores the need to incorporate both archaeological and geological methods of stratigraphy in the observation and interpretation of archaeological deposits.

First Stratigraphers: "Deep Time" and Uniformitarianism

Stratigraphy's intellectual roots lie with a great number of geologists of the late seventeenth through early nineteenth centuries. Several excellent summaries of the events leading to the development of geological and archaeological stratigraphy have been published, including those of Grayson (1983), Gould (1987), Harris (1989), and Stein (2000). When reading about the accomplishments of early geologists, the immense conceptual hurdles present at the time must be appreciated. The earth's history was viewed within a compressed scale of a few thousand years, specific deposits were usually explained in terms of biblical events that were catastrophic in scale, and the possibility of biological extinction was unrecognized until the early nineteenth century. All three of these assumptions were to be dismantled as part of the early history of stratigraphy.

The Danish scientist Nicolaus Steno (1916) is credited with the first explicitly scientific treatise on stratigraphy, *Prodromus*, originally published in 1669. His initial problem was to understand how fossil shark's teeth (called "tongue stones") became embedded within solid deposits. He articulated what we now call the *law of superposition*, in which layers are successively deposited, one after another, such that the oldest layers are on the bottom and the youngest on the top. In addition, he reasoned that many of the deposits were the result of settling out from water and, because they were originally deposited in a fluid, that they must have been laid down horizontally. Harris (1989:31) discusses this more explicitly as the *law of original horizontality*. Steno also proposed that deviations from horizontal strata must have been caused by either uplifting or downfall, providing a concise theory of the various processes responsible for the earth's depositional history (Grayson 1983:14–16). His classic diagram of the original layering and subsequent cutting and filling of geological deposits (Figure 6.1) is familiar to legions of students in the geosciences.

Steno worked within a time in which the age of the earth still was assumed to be relatively young and one in which geological events were reckoned according to biblical tradition. Two eminent geologists of the late eighteenth and early nineteenth centuries, John Hutton and Charles Lyell, significantly helped to change these views. Hutton's *Theory of the Earth* (1788) presented the first discussion of erosion to account for *unconformities*, or fossil erosional surfaces, that appeared in the earth's strata (Figure 6.2). On the basis of observations of erosional processes in the present, he noted the immensity of time that was required to create the observed deposits. He also proposed that there must be processes of repair to counteract erosional processes, especially those of igneous origin. Although he did not know the absolute age of the earth, his work began to challenge the idea that the age of the earth could be reckoned according to how many generations were discussed in biblical genealogies.

Charles Lyell's *Principles of Geology* (three volumes, published between 1830 and 1833) developed these geological principles in more detail and applied them to specific sequences in Europe. It was not until a later review of his work that the term *uniformitarianism* was first used (Grayson 1983:79), but it is this principle that is most closely associated with Lyell's contribution. This principle states that the processes responsible for the

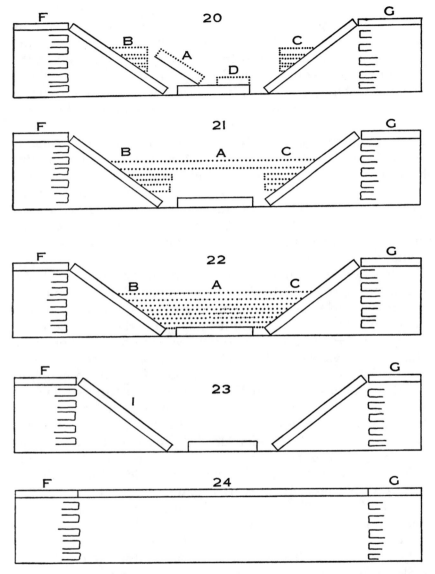

Figure 6.1.   Cross sections made by Nicolaus Steno (1669) illustrating different points in the geologic sequence of Tuscany. (Reproduction from English translation by John Garrett Winter, University of Michigan Humanistic Studies, Vol. XI, pt. 2, 1916.)

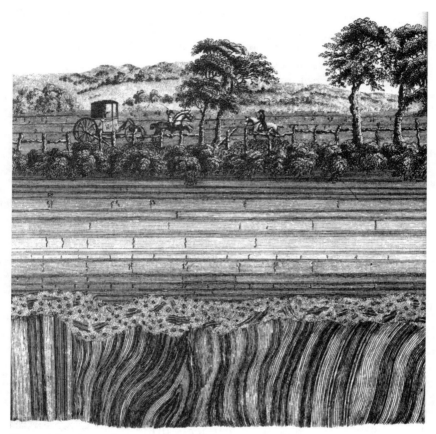

Figure 6.2. Unconformity at Jedburgh, Borders. Lithograph by John Clerk, 1787, published by James Hutton (1788) in his Theory of the Earth. *(Reproduction from Gould [1987] reprinted by permission of Sir Robert M. Clerk, Bt. of Penicuik.)*

production of deposits in the past are those that can be observed in the present. Although a strict use of a uniformitarian principle in archaeological research has been criticized because of the possibility that past processes have no modern analog, this is less of a problem for the application of the principle to geological deposits.

These early geologists provided the foundation for understanding the history of the earth in terms of what John McPhee (1980) has called "deep time." Their efforts significantly shifted how people thought about the relative age of geological deposits and led to an appreciation of the great age of the earth. But as many historians have pointed out (e.g., Grayson 1983; Gould 1987), one of the major problems with early geological works such as Hutton's and Lyell's was that, to promote a uniformitarian theory for geological accumulation, it was assumed to be synonymous with a constant *rate* of accumulation. This constant rate was contrasted with the prevailing idea of catastrophism. It was not until much later that Eldredge and Gould (1972) would disentangle this knot by providing a cogent argument for punctuated equilibria, thus opening up the possibilities for different models of rates of change, without rejecting the basic tenet of uniformitarianism: that processes in the past could be modeled from processes observed in the present.

Thus, by the early nineteenth century, many of the principles of stratigraphy that form the basis of contemporary stratigraphic research had been developed. However, the major element that was missing was the application of these principles to archaeological settings. Although geologists observed deposits with fossil remains, more concerted effort on the dating of these remains and their different associations needed to be developed.

History of Archaeological Applications of Stratigraphy

Steno's recognition of fossilized shark's teeth within geological layers was later extended to artifacts during the late eighteenth century by John Freere who found stone tools in association with extinct fauna in 1797. Freere's discovery was ignored until the mid-nineteenth century, however, when geologists such as Lyell verified these associations. Another important archaeological milestone was the exhibit mounted by Christian Thomsen at the National Museum of Denmark in 1819, which arranged artifacts according to three ages: stone, bronze, and iron (Daniel 1967; Harris 1989:7–8). This sequence was based on field collections of artifacts, and especially, the recognition of associations of artifacts in different archaeological contexts. The significance of the Three Age System is that it caused others interested in the past to consider how their material related in sequences of time. However, these observations were not accompanied by the incorporation of stratigraphic methods in archaeological excavations, only the observation of stratigraphic differences and associations of artifacts.

Boucher de Perthes's work near Abbeville, France, was one of the first to combine the stratigraphic approach of nineteenth-century geologists with archaeological excavations (see Grayson 1983). In his work at open sites in the area, de Perthes produced detailed stratigraphic drawings (e.g., Figure 6.3) that showed the context of chipped stone artifacts and demonstrated that they were at found at great depths *and* in the same beds as extinct animals such as elephant and rhinoceros. Many of his ideas were out of date by the time he wrote his book *Antiquities* in 1897, because he still adhered to theories of catastrophism. Nonetheless, he did recognize that human life on earth had great antiquity and pointed the way to archaeological approaches to deep time in which detailed artifact analyses and geological observations of stratigraphy were combined. Unfortunately, de Perthes engaged in heavy rewriting of his own interpretations that bordered on scholarly misrepresentation and he was the victim of deception by his own workers that lessened the impact of his research (Grayson 1983:118–132).

Although the application of stratigraphic methods to archaeological deposits occurred in the Americas and Europe in the late nineteenth and early twentieth centuries, an important distinction should be made between the observation of archaeological stratigraphy and the actual use of stratigraphic methods during excavation. Another important distinction is between stratigraphic excavation and stratigraphic dating (Lyman and O'Brien 1999). Stratigraphic excavation is "removing artifacts and sediments from vertically discrete three-dimensional units of deposition and keeping those artifacts in sets based on their distinct vertical recovery proveniences for the purposes of measuring time" (O'Brien and Lyman 1999:149). Stratigraphic excavation may be in either natural (geological) or arbitrary (metric) units. At a gross level, stratigraphic dating can be based on the observation of archaeological stratigraphy, but it was the onset of stratigraphic excavations that provided greater accuracy in stratigraphic dating.

There is much debate on when the first stratigraphic excavations were conducted. In Europe, stratigraphic observations

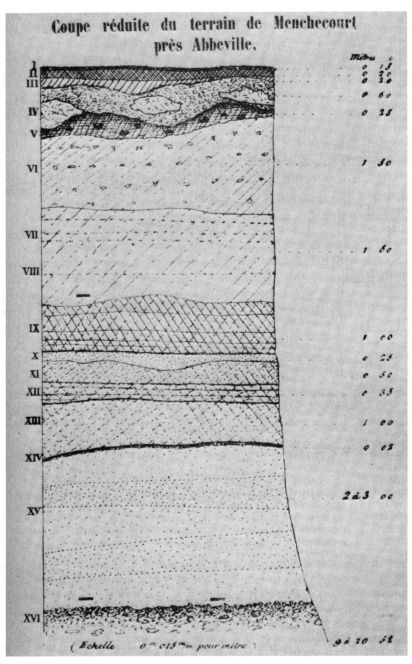

Figure 6.3.   Boucher de Perthes's profile of Hospital strata, originally published in 1847, showing the stratigraphic positions of artifacts. (Reproduction from Grayson [1983], reprinted by permission of Academic Press.)

were made by many archaeologists in the late nineteenth and early twentieth centuries (see Daniel 1967; Harris 1989; Praetzellis 1993 for summaries). Pitt-Rivers (1887–1898), in his four-volume report *Excavations in Cranborne-Chase* (southern England), incorporated explicit consideration of stratigraphic principles in archaeology. Despite its title, Sir Flinders Petrie's (1972 [1904]) *Methods and Aims in Archaeology* scarcely mentions archaeological stratigraphy (Harris 1989:4). J. P. Droop published *Archaeological Excavation* in 1915, which contained a few section drawings illustrating the nature of later constructions on existing strata and advocated the use of arbitrary excavation levels. Sir Mortimer Wheeler produced section drawings in the 1920s and first used a system of numbering layers in 1934 at Maiden Castle, Dorset (Figure 6.4). The earliest of Wheeler's excavations did not use natural strata, but incorporated arbitrary units. It was not until the excavations at Maiden Castle that he excavated in natural, stratigraphic layers. His 1954 handbook, *Archaeology from the Earth*, summarizes many of the recording techniques that he developed, and it discusses the priority of understanding layering to develop sequences and the distinction between horizontal and vertical excavation.

Historians of archaeology sometimes refer to the "stratigraphic revolution" in Americanist archaeology that was initiated by the work of Manuel Gamio, Alfred V. Kidder, and Nels C. Nelson in the 1910s. This revolution is seen as a paradigm shift by Browman and Givens (1996), who point out that it was even recognized as such by archaeologists of the time (but see Lyman and O'Brien 1999). As they note (Browman and Givens 1996:80), the first use of the term "the new archaeology" was made by Clark Wissler in 1917 to refer to the incorporation of the new stratigraphic excavation methods of the 1910s. They also point out that, like many scientific revolutions, there were many protagonists and a convergence in goals that reached across continents. Indeed, they argue that each of the major Americanists who are attributed with revolutionizing excavations methods had strong European ties and influences.

Manuel Gamio, Nels Nelson, and Alfred Kidder are usually credited as the three major Americanists who initiated the stratigraphic revolution, even though it has been pointed out that

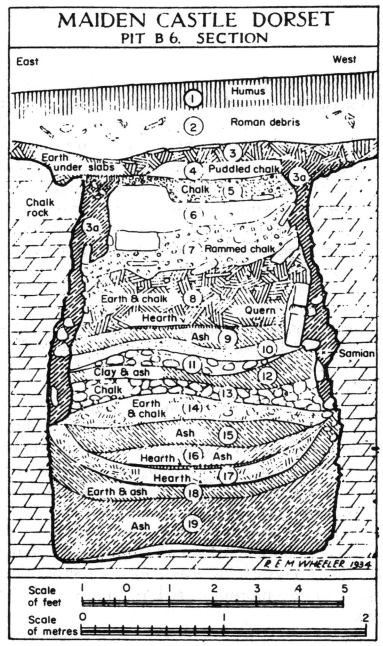

Figure 6.4. Sir Mortimer Wheeler's (1954) section of Pit B.6 at Maiden Castle, Dorset, one of the first archaeological sections to use layer numbers. (Reproduction from Archaeology from the Earth, reprinted by permission of Oxford University Press.)

"trying to figure out who was the first archaeologist to excavate stratigraphically is akin to figuring out when and where the first baseball game was played" (O'Brien and Lyman 1998:8). Before their work, stratigraphic *observations* had been made by many archaeologists in the Americas. For example, Max Uhle revealed the chronological depth of the Andean sequence through the association of burial contexts with what he called *geological stratification*, during his excavation at the Old Temple of Pachacamac, in Peru (Kaulicke 1998). W. H. Dall (1877:49) distinguished several levels in "a gradual progression" during the excavation of a shell mound in the Aleutian Islands, Alaska. But it was Gamio, Nelson, and Kidder who really brought stratigraphic excavations to the forefront of American archaeology. Because of their connections with Europeanists and because they read and knew of each other's work, they were arguably part of a broader international shift in the paradigm of archaeology.

Manuel Gamio conducted stratigraphic excavations in the Americas during his work at Atzcapotzalco, Mexico City, in 1911–1912 (1913). He used arbitrary units, but his units were variably sized, presumably to conform to some of the natural variation he observed in the deposits (Figure 6.5). Nels Nelson conducted stratigraphic excavation of the shell mounds at Emeryville, near San Francisco, Ellis Landing in New York, and in the Pueblo site of San Cristobal in the Galisteo basin of New Mexico. The latter excavations employed arbitrary, consistent 0.3-m (1-ft) units. At Pecos, Alfred Kidder (1962 [1924]) was the first to excavate using natural stratigraphic units (Figure 6.6). These three innovations were the basis for the stratigraphic revolution, but each approached archaeological stratigraphy in different ways (O'Brien and Lyman 1999).

Lyman and O'Brien (1999:70; see also Lyman et al. 1997; O'Brien and Lyman 1999) suggest that it was not how artifacts were collected that made up the stratigraphic revolution, but how those artifacts were used to measure change. Up until the 1910s, stratified sites were thought to be rare in North America because of the absence of clearly demarcated levels with distinct artifact assemblages, as had been found in Europe. An important shift in approach occurred when the idea that each stratum must contain qualitatively different assemblages was replaced by the

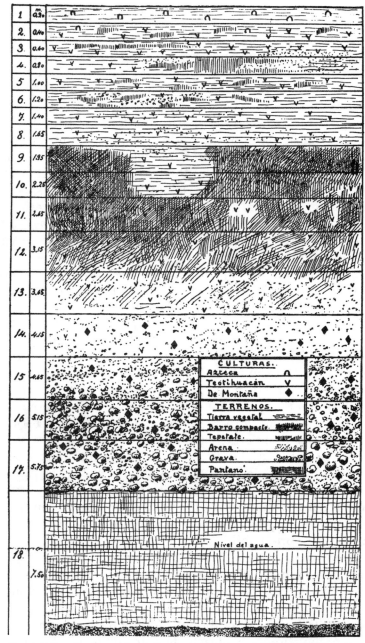

Figure 6.5.   Stratigraphic section made by Manuel Gamio (1913) at Atzcapotzalco, Mexico City, in 1911–1912, based on one of the earliest stratigraphic excavations in the New World. (Reproduction from Willey and Sabloff [1980:figure 76].)

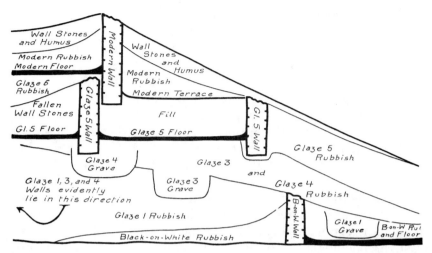

Figure 6.6. *Kidder's cross section through the North Terrace at Pecos Pueblo. (Reproduction from* An Introduction to the study of Southwestern Archaeology, *by Alfred Vincent Kidder [1924: figure 8], reprinted by permission of Yale University Press).*

idea that change could be measured analytically. Alfred Kroeber's and Leslie Spier's use of frequency seriation, or percentage stratigraphy, to build a sequence of Zuni sites that was verified through stratigraphic excavations is exemplary of this approach. Lyman and O'Brien (1999) consider this to be the "real" revolution of early archaeology in the Americas because it transcended traditional, essentialist notions of progress from one stage to another and opened up new methods for the measurement of culture change.

Lyman and O'Brien (1999:97–98) also outline some of the negative impacts of this revolution. First they note that archaeologists of the time considered each stratum or depositional unit as a chunk of a cultural continuum, each unit somehow real in an ethnographic sense. A set of associated artifacts recovered from vertically discrete units represented a steady state in a cultural lineage. In this context, the use of a depositional record to confirm apparent changes in culture was based on the varying popularities of particular culture traits, expressed in frequencies of artifact types. Since then, the discipline has adopted the superpositional component of the "stratigraphic revolution," using concepts such as components and phases and a discontinuous model of culture change. They argue that the potential of the measurement of continuous cultural change rendered as fluctuations in frequencies of artifact types has not yet been fully exploited (Lyman and O'Brien 1999:101).

Another historical trend of the twentieth century was the creation of a gap between geoarchaeological and behavioral approaches to understanding general processes of stratification. This gap is not just in the application of methods but in the very kinds of archaeological sites that are studied. A divergence between those who study Paleolithic and Paleoindian archaeology versus those working with complex architectural sites was entrenched by the early twentieth century (Stein 2000). Archaeologists working on Paleolithic and Paleoindian sites were more likely to incorporate geoarchaeologists on their projects. By contrast, archaeologists working with complex architectural deposits relied more heavily on other techniques of analyzing architecture and artifactual data for the identification and interpretation of different strata (Stein 2000). The latter has included several innovations, including the Harris matrix (Harris 1989), discussed in more detail later. The contrasts in the kinds of deposits that archaeologists need to address are illustrated in Figures 6.7 and 6.8, which show stratigraphic sections of a buried hunter-gatherer site in southeastern Arizona and a Maya architectural complex, respectively.

The contrast between archaeologists excavating sites produced by forager-collectors and archaeologists studying large, complex societies with abundant architectural remains is still true in archaeology today. This has affected both archaeological training and practice in Europe and the Americas. In the remainder of this chapter we discuss current approaches to sequence and stratigraphy, including points of divergence and convergence between geoarchaeological and behavioral approaches.

Geoarchaeological Approaches to Stratigraphy

Several geoarchaeologists (e.g., Courty 2001; Stein 1992, 2000) have noted the divergence in approaches to stratigraphy used in

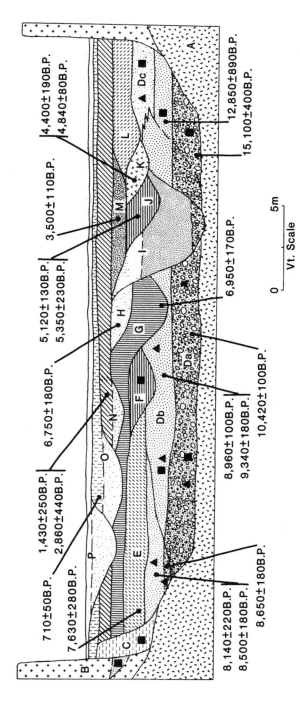

Figure 6.7. *Example of section showing alluvial stratigraphy and radiocarbon dates from Whitewater Draw, southeastern Arizona. (Reproduction from Waters [1990:Figure 3], in Archaeological Geology of North America, Centennial Special Volume 4, Geological Society of America.)*

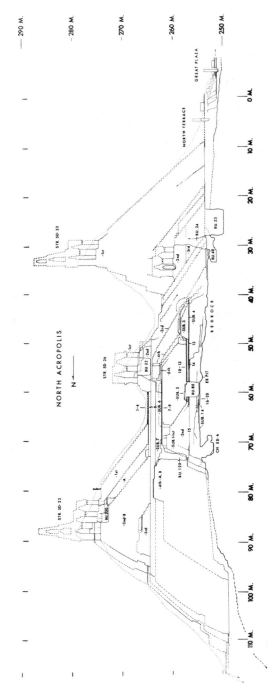

Figure 6.8. Construction sequence, North Acropolis and North Terrace at Tikal, Guatemala. (Reproduction from Coe [1967], reprinted by permission of University of Pennsylvania Museum, Tikal Project Neg. 67-5-113.)

the geosciences and archaeology. Stein, in particular, argues that contemporary archaeological use of the concept of stratigraphy has not kept pace with its use in the geosciences. Geologists approach stratigraphy using "the principles of superposition, cutting relationships, inclusions, and unconformities," not just the observation and description of layers (Stein 1992:72, citing Matthews 1984). Stein points out that strata can be identified and described in a number of different ways, including the presence, type and number of artifacts; age; magnetic properties; degree of weathering; and the floral and faunal material found in association. Three major classes of stratigraphic information—physical lithology, age, and artifactual content—are used by geologists to analyze stratigraphy. Each of these has a standard nomenclature and methodology, as discussed in the *International Stratigraphic Guide* (Hedberg 1976) and the *North American Stratigraphic Code* (NACOSN 1983). The geologic units are referred to as *lithostratigraphic, biostratigraphic,* and *chronostratigraphic* (also geochronologic or geochronometric) units.

Rather than the construction of an entirely new guide for archaeologists, Stein (1990, 1992) advocates additions to the use of lithostratigraphic and chronostratigraphic units so that they can be more widely applicable to archaeological sites. Lithostratigraphic units are defined on the basis of lithologic characteristics. To the current subdivisions of lithostratigraphic units into formation, member, and bed (in descending scale), Stein adds the term *layer*. A layer is a synthetic grouping of smaller strata that are combined to form a recognizable unit across the site. Just as there may be multiple levels within a stratum, multiple strata may make up a layer. Some archaeological protocols use a similar concept to the layer called the *analytic unit*, which is a three-dimensional unit that is used to group strata in later analysis. Layers need not be continuous across the site, and many layers are discrete because they are bounded by the edges of features or architecture. Chronostratigraphic units are based on the interpretation that rocks were formed at the same time. In geology they are not based on the interpretation of artifacts, but Stein argues that this addition is needed to make the current nomenclature flexible enough to apply to archaeological stratigraphy.

One additional unit has been suggested by geoarchaeologists for archaeological sites, the *ethnostratigraphic* unit (Gasche and Tunca 1983; Stein 1990, 1992). The ethnostratigraphic unit is based on the content of archaeological strata, especially artifacts. It is similar to the biostratigraphic unit, but different in important ways. One of the most important differences is that artifacts are not fossils. Another is that artifacts are classified and analyzed in many ways, different from the Linnaean classification of animals. A major problem in the use of the ethnostratigraphic unit, however, is the lack of a standard for classifying artifacts, which can make correlations between sites impossible (Stein 1990:516–517). The latter factor is probably the major reason why standardized use of ethnostratigraphic layers has never been widely applied by archaeologists.

Other approaches from the geosciences have been incorporated more widely in the study of archaeological stratigraphy. This is especially true of the use of techniques to identify the formation and dating of particular deposits. These techniques have largely been drawn from soil science, micromorphology, and geochronology and have a long history in the interpretation of archaeological stratigraphy—especially in the analysis of cave sites (e.g., Bordes 1972; Laville et al. 1980). Chronometric methods are discussed in more detail in chapters 9 and 10 and are not discussed in detail here.

The application of soil science has had a long history in the study of stratigraphy. As Holliday and his colleagues (1993:31–32) discuss, the utility of soils to archaeologists is limited only by the temporal scale of human occupation. Buried soils can be useful chronological markers that help to bracket human occupations. They are even more useful if they are correlated with human occupation and can be further sampled to understand the environmental context of that occupation. In either case, accurate identification and description of soils during archaeological excavation is an important contribution to understanding site stratigraphy (Mandel and Bettis 2001). As landscape archaeology becomes more important for understanding archaeological sites in their broader contexts, these approaches undoubtedly will have greater applications in the future.

Micromorphological studies are used by a variety of scientists in soil sciences and archaeology (Courty 2001; Courty et al. 1989; Goldberg 1983; Holliday et al. 1993; Macphail and Cruise 2001). The application of these studies to archaeological stratigraphy has resulted in several insights into intrasite formation processes and microstratigraphy. Seemingly homogeneous layers can be formed through several distinct events and detected through micromorphology. Using this technique, anthropogenic deposits can also be distinguished from those formed through natural formation processes. The residues of burning, organic refuse, construction materials, and activity surfaces may not be indicated by visual inspection, especially after long periods of time, but can be identified through the techniques of optical microscopy that are the backbone of micromorphological analyses (Courty et al. 1989). These techniques may also be combined with complementary microchemical instrumental analyses to confirm the identification of deposits. Micromorphological techniques can also be useful for identifying the specific processes responsible for postoccupational alterations to buried deposits, or diagenesis, and have been especially useful in the analysis of cave deposits (e.g., Bar-Yosef 2001).

Like all archaeometric techniques, the appropriate application of micromorphology and microchemical analyses to microstratigraphic interpretation depends on a number of interrelated factors. One of the most important is bringing in specialists early in the research design process to ensure that the research questions posed can be addressed with the technique and that important questions that could be addressed are not overlooked (Courty 2001:209–211). Two other important factors are an appropriate sampling design and correct sample collection in the field (Macphail and Cruise 2001:243–244). Ideally, samples from the same deposit should be taken for complementary analytic techniques such as palynology, micromorphology, chronometric dating, and soil chemistry. A single bulk sample cannot be later subdivided for these analyses because of contamination. Similarly, a single specialized sample that has been consolidated for a microscopic analysis cannot later be subsampled for other analyses. Ideally, complementary analyses of the same deposits will be performed to provide the best interpretation of stratigraphic and microstratigraphic relationships and the construction of archaeological sequences.

Harris Matrix

Some archaeologists argue that cultural deposits require their own approaches and their own theories of accumulation (Harris 1989; Brown and Harris 1993). Harris (1989:29–30) points out that there are two reasons why a strictly geological approach to stratigraphy is inappropriate for archaeological deposits. First, geological stratigraphy was developed for alluvial situations and in settings that are highly consolidated. Second, artifacts are not analogous to the noncultural inclusions found in geological contexts that might be used to identify a specific deposit. What Harris emphasizes instead are the many ways in which strata and their contents (especially artifacts) might deviate from the expected because of the intervention of natural and cultural site formation processes (see also Schiffer 1987).

One of the major contributions of Harris's work is the recognition of two different stratigraphic components: the *stratum* (or deposit), and the *interface*. Whereas the stratum is any deposit of sediments, the interface is the dividing line between deposits, or their surfaces (Harris 1989:xiv; see also Brown and Harris 1993). Features and feature interfaces are special classes of deposits and interfaces that are created through human intervention (Smith 2000:125). Using these definitions, Harris summarizes the main laws that govern stratification in archaeological contexts:

- The law of superposition, which indicates that in a series of layers and interfacial features the upper units of stratification are younger and the lower are older (Harris 1989:30).
- The law of original horizontality, which indicates that any archaeological layer deposited in an unconsolidated form will tend toward a horizontal position (Harris 1989:31).
- The law of original continuity, according to which any archaeological deposit as originally laid down, or any inter-

facial feature, will be bounded by a basin of deposition or may thin down to a feather edge (Harris 1989:32).

- The law of stratigraphic succession, which implies that a unit of archaeological stratification takes its place in the stratigraphic sequence of a site from its position between the undermost of the units that lie above and the uppermost of all the units that lie below (Harris 1989:34).

Harris has developed an analytic technique based on the above laws that consists of a chart of boxes that represent the different depositional units identified during an excavation—the Harris matrix. Harris matrices have great advantages for recording and displaying stratigraphic sequences because they show the relationship of strata across the entire site. Stratigraphic sections can show only a portion of the site at a time, represented as a cut through different layers. These sections are two-dimensional representations. Plan views are also two-dimensional representations of the site that usually illustrate one surface or exposure at a time. By contrast, the Harris matrix presents information on four dimensions combining information on the depth, extent, and chronological relationships of the strata (Harris et al. 1993:1). In this way, the matrix can present a complete stratigraphic sequence of the entire site.

The matrix admits only three possible kinds of relationships between given units of stratification: of no direct stratigraphic relationship, of superposition, or of correlation (Harris 1989:36). Each relationship is denoted by a different graphic convention for connecting the boxes (Figure 6.9). If one unit is superposed over another, then there are two other possibilities, depending on which unit is older. If the unit that is above the other is the oldest, then this would be an example of reverse stratification.

Once the relationship between several pairs of units is determined, these individual relationships can be combined to construct a stratigraphic sequence. Figure 6.10 illustrates how the matrix is built based on these individual decisions. Figure 6.10a shows how the order of superposition of three units may be determined, Figure 6.10b how two units are logically correlated with each other (i.e., have the same date), and Figures 6.10c and 6.10d how units may have no relationship to each other but are

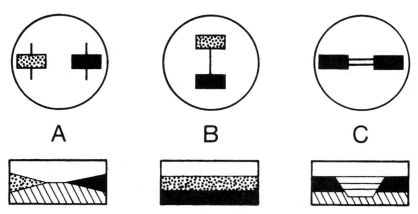

Figure 6.9. The three stratigraphic relationships recognized by the Harris matrix system. (Reprinted from Principles of Archaeological Stratigraphy, *by Edward Harris, p. 36, figure 9, copyright 1989, with permission of Elsevier.)*

related to other units through superpositioning. Last, in Figures 6.10e$_i$ and 6.10e$_{ii}$, one correct and one erroneous decision in the construction of the sequence are shown. To avoid errors such as the latter, the sequence diagram should be constructed in the field as part of the excavation recording process (Bibby 1993). An example of a Harris matrix constructed for one excavation unit at the Hoko River shell-mound site shows how complex stratigraphy is summarized (figure 6.11).

Paice (1991) identifies several problems with the presentation and use of the Harris matrix. One problem is that of recognition, as particular loci are hard to find in a "sea of numbered boxes." A second problem is the impossibility of noting whether a particular locus lasts through the deposition of a series of other loci. Finally, there is a problem in the display or exposition of information in broad-scale three-dimensional space (Paice 1991:17–18). She suggests that the first problem can be solved through different notations for each locus. Thus, square boxes should represent only walls. Other loci would remain unboxed until after new symbols are provided. For example, a U symbol for a pit locus, a mounded symbol for a fill locus, a lower horizontal line for a floor, and a "box without a lid" for an installation (Paice 1991:19–20). To define the longevity of loci, the author proposes that one locus never be placed directly above another

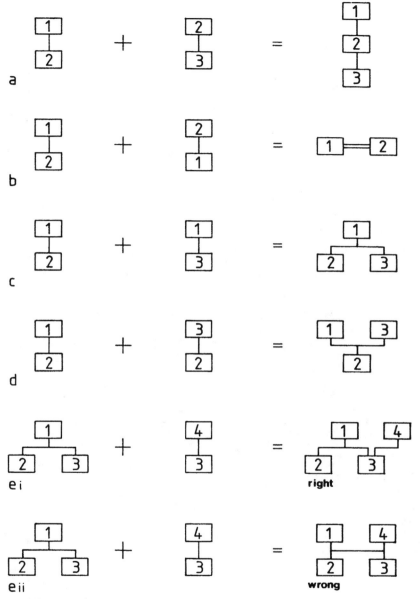

Figure 6.10. Examples of how individual stratigraphic relationships are combined to form a stratigraphic sequence, based on Orton (1980:Figures 3.2 and 3.3). (Reprinted from Practices of Archaeological Stratigraphy, *Harris et al., editors, "Building stratigraphic sequences on excavations: An example from Konstanz, Germany," by David I. Bibby, p. 107, figure 7.2, copyright 1993, with permission of Elsevier.)*

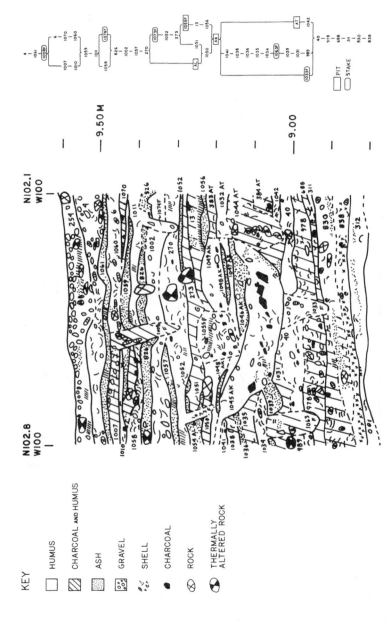

Figure 6.11. A stratigraphic profile and Harris matrix for unit in the Hoko River Rockshelter. (Reprinted from Practices of Archaeological Stratigraphy, Harris et al., editors, "Three-dimensional assessment of activity areas in a shell midden: an example from the Hoko River Rockshelter, State of Washington," by Barbara Stucki, p. 128, Figure 8.2, copyright 1993, with permission of Elsevier.)

in the matrix unless it physically overlies that locus. As a result, it is possible to modify boxes into vertical columns (especially with walls). Paice (1991:21–26) also presents several graphical techniques to represent three-dimensional structures in two dimensions, through the linking of several stratigraphic sections on the basis of discontinuous lines that denote contemporaneity.

The construction of Harris matrices has been aided through the ArchED computer program. This program was written by a group of students as part of the practical programming course Automatic Graph Drawing at the MPII, Saarbrücken, Germany (Hundack et al. 2001). As of this writing, the program is free and downloadable from the web (http://www.mpi-sb.mpg.de/~arche/).

Harris matrixes have been used to produce stratigraphic sequences on many projects, ranging from the ancient Maya to Colonial Williamsburg to medieval Europe (Harris et al. 1993). The method has been particularly useful for complex archeological stratigraphy bounded by architectural units and thus has been used widely by historical archaeologists—not too surprisingly as Harris himself is a historical archaeologist. Harris developed this method to link strata that were separated by balks, which are areas not excavated so that the stratigraphic section can be seen from two sides. The method of excavation using balks, originally advocated by Sir Mortimer Wheeler, is no longer used on most projects. Nonetheless, architecture essentially does the same thing by breaking up continuous strata, and the Harris matrix remains an excellent way to correlate and sequence strata, especially those in complex architectural sites.

Standing architecture has also been recorded using Harris matrices, but with some modification of terminology. Smith (2000:125) notes that Harris's concept of feature interfaces was largely based on subsurface stratigraphy and defined on the basis of the removal or modification of stratigraphic deposits. In aboveground architecture, fenestrations are analogous to feature interfaces in Harris matrices. Smith argues, however, that these are not merely interfaces but should be treated as separate stratigraphic units, that is, as features. Treating fenestrations as merely interfaces places them within the same units as the wall, even though they may be a later modification of that wall and important for interpreting changes in the use of the structure.

The application of Harris matrices to nonarchitectural sites is more limited. Nonetheless, even rock art has been successfully graphed. Chippindale and his colleagues (2000), studying a rock-painting panel at Garnawala, Innesvale Station (Northern Territory), Australia, showed how a sequence of figures can be interpreted through superpositioning and the use of Harris matrices. In this case, 58 separate superpositions were discerned involving 32 different figures. Stylistic similarities in some of the figures allow different panels to be tied together. Absolute dating of rock art is still not well developed and relative sequences through superpositioning of different styles of figures will remain one of the most important means of relatively dating rock art images. In this novel application of the Harris matrix (see also Chippindale and Taçon 1993), it was striking how much this systematic method increased the information gained over a more casual field observation.

One goal of many proponents of the Harris matrix is to phase and correlate sequences (see especially Bibby 1993; Harris 1989:105–119; Pearson and Williams 1993). Much of this is done in the postexcavation analysis of stratigraphy. Once the sequences for individual excavation units have been constructed, the longest sequence of contexts is selected as the primary route. Then, that sequence is phased by grouping contexts that represent the same set of activities—also called a context series. Examples of sets of activities include the construction of floors, deposition of specific kinds of debris, or repair events. Then, the next-longest sequence of contexts is added to the matrix and so forth until all contexts have been similarly phased. Figure 6.12 illustrates a Harris matrix from the Fischemarkt excavations in Germany that has been subdivided into major phases (shown with Arabic numbers), subphases (letters), and two period interfaces (PiI and PiII). The period interfaces "are considered to represent surfaces that remained in existence for periods of time in which little or no activity took place to cause the build-up of stratification" (Bibby 1993:115–117). As Harris (1989:115) points out, one of the major problems with excavation phasing is that it emphasizes periods of deposition. There will also be periods of human activity at the site that do not result in the deposition of strata, which are these interfacial periods.

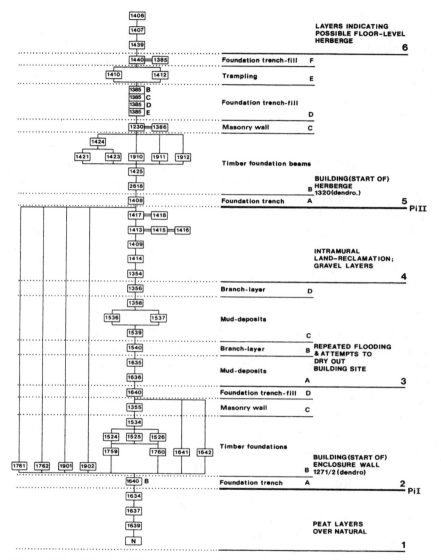

Figure 6.12. (Reprinted from Practices of Archaeological Stratigraphy, Harris et al., editors, "Building stratigraphic sequences on excavations: an example from Konstanz, Germany," by David I. Bibby, p. 116, figure 7.10, copyright 1993, with permission of Elsevier.)

Triggs (1993) provides an excellent example of how the Harris matrix improves the objective identification of phases across an excavation unit or site. Using one of Kenyon's (1981) stratigraphic profiles, he constructed a Harris matrix and then showed how her phases crosscut units that logically could not be in the same stratigraphic relationship. Although her work at Jericho is admirable, the complexity of the stratigraphy and the lack of an objective method of analysis inhibited the most accurate construction of phases.

Critics of the Harris matrix approach have largely come from the ranks of geoarchaeologists. These critiques center on the use of the concept of the interface, a necessary part of the construction of the Harris matrix because individual deposits must be able to be related to each other. Nonetheless, defining an interface is not an easy matter. Many kinds of interfaces are easy to distinguish, such as walls and floors. Other surfaces and the interfaces of natural strata may be more difficult to demarcate clearly. Archaeological fieldwork requires that strata be identified, and archaeological stratigraphers can often define the edges of strata in the field, especially strata in younger deposits that have not been subjected to extensive postoccupational disturbance and diagenesis. Depending on the temporal and spatial scale of inquiry, however, strata boundaries can be more difficult to demarcate firmly. With the current emphasis on microstratigraphic variation in the geosciences, it is not surprising, then, that there has been debate about the objective identification of interfaces in the field.

What has not been as widely discussed in this debate is that the two approaches can be used in a complementary way. The Harris matrix allows the four-dimensional representation of different deposits based on the field excavators' observations of extent and depth. Microstratigraphic approaches allow the refinement of the identification of deposit content and boundaries, the natural and cultural processes that formed them, and how they have been transformed through time. Feedback between the two can be incorporated and would enhance interpretations of any project. A tension between the two is only partly a pragmatic one—there are some fundamental philosophical differences in their approach to stratigraphy. Use of the Harris matrix inevitably focuses on boundaries and a superpositional approach, whereas many contemporary microstratigraphic analyses focus on strata content.

Formation Processes and Depositional Practice

Another approach to stratigraphy has been fostered through more explicit consideration of cultural and natural formation processes. The most explicit discussion of this approach has been by Michael Schiffer (1972, 1976, 1983, 1987). He recognized that a balanced view of both cultural and natural formation processes was needed to understand archaeological stratigraphy. He noted that many archaeologists took for granted that past behaviors were the sole determinants of the present-day properties of the archaeological record. Instead, Schiffer argued that the archaeological record is transformed through time and could not be interpreted without taking into account the many different transformational processes. Although some of these transformations are aided by application of methods from the geosciences, other transformations had to be understood through the study of behavior—during and after the deposition of archaeological materials. He therefore developed a methodological framework to address the different processes of alteration that conclude in the formation of the archaeological record.

The basis of Schiffer's (1987) methodology was the idea that formation processes do not just degrade artifacts and deposits but introduce patterning of their own. These patterns can be understood using appropriate analytic and inferential tools. He described the nature of cultural depositions in sites as the product of discard processes generated in the breakage or deterioration of artifacts (Schiffer 1987:47–48). Cultural deposits could be primary or secondary refuse according to whether artifacts were discarded in place or moved to other places (Schiffer 1987:58–59). Another form of discard, de facto refuse, is produced when activities cease in an area and things are left behind in the place that they were being used (Schiffer 1987:89–97).

Besides cultural variables in the formation of the archaeological record, Schiffer also described processes of natural origin.

These included disturbances on sediments and soils (pedoturbation), the activity of animals (faunalturbation) or plants (floralturbation), freeze-thaw action (cryoturbation), slope movement (graviturbation), swelling and shrinking in clay (argilliturbation), and soil gas disturbance in soils (aeroturbation) (Schiffer 1987:207–217).

The influence of formation-process research on archaeological studies of stratigraphy has been considerable (e.g., papers in Goldberg et al. 1993). Some of these have taken a more artifact-based approach to understand the accumulation of artifact assemblages over time (see Varien and Mills 1997 for an overview). Others have incorporated geoarchaeological methods to understand cultural and natural formation processes (e.g., Goldberg et al. 2001). Still others have looked at specific kinds of activities and their impact on the stratigraphic record, such as abandonment behavior (e.g., Cameron and Tomka 1993).

A number of students and colleagues of Michael Schiffer's have taken a life history approach to understand how artifacts are used and deposited (e.g., Walker 1995; Walker et al. 2000). Of primary interest in these studies is the recognition of special kinds of discard behavior that help to identify deposits that were produced through specific activities such as ritual or violence. Walker argues that objects that were used in ritual contexts are not likely to be discarded in "normal" trash but as "ceremonial trash." He (Walker 2002) has made the argument that archaeologists need to get away from "practical reason" in the interpretation of stratigraphy, pointing out that some behaviors span multiple strata; a stratigraphic approach that treats each layer separately (the practical approach) is therefore incomplete. Examples include the ritual burning of structures and discard of certain classes of artifacts before and after burning. Other examples are the ritual discard of objects that demarcate earlier ritual use of a structure but are separated from floor assemblages by other layers of intentionally and naturally deposited material.

Walker's insights are valuable in that they recognize that different strata may be related to each other in what he calls a "trans-temporal" manner. His approach is one that is also used in the work of social scientists focusing on social memory and landscapes (e.g., Connerton 1989), which are writ small within the deposits of individual structures. Nonetheless, this approach does not replace a more traditional stratigraphic approach. What it does is point out the importance of understanding the cultural basis for different kinds of depositional practices—practices that can be only inferred based on accurate and detailed analyses of stratigraphic relationships.

In recent years there has been a growing interest in understanding intentional depositional processes or practices. Although it comes out of a very different intellectual tradition than the behavioral archaeologists', there has been a convergence of interest in special deposits—those that are "out of character for everyday household waste" (Thomas 1999:66). Most important in their recognition is distinguishing the intentional from the inadvertent (Needham and Spence 1997).

The concept of formal or structured deposits recognizes that the intentional discard of certain objects can be a window into specific kinds of activities and, more importantly, their change through time (Chapman 1981; Hill 1995; Richards and Thomas 1984; Thomas 1999). Many of these deposits are viewed by archaeologists as a way in which people made places more meaningful through their placement in or near buildings, monuments, or features. Structured deposits have been particularly popular in the interpretation of Neolithic societies of Great Britain (e.g., Bradley 1990, 2000; Pollard 2001; Thomas 1999), but other applications are becoming increasingly popular in the archaeological literature. These deposits are not caused by a single kind of activity, however, and current research now focuses on differentiating the various kinds of deposits intentionally created and modified through the occupation of sites, including dedicatory caches, votive offerings, and the discard of retired objects used in ritual contexts (Mills 2004; Walker 1995). Although most (but not all) of these are artifact-centered studies, they are based on an understanding of the stratigraphic contexts of both artifactual and nonartifactual materials combined with interpretations of their social context of use and discard.

Current Issues

The current status of methods in sequence and stratigraphy raises four issues in how archaeologists think about time and how we approach archaeological deposits.

The first issue focuses on the models of change that are used to interpret the archaeological record. Time is viewed in discontinuous packages when using stratigraphy, especially the interfacial approach that is the backbone of the Harris matrix. This discontinuous approach to time is especially apparent in the goal of the Harris matrix to produce phases. In contrast to this approach is a more continuous approach to time that is most evident in the use of frequency seriation of artifacts. Whether archaeologists use frequency seriations in a continuous or discontinuous model is another issue. In fact, neo-Darwinian evolutionary archaeologists argue that a setback in the use of seriation has been in evidence since the 1950s because archaeologists have interpreted artifact seriations in terms of cultural stability and change within a model of discontinuous change (see especially O'Brien and Lyman 1999:224–225).

The second issue is the complementary, yet independent nature of different methods of chronological ordering. Stratigraphy and seriation are complementary because the most accurate seriations will result from the use of stratigraphic excavations. This was the most important contribution of archaeologists who contributed to the stratigraphic revolution of the early twentieth century—they excavated stratigraphically *and* they used frequency seriation. The best chronological sequences will be produced by incorporating and combining as many methods of chronological control as possible: stratigraphy, seriation, cross-dating, and chronometric dating. In constructing these sequences, however, each chronological method must be recognized as being independent of the others. The conflation of stratigraphic position with the age of the content of those strata is one of the biggest mistakes made by archaeologists (O'Brien and Lyman 1999:145). The age of the depositional event is different from the age of the contents of the deposit—and needs to be assessed independently.

A third issue is the gulf that still exists between archaeologists who work with deeply stratified nonarchitectural sites and those working with extensive architectural remains. This contrast generally corresponds with both the social scales of investigation (hunter-gatherer vs. complex societies) and in the kinds of techniques that will be employed to record, analyze, and interpret stratigraphic variability (Stein 2000). The former are more likely to incorporate geoarchaeologists into their projects, whereas the latter are more likely to use Harris matrices to order, correlate, and sequence units. All of these approaches are possible to incorporate in most archaeological projects and would enhance the interpretation of deposits from archaeological sites.

Finally, we note that some of the most interesting new research on stratigraphy is in the analysis of intentional depositional processes. This approach combines a recognition of cultural formation processes with an interest in human agency to produce new interpretations about past landscape use, ritual practices, and the construction of social memory. These studies use both stratigraphic position and content to make inferences demonstrating that the value of stratigraphic interpretation is not limited to chronology alone.

References

Bar-Yosef, Ofer
   2001   A personal view of earth sciences' contributions to archaeology. In *Earth Sciences and Archaeology*, edited by Paul Goldberg, Vance T. Holliday, and C. Reid Ferring, pp. 473–488. Kluwer Academic/Plenum Publishers, New York.

Bibby, David I.
   1993   Building stratigraphic sequences on excavations: An example from Konstanz, Germany. In *Practices of archaeological stratigraphy*, edited by Edward C. Harris, Marley R. Brown III, and Gregory J. Brown, pp. 104–121. Academic Press, New York.

Bordes, François
   1972   *A tale of two caves.* Harper and Row, New York.

Bradley, Richard
   1990   *The passage of arms: An archaeological analysis of prehistoric hoards and votive deposits.* Cambridge University Press, Cambridge.
   2000   *An archaeology of natural places.* Routledge, New York.

Browman, David L., and Douglas R. Givens
1996   Stratigraphic excavation: The first "new archaeology." *American Anthropologist* 98:80–95.

Brown, Marley R., and Edward C. Harris
1993   Interfaces in archaeological stratigraphy. In *Practices of archaeological stratigraphy*, edited by Edward C. Harris, Marley R. Brown III, and Gregory J. Brown, pp. 7–20. Academic Press, New York.

Cameron, Catherine M., and Steve Tomka (editors)
1993   *Abandonment of settlements and regions: Ethnoarchaeological and archaeological approaches*. Cambridge University Press, Cambridge.

Chapman, Robert
1981   The emergence of formal disposal areas and the 'problem' of megalithic tombs in prehistoric Europe. In *The archaeology of death*, edited by I. Kinnes, pp. 71–81. Cambridge University Press, Cambridge.

Chippindale, Christopher, and Paul S. C. Taçon
1993   Two old painted panels from Kakadu: Variation and sequence in Arnhem Land rock art. In *Time and space: Dating and spatial considerations in rock art research*, edited by J. Steinbring (papers of Symposia F and E, AURA Congress Cairns 1992), pp. 32–56. Occasional AURA Publication 8. Australia Rock Art Research Association, Melbourne.

Chippindale, Christopher, Joané De Jongh, Josephine Flood, and Scott Rufolo
2000   Stratigraphy, Harris matrices, and relative dating of Australian rock-art. *Antiquity* 74:285–6.

Connerton, Paul
1989   *How societies remember*. Cambridge University Press, Cambridge.

Courty, Marie-Agnès
2001   Microfacies analysis assisting archaeological stratigraphy. In *Earth sciences and archaeology*, edited by Paul Goldberg, Vance T. Holliday, and C. Reid Ferring, pp. 205–239. Kluwer Academic/Plenum Publishers, New York.

Courty, Marie-Agnès, Paul Goldberg, and Richard Macphail
1989   *Soils and micromorphology in archaeology*. Cambridge University Press, Cambridge.

Dall, W. H.
1877   On succession in the shell-heaps of the Aleutian Islands. In *Contributions to North American ethnology* 1:41–91. U.S. Department of the Interior, Washington, D.C.

Daniel, Glyn
1967   *The origins and growth of archaeology*. Penguin Books, Baltimore.

Droop, J. P.
    1915   *Archaeological Excavation.* Cambridge University Press, Cambridge.

Eldredge, Nils, and Stephen Jay Gould
    1972   Punctuated equilibria: An alternative to phyletic gradualism. In *Models in paleobiology,* edited by T. J. M. Schopf, pp. 82–115. Freeman, Cooper, San Francisco.

Gamio, Manuel
    1913   Arqueologia de Atzcapotzalco, D.F., Mexico. *Eighteenth International Congress of Americanists, Proceedings*:180–187. London.

Gasche, Hermann, and Önhan Tunca
    1983   Guide to archaeostratigraphic classification and terminology: Definitions and principles. *Journal of Field Archaeology* 10:325–335.

Goldberg, Paul
    1983   Applications of soil micromorphology in archaeology. In *Soil micromorphology, Volume 1: Techniques and applications,* edited by P. Bullock and C. P. Murphy, pp. 139–150. Academic Publishers, Kerkhamsted: A. B.

Goldberg, Paul, David T. Nash, and Michael D. Petraglia (editors)
    1993   *Formation processes in archaeological context.* Monographs in World Archaeology No. 17. Prehistory Press, Madison, Wisconsin.

Goldberg, Paul, Vance T. Holliday, and C. Reid Ferring (editors)
    2001   *Earth sciences and archaeology.* Kluwer Academic/Plenum Publishers, New York.

Gould, Stephen Jay
    1987   *Time's arrow, time's cycle: Myth and metaphor in the discovery of geological time.* Harvard University Press, Cambridge.

Grayson, Donald K.
    1983   *The establishment of human antiquity.* Academic Press, New York.

Harris, Edward
    1989   *Principles of archaeological stratigraphy.* 2nd ed. Academic Press, New York.

Harris, Edward C., Marley R. Brown III, and Gregory J. Brown (editors)
    1993   *Practices of archaeological stratigraphy.* Academic Press, New York.

Hedberg, Hollis Dow
    1976   *International stratigraphic guide: A guide to stratigraphic classifications, terminology, and procedure.* Wiley, New York.

Hill, J. D.
    1995   *Ritual and rubbish in the Iron Age of Wessex: A study on the formation of a specific archaeological record.* British series 242. British Archaeological Reports, Oxford.

Holliday, Vance T., C. Reid Ferring, and Paul Goldberg
1993   The scale of soil investigations in archaeology. In *Effects of scale on archaeological and geoscientific perspectives*, edited by Julie K. Stein and Angela R. Linse, pp. 29–37. Special Paper 283. Geological Society of America, Boulder, Colorado.

Hundack, Christoph, Petra Mutzel, Igor Pouchkarev, and Stefan Thome
2001   ArchED: A program for drawing Harris Matrices. Electronic document, http://www.mpi-sb.mpg.de/~arche/.

Hutton, James
1788   Theory of the earth. *Transactions of the Royal Society of Edinburgh* 1:209–305.

Kaulicke, Peter
1998   Max Uhle y el Perú antiguo: Una introducción. In *Max Uhle y el Perú antiguo*, edited by Peter Kaulicke, pp. 25–46. Pontificia Universidad Católica del Perú, Lima.

Kenyon, Kathleen M.
1981   *Excavations at Jericho, volume three: The architecture and stratigraphy of the tell*, edited by T. A. Holland. British School of Archaeology in Jerusalem, London.

Kidder, Alfred Vincent
1962   [1924] *An Introduction to the Study of Southwestern Archaeology*. Rev. ed. Yale University Press, New Haven, Connecticut.

Laville, Henri, Jean-Philippe Rigaud, and James Sackett
1980   *Rock shelters of the Perigord: Geological stratigraphy and archaeological succession*. Academic Press, New York.

Lyell, Charles
1830–1833. *Principles of geology, being an attempt to explain the former changes of the earth's surface by reference to causes now in operation*. John Murray, London.

Lyman, R. Lee, and Michael J. O'Brien
1999   Americanist stratigraphic excavation and the measurement of culture change. *Journal of Archaeological Method and Theory* 6(1):55–108.

Lyman, R. Lee, Michael J. O'Brien, and Robert C. Dunnell
1997   *The rise and fall of culture history*. Plenum Press, New York.

MacPhail, Richard I., and Jill Cruise
2001   The soil micromorphologist as team player. In *Earth sciences and archaeology*, edited by Paul Goldberg, Vance T. Holliday, and C. Reid Ferring, pp. 241–267. Kluwer Academic/Plenum Publishers, New York.

McPhee, John
   1980   *Basin and range*. Farrar, Straus, and Giroux, New York.

Mandel, Rolfe D., and E. Arthur Bettis III
   2001   Use and analysis of soils. In *Earth sciences and archaeology*, edited by Paul Goldberg, Vance T. Holliday, and C. Reid Ferring, pp. 173–204. Kluwer Academic/Plenum Publishers, New York.

Matthews, R. K.
   1984   *Dynamic stratigraphy: An introduction to sedimentation and stratigraphy*. 2nd ed. Prentice-Hall, Englewood Cliffs, New Jersey.

Mills, Barbara J.
   2004   The establishment and defeat of hierarchy: Inalienable possessions and the history of collective prestige structures in the Pueblo Southwest. *American Anthropologist* 106(2):238–251.

NACOSN (North American Commission On Stratigraphic Nomenclature)
   1983   North American stratigraphic code. *American Association of Petroleum Geologists Bulletin* 67:841–875.

Needham, Stuart, and Tony Spence
   1997   Refuse and the formation of middens. *Antiquity* 71:77–90.

O'Brien, Michael J., and R. Lee Lyman
   1998   *James A. Ford and the growth of Americanist archaeology*. University of Missouri Press, Columbia.
   1999   *Seriation, stratigraphy, and index fossils: The backbone of archaeological dating*. Kluwer Academic/Plenum Publishers, New York.

Paice, Patricia
   1991   Extensions to the Harris Matrix system to illustrate stratigraphic discussion of an archaeological site. *Journal of Field Archaeology* 18:17–28.

Pearson, Nicky, and Tim Williams
   1993   Single-context planning: Its role in on-site recording procedures and in post-excavation analysis at York. In *Practices of archaeological stratigraphy*, edited by Edward C. Harris, Marley R. Brown III, and Gregory J. Brown, pp. 89–103. Academic Press, New York.

Petrie, Sir Flinders
   1972   [1904] *Methods and aims in archaeology*. B. Blom, New York.

Pitt-Rivers, General Augustus Henry Lane-Fox
   1887–1898   *Excavations in Cranborne Chase*. Privately printed.

Pollard, Joshua
   2001   The aesthetics of depositional practice. *World Archaeology* 33(2):315–333.

Praetzellis, Adrian
    1993   The limits of arbitrary excavation. In *Practices of archaeological stratigraphy*, edited by Edward C. Harris, Marley R. Brown III, and Gregory J. Brown, pp. 68–86. Academic Press, New York.

Richards, C., and Julian Thomas
    1984   Ritual activity and structured deposition in later Neolithic Wessex. In *Neolithic studies: A review of some current research*, edited by R. Bradley and J. Gardiner, pp. 189–218. BAR British Series No. 133, Oxford.

Schiffer, Michael B.
    1972   Archaeological context and systemic context. *American Antiquity* 37:156–165.
    1976   *Behavioral archaeology*. Academic Press, New York.
    1983   Toward the identification of formation processes. *American Antiquity* 48:675–706.
    1987   *Formation processes of the archaeological record*. University of New Mexico Press, Albuquerque.

Smith, Rebecca
    2000   Recording for recording's sake. In *Interpreting stratigraphy: Site evaluation, recording procedures and stratigraphic analysis, BAR International Series*, edited by Steve Roskams, 910:125–128. Archaeopress, Oxford.

Stein, Julie K.
    1990   Archaeological stratigraphy. In *Archaeological Geology of North America*, Norman P. Lasca and Jack Donahue, pp. 513–523. Geological Society of America Centennial Special Vol. 4. Geological Society of America, Boulder, Colorado.
    1992   Interpreting stratification of a shell midden. In *Deciphering a shell midden*, edited by Julie Stein, pp. 71–93. Academic Press, New York.
    2000   Stratigraphy and archaeological dating. In *It's about time: A history of archaeological dating in North America*, edited by Stephen E. Nash, pp. 14–40. University of Utah Press, Salt Lake City.

Steno, Nicolaus
    1916   [1669] *The prodromus of Nicolaus Steno's dissertation concerning a solid body enclosed by process of nature within a solid*. (An English version with an introduction and explanatory notes by John Garrett Winter, University of Michigan Humanistic Studies, Vol. XI, pt. 2.)

Thomas, Julian
    1999   *Understanding the Neolithic*. Routledge, London. [Revised 2nd ed. of *Rethinking the Neolithic*, 1991].

Triggs, John
    1993   The seriation of multilinear stratigraphic sequences. In *Practices of archaeological stratigraphy*, edited by Edward C. Harris, Marley R.

Brown III, and Gregory J. Brown, pp. 250–273. Academic Press, New York.

Varien, Mark D., and Barbara J. Mills
    1997   Accumulations research: Problems and prospects for estimating site occupation span. *Journal of Archaeological Method and Theory* 4:141–191.

Walker, William H.
    1995   Ceremonial trash? In *Expanding archaeology*, edited by James M. Skibo, William H. Walker, and Axel E. Nielsen, pp. 67–79. University of Utah Press, Salt Lake City.
    2002   Stratigraphy and practical reason. *American Anthropologist* (104) 1: 159–177.

Walker, William H., Vincent M. Lamotta, and E. Charles Adams
    2000   Katsinas and kiva abandonment at Homol'ovi. In *The archaeology of regional interaction*, edited by Michelle Hegmon, pp. 341–360. University Press of Colorado, Boulder.

Wheeler, Sir Mortimer
    1954   *Archaeology from the earth*. Oxford University Press, Oxford.

7

Ethnoarchaeology

John W. Arthur
Kathryn J. Weedman

In November 1996 we drove toward Chencha, the central town of the Gamo highlands, in our tightly packed 1988 Toyota Land Cruiser. We thought we were well prepared to begin our 2-year ethnoarchaeological studies. For almost 3 years we had been reading, writing our grant proposals, and preparing our minds for the intellectual expedition at hand. We spent the summer months immediately preceding our 2-year stay carefully making lists and acquiring the equipment we would need to carry out our fieldwork. Finally, excited and confident, we said good-bye to our families and boarded the plane. After a month of paperwork in Addis Ababa to acquire permits and a vehicle, we began our overland journey to the Gamo people, who were yet unaware of the two foreigners about to enter their lives.

As the two of us, alone in this foreign country, drove up the mountain to Chencha, the enormity of our project began to sink in. For the next 2 years of our lives we would be living outside our own culture among a people who at that moment seemed immensely different from us. Our stomachs fluttered. How could we be such naive realists? Were there really any cross-cultural uniformities—regularities—or lawlike generalizations to help us bridge the gap between our worldview and that of the Gamo? Would we find a cross-cultural common ground in securing our basic needs of food, water, and shelter, or would a new physical environment force us to change our behavior entirely? Would our need to share our inner thoughts and establish rapport and friendships supersede our biological needs? Perhaps all aspects would blend, reflecting both our individuality and our own culture and the individuals and aspects of the new culture we were entering. How would we resolve the long-term day-to-day issues of living in and studying the material culture of another society? How would we formulate questions about the material world in ways that would translate easily into another worldview? Most importantly, how would we preserve a sense that what we learned was extraordinary once it had become mundane in our own minds and then translate it into a meaningful discourse that could be used as a reference capable of transcending and linking the past and the present?

Many of our methodological solutions came to us as we learned more about the Gamo people. Some solutions were uniquely situated to the issues and practices we studied, but many others may be useful in other contexts and thus applicable for a wider audience. Although numerous important overviews of the history of ethnoarchaeology exist (Agorsah 1990; Ascher 1961; Atherton 1983; Chang 1967; Cunningham 2003; David 1992; David and Kramer 2001; Gould and Watson 1982; Longacre 1970, 1978; MacEachern 1996; Wylie 1982, 1985), still absent is a brief text that ties together analytic method, interpretation, and field methods. We hope to offer here a concise and stimulating outline of ethnoarchaeological paradigms, their dependent methods, and advice for the novice conducting field research.

Recipes for the Past: Ethnoarchaeology Defined

Ethnoarchaeologists use the living context as a recipe for stirring up the past—in more formal terms, we appreciate the definition provided by David and Kramer (2001):

> Ethnoarchaeology is neither a theory nor a method, but a research strategy embodying a range of approaches to understanding the relationships of material culture to culture as a whole, both in the living context and as it enters the archaeological record, and to exploiting such understandings in order

to inform archaeological concepts and to improve interpretation. (David and Kramer 2001:2)

The term ethnoarchaeology was first used in 1900 by Fewkes (1900:579), and then variously renamed as action archaeology (Kleindienst and Watson 1956), ethnography for archaeology (Ascher 1961), archaeo-ethnography (Oswalt 1974), archaeological ethnography (Watson 1979), living archaeology (Gould 1980:x), and ethnoanalogy (Owen and Porr 1999).

Discussions of ethnoarchaeology are spiced with misuse of the term analogy, which is supposedly the method that blends and distills ethnoarchaeological research. However, archaeologists usually extend "analogies" beyond what they can see as similar, and hence there is an active debate over what ingredients are appropriate for creating "the perfect analogy," including the presence of direct-historical ties (Ascher 1961), technological similarity (Hawkes 1954), similar environment (Gould and Watson 1982), adaptive processes (Binford 1967), or ideological continuity (Hodder 1982:217–220). While debating over when an analogical reference is appropriate, most seem to miss the meaning of analogy itself. Gould defined analogy in narrow terms, as consisting of only a comparison for similarity, which he rejects immediately, and pursues *argument by anomaly* (1980:32; Gould and Watson 1982). Gould advocated interpretation by anomalies as the tool for discovering behavioral relationships and better explanations for the variability witnessed in the past. As Wylie (1982, 1985) pointed out, Gould sets up a "fallacy of the perfect analogy." She (Wylie 1982:393) quoted Fischer's (1970:257–259) statement that "an analogy, by its very nature, is a similarity between two or more things which are in other respects unalike. A 'perfect analogy' is a contradiction in terms. . . . If there are no dissimilarities then we would have identity rather than analogy." The literature on analogy demonstrates that analogy is not exclusively a relation of similarity (Wylie 1985). In fact, because change is a constant factor in society, then the differences are as important as the similarities when we are comparing aspects of culture through time and across space.

Furthermore, in an important paper, Schmidt (1985, and again 1997:28–30) argued that archaeologists are actually engaged in metonymy. Metonymy differs from analogy in that analogies share some similar attributes but metonymy mixes domains: one object is referred to as another. Although at first this may seem to be a simple matter of semantics, in truth we are masking what we actually do. Metonymy has several aspects: (1) parts represent the whole, (2) when names change the part named takes on the attributes of the name attached to it, which implies a relationship without stating it, and (3) it brings together two attributes that each represent two different domains and collapses them into a single domain. Archaeologists use artifacts (parts) to create a past culture (whole). We further ascribe names to the artifacts, which imply an unspoken meaning such as scraper or point. In addition, we describe the past as we see it in the present, thus reducing past and present to sameness (mixing two separate domains). Hence we engage the past through metonymy. We try to create a past recipe from a present one without knowing which or if all or even some of the ingredients are the same; the result is either a duplicate of the current recipe or a new concoction.

The use of metonymy unites ethnoarchaeology, but the renaming of ethnoarchaeology and the various roles or approaches (demonstrated below) associated with this subdiscipline demonstrate the paradigmatic changes in anthropological thought in the last century and the complexity of recreating the past for present understanding. The only means that we have for understanding the preliterate past are the material remains and their spatial patternings left by our ancestors. There is little room to question the idea that the translation of artifacts, features, and landscapes into a story of the human past depends on our current understanding of the present human condition. Hawkes (1954:168; and later Schmidt 1997) compared the study of prehistory to the uncertainty of an onion: "It works as one peels onions, and so it reaches the final question, has the onion in fact got a central nucleus at all or is it just all peel?" As will be demonstrated in this chapter, whether prehistory consists of different layers or has a core is still one of the primary debates among ethnoarchaeologists and archaeologists. In the direct-historical approach, each period of prehistory represents a unique layer of the past. The best analogies, according to the direct-historical approach, are those linking the present layer to past layers when examining the same cultural group through time. In contrast, processualists, structuralists, and behavioral ecologists believe there is a core of similarity for all of humanity, making cross-cultural (temporal and spatial) comparisons possible. The processualists believed that the core ingredients are functional; the structuralists, ideological; and behavioral ecologists, environmental. Most recently, those who espouse practice theory consider human behavior to be highly variable and not reducable to a core or cross-cultural laws. Thus they contend that we can obtain only a taste or flavor of the past. Hence all archaeological and ethnoarchaeological methods depend on metonymy. How this is achieved has been debated since the foundations of archaeological studies.

Direct-Historical Approach: Layers of an Onion

The direct-historical (Fenton 1949, 1952; Steward 1942) or continuous (Gould 1974, 1978) approach accepted that there is cultural continuity, a historical relationship, between a living culture and a past culture. Methodologically, the direct-historical approach proceeded from the present (known layer) into the past (unknown layers) and focused on those elements that agree throughout all layers of the timescale. The use of the direct-historical approach initially aligned with and mirrored popular contemporary notions and cultural anthropological research, that is, unilineal evolution (Tylor 1871) followed by functionalism (Malinowski 1961) and structural functionalism (Radcliffe-Brown 1952). These paradigms adhered to the notion that there had been little if any cultural change or progress outside Europe and even went to the extent of re-creating an "ethnographic present" by describing cultures as they supposedly were before European contact (Moore 1994:40). The direct-historical approach, although not specifically so named in its earliest use, was the first approach implemented for understanding the archaeological record.

Imperial Tradition

Gamble (1993) revealed the agenda behind the earliest archaeological reconstructions when he labeled it the imperial tradition, in which species arise in centers and then disperse. He highlighted a parallel between European imperialistic colonial actions and archaeological interpretations, such that the perceived hinterlands of Africa, Asia, and America paradoxically were rendered stagnant while serving as cradles (Gamble 1993). These hinterlands experienced change and complexity only when exposed to Europeans. Europeans equated prehistoric societies with contemporary non-European societies and, using evolutionary paradigms in archaeological interpretations, relegated people outside the Western world to inferior social positions (Priest 1833; Stow 1905). They attributed the amazing architectural remains and abundant artifacts from the Nile and Indus valleys, the highlands of Ethiopia, the Zimbabwean plateaus, and the mound complexes of North America to prehistoric contact with European peoples (Orme 1981:1–16; Robertshaw 1990; Trigger 1989:110–114; Willey and Sabloff 1974:12). Prehistorians assigned European terminology to Stone Age assemblages in Africa, Asia, and the Americas to instill a sense of change within European history. Since the day objects were recognized as products of past human activities, we have been engaged in a process of metonymy (Schmidt 1985). The choice of the word "we" is crucial because it puts into context the cradling and nurturing of the discipline of archaeology within the Westerner's world that served to legitimate European power.

Cushing (1886) was the first to allow for a direct connection between prehistoric and modern populations of Native Americans. Methodologically he employed living Zuni, their language, and material culture to re-create the origin of house and ceramic forms. This could be possible only in a worldview that believed little cultural change was associated with non-European societies. For example, he requested that a Zuni woman produce particular ceramic forms so that he could learn how they were made in the past! (Cushing 1886:500–501). There was no doubt in Cushing's mind of a direct-historical connection:

> In the times when his was a race of cliff and mesa dwellers, the most common vessel appertaining to his daily life was the flat-bellied canteen or water-carrier. This was suspended by a band

across the forehead, so as to hang against the back, thus leaving the hands as well as the feet free for assistance in climbing. It now survives only for use on long journeys or at camps distant from water. (Cushing 1886:512)

Soon afterward, Jesse Walter Fewkes (1900:579) in his study of Hopi Pueblos first enlisted the term "ethno-archaeologist" to refer to the work of comparing the present to the past. Fewkes stated (1900:578–579),

There remains much material on the migrations of Hopi clans yet to be gathered, and the identification by archeologic methods of many sites of ancient habitations is yet to be made. This work, however, can best be done under guidance of the Indians by an ethno-archaeologist, who can bring as a preparation for his work an intimate knowledge of the present life of the Hopi villagers.

In the Americas (Murdoch 1892:294–301; Nelson 1899:112–118; Nelson 1914; Swanton and Dixon 1914) and later in Africa and Asia (Allchin 1957; Elkin 1948; Stow 1905:62), the use of the direct-historical approach was acceptable because it reflected popular contemporary notions and cultural anthropological research. Non-Western societies could be used as models for the past because they had experienced little to no cultural change. The underlying premise was an ideology that portrayed non-Europeans as stagnant, unsophisticated, and primitive and Europeans as developing, refined, and advanced (Orme 1981:1–16). However, during this period we gained an important understanding of ancient material objects, because for the first time they were recognized as the products of human behavior.

"Upstreaming" in Troubled Waters

From the late 1930s to the 1950s, archaeologists began to recognize that little attention was given to the methodology through which the past and present were compared (Kluckholm 1939). Thompson (1956) felt that archaeological inferences were inherently subjective on two accounts: (1) formulating the hypothesis and (2) selecting ethnographic analogs. He argued that both the probative (ethnographic) and indicative (archaeological) "ingredients" (time, space, and culture) should be clearly defined in the comparison to establish cultural contexts and the compatibility of the comparison. Fenton (1949, 1952) called for cultural anthropologists and archaeologists to "bridge the gap between anthropology and history" through the direct-historical approach, a methodological approach that he termed *upstreaming*.

> Archaeology is perhaps the most difficult proving ground for the method and requires the most exacting and critical techniques. . . . "Upstreaming" . . . rests on three premises: 1) major patterns of culture tend to be stable over long periods of time, so that one should watch out lest he commit the fallacy of assumed acculturation, 2) "upstreaming" proceeds from the known to the unknown, concentrating on recent sources first because they contain familiar things, and thence going to earlier sources, 3) a preference for those sources in which the descriptions of the society ring true at both ends of the time scale. (1952:334–335)

Concurrently in Old World archaeology, Hawkes (1954) asserted that archaeologists must work backward, from the historical to the "ante-historic." Although the call for the direct-historical approach seemed benign, archaeology continued to be a political tool. In the Americas archaelogy reinforced the idea that Native American cultures were stable and unchanging in contrast to Anglo-American cultures. In Europe archaeology justified the construction and legitimation of contemporary ethnic and national identities referred to as tribal research or settlement archaeology (Jones 1997:2–3, 16; Trigger 1989:161–167; Veit 1989). In particular, the culture-historical approach aligned artifactual similarity through time with cultural continuity and ethnic continuity. This is most apparent in the work of Gusraf Kossinna, who believed it was possible to directly trace the presence of German peoples as far back as the Mesolithic (Veit 1989). He worked backward, directly tracing material similarity from the historical to the prehistoric within particular settlement regions.

American archaeologists reinforced their culture-historical reconstructions of the past using the direct-historical approach (Ford and Willey 1940; Kroeber 1916; Mason 1964; Parsons 1940;

Strong 1933). In the American Southwest and Midwest, archaeologists sought to justify their ceramic typologies as representative of culture groups through drawing parallels with the present (Brew 1946; Ford 1954; Gifford 1960; Krieger 1944; Rouse 1960). For example, Colton (1953) believed that archaeological types were inherent and representative of prehistoric variation and demonstrated it through the study of living Hopi pottery production. He claimed that the Hopi methods and sequence of production were similar enough to prehistoric methods to be useful for deriving typological studies. He enlisted color, surface treatment, paint, decoration, core (cross section), strength, porosity, rim, handle, and vessel forms as important attributes ethnographically and thus applicable to create archaeological typologies. The origins of the taxonomic system employed in archaeology rest with an interest in the classification of cultural history and ultimately evolutionary models (Childe 1950; Service 1962; White 1959).

Beginning in the 1950s, nations began to regain their independence from the clutches of colonialism. Archaeologists working in Africa and other non-European-American contexts gained a new political agenda. They were searching to decolonize history and to demonstrate indigenous progress. Thus the direct-historical method was used to demonstrate indigenous innovation, contribution, and progress. The approach broadened methodology by combining oral history, historical linguistics, and archaeology. For instance, Oliver (1966), Huffman (1982), Phillipson (1976, 1977), and Vansina (1990) argued, on the basis of the present-day distribution of Bantu speakers in sub-Saharan Africa, settlement patterns, and linguistic history that Iron Age sites in eastern, western, and southern Africa were populated by ancestors of living Bantu speakers. They paralleled archaeological Iron Age site-settlement organization with that of living Bantu speakers, known as "Central Cattle Kraal Pattern." However, most notably they focused on ceramic styles as indicators of ethnicity or culture. Although they acknowledged indigenous development they failed to recognize that the recipe for progress was a concoction of Western ideology, and their comparisons only served to emphasize stagnation between past and present (Fabien 1983:16; Stahl 2001:9–11; Trigger 1989:174–185). Furthermore, those arguing for an "Iron Age package" were narrowly focused on a few attributes across large time and spatial realms, creating "walking pots" rather than developing local histories (Schmidt 1975, 1990).

The key to the direct-historical or upstreaming methodology was a search for a "perfect analogy"; hence ethnoarchaeologists emphasized only the similarity between the past and the present and rarely acknowledged cultural change. Few ethnoarchaeologists in the past or even today heeded Clark's (1953:116) insightful warning that where historical continuity can be demonstrated "it is in the highest degree unlikely that the peasants, herdsmen or fishers concerned will have remained uninfluenced by usages and ideas from the economically dominant urban stratum." Upstreaming ignored cultural change and focused solely on continuity through time, thus blurring the line between the different layers of the onion. Yet, importantly, for the first time non-Western peoples were recognized for their prehistoric and historical achievements. Although racist interpretations of the past were declining, as Stahl (2001:14) emphasized, these achievements were still measured against Western ideas of progress.

General Comparative Approach: An Onion with a Core

The general comparative approaches (Clark 1953; Willey 1953)—discontinuous (Gould 1974, 1978) or universal core (Cunningham 2003)—were a reaction against evolutionary models and diffusionist models that failed to appreciate the uniqueness of the past. The purpose of the comparative method was to stimulate and to give direction rather than replace prehistory (Clark 1953). In the mid-twentieth century, anthropology reached a pivotal point when scientific, or neoevolutionary; cultural-ecology; and cultural-materialism paradigms were at odds with structural and symbolic anthropology (Geertz 1973; Harris 1979; Lévi-Strauss 1963; Steward 1955; White 1959). The general comparative approaches were similar in that they shared a belief in prime movers or single regularities that drive culture and transcend time; however, what structures behavior is disputed, especially between processually or ecologically derived models and contextual or ideological models (Cunningham 2003; David 1992; Kosso 1991; Wylie 2000:228).

Functional Uniformitarianism—Middle Range Theory

Processualists drew heavily on earlier works (see, for instance, Childe 1958: 51; Clark 1953; Hawkes 1954; Willey 1953) that argued that general laws and cultural processes (now termed processualism), particularly those in the functional realms, provide better models for the past than the direct-historical, taxonomic, or culture-historical approaches. To eliminate any speculation concerning reconstructions of the past, processualists advocated a dedication to positivism and enacting proper scientific research programs. Processual studies often relied on detailed quantitative and statistical studies rather than focusing on context (David 1992). Binford (1962:217), a leading proponent of processual studies, insisted on an archaeology based on anthropology because both were "striving to explicate and explain the total range of physical and cultural similarities and differences characteristic of the entire spatial-temporal span of man's existence." Processualists believed in the use of ethnographic references to formulate a hypothesis but not in the evaluative interpretive conclusions (Binford 1967). This echoes Clark's (1953:118) earlier statement that "comparative ethnography can promote the right questions, only archaeology, in conjunction with the various natural sciences on which prehistorians freely draw can give the right answers." Hence ethnography should not be used directly but only as a source for sifting out general models of behavior that then can be used to test against the past to see which has the best fit (Binford 1967; Watson et al. 1971). Many processualists invoked middle-range theory to describe the process of discovering what created the arrangement of archaeological remains, in essence transforming the static into a dynamic (Binford 1981; Schiffer 1972). In the search for the dynamic, processualists turned to ethnographic and actualistic studies of modern material culture, rejuvenating ethnoarchaeological studies.

One of the major goals of processual ethnoarchaeologists was the construction of general lawlike models, either by testing archaeological assumptions in a present context or through ethnoarchaeological discovery (Cunningham 2003; Yellen 1977:6–8). Often processual ethnoarchaeological studies did not contain an archaeological component. This is because the ethnographic fieldwork was conducted with a broad rather than a contextualized archaeological question. For instance, many processual-oriented ethnoarchaeological studies focused on testing archaeological questions in an ethnographic context before applying them to archaeological contexts (Binford 1967, 1978a, 1978b, 1981; Hitchcock 1982; Hayden and Cannon 1984:2; Kent 1995, 1998; Wiessner 1983, 1984; Yellen 1977); others borrowed ethnographic texts from other parts of the world and applied them to specific archaeological problems (Deetz 1968; Jarman et al. 1972; Longacre 1974). Binford's study of the Nunamiut (1978b) provides an example of a general model. It was propelled by his interest, not in Eskimo prehistory, but in the Paleolithic and by his desire to "seek [relevant] experiences in the world, experiences that can elucidate the usefulness and accuracy of our tools for comprehending and describing reality" (1978b:5). Binford argued that the formation process, in this instance procurement, processing, and consumption strategies, of the past and the present are one and the same when he borrowed geology's concept of uniformitarianism. In his study of nine Nunamiut butchering events, he noted an immense amount of variability (Binford 1978b:47–86). He explained this Nunamiut variation through cross-cultural comparisons of butchering for need, which creates standardization (!Kung, Alawayra, Navajo), vs. butchering for anticipated need (Eskimo and Plains peoples), which creates internal variability. Rather than seeking explanation within the context of each butchering event, Binford focused on creating an ability to recognize activities that would remain the same through time and space. This functionalist approach was deeply embedded in rational-choice theory. Binford maintained that "the Nunamiut behave rationally in their treatment of animal foods" (Binford 1978b:453) and "a major component of man's adaptive success has been his ability to behave rationally" (Binford and Binford 1966:289). Material culture was accepted as an expression of human beings' rational ability to maintain and perpetuate human groups. The nomothetic functionalist approach was thought to eliminate any dependence on analogies and on any other broadly inductive form of inference.

Spoiler or cautionary tales test archaeological assumptions and alert archaeologists to the wide variety of human behaviors that can produce results that differ from entrenched archaeological ideas (Binford 1979; Bonnichsen 1973; Hill 1968; Longacre and Ayers 1965; Thomson 1939). These studies are important because they often illustrate equifinality by showing that different behaviors or other processes may have similar material consequences. They serve to reacquaint archaeologists with the people behind the materials (David 1992). The first cautionary ethnoarchaeological study was Thomson's (1939) study of the Wik Monkan of Australia. He questioned archaeological interpretations of material culture as representative of cultural groups and highlighted seasonality as influential in creating artifact diversity across space. Heider's (1967) ethnographic study of the Dungum Dani of Papua New Guinea is also a classic cautionary tale because it disputed archaeological assumptions concerning artifact typology, settlement organization and activity areas, meaning of rock art, and trade relationships. Heider argued that archaeologists need to seek a wide range of ethnographies for their analogies.

Taphonomic or actualistic studies helped us to translate the archaeological record (Cunningham 2003) and aided in sharpening or refining our techniques, referred to by Yellen (1977:11–12) as the laboratory approach. The advent of the nomothetic approach to archaeology led archaeologists to focus their interests in deciphering site-formation processes, classically divided into N-transforms (noncultural transforms) and C-transforms (cultural transforms) by Schiffer (1983, 1988). The emphasis of actualistic studies was on decoding the effects of noncultural agents, such as hyenas (Binford et al. 1988; Blumenschine 1987; Crader 1974), dogs (Binford and Bertram 1977; Hudson 1993), and chimpanzees (Sept 1992; Toth et al. 2002). For example, Blumenschine (1987) approached the question of whether Pliocene and Pleistocene humans were scavengers or hunters through a study of scavenging in Tanzania's Serengeti National Park and Ngorongoro crater. He believed that spotted hyenas, as initial consumers, were responsible for the vast majority of carcasses that were eaten completely, usually depriving other scavengers of the carcass. Spotted hyenas preferred open plains or lightly wooded habitats rather than riparian woodlands. Blumenschine noted that all known Olduvai archaeological sites are located near ephemeral or perennial watercourses that supported riparian woodlands, where a carcass would be safe from scavengers such as hyenas, increasing the potential for human consumption. This study suggested that carcass bone marrow and head contents were probably more frequently available for hominids in this environment because of a shortage in the hyena population, and as a result the east Turkana and Olduvai environments were conducive to hominid scavenging. The goal of taphonomic studies was to shed light on the processes that affect artifact distribution in the archaeological record. With few exceptions, however, they failed to replicate true formation processes because they primarily focused on a singular process rather than interaction or multiple processes (as exceptions see Blumenschine and Marean 1993; Gifford 1978).

In a manner reminiscent of concepts set forth by Clark (1953) and Steward (1942), some scientific ethnoarchaeologists believed that, to avoid speculation, the past and present cultures should be contextualized within similar physical environments (Gould 1974, 1980; Gould and Watson 1982; Spiess 1979). In the search to create cross-cultural laws that would span time and space, many focused on how humans adapt to their environment, a neoevolutionary perspective that accepts a high degree of regularity in behavior through time and space. In particular, Gould (1974; 1980:48–53; 1990) held that humans are constrained by the natural environment and in turn have certain determinate adaptive options opened to them in given environments. Any ethnoarchaeological study that separated humans and their culture from the natural world was rendered misleading (Gould 1978). Although Yellen (1977:49–51) did not take as strong a stance as

Gould, he argued that models based on environmental, geographical, or locational models are less problematic than those based on "normative models." Gould (1980:138–142), for example, noted the presence of stone adzes made of exotic inferior materials in the lithic assemblage at Puntutjarpa rockshelter. Ethnographic studies among the Australian Aborigines found that exotic cherts were carried by men who collected them personally or acquired them as gifts. Men gave other men chert as a token of their mutual affiliation to the same patrilineal clan and cult lodge. Gould (1980:156) argued through anomaly (the exotic chert being the anamaly) that this type of exchange is an adaptive strategy for survival in a harsh environment and can be found cross-culturally in both time and space.

Processual archaeologists believed that we can access the past through generalized laws, or scientific methods, of human behavior because all human actions are based on rationality, which is held to be universally similar. Function or adaptation (sometimes contextualized in specific environments) is viewed as the core ingredient for blending up the past from the present. Importantly, the processual approach to ethnoarchaeological studies enlisted a scientific method and principles of uniformitarianism, espousing the view that only these methodologies allow us to escape speculation when re-creating the past. Processualists were instrumental in insisting on the use of scientific methods in archaeology and ethnoarchaeology.

Contextualized Studies

An alternative to the processualist's view of ethnoarchaeology can be found in a contextual approach to ethnoarchaeology. Contextual ethnoarchaeology emphasized social practices and the reading of symbols, in other words, material culture as a specific system of signs that reflect the structure (Hodder 1982). Hence it is based in the structural and symbolic paradigms of Lévi-Strauss (1963) and Geertz (1973). While processualists viewed structure as a system and believed it to be a tool for adapting to the environment, the contextual concept of structure viewed it as a code (Hodder 1989). The goal was not to find regularities but understand the structure and deep meanings, that is, Geertzian thick description (1973), through material culture and its spatial distribution (Gabrilopoulos 1995:2; Porr 1999:195). In essence, this meant knowing what the symbol means, which is inferred through the context.

Contextual ethnoarchaeology also stressed symbolic continuity through time by relying on structuralism. Structuralism provided that the inherent structure of the human mind is responsible for social facts (behavior and material objects). As Leone (1982:742–743) explained well, Lévi-Strauss's structuralism indicated that

> the human mind categorizes and divides, creates contrast and oppositions. . . . The mind uses a limited repertoire of contrastive categories. . . . The benefit for the archaeologist is . . . that all artifacts can be treated as having equal significance . . . no class of artifacts . . . is any further from the root of culture than any other, the human mind ordered them all.

Thus it followed that because all humans have the same biological networking in their minds it should be possible to discover rules for how the categories are applied to the world. The categories are universal and cannot be lost through time even though the details of a culture may be. Hence structuralism made cultures comparable across time and space. For example, Schmidt (1997, 1998) outlined the symbolic meaning of iron smelting in central and eastern Africa among the Haya, Pangwa, Fipa, Lungu, and Barongo. Predominately, they used iron tools in agricultural production; a "fertile" furnace produced large amounts of iron that through use increased the fertility of the land, which in turn enhanced human reproduction. Iron served, and still serves, as a symbol of fertility, human as well as agricultural. Cross-culturally the symbolic meaning of iron is reproduced through the practice of iron smelting, the shape and attributes of the furnace, and the presence of medicine pots inside the furnace containing plants or clay liquids known to cure human infertility. Schmidt (1997, 1998) has recovered similar material symbols of fertility associated with Iron Age furnaces. Although he recognized an ideological continuity relating smelting to fertility, he went further and noted differences in time and space affiliated with male or female symbols outlining changes in the level of tension between genders as a concurrent reflection of changing economic and political spheres (Schmidt 1998).

Contextualists criticized processual archaeologists for placing a higher value on etic observations and trivializing or ignoring emic considerations (Trigger 1990). Harris (1979:36) first applied the distinction between the observer's (etic) behavioral domain and the observed native mental activity (emic) to ethnographic studies. The overarching rationale is derived from the biological model of selection, whereby the particular means of adaptation (emic) is of minor importance so long as the structural adaptive success (etic) is approximated. Harris (1979:36) believed both emic and etic perspectives were of value and should be incorporated. Ethnoarchaeological studies have the potential to escape Eurocentric interpretations and reconstructions of the past by focusing on emic perspectives (David 1992; Schmidt 1985). A contextual approach to ethnoarchaeology allowed us to explore the ideologies of living populations and how they invoke meaning through materials (Hodder 1989, 1990; Schmidt 1985).

Archaeologists who attempted to take a conjunctive approach (Taylor 1948), examining history and context and incorporating human ideas, were accused of pure speculation (Binford 1962; Leach 1973). Ironically, it is this context that processualists ignored, which allowed contextual ethnoarchaeology to be scientific rather than speculative (Taylor 1948; Wylie 1982, 1985). The context of the material remains provided the background knowledge for informed, plausible explanations. Contextual models were not speculative because they were constrained by the material record left by the past and because plausible explanations were based on informed analysis of how they could have been generated. Giddens (1979:242–245) similarly stated that all laws operate within a boundary and that we can rationalize action only in its context, as history dictates. Archaeologists test the relationships they posit through a variety of mediums and contexts, including the ethnographic present, historical documents, oral history, and archaeological material culture (Schmidt 1983; 1997:27–28). Contextualists posited that examining the differences as well as the similarities in different contexts (social, environmental, space, object, and text) would expand rather than reduce culture and people to a set of unchanging rules (Hodder 1982:217–220). Contextual ethnoarchaeological studies avoided the inherent contradiction of creating ladders to reach the "perfect analogy." Because change is a constant factor in society, the differences were as important as the similarities when comparing aspects of culture through time and across space (Schmidt 1985; Wylie 1985).

Like processualists, contextualists believed that there are human universals. But for contextualists, the core existed because human minds are biologically structured alike, which results in a similar categorization of the material world. Contextualists also argued for objectivity; similar to rational theory, it is objectivity that allows us to bridge the past with the present (Hodder 1986:170; 1987:10; Johnsen and Olsen 1992). In this case, the core of the onion—culture—is a structured ideology, which repeats itself in the cross-cultural layers in time and space. The contextual approach is scientific because it focuses on context and acknowledges the differences as well as the similarities, which constrained speculative interpretation (Giddens 1979:242–245; Schmidt 1985; Wylie 1982, 1985).

Behavioral Ecology

Today, behavioral ecologists criticize earlier scientific ethnoarchaeologists because they did not advocate a general theory or answer the critical question of why a particular cultural system worked the way it did (Bettinger 1987; Broughton and O'Connell 1999; Kelley 1999; O'Connell et al. 1988; O'Connell 1993, 1995; Simms 1992). They take to task processual ethnoarchaeological studies because they tend to be descriptive or cautionary tales, causing ethnoarchaeologists to be viewed historically as "obnoxious spectators" (Simms 1992) with "trivial pursuits." Behavioral ecology posits that variation is the result of differences in the decisions of people based on their local environment. This perspective holds that all human actions are rational and that "people weigh their options and opt for those that provide the highest benefit:cost ratio given opportunity cost" (Kelley 1999:69). Hence individuals make their decisions on the basis of efficiency and effectiveness. Although individuals make decisions, the archaeological record contains assemblages that are the result of many individuals. Thus the focus is on building models for interaction between people as a collective and their natural environment in ways that enhance fitness, whether genetic, physiological, or cognitive (Broughton and O'Connell 1999). They offer a unifying theory of behavior ecology, or neo-Darwinism: "the basic premise is that all living organisms are shaped by natural selection" (O'Connell 1995:209). For example, in Paleolithic studies there is considerable debate over the variability in faunal assemblages and how or if this relates to human behavior (Binford 1984; Blumenschine 1987; Hudson 1993). O'Connell (1993, 1995) argues that the Hadza foragers' prey selection and transport depends on taxonomy, processing techniques, encounter rates, and seasonality. Thus individual cases vary greatly, and it is difficult to define a pattern or ideal case. However, each individual event does share a common rationale, that ultimately all decisions are fitness related.

Ecological behaviorists believe that the strongest comparisons are between cultures that share a similar environment. They, like processualists, adhere to the hypodeductive or nomothetic approach. Behavioral ecologists, however, suggest that they hold the only theory that unites all of humanity: natural selection, in which humans strive to maximize their fitness. This theory serves to account for all behavior (and material correlates) regardless of the context. According to behavioral ecologists, the core of the onion—culture—may vary in its ingredients, but the reason it is there is a result of natural selection!

Processualists, contextualists, and behavioral ecologists all argue for human universals using a nomothetic approach. They believe that their respective approaches bring us closer to the truth of the past through reference to the present. These studies have served to unify humanity through cross-cultural comparisons during eras of war and Cold War tensions (1960s to 1980s). Today many archaeologists and ethnoarchaeologists have adapted a scientific perspective, but they often combine it with a direct-historical approach to obtain a "more perfect analogy" (Cribb 1991; Ebert 1968; Hill 1968; Horne 1994; Janes 1991; Kramer 1982; Kuznar 1995; Longacre 1968; Thomas 1983; Yakar 2000).

Practice and Taste: The Flavor of the Onion

Ethnoarchaeologists have recently turned to the concept of practice, or social agency as it is known in archaeology (Dobres and Hoffman 1999; Dobres and Robb 2000), which is grounded in the concept that all actions, including human motions and practices such as technology are learned and enacted in a social context. It is a paradigm that relies heavily on the writings of Pierre Bourdieu (1977, 1984). Porr (1999:9) summarizes this paradigm:

> It contains self-conscious and active individuals and their practices and the existence of objects, buildings, paths, tracks and so on. The principles structuring a society are not only existent in abstract, discursive values, meanings or norms, but also in daily practices and habits, which are in turn inseparable from their material environment.

The concept of practice refuses to dichotomize the world into society and individual or materialism and mentalism but rather states that the social world encompasses all these tensions. Adherents of social agency criticize the earlier approaches for their environmental or cultural and symbolic metonymies, which are abstractions that neglect practice (Porr 1999). Social agency advocates that although material culture provides us with information about collective agents/normative behavior, material culture can take us further to understand social contexts at a variety of scales including individual actions and experiences. The individual is the source of variation and change, and a prehistory with agency allows us to view human will, free of adaptation or forced mechanistic behavior.

Practice theory also draws heavily on postmodern trends in ethnography that argue that science is culturally bound, as are the observers. Ethnographers cannot have a neutral or objective knowledge about a culture, as all observations are filtered through the observer's own language, cultural background, and personal experiences (Rosaldo 1989). Hence middle-range and structural approaches are not low-level methodological work as indicated by Raab and Goodyear (1984) but informed by hermeneutics (layers of meaning), and they are not independent of archaeological theory or interpretation (Kosso 1991; Tilley 1993; Wylie 1993). Cunningham (2003) suggests that universal-core approaches should receive more critical analysis, and its advocates need to accept that there are not eternal truths but regularities or processes that may vary with context. The terms and phrases we ascribe to material culture are contextualized within a current understanding and are a dialectical, or a continuous interplay, between past and present (Johnsen and Olsen 1982). Many ethnoarchaeological approaches tend to introduce history after culture, which is reminiscent of salvage ethnography or the ethnographic present (Wobst 1978; Stahl 2001:27–30). They are unidirectional in acknowledging that the past can affect the present, and often overlook how the use of the present as a baseline can affect interpretations of the past. The trajectory then of ethnographic and archaeological reasoning must be viewed in terms of not only how we transform the past from present knowledge and past material culture but also how we affect the present with our interpretations (Schmidt 1985; Wilmsen 1989:xiii).

Hence many ethnoarchaeologists are naive realists in the sense that they believe there is a single, obtainable real truth, ignoring the way theory and context inform their explanation and believing that all people define the real world of objects, events, and living creatures in the same way (David 1992). David (1992:332) suggests that ethnoarchaeologists should engage in a subtle realists' perspective in which all social structures are open because "societies are continuously being transformed in practice, are only relatively enduring, and are thus irreducibly historical" (David 1992:332). The goal is to recognize transcultural regularities so we may be able to explain but not predict linkages between ideational (unobserved) and phenomenal (observed) orders of reality. For instance, as part of the Mandara Archaeological Project, David studied the mortuary practices of seven different cultural groups and found that in all of them the practice and material culture of the disposal of the dead was an "on going invention of society" (David 1992:350). This transcultural regularity existed despite each of these cultures having unique materials and practices. He believes that, rather than focusing on outlining regularities that can transcend time and space, an ethnoarchaeologist's primary goal is "to raise the analogical consciousness of archaeologists" and ultimately to open up other worldviews.

Furthermore, followers of practice theory do not seek meaning in the contextual sense, because meaning varies in time and space (David 1992; Stahl 2001:36). In the absence of text to decipher meaning, we are dependent on present-day cultures that ascribe their own contextual meanings to the material world. Stahl (2001:35) prefers to search for *taste*, which is based on Bourdieu's distinctions (1984:190). Taste is embodied in objects that "reflect choices and preferences that are socially conditioned and suppositions (habitués)" (Stahl 2001:35). Taste is shaped by proximity to source, diversity, quantitative dimensions, and production (Stahl 2001:141). For example, Stahl suggests that the presence of imported glass beads, smoking pipes, and maize phytoliths indicate newly acquired tastes for imported objects at Kuulo Kataa, Ghana, a 69-acre site occupied between the early fourteenth and mid-seventeenth centuries. She also argues that shifts in taste drew them into wider exchange networks and served as a practice of distinction for those who possessed them, which eventually led to larger economic and political changes. Her study of the Banda, although it begins with a study of contemporary culture, is not a static study but a "view of culture-in-the-making" (Stahl 2001:30) and incorporates artifacts, documents, and oral histories, tacking as per Wylie (1989) between source, or ethnographic, and subject, or archaeological-side, concerns.

Another social-practice methodology engaged in by ethnoarchaeologists is exemplified in the work of Roux (1999), Lemonnier (1992), and Gosselain (1992) and their use of *chaînes opératoires*. This method examines material culture through the process or practice of its production, use, and discard. It differs from life-cycle or behavioral approaches (Schiffer and Skibo 1997) in that it stresses free cultural choice and an absence of either strict cultural or environmental determinism (David and Kramer 2001:148–150). Society and objects are never in stasis but always embedded in a larger dynamic context. Roux's (1999) study of classic Harappan stone beads, which are highly homogeneous and rare, combines transcultural regularities while maintaining that cultural choice and historical diversity are complementary approaches. She studied the present-day bead manufacturing process in India, including heating, knapping, grinding, drilling, polishing, and shining of stone beads and the skills involved. Roux tested skill by introducing a new material, glass, and a new bead dimension. The more-skilled craftspersons were able to produce much higher quality beads from the glass than the less skilled. The most competent knappers required more than 10 years of practice to master the production of beads of all shapes and sizes. Roux notes that this time length is a transcultural regularity for attaining expertise in a craft. She thus argues that the small number of high-quality classic Harappan beads was made by a few highly skilled craftspersons, who produced other items as well. Bead production was probably not a commercial enterprise but rather a demand of a small elite population.

Followers of social agency believe that we need to recognize that we are influenced by our own historical context and that no two onions are exactly the same. Humans and their material products are variable and we cannot advocate the use of generalized laws for humanity—there may be some regularities in specific contexts but not universal uniformitarian laws. As a consequence of this belief we can obtain only the flavor or a taste of history and prehistory, because our own context and flavor or taste will always permeate the reconstruction.

All of the approaches to ethnoarchaeology—the direct-historical approach, the general-comparative approach (processualism, behavioral ecology, and contextual), and social agency—are united under the use of metonymy. Through each of these approaches we have added a new structure or structuration (layer, core, or taste) that serves to broaden our understanding of the past (onion). Most of the paradigms contend that humans behave similarly across time and space because of the presence of one or more of the following "ingredients": cultural continuity (direct-historical approach), functionality (processualism), ideology (contextual or structuralism), or environment (behavioral ecology). Only practice theory holds that, although human behavior may have some temporal and spatial regularities, there are no universals, hence no perfect ingredients to re-create the past—we can get only a taste of the different flavors. The methods we use to engage metonymy in reconstructing the past directly reflect broader paradigmatic trends. Hence the era of interpretation infuses our recipes for peeling, processing, and consuming the onion of life.

Ethnoarchaeological Field Methods

We find that, although ethnoarchaeologists debate extensively over the use of metonymy, unlike archaeologists they rarely discuss their field methods (see as an exception Hayden and Cannon 1984:11, 21–39; Kuznar 1995; Yellen 1977:54–64; and a general overview in David and Kramer 2001:71–90). The type and quality of the model created by ethnoarchaeological methods is directly dependent upon when the fieldwork is conducted (i.e., the era of the research and more specifically the years, seasons, months, or days spent in the field) and the attention that the ethnoarchaeologist gives to understanding the history, language, and customs of the people being studied. Thompson (1956) and later Stahl (2001:30–40) emphasized the importance of clearly delineating the ethnographic probative, or source-side, and the archaeological indicative, or subject-side, context. It is immensely helpful to review previous researchers' works (ethnographic, historical, and archaeological) to develop a better understanding of the culture and historical changes that may influence your research. The majority of ethnoarchaeological studies do not engage in the standard archaeology of excavation and analyses (see Schmidt 1997 for an exception) but are limited to studying present-day societies with a focus on their material culture. Usually archaeological research follows an ethnoarchaeological project, such as the case of Yellen's (1977) study of settlement organization of the !Kung and later Stone Age sites in Botswana (Yellen and Brooks 1988).

One of the most important aspects of ethnoarchaeology is to conduct research that will be useful to archaeologists as they interpret sites and material culture. Simms (1992) labeled ethnoarchaeologists the "obnoxious spectator" because they tend to point out inconsistencies in the archaeological interpretation although failing to outline analytic methods that would be useful to archaeologists. Although this is a valid point, several new studies have bridged this gap between archaeology and ethnoarchaeology, including ceramic-use-alteration studies (Arthur 2003; Kobayashi 1994; Skibo 1992) and lithic-use-wear and morphological studies (Hayden 1979, 1987; Rots and Williamson 2003; Weedman 2002a), which systematically document types of use wear with specific behaviors. Although ethnoarchaeology shares some of the methods employed by archaeologists and ethnographers, ethnoarchaeologists have their own, unique approaches because they are focusing on the relationship between living people and their material culture. As noted by David and Kramer (2001:411), few researchers have dedicated their lives to ethnoarchaeology (D. Arnold, David, Kent, Kramer, and Longacre are exceptions). Thus many ethnoarchaeological studies are conducted by archaeologists who are well aware of archaeological methods, but, in the age of the dying four-field approach, they probably have not studied ethnographic methods. Hence we strongly urge researchers to participate in ethnoarchaeological and ethnographic readings and courses before they undertake an ethnoarchaeological project (see Babbie 2001; Bernard 1988; David and Kramer 2001; Spradley 1979). This section attempts to address major issues related to ethnoarchaeological fieldwork by discussing ethics, daily life, assistants, census and interviewing, participant observation, mapping, and material culture.

Ethnoarchaeological Ethics

Often ethnoarchaeological research is conducted among non-Western peoples in a rural setting, where values may be vastly different from the ethnoarchaeologist's, and therefore ethnoarchaeologists need to be aware of their ethical responsibility. The American Anthropological Association (1998) has stated that researchers are obliged to guarantee the safety, dignity, and privacy of the people with whom they work. When conducting an ethnoarchaeological project funded by a U.S. federal grant, the researcher must complete an institutional review board (IRB) application. This application is reviewed by an IRB, which ensures that the research respects the participants; minimizes physical, psychological, economic, and social harm to individuals; treats all participants fairly; and respects the privacy and confidentiality of all participants. The IRB often requires that the researcher obtain formal consent in the form of a signature from each participant, which can be problematic in nonliterate societies. Before the researcher begins an interview, she or he is socially obligated to explain the purpose of the project and obtain permission to use the knowledge, name, and videotape, and photograph images of the participant. In addition, each participant should be told that they can stop the interview whenever they wish.

In many communities, elders and local leaders are highly respected and trusted. It behooves the ethnoarchaeologist to seek out these individuals when beginning research. Not only does it help to establish rapport in a community but it is important when studying or discussing potentially sensitive topics or areas such as shrines (Brown 2002:65–67). Often during the research project a situation will arise that warrants the aid of an elder or leader, and if the researcher has already shown respect to the elders and leaders in the community, then they are more likely to assist a researcher conducting field research. In addition, by building rapport with the community's elders, other community members are more likely to assist you in your research objectives.

The practice of ethnoarchaeology is intrusive to the host community, and therefore researchers should attempt to make as little negative impact upon the community as possible. This means as few people as possible should be brought into a community to conduct the research. This includes having no more than three people conduct interviews so as to not attract attention allowing the participant to feel his or her statements are protected from other people in the community. Hayden and

Cannon's (1984:11) research among the Maya of Mexico and Weedman and Brandt's study of the Konso of Ethiopia broke their research group into distinct teams with specific jobs (e.g., mapping and interviewing) to reduce the impact on their participants and the community. As David and Kramer (2001:89) state, "Ethnoarchaeologists face the same ethical dilemmas and challenges that confront ethnographers, and it would be fatuous to claim immunity because one is really 'just an archaeologist.'"

Ethnoarchaeologists have a responsibility to give back to the community that has accepted the researcher. This can be accomplished by donating gifts such as books and supplies to the local school. In our case and in others (Deal 1998:5), we took a Polaroid snapshot of the family and gave it to them, which they appreciated. Often while conducting an interview, we noticed that someone was ill and so we gave rides to the clinic and paid for medical costs. By engaging in long-term ethnoarchaeological research, the researcher will learn the specific needs of the people living in the host community. Researchers who give back to the host community strengthen their rapport, which is essential to ethnoarchaeological research.

Daily Life as an Ethnoarchaeologist

Although daily life is not discussed with much detail in the ethnoarchaeological literature (see as exception Skibo 1999), several points that we learned during our own fieldwork should be brought forward. A preliminary visit to the research area is essential to begin understanding all the basic steps before fieldwork begins. Previous knowledge of the host country's permit regulations and local infrastructure such as electricity, water, and roads is invaluable. This may not seem very important, but when dealing with electrical equipment such as camcorders, computers, and printers, you will want to know if you need to bring a generator or solar equipment. Knowing about the roads is essential for developing a research strategy that either encompasses or bypasses the road network. For example, for Weedman's study (2000) of the Gamo hideworkers, she had to backpack her equipment and walk, which limited the type and amount of equipment she could take. Knowing the available infrastructures limits frustration and the amount of time it will take to conduct the research in a given area. Knowing what kind of health system is in place is also important, especially when in an area prone to certain medical conditions, such as malaria. We recommend, as have others (David and Kramer 2001:71), having a general medical guide for traveling in remote, rural areas of the world, such as *Where There Is No Doctor* (Werner 1992); in some cases medical guides are written for a specific country.

As David and Kramer (2001:71) discuss, time is one of the more important issues facing an ethnoarchaeological research project. Time is constantly an enemy to a fieldworker, whether an ethnoarchaeologist or an archaeologist. The three biggest time eaters are routine paperwork, vehicle problems, and illness. A good day for us was when we woke up feeling well, the Land Cruiser started, we were able to drive easily to our research area on a dry dirt road, we obtained valuable information from willing participants, and we returned home without any truck problems or illnesses. Routine paperwork can be shortened if the researcher knows the procedures from a preresearch visit. Although going through the process of obtaining official letters does take time, once you have these letters they will facilitate your research. Vehicle problems are a constant exercise in frustration; you develop a love-hate relationship with your transportation. If the project is without hired professional drivers and is in a remote area, we suggest that at least one of the field crewmembers take a mechanic course.

The practice of ethnoarchaeology takes longer to obtain meaningful information than archaeological research, because the ethnoarchaeologist needs to establish rapport, learn the language, and obtain key participants, all before beginning the research. For a dissertation project, most ethnoarchaeologists should conduct an 18- to 24-month project similar to ethnographic research, in contrast to most archaeological dissertations, which can be conducted in 12 months.

Assistants

A good assistant can significantly improve your quality of life in the field. Assistants can facilitate the intricacies of permits, find you a place to live, translate between you and participants, and most importantly be someone you can trust and develop a friendship with. Even if the researcher is fluent in the local language, we recommend traveling with a local assistant. In areas where a participant may have some trepidation about a stranger, the local assistant provides a reassuring quality that the foreign researcher is someone who will not harm or create problems for the household. Assistants must show respect to all informants, no matter the race, gender, or social status of the informant. This could potentially be an issue, for instance, if the assistant is well educated and a high caste member and the majority of the participants lack a formal education or belong to a low caste, such as an artisan. Contacting previous researchers who have worked in your proposed research area can provide the quickest and most helpful way of finding an appropriate assistant.

The researcher should try to become fluent in the host language. That might not be possible if there is insufficient time to learn the host language or if it is only an oral language and classes are not available. An assistant who translates needs to know to translate as much as possible word by word and not try to condense the participant's words. In addition, the assistant should allow the participant to give the answer and not try to give their own interpretation or answer to the question. A camcorder or tape recorder allows the assistant and researcher to transcribe interviews. We as did Deal (1998:5) conducted interviews with translators before they did interviews with participants to acquaint translators with the proposed questions. If the research requires collecting information from a number of participants, assistants may become bored by the redundant questions and answers. The researcher should explain that the compiled information could reveal a trend entrenched in that society. Also, one way to alleviate boredom is to work on another part of the project, which may relieve both you and your assistants from the repetition of fieldwork.

Working in Ethiopia, as in our case, a researcher must have at all times a government representative from the cultural office. The government representative usually does not know the local language; thus having a local assistant still is necessary to inter-pret interviews with informants. Both the local assistant and government representative should be treated as equal partners in the research. Another issue is per diem for both. Researchers should consut the proper government authorities concerning the regulations and standards for salary, per diem, and participant reimbursement in their respective research country.

Assistants do not have to stop work when the researcher is not present within the host community. William Longacre's (1974, 1981, 1991, 2000) longitudinal study among the Kalinga of Luzon, Philippines, trained a group of Kalinga assistants to gather information when the researchers returned to their uni-versity or left to avoid political turmoil (Longacre and Skibo 1994:xv; Stark 1994:172). This enables the researcher to continue the work and document changes within the society and its mate-rial culture that would otherwise not be known to the academic community. Longitudinal projects also have the potential to gen-erate deeper local interests in anthropology and ethnoarchaeol-ogy. Indigenous assistants may seek to pursue an academic education in the host country or at a Western institution, thereby strengthening the field of ethnoarchaeology by encouraging non-Western participation. Furthermore, we suggest that assistants be given the opportunity to coauthor texts, if they so desire, and minimally be acknowledged for their conributions to any text.

Census and Interviewing

As an anthropologist and representative of your nation and field, you should show immense respect for the people whose lives you are studying. During the initial interview or census it is essential to convey to your participants your project goals, methodology, and the types of knowledge you wish the indi-vidual to share. When conducting interviews, make an appoint-ment so that the person has a scheduled time to share their knowledge. A scheduled interview demonstrates to the partici-pant that you respect that they have primary responsibilities outside the anthropological research. We found that most in-formants reacted very positively when we respected their schedules and formally requested their participation in the project rather than just assuming they had the time and interest to take part in our studies.

The important criterion for assessing the type of census and interviewing questions to use is whether this information is relevant for archaeologists. The responsibility of the ethnoarchaeologist is to have a research design that will yield results that make a significant contribution to the archaeological community. Whether working in a foraging, pastoral, agrarian or urban society, compiling a census of the people provides an essential part of knowing the diversity within a community. This builds rapport as you introduce yourself to each family or household and discuss your objective. The census becomes the bedrock for your research, as you begin to understand the makeup of a community: for example, that it is predominantly widows or that a household belongs to a potter or an elite ritual sacrificer. In addition, when taking a census you meet and talk with most of the members in your specific research area, and you begin to realize who will be valuable participants and who may not want to work with you later in your research. We were fortunate that the vast majority of people were willing to participate in our research.

During the interview, avoid asking leading questions but rather have the participant come up with her or his answers independently (Spradley 1979). When conducting the interview, keep eye contact and listen to the answers. If you are constantly writing the person's answers and not taking part in the conversation, the participant may lose interest. With any social situation, every interview will be slightly different, some easier than others. When a participant is shy or does not provide a lot of detail, it may be necessary to ask questions that are more detailed, but we still suggest that it is best not to ask leading questions. One may ask many different types of questions (e.g., structural, contrasting, and descriptive), and we refer to Spradley (1979:60) for a concise discussion on interviewing methods.

Not every informant is going to provide you with golden information every day, and sometimes you will not recognize it as golden until later. Managing your time well and being flexible and patient are important during research. Interviewing can be tiring for both the interviewer and interviewee, and we suggest that interviews not continue longer than 2 hours before a break.

Sometimes it is better to have short interviews with the same individual extended over several days. This allows you to go over the information previously given to find gaps in your knowledge and better prepare for the next interview with the individual. Each interview is different, and you may decide that it would be better to end the interview earlier than expected or you may need to change the interview time. Even with a prescheduled interview time, sometimes the time is not right for an interview, for instance, because of illness or an external situation that disrupts the rhythm of the area where you are working. This should not be seen as a negative occurrence but as an exciting time to learn about the nuances of the society. Each day for an ethnoarchaeologist is different and seldom a bore.

The use of questionnaires remains a popular technique for gathering information. The positive aspects of a questionnaire are that it allows the researcher to organize the questions for each informant and not forget to ask an important question. However, questionnaires should be continually revised to remove questions that are confusing or not relevant, and a researcher should not be afraid to discuss topics that are not part of the questionnaire. Divergence from the questionnaire should be encouraged when the informant begins to discuss something in detail or the researchers think of, in the middle of the interview, an important topic that had not occurred before but now seems relevant and critical to the research problem. As the research progresses, questionnaires will most likely be phased out and the researcher will conduct more of an open interview, which tends to allow more detailed information than a questionnaire can offer. However, questionnaires can substantially add to the detailed ethnographic information that one gathers, and Bernard (1988:146–147) suggests that the researcher do a simple survey questionnaire in the first 2 weeks of the project and another one pertaining to specific issues at the end of the project.

Participant Observation

Ethnoarchaeologists are primarily concerned with the interaction between people and their materials, so participant observation is essential. Engaging in participant observation allows the ethnoarchaeologists to obtain valuable information that otherwise may be skewed by the informant. What is participant observation? Bernard's (1988:148–179) valuable insights concerning participant observation note that it allows one to take part in daily activities that otherwise would be difficult for a stranger to observe. Furthermore, learning the language of the host community allows the participant observer to understand important nuances within the culture. Participant observation also means that people do not change their behavior when the ethnoarchaeologists are around, which helps a researcher knowledgeable about the culture to formulate valuable questions and make informed statements about cultural behavior. Being a participant observer means also that you should engage in as many activities as possible that involve births, feasts, marriages, deaths, and everyday events.

Living within a community as an outsider makes you "the center of the village stage" (Boissevain 1970:71). This can be daunting when it goes on for an extended time, because of the lack of privacy and being observed (Denton 1970:104–105). Personal privacy is very important to most North Americans but a foreign concept in many parts of the world. However, as you begin to assimilate into the society and become used to being observed (as you are observing others), this becomes less and less of a nuisance. Being constantly observed was one of the most difficult aspects of culture shock for us and others working in Ethiopia. In particular, children are fascinated with foreigners and followed us everywhere, which posed some difficulties during interviews. However, time remedies this problem because even the children lose their interest in you and you begin to partially blend into the host community.

Mapping Places and Things

Mapping allows you to develop a spatial picture of your research area, which is important for assessing activity areas and the use of space delineated by particular social groups. This can be one of the more time-consuming activities if you are mapping each artifact with the piece-plotting method within a household (see Yellen 1977:59). This type of mapping has come under scrutiny for sacrificing the study of a larger area for "the illusion of precision" (O'Connell 1995:227). Coverage of large areas to understand the diversity is compromised if the researcher focuses on specific elements or artifacts in a limited area without researching the variation of space in relation to behavior. Another type of mapping consists of recording the location of households and the footpaths within each community to show the spacial diversity of socioeconomic status within a village (see Arthur 2000). With the present-day technology of global positioning systems (GPSs), mapping of large areas such as households within a community can be done quickly. Mapping of households, activity areas, and material culture provides substantial interaction with the host community that builds on the time you spend compiling census information. People become accustomed to having the researcher around their village each day. Also you can observe the daily activities of the people, which is important in figuring out which days are best for conducting more-extensive interviews. Within our fieldwork, half the village would be absent on days that correspond to markets and to important holidays. Therefore mapping activities aid in understanding your informants' temporal activities and their weekly schedule, which helps you manage and organize your time.

Material Culture

Ethnoarchaeology encompasses many different types of material culture studies, and from 1990 to 1998 most of the research has focused on ceramics, space and architecture, and theory and methods (David and Kramer 2001:29). Each study has its own methods—there is not a single way to conduct ethnoarchaeology on a specific material or question. The types of ethnoarchaeological studies have changed over the last five decades. Initially researchers attempted to record the complete inventory of materials and their associated activities within one culture (Kleindienst and Watson 1956). Today most ethnoarchaeologists focus on a single material culture to address a specific research question. Recent studies indicate a vast array of different types of research questions that are formulated from the same type of material. For example, among ceramic studies, investigations range from use alteration (Arthur 2002, 2003; Kobayashi 1994; Reid and Young 2000; Skibo 1992) to style through the *chaîne opératoire* approach (Gosselain 1992, 2000), looking at the relationship between performance and style (Longacre 2000), exchange (Kramer 1997; Mohr Chavez 1992; Stark 1992, 1994; Stark and Longacre 1993) or use life (Neupert and Longacre 1994; Shott 1989; Tani 1994). Ceramic studies in ethnoarchaeology continue to be one of the most intensively studied materials in ethnoarchaeology (David and Kramer 2001:14–29). The study of architecture in ethnoarchaeology has grown in popularity since 1982 (David and Kramer 2001:24–29) and has involved formation processes (Janes 1989), gender (Donley 1982, 1987; Donley-Reid 1990), space and inheritance (Horne 1994), socioeconomic wealth (Kramer 1982), and political organization (Smith and David 1995). Other studies of material culture have included fauna (Bunn 1993; Hudson 1993; O'Connell 1993), flora (D'Andrea et al. 1999; Reddy 1997), stone tools (Brandt et al. 1996; Brandt and Weedman 1997, 2002; Gallagher 1977; Hayden 1979, 1987; Weedman 2000, 2002a, 2002b), and iron production (Kusimba 1996; Schmidt 1996, 1997).

The ethnoarchaeologist also will need to make assessments concerning the collection of the material under study. In some cases, it is unreasonable to collect the material, as in the case of Arthur's (2000, 2002, 2003) research, because people were using their household ceramic assemblages everyday and so analysis had to be conducted within each household. This compares to Weedman's analysis of stone scrapers, in which she collected unused and discardable stone tools from Gamo and Konso hideworkers. Several years later, other researchers (Rots and Williamson 2003) were able to study the Gamo collection for microwear and residues and added substantially to our knowledge concerning the effectiveness of these methods as interpretive tools. Whether to collect or not is also under the purview of the governmental regulations that may designate ethnographic and archaeological materials to the same status. If this is the case, then the researcher should make sure there is adequate storage in the national museum or another appropriate facility to house the collection. This is important for not only the host country

and community but also future ethnoarchaeologists and archaeologists who may want to reanalyze the material.

Conclusion

Ethnoarchaeology is essential for developing archaeological interpretations because it provides our only recourse for exploring
new positions concerning the similarities and differences in objects in association with their environmental, social, and spatial
contexts. Although some seem adamant in creating a unified ethnoarchaeological practice and theory (Cunningham 2003; David
1992; O'Connell 1995; Simms 1992), these multiple views all contribute to a better understanding of the past, the present, and
ourselves. Culture is self-perpetuating, yet it constantly changes
as human actions and expressions represent their unique individual context in the world. Thus, all material items and lifeways both past and present never follow the exact same recipe
but are unique blends of ancestors and the present context.

References

Agorsah, E. Kofi.
    1990   Ethnoarchaeology: the search for a self-corrective approach to the
           study of past human behavior. *The African Archaeological Review*
           8:89–208.

Allchin, Bridget
    1957   Australian stone industries, past and present. *Journal of the Royal
           Anthropological Institute* 87:115–136.

American Anthropological Association
    1998   Code of Ethics of the American Anthropological Association.
           http://www.aaanet.org/committees/ethics/ethcode.htm.

Arthur, John W.
    2000   *Ceramic ethnoarchaeology among the Gamo of southwestern Ethiopia.*
           PhD dissertation. University Microfilms, University of Florida, Ann
           Arbor.

2002   Brewing beer: Status, wealth, and ceramic use-alteration among the Gamo of southwestern Ethiopia. *World Archaeology* 34:516–528.

2003   Beer, food, and wealth: An ethnoarchaeological use-alteration analysis of pottery. *Journal of Archaeological Method and Theory* 9:331–355.

Ascher, Robert
   1961   Analogy in archaeological interpretation. *Southwestern Journal of Anthropology* 17:317–325.

Atherton, John
   1983   Ethnoarchaeology in Africa. *The African Archaeological Review* 1: 75–104.

Babbie, Earl R.
   2001   *The practice of social science research.* Wadsworth Thomson Learning, Belmont, California.

Bernard, H. Russell
   1988   *Research methods in cultural anthropology.* Sage Publications, London.

Bettinger, Robert L.
   1987   Archaeological approaches to hunter-gatherers. *Annual Review of Anthropology* 16:121–142.

Binford, Lewis R.
   1962   Archaeology as anthropology. *American Antiquity* 28:217–225.

   1967   Smudge pits and hide smoking: The use of analogy in archaeological reasoning. *American Antiquity* 32:1–12.

   1978a Dimensional analysis of behavior and site structure: Learning from an Eskimo hunting stand. *American Antiquity* 43:330–361.

   1978b *Nunamiut ethnoarchaeology.* Academic Press, New York.

   1979   Galley pond mound. In *An archaeological perspective*, edited by Lewis Binford, pp. 390–420. Academic Press, New York.

   1981   *Bones: Ancient men and modern myths.* Academic Press, New York.

   1984   *Faunal Remains from Klasies River Mouth.* Academic Press, Orlando.

Binford, Lewis R., and Sally Binford
   1966   A preliminary analysis of funtional variability in the Mousterian of Levallois facies. *American Anthropologist* 69:238–295.

Binford, Lewis R., and Jack R. Bertram
   1977   Bone frequences and attritional processes. In *Background studies for theory building*, edited by Lewis R. Binford, pp. 77–153. Academic Press, New York.

Binford, Lewis R., M. G. L. Mills, and Nancy Stone
    1988   Hyena scavenging behavior and its implications for the interpretation of faunal assemblages from FLK 22 (the zinj floor) at Olduvai Gorge. *Journal of Anthropological Archaeology* 7:99–135.

Blumenschine, Robert J.
    1987   Characteristics of an early hominid scavenging niche. *Current Anthropology* 28:383–407.

Blumenschine, Robert J., and Curtis W. Marean
    1993   A carnivore's view of archaeological Bone Assemblages. In *From bones to behavior: Ethnoarchaeological and experimental contributions to the interpretation of faunal remains,* edited by Jean Hudson, pp. 273–300. Center for Archaeological Investigations, Southern Illinois University, Carbondale.

Boissevain, Jeremy
    1970   Fieldwork in Malta. In *Being an anthropologist,* edited by George D. Spindler, pp. 58–84. Holt, Rinehart, and Winston, Inc., New York.

Bonnichsen, Robson
    1973   Mille's camp: An experiment in archaeology. *World Archaeology* 4:277–291.

Bourdieu, Pierre
    1977   *Outline of a theory of practice.* Cambridge University Press, Cambridge.
    1984   *Distinction: A social critique of the judgment of taste.* Routledge and Kegan Paul, London.

Brandt, Steven A., and Kathryn J. Weedman
    1997   The ethnoarchaeology of hide working and flaked stone tool use in southern Ethiopia. In *Ethiopia in broader perspective: Papers of the XIIth International Conference of Ethiopian Studies,* edited by Katsuyoshi Fukui, Elsei Kurimoto, and Masayoshi Shigeta, pp. 351–361. Shokado Book Sellers, Kyoto.
    2002   The ethnoarchaeology of hide working and stone tool use in Konso, southern Ethiopia: An introduction. In *Le travail du cuir de la prehistoire à nos jours,* edited by Frédérique Audoin-Rouzeau and Sylvie Beyries, pp. 113–130. Editions APDCA, Antibes.

Brandt, Steven A., Kathryn J. Weedman, and Girma Hundie
    1996   Gurage hide working, stone tool use and social identity: An ethnoarchaeological perspective. In *Essays on Gurage language and culture: Dedicated to Wolf Leslau on the occasion of his 90th birthday November 14, 1996,* edited by Grover Hudson, pp. 35–51. Harrassowitz, Verlag.

Brew, John Otis
1946   *The uses and abuses of taxonomy: The archaeology of alkali ridge, south-east Utah*. Papers of the Peabody Museum of American Archaeology and Ethnology, vol. 21, 44–66. Harvard University Press, Cambridge.

Broughton, Jack M., and James F. O'Connell
1999   On evolutionary ecology, selectionist archaeology, and behavioral archaeology. *American Antiquity* 64:153–165.

Brown, Linda Ann
2002   The structure of ritual practice: An ethnoarchaeological exploration of activity areas at rural community shrines in the Maya highlands. Unpublished PhD dissertation, University of Colorado, Denver.

Bunn, Henry T.
1993   Bone assemblages at base camps: a further consideration of carcass transport and bone destruction by the Hazda. In *From bones to behavior: ethnoarchaeological and experimental contributions to the interpretation of faunal remains*, edited by Jean Hudson, pp. 156–168. Occasional Paper 21. Center for Archaeological Investigations, Southern Illinois University, Carbondale.

Chang, Kwang-Chih
1967   Major aspects of the interrelationship of archaeology and ethnology. *Current Anthropology* 8:227–243.

Childe, Vere Gordon
1950   The urban revolution. *Town planning review* 21:3–17.
1958   *The prehistory of European society*. Penguin, Harmondsworth.

Clark, John Graham D.
1953   Archaeological theories and interpretation: Old world. In *Anthropology Today: Selections*, edited by Sol Tax, pp. 104–121. University of Chicago Press, Chicago.

Colton, Harold S.
1953   *Potsherds*. Bulletin 25. Museum of Northern Arizona, Flagstaff.

Crader, Diana C.
1974   The effects of scavenger on bone material from a large mammal: An experiment conducted among the Bisa of the Zuangusa Valley, Zambia. In *Ethnoarchaeology*, edited by Christopher Connan and C. W. Clewlew Jr., pp. 161–176. Monograph IV. Institute of Archaeology, University of California, Los Angeles.

Cribb, Roger L. D.
1991   *Nomads in archaeology.* Cambridge University, Cambridge.

Cunningham, Jeremy
2003   Transcending the "obnoxious spectator": A case for processual pluralism in ethnoarchaeology. *Journal of Anthropological Archaeology* 22:389–410.

Cushing, Frank H.
1886   A study of pueblo pottery as illustrative of Zuni culture growth. *Washington Bureau of American Ethnology, Annual Report* 4:467–521.

D'Andrea, A. Catherine, Diane E. Lyons, A. C. Mitiku Haile, and E. A. Butler
1999   Ethnoarchaeological approaches to the study of prehistoric agriculture in the Ethiopian highlands. In *The explorations of plant resources in ancient Africa,* edited by Marjike van der Veen, pp. 101–122. Plenum Publishing Corp., New York.

David, Nicholas
1992   Integrating ethnoarchaeology: A subtle realist perspective. *Journal of Anthropological Archaeology* 11:330–359.

David, Nicholas, and Carole Kramer
2001   *Ethnoarchaeology in action.* Cambridge University Press, Cambridge.

Deal, Michael
1998   *Pottery Ethnoarchaeology in the Central Maya Highlands.* University of Utah Press, Salt Lake City.

Deetz, James
1968   Cultural patterning of behavior as reflected by archaeological materials. In *Settlement archaeology,* edited by Kwang-chih Chang, pp. 31–42. National Press Books, Palo Alto, California.

Dentan, Robert K.
1970   Living and working with Semai. In *Being an anthropologist,* edited by George D. Spindler, pp. 85–112. Holt, Rinehart, and Winston, Inc., New York.

Dobres, Marcia-Anne, and Christopher R. Hoffman
1999   Introduction: A context for the present and future of technology studies. In *The social dynamics of technology,* edited by Marcia-Anne Dobres and Christopher R. Hoffman, pp. 1–22. Smithsonian Institution Press, Washington, D.C.

Dobres, Marcia-Anne, and John E. Robb
2000   Agency in archaeology: Paradigm or platitude? In *Agency in archaeology,* edited by Marcia-Anne Dobres and John E. Robb, pp. 1–18. Routledge, London.

Donley, Linda Wiley
  1982   House power: Swahili space and symbolic markers. In *Symbolic and structural archaeology*, edited by Ian Hodder, pp. 63–73. Cambridge University Press, Cambridge.
  1987   Life in the Swahili town house reveals the symbolic meaning of spaces and artefact assemblages. *African Archaeological Review* 5:191–192.

Donley-Reid, Linda Wiley
  1990   The power of Swahili porcelain, beads, and pottery. In *Powers of observation: alternative views in archaeology*, edited by Sarah M. Nelson and Alice B. Kehoe, pp. 47–59. Archaeological Papers of the American Anthropological Association 2, Washington, D.C.

Ebert, James I.
  1968   An ethnoarchaeological approach to reassessing the meaning of variability in stone tool assemblages. In *Ethnoarchaeology: Implications of ethnography for archaeology*, edited by Carol Kramer, pp. 59–74. Columbia University Press, New York.

Elkin, Adolphus P.
  1948   Pressure flaking in the northern Kimberly, Australia. *Man* 130:110–112.

Fabien, Johannes
  1983   *Time and the other: How anthropology makes its objects*. Columbia University Press, New York.

Fenton, William N.
  1949   Collecting materials for a political history of the six nations. *Proceedings of the American Philosophical Society* 93:233–238.
  1952   The training of historical ethnologists in America. *American Anthropologist* 54:328–339.

Fewkes, Jesse Walter
  1900   *Tusayan migration traditions*. Washington Bureau of American Ethnology, Washington, D.C.

Fischer, David Hackett
  1970   *Historians' fallacies: Toward a logic of historical thought*. Harper and Row, New York.

Ford, James, A.
  1954   On the concept of type. *American Anthropologist* 56:42–57.

Ford, James A., and Gordon Willey
1940   *Crooks site, a marksville period burial mound in La Salle Parish, Louisiana.* Anthropological Study No. 3. State of Louisiana, Department of Conservation.

Gabrilopoulos, Nick
1995   Ethnoarchaeology of the tallensi compound (upper east region, Ghana). PhD dissertation. Department of Archaeology. University Microfilms, Ann Arbor.

Gallagher, James P.
1977   Contemporary stone tool use in Ethiopia: Implications for Archaeology. *Journal of Field Archaeology* 4:407–414.

Gamble, Clive
1993   Ancestors and agendas. In *Archaeological theory: Who sets the agenda,* edited by Norman Yoffee and Andrew Sherratt, pp. 39–52. Cambridge University Press, Cambridge.

Geertz, Clifford
1973   *The interpretation of cultures.* Basic Books, New York.

Giddens, Anthony
1979   *A central problem in social theory.* University of California Press, Berkeley.

Gifford, Diane P.
1978   Ethnoarchaeological observations of natural processes affecting cultural material. In *Explorations in ethnoarchaeology,* edited by Richard A. Gould, pp. 77–101. University of New Mexico Press, Albuquerque.

Gifford, James C.
1960   The type variety method of ceramic classification as an indicator of cultural phenomena. *American Antiquity* 25:341–347.

Gosselain, Olivier P.
1992   Technology and style: Potters and pottery among the Bafia of Cameroon. *Man* 27:559–586.

Gosselain, Oliver P.
2000   Materializing identities: an African perspective. *Journal of Archaeological Method and Theory* 7:187–217.

Gould, Richard A.
1974   Some current problems in ethnoarchaeology. In *Ethnoarchaeology,* edited by C. William Clewlow, Jr., pp. 29–48. University of California, Los Angeles.

1978   Beyond analogy in ethnoarchaeology. In *Explanations in Ethnoar-chaeology*, edited by Richard A. Gould, pp. 249–293. University of New Mexico Press, Albuquerque.
1980   *Living Archaeology.* Cambridge University Press, Cambridge.
1990   *Recovering the Past.* University of New Mexico Press, Albuquerque.

Gould, Richard A., and Patty Jo Watson
1982   A dialogue on the meaning and use of analogy in ethnoarchaeolog-ical reasoning. *Journal of Anthropological Archaeology* 1:355–381.

Harris, Marvin
1979   *Cultural materialism.* Random House, New York.

Hawkes, Christopher
1954   Archaeological theory and method: Some suggestions from the Old World. *American Anthropologist* 56:155–168.

Hawley, Florence M.
1936   Field manual of prehistoric southwestern pottery types. *University of New Mexico Anthropological Series Bulletin 291.* University of New Mexico Press, Albuquerque.

Hayden, Brian
1979   *Paleolithic reflections.* Humanities Press, Atlantic Highlands, New Jersey.
1987   Use and misuse: The analysis of endscrapers. *Lithic Technology* 16:65–70.

Hayden, Brian, and Aubrey Cannon
1984   *The structure of material systems: Ethnoarchaeology in Maya highlands.* Society for American Archaeology Papers No. 3. Washington, D.C.

Heider, Karl G.
1967   Archaeological assumptions and ethnographical facts: A cautionary tale from New Guinea. *Southwestern Journal of Anthropology* 23:52–64.

Hill, James N.
1968   Broken K pueblo: Patterns of form and function. In *In pursuit of the past*, edited by Sally R. Binford and Lewis R. Binford, pp. 103–142. Aldine, New York.

Hitchcock, Robert K.
1982   *The ethnoarchaeology of sedentism: Mobility strategies and site structure among foraging and food production populations in the eastern Kalahari Desert, Botswana.* PhD dissertation, University of New Mexico. University Microfilms, Ann Arbor.

Hodder, Ian
  1982   *Symbols in Action*. Cambridge University Press, Cambridge.
  1986   *Reading the past*. Cambridge University Press, Cambridge.
  1987   The contextual analysis of symbolic meanings. In *The archaeology of contextual meaning*, edited by Ian Hodder, pp. 1–10. Cambridge University Press, Cambridge.
  1989   This is not an article about material culture as text. *Journal of Anthropological Archaeology* 8:250–269.
  1991   Interpretive archaeology and its role. *American Antiquity* 56:7–8.

Horne, Lee
  1994   *Village spaces: Settlement and society in Northeastern Iran*. Smithsonian Institution Press, Washington, D.C.

Hudson, Jean
  1993   The impacts of domestic dogs on bone in forager camps: Or, The dog-gone bones. In *From bones to behavior: Ethnoarchaeological and experimental contributions to the interpretation of faunal remains*, edited by Jean Hudson, pp. 301–323. Center for Archaeological Investigations, Southern Illinois University, Carbondale.

Huffman, Thomas
  1982   Archaeology and ethnohistory of the African iron age. *Annual Review of Anthropology* 11:133–150.

Janes, Robert R.
  1991   *Preserving diversity: Ethnoarchaeological perspectives on culture change in the western Canadian subartic*. Garland Publishing, New York.

Jarman, Michael E., Claudio Vita-Finzi, and Eric S. Higgs
  1972   Site catchment analysis in archaeology. In *Man, settlement and urbanism*, edited by Peter J. Ecko, Ruth Tringham, and G. W. Dimbleby, pp. 61–66. Schenkman, Cambridge, Massachusetts.

Johnsen, Harald, and Bjørnar Olsen
  1992   Hermeneutics and archaeology: On the philosophy of contextual archaeology. *American Antiquity* 57:419–436.

Jones, Siân
  1997   *The archaeology of ethnicity*. Routledge, London.

Kelley, Robert L.
  1999   Elements of the behavioral ecological paradigm for the study of Prehistoric Hunter-Gatherers. In *Social theory in archaeology*, edited by Michael B. Schiffer, pp. 63–78. University of Utah Press, Salt Lake City.

Kent, Susan
    1995   Ethnoarchaeology and the concept of home: A cross-cultural analy-
            sis. In *The concept of home: An interdisciplinary view*, edited by David
            Benjamin and David Stea, pp. 163–180. Avebury, London.
    1998   Invisible gender-invisible foragers; southern African hunter-
            gatherer spatial patterning and the archaeological record. In *Gender
            in African Prehistory*, edited by Susan Kent, pp. 69–82. AltaMira,
            Walnut Creek, California.

Kleindienst, Maxine, and Patty Jo Watson
    1956   Action archaeology: The archaeological inventory of a living com-
            munity. *Anthropology Tomorrow* 5:75–78.

Kluckholm, Clyde
    1939   The place of theory in anthropological studies. *Philosophy of Science*
            6:328–344.

Kobayashi, Masashi
    1994   Use-alteration analysis of Kalinga pottery: Interior carbon deposits
            of cooking pots. In *Kalinga ethnoarchaeology: Expanding archeological
            method and theory*, edited by William A. Longacre and James M.
            Skibo, pp. 127–168. Smithsonian Institution Press, Washington, D.C.

Kosso, Peter
    1991   Method in archaeology: Middle range theory as hermeneutics.
            American Antiquity 56:621–627.

Kramer, Carol
    1982   *Village ethnoarchaeology: Rural Iran in archaeological perspective*. Acad-
            emic Press, New York.
    1997   *Pottery in Rajasthan: ethnoarchaeology in two Indian cities*. Smithsonian
            Institution Press, Washington, D.C.

Krieger, Alex D.
    1944   The typological concept. *American Antiquity* 9:271–287.

Kroeber, Alfred L.
    1916   Zuni Potsherds. *American Museum of Natural History Anthropological
            Papers* 18:7–21.

Kusimba, Chaparukha M.
    1996   Social context of iron forging on the Kenya coast. *Africa* 66:386–410.

Kuznar, Lawrence A.
    1995   *Awatimarka: The ethnoarchaeology of an Andean herding community*.
            Harcourt Brace, Fort Worth.

Leach, Edmund R.
   1973   Concluding address. In *The explanation of culture change: Models in prehistory*, edited by Colin Renfrew. University of Pittsburgh Press, Pittsburgh.

Lemonnier, Pierre
   1992   *Elements for an anthropology of technology*. University of Michigan, Ann Arbor.

Leone, Mark P.
   1982   Some opinions about recovering mind. *American Antiquity* 47:742–760.

Lévi-Strauss, Claude
   1963   *Structural anthropology*. Basic Books, New York.

Longacre, William
   1968   Some aspect of prehistoric society in east-central Arizona. In *New perspectives in archaeology*, edited by Sally R. Binford and Lewis R. Binford, pp. 89–102. Adline, Chicago.
   1970   *Archaeology as Anthropology*. University of Arizona, Anthropological Papers Vol. 17. University of Arizona, Tucson.
   1974   Kalinga pottery making: The evolution of a research design. In *Frontiers of anthropology: An introduction to anthropological thinking*, edited by Murray J. Leaf, pp. 51–67. Van Nostrand Company, New York.
   1978   Ethnoarchaeology. *Reviews in Anthropology* 5:357–363.
   1981   Kalinga pottery: an ethnoarchaeological study. In *Pattern of the past: studies in honor of David Clarke*, edited by Ian Hodder, Glenn Isaac, and Norman Hammond, pp. 49–66. Cambridge University Press, Cambridge.
   1991   Sources of ceramic variability among the Kalinga of northern Luzon. In *Ceramic ethnoarchaeology*, edited by William A. Longacre, pp. 95–111. The University of Arizona Press, Tucson.
   2000   I want to buy a black pot. *Journal of Archaeological Method and Theory* 7:273–293.

Longacre, William, and James E. Ayers
   1965   Archaeological lessons from an Apache Wickiup. In *Pursuit of the past*, edited by Sally R. Binford and Lewis R. Binford, pp. 151–160. Aldine, New York.

Longacre, William A., and James M. Skibo
   1994   *Kalinga Ethnoarchaeology: Expanding archaeological method and theory*. Smithsonian Institution Press, Washington, D.C.

MacEachern, Scott
1996   Foreign countries: The development of ethnoarchaeology in sub-Saharan Africa. *Journal of World Prehistory* 10:243–304.

Malinowski, Bronsilaw
1961   *Argonauts of the Western Pacific*. E. P. Dutton, London.

Matson, Frederick R. (editor)
1964   *Ceramics and man*. Viking Fund Publications in Anthropology No. 41, Chicago.

Mohr Chavez, Karen L.
1992   The organization of production and distribution of traditional pottery in South Highland Peru. In *Ceramic production and distribution: an integrated approach*, edited by George J. Bey III and Christopher A. Pool, pp. 49–92. Westview Press, Boulder, Colorado.

Moore, Sally Falk
1994   *Anthropology and Africa*. University Press of Virginia, Charlottesville.

Murdoch, John
1892   Ethnological results of the point barrow expedition. *9th annual report of the bureau of American ethnology for the years 1887–1888*. William W. Fitzhugh, ed., 19–441 U.S. Government Printing Office, Washington, D.C.

Nelson, Edward William
1899   *The Eskimo about Bering Strait*. Smithsonian Institution Press, Washington, D.C.

Nelson, Nels C.
1914   *Pueblo ruins of the Galisteo Basin, New Mexico*. Anthropological Papers of the American Museum of Natural History 15(1), New York.

Neupert and Longacre
1994   Informant accuracy in pottery use-life studies: a Kalinga example. In *Kalinga ethnoarchaeology: expanding archaeological method and theory*, edited by William A. Longacre and James M. Skibo, pp. 71–82. Smithsonian Institution Press, Washington, D.C.

O'Connell, James F.
1993   Discussion: Subsistence and settlement interpretations. In *From bones to behavior: Ethnoarcaheological and experimental contributions to the interpretation of faunal remains*, Jean Hudson, ed., 169–178. Center for Archaeological Investigations, Southern Illinois University, Carbondale.
1995   Ethnoarchaeology needs a general theory of behavior. *Journal of Archaeological Research* 3:205–255.

O'Connell, James F., Kristen Hawkes, and Nicholas Burton Jones
1988 Hadza scavenging: Implications for Plio-Pleistocene hominid subsistence. *Current Anthropology* 29:356–363.

Oliver, Roland
1966 The problem of Bantu expansion. *Journal of African History* 7:361–376.

Orme, Bryony
1981 *Anthropology for archaeologists.* Cornell University Press, Ithaca, New York.

Oswalt, Wendell H.
1974 Ethnoarchaeology. In *Ethnoarchaeology*, edited by Christopher B. Donnan and C. William Clewlow Jr., pp. 3–14. Institute of Archaeology Monograph 4. University of California, Los Angeles.

Owen, Linda R., and Marting Porr
1999 Ethno-analogy in theory and practice: An introduction. In *Ethno-Analogy and the reconstruction of prehistoric artefact use and production,* edited by Linda R. Owen and Martin Porr, pp. 1–2. Verlag and Vertrieb, Tubingen.

Parsons, Elise Clews
1940 Relations between ethnology and archaeology in the Southwest. *American Antiquity* 5:214–220.

Phillipson, David
1976 Archaeology and Bantu linguistics. *World Archaeology* 8(1):66–82.
1977 *The later prehistory of eastern and southern Africa.* Africana Publishing, New York.

Porr, Martin
1999 Archaeology, analogy, material culture, society: An exploration. In *Ethno-Analogy and the reconstruction of prehistoric artefact use and production,* edited by Linda R. Owen and Martin Porr, pp. 3–16. Verlag and Vertrieb, Tubingen.

Priest, Josiah
1833 *American antiquities and discoveries in the west.* Hoffman and White, Albany, New York.

Raab, L. Mark, and Albert C. Goodyear
1984 Middle range theory in archaeology: a critical review of origins and applications. *American Antiquity* 49(2):255–268.

Radcliffe-Brown, A. R.
1952 *Structure and function in primitive society.* Free Press, New York.

Reddy, S. N.
    1997   If the threshing floor could talk: integration of agriculture and pas-
            toralism during the Late Harappan in Gujarat, India. *Journal of An-
            thropological Archaeology* 16:162–187.

Reid, Andrew, and Ruth Young
    2000   Pottery abrasion and the preparation of African grain. *Antiquity*
            74:101–111.

Robertshaw, Peter
    1990   A history of African archaeology: An introduction. In *A history of
            African archaeology,* edited by Peter Robertshaw, pp. 3–12. James
            Currey, London.

Rosaldo, Renato
    1989   *Culture & Truth: The remaking of social analysis.* Beacon Press, Boston.

Rots, Veerle, and Bronwynne Williamson
    2003   Microwear and residue analysis in perspective: the contribution of
            ethnoarchaeological evidence. *Journal of Archaeological Science*
            31:1287–1299.

Rouse, Irving
    1960   The classification of artifacts in archaeology. *American Antiquity*
            25:313–323.

Roux, Valentine
    1999   Ethnoarchaeology and the generation of referential models: The
            case of Harappan canelian beads. In *Ethno-Analogy and the recon-
            struction of prehistoric artefact use and production,* edited by Linda R.
            Owen and Martin Porr, pp. 153–170. Verlag and Vertrieb, Tubingen.

Schiffer, Michael B.
    1972   Archaeological context and systematic context. *American Antiquity*
            37:156–165.
    1983   Toward the identification of formation processes. *American Antiq-
            uity* 48:675–706.
    1988   The structure of archaeological theory. *American Antiquity*
            53:461–485.

Schiffer, Michael B., and James Skibo
    1997   The explanation of artifact variability. *American Antiquity* 62:27–50.

Schmidt, Peter R.
    1975   A new look at interpretations of the early iron age in East Africa.
            History in Africa 2:127–136.
    1983   An alternative to a strictly materialist perspective: A review of his-
            torical archaeology, ethnoarchaeology and symbolic approaches in
            African archaeology. *American Antiquity* 48:62–75.

1985   Symboling in archaeology: Towards a more humanistic science. Paper presented at the 51st Annual Meetings of the Society for American Archaeology, New Orleans, Louisiana.

1990   Oral traditions, archaeology and history: A short reflective history. In *A History of African Archaeology*, edited by Peter Robertshaw, pp. 252–270. James Currey, London.

1996   Reconfiguring the Barongo: Reproductive symbolism and reproduction among a work association of iron smelters. In *The culture and technology of African iron production*, edited by Peter R. Schmidt, pp. 74–127. University Press of Florida, Gainesville.

1997   *Iron technology in east Africa: Symbolism, science, and archaeology.* Indiana University Press, Bloomington.

1998   Reading gender in the ancient iron technology of Africa. In *Gender in African Prehistory*, edited by Susan Kent, pp. 139–162. AltaMira Press, Walnut Creek, California.

Sept, Jeanne M.

1992   Was there no place like home? A new perspective on early hominid archaeological sites from the mapping of chimpanzee nests. *Current Anthropology* 33:187–208.

Service, Elman R.

1962   *Primitive Social Organization.* Random House, New York.

Shott, Michael

1989   On tool-class use lives and the formation of archaeological assemblages. *American Antiquity* 54:9–30.

Simms, Steven R.

1992   Ethnoarchaeology: Obnoxious spectator, trivial pursuit, or the keys to a time machine? In *Quandaries and Quests: Visions of Archaeology's Future*, edited by LuAnn Wandsnider, pp. 186–198. Occasional Paper No. 20, Center for Archaeological Investigations, Southern Illinois University, Carbondale.

Skibo, James M.

1992   *Pottery function: a use-alteration perspective.* Plenum, New York.

1999   *Ants for Breakfast: Archaeological adventures among the Kalinga.* University of Utah Press, Salt Lake City.

Smith, Adam, and Nicholas David

1995   The production of space and house of Xidi Sukur. *Current Anthropology* 36:441–471.

Spiess, Arthur E.

1979   *Reindeer and caribou hunters.* Academic Press, New York.

Spradley, James P.
1979   *The ethnographic interview*. Holt, Rinehart, and Winston, Inc., New York.

Stahl, Ann Brower
2001   *Making history in Banda*. Cambridge University Press, Cambridge.

Stark, Miriam T.
1992   From sibling to suki: social relations and spatial proximity in Kalinga pottery exchange. *Journal of Anthropological Archaeology* 11:137–151.
1994   Pottery exchange and the regional system: A Dalupa case study. In *Kalinga ethnoarchaeology: Expanding archeological method and theory*, edited by William A. Longacre and James M. Skibo, pp. 169–198. Smithsonian Institution Press, Washington, D.C.

Stark, Miriam T., and William A. Longacre
1993   Kalinga ceramics and new technologies: social and cultural contexts of ceramic change. In *The social and cultural contexts of new ceramic technologies*, edited by W. David Kingery, pp. 1–32. American Ceramic Society, Westerville, Ohio.

Steward, Julian H.
1942   The direct historical approach to archaeology. *American Antiquity* 7:337–343.
1955   *Theory of culture change*. University of Illinois Press, Urbana.

Stow, George William
1905   *The native races of South Africa*. London: Swan Sonneschien.

Strong, William D.
1933   The plains culture area in the light of archaeology. *American Anthropologist* 35:271–287.

Swanton, John R., and Roland B. Dixon
1914   Primitive American History. *American Anthropologist* 16(3):376–412.

Tani, Masakazu
1994   Why should more pots break in larger households? Mechanisms underlying population estimates from ceramics. In *Kalinga ethnoarchaeology: Expanding archeological method and theory*, edited by William A. Longacre and James M. Skibo, pp. 51–70. Smithsonian Institution Press, Washington, D.C.

Taylor, Walter W.
1948   *A study of archaeology*: Memoir 69 of the American Anthropological Association, Washington, D.C.

Thomas, David Hurst
1983   *The archaeology of Monitor Valley 1. epistemology*. Anthropological Papers of The American Museum of Natural History 58(1), New York.

Thompson, R. H.
1956   The subjective element in archaeological inference. *Southwestern Journal of Anthropology* 12:327–332.

Thomson, Donald F.
1939   The seasonal factor in human culture, illustrated from the life of a contemporary nomadic group. *Proceedings of the prehistoric society* 5:209–221.

Tilley, Christopher
1993   Introduction: Interpretation and a poetics of the past. In *Interpretative Archaeology*, edited by Christopher Tilley, pp. 1–29. Berg, Oxford.

Toth, Nick, Kathy Schick, and Selassie Semaw
2002   *A technological comparison of the stone tool-making capabilities of Australopithicus/early Homo, Pan paniscus, and Homo sapiens, and possible evolutionary implications.* Paper presented at the Paleoanthropological Society meeting, Denver, Colorado, March 19–20.

Trigger, Bruce G.
1989   *A History of Archaeological Thought.* Cambridge University Press, Cambridge.
1990   The history of African archaeology. In *A history of African archaeology*, edited by Peter Robertshaw, 309–319. London: James Currey.

Tylor, Edward Burnett
1871   *Primitive Culture.* J. Murray, London.

Vansina, Jan
1990   Paths in the rainforest. University of Wisconsin Press, Madison.

Veit, Ulrich
1989   Ethnic concepts in German prehistory: A case study on the relationship between cultural identity and archaeological objectivity. In *Archaeological approaches to cultural identity*, edited by Stephen J. Shennan, pp. 33–56. Routledge, London.

Watson, Patty Jo
1979   *Archaeological ethnography in Western Iran.* Viking Fund Publications in Anthropology 57. University of Arizona Press, Tucson.

Watson, Patty Jo, Steven A. LeBlanc, and Charles L. Redman
1971   *Explanation in archaeology: An explicitly scientific approach.* Columbia University Press, New York.

Weedman, Kathryn J.
2000   *An ethnoarchaeological study of stone scrapers among the Gamo people of southern Ethiopia.* PhD dissertation. University Microfilms, Ann Arbor, University of Florida.

2002a   On the spur of the moment: Effects of age and experience on hafted stone scraper morphology. *American Antiquity* 67:731–744.

2002b   An ethnoarchaeological study of stone-tool variability among the Gamo hide workers of southern Ethiopia. In *Le Travail Du Cuir de La Prehistoire à nos jours*, edited by Frédérique Audoin-Rouzeau and Sylvie Beyries, pp. 131–142. Editions APDCA, Antibes.

Werner, D., C. Thurman, and J. Maxwell
1992   *Where there is no doctor: a village health care handbook.* Hesperian Foundation, Palo Alto, California.

White, Leslie A.
1959   *The Evolution of Culture.* McGraw-Hill, New York.

Wiessner, Polly
1983   Style and social information in Kalahari San projectile points. *American Antiquity* 48:253–276.
1984   Reconstructing the behavioral basis for style: A case study among the Kalahari San. *Journal or Anthropological Archaeology* 3:190–234.

Willey, Gordon R.
1953   Archaeological theories and interpretation: New world. In *Anthropology Today: Selections*, Sol Tax, ed., 170–194. The University of Chicago Press, Chicago.

Willey, Gordon R., and Jeremy A. Sabloff
1974   *A history of American archaeology.* Thames and Hudson, London.

Wilmsen, Edwin
1989   *Land Filled with Flies.* Chicago University Press, Chicago.

Wobst, H. Martin
1978   The Archaeo-Ethnology of hunter-gatherers or the tyranny of the ethnographic record in archaeology. *American Antiquity* 43:303–309.
2000   Agency in (spite of) material culture. In *Agency in archaeology*, edited by Maria Dobres and John E. Robb, pp. 40–50. Routledge, London.

Wylie, Alison
1982   An analogy by any other name is just as analogical: A commentary on the Gould-Watson dialogue. *Journal of Anthropological Archaeology* 1:382–401.
1985   The reaction against analogy. *Advances in Archaeological Method and Theory* 8:63–111.
1989   The interpretative dilemma. In *Critical traditions in contemporary archaeology*, edited by V. Pinksy and A. Wylie, pp. 18–27. Cambridge University Press, Cambridge.
1993   A proliferation of new archaeologies. In *Archaeological theory: Who sets the agenda*, edited by Norman Yoffee and Andrew Sherratt, pp. 20–26. Cambridge University Press, Cambridge.

2000 Questions of evidence, legitimacy, and the (dis)unity of science. *American Antiquity* 65:227–237.

Yakar, Jak
2000 *Ethnoarchaeology of Anatolia.* Tele Aviv University Monograph series Number 17. Emery and Claire Yass Publications in Archaeology. Graphit Press, Jerusalem.

Yellen, John E.
1977 *Archaeological approaches to the present.* Academic Press, New York.

Yellen, John E., and Alison S. Brooks
1988 The Late Stone Age archaeology of the !Kangwa-/Xai/Xai Valleys, Ngamiland. *Botswana Notes and Records* 20:5–27.

8

Maritime Archaeology

Mark A. Feulner
J. Barto Arnold III

Broadly stated, maritime archaeology is the scientific study of humanity's seafaring past through the interpretation of material remains (Muckelroy 1978:4). Maritime culture has always been an important part of our ancestors' lives, influencing every aspect of social organization. Political power, economic strength, social order, and even the spread of religious beliefs have all been closely tied to maritime activities. The seafarers of the past, as well as the industries that supported their activities, created a subculture that influences modern society (Muckelroy 1980:24–25). Maritime archaeology studies every aspect of our seafaring heritage, examining the vessels, their cargoes, the ports they used, and the industries that supported maritime activities, as well as the people who went to sea (Babits and Tilburg 1998:25–26).

A more narrowly defined discipline within maritime archaeology is that of nautical archaeology, a specialty that focuses on maritime technology, in effect, the vessels of seafaring cultures and the equipment needed to operate them (Babits and Tilburg 1998:24). As the primary material remains of maritime activity, ships are testimony to the technological achievements of the societies that produced them. Watercraft, the most practical and economical form of long-distance transportation in preindustrial societies, were often the most sophisticated and advanced machines they produced (Muckelroy 1980:24). As a significant financial commitment, they also serve as indicators of the economic strength of the societies that produced them. The study of ships and ship technologies is a powerful tool in understanding cultures involved in maritime activities.

Both maritime and nautical archaeology are closely wed to the relatively new field of underwater archaeology. This discipline is exactly what the name implies, archaeology conducted in an underwater environment or, more precisely, the scientific study of submerged cultural resources. It encompasses a large portion of the work done in maritime archaeology, as well as a host of other archaeological pursuits. Studies of submerged Paleolithic settlements, fossilized remains from springs, sacrificial wells, and sunken cities all fall within the realm of underwater archaeology, but are not part of maritime archaeology. Maritime archaeology and underwater archaeology are virtually synonymous because most of the cultural remains from seafaring activities are to be found beneath the waters of the world (Babits and Tilburg 1998:27–28).

Doing Archaeology Underwater

Archaeology is a demanding, and often unforgiving, endeavor. A great deal of labor goes into every survey and every excavation, whether the site is terrestrial or submerged. Both environments pose similar difficulties to the archaeologist; each possesses its own unique problems and offers different advantages. Every excavation is subject to its environment, the weather, and the remoteness of its location. An archaeologist faces three primary problems in the field: cost, time, and human limitations. When conducting studies in an underwater medium, these factors become more intense and take on a special character.

The cost of funding an underwater project can be staggering and often prohibitive. A land archaeologist's logistical concerns are normally limited to transport to the site, shelter, supplies, and archaeological tools. The underwater archaeologist has the same concerns, to which he adds more complex and expensive equipment and specialized training requirements.

Figure 8.1.   An archaeologist gently fans away sediment from the remains of a hull.

In addition to the boat normally required to reach a site, some form of life-support gear is needed, either surface supply or scuba (self-contained underwater breathing apparatus) (Muckelroy 1980:12). A surface-supply system pumps air from the surface to the diver below by means of a hose. It has the advantage of keeping a diver supplied with air for extended periods and is often less expensive than scuba. However, movement is restricted by the hose, and in most cases surface supply is practical to use only in shallow depths, usually in less than 20 m of water. For deeper investigations and greater freedom of movement, divers use scuba, carrying their air supply in a cylinder of compressed air. This allows much greater maneuverability in the water, but time underwater is restricted by the amount of air in the cylinder.

Both underwater breathing systems require ancillary equipment; air compressors, exposure suits, buoyancy compensation devices (BCDs), weighting systems, compressed air cylinders, masks, fins, and additional diving equipment add substantially to the cost of working on a submerged site. Divers also require specialized training in the use and maintenance of their gear, both for safety and for the archaeology to be performed competently. Because of the particular hazards of diving, especially in deeper waters and remote locations, safety equipment such as medical-grade oxygen, a hyperbaric chamber, and an on-site dive physician can become necessary and greatly increase expenses.

The archaeological tools for work underwater also influence the cost. Many standard tools need to be adapted for work underwater or suitable replacements found. Every piece of equipment, from measuring tapes to photographic cameras, must be able to withstand the rigors of constant immersion in water, most often saltwater, at various depths. There are also specialized tools used only on underwater sites that are not found on terrestrial sites that take advantage of, and deal with, the characteristics of submerged environments. Archaeological tools used underwater require a great deal of care and maintenance, and usually need to be repaired or replaced very often.

All of these factors combine to make underwater archaeology very expensive. Frequently an important factor in contemplating an underwater investigation is whether what can be learned justifies the expense.

Time is another aspect of working underwater that can hamper the archaeologist. Divers are limited in the amount of time they can stay submerged by several factors. Scuba has a limited air supply, which requires a diver to surface periodically to replenish air. Air consumption rates vary from diver to diver and increase as the diver descends into deeper waters. Most dives last between 20 minutes and an hour, and the underwater archaeologist must do the work within this time. In contrast, the archaeologist working on a terrestrial site often labors for several hours at a stretch, limited only by personal stamina.

Dive time is also limited by the risk of decompression sickness (DCS), or the bends, which can afflict both scuba and surface-supply divers. If enough nitrogen is absorbed from the compressed air breathed by the diver, the gas can form bubbles when the diver rises as it comes out of solution in the bloodstream. The effects of DCS can range from minor skin irritation and joint pain to paralysis and death (Muckelroy 1978:38). The deeper and longer the dive, the greater the chance of DCS.

There are three ways to prevent DCS. The primary method is the use of dive tables that indicate the amount of time an individual can remain at specified depths without absorbing an unsafe amount of nitrogen. The second technique is to perform decompression stops, where the diver lingers at shallow depths to allow nitrogen to be safely released by the body before surfacing. The final and most costly way of preventing DCS is to use a hyperbaric chamber at the surface to maintain a high ambient air pressure and gradually bring the diver to normal air pressure, allowing nitrogen to be slowly and safely released by the body (Muckelroy 1978:38). However, each method severely limits the archaeologist's time working on a site.

The restricted amount of time an underwater archaeologist can actually work on a site is a glaring disadvantage. In a submerged environment, an archaeologist can be limited to as few as two sessions of 20 minutes apiece each day, allowing only 40 minutes a day to work. This limitation greatly hampers work underwater and can greatly increase operating costs. It can take three to five times the number of people as much as five to seven times longer to do a comparable amount of work on a submerged site (Muckelroy 1978:48).

The final major problem faced by the archaeologist working underwater is human limitations. Submerged environments are inherently alien, where human adaptability has its limits. The physical effects of greater-than-normal ambient pressures combined with heat loss can have a deleterious effect on the human body if not addressed. Deepwater diving can have an additional physiological effect that bears a psychological impact. At depths greater than 30 m a diver may experience a condition called nitrogen narcosis, "the rapture of the deep" (Muckelroy 1978:25). Its overall effect varies, from a feeling of rapture and intoxication to fear and confusion. Problems with visibility can also disorient divers, particularly in blackout conditions. In the best diving conditions, the refraction of light through water and the diver's mask distorts the appearance of objects, making them seem closer and larger than they actually are (Muckelroy 1978:24). These various problems can attack a diver singly or in combination, and the reduced intellectual capacities caused by these physiological factors can be hazardous, as well as hampering archaeological recording.

Despite these various difficulties, archaeology can be performed underwater, where the environment does provide a few advantages over terrestrial archaeology. Vertical movement in the water column can allow the archaeologist to get a bird's-eye view of the site. The diver can hover over the area being excavated, which limits disturbance of remains. Spoil can be removed with the wave of a hand, to be carried away by currents or by simple suction devices (Muckelroy 1978:49). Larger pieces of overburden and heavier artifacts that would require heavy machinery on land can be moved by a few divers using a lift bag, which uses air to lend buoyancy to an object. These factors can greatly aid an archaeologist's efforts underwater.

The primary advantage of working underwater is the richness of submerged sites. Most submerged sites are single-component sites, exhibiting less contamination from later periods than terrestrial sites. Many artifacts enjoy greater protection from the ravages of time in an underwater environment than on land (Muckelroy 1978:52–55). Objects can be found in a submerged site that have never been recovered terrestrially, and often they are of museum exhibit quality. Also, the wrecking of a ship or the flooding of a harbor town is a disaster that can happen in an instant. When such calamities occur, even those who survive leave many of their belongings behind when they escape, which can provide the archaeologist with substantial clues as to what their daily life was like. In effect, a shipwreck or sunken city forms a time capsule that provides a frozen picture of the past (Muckelroy 1978:56–57). This means that a submerged site often has a chronological sharpness as a group of artifacts belonging to a particular moment in time.

Brief History of Maritime Archaeology

Humanity has been losing material culture to the sea for as long as it has been attempting to cross it. And, for just as long, humanity has endeavored to reclaim what the sea has taken away. Until recent centuries, the only tools available to those attempting to salvage objects from the sea were hooks, nets, and free divers (Muckelroy 1978:10). Early attempts were made to extend

Figure 8.2.   A diver using a lift bag to raise a heavy stone anchor. On the surface, it would require four to six people to move the anchor.

a free diver's time on the bottom. Crude devices such as long tubes and leather bags filled with air were tried with little success (Babits and Tilburg 1998:343–344). However, technological innovations over the past four centuries have greatly improved our ability to work on the bottom of the ocean.

Between A.D. 1500 and 1800, bells extended divers' time on the bottom by trapping a supply of air for breathing as needed. This idea of trapping air was improved upon with the practice of submersing enclosed barrels of air in the eighteenth century. The nineteenth century saw the development of the more familiar hard-hat diving gear, which kept a diver on the bottom for considerable periods by means of a constant supply of fresh air pumped from the surface to the diver through a hose (Babits and Tilburg 1998:345–348).

The nineteenth century also saw the establishment of archaeology as a scientific discipline, and with it maritime archaeology soon emerged. In the early nineteenth century, the first scientific consideration of the potential of submerged cultural remains was made by a geologist, Charles Lyell. In a chapter of *Principles of Geology* (1832), he analyzed accounts of well-preserved artifacts recovered from the sea and listed contemporary shipping losses to demonstrate the amount of cultural material being deposited on the ocean floor. Lyell concluded that, in time, the number of artifacts on the bottom of the ocean would exceed those on land (Lyell 1832:258).

Incongruously, and despite Lyell's enthusiasm for the archaeological potential underwater, maritime archaeology began on land, with terrestrial excavations of early vessels in Scandinavia. One of the first was a boat dated to the fourth century A.D. found in Nydam, Denmark, investigated by Conrad Engelhardt in 1863 (Engelhardt 1865). This was soon followed by the recovery of several Viking ships in Norway; the first was from Tune and another from a burial mound in Gokstad (Nicolaysen 1882). The Gokstad find, whose investigation was begun in 1880 by Nicolay Nicolaysen, is considered a classic vessel from the Viking era. The most notable of these buried ships, discovered in Oseberg in 1904 (Brögger et al. 1917), presented a rich find, not just for the high level of preservation of the ornately designed vessel but also for the extraordinary collection of burial goods of remarkable craftsmanship and quality recovered in fine condition.

Around this time, archaeologists began to exhibit a growing interest in what lay beneath the surface of the ocean. However, archaeologists remained mostly land bound in the early twentieth century, not venturing much into the underwater realm largely because of the physical demands, risks, and intensive training required by diving in the cumbersome equipment then available. Still, some fantastic discoveries were made in this period.

In 1900 Greek sponge divers found a collection of marble and bronze statues in 60 m of water near Antikythera, a Mediterranean island situated midway between Crete and the Greek mainland. Seven years after that find, sponge divers discovered a collection of sunken treasures off the Tunisian coast near Mahdia. Recovery operations at both sites were supervised from the surface by archaeologists. Using vessels from the Greek navy and professional divers, these projects yielded a spectacular collection of Greek statuary and other artifacts, the most prominent being the famous Antikytheran youth (Weinberg et al. 1965; Frondeville 1956). The discoveries at Mahdia and Antikythera, combined with numerous smaller finds in the Mediterranean dragged up by fishing nets or located by sponge divers, served to illustrate the great potential for classical archaeology that lay underwater. Yet the archaeologist remained a passive observer on the surface, leaving the underwater work to professional divers.

There were limited advances in maritime archaeology during the years between World Wars I and II. One was the draining of Lake Nemi in Italy, at the order of Benito Mussolini, exposing for excavation the palatial Roman barges known to lie on the bottom of the lake (Ucelli 1950). Though specialized craft, they yielded much information on Roman ship construction.

World War II produced a new underwater technology that had a profound effect on maritime archaeology and upon underwater research in general. In 1942 Jacques-Yves Cousteau, an officer in the French navy, and an industrial-gas equipment engineer by the name of Émile Gagnan invented the aqualung, the first completely automatic self-contained breathing apparatus (Cousteau 1953, 3–8 and 19–20). The aqualung quickly supplanted the cumbersome hard-hat diving-gear of sponge divers and began a revolution in undersea exploration. It allowed anyone of reasonable health to dive with less training, lower expenses, and greater freedom of movement than surface-supplied divers. This device both paved the way for future underwater archaeological investigations and facilitated the activities of salvors and treasure hunters.

The invention of the aqualung soon led to attempts at underwater archaeological investigation. In 1948 Cousteau led his Undersea Research Group (GERS) in an investigation of an amphora mound near Grand Congloué, close to the French town of Marseilles (Taylor 1965:66–75). Later, in 1957, Cousteau's friend and associate Philippe Taillez organized an expedition to excavate a first-century B.C. Roman wreck off Titan near Lavandon, France. Working with Fernand Benoit, director of Antiquities for Provence, the project resulted in the recovery of the merchant ship. Although some excavation tools and techniques, such as the use of an airlift, were realized on these projects, the archaeology was inadequate when compared with the standards held on land. Taillez, recognizing the inadequacy of the work, noted that a wreck was archaeologically important as the "frozen slice of time" it represented and that much more could be learned by an archaeologist doing a personal inspection of the site at the bottom (Taylor 1965:76–91).

Underwater archaeology moved closer to the standards of terrestrial digs with the Italian-led excavation of a late-second-century B.C. wreck at Spargi, near the Sardinian coast, in 1958 and 1959. Led by Nino Lamboglia, the Italians used a grid system and exhaustive photographic planning and solved some problems with underwater surveying. However, there remained recording inaccuracies that made site plans difficult to produce. Removal of material and artifacts, particularly amphorae, had a profound impact on site characteristics that were difficult for the divers to note and introduced imprecision in mapping (Taylor 1965:103–118.)

As the excavation at Spargi entered its third season in 1960, the University Museum of the University of Pennsylvania sent an expedition to excavate the remains of a Bronze Age ship from about 1200 B.C., located by Peter Throckmorton at Cape Gelidonya on the southwestern Turkish coast. Led by then-student George Bass, the excavation yielded spectacular finds and controversial conclusions, suggesting that Phoenician merchants had been making contact with Greece centuries earlier than previously thought (Bass 1975:25–59). More importantly, the project demonstrated that an archaeologist could direct an underwater excavation from the bottom and apply strict scientific methodology. This proved that the accuracy of a land excavation could be achieved under the sea.

At the first conference on underwater archaeology held at Cannes in 1955, Professor Lamboglia had outlined five questions faced by the underwater archaeologist: (1) Could excavations be conducted underwater with the scientific accuracy found on land without exorbitant costs? (2) Should scuba or helmeted divers be employed? (3) What is the position of an archaeologist on an underwater excavation, and how does he or she interact with divers and technicians? (4) After initial recording, could a wreck be excavated in the same manner as a land dig, with observable stratigraphy? (5) Can a wreck be raised to the surface? (Taylor 1965:190). By 1960 three of the questions had been satisfactorily answered. The work done at Spargi and Gelidonya suggested that the other two, the first and fourth, would soon be answered. Bass would soon provide definitive answers to those questions.

Bass returned to Turkey in the summer of 1961, this time to excavate a Byzantine shipwreck near Yassi Ada. He brought with him a selected team, possessing the skills needed on a terrestrial dig and also trained as divers to bring those talents to the sea floor. Again, new tools were employed and new techniques developed to augment those proven before, including the use of a submersible vehicle to observe the excavation (Bass 1975:112–122). The wealth of cultural material recovered from this site included the wreck itself. After four seasons of excavation the project had proved that underwater archaeology was a fully viable exercise and that the artifacts and knowledge recovered certainly justified the costliness of the endeavor. Shipwrecks not only provided a greater understanding of maritime culture, but had proven to be uniquely informative about more general aspects of ancient societies.

Locating a Site

Archaeological sites, on land or underwater, are discovered by either deliberate searches or accidents. Many submerged sites have been located by chance, by fishermen and sponge divers going about their usual business, and many by professionals who have endeavored to find them.

Although submerged sites may be located during a comprehensive survey, they are often found through intensive prior research. Archival records can provide a significant amount of information regarding site locations, often quite useful for relatively modern wrecks (Muckelroy 1980:14). Historical documents can also provide relevant information, such as the size of the vessel and the cargo it was carrying, which can aid the archaeologist in preparing for survey and excavation. An understanding of site formation processes can combine with the knowledge of an area's geography and tidal conditions to narrow a search field (Babits and Tilburg 1998:243, 268–269). Research conducted before a field investigation is invaluable.

Whether knowledge of a site is gained by reports or research, the detective work must continue with a systematic search of the area that has been indicated. The simplest way to accomplish this is by divers conducting a visual reconnaissance of the bottom. However, the search area must be small and well defined, because a diver can cover only a limited area while swimming with a restricted air supply (Muckelroy 1980:14). A diver's search efficiency can be marginally improved by towing the diver with a boat or by using a powered underwater sled. Various search patterns can be employed, similar to those used on land, but visual reconnaissance remains restricted by the constraints of the marine environment: low underwater visibility, varying sea conditions, and weather combine with the issues of time, fatigue, and decompression concerns to make diver searches a very limited tool.

Remote Sensing

An alternative to diver reconnaissance is electronic remote-sensing equipment, devices that allow much larger areas to be searched rather quickly (Muckelroy 1980:14). They come in several forms—photographic, acoustical, magnetic. Visual searches can be done remotely with underwater still photography and video cameras towed behind a vessel or mounted on a submersible vehicle (Muckelroy 1980:15). These have the benefit of a visual search without the need of employing divers and the bonus of providing a record of the search that can be reviewed. Cameras may also be used for aerial reconnaissance from aircraft, where higher elevations allow features to become more visible in good conditions.

Acoustical searches can also scrutinize large areas. Acoustical equipment, or sonar, propagates sound waves and measures their reflections to generate images of three-dimensional features on the sea bottom (Muckelroy 1980:14). Sonar equipment has several forms, the two most useful being the side-scan sonar and the sub-bottom profiler. Side-scan sonar "looks" to the left and right of the sensing device and detects features that project from the sea floor with a high degree of detail. A sub-bottom profiler "looks" downward to find features different from the sea bottom and sometimes may detect objects buried by a thin layer of sediment (Dean et al. 1992:143–144).

Magnetic searches employ a magnetometer to detect variances in the magnetic field caused by the presence of ferrous materials (Muckelroy 1980:14). The variance is proportional to the amount of ferrous material encountered and its distance from the sensing device. Although it does not produce a picture of the appearance or shape of an object, this method can accurately pinpoint an object and provide an idea of its size (Dean et al. 1992:142–143). A magnetometer is also useful in locating buried sites because a covered anomaly still changes the magnetic field.

Remote-sensing equipment is an invaluable tool, allowing large underwater areas to be searched relatively quickly, and can be deployed in situations and conditions that would be hazardous to divers (Dean et al. 1992:136). Magnetometers and sonar equipment have the added advantage of being able to "see" what the human eye may miss, particularly in waters with poor visibility. Different systems can be combined in different configurations to gather an even greater amount of data during a single search.

Navigational Tools

Any search needs to be conducted systematically and requires reliable navigation. Traditional navigation techniques using optical methods of fixing position are still used today. Compasses and transits are simple tools for determining position visually, requiring only accurate charts, a good compass, and practice to be effective (Dean et al. 1992:112–113). However, these are line-of-sight techniques that depend on charted features that may not be convenient for fixing the site location. Also, error can be introduced when fixes are taken from a moving boat, and inaccuracy increases as the observer moves farther away.

Greater accuracy can be achieved using a sextant or theodolite, precise and relatively cheap tools that measure angles to establish position. The sextant can be used to establish global position by measuring vertical angles between the horizon and celestial bodies but is more often used archaeologically to measure angles between features in the horizontal plane (Dean et al. 1992:113–115). It is a very portable, and delicate, instrument that can be quite accurate in the hands of an experienced user. A theodolite is an excellent surveyor's tool that measures angles in both planes simultaneously. Although it cannot be used on a boat, because it requires a stable base, it can give definite positions from shore once its location is established to known landmarks (Dean et al. 1992:118–119). Being optical tools, the sextant and theodolite also rely on line-of-sight operation and require accurate charts.

Technological advances have now produced electronic survey tools of great use to the archaeologist. Although more expensive than low-technology methods and requiring more maintenance, electronic survey tools have significant advantages over optical ones. Most have greater ranges than optical tools and frequently greater accuracy. Electronic systems can also be used with remote-sensing equipment to rapidly gather large amounts of data that can be combined with other digital information for analysis with computers (Dean et al. 1992:120). Of the numerous forms of electronic positioning tools, three are most useful in a marine environment.

The simplest electronic system is the electronic distance measurer (EDM), a line-of-sight tool that uses electromagnetic waves, usually infrared, to measure the distance to a target. EDMs require a stable platform to be effective and are often combined with a theodolite for survey work performed close to shore (Dean et al. 1992:122–123). Handheld models can be employed on a boat but are not as accurate.

A system that uses a similar principle, in a more sophisticated manner, employs microwave shore stations. A mobile distance measuring unit (DMU) reads the radio signals transmitted from three or more stations established on shore in different locations and calculates the distance to each, information by which a computer triangulates position instantaneously (Dean et al. 1992:120–121). Although this system is very accurate and does not rely on line of sight, the equipment is costly and often requires the permission of government agencies to establish stations in areas without public ones. The system must be calibrated daily against a known distance, and the positions of the shore stations must be fixed before the survey begins. Signal problems and atmospheric phenomena can cause range holes, gaps in the positioning data (Dean et al. 1992:121). A DMU can aid in maintaining a planned course and record the vessel's track with a plotter, useful for the systematic coverage of a search area. The rapid collection of information and instantaneous display of accurate navigational data greatly increase the efficiency of a survey (Dean et al. 1992:121–122). A DMU also has a much greater range than the other tools, and shore stations can be placed in locations that are most advantageous.

Perhaps the most popular form of electronic positioning is offered by satellite navigation systems, such as the now ubiquitous global positioning system (GPS), originally established by the U.S. government for military purposes but long available for public use (Dean et al. 1992:123). In these systems, a receiver interrogates signals transmitted by satellites orbiting Earth to calculate its position. GPS has many of the advantages of microwave shore stations, such as instantaneous navigational information and the ability to directly send positioning data to a plotter or computer. It also does not require any setup by the surveyor. Navstar GPS, maintained by the U.S. government, has an almost complete coverage of the world and a virtually unlimited range. The cost of GPS receivers varies with the quality of the units, but they are not overly expensive, and their accuracy and ease of use make them exceptionally fine survey tools.

The advantages offered by GPS have led to their almost complete adoption by the archaeological community. Many boats carry GPS receivers as standard equipment, units that are normally greatly superior to handheld models, and it is one of many features an underwater archaeologist will look for when acquiring a vessel. It is important to note that GPS receivers do not function underwater. Submerged sites are located by markers on the surface of prominent features on the bottom. Objects on the site are then located by relating them to these features.

Search Methods

The goal of most searches is total coverage of a selected area to locate a specific target, to dismiss a region from the search parameters, or to identify targets in a given area (Babits and Tilburg 1998:319–321). However, though total coverage is the ideal, it is impossible to achieve. A visual search that scrutinizes every square meter of an area may still miss objects that are buried or otherwise obscured. A remote-sensing survey may fully cover a region and identify some targets but may miss other important features because of their size or nature. In the end, even the most rigorous searches cannot definitively say that an area is devoid of archaeological materials (Dean et al. 1992:128). They can only report what is found.

Remote-Sensing Searches

Most remote-sensing equipment needs to be employed in straight lines and at level depths to be effective. Changes in course headings and depth skew the data gathered by these systems, particularly with acoustical gear. "Mowing the lawn" is a technique employed to reduce the amount of error introduced to a survey. It refers to a pattern of straight parallel tracks that ensures that good data are gathered. The distance between each parallel track, predetermined by operator and pilot, depends on the size of the target, the coverage desired, and the equipment being used. Total coverage is achieved when there is a sufficient amount of overlap between each track. It can be improved upon by making a few perpendicular tracks over the area to tie the data from the parallel tracks together (Dean et al. 1992:137–139).

At times, it may be desirable to gather data on a target from different angles. In these cases, multiple passes on different tracks are made over the target's position, providing additional data and revealing features that may have been obscured during the original search.

The key to an effective search is good navigation. Almost all remote-sensing equipment can be directly linked to digital navigational data via a computer, with a great deal of compatibility with GPS. Instantaneous navigational data is invaluable in remote-sensing searches, ensuring good coverage and accurate positioning data on targets (Dean et al. 1992:139). Once targets are identified by remote sensing, visual confirmation is required to guarantee that the search has been successful.

Diver Searches

Of the numerous methods for searching with divers, each has advantages and disadvantages in relation to cost, time, coverage, and fixing position. Most can be augmented by using handheld metal detectors to locate artifacts buried in the seabed (Dean et al. 1992:128). All require competent divers with trained eyes and an appropriate search plan.

One method that permits rapid coverage is a towed search, in which the diver is towed by a surface vessel or rides a personal underwater vehicle, such as a diver sled or a wet submersible (Dean et al. 1992:130–132). Large areas can be covered with significantly less fatigue to the diver and at much greater speed. The major problem with towed searches is the difficulty of fixing positions accurately, especially when multiple targets are identified. Also, its effectiveness is limited by visibility and the diver's speed.

Swimming searches allow more intensive reconnaissance of the bottom and make the use of metal detectors more feasible. These searches can be as simple as having a diver swim around a defined area of the seabed or along a prescribed track, navigating by the use of bottom contours, currents, or a submersible compass. Any targets identified are marked by securing to them small floats carried by the diver.

Swimming searches are more efficient when lines are used to guide the search. The simplest use of a line is the circle search, useful in areas with a flat bottom. One end of the line is fixed at a stationary position to form the focus of the circle, and the other end is held by the swimmer. Using the line to remain a constant distance from the focus, the diver can swim in expanding or shrinking concentric circles to cover an area (Dean et al. 1992:134–135). This technique does not require a great deal of setup, and the line will snag on any objects projecting from the seabed, facilitating the discovery of features the diver may not see.

Other swimming searches use straight ground lines to guide the search. In a swimline search a string of divers swims a course parallel to a single ground line, marking targets with small buoys as they are discovered (Dean et al. 1992:132–133). A jackstay search uses two parallel ground lines fixed a distance apart, between which a pair of divers swims along either side of a mobile third line, or stay, running perpendicular to the ground lines in opposite directions. After each pass, the stay is moved along the lines a certain distance and the next pass begins (Dean et al. 1992:133–134). These searches provide effective visual reconnaissance, particularly in shallow, clear water. Difficulties arise in maintaining adequate communications between divers, from limits in time on the bottom, and from bottom topography.

Other patterns, such as a grid search, are rarely used because they involve more setup and greater difficulty for the divers. Such patterns are reserved for tightly defined areas where large sections of the bottom do not need to be covered, for example, around established sites to search for small artifacts and other features moved off-site by currents or surge and to determine if the excavation area should be expanded (Dean et al. 1992:134).

Site Survey

Once an underwater site has been located and identified, the next step in an archeological investigation is a predisturbance survey, just as it is in a terrestrial site. Making an initial site plan is crucial to developing a complete record of a site. Information gathered at the outset of an investigation not only records the original site condition, but also aids in developing excavation strategy and forms the basis of all subsequent recording (Dean et al. 1992:148). The various techniques for developing a site plan can be used singly or in combination, with the methodology at the discretion of the investigator and influenced by the condition of the site, its environment, and the level of accuracy desired (Muckelroy 1980:16–17).

The most basic technique to develop a site plan is to take direct measurements that, when combined with sketches and other survey methods, provide significant detail to a site plan. Direct measurements also serve as a check against errors introduced by other surveying techniques. The basic tools for measuring and orienting features are a tape measure and a compass, and the data gathered can be further enhanced by measuring angles with a goniometer or inclinometer (Dean et al. 1992:155–156). Noting the angles of features in relation to each other, in both the horizontal and vertical planes, provides a site plan with depth and defines specific details, such as hull curvature.

A method for developing an overall site plan uses offset measurements. A baseline is set over a site or to one side, and distances are measured in the horizontal plane at right angles from the baseline at various increments to site features (Dean et al. 1992:163). A plumb bob is employed, reaching from the measuring tape to the feature, to ensure accuracy. Normally two divers are required to perform offsets and, for accurate measurements, both must take care to keep the tape level and at a right angle to the baseline (Dean et al. 1992:163). This method can provide good information about the size, shape, position, and orientation of site features in relation to the baseline. It is a flexible tool that requires minimal setup time, and the baseline can be placed at a height that clears obstructions and projecting features. Measurements can also be taken in the vertical plane

Figure 8.3.   An archaeologist leans over part of a site as he sketches a plan view.

Figure 8.4.   A baseline has been set parallel to the keel on this site. This placement is often favored because it facilitates the drawing and measuring of various components.

with a calibrated plumb-bob line, to measure slopes and hull curvatures.

A technique somewhat easier for the individual taking measurements but requiring a great deal of prior work, is trilateration. A tape and plumb bob, but not a baseline, are again used to take measurements of features in the horizontal plane. Instead, measurements are taken from a minimum of two fixed datum points to each feature, and the distances are used to triangulate their positions (Dean et al. 1992:162). The use of three or more points and additional calculations increases accuracy. The datum points are arrayed in a rough circle around the site, set in positions advantageous to measuring, and their number is determined by the size of the site. Substantial preliminary work is needed to fix the positions of the points in relation to each other (Dean et al. 1992:157–158). Once the datum points are set and measured in relation to each other, measurements can be made quickly by a single diver and a detailed site plan developed with simple mathematics.

Figure 8.5.   The ability to juggle a plumb bob, measuring tape, and writing materials while balanced on a slope is one of the many skills an underwater archaeologist must master.

A system very similar to trilateration is the direct survey method (DSM), which also uses an array of established datum points circling the site and measured to each other so as to fix their positions. Measurements are taken directly from the datum points to the features without a plumb bob, making the diver's work much simpler (Dean et al. 1992:175). Because measurements in DSM include a vertical component, a minimum of three points are used instead of two, and greater accuracy is achieved with four or more points. Normally a computer is used to determine positions from the measurements, using a program to calculate best fit. The operator can manipulate the data to make refinements or to determine if the measurements are in error and need to be repeated (Dean et al. 1992:175–177). DSM generates a three-dimensional plan of a site, with detailed plotting of points on slopes and other differences in depth. Although this technique is limited to line-of-sight measurements and requires as much prior preparation as trilateration, it is highly flexible, quick, and extremely accurate (Dean et al. 1992:178).

A grid is another popular surveying tool, established by dividing the site into quadrants of a chosen size, commonly around 1 m^2. The divisions are marked by various means, ranging from rigid metal tubing fixed over a site to intersecting ropes secured to each other across the site and staked down around its perimeter (Dean et al. 1992:157). The use of a grid makes underwater drafting simple by allowing the diver to focus on a small portion at one time. Each square is given a designation and marked, so that the record of each area can be absorbed into the overall site plan. Each square can be subdivided into smaller quadrants with a planning frame to facilitate the recording of smaller details. For example, a 1-m square can be divided into 100 squares, each 10 × 10 cm, creating a 10 × 10 grid within the square. Clear plastic can be suspended over a square to trace features (Dean et al. 1992:164–166). If stable and rigid, grids provide baselines and datum points from which measurements can be taken. Grids can also guide site photography. However, grids can be very time-consuming to install, and any shifting of the grid because of diver activity or environmental factors can fatally affect its accuracy (Dean et al. 1992:157).

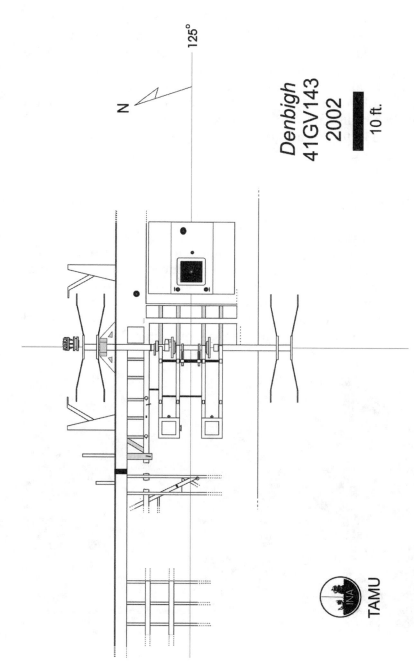

N

125°

Denbigh
41GV143
2002

10 ft.

TAMU

Figure 8.6. This plan of a Civil War steamship was produced with computer software utilizing information from historical studies and archaeological investigations of the wreck.

Underwater photography is another useful means of recording a site. The ability of the diver to hover over a site provides a simple way to photograph a plan view. However, cameras have to be adapted for underwater use, and the photographer must be skilled at taking pictures in submerged environments. With proper equipment and lighting techniques, a photographer with good dive skills can produce an excellent visual record (Dean et al. 1992:183–195). In addition, the images obtained from underwater photography can be quite stunning, and often are useful in education and increasing public awareness (Dean et al. 1992:182).

Conditions in the underwater environment are normally such that an entire site cannot be encompassed in a single photograph. To gain an overall view, the investigator can use photomosaics, overlapping pictures joined to form a single image (Muckelroy 1978:33). These can be produced by means as complex as a photographic tower placed on a rigid grid and as simple as a diver swimming over the site with the camera (Dean et al. 1992:189). The pictures in a photomosaic can be arranged either by hand or digitally on a computer. With computer

Figure 8.7.   Divers use a rigid grid to identify their work areas while hovering over a site.

Figure 8.8. A smaller grid has been employed on a portion of a site so that the archaeologist can produce a more accurate scale drawing.

Figure 8.9. An underwater photographer taking a picture of a site feature.

manipulation, underwater video can also produce photomo-saics. A good final image requires that the photographer main-tain a constant distance over the site and that each photograph provide sufficient overlap to piece it with its neighbors.

These are some of the more common techniques for site recording. Many others can be, and have been, employed on un-derwater sites. Virtually any survey method available to the ar-chaeologist working on land can be adapted for use in submerged environments.

Excavating Underwater

The excavation of a submerged site follows the same basic rules of digs conducted on land and employs similar methods. Arti-facts are exposed and recovered in the same manner, with dili-gence given to protect the objects and record their positions and associations within the site's context. Trenches, boxes, open areas,

Figure 8.10.   A diver using a pipe draped across a site so that he may take a series of photographs at a constant elevation.

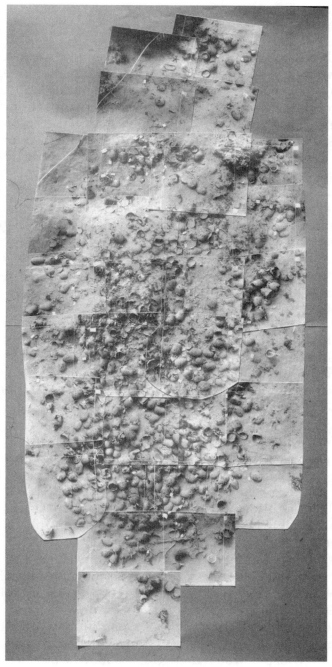

Figure 8.11.   This is a photomosaic of an amphora mound excavated on the coast of Turkey.

and other strategies used on land can be employed underwater effectively to excavate a site (Muckelroy 1978:31). Exceptional care must be taken by the underwater excavator, because physical contact is not required to disturb exposed artifacts in this environment. A diver's movements alone can cause currents that can move or damage fragile objects. However, skilled investigators can excavate a submerged site to the same standards as on land.

The tools for loosening sediment underwater are also the same as those used on land: trowels, brushes, dental picks, knives, hammers, and chisels can all be employed to break up sediments. The most sensitive and useful tool for moving silt around is the diver's hand (Dean et al. 1992:208). Underwater, the archaeologist can gently fan away sediments to expose an artifact with minimal disturbance.

The removal of spoil from a site is where the underwater archaeologist gains a significant advantage. Sediments can be removed in bulk using a shovel and bucket underwater, but this unwieldy method does not take advantage of the environment. Underwater, the archaeologist's bucket and wheelbarrow can be replaced with the airlift and water dredge (Muckelroy 1980:20).

The airlift, a simple device that operates like a vacuum cleaner, consists of a lengthy rigid tube in a vertical or near-vertical position over the area being excavated. As air is injected into the lower end of the tube, the expanding bubbles rising through its length create a suction that draws in water and material behind them, carrying sediments away from the site (Dean et al. 1992:209). The air is usually pumped from the surface by a low-pressure compressor, the size dependent on the depth of the site and the diameter of the airlift (Dean et al. 1992:209–210). Airlifts can be deployed in numerous configurations tailored to the site needs; divers can place the airlift in a position most beneficial to their work, locating the intake near the area of concentration and orienting the discharge to an off-site location.

Although the discharge end of an airlift may project out of the water on a shallow site and still work effectively, it is more common to use a water dredge in shallow water. The water dredge lies horizontally on the seabed and uses water jetted across the mouth of the intake in the direction of the discharge.

Figure 8.12.   Using an airlift, an archaeologist carefully removes sediment from around a cluster of amphorae.

Figure 8.13.   Divers employ a water dredge to remove spoil from a site.

The water must be pumped at a sufficient speed and volume to cause the induction needed for the dredge to work effectively (Dean et al. 1992:211–212). Like an airlift, the dredge can be configured in a number of arrangements, and it is up to the investigator to determine which is appropriate for a site.

Recovering Artifacts

The recovery of artifacts from a submerged site can be difficult, because the removal of sediments may not free an object because of unique processes that can occur in a marine environment. Artifacts are often found in conglomerates, encrustations composed of rock-hard layers of calcium carbonate, marine life, sediments, and corrosion products (Hamilton 1976:4). One of the more frequently encountered is formed by concretions made as iron artifacts deteriorate (Muckelroy 1978:34). These conglomerates must be carefully freed, and large ones with multiple artifacts embedded within them must be judiciously broken into manageable pieces before being raised to the surface, a complex operation where caution must be employed.

Artifacts found on submerged sites are often noteworthy for their high level of preservation. Even iron objects that have completely corroded away have frequently left behind a "ghost," a perfect mold of their features within the concretions formed around them (Muckelroy 1980:178). These exceedingly fragile objects must be handled with great care when brought to the surface. For smaller artifacts, packing in a container with sediments and water surrounding them is sufficient protection during raising and transport (Muckelroy 1978:33). Wrappings, bandages, and other packing materials protect delicate objects. Large artifacts are secured to rigid supports to maintain their shapes, and heavier objects are attached to air-filled containers to make them buoyant during raising (Muckelroy 1978:33–34). More resilient finds can be raised without a great deal of protection, but efforts to conserve them must begin immediately when they reach the surface.

The conservation of recovered artifacts, often the most important aspect of an archaeological investigation, is particularly

Figure 8.14.   Fragile timbers are placed in padded crates before removal to the surface.

so in a marine environment (Muckelroy 1980:180). Conservation preserves the information that artifacts represent, as well as assuring the opportunity for additional study of the original objects in the future. A conservation plan for recovered artifacts is an essential part of any underwater excavation strategy (Hamilton 1976:4).

Although the conservation of waterlogged materials is a distinct science in and of itself, some issues must be addressed by the archaeologist in the field. Because finds are immediately exposed and vulnerable to new destructive elements that prompt decay and chemical changes when brought to the surface, immediate steps must be taken to properly store and protect artifacts. The primary concerns and basic tenets are to keep the objects cool, wet, and out of unnecessary light (Robinson 1998:91).

A conservation workshop in the field is often beneficial, where artifacts are logged, assessed, and placed into temporary storage (Robinson 1998:93). With an archaeological conservator present, a workshop in the field can serve like a hospital emergency

room, appraising the condition of finds, identifying critical artifacts that need special attention, providing initial cleaning and
treatment, and providing suitable stabilization and protection
for shipment to a conservation laboratory (Robinson 1998:92). It
is an elaborate effort, expensive and time-consuming, but gives
results that greatly outweigh the expense in the long run.

Future of Maritime Archaeology

Maritime archaeology has greatly evolved in the past few
decades, as its basis in early classical studies has expanded to
cover all eras and aspects of maritime cultural heritage. Special-
ties in medieval, postmedieval, and New World maritime archaeology have long been established, as have regional studies
in Europe and the Americas. Newer areas of investigation in the
Pacific and Asia have also developed.

Over the years, maritime archaeology has also formalized itself as a discipline. The use of scientific methodology in its practice has been proven, and the techniques and standards by
which a maritime archaeologist operates have been firmly defined. Most importantly, maritime archaeology has gained the
acceptance within the academic community that it vainly sought
during its early years.

What will be the next evolution for maritime archaeology?
Several years ago, researchers used a small robot to explore a region of one of the pyramids at Giza that was inaccessible to humans. Similar technologies are beginning to be employed
underwater. Submersible remotely operated vehicles (ROVs)
and autonomous underwater vehicles (AUVs) have been used
for years to inspect oil rigs, pipelines, and other structures in regions that were too hazardous for divers. These technologies can
be adapted to conduct archaeological investigations. ROVs and
AUVs have already been successfully used to conduct shipwreck surveys in waters too deep for divers. The next step is
proving that they can be employed to conduct an excavation to
archaeological standards. However, the use of these technologies
to do so would exact an exorbitant, if not prohibitive, cost. Only
time will tell if the ends will justify the means, as it has with
divers performing archaeology underwater.

*Figure 8.15.   A diver uses a lift bag to raise a basket filled with artifacts to the sur-
face.*

Acknowledgments

The authors would like to thank the Archives Office of the Institute of Nautical Archaeology for its assistance in the preparation of this work. All images courtesy of the Institute of Nautical Archaeology.

References

Babits, Lawrence E., and Hans Van Tilburg (editors)
1998   *Maritime archaeology: A reader of substantive and theoretical contributions.* Plenum Press, New York.

Bass, George F.
1975   *Archaeology beneath the sea.* Walker, New York.

Brögger, A. W., H. J. Flak, and Haakon Schetelig
1917   *Osebergfundet Utgit av den Norske Stat.* Universitetets Oldsaksamling, Kristiania, Norway.

Cousteau, Jacques-Yves, and Frédéric Dumas
1953   *The silent world.* Harper, New York.

Dean, Martin, Ben Ferrari et al. (editors)
1996   *Archaeology underwater: The NAS guide to principles and practice.* Nautical Archaeology Society and Archetype Publications, London.

Engelhardt, Conrad
1865   *Denmark in the early Iron Age.* Williams and Norgate, London.

Frondeville, Guy de
1956   *Les visiteurs de la mer.* Le Centurion, Paris.

Hamilton, Donny L.
1976   *Conservation of metal objects from underwater sites: A study in methods.* Miscellaneous Papers 4, Publication 1. Memorial Museum and the Texas Antiquities Commission. Austin.

Lyell, Charles
1832   *Principles of geology.* J. Murray, London.

Muckelroy, Keith W.
1978   *Maritime archaeology.* Cambridge University Press, Cambridge.
1980   (editor) *Archaeology under water: An atlas of the World's submerged sites.* McGraw-Hill, New York.

Nicolaysen, Nicolay
1882   *Langskibet fra Gokstad ved Sandefjord.* A. Cammermeyer, Kristiania, Norway.

Robinson, Wendy
 1998 *First aid for underwater finds.* Nautical Archaeology Society and Archetype Publications, London.

Taylor, Joan du Plat (editor)
 1965 *Marine archaeology: Developments during sixty years in the Mediterranean.* Hutchinson, London.

Ucelli, Guido
 1950 *Le navi di Nemi.* La Libreria dello Stato, Rome.

Weinberg, Gladys D., Virginia R. Grace et al.
 1965 *The Antikythera shipwreck reconsidered.* American Philosophical Society, Philadelphia, Pennsylvania.

PART 2

ANALYTIC METHODS

9

Radiocarbon Dating

Paul B. Pettitt

Radiocarbon dating has rightly been referred to as "a godsend to archaeology" (Renfrew 1973) because a little more than a half century ago it truly revolutionized the discipline (Clark in Gillespie 1984) and in doing so "opened a new era" (Wheeler 1958). With the announcement of the first radiocarbon dates in 1949 and the widespread availability of the technique from 1950, archaeologists could for the first time test the accuracy of their stylistically based relative-dating systems. There were many surprises. The origins of agriculture and metallurgy were pushed back considerably, and the antiquity of the European Neolithic, for example, almost doubled overnight, so much so that Stuart Piggott (1959) famously dismissed the first ^{14}C dates for British Neolithic monuments as being "archaeologically inacceptable" because they did not agree with his setting of the beginning of the Neolithic at 2000 B.C. Before the advent of this first chronometric dating technique, no independent means were available for archaeologists to test their seriation-based relative-dating methods. The chronological flexibility that obtained before the 1950s is epitomized by Gordon Childe's famous joke that chronology was like a bellows, that is, it could be expanded or contracted depending on how best it would fit one's theories.

In theory, anything that once lived, anything that exchanged carbon with the biosphere, can be dated with the ^{14}C technique. Materials differ chemically, however, and those that are relatively "open" chemically are more susceptible to contamination, which will affect the resulting age calculation. Contamination is a serious issue and bears on the accuracy of the technique. In addition, many organic materials rarely survive on archaeological sites. Many of the ^{14}C dates that exist today, therefore, have been measured on samples of charcoal, bone, and antler, the most commonly occurring organic material remains. Materials such as wood, parchment (paper), vellum (skin), hair, textiles, shell, and macroscopic seed and plant remains may be dated if recovered. Modern techniques of measurement require very small samples and because of this have opened up the possibility of dating small items, such as lipids found on the surfaces of ceramic vessels, pollen from archaeological sites, and the pigments used in rock art. In addition, they have facilitated the direct dating of precious artifacts, artworks, and religious relics such as the bones of saints and the Shroud of Turin. The greater majority of ^{14}C dates, however, are measured on the prosaic refuse of everyday life—animal bones from past meals and charcoal from hearths.

Since its discovery, it can be broadly said that ^{14}C dating has been through four main developmental phases, which parallel the general way that relative and absolute dating techniques have evolved (Pettitt 2005). We are still in the fourth of these phases.

- *Infancy* (1947–1960). The discovery of the technique and application to archaeological and geologic materials.
- *Refinement* (1960–early 1980s). The discovery that atmospheric production of ^{14}C has not been constant, and first attempts to correct (calibrate) the effects of this using dendrochronology (tree-ring dating). Also, the realization that sampling methods and archaeological concerns are just as important as chemical and physical factors (chronometry), with Waterbolk (1971) publishing date evaluation criteria.
- *AMS developmental* (1983–1990s). Accelerator mass spectrometry (AMS) techniques begin to be used for direct measurement of ^{14}C and open up a new range of samples to the technique in addition to new problems.

- *Frontiers* (1990s–present). Correction by uranium-series dating of corals and flowstones begins to extend beyond dendrochronological curves and demonstrates potential problems with accuracy in the older age range of the technique. Although problems become more apparent, developments in sample pretreatment and measurement facilitate the dating of extremely small and chemically complex samples.

Four main methodological phases in the ^{14}C dating process take the sample from the archaeologist through chemists and physicists to final interpretation, which ideally involves all three. First, samples are selected for dating in the field or during post-excavation analysis. A phase of chemical pretreatment follows, to prepare the sample for the third, measurement, phase. Finally, results are interpreted in the light of the archaeological questions the samples were selected to address. Each phase has potential pitfalls. Before outlining these, a brief consideration of the discovery and early history of the technique is given.

Brief History

Cosmic radiation was discovered in 1911, and during the development of the atomic bomb in the 1940s a weak radioactive isotope in the Earth's biosphere—^{14}C—was known to exist. In 1947 naturally occurring ^{14}C was detected for the first time by E. C. Anderson. He and his PhD supervisor at the University of Chicago, Willard F. Libby, were measuring extremely low levels of radioactivity in living materials, having famously perfected their techniques on methane gas from the Baltimore sewage plant. Because ^{14}C is radioactive it is unstable, and Libby soon realized that the decay of ^{14}C in organic items could be used as a dating technique. This would be possible as long as the ratio of ^{14}C activity in a given sample could be compared with that in contemporary material that was in dynamic equilibrium with the biosphere, that is, the ratio of unstable ^{14}C to stable ^{12}C and ^{13}C remained approximately the same. Libby began to test the new dating method in 1948 and soon after published a major statement on the technique's efficacy and potential (Libby et al. 1949). Proving the reliability and consistency of ^{14}C dating relied on being able to date samples for which an age was known by independent means within acceptable degrees of confidence. Using a half-life of 5568 ± 30 years (see following discussion of principles), Libby and his team could predict the levels of ^{14}C that should remain in samples of known age. Artifacts from the tombs of Egyptian rulers, for which a relatively tight chronology was suspected through artifactual and historical cross-checking, were ideal to test the method. Preserved timbers from tomb architecture and coffins could be used to provide the relatively large-size samples required by the measurement techniques of the day. Initial results, to everyone's elation, proved encouragingly accurate and a golden decade of early measurements ensued. Samples from around the Old and New Worlds for which an age was suspected flooded to the Chicago laboratory, and by the end of the 1940s Libby was publishing date lists, a tradition in the ^{14}C community ever since.

The importance of the technique was grasped immediately by archaeologists. In the editorial to *Antiquity* for September 1949, O. G. S. Crawford headlined the issue with the news that "a discovery has been made in America which may be of the greatest use to archaeologists." Recollecting how he had been told the news, Sir Mortimer Wheeler could barely contain his excitement. "Lord Cherwell, who had just come back from America, told us for the first time of the new radiocarbon method of dating ancient organic substances. . . . I remember how Crawford's eyes lighted up as the conversation proceeded, and how under his breath he whispered 'it's a scoop.' And so it was" (Wheeler 1958).

Soon, the effects of the new dating technique were having considerable impact on prehistoric and historical archaeology, which Renfrew (1973) has referred to as the "First Radiocarbon revolution." Some of the first samples measured at Chicago derived from Near Eastern sites with some of the earliest indications of agriculture in the world. The origins of agriculture were at the time thought to date to around 4500 B.C., or around 6,000 years ago.

Early interest in establishing a radiocarbon dating laboratory was expressed in the British Museum (Bowman 2002), for which planning began in 1949, and other laboratories began measuring ^{14}C dates almost immediately. By the mid-1950s a number of laboratories in Europe and the United States were producing radiocarbon measurements and publishing them routinely. Problems did emerge from the outset, however, notably when ^{14}C dates did not agree at all with the suspected ages of samples derived from historical sources or logical expectation, in particular with the early dynastic period in Egypt. Libby recognized that for some periods ^{14}C measurements and expected ages agreed, for others they were divergent. In 1957 a detailed critique of the method—and in particular its application to European prehistory—was published by Milojčić that pointed out the numerous assumptions necessary for the technique to work and the fact that these had not been tested experimentally. Piggott's own objections surfaced also at this time.

Renfrew (1973) has singled out 1960 as a decisive year in the development of ^{14}C dating, because it saw the publication of a conference's proceedings in which many problems were addressed and a number eliminated (Waterbolk 1960). Here, one enters the refinement phase, in which the scope and limitations of the technique were largely defined. Most importantly, it was recognized at the conference that atmospheric production of ^{14}C had not been constant over time, and had in fact varied with fluctuations in the intensity of the Earth's magnetic field. This seemed to explain the discrepancies that had come to light with the accuracy of the technique. In addition, the contribution of the Suess effect to accuracy (see later discussion on artificial production of ^{14}C) was appreciated. Some presentational conventions had also arisen, notably whether dates should be presented with respect to Christian time (B.C.) or before the present (B.P.).

By 1966 a number of laboratories—but especially in Arizona and La Jolla, California—had measured samples of wood that could be identified to specific tree rings, notably from California bristlecone pines. These were now demonstrating the effects of fluctuating ^{14}C production on dates and permitted calibration, a conversion to calendrical ages at least back to the mid-sixth millennium B.C. The 1970s can be seen as a period of mainly improvements to dendrochronologically based calibration. By the late 1970s AMS techniques began to be used for ^{14}C dating. Although this is a relatively costly means of undertaking dating and only about a dozen laboratories undertake it, industry was rapid and by 1990 an estimated 10,000 AMS ^{14}C dates had been produced (Hedges 1990).

Principles

The chemical and physical principles underlying radiocarbon dating are now well understood (e.g., Gillespie 1984; Aitken 1990; numerous papers in *Radiocarbon*). Carbon occurs in three isotopes of similar chemical properties but each with a different atomic weight—^{12}C, ^{13}C, and ^{14}C. Of these, ^{12}C and ^{13}C are stable, whereas ^{14}C (alternatively, radiocarbon or carbon-14) is unstable because it is radioactive. ^{14}C is the main product of the continual flux of cosmic rays into the Earth's atmosphere. It is created continuously in the upper atmosphere in several ways as neutrons (n) produced by cosmic rays interact with nitrogen atoms. The resulting ^{14}C is radioactive and consequently subject to ultimate decay to the stable ^{14}N. As this decay occurs a beta particle (β) is emitted. The process of creation and decay can be expressed as follows:

$$^{14}N + n \rightarrow\ ^{14}C \rightarrow\ ^{14}N^+ + \beta^-.$$

Because the chemical behavior of ^{14}C is the same as ^{12}C with the exception of its isotopic fractionation (see later discussion) it is incorporated in the global carbon cycle. It combines with oxygen to form CO_2, which mixes with inactive atmospheric carbon and becomes rapidly distributed through the atmosphere. The CO_2 becomes incorporated into the aquatic biosphere through dissolution in water and into the terrestrial biosphere through incorporation into plants through photosynthesis. From there it is transmitted up food chains through feeding organisms, and in this sense we are to a large extent what we eat. Because of this, the stable isotopes of carbon and nitrogen are of use to paleodietary reconstruction as will be seen in the later discussion. Through these routes carbon is mixed through the entirety of the Earth's biosphere and exists at an equilibrium that is maintained through production and decay. During the life of an organism, decayed ^{14}C is constantly replenished, but because this depends on photosynthesis or feeding this exchange ceases with the biological death of an organism. From this point on, decayed ^{14}C will not be replaced, and the process begins to have direct relevance to chronology. The proportion of ^{14}C to stable carbon will decay logarithmically according to the principles of the law of exponential decay. When interpreting ^{14}C dates therefore, it is important to realize that a measurement relates to the time an organism ceased exchanging carbon with the biosphere—the time of its death. A ^{14}C date on a textile, for example, relates to the time at which the plant used to make the textile was harvested, and a measurement of a wooden object dates the time at which the source tree was felled to produce usable timber.

The speed of decay of radioactive isotopes is expressed as the *half-life,* which is the amount of time in which half the radioactive atoms present in a given molecule disappear, as in the case of ^{14}C back to ^{14}N. Libby originally estimated the half-life of ^{14}C to be 5568 ± 30 years. This is known as the "Libby half-life." Soon, however, it became apparent that he had underestimated this by approximately 3 percent, and the half-life is now known to be approximately 5730 years. Because radiocarbon dates had been produced and published before this realization, for consistency the discipline has retained the use of the old (and incorrect) Libby half-life, and laboratories simply correct for the error (by multiplying the old half-life by 1.03) when calibrating raw dates. Figure 9.1 plots the amounts of remaining ^{14}C in a sample by half-life. By about nine half-lives, the remaining ^{14}C is approximately 0.19 percent of its original abundance, making it difficult to separate from background ^{14}C. Thus the age limit of the technique is about 55,000 years (see later discussion of measurement methods). Early promises of the AMS technique to extend this limit back perhaps to 60,000 years or more have not been realized and the useful limits are essentially fixed at this point.

Fortunately, the ratios of the two stable and one unstable isotopes of carbon remain constant. In any given carbon molecule, about 99 percent will be ^{12}C, about 1 percent will be ^{13}C, and about 1×10^{-12}, or one in a million million atoms, will be ^{14}C. Because of this, and because decay occurs according to the principles

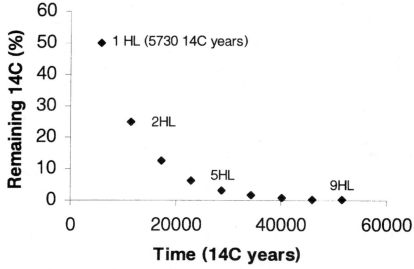

Figure 9.1. *Decay of 14C over time, expressed as percentage 14C remaining. HL = half life.*

of a known physical law, it follows that, by predicting the original amounts of ^{14}C in a sample from its known levels of stable carbon and by measuring the amounts of ^{14}C remaining, the amount of ^{14}C that has decayed can be ascertained. Because this decay occurs at a rate that is stable, at least in the long term, a date can therefore be calculated. The decay process can be expressed as follows:

$$R = A\exp(-T/8033),$$

where R is the measured ratio of $^{14}C/^{12}C$ in the sample, A is the original ratio of $^{14}C/^{12}C$ in the living organism, T is the amount of time that has passed since the organism's death, and 8033 is the average age of a ^{14}C atom as computed from the half-life. Thus the age of a sample is

$$T = 8033 \ln (R/A).$$

Although the rationale of the technique is straightforward, a number of problems affect its accuracy. One of the major assumptions in the early days of ^{14}C dating was that cosmic ray flux, and therefore ^{14}C production, had been constant. It was discovered early on in the method's infancy that this was not so, and that accuracy was a potentially major issue. That it is a continued concern today is discussed later.

Selection of Samples for Dating

Considerable thought has to be put into the selection of samples appropriate for dating. The technique is costly, and in particular, demonstrating a clear and meaningful relationship between the sample dated and the archaeological event for which the date is sought is crucial. For older periods, demonstrating that a sample pertains to human activity may be an issue. Bones bearing stone-tool cut marks are particularly useful in this light, especially with the AMS technique (see later discussion). Seeds of a particular cultivar or bones of a specific domesticate may be dated directly, providing unambiguous evidence for agriculture and animal husbandry. Charcoal may be sampled from within clear hearths or from features such as pits or occupation spreads. In addition, specific items, perhaps those of typological or other value, can be dated directly. Because AMS samples are relatively small, chemical pretreatment of these can be more rigorous than that used for conventional ^{14}C dating, enabling greater confidence of removing contamination.

Concern should be given to maximize the information return for each sample selected for dating. For example, a reindeer bone bearing the engraved depiction of a horse will date human activity at the site, the existence of reindeer in the region, and perhaps even an artistic style. Dating charcoal from a hearth will date not only the human activity but the presence of whatever species it came from in the region.

Although in ideal circumstances archaeologists will have a variety of samples available for which information return will be maximized, in reality the specific samples submitted for ^{14}C dating will typically reflect a compromise among (1) the archaeological questions being addressed by a dating project, (2) the available organic materials on site that pertain to these, and (3) issues of what precious artifacts may be sampled and how much material may be removed from them. As archaeological materials are a finite resource, destruction should be kept to a minimum and sampling should be sympathetic to the needs of other scholars both now and in the future. In particular, landmarks on bone should be avoided, particularly those that facilitate identification or are important in determining the sex, age, or reconstruction of stature in animals. Concern should also be given to how samples might be displayed in the future, and sampling should be undertaken from a location that will probably not be visible. For example, human remains are usually displayed extended and supine or, if they originated in burials, in the burial position. Drilling from natural breaks or on the back (posterior) parts of long bones should be invisible when the sample is displayed in these cases. The sampling of human bone should, without exception, be undertaken with due concern for all these issues and with respect.

When storing samples for dating, care should be given to protecting the sample and to avoiding potential contamination. Ideally, samples should be wrapped in aluminum foil or housed in glass containers such as Wheaton vials. Carbon-bearing materials such as tissue paper should not come into direct contact with the samples. When preparing very small samples, gelatin capsules should be particularly avoided. Whatever storage and protection medium is used, this should be placed in a sealed plastic bag and clearly labeled. Plastic containers are acceptable, although they do contain carbon: it is recommended that samples stored in these be wrapped in foil first. Samples should be identified as closely as possible, ideally to genus, but at least to family. For wood or charcoal samples such an identification would demonstrate whether an old-wood effect (see later discussion of interpretation) might pertain.

Preparing Samples for ^{14}C Dating

Pretreatment, the means by which ^{14}C is isolated in samples, extraneous materials and contaminants removed, and the sample made into a form appropriate for measurement, is a crucial stage of the dating process. Without rigorous chemical procedures, technicians would not understand the nature of the samples they are dating, and consequently interpretation of resulting dates would be impossible because it would not be clear and beyond reasonable doubt that the carbon date pertains only to the death of the organism concerned.

Samples for AMS ^{14}C dating are typically in the order of 500 mg or less. The amount of sample required does vary by material, and Table 9.1 notes the typical required sizes for the most commonly dated materials for AMS measurement. Samples that are wet upon submission to radiocarbon laboratories will need to be of considerably larger size because much of their weight will be water. For samples of bone, antler, and ivory, all essentially chemically similar, the sample may be removed as a lump, for example, from a natural break, but the preferred means of removal is by drilling. Although any anatomical element may be used, the dense cannon bone in midshaft regions of long bones is best, because trabecular bone will contain sediment and potentially more contamination and, as a result of its open nature, material will need to be removed over a larger area causing more visible damage to the bone than necessary. By contrast, small, discrete holes can be drilled into cannon bone, ideally at locations that are not anatomical landmarks or will not be visible when the object is put on display. Needless to say, a process of

Table 9.1. Average (Optimum) and Lowest-Limit Sample Sizes Required for AMS Radiocarbon Measurement

Material	Weight (mg)	Lowest Limit (mg)
Bone, antler, ivory	500	100
Charcoal	20	5
Bulk peat, dry	40	20
Peat, wet	80	40
Plant macrofossils, wood	40	20
Shell carbonates	25–30	10
Paper, parchment	20	10

Source: Courtesy of Dr. Tom Higham, Oxford radiocarbon accelerator unit.
Note: Optimum and limit sample sizes vary depending on quality of preservation and pretreatment methods. These numbers give a reliable indication of the general size ranges.

consultation among museum curators responsible for samples, radiocarbon specialists, and the archaeologist submitting the sample for dating is a crucial first step of this process.

After the sample for dating has been removed from its parent object, it undergoes chemical treatment designed to remove superfluous elements (such as the mineral component in bone) and contamination sources of carbon. The exact treatment a sample undergoes and the chemicals used will vary by material. Ivory, for example, is tough and requires strong acid; charcoal on the other hand would be destroyed if anything other than weak dilute acid were used. For bone, acid (typically HCl) is used to demineralize the sample, reducing it to collagen, the bulk carbon desired for dating. Following this, the sample is washed in alkali to remove humic acids the sample may have taken up from its burial environment. The purified collagen is then heated to convert it to gelatin and freeze-dried to facilitate combustion to turn it to CO_2. Combustion occurs above 1,000°C in a flash-combustion oven. Part of the resulting gas will then be bled off into a conventional mass spectrometer to measure its stable isotopes of carbon and establish whether any contamination remains. With the same rationale that allows the use of stable isotopes in dietary reconstruction (see later discussion on isotopic fractionation), their ratio indicates whether the sample is chemically what it should be. Stable isotope ratios characteristic of marine organisms measured from a human bone could demonstrate, for example, that the individual consumed considerable amounts of marine foodstuffs and a correction for a reservoir effect will be necessary. Conversely, they may indicate that a fish-based consolidant to preservative applied to the bone has not been successfully removed and is therefore contaminating the sample. If samples look chemically suspicious at this stage, laboratories will fail them or begin pretreatment afresh.

Measurement Methods

The detection or measurement of ^{14}C has always been difficult given that its abundance is only one part in 1×10^{12} parts of atmospheric CO_2. During the infancy of the technique, measurement methods were not advanced enough to detect ^{14}C at such low levels of abundance, so indirect methods of estimating the levels of ^{14}C in samples were necessary. This can be undertaken by measuring the radioactivity of a sample. Because each decay of ^{14}C into ^{14}N produces a beta particle emission, the amount of beta particles will reflect the amount of residual ^{14}C in a sample and therefore the amount of decay that has occurred. The counting of beta particles therefore has formed the mainstay of measurement techniques since the discipline's infancy and is referred to as conventional radiocarbon dating. Although ^{14}C dating by AMS has now become the most common technique, a number of conventional dating laboratories are still in operation.

Two main conventional methods exist for counting beta particles: gas proportional counting and liquid scintillation counting. The former, which was by far the most commonly employed method up to the 1970s, involves the introduction to a counter of the sample as gas (CO_2). The particles are attracted to a wire within the counter carrying a high-voltage charge. As the particles are attracted to the counter, neutralization occurs, which can be detected and registered electronically.

By contrast, liquid scintillation involves the conversion of CO_2 gas into benzene (C_6H_6) and the subsequent mixing of this with a stable (nonradioactive) scintillator that is activated by beta emissions. The resulting light pulses (scintillations) can be counted electronically. The measurement capabilities of both conventional techniques allow the counting of ^{14}C levels low enough to correspond to ages up to approximately 50,000 B.P., that is, approaching nine half-lives.

In 1977 measurement methods used in nuclear research were for the first time applied to ^{14}C dating and became commercial by 1983. AMS enabled the direct counting of carbon atoms for the first time. Because the concentration of ^{14}C is very low, a particle accelerator can assist the measurement process by separating ions that may be confused with ^{14}C before final measurement. The basic principle of AMS is to separate atoms of different atomic weights and thereby facilitate their individual detection and counting. This is possible because atoms will behave in relatively predictable ways when given a charge and accelerated at high speed through a magnetic field. Their differing atomic masses cause each of the three relevant carbon isotopes to accelerate with a different degree of curvature, allowing their separation. Because of its relative sensitivity, AMS detection requires only small samples of carbon, typically less than 3 mg. In some cases, samples as small as 30 μm can be measured and thus archaeological materials up to one-thousandth the size of those required by conventional techniques are suitable. Given this, there are considerable advantages to AMS dating. Small or precious samples that would be mostly destroyed in conventional dating are now datable, and archaeologists can now employ well-informed sample selection strategies in the field that maximize the relevance of samples selected for dating to their specific archaeological concerns. In addition, the wide range of small items available for dating makes it more likely that these will survive on archaeological sites and therefore improves considerably the chances of dating sites on which organic preservation is not good.

To do this, samples are introduced into an ion source as elemental carbon (in the form of graphite) or CO_2 gas. The sample is then bombarded with heavy cesium ions. The effect of this is to produce a negative charge. This is the first step to isolating ^{14}C for detection because it enables a distinction to be made between it and ^{14}N, which does not have a negative charge. Following ionization, the sample is directed into a tightly focused beam moving at high energy (approximately 25 kilo-electron volts [keV]) and high speed. The beam passes the first of two magnets, which selects all ions in the sample with an atomic mass of 14. This facilitates the separation of ^{14}C from superfluous isotopes that will dominate the sample such as ^{12}CH and ^{13}CH. The separation is crucial given the very low numbers of ^{14}C atoms present. After this, the ions are introduced into the particle accelerator and travel toward a terminal operating at approximately 2 megavolts (MV). As they travel into this, their acceleration increases to very high speed, generally around one-tenth the speed of light. In the center of the accelerator is a cloud of gas, usually argon, which acts as a stripper. Because they are traveling at high speed, when they encounter the gas stripper, the molecular ions such as ^{12}CH and ^{13}CH are broken up. This process also affects the carbon ions, by removing four electrons and therefore turning their charge positive. This sudden change of charge has the effect of repulsing them from the central part of the accelerator, and because of this, their energy as they travel through the second half of the accelerator reaches approximately 8 MV. At this point a second magnet is used to select ions with the momentum that is expected of ^{14}C under such conditions, and a specific filter arrests the ions selected by the magnet. Having been filtered out in this way, the ^{14}C ions are introduced into a detector where they are detected as electrical current and their number can be counted directly.

The end result of the AMS technique is to produce counts of ^{12}C, ^{13}C, and ^{14}C. Some of the ^{14}C atoms introduced into the accelerator will be lost, and not all will reach the detector. The same is true for the stable isotopes, ^{12}C and ^{13}C, and the observed deficiencies in these can be used to correct for missing ^{14}C. All measurements of ^{14}C are undertaken relative to two others: a modern reference standard and background levels of ^{14}C. The reference standard is used to comprehend isotopic fluctuation over time, and to control for this, an artificial standard is used. The internationally agreed standard is 95 percent of the $^{14}C/^{12}C$ ratio in oxalic acid prepared by the U.S. National Bureau of Standards. Only this reference standard, formally known as 0.95 NBS oxalic acid, should be used in the calculation of ^{14}C dates.

Background levels of ^{14}C can never be completely eliminated, although the shielding of detection systems and their siting underground certainly removes some of this material. With samples approaching the limitations of the technique, in which levels of ^{14}C are extremely low, it may be difficult to distinguish between these and the background ^{14}C. When this is the case, measurements are expressed as infinite ages, for example, > 50,000 B.P. Interpretation of infinite ages is difficult. In theory the true age of a sample could be older than the stated minimum, and there is no a priori reason to believe that it need lie relatively close to the minimum.

Isotopic Fractionation: Quality Control and Dietary Studies

The general ratio of ^{12}C, ^{13}C, and ^{14}C in carbon molecules, previously given, does not necessarily remain stable, and can vary through a number of processes. The degree of uncertainty in estimating true ages because of this is reflected in relatively coarse precision in certain periods, that is, a large error (see discussion of interpretation). The enrichment or depletion of one carbon isotope relative to the others is known as isotopic fractionation. The stable carbon isotope ratio—$\delta^{13}C$—expresses such variation as the ratio of ^{13}C to ^{12}C against an internationally accepted standard. The standard is Cretaceous carbonate from the Pee Dee belemnite formation in South Carolina, known as PDB. The measurement of the $\delta^{13}C$ is precise, with errors typically about plus or minus 0.3 per mil.

The stable isotope ratio can be used in three ways. First, small corrections to ^{14}C date calculation can be made on the basis of fluctuations from the mean ratio relative to the PDB standard. Secondly, the $\delta^{13}C$ acts as a quality control; if samples fall outside the expected range by material type, fractionation has occurred through the incorporation of foodstuffs from another carbon biome, for example, aquatic foods into the diet of a terrestrial organism or contamination (see later discussion on interpretation). Radiocarbon laboratories should publish the $\delta^{13}C$ ratio for each date, so it is apparent to the reader that the sample falls within the expected range. In addition, it should be made clear that the laboratory concerned has corrected for isotopic fractionation in the age calculation.

Related Issues: Dendrochronology and Stable Isotope Dietary Studies

Early in the history of radiocarbon dating it was realized that radiocarbon measurements would need to be converted to true, calendrical dates. Such a process, generally referred to as calibration, requires an independent means of establishing the age of a particular sample, which can then itself be dated by radiocarbon. Some samples' ages are known through historical information, for example, bones from graves with such information on the headstone, but in prehistory this information is unavailable. Dendrochronology, the dating of felled trees by counting of annual growth rings, was developed before radiocarbon dating, in fact in the early decades of the twentieth century. Tree rings are created in annual growth phases, and the trunk cross section of every tree contains a year-by-year record of growth. Tree rings are not uniform—their thickness varies because of their age, climate, and growing conditions. Sharp climatic events, such as brief cold snaps, produce specific markers, in this case very thin rings reflecting the restricted growth. Given this, it follows that rings in a given tree may be linked to others through matching their sequence, rather as modern bar codes or strands of sequence DNA may be linked. Through this, in theory at least, tree-ring sequences may be correlated back from the present day as far as preserved tree remains allow. Long-lived trees such as the California bristlecone pine (*Pinus aristata* and *P. longaeva*) and oaks preserved in peat bogs (notably in Germany and Ireland) are useful because they minimize the number of individual trees required to link to the earliest possible periods. So far, a continuous dendrochronological sequence is available to about 14,000 years ago.

From the 1960s, the potential of tree-ring dating for calibrating radiocarbon measurement was realized. Samples that had been dated to the nearest year by dendrochronology were dated by radiocarbon. The resulting twinned dates for each of a number of samples could then be plotted, resulting in a calibration curve. From this point on, the curve, nowadays highly precise and full of data points, could be used to find a radiocarbon date, which is its calendrical age range (see later discussion on calibration and correction).

A second related area of increasingly important research involves the stable isotopes of carbon, in addition to nitrogen, that in addition (in the case of carbon) to being crucial for the calculation of a radiocarbon date and to the evaluation of contamination in samples, yield information on past diets. The stable isotopes of carbon (^{12}C and ^{13}C) and nitrogen provide information about protein intake (alone) in two ways. First, the amounts of meat as opposed to vegetal resources that provide protein (nitrogen), and second, the relative contribution of aquatic (marine and riverine) organisms to protein (carbon). $\delta^{13}C$ values measure the relative amounts of marine vs. terrestrial protein in diets, on a sliding scale from totally marine diets (approximately –12 per mil) to totally terrestrial (approximately –21 per mil). In addition, because marine trophic pyramids are longer than terrestrial ones, the $\delta^{15}N$ values—which rise 2–4 per mil per trophic level—will reflect the position of the organism in a trophic pyramid. The combination of the two has been used to demonstrate, for example, significant levels of meat consumption among the Neanderthals (Richards et al. 2000) and a mid–Upper Paleolithic antiquity at least for a broad-spectrum gathering economy in which aquatic resources contributed up to 50 percent of protein intake in Europe (Richards et al. 2001).

Interpretation: Accuracy and Precision

In contrast to all other chronometric dating techniques, at least at present, ^{14}C dating is relatively precise, given that fewer assumptions need to be made for measurements to be turned into dates. Errors are typically in the region of plus or minus 1 percent. However, its accuracy can vary significantly and may be very poor beyond about five half-lives. It is important to distinguish between these two criteria, because by these all chronometric techniques are evaluated. They may be defined as follows (from Gillespie 1984, with modifications):

Accuracy: the closeness of a chronometric age determination to the real age.
Precision: the total chronometric age range the true age should lie within, with a given level of confidence, that is, the size of the error.

A number of factors may affect the accuracy of ^{14}C dates, and some of these are still very problematic. Laboratory measurement techniques determine the precision of a date. The error of a date is a statistical reflection of the uncertainty of the measurement; thus in situations where uncertainty is relatively large, for example, when the amount of carbon available for measurement is very small and counting statistics therefore not good, the error will be relatively large or imprecise. Figure 9.2 uses a dartboard as an analogy to clarify accuracy and precision and illustrate how they interact.

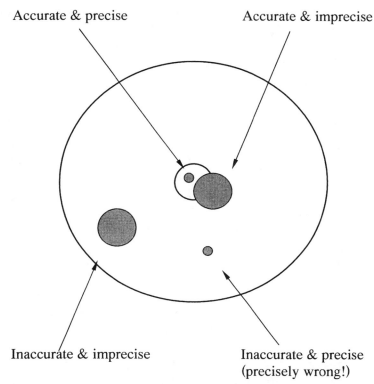

Accurate & precise   Accurate & imprecise

Inaccurate & imprecise   Inaccurate & precise
                            (precisely wrong!)

Figure 9.2. Dartboard analogy for chronometric accuracy and precision. Assume that the real age of a sample is the bull's-eye (open circle). The arrows reflect the dating technique of concern, in this case radiocarbon. The goal of the exercise is to establish the real age of the sample, i.e., hit the bull's-eye. Any arrow that hits part or all of the bull's-eye is accurate. The size of uncertainty of the measurement, in this case the thickness of the arrows, will affect the result. Thin arrows (narrow time ranges) are precise, thick arrows imprecise. Thus it is possible to be accurate but imprecise (thick arrow hitting part of the bull's-eye) or inaccurate but precise (precisely wrong!). Ideally, accurate and precise dates are what chronometrists aim for.

Three phenomena affect the accuracy of ^{14}C dates: changes in the atmospheric production of ^{14}C (cosmogenic variation; previously discussed), differential isotopic fractionation of carbon in certain biotopes (reservoir effects), and extraneous carbon introduced into samples after death (contamination). In addition, the relatively small amounts of ^{14}C in samples older than about six half-lives may cause a clustering of dates around 40,000 B.P. This is known as an asymptotic effect. This is still poorly understood and may have serious effects on our understanding of archaeological events that happened within a few millennia of this time, for example, the colonization of Australia or Europe by anatomically modern humans.

What Is in a ^{14}C Date?

The rate of ^{14}C decay is never constant. To use ^{14}C for dating one must make the assumption that this random process will average out in the long term. Results, therefore, express a deviation from the mean rather than an absolute age estimation and thus ultimately depend on counting statistics. This uncertainty is reflected in the error of a date. Longer counting times produce greater confidence in resulting ages because more atoms are counted and thus reduce the error. This is the rationale of high-precision dating as practiced, for example, at the University of Belfast.

For purposes of presentation and comprehension, dates are expressed as a mean (the correctness of which reflects accuracy) and an error (the precision of the measurement). It is important to remember that this is merely a presentational convention, and there is no necessarily higher probability that the true age of the sample is close to the mean. Errors are expressed at 1 standard deviation (1σ), or a 68 percent chance that the real age of the sample lies within the range of the date. From this it is easy to see that up to one-third of ^{14}C dates will be incorrect at 1σ. To have greater confidence in results, however, dates should be used and compared at 2σ (95 percent confidence), which simply entails doubling the error and taking it into account. For ^{14}C dates that are beyond calibration and correction curves, there are no means of ascertaining where within an age range the real age of a sample is most likely to lie. The correct use of errors and confidence levels can be explored with the following example, using a date measured at Oxford:

OxA-8296 δ^{13}C = –20.5 per mil   29,080 ± 400

The sample dated was from a Neanderthal bone from the site of Vindija, Croatia (Smith et al. 1999). Because the error is to a large extent the function of the mean age, as sample age gets older, the associated error will increase, which explains the relatively coarse precision for this measurement. At 1σ, the age range for this sample in uncalibrated years is 28,680–29,480 B.P., a range of just under one millennium. At 2σ, however, with which one can talk more confidently about the result, the age range increases to 28,280–29,880 B.P., some one and a half millennia. Because there is no currently accepted correction curve for this time period, there is no a priori reason to suspect that the real age of the sample lies at any particular point within this age range. Needless to say, this degree of imprecision has major implications when archaeologists discuss, for example, whether Neanderthals overlapped in time with modern humans.

With sample ages that fall into the range of calibration curves, however, it is often possible to refine the result further and isolate a part of the age range within which the real age is most likely to fall. This relates to the nature of the calibration curve and the best fit of the age measurement with it.

Artificial Production of ^{14}C: Nuclear Bombs and Fossil Fuels

In addition to its natural production in the upper atmosphere, ^{14}C can also be produced artificially, for example, in nuclear reactions. Nuclear power produces some ^{14}C, but monitoring has demonstrated that these levels are too small to have an effect on dating accuracy. The testing of nuclear bombs in the 1950s and 1960s, on the other hand, produced very large amounts of ^{14}C, which do affect the dating of samples in this time range, for example, forensic samples. The amounts of ^{14}C in the atmosphere were almost doubled during this period and have been decreasing steadily ever since. Because of this, the specific levels of ^{14}C activity in samples can be related very specifically to periods in the middle part of the twentieth century, producing a highly precise part of the calibration curve.

The burning of fossil fuels also has a major effect on accuracy, at least from the mid-seventeenth century A.D. to the mid-twentieth. This process releases large amounts of CO_2. Fossil fuels are so old that the ^{14}C they once contained is absent, so they are relatively enriched in ^{12}C and ^{13}C. The net effect is to reduce the ratio of ^{14}C to stable carbon in the atmosphere, the so-called Suess effect, which will cause an overestimation of age.

Calibration and Correction

Changes in atmospheric production of ^{14}C can be considerable. In the period between approximately 25,000 and 60,000 B.P., for example, production levels seem to have been 20–40 percent higher than today. The higher ratio of ^{14}C to ^{12}C will result in considerable underestimation of ages (Duplessy 1996). The rate of underestimation may be as high as 6 ka. Discrepancies can be observed, for example, in the sediments of Lake Suigetsu, Japan, which have been dated by counting varves in addition to ^{14}C (Kitagawa and van der Plicht 1998). The recognition of this fluctuation has understandably led to the desire to correct the accuracy of ^{14}C dates by comparing ^{14}C results with those measured on the same samples using other, independent means. Most commonly, dendrochronological dates have served this purpose, facilitating the construction of *calibration* curves. The rationale behind this is that annual growth rings in long-lived trees can be estimated to exact years as long as tree-ring sequences can be linked to modern ones for which exact years are known. The fluctuation in tree-ring width due to environmental conditions prevailing at the time of growth allows the matching that is required to do this. The use of this technique depends on the survival of trees of useful antiquity, and in addition to the California bristlecone pine, Irish bog oaks and German oak and pine chronologies have been most important. Such curves take us back only as far as tree parts survive, to about 13,000 B.P., yet have produced finely tuned sawtooth calibration curves.

Beyond this, other methods and materials, such as the uranium-series dating of corals and flowstones, take us further back (e.g., Richards and Beck 2001), although such comparisons are in their infancy and it is premature to use these as formal correction curves. Van Andel (1998) has suggested that curves produced by these latter techniques should be referred to as *correction,* to distinguish them from the dendrochronologically based calibration. The current internationally accepted calibration curve is INT-CAL04 (Reimer et al. 2004). Dendrochronologically dated tree-ring samples take this back to 14,500 calendar years before present; and before this data from marine corals and small organisms (forams) take the calibration curve back to around 26,000 calendar years before present. Corals, as with flowstones, are laid down annually and provide the same rationale for use in age correction. Because, however, of the number of assumptions needed when using radiometric dating methods other than ^{14}C (see chapter 10 for other dating methods), the resulting uncertainty is large, with errors typically in the plus or minus 10 percent range. The effect of this imprecision is to produce a much smoother correction curve in which more time is encapsulated in age ranges. At present only two data points exist beyond 24,000 B.P., yet they suggest considerable deviations between calendrical and ^{14}C dating.

Contamination

Contamination is a frequently used term in ^{14}C dating, although like *accuracy* and *precision* it may on occasion be misused. Contamination refers to any carbon that was not an original component of the sample of interest in life. Formally speaking, a sample may be described as contaminated if its $^{14}C/^{12}C$ ratio has changed since deposition by any process other than radioactive decay (Gillespie 1984). Contamination most likely involves the introduction of extraneous carbon into the chemical matrix of the sample and a laboratory's failure to remove it.

In contrast to reservoir effects, which relate to a sample's biotope in life, contamination may be introduced to the sample only after death, either through taphonomic processes in the ground or through the way a sample has been treated after excavation. Typical taphonomic sources of carbon contamination include humic acids—the products of the biological breakdown of plant products—small organic items that may penetrate a sample such as plant rootlets, and carbonates. All of these can be highly mobile in soils and sediments.

Reservoir Effects

The relatively long food chains in aquatic environments will bring about isotopic fractionation and consequently affect ^{14}C

ages. This problem applies to all marine and riverine organisms, perhaps the most pertinent archaeologically speaking being shells. Slower transmission through aquatic biomes results in relatively old carbon, referred to as a *reservoir effect*. The marine reservoir effect is approximately 400 years, but at present the riverine effect is unknown. In addition, individuals whose diet consists partly of aquatic resources will also be subject to a reservoir effect equal to the percentage contribution of the aquatic foodstuff. For example, a ^{14}C date on the bone of a medieval monk who ate fish every Friday would need to be corrected to account for the approximately 14 percent of carbon taken up that includes reservoir carbon. Such correction can be undertaken by combining marine and terrestrial correction curves and calibration and is beyond the scope of this chapter.

Interpretation: Issues of Archaeological Association

Dates serve archaeology, not the other way around, and a date is only as good as the quality and integrity of the samples actually dated and their archaeological relevance. Although such issues of context were readily apparent to Waterbolk four decades ago (1960), they are often ignored by archaeologists, which has resulted in a burgeoning database of dates of dubious value. Only in recent years are archaeologists paying particular attention to these issues of chronometric hygiene (e.g., Spriggs 1989; Pettitt et al. 2003).

To an archaeologist, a date is only as good as its association with the object or event that it is intended to date. The chronometry (i.e., the chemistry and physics used to measure) of a ^{14}C date may be perfectly good, but the date is of little use if it cannot be associated confidently to a relevant archaeological level or feature. In addition, the nature of the sample itself may create problems and alter the accuracy of the measurement, that is, overestimate or underestimate true age. With some wood samples, for example, the problem of age overestimation is an issue. Because dates on wood reflect the age of the tree's felling, it follows that samples taken from the heartwood of long-lived trees such as oak may seriously overestimate the age of construction of wooden items. This *old-wood effect* can overestimate by up to 400 years. To avoid this, either short-lived species should be selected for dating or elements of wood that are known not to have lived very long should be used, for example, twigs and branches.

Sample materials will also vary in their reliability for varying chemical or stratigraphic reasons. Charcoal, although a good sample chemically because it is virtually pure carbon and for which therefore measurement will be relatively easy, may have been highly mobile stratigraphically. Small fragments of charcoal and other substances can move vertically and horizontally in sediments through the action of worms and other burrowing animals and even climatic phenomena such as frost wedging.

Mobile samples may be described as being residual or invasive, respectively causing an overestimation or underestimation of the age of an archaeological level. The action of both is demonstrated in Figure 9.3. It is the archaeologist's task to minimize the chances of submitting either residual or invasive samples for dating. In ideal circumstances, archaeologists will select a variety of sample materials from secure contexts when dating

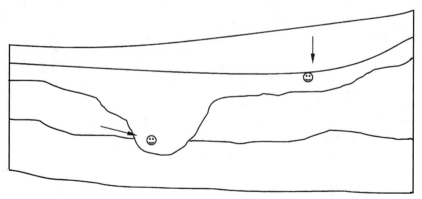

Figure 9.3.   Residual and invasive samples in archaeology. Upper sample to the right is invasive, as it has moved stratigraphically from the upper horizon into the next lower. It will therefore cause an underestimation of this horizon's age. Lower sample to the left is residual, because it has eroded into a pit from a lower horizon. The sample will cause an overestimation of the age of the pit contents. Both samples would be excavated from the same horizon, but resulting age ranges—one an overestimation, one an underestimation—would be very different.

archaeological levels. Identifying samples to genus, and thereby eliminating old wood, or avoiding marine samples are obvious strategies to minimize the risk of stratigraphic mobility while maximizing information return.

The Future

The developmental history of radiocarbon dating follows a logical and cautious extension of its scope from its initial development in the 1950s, calibration from the 1960s and 1970s, and revolutionary change through AMS technology from the 1980s. At the start of the twenty-first century it is at an exciting stage in its development and should certainly not be seen as a static field in which all problems have been overcome or its scope easily defined. It takes us back to around 50,000 years ago and will not take us farther back in time; for earlier ages we depend on various relative-dating techniques and other radiometric techniques that, for the moment at least, have a far poorer precision than radiocarbon (see chapter 10 for other dating techniques). Modern research aimed at extending the process of correction of radiocarbon measurements (termed *calibration* if using tree rings, *correction* when using other dating techniques) to 50,000 B.P. is in progress. This will bring about the exciting possibility of using real calendrical dates for the Upper Paleolithic and later part of the Middle Paleolithic, which will allow the direct comparison of archaeological data to climate as reflected by the calendrically dated ice cores and deep-sea cores. Such studies are, however, also revealing significant problems beyond 30,000 B.P., such as large plateaus probably caused by extraterrestrial phenomena, such as supernovas, and changes in the Earth's orbit, axis, and wobble. The recognition of problems during a frontier phase is not surprising. Frontiers involve as much learning about barriers and limitations as they do about pushing the scope of techniques. As necessary sample sizes become much smaller and minuscule amounts of carbon are extracted from samples that were never traditionally thought suitable for radiocarbon dating (e.g., iron), specialists learn more about the complex chemistry and physics of old carbon. For a carbon-based life-form, it is fitting that radiocarbon has been critical to our understanding of our own prehistory. As we continue to unlock the secrets of carbon in circulation today, and that still contained in the remains of people, animals, and plants that once lived, there are certainly more surprises in store.

References

Aitken, M. J.
   1990   *Science Based Dating in Archaeology.* Longman, London.

Bowman, S.
   2002   Radiocarbon dating at the British Museum—the end of an era. *Antiquity* 76:56–61.

Duplessy, J.-C.
   1996   Chronology problems in Stage 3. Paper presented to the conference on Palaeoclimatology and palaeoceanography of Europe and the North Atlantic between 60,000 and 25,000 BP (Oxygen Isotope Stage 3). University of Cambridge, Godwin Institute for Quaternary research, July 1996.

Gillespie, R.
   1984   *Radiocarbon User's Handbook.* Oxford University Committee for Archaeology Monograph 3, Oxford.

Hedges, R. E. M.
   1990   A review of the application of AMS-^{14}C dating to archaeology. *Nuclear Instruments and Methods in Physics Research* B52:428–432.

Kitagawa, H., and J. van der Plicht
   1998   Atmospheric radiocarbon calibration to 45,000 yr BP: Late Glacial fluctuations and cosmogenic isotope production. *Science* 279:1187–1190.

Libby, W. F., E. C. Anderson, and J. R. Arnold
   1949   Age determination by radiocarbon content: Worldwide assay of natural radiocarbons. *Science* 109:227–228.

Pettitt, P. B.
   2005   Relative and absolute dating. In *Archaeology: The Key Concepts,* edited by C. Renfrew and P. Bahn. Fitzroy Dearborn, London, in press.

Pettitt, P. B., Davies, S. W. G., Gamble, C. S. and Richards, M. B.
   (2003)   Palaeolithic radiocarbon chronology: quantifying our confidence beyond two half-lives. *Journal of Archaeological Science* 30:1685–1693.

Piggott, S.
   1959   The radiocarbon date from Durrington Walls. *Antiquity* 33, 289.

Reimer, Paula J.; Baillie, Mike G.L.; Bard, Edouard; Bayliss, Alex; Beck, J Warren; Bertrand, Chanda J.H.; Blackwell, Paul G.; Buck, Caitlin E.; Burr, George S.; Cutler, Kirsten B.; Damon, Paul E.; Edwards, R Lawrence; Fairbanks, Richard G.; Friedrich, Michael; Guilderson, Thomas P.; Hogg, Alan G.; Hughen, Konrad A.; Kromer, Bernd; McCormac, Gerry; Manning, Sturt; Ramsey, Christopher Bronk; Reimer, Ron W.; Remmele, Sabine; Southon, John R.; Stuiver, Minze; Talamo, Sahra; Taylor, F.W.; van der Plicht, Johannes; Weyhenmeyer, Constanze E. (2004) IntCal04 Terrestrial Radiocarbon Age Calibration, 0–26 Cal Kyr BP *Radiocarbon* 46(3):1029–58.

Renfrew, C.
1973   *Before Civilisation: The Radiocarbon revolution and Prehistoric Europe.* Jonathan Cape, London.

Richards, D. A., and J. W. Beck
2001   Dramatic shifts in atmospheric radiocarbon during the Last Glacial period. *Antiquity* 75:482–485.

Richards, M. P., P. B. Pettitt, M. C. Stiner, and E. Trinkaus
2001   Stable isotope evidence for increasing dietary breadth in the European mid Upper Palaeolithic. *Proceedings of the National Academy of Sciences USA* 98(11):6528–32.

Richards, M. P., P. B. Pettitt, E. Trinkaus, F. H. Smith, M. Paunovic, and I. Karavanic
2000   Neanderthal diet at Vindija and Neanderthal predation: The evidence from stable isotopes. *Proceedings of the National Academy of Sciences USA* 97(13):7663–6.

Smith, F. H., E. Trinkaus, P. B. Pettitt, I. Karavanic, and M. Paunovic
1999   Direct radiocarbon dates for Vindija G1 and Velika Pecina Late Pleistocene human remains. *Proceedings of the National Academy of Sciences USA* 96:12281–12286.

Spriggs, M.
1989   The dating of the island southeast Asian Neolithic: An attempt at chronometric hygiene and linguistic correlation. *Antiquity* 63:587–613.

Van Andel, T.
1998   Middle and Upper Palaeolithic environments and the calibration of ^{14}C dates beyond 10,000 BP. *Antiquity* 72:26–33.

Waterbolk, H. T.
1960   The 1959 carbon-14 symposium at Groningen. *Antiquity,* 34:s 14–18.
1971   Working with radiocarbon dates. *Proceedings of the Prehistoric Society* 37:15–33.

Wheeler, M.
1958   Crawford and *Antiquity. Antiquity* 32:4.

10

Other Dating Techniques

Alistair W. G. Pike
Paul B. Pettitt

Time is a continuum that humans generally see as a succession of events. In archaeology our points of reference are those events that we see as marking some kind of change in human behavior. Change is therefore a chronological landmark for the archaeologist: it permits us to divide time into discrete and understandable temporal segments, or periods, such as the Bronze Age. Such periods are often seen as having no significant change within them and are therefore often treated as synchronic segments, or periods in which all temporal points are regarded as contemporaneous. In this sense our understanding of the human past is analogous to geology, whereby certain strata mark changes in depositional activity that can be correlated from site to site, and therefore dating in archaeology helps us to establish regional cultural stratigraphies.

Regrettably, the methods of dating available to archaeologists, at least at present, limit the precision with which time can be estimated and segmented. Many dating methods require measurements and observations that can never be exact. Our observations, therefore, usually have an uncertainty associated with them, and there will always be uncertainties on any date calculation. This is expressed as an error, and the greater the uncertainties, the larger the error. The magnitude of these vary from technique to technique. Some techniques require the estimation of processes that are generally unknown or unknowable, further increasing the uncertainty of a date. For example, the water content of sediment averaged over long times affects a luminescence date; likewise, the average temperature must be estimated to calculate a date from measurements of amino acid racemization in shells. Some methods even require assuming the physical processes on which the calculated date entirely depends, for example, rates of uranium uptake for uranium-series (U-series) dating of bones and teeth (see later discussion). Because the uncertainty associated with such assumptions is rarely quantifiable, it is rarely possible to express this as an error. This is a question of accuracy rather than precision (see chapter 9 for an explanation of these concepts). Our assumptions can on occasion be inappropriate, and the resulting date therefore inaccurate, irrespective of the precision associated with it.

Even when we can be fairly confident that dates are accurate, the resulting imprecision may, when read at 95 percent confidence (2σ), be itself limiting. The main problem is how useful imprecise dates are to archaeological inquiry, and scholars have to ask questions of their data that can be met by the chronological resolution available to them. The precision of dating African Plio-Pleistocene sites (i.e., the period 1.5–2.5 million years before the present [B.P.]) by paleomagnetism and potassium-argon (K-Ar) dating, for example, means that they can be dated only to within 100,000 years of each other, requiring an assumption, if the dates overlap within error, that they are contemporary before they can be compared and then interpreted (Stern 1993). Such circumstances need to be reconciled with exceptionally well preserved sites where, for example, knapping scatters may represent only 15 minutes of activity, and an understanding of the different sources of information contained in these data is necessary to reconstruct early human behavior (Gamble 1996, 1999). At the other extreme, in complex societies it may be that no period can be treated as a stationary state, and attempts must therefore be made to subdivide these into ever-smaller subperiods, for example, Early, Middle, and Late Bronze Age. Here, chronometric dating meets archaeologically based periodizations based on typological changes in artifacts over time, for example, pottery seriation. With dating, therefore, we generally can possess only windows of limited and varying opacity and size, which produce a restricted view of the fluctuating pace of behavioral change.

Dating: What It Addresses and How It Developed

All dating objectives fall into three main types: periodization, determination of relative age, and absolute (chronometric) dating. The earliest uses of dating therefore amounted to the recognition of basic periods, for example, Roman, on the basis of historical information or similarities in material culture across space. The use of simple stratigraphic observations, such as those of the eighteenth-century British antiquarian William Stukeley, enabled the ordering of periods in time, for example, pre-Roman, Roman, and medieval. By the mid-nineteenth century this resulted in the Three Age System of Christian Thomsen, a broadly applicable scheme of successive stone, bronze, and iron ages. By the 1860s, a flurry of excavations in Europe revealed that these periods were themselves divisible into subperiods, and this relative development resulted in the Stone Age being subdivided into an Old Stone Age (Paleolithic) and a New Stone Age (Neolithic) (Lubbock 1865). Archaeologists were preoccupied with establishing regional chronologies throughout the nineteenth and early twentieth centuries. It was realized by the early nineteenth century that some artifacts and documents inherently contained chronological information, such as coinage or Egyptian King Lists. The presence of artifacts attributable to regional periods was used ingeniously to establish schemes for cultures in which such did not exist, notably the European Iron Age (using Roman coinage) or civilizations of the Aegean Bronze Age (using Egyptian imports). Where artifacts with inherent chronological information were unavailable, artifact seriation produced many schemes that still have currency today, for example, that of Flinders Petrie for the Egyptian Predynastic.

Through the nineteenth century, geologists were radically transforming our understanding of the antiquity of the Earth and the processes that shaped it. Planets usually have a variety of climatic and environmental phenomena operating at differing scales, from small-scale repetitive phenomena such as Earth's days and seasons to the larger-scale fluctuations in ice buildup in the Pleistocene. These may be due to the eccentricity of planetary orbits and how they tilt (axis angle) and wobble (precession). In addition to this, changes in planetary geomagnetic fields and planetary albedo will dramatically affect climate and concomitant environments. Geologists were quick to realize the potential of how such changes were recorded in the geologic record. Sir Charles Lyell inferred on the basis of uniformitarianism—the principle that the geologic processes occurring today must have been the same in the past—that the Earth had a considerable antiquity. In the 1880s Albrecht Penck devised a relative-dating scheme for Pleistocene glacial and interglacial cycles on the basis of stratigraphic observations of Bavarian river terraces, which was subsequently expanded elsewhere. Around the same time, the potential of annual depositional layers in lake sediments—varves—was realized, and in the 1930s pollen preserved in such sediments were used to construct relative-dating periods (pollen zones) that are still used today.

Although these relative-dating schemes developed quickly, no appreciation of the real ages of periods before the Roman would be available until the mid-twentieth century. Even the influential prehistorian Gordon Childe famously used different assumptions about the duration of the Neolithic and Bronze Age depending on how best they fitted certain theories (McNairn 1980). Until the mid-nineteenth century, James Ussher's relative-dating scheme for the Earth was a chronological mainstay for most people. This was based on a literal interpretation of the "begats" of Genesis chapter five, resulting in the long-held view that the world was created in 4004 B.C. The emerging geologic observations previously noted, however, challenged this. By the end of the nineteenth century, the recognition of the great antiquity of the Earth and a long period of human prehistory was generally accepted in scientific circles. Regional schemes had been developed and the resulting periods correlated with others with varying degrees of success.

The first archaeological applications of absolute-dating methods—chronometric techniques—came only after World War II, not surprisingly in a period in which research into radioactivity was intensive. The first use of radioactive decay for archaeological dating was radiocarbon, by Willard Libby in the late 1940s and early 1950s (see chapter 9). By the 1960s the principles of radioactive decay and their use for dating were extended to several other radioactive isotopes that considerably lengthened the time range over which they were applicable. The effect was dramatic: in the 1920s the period over which humans evolved was thought to be around 1 million years at most; by the 1960s scholars were routinely dealing with 4 or 5 million years of human history.

Relative Dating

Although relative dating understandably has historical precedence over chronometry, it should not be thought of as the "poor relative" of absolute methods. On the contrary, some relative-dating methods form today the backbone of Quaternary science, such as biostratigraphy, and new developments rely on it to provide a global chronological scheme, i.e., oxygen isotope stratigraphy. Much dating in archaeology relies on the correlation of multiple and independent sources of chronological information, from coins, pottery styles, and tombstone inscriptions for Roman sites to biostratigraphic, paleomagnetic, and chronometric data for human evolution. Ideally then, current research emphasizes the interrelation between diverse data sets so as to minimize potential error. These sources conflict from time to time and often relate to the assumptions one has to make for chronometry (see previous discussion).

Amino Acid Racemization and Aminostratigraphy

Amino acids, the building blocks of protein in living beings, exist in two distinct forms, L-enantiomer and D-enantiomer. During the formation of tissue (i.e., during the development of an organism) only the L-enantiomer is present, and slowly this converts to the D-enantiomer form until an approximately 50:50 equilibrium is reached at which point the amino acid is said to be racemic. The processes of conversion are known as racemization or epimerization (e.g., Bowen 1978; Lowe and Walker 1984; Aitken 1990).

Ratios of L- to D-enantiomers can be used to correlate strata at different sites and thereby arrange them into relative-dating schemes. This is the rationale of aminostratigraphy, and it has been successfully used to construct regional chronological schemes such as that for the British Middle Pleistocene (Figure 10.1). In theory, amino acid measurements can be made on any sample materials that contain proteins, although in practice measurement is usually restricted to those samples that trap the proteins in hard carbonate skeletons. For this reason, shell is particularly appropriate and benefits from additional biostratigraphic information on the mollusks themselves. There are pitfalls that render the technique problematic. Because racemization is affected by temperature, it must be assumed that temperature has remained constant since the time of deposition of the measured sample. This will clearly not have been the case through the glacial and interglacial cycles of the Pleistocene. Because of this, attempts have been made to correct (calibrate) the technique using radiocarbon dating. Samples within the range of the radiocarbon method are dated, and with this resulting

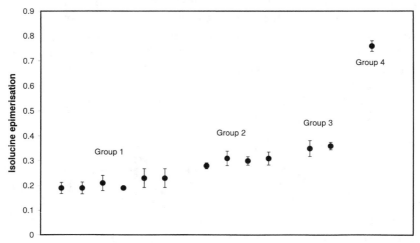

Figure 10.1. Aminostratigraphy (isoleucine epimerization) of British Middle Pleistocene Corbicula fluminalis according to Miller et al. (1979). Group 1, youngest sites (left to right): Aveley, Stutton, Crayford, Clacton, Ilford, Shoeburyness. Group 2: Clapton, Grays, Swanscombe, Stoke Newington. Group 3: Purfleet A, Purfleet B. Group 4, the oldest site: Wangford.

known age, the racemization rate is calculated. This rate is then applied to calculate dates for older samples from the same site, those out of radiocarbon range. This still, of course, requires the assumption that the temperature over the last 20,000 to 30,000 years is representative of the temperature over the entire time span of the site. The technique has produced various controversial results. For example, the racemization dates of > 40,000 years period for the initial colonization of the Americas were later revised to just 5,000 years (Bada et al. 1984), and results of the technique are rarely accepted without additional corroborative evidence.

Oxygen Isotope Record

The study of deep-sea sediments has revolutionized our understanding of Quaternary climatic change (Shackleton 1967). This is because ocean sediments usually preserve a continuous record of sedimentation, rather than the discontinuous, partial record characteristic of land-based data (e.g., Bowen 1978). The process involves examining the oxygen isotopic composition of microorganisms recovered from deep-sea sediments called foraminifera. The ratio of ^{16}O and ^{18}O in foraminifera reflects the ratio of oxygen isotopes in the oceans at the time of deposition. Glacial and polar ice are preferentially enriched in ^{16}O; thus the larger the polar ice caps, the greater the amount of ^{16}O incorporated and therefore the more depleted the oceans. Thus in glacial periods ocean surface waters become enriched in ^{18}O, implying a smaller ocean volume with water locked up as polar ice. The reverse occurs in warmer periods: lowered ^{18}O levels relative to ^{16}O in foraminifera imply larger oceans and smaller masses of polar ice. The ratios of these isotopes are expressed relative to an international standard—the Pee Dee belemnite (PDB) formation identical to that used for radiocarbon (see chapter 9). The resulting $\delta^{18}O$ fluctuates over time (i.e., throughout a core sample) and its levels reveal periods in which the oceans were relatively small and polar ice relatively large (glacials) and periods in which the reverse obtained (interglacials). Called oxygen isotope stages (OISs; increasingly called marine isotope stages [MISs]), long and shorter cold periods (glacials and stadials, respectively) are given ever numbers, longer and shorter warm periods (interglacials and interstadials) odd, counting back from OIS, or MIS, 1 (the Holocene). A similar record has now been produced from ice cores drilled through Greenland and Antarctica (e.g., Barnola et al. 1987; Leuenberger et al. 1992; Petit et al. 1999; Johnsen et al. 2001). The ice and deep-sea cores are increasingly revealing unstable, high-amplitude (marked change in brief periods) shifts in climate during the Pleistocene (Figure 10.2).

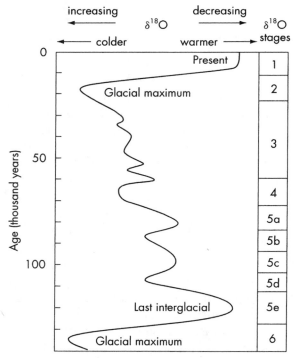

Figure 10.2.   The oxygen isotope record preserved in ice cores and deep-sea sediments shows fluctuations in δ¹⁸O indicative of warm (interglacial and interstadial) and cool (glacial and stadial) conditions. The climatic fluctuations are divided into isotope stages: warm periods with an even number, cold periods with odd numbers. (From The Great Ice Age: Climate Change and Life, by R. C. L. Wilson et al., figure 4.3, Taylor and Francis, 2000).

Paleomagnetism

The rotation of the liquid core of the Earth has a dynamo effect that generates the Earth's magnetic field. Fluctuations in the dynamo effect can cause variations in the strength of the magnetic field, the position of magnetic north, and even a reversal of the north and south magnetic poles. Sediments containing magnetic minerals such as volcanic tuffs preserve a record of the paleomagnetic properties of the Earth at the time of their deposition, and like oxygen isotope cores, have been used to build up a long relative-dating scheme of paleomagnetic data. Of particular importance are the reversal events where the Earth's dipole flips, and the magnetic north pole becomes the south pole. From about 730,000 B.P. to about 2.5 million B.P. the Earth's magnetic polarity was reversed in the so-called Matuyama reversed chron. Within this and our current normal-polarity chron (the Brunhes), short periods of reversal define subchrons, for example, the Blake (104,000–117,000 B.P.) and Olduvai (1.67–1.87 million B.P.) reversals. On sites where no additional dating is available, the identification of sediments formed during a period of reversed polarity provides a broad estimate of their age. For larger sequences of sediment that witness several reversals, more precise dates can be provided. For example, a stratigraphic sequence of sediments at Koobi Fora, Kenya, with reversed–normal–reversed polarity, allowed the Olduvai subchron to be identified, which dated the *Homo ergaster* fossils within the sediments at 1.7 to 1.8 million years old (McDougal et al. 1985).

A related technique that can provide absolute dates for the last few millennia is archaeomagnetic dating. The effective position of the magnetic north is continually changing without necessarily reversing. This phenomenon has been used to provide archaeomagnetic dates for the last few thousand years. At a point on the Earth's surface, the position of the effective magnetic north pole is defined by the angle of dip (inclination) of the magnetic force lines—the angle of intersection of these lines with the Earth's surface—and the angle of declination, the angle between true North (axis of spin) and magnetic north. Magnetic materials align to the direction of the Earth's magnetic field and if undisturbed will preserve this signal. This effect is especially pronounced if the materials are fired (e.g., in kilns or hearths). The direction of remnant magnetism in samples carefully removed from the walls of kilns can be compared to reference curves. Local effects may cause variation in the Earth's magnetic field from region to region, so a reference curve is necessary for a particular region to calculate a date. The reference curves are constructed from known-age (usually radiocarbon dated) samples or, for more recent periods, historical records of the position of the geomagnetic pole.

This method was used on a series of iron-smelting furnaces at the site of Crawcwellt West in Wales. Magnetic dating indicated that the furnaces were last fired between 250 and 50 B.C., or wholly within the Iron Age (Crew 1989). It is rare, however, to find a site where no other dateable material is available and archaeomagnetic dating must be solely relied upon.

Biostratigraphy

Since Georges Cuvier demonstrated that certain animals had become extinct in the past and others had appeared, the potential of animal bones for relative dating has been appreciated by prehistorians. In the nineteenth century the French prehistorian Gabriel de Mortillet constructed a relative-dating scheme of successive epochs that were defined by the dominant fauna of the time, for example, the reindeer age. Mammalian biostratigraphy forms a crucial underpinning to the dating of Plio-Pleistocene sites, and has on occasion played a role in refining chronometric techniques such as K-Ar dating did with the KBS-tuff controversy (see later discussion of K-Ar dating). The rationale behind biostratigraphy is that evolutionary grades of animals will have an inherent relative chronology. If, for example, a line of pigs evolved over time from type A (the earliest) through B to C (the latest) one might infer that sites with pigs of type C are younger than those with pigs of type A or B. Entire suites of mammals can be used in this way, particularly African pigs and bovids that went through considerable evolutionary diversification in the Pliocene-Pleistocene. Small animals are of particular use for the Pleistocene, because their generations are short and consequently they evolve relatively rapidly. The water vole has been important in dating the British Lower Paleolithic site of Boxgrove to around 500,000 B.P. In the Middle Pleistocene the water vole evolved from an early form with rooted teeth (*Mimomys savini*) to the extant water vole with unrooted teeth (*Arvicola terrestris cantiana*). The transition to the latter occurred about 500,000 B.P. in northern Europe; thus the dominance of unrooted forms at Boxgrove alongside a residual 20 percent with root development clearly places the site close to this time (Roberts and Parfitt 1997).

In addition to evolutionary changes within distinct animal lines, the fluctuating climatic conditions of the Pleistocene brought about unique associations of animal species. Glacial and interglacial periods can be distinguished on the basis of these associations. The warmth-loving mollusk *Corbicula fluminalis* is, for example, found only in interglacials, and its dating can be further refined by amino acid racemization (see Figure 10.1). In Britain, the presence of the hippopotamus is restricted to the last interglacial (OIS 5e) and forms an important biostratigraphic marker. Subsequent faunal associations are being recognized that distinguish OISs 5, 4, and 3 (Currant and Jacobi 1997).

Radioactivity—Nature's Clock

The majority of chronometric (absolute dating) techniques measure time through the decay of radioactive elements or measure the cumulative effect of radioactivity on certain materials. Radioactivity is a process that operates at the atomic scale. Atoms can be thought of as consisting of a nucleus made up of protons and neutrons surrounded by a shell of electrons. Protons and electrons carry a positive and negative charge, respectively, and in an uncharged atom the number of electrons is equal to the number of protons. The number of protons (and hence also the number of electrons) defines the chemical properties of an element. Nitrogen differs from carbon, for example, in having an additional proton (seven protons to carbon's six, and in its uncharged state seven electrons). Neutrons have no charge and do not affect the chemical properties of an atom but change the mass. Isotopes are atoms of an element that possess similar chemical properties, but they differ in the number of neutrons in the nucleus and hence differ in atomic mass. For example, the three isotopes of carbon, ^{12}C, ^{13}C, and ^{14}C, all have six protons but have six, seven, and eight neutrons, respectively. Note that the atomic mass of each is denoted by the superscript and represents the number of protons and neutrons (e.g., ^{12}C has six protons and six neutrons, which total to equal its atomic mass). ^{12}C and ^{13}C are both stable atomic configurations, but ^{14}C is radioactive.

Radioactive isotopes have a configuration of protons and neutrons in their atomic nucleus that makes them inherently unstable. From this instability there is a probability that the atom will spontaneously decay. For any single atom, decay is seemingly random and unpredictable, but when a large number of atoms are considered together the decay proceeds in a predictable manner. The rate of decay of an isotope is defined by this probability of decay, although the half-life of an isotope is a more convenient number to deal with.

The more atoms of a radioactive isotope present in a sample, the more that will decay in a given time. The half-life of an isotope represents the time taken for half the atoms in a sample to decay. Thus, for radiocarbon, half the original atoms will be left

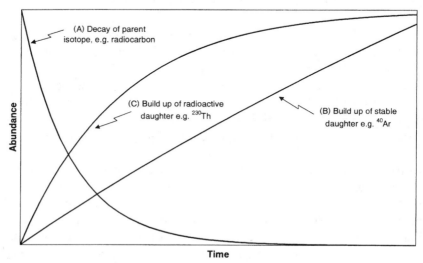

Figure 10.3. Radioactive schemes that can be used for dating.

after 5,730 years, a quarter after 11,460 years, one-eighth after 17,190 years, and so on (see Figure 10.3a). A radiocarbon date can therefore be calculated by measuring the amount of radiocarbon present in the sample today, if the amount of radiocarbon at time zero (the death of the organism) is known. Originally the amount of radiocarbon in a sample at time zero was assumed to be the same for all samples, but later it was realized that radiocarbon production in the atmosphere was not constant and calibration was necessary using dendrochronology (tree-ring dating; see chapter 9). For other radioactive-dating methods it is not necessary to know the initial concentrations of the parent isotope because the daughter isotope (the product of the radioactive decay) can be measured. Whereas radiocarbon dating measures the decay of a radioisotope, K-Ar dating measures the buildup of the decay product of ^{40}K (potassium-40), which is ^{40}Ar (argon-40; Figure 10.3b). Some daughter isotopes are themselves radioactive and can be members of long decay chains. These chains, notably the uranium, actinium, and thorium series (with ^{238}U, ^{235}U, and ^{232}Th as their parent isotopes), have a multitude of dating applications. Chains of radioactive elements eventually reach a state of equilibrium where the decay rate of each member of the chain is the same. Natural processes, however, can remove or isolate a member of the chain and disrupt this equilibrium. Chronological information can be obtained either from the buildup of a daughter isotope or through the decay of a parent isotope that is in excess (Figure 10.3c).

Some dating methods, notably luminescence and electron spin resonance dating, do not measure the parent isotopes or decay products. Instead, they measure the cumulative effect of radioactivity on materials, which is an indirect measure of how much radioactivity a sample has received since it was buried. The sources of radioactivity in an archaeological layer are varied and come from radioactive elements in the sediments and cosmic radiation from space. The pulverized rocks that make up sediments will be of geologic age, and any short-lived radioisotopes will have decayed away leaving only the very long-lived isotopes. The change in radioactivity of these long-lived isotopes (e.g., ^{238}U has a half-life of 4.5 billion years) over the burial time of an archaeological layer will be insignificant, and it is generally assumed that the levels of radioactivity measured today are representative of those of the past.

Radioactivity is a natural process and continues at an immutable rate independent of temperature or chemical reactions. Most materials will contain some natural radioactivity from impurities such as uranium. But for chronologies to be meaningful, the clock has to be set ticking at an archaeologically relevant event (time zero). A flint nodule, if it could be dated, would yield a far older date than the age at which it was picked up and knapped into a hand ax. Many dating methods are constrained, when applied to archaeology, to materials from contexts where a meaningful zeroing event has occurred. For radiocarbon this is the death of an organism, when it ceases to exchange carbon with the atmosphere, but for other techniques it can be more specific. For example, a thermoluminescence signal from flint requires heating to above 450°C to reset the geologic signal (Valladas 1992), and K-Ar dating requires volcanic material that has been heated to even higher temperatures. The possible incomplete resetting of the clock has spawned many dating controversies.

Radioactive decay involves the emission of an alpha particle, a beta particle, or gamma rays. These can be detected and have an energy specific to the isotope decaying. Hence the amount of ^{238}U or ^{235}U in a sample can be measured by counting the number of alpha particles of a specific energy emitted over a given time. But both these elements have long half-lives, so large samples and long counting times are required to give a useful precision on the measurement. In the last 20 years, however, techniques of mass spectrometry allow the direct measurement of many of the radioisotopes, substantially increasing the precision and reducing the sample sizes required.

The basis and applications of each dating technique are discussed in the following sections.

U-Series Dating

Three decay series are of importance in radioactive dating methods: the thorium series (^{232}Th and daughter isotopes), the uranium series (^{238}U and daughter isotopes), and actinium series

(^{235}U and daughter isotopes); see Figure 10.4. The thorium series finds more geologic application (e.g., Ivanovich and Harmon 1982; Henderson and Anderson 2003) and will not be discussed here. The uranium and actinium series, on the other hand, are of more relevance to archaeological chronology with application to the dating of calcium carbonate (speleothem) deposits (e.g., Schwarcz 1980; Edwards et al. 1997; Richards and Dorale 2003),

The uranium series		The actinium series	
Nuclide	*Half-life*	*Nuclide*	*Half-life*
^{238}U	**4.47 x 10^9 yrs**	^{235}U	**7.04 x 10^8 yrs**
^{234}Th	24.1 days	^{231}Th	1.1 days
^{234}Pa	6.69 hours	^{231}Pa	**3.28 x 10^4 yrs**
^{234}U	**2.54 x 10^5 yrs**	^{227}Ac	21.8 yrs
^{230}Th	**7.57 x 10^4 yrs**	^{227}Th	18.7 days
^{226}Ra	1600 yrs	^{223}Fr	22 mins
^{222}Rn	3.8 days	^{223}Ra	11.4 days
^{218}Po	3.0 mins	^{219}At	50 secs
^{218}At	1.6 secs	^{219}Rn	4.0 secs
^{218}Rn	0.035 secs	^{215}Bi	7.7 mins
^{214}Pb	26.9 min	^{215}Po	1.8 x 10^{-3} secs
^{214}Bi	19.7 min	^{215}At	10^{-4} secs
^{214}Po	1.6 x 10^{-4} secs	^{211}Pb	36.1 min
^{210}Tl	1.3 mins	^{211}Bi	2.1 min
^{210}Pb	22.6 yrs	^{211}Po	0.52 secs
^{210}Bi	5.0 days	^{207}Tl	4.8 mins
^{210}Po	138.4 days	^{207}Pb	stable
^{206}Hg	8.2 mins		
^{206}Tl	4.2 ins		
^{206}Pb	stable		

Figure 10.4. The uranium and actinium decay series. The decay chain starts at the top with the parent isotope (e.g., ^{238}U or ^{235}U). Each nuclide decays to the one below it. The long-lived nuclides marked in bold are those used in archaeological dating.

corals and shells (e.g., Bard et al. 1993; Szabo and Rosholt 1969; Edwards et al. 2003), peat (e.g., Vogel 1980), and bone (see later discussion).

If a system is closed to the migration of daughter or parent isotopes (i.e., there is no loss or gain of any of the isotopes in the decay chain), the decay series will build up to radioactive equilibrium such that, for every parent isotope that decays, a daughter isotope decays for all isotopes down the decay series. If this equilibrium is disrupted, for example, by the removal of one of the daughters in the series, gradual ingrowth of the daughter will occur at a predictable rate until equilibrium is once again established. This is the principle behind exploiting the U-series decay chain for dating. A number of processes can cause this disequilibrium, but of primary importance to archaeological materials is the differential solubility of U, Th, and Pa. The difference in solubility leads to a separation of ^{238}U (and also ^{234}U) and ^{235}U from their daughter isotopes ^{230}Th and ^{231}Pa in groundwater. Material precipitated from the groundwater (e.g., the formation of flowstones in caves) will contain the U isotopes but little or no ^{230}Th or ^{231}Pa. Gradually, however, these daughters build up from the decay of their parent isotopes.

Making the closed-system assumption that there has been no gain or loss of the isotopes except through radioactive decay, the time elapsed, t, since the formation of the material can be calculated from a measurement of the isotope activities, for example,

$$\frac{^{230}Th}{^{234}U} = \frac{1 - e^{(-\lambda_{230}t)}}{^{234}U/^{238}U} + \left(1 - \frac{1}{^{234}U/^{238}U}\right)\frac{\lambda_{230}}{\lambda_{230} - \lambda_{234}}(1 - e^{(-(\lambda_{230} - \lambda_{234})t)}).$$

where λ_{23x} is the decay constant for isotope of mass $23x$. Account is made for potential disequilibrium between ^{238}U and ^{234}U, which is usually the case, and it can be seen that if $^{234}U/^{238}U = 1$, the equation simplifies to its first term, which is the form of the $^{231}Pa/^{235}U$ dating equation

$$\frac{^{231}Pa}{^{235}U} = 1 - e^{(-\lambda_{231}t)}.$$

The $^{231}Pa/^{235}U$ ratio is a useful corroboration of a $^{230}Th/^{234}U$ date. Because of the different half-lives of ^{231}Pa and ^{230}Th, any gain or loss of uranium will affect the calculated dates to a different extent. Thus discordance between dates calculated by the two methods is an indication that the system has not remained closed (Cheng et al. 1998). However, ^{231}Pa is difficult to measure with the precision required to identify discordance.

The age limit of the method is defined by the precision of the measurement of the isotope ratios. An infinitely old sample will have a $^{230}Th/^{234}U$ activity of 1, and thus the upper limit for dating is constrained by our ability to differentiate an activity slightly less than this from unity. Early U-series studies measured the isotope ratios by measuring the alpha radiation emitted by their decay. This is a slow and relatively imprecise method, giving perhaps 3 to 5 percent precision. In general, a limit of 350,000 years is cited ($^{230}Th/^{234}U = 0.96$, $^{234}U/^{238}U = 1.0$), but high-precision mass spectrometry has produced dates as old as 500,000 years ($^{230}Th/^{234}U = 0.99$; e.g., Goldstein and Stirling 2003).

Dating of Speleothem Deposits

Calcium carbonate deposits in caves (e.g., stalactites or flowstones, collectively known as speleothem) are an ideal material for U-series dating. Because they precipitate from cave drip water they contain U but no Th or Pa at formation (if no sediment is incorporated). In general they remain a closed system.

In cases where archaeological deposits are interstratified with flowstones, a precise chronology can be produced. At the French cave of La Chaise de Vouthon, one of the phases of Neanderthal occupation was dated to between 98,000 and 102,000 years ago from flowstones immediately above or below the deposit (Blackwell et al. 1992). In most cases, however, only minimum or maximum ages can be provided. For example, a stalagmite found above two hominid phalanges at the Sima de Los Huesos at Atapuerca, Spain, gave dates consistent with the hominids entering the cave more than 350,000 years ago (Bischoff et al. 2002). Similarly, U-series dates from a flowstone above the youngest *H. erectus* fossils at Zhoukoudian I in China revealed them to be older than about 400,000 B.P. (Shen et al.

2001). This is particularly significant because a previous study using U-series dating on bones and teeth had suggested that *H. erectus* from this site and *H. sapiens* from the sites of Dali and Chaou may have been contemporary in China at around 200,000 B.P. (Chen and Yuan 1988).

For U-series dating, about a gram of sample is required, although this depends on the uranium concentration and the age of the sample. Problems may be encountered with the incorporation of detrital thorium, usually from sediment incorporated into the speleothem. The sediment will contain ^{230}Th that, if undetected, can lead to erroneous U-series dates. High levels of common thorium (^{232}Th) in the sample indicate such contamination, and there are methods for subtracting the detrital contribution to the final date (Bischoff and Fitzpatrick 1991).

Dating Teeth and Bones with U Series

Although minimum or maximum ages provided by U-series dates on speleothems above or below cultural deposits have played an important role in providing a chronology for the middle and upper Pleistocene, there are many sites where suitable material is not present or where a minimum or maximum date does little to improve our understanding. Hence attempts have been made to apply U-series dating directly to bones or teeth.

The difficulty is that bones and teeth are not closed systems. They take up uranium from the burial environment that can also be subsequently lost. To calculate a U-series date from measured isotopes, an assumption about U uptake needs to be made. The simplest assumption (the early uptake, or EU, assumption) is an approximation to the closed system assumption. U is assumed to enter the bone shortly after burial, and the bone becomes closed to further migration. An early attempt at U-series dating of teeth and bone used the EU assumption to calculate dates for Neanderthal and modern *H. sapiens* sites in Israel. The results showed that Neanderthals and modern humans were approximately coeval at about 100,000 B.P. As well as demonstrating the great antiquity of modern human occupation in Israel, the results differed from previously held views that the modern human postdated the Neanderthals and the early view that Neanderthals evolved into modern humans (McDermott et al. 1993).

But with further U-series studies on bone there was a gradual realization that the EU assumption was not universally applicable and gave results sometimes greatly at odds with the perceived age of the site (e.g., Szabo et al. 1973; Rae et al. 1989; Michel et al. 2000; Pike and Pettitt 2003). An alternative model was proposed, the linear uptake (LU) model, in which the uranium was taken up at a constant rate. The LU model will produce a date a little more than twice as old as that of the EU model for the same bone (Bischoff et al. 1994). However, this also did not prove to be universally applicable, and there were no independent means to determine which of the two models should be employed for a particular bone.

Recent advances have been made that look set to make U-series dating of bone more reliable. Using a diffusion model of U uptake (Millard and Hedges 1996) that predicts the development of spatial distribution of U and U-series isotopes across a bone section, Pike et al. (2002) were able to show how the U-uptake history of a bone can be reconstructed from measurements of these distributions. Preliminary studies have shown a good agreement between radiocarbon and other control dates and U-series dates calculated by this method.

Luminescence Dating

Radiocarbon, U-series, and K-Ar techniques directly measure radioisotopes or their decay products to obtain age information. But the measurement of the effect of radiation on a sample, rather than the radiation itself, can also provide a date. Luminescence dating measures the changes caused in the crystal lattice of a mineral when it is exposed to natural background radiation. If the annual dose of radiation can be estimated (from on-site measurements) and the total radiation dose received is known, it is a simple matter of dividing one by the other to calculate the age of the sample.

When a sample such as quartz is exposed to radiation, electrons are liberated from the crystal lattice. Some of these free electrons are captured in lattice deficiencies that act as electron traps. The number of trapped electrons thus increases as the material is exposed to radiation over time. When energy is supplied to the lattice, in the form of heat or light, some of these traps evict their electrons. Some of these evicted electrons are conducted to and combine with luminescence centers (impurities in the lattice) and emit light (Figure 10.5). Thus the light emitted is proportional to the number of trapped electrons, which is in turn proportional to the amount of radiation received by the sample, which is in turn proportional to the time elapsed since the traps were last emptied (e.g., Aitken 1990).

The last point is an important one, because many raw materials (e.g., flint) and sediments contain a geologic luminescence signal, and this signal needs to be zeroed at an archaeologically meaningful event for the luminescence date to be meaningful. Heating of flint or the firing of a pot will zero the signal, as will the exposure of sediment to sunlight (although the method of measurement of the luminescence signal will differ between the two).

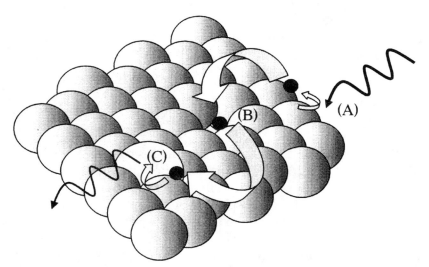

Figure 10.5. Schematic of the luminescence phenomenon. Exposure of the mineral to radiation produces free electrons (a), some of which conduct to electron traps (b). Exposure of the sample to sufficient heat or light evicts the electrons from the traps, some of which will conduct to luminescence centers. The recombination of the electron with the luminescence center (c) emits light that is measured. Thus the measured luminescence is proportional to the number of trapped electrons, which in turn is proportional to the total radiation dose received.

The luminescence signal is measured by applying energy, either by heating the sample in the case of thermoluminescence (TL) dating or in optically stimulated luminescence (OSL); exposing the sample to laser light of a narrow wavelength; and measuring the light emitted as the evicted trapped electrons combine with luminescence centers. The luminescence signal for a given radiation dose will vary from sample to sample, material to material, and even mineral grain to mineral grain, so the sensitivity of the sample is measured by giving increasing doses of a known amount of radiation and measuring the increase in signal (Figure 10.6).

The annual radiation dose has three components. The external dose derives from radioactive elements such as ^{238}U, ^{232}Th, and ^{40}K in the surrounding sediments, the internal dose comes from similar radioactive elements within the sample itself, and a cosmic radiation dose comes from space.

Because gamma radiation reaching the sample may originate as much as 50 cm away from the sample, possibly even from the stratigraphic layers above or below, the gamma dose rate is

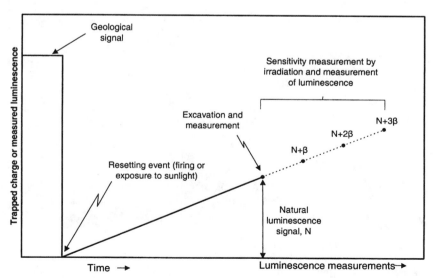

Figure 10.6. Schematic showing the buildup of trapped charge during burial, then measurement of the natural luminescence and sensitivity of the sample by further irradiation.

generally evaluated on site. Portable gamma spectrometers can be used (which can make a measurement in an hour or two), or capsules of minerals with high luminescence sensitivity can be inserted where the sample was removed and left for several months (Figure 10.7). Alpha and beta radiation are less penetrating, and beta doses can be evaluated from laboratory measurement of U, Th, and K concentrations in a sample of the bulk sediment that makes up the burial matrix. For thick samples such as pottery and flint, the internal dose becomes more important than the external dose (because of absorption of the alpha- and beta-dose by the outer 2 mm, which can be removed before dating). In such cases the U, Th, and K concentrations of the sample need to be determined to estimate the dose rate. Because of the need for on-site measurement, samples are gener-

Figure 10.7. Excavated section at Old Scatness Broch, Shetland, United Kingdom, showing sediment samples being removed for OSL dating. Plastic tubes visible in the section have been hammered into the sediments and sealed with lids to prevent exposure to light before being removed. The gamma dose is then measured using a gamma spectrometer placed in the holes left by the samples. (Photo: Jean-Luc Schwenninger)

ally removed by a specialist. It is essential that archaeologists plan their luminescence-dating strategy so that the dating specialist can remove samples and make measurements while the site is still accessible.

The chronological limit of luminescence dating depends on the material dated and the levels of ambient radioactivity that may cause saturation of the electron traps. However, dates as old as 300,000 B.P. are routinely produced, and techniques are being developed that may allow much older samples to be dated (Singarayer et al. 2000).

TL dating has been applied to the dating of burned flint that has been heated to above 450°C (e.g., Valladas 1992). The Middle Paleolithic site of Tabun in Israel has yielded a long sequence of layers containing stone tools, and a near-complete skeleton of a Neanderthal, and a second Neanderthal jaw. Burned flints have provided a chronology for the lower layers to 320,000 B.P., although such material was lacking from the uppermost layers, which may have contained the Neanderthal remains (Mercier et al. 1995; Mercier and Valladas 2003).

Pottery can also be dated by TL, from the luminescence of either the coarse quartz grain inclusions, or sometimes feldspar separated from the body of the pot, or from the fine-grain technique, which dates the polymineral matrix of the clay. OSL dating has recently been applied to pottery that has the advantage of requiring a smaller sample size than TL dating, and in conjunction with TL dating has been used to test the dating of pottery on stylistic grounds (Barnett 2000). The results showed that in general the date assumed on the basis of surface decoration agreed well with luminescence dates, but dates based on fabric type could be significantly in error.

Small grains of quartz and sometimes feldspar are the most common minerals dated in sediments by OSL. The signal is reset (bleached) by exposure to sunlight during transport by wind or water. OSL dating of sediments is finding increasing application to archaeology because suitable sediments are generally more prevalent than burned flints. OSL dating was one of the techniques used to date the deposits that allegedly formed the burial of the Lake Mungo 3 skeleton in Australia. The OSL date of 61,000 ± 2000 B.P., in broad agreement with U-series and electron spin resonance measurements on the skull, backdated the arrival of humans to Australia by about 20,000 years (Thorne et al. 1999). The study generated considerable controversy, in particular revealing one of the weaknesses of OSL dating: the difficulty in some cases of securing the relationship between the datable sediments and the archaeological deposits (e.g., Bowler and Magee 2000). A second study of a more complete sequence of the Lake Mungo sediments obtained a considerably younger date of 40,000 ± 2000 B.P. for the deposits that contained the Lake Mungo 3 burial (Bowler et al. 2003).

Another potential problem with OSL (and TL) dating is the incomplete zeroing of the geologic signal (known as partial resetting). This may have been the case in the Jinmium controversy. An early OSL study dated the artifact-bearing sediments from the Jinmium rockshelter in the far north of Australia at 116,000 to 176,000 B.P., at least 50,000 years older than previously thought (Fullagar et al. 1996). But the technique used by Fullagar et al. measured the luminescence of groups of about 3,000 grains. A later study by Roberts et al. (1999) measured the luminescence of single grains and found a wide distribution of ages for grains from an individual layer, some as young as 10,000 B.P. Their interpretation was that the old date of Fullagar et al. was calculated from the average luminescence of these younger grains mixed with partially reset grains that had fallen off the walls of the rock shelter and retained their geologic luminescence. They conclude that the youngest grains gave the best estimate of the age of the deposits, probably closer to 10,000 B.P. than 100,000 B.P.

More recent deposits have been dated with considerable precision using OSL (Rhodes et al. 2003), and in some cases OSL dates may provide an alternative to radiocarbon dating for young deposits, especially for periods where fluctuations in atmospheric ^{14}C production make calibrated radiocarbon dates imprecise.

Electron Spin Resonance Dating

Electron spin resonance (ESR) dating is related to luminescence dating in that it also measures the effect of ionizing radiation on a crystal lattice. In a classical model, paired electrons in an atom are magnetically neutral, but single electrons have a magnetic moment that arises from their unpaired spin (i.e., they behave like tiny bar magnets). Unpaired free electrons are liberated from the lattice by the effect of ionizing radiation, and these free electrons can be trapped at lattice deficiencies or by impurities. As for luminescence dating, the number of trapped electrons is proportional to the radiation dose received, and this measurement combined with an estimation of the annual radiation dose yields the time elapsed—in most materials dated by ESR—since the formation of the material.

The number of trapped electrons is measured, without eviction from the trap, by their absorption of microwave radiation in a given magnetic field. In simple terms, the energy of the microwave is absorbed when the unpaired electron flips its axis of spin and reverses the direction of its magnetic field. The amount of absorption is proportional to the population of trapped unpaired electrons and hence the total radiation dose received in antiquity. Measurements of the sensitivity of the material to radiation dose are made by exposing the sample to additional radiation and measuring the increase in the ESR signal. An age is calculated simply by dividing the calculated total dose received in antiquity (also known as the equivalent dose) by the estimated annual dose.

There are many materials that exhibit ESR, ranging from organic molecules found in potato chips to silicates in volcanic rocks (e.g., Ikeya 1993), but of most importance to archaeology is the application of ESR dating to tooth enamel.

The measurement of an ESR signal in tooth enamel is relatively straightforward. The enamel is separated from the dentine, and about 50 to 100 µm (0.05–0.1 mm) is ground away from the outer and inner surfaces. The remaining enamel is powdered and placed in the ESR spectrometer. After measurement a portion of the powdered enamel is analyzed for U, Th, and K to calculate the internal dose. The external dose is evaluated in a similar fashion as for luminescence, but determination of the overall dose rate is a little more complex. This is because, in addition to the external dose, the sample receives an internal dose that may be changing over time. Teeth, like bones, take up radioactive uranium from the burial environment, and an ESR date has to be calculated with an assumption for U uptake in both the enamel and the dentine.

The first attempts at accounting for uranium uptake used both the EU and LU models that have been used for U-series dating of bones as previously discussed (e.g., Ikeya 1982). For teeth with low uranium concentrations, there will be little difference between the date calculated using the EU and LU assumptions, but for teeth with high U concentration, the annual dose is dominated by the dose from the migrating U, and the LU date will be up to twice as old as the EU date. Often dates calculated by both uptake assumptions are quoted for a sample, with the implication that these represent the maximum and minimum possible ages.

However, a more sophisticated model of U uptake for ESR dating is increasingly employed. Grün et al. (1988) proposed the p-parameter model to combine ESR and U-series measurements from the same tooth. Because uranium uptake affects both the ESR date and the U-series date, the correct uptake model when applied to both should give the same calculated age. Grün et al. identified a series of uptake regimes defined by the parameter p (figure 10.8). A value of p is found so that U-series and ESR ages calculated for the uptake, defined by p, are in agreement. This model is considerably more flexible than the EU or LU models because it can describe U uptake late in the burial history of a tooth. For example, Grün et al. were able to apply the model to obtain a date of 319,000 ± 38,000 B.P. for a tooth from the British Lower Paleolithic site of Hoxne. This is in general agreement with the biostratigraphic data that places Hoxne in OIS 9 or 11. This should be compared with the U-series dates for the same site, calculated using the EU assumption, of just 27,000 to 56,000 B.P.

The dating limit for ESR is again dependent on the level of background radioactivity, but dates as old as 2 million years have been produced on bovid teeth from the australopithecine site of Sterkfontein in South Africa (Schwarcz et al. 1994). As for luminescence dating, it is better to have a specialist visit the site to remove samples, although some previously excavated museum specimens have been dated by using measurements of U, Th, and K in sediment adhering to the surface of the tooth to evaluate the external dose.

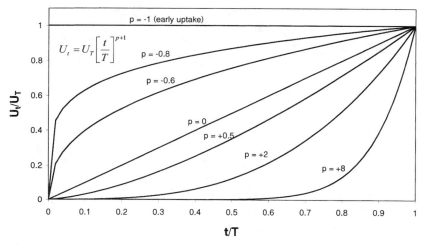

Figure 10.8. *Uranium uptake regimes defined by the p-parameter model. U_t represents the uranium concentration at time t, U_T represents the measured uranium concentration, and T represents the age of the tooth. A value of p is found to give agreement between both the U-series date and the ESR dates calculated using U uptake according to the model.*

ESR dating has been applied to many of the African sites important to the understanding of the origins of modern humans (see summary in Grün and Stringer 1991). For example, an ESR chronology for the complete sequence at Border Cave has been produced, including a direct ESR date on a hominid tooth (Grün and Beaumont 2001; Grün et al. 2003). These results show the Middle Stone Age at Border Cave extends beyond 200,000 BP, and perhaps that modern humans were present as early as 170,000 B.P. Another group of important South African sites are the caves at Klasies River mouth. These have yielded LU ESR dates on teeth associated with modern human remains older than 90,000 B.P. The teeth, however, have high U concentrations, and the EU dates are close to half this value (Grün et al. 1990).

Combined ESR and U-series dating using the *p*-parameter model has provided a chronology for the Middle Paleolithic sequence at Tabun in Israel. Layers B and C date somewhere within 86,000 to 137,000 B.P. and 105,000 to 195,000 B.P., respectively (Grün and Stringer 2000) and are the layers from which the Neanderthal skeleton reputedly came. ESR dates from lower in the sequence are considerably younger than the TL dates on burned flints (Mercier and Valladas 2003), and it is not clear whether the difference is due to problems with the assessment of the annual dose rates for either technique or the luminescence signal not being completely zeroed for the flints.

K-Ar and Ar-Ar Dating

With a half-life of 1.25 billion years, ^{40}K decays to ^{40}Ar. Extreme heating events such as volcanic eruption will drive off the gaseous ^{40}Ar. Subsequent buildup of ^{40}Ar from the decay of ^{40}K allows determination of the time elapsed since heating from measurement of $^{40}K/^{40}Ar$. In the traditional approach, the K content of a sample was measured using techniques such as atomic absorption spectrometry and the ^{40}Ar in a high-resolution gas-source mass spectrometer. Greater precision, however, can be achieved by irradiating the sample in a neutron flux to convert some of the K to ^{39}Ar and measuring $^{39}Ar/^{40}Ar$ in the mass spectrometer.

Single grains of K-rich minerals can be heated with a laser to release the Ar, allowing detection of older contaminating grains. The possibility of contamination of the sample with atmospheric Ar can be identified by measurement of another isotope of argon, ^{36}Ar, which is present in small quantities in the air. An additional complication is identifying whether all the argon was removed during the heating event. The sample can be heated stepwise and the $^{39}Ar/^{40}Ar$ measured at each step. If the $^{39}Ar/^{40}Ar$ is consistent for each fraction of argon released, the age is likely to be reliable. However, if excess argon remained in the sample after the heating event or a subsequent heating event or weathering of the mineral has released some of the argon, the $^{39}Ar/^{40}Ar$ dates for different heating steps are likely to be different.

Archaeological applications of K-Ar dating require volcanic material associated with cultural layers. This limits its application, but there are areas of the world where volcanic activity has been frequent enough to provide archaeologically relevant chronologies. K-Ar measurement on volcanic tuffs within Bed 1 at Olduvai Gorge, Tanzania, provided a date of about 1.8 million years for *Homo habilis* and was also used to calibrate the Olduvai magnetic event (e.g., Evernden and Curtis 1965; Walter et al. 1991). During the early development of the technique, however, initial results overestimated the age of the KBS tuff at Koobi Fora, apparently providing a surprisingly early date of ca. 2.6 million years for the emergence of the genus *Homo*, fossils of which were stratified below the dated KBS tuff. These results were at odds with mammalian biostratigraphy, which instead suggested an age closer to that of Olduvai Bed 1: 1.8 million years. Upon reanalysis the K-Ar results were modified and agreed with the biostratigraphy—a good example that complex scientific techniques are not always right. The KBS-tuff controversy stands as a warning to maximize the number of dating techniques applied to early sites.

The older the sample, the more radiogenic Ar produced in the sample and the easier it is to measure. Given the very long half-life of ^{40}K, the older limit of the technique is beyond the age of the Earth. Of interest to archaeologists is the younger limit of the technique, which can be reached for very K-rich minerals in volcanic deposits. Such minerals were found in pumice that fell on Pompeii, and an $^{40}Ar/^{39}Ar$ date of 1,925 ± 94 years (since 1997) was in impressive agreement with the account of the eruption given in A.D. 79 by Pliny the Younger, or 1,918 years since 1997 (Renne et al. 1997).

This is an exceptional study, but archaeological applications are increasing with the increasing sensitivity of the technique. For example, $^{40}Ar/^{39}Ar$ was used to date anatomically modern *Homo sapiens* fossils from Herto, Ethiopia, to 154,000 to 160,000 B.P. If these dates are reliable, according to current morphological classification, these fossils represent the earliest known examples of modern humans (Clark et al. 2003). Others see the date of 160,000 B.P. as representing only a maximum age for the fossils. The stratigraphic unit directly above the fossils could not be dated because of contamination with older feldspar. So Clark et al. dated a volcanic deposit 500 km away to 154,000 B.P. and inferred on the basis of major and trace element analysis of glass shards that it represented the same volcanic event present at Herto. Faupl et al. (2003), however, reject this "geochemical correlation," stating that similarities in glass composition do not definitely imply the two deposits belong to the same volcanic event but that they simply share similar petrogenic conditions. This debate again reveals the need to ensure stratigraphic integrity for the application of these indirect dating methods.

Conclusion

Currently, a wide range of relative- and absolute-dating methods are available to the archaeologist. Each can be described by its scope and limitations. Some are appropriate for only very specific materials or circumstances, and others have broader application to most archaeological sites. Limitations and pitfalls, which in some circumstances are only beginning to be understood, can lead to erroneous results, that is, inaccuracy. The controversial dates we have outlined in this chapter are examples of this. Thus the archaeologist should be aware of what these limitations might be, and that, just because dating might be scientific, it may not always be correct.

Dating methods are continually evolving. New approaches to existing methods, such as luminescence dating of single grains of sediment or the measurement of radioactive isotopes in extremely small samples using laser ablation, are becoming more routine. In addition to such improvements, which are bringing down the required size of sample, improvements in technology have allowed the rarest of isotopes to be measured, for example, ^{26}Al and ^{10}Be, formed from cosmic radiation. Some of these will form the basis of future dating methods.

References

Aitken, M. J.
  1990   *Science-Based Dating in Archaeology.* Longman, London.

Bada, J. L., R. Gillespie, J. A. J. Gowlett, and R. E. M. Hedges
  1984   Accelerator mass spectrometry radiocarbon ages of amino acid extracts from Californian palaeoindian skeletons. *Nature* 312:442–444.

Bard, E., M. Arnold, R. G. Fairbanks, and B. Hamelin
  1993 ^{230}Th-^{234}U and ^{14}C ages obtained by mass spectrometry on corals. *Radiocarbon* 35:191–199.

Barnett, S. M.
    2000   Luminescence dating of pottery from later prehistoric Britain. *Archaeometry* 42:431–458.

Barnola, J. M., D. Raynaud, Y. S. Kortkevich, and C. Lorius
    1987   Vostok ice core provides 160,000-year record of atmospheric CO_2. *Nature* 329:408–414.

Bischoff, J. L., and J. A. Fitzpatrick
    1991   U-series dating of impure carbonates: An isochron technique using total-sample dissolution. *Geochimica et Cosmochimica Acta* 55:543–554.

Bischoff, J. B., D. D. Shamp, A. Aramburu, J. L. Arsuaga, E. Carbonell, and J. M. Bermudez de Castro
    2002   The Sima de Los Huesos Hominids date to beyond U/Th equilibrium (>350ky) and perhaps to 400–500 ky: New radiometric dates. *Journal of Archaeological Science* 29:275–280.

Bischoff, J. L., R. J. Rosenbauer, A. F. Moench, and T.-L. Ku
    1994   Derivation of age equations for early uptake and linear uptake of uranium by fossil bone. U.S. Geological Survey open-file report 94–628, U.S. Department of the Interior.

Blackwell, B., N. Porat, Schwarcz, H., and A. Debenath
    1992   ESR dating of tooth enamel: Comparison with $^{230}Th/^{234}U$ speleothem dates at La Chaise de Vouthon, France. *Quaternary Science Reviews* 11:231–244.

Bowen, D. Q.
    1978   *Quaternary Geology.* Pergamon, Oxford.

Bowler, J. M., H. Johnston, J. M. Olley, J. R. Prescott, R. G. Roberts, W. Shawcross, and N. Spooner
    2003   New ages for human occupation and climatic change at Lake Mungo, Australia. *Nature* 421:837–840.

Bowler, J. M., and J. W. Magee
    2000   Redating Australia's oldest human remains: A sceptic's view. *Journal of Human Evolution* 38:719–726.

Chen, T., and S. Yuan
    1988   Uranium-series dating of bones and teeth from Chinese Paleolithic sites. *Archaeometry* 30:59–76.

Cheng, H., Lawrence Edwards, R., M. T. Murrell, and T. M. Benjamin
    1998   Uranium-thorium-protactinium dating systematics. *Geochimica et Cosmochimica Acta* 62:3437–3452.

Clark, J. D., Y. Beyene, G. Wolde-Gabriel, W. K. Hart, P. R. Renne, H. Gilbert,
A. Defleur, G. Suwa, S. Katoh, K. Ludwig, J.-R. Boisserie, B. Asfaw, and T. D.
White
    2003   Stratigraphic, chronological and behavioural contexts of Pleis-
tocene Homo Sapiens from Middle Awash, Ethiopia. *Nature*
423:747–752.

Crew, P.
    1989   Excavations at Crawcwellt West, Merioneth, 1986–1989, A prehis-
toric upland iron working settlement. *Archaeology in Wales* 29:11–16.

Currant, A., and R. Jacobi
    1997   Vertebrate faunas of the British Late Pleistocene and the chronology
of human settlement. *Quaternary Newsletter* 82:1–8.

Edwards, R. L., J. H. Cheng, M. T. Murrell, and S. J. Goldstein
    1997   Protactinium-231 dating of carbonates by thermal ionization mass
spectrometry: Implications for Quaternary climate change. *Science*
276:782–786.

Edwards, R. L., C. D. Gallup, and H. Cheng
    2003   Uranium-series dating of marine and lacustrine carbonates. *Reviews
in Mineralogy and Geochemistry* 52:363–405.

Evernden, J. F., and G. H. Curtis
    1965   The potassium-argon dating of Late Cenozoic rocks in East Africa
and Italy. *Current Anthropology* 6:343–385.

Faupl, P., W. Richter, and C. Urbanek
    2003   Dating of the Herto hominid fossils. *Nature* 426:621–622.

Fullagar, R. L. K., D. M. Price, and L. M. Head
    1996   Early human occupation of northern Australia: Jinmium rock-shel-
ter. *Antiquity* 70:751–773.

Gamble, C. S.
    1996   Hominid behaviour in the Middle Pleistocene: An English perspec-
tive. In *The English Palaeolithic Reviewed,* edited by C. S. Gamble and
A. J. Lawson, pp. 63–71. Trust for Wessex Archaeology, Salisbury.
    1999   *The Palaeolithic Societies of Europe.* Cambridge University Press,
Cambridge.

Goldstein, S. J., and C. H. Stirling
    2003   Techniques for measuring uranium-series nuclides, 1992–2002. *Re-
views in Mineralogy and Geochemistry* 52:23–57.

Grün, R., and P. Beaumont
    2001   Border Cave revisited: A revised ESR chronology. *Journal of Human
Evolution* 40:467–482.

Grün, R., P. Beaumont, P. V. Tobias, and S. Eggins
2003 On the age of the Border Cave 5 human mandible. *Journal of Human Evolution* 45:155–167.

Grün, R., H. P. Schwarcz, and J. Chadham
1988 ESR dating of tooth enamel: Coupled correction for U-uptake and U-series disequilibrium. *Nuclear Tracks and Radiation Measurement* 14:237–241.

Grün, R., N. J. Shackleton, and H. J. Deacon
1990 Electron spin resonance dating of tooth enamel from Klasies River Mouth Cave. *Current Anthropology* 31:427–432.

Grün, R., and C. Stringer
2000 Tabun revisited: Revised ESR chronology and new ESR and U-series analyses of dental material from Tabun C1. *Journal of Human Evolution* 39:601–612.

Grün, R., and C. B. Stringer
1991 Electron spin resonance dating and the evolution of modern humans. *Archaeometry* 33:153–199.

Henderson, G. M., and R. F. Anderson
2003 The U-series toolbox for palaeoceanography. *Reviews in Mineralogy and Geochemistry* 52:493–531.

Ikeya, M.
1982 A model of linear uranium accumulation for ESR age of Heidelberg Mauer and Tautavel bones. *Japanese Journal of Applied Physics Letters* 21:690–692.
1993 *New Applications of Electron Spin Resonance, Dating, Dosimetry and Microscopy.* World Scientific Publishing, Singapore.

Ivanovich, M., and R. S. Harmon
1982 *Uranium Series Disequilibrium: Applications to Environmental Problems.* Clarendon Press, Oxford.

Johnsen, S., D. Dahl-Jensen, N. Gundestrup, J. Steffensen, H. Clausen, H. Miller, V. Masson-Delmotte, A. Sveinbjornsdottir, and J. White
2001 Oxygen isotope and palaeotemperature records from six Greenland ice core stations: Camp Century, Dye-3, GRIP, GISP2, Renland and NorthGRIP. *Journal of Quaternary Science* 16(4):299–307.

Leuenberger, M., U. Siegenthaler, and C. C. Langway
1992 Carbon isotope composition of atmospheric CO_2 from an Antarctic ice core. *Nature* 357:488–490.

Lowe, J. J., and M. J. C. Walker
1984 *Reconstructing Quaternary Environments.* Longman, London.

Lubbock, J.
1865   *Pre-Historic Times.* Williams and Norgate, London.

McDermott, F., R. Grün, C. B. Stringer, and C. J. Hawkesworth
1993   Mass-spectrometric U-series dates for Israeli Neanderthal/early hominid sites. *Nature* 363:252–255.

McDougal, I., Davies, T., Maier, R. and Rudowski, R.
1985   Age of the Okote Tuff Complex at Koobi Fora, Kenya. *Nature* 316:793–794.

McNairn, B.
1980   *The Method and Theory of V. Gordon Childe.* Edinburgh: University Press.

Mercier, N., and A. Valladas
2003   Reassessment of TL age estimates of burnt flints from the Palaeolithic site of Tabun Cave, Israel. *Journal of Human Evolution* 45:401–409.

Mercier, N., H. Valladas, J.-L. Reyss, A. Jelinek, L. Meignen, and J.-L. Joron
1995   TL dates of burnt flints from Jelinek's excavations at Tabun and their implications. *Journal of Archaeological Science* 22:495–509.

Michel, V., Y. Yokoyama, C. Falgues, and M. Ivanovich
2000   Problems encountered in the U-Th dating of fossil red deer jaws (bone, dentine, enamel from Lazaret Cave: A comparative study with early chronological data. *Journal of Archaeological Science* 27:327–340.

Millard, A. R., and R. E. M. Hedges
1996   A diffusion-adsorption model of uranium uptake by archaeological bone. *Geochimica et Cosmochimica Acta* 60:2139–2152.

Miller, G. H., J. T. Hollin, J. T. Andrews
1979   Aminostratigraphy of UK Pleistocene deposits. *Nature* 281: 539–543.

Petit, J., J. Jouzel, D. Raynaud, N. Barkov, J-M. Barnola, I. Basile, M. Benders, J. Chappellaz, M. Davis, G. Delaygue, M. Delmotte, V. Kotlyakov, M. Legrand, V. Lipenkov, C. Lorius, L. Pepin, C. Ritz, E. Saltzman, and M. Stievenard
1999   Climate and atmospheric history of the past 420,000 years from the Vostok ice core, Antarctica. *Nature* 399:42936.

Pike, A. W. G., R. E. M. Hedges, and VanCalsteren, P.
2002   U-series dating of bone using the diffusion-adsorption model. *Geochimica et Cosmochimica Acta* 66:4273–4286.

Pike, A. W. G., and P. B. Pettitt
2003   U-series dating and human evolution. *Reviews in Mineralogy and Geochemistry* 52:607–630.

Rae, A., R. E. M. Hedges, and M. Ivanovich
1989 Further studies for uranium-series dating of fossil bones. *Applied Geochemistry* 4:331–337.

Renne, P. R., W. D. Sharp, A. L. Deino. G. Orsi, and L. Civetta
1997 $^{40}Ar/^{39}Ar$ dating into the historical realm: Calibration against Pliny the Younger. *Science* 277:1279–1280.

Rhodes, E. J., C. Bronk-Ramsey, Z. Outram, C. Batt, L. Wilis, S. Dockrill, and J. Bond
2003 Bayesian methods applied to the interpretation of multiple OSL dates: High precision sediment age estimates from Old Scatness Broch excavations, Shetland Isles. Quaternary Science Reviews, 22:1231–1244.

Richards, D. A., and J. A. Dorale
2003 Uranium-series chronology and environmental applications of speleothems. *Reviews in Mineralogy and Geochemistry* 52:407–460.

Roberts, R. G., R. F. Galbraith, J. M. Olley, H. Yoshida, and G. M. Laslett
1999 Optical dating of single and multiple grains of quartz from Jinmium rock shelter, northern Australia: Part II results and implications. *Archaeometry* 41:365–395.

Roberts, M. B., and S. Parfitt
1997 *The Middle Pleistocene Hominid site at ARC Eartham Quarry, Boxgrove, West Sussex, UK.* English Heritage, London.

Schwarcz, H. P.
1980 Absolute age determination of archaeological sites by uranium series dating of travertines. *Archaeometry* 22:3–24.

Schwarcz, H. P., R. Grün, and P. V. Tobias
1994 ESR dating studies of the australopithecine site of Sterkfontein, South Africa. *Journal of Human Evolution* 26:175–181.

Shackleton, N. J.
1967 Oxygen isotope analyses and Pleistocene temperatures reassessed. *Nature* 215:15–17.

Shen, G., T.-L. Ku, H. Cheng, R. L. Edwards, Z. Yuan, and Q. Wang
2001 High-precision U-series dating of Locality 1 at Zhoukoudian, China. *Journal of Human Evolution* 41:679–688.

Singarayer, J., R. M. Bailey, and E. J. Rhodes
2000 Age determination using the slow component of quartz OSL. *Radiation Measurements* 32:873–880.

Stern, N.
1993 The structure of the Lower Pleistocene archaeological record. *Current Anthropology* 34(3):201–225.

Szabo, B. J., and J. N. Rosholt
1969 Uranium-series dating of Pleistocene molluscan shells from southern California—an open system model. *Journal of Geophysical Research* 74:3253–3260.

Szabo, B. J., A. M. Stalker, and C. S. Churcher
1973 Uranium series ages from some quaternary deposits near Medicine Hat, Alberta, Canada. *Canadian Journal of Earth Sciences* 109:1464–1469.

Thorne, A., R. Grün, N. A. Spooner, J. J. Simpson, M. McCulloch, and D. Curnoe
1999 Australia's oldest human remains: Age of the Lake Mungo 3 skeleton. *Journal of Human Evolution* 36:591–612.

Valladas, H.
1992 Thermoluminescence dating of flint. *Quaternary Science Reviews* 11:1–5.

Vogel, J. C.
1980 A new method of dating peat. *South African Journal of Science* 76:557–558.

Walter, R. C., P. C. Manega, R. L. Hay, R. E. Drake, and G. H. Curtis
1991 Laser fusion $^{40}Ar/^{39}Ar$ dating of bed I, Olduvai Gorge, Tanzania. *Nature* 354:145–149.

11

Geographic Information Systems

Mark Gillings
David Wheatley

Much, if not all, of the information that archaeologists set out to interpret is wholly or partially spatial in nature. That information varies in scale and character from the locations of sites within continents to the positions of individual artifacts within excavated contexts. Virtually everything archaeologists are interested in was found somewhere, and through their location in space, archaeological features and artifacts are related to other features of the natural or cultural environment. These are generally not random, but are structured in such a way as to encode meanings that require interpretation. It is therefore not surprising that archaeology has had a long tradition of interest in methods for the analysis and interpretation of explicitly spatial information and that the availability of new technological tools such as geographic information systems (GIS) has had a profound impact on the discipline. Introduced to archaeology in the mid-1980s, GIS have taken less than a decade to become a standard part of the archaeological toolkit. This chapter will briefly outline the historical reasons why this particular technology has become so ubiquitous and then discuss basic forms of analysis that it permits.

GIS in Archaeology and Anthropology

Although cartographic and spatial analysis software first began to be used for archaeological analyses during the 1970s, the use of the integrated set of approaches we now refer to as GIS really began in the early 1980s. GIS appeared first in the United States (e.g., Kvamme 1983a, 1983b) and then slightly later in the United Kingdom (e.g., Harris 1985, 1986), the Netherlands (Wansleeben 1988), and other parts of Europe (e.g., Arroyo-Bishop and Lantada Zarzosa 1995; Biro and Fejes 1995; Blasco et al. 1996; Neustupny 1995). In the United States it was in large part the potential for predictive modeling that initially provided the greatest impetus to its widespread adoption (see papers in Allen et al. 1990; Judge and Sebastian 1988; Westcott and Brandon 2000).

As the potential applications of GIS became more clear and software became more widely available, so the number of applications increased. A number of conferences and seminars resulted in a series of edited volumes with examples of GIS applications and discussions of theory and method (Aldenderfer and Maschner 1996; Allen 1990; Lock and Stancic 1995; Maschner 1996a). Since then there has been a continuing growth in the number of archaeological projects that make use of GIS, to the extent that it would now be difficult to conceive of a regional survey project or spatial modeling exercise that did not. At the same time some debate about the relationship between GIS-based archaeological analyses and wider issues of archaeological theory has also surfaced (Harris and Lock 1995; Wheatley 1993; Wheatley 2000; Wise 2000; Zubrow 1990b), often centered on predictive modeling (Gaffney and van Leusen 1995; Kvamme 1997; Wheatley 1998).

One notable characteristic of the adoption of GIS within archaeology has been the parallel recognition of the importance of the technology by both research archaeologists and cultural resource managers. Considerable impetus was given to the adoption of GIS by archaeologists involved in national or regional archaeological inventories because existing archaeological records were based on a system of maps linked by identifiers to record cards. Many archaeologists found that maps of archaeological remains were an intuitive and useful method of representation, two qualities that were often lost when records were translated into database systems of the then conventional kind. GIS, which offer a map-based representation of site locations as a primary interface, have therefore proved a particularly attractive technology throughout the world (Amores et al. 1999; Boaz and Uleberg 1993; Garcia-Sanjuan and Wheatley 1999; Guillot and Leroy 1995; Harris and Lock 1992; Kincaid 1988; Lock and Harris 1991).

Types of Geographic Information Systems

GIS are computer systems whose main purpose is to store, manipulate, analyze, and present information about geographic space. It is important to understand that a GIS is not a single, monolithic computer program but rather a spatial toolbox made up of different software and hardware-component technologies. As a result of this, software systems that are referred to as GIS are extremely varied, and the boundaries between GIS, remote sensing, computer-aided mapping, and database management are becoming increasingly blurred. Marble (1990) considers that GIS comprise four major subsystems, which we can summarize as follows:

- The *data entry* subsystem handles all of the tasks involved in the translation of raw or partially processed spatial data into an input stream of known and carefully controlled characteristics.
- The *spatial database* (which corresponds to Marble's data storage and retrieval subsystems) is responsible for storing spatial, topological, and attribute information and maintaining links with external database systems.
- The *manipulation and analysis* subsystem takes care of all data transformations and carries out spatial-analysis and modeling functions.
- The *visualization and reporting* subsystem returns the results of queries and analyses to the user in the form of maps and other graphics as well as text.

Today we might add the *user interface*, which although not itself part of the flow of data, is an essential component of a modern GIS because it is through this that users submit instructions to the other subsystems and obtain feedback on the progress of commands.

Many GIS will allow their internal spatial database to be linked to an external database management system (DBMS) so that information stored in the DBMS is made available to the GIS. In turn the GIS can be used to make additions or modifications to the data in the external database. This is especially useful in larger organizations that may already have a substantial investment in their database system and who therefore wish to integrate a GIS into their existing information technology strategy. The visualization and reporting system is frequently bound up closely with the interface to the GIS, because the most intuitive method of interacting with spatial data, and constructing queries, is often simply to point at a visual representation of a map. GIS all provide functions for the creation of on-screen maps, allowing the user to specify which data layers are displayed and how they are to be represented. In addition, many systems provide functions for producing printed maps, Internet-ready graphics files, and alternative methods of representing the data on screen or paper. Manipulation and analysis tools are what give a GIS its unique identity. In more advanced systems, the manipulation and analysis functions will be available directly, and users will also have a programming interface available to automate repetitive sequences of tasks and to write new analysis functions.

Databases for Spatial Data

The central component of a GIS is a database specifically configured to represent geographic space. This must store three distinct components:

- position in geographic space: the *locational* component
- the logical relationships between objects: the *topological* component
- their characteristics: the *attribute* component

To which we might add a description of the contents of the database: the *metadata* component. This is distinct from traditional (nonspatial) databases that are concerned only with the attribute and metadata components and so make no explicit distinction between the location of a stored object (e.g., an archaeological site) and its other attributes (date range, finds, structural evidence, etc.).

Thematic Mapping and Georeferencing

The way that information is classified and stored in a GIS is quite different from a conventional map. Maps contain information relating to many different themes—contours, rivers, communications, boundaries, and the locations of archaeological sites. GIS break this information down into themes and then store and manage each of these as a different theme relating to a particular facet of the region under study. The precise terminology used for these discrete slices of thematic data varies, with some systems using the term *layer* and others *theme, coverage,* or *image.* This form of organization is also unrelated to the way that the theme is represented: themes will usually be either *vector* or *raster* representations of space (see discussion on spatial data models).

The use of thematic layers makes conceptual sense, particularly in the management and organization of data. For the concept to work, however, we have to be able to combine and overlay the individual layers in our database while maintaining the original spatial relationships held between the component features. To ensure that this is so, at the heart of the spatial database is a mechanism whereby every location in each data layer can be matched to a location on the earth's surface and hence to information about the same location in all the other data layers. This makes it possible for the user of the GIS to identify the absolute location of, for example, a pottery density held in a field-walking theme, the limits of a protected archaeological site, a river in an hydrology layer, and any other archaeological or nonarchaeological information within the overall spatial database.

This registering of the spatial locations of features in the individual thematic layers to the surface of the earth relies upon *georeferencing.* This refers to data that have been located in geographic space, their positions being defined by a specified coordinate system. Systems of reference for geographic space can be distinctly *local,* in that they can be used only to correlate a small group of objects, or very *global* if they can be used to represent objects from anywhere in the world. A good example of a local system would be the grid of an archaeological site, and the best example of a truly global system is the WGS84 system of coordinates used by the global positioning system of satellites. Between these two extremes are national or regional map grids that are in turn based on map projections.

Projection refers to the mathematical transformation that is used to translate the three-dimensional reality of a position on the earth's surface into the two-dimensional coordinate system of a map. Such a translation cannot be undertaken without some compromise in such properties as area, shape, distance, and compass bearing. Needless to say, the precise projection used has an important influence on the properties of the map derived from that process. As a result, understanding which projection has been used in the creation of a map is an essential first step in incorporating it into a spatial database. For small study areas, it is sometimes acceptable to ignore projection and to assume that the region of interest on the earth's spherical surface does correspond to a flat two-dimensional plane. However, if the study region is larger than a few kilometers or if information is to be included from maps that have been constructed with different projections, then the GIS needs to understand the projections used for each layer. This is used to georeference the thematic layers held within the overall spatial database and so relate it back to a truly global reference system. Most GISs allow data to be collected in a variety of different coordinate reference systems and then provide mechanisms for each of those systems to be related to a more global system.

Spatial Data Models: Vectors and Rasters

The precise way a given GIS conceptualizes, stores, and manipulates spatial information is referred to as its spatial data model. Although a variety of different conceptual models of space are possible, only two are in common archaeological usage. These are termed *vector* GIS and *raster* GIS. The essential difference is that vector data is a formal description of something in the real world, usually in the form of geometric shapes, whereas raster data comprises a number of samples of something, usually taken at regularly spaced intervals.

In a vector data file (Figure 11.1, left), the information is represented in terms of geometric objects, or primitives. These primitives are defined in terms of their locations and properties within a given coordinate system, or model space. The most common origin of vector data is from digitized maps, where the various features inscribed upon the surface of the paper map are converted into coordinates, strings of coordinates, and area structures, usually using a digitizing tablet. Vector data may permit a complete description of the topological connections between geographical lines and areas using *arc-node topology*, in which case the relationships of (for example) adjacency between administrative units or between roads in a road network can be explicitly represented. However, vector data can be expensive to generate or purchase because it is highly labor intensive to collect them and ensure that they are error free.

Raster data files (Figure 11.1, right) store information as a rectangular matrix of cells, each of which contains a measure-

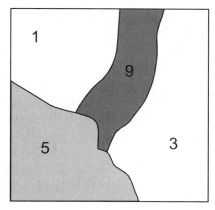

Figure 11.1. Vector (left) and raster (right) forms of representation. In the vector model, the geographic characteristics are modeled as geometric forms, described in terms of points, lines, and areas. In this example, the lines are joined to enclose the areas in what is called arc-node topology. *The raster model simply breaks the geographic area up into equally sized samples—in this case squares—and allocates each square to one of the categories.*

ment that relates to one geographic location. This is a sampling approach to the representation of spatial information: the more samples taken, the closer the representation will be to the original. One widespread form of raster data used in GIS is remotely sensed imagery. In this case, each of the raster cells in the resulting matrix is a measurement of the amount of electromagnetic radiation in a particular waveband that is reflected from a location to the sensor. Raster storage is simple but typically data-intensive unless the storage is at a low resolution or mitigated through the use of compression. Unless the resolution of a data theme is predetermined—for example, the cell samples' derivation from geophysical survey or field walking—then a compromise is necessary between a high resolution, which provides better definition of features, and the decreased storage requirement and processing time offered by lower-resolution representations. Analysis of raster data is relatively straightforward to undertake, although it is more limited than for vector data because the spatial relationships between geographical areas are not explicitly represented.

Many contemporary GIS allow both raster and vector representations of space to be used and provide mechanisms for converting data between the two where that is possible. The choice of representation for any given archaeological project will depend primarily on the purpose for which the data is required: although many tasks can be undertaken with either, many more are better suited to either vector or raster representation. The vector model, much better at working with clearly bounded entities and network-based analyses (e.g., shortest distance between points on a road system), is ideally suited to database-intensive applications such as sites and monuments inventory work. Raster storage tends to require far more data storage because sampling, particularly at higher resolutions, can introduce significant levels of redundant information. Raster data structures, ideally suited to problems that require the routine overlay, comparison, and combination of locations within thematic layers, are essential for storage and analysis of satellite and aerial-photographic data. Additionally, the raster model copes better with data that change continuously across a study area such as elevation, slope, or changing artifact densities in the plow soil (n).

Elevation Modeling

Elevation models—representations of the surface of terrain—are a widespread and useful theme stored within a GIS. They differ from many other forms of spatial data (such as geology and soil maps, political areas, or vegetation maps) in that the latter generally involve discrete variables. An elevation model, on the other hand, represents continuous variation over the land surface. The importance of elevation models to archaeological analysis is that elevation can produce many derivatives. These may include commonly used estimates of slope and aspect but also more sophisticated measures of terrain form that are more directly relevant to human occupation, such as ridge-drainage indices (Kvamme 1992). Elevation models and their derivatives in turn underpin a very wide variety of other analytic methods including the following:

- visualization of topography and of other data in relation to terrain
- cost-distance and least-cost pathway analyses
- predictive modeling for research or management
- analysis of visibility and intervisibility
- simulation of natural processes such as flooding and erosion
- virtual reality and the visual re-creation of archaeological landscapes

Types of Elevation Data and Elevation Models

The simplest form of elevation source data consists of point entities that have height as an attribute. This type of data, a common product of field survey, can be in the form of either regularly spaced points, *gridded point data*, or irregularly spaced points, generally called *spot heights*. On paper maps, terrain is usually represented by *contour lines*, which provide a visual representation of terrain form but in many ways are far from an ideal way of representing terrain. Variation between the contour intervals can be fully represented only by adding supplementary contours or including additional representations of terrain such as break-of-slope lines or spot heights.

The storage of contours in a GIS database presents no new problems that have not already been discussed. Contour lines can be regarded as lines with an attribute corresponding to known height or as nested polygons, again with height as a single attribute. Contour plans can therefore be stored in the same way as many other types of data. However, although contours are easy to store, they do not really constitute an elevation model per se because a contour map does not form a continuous model of the terrain. Contours do commonly form the first stage in the process of generating an elevation model, and predigitized contours are available from a number of mapping agencies.

The most common form of digital elevation model (DEM) involves a regular rectangular grid of altitude measurements in which each cell is assigned its corresponding altitude value, called an *altitude matrix* (Figure 11.2). Many mapping agencies now supply topographic data in this format, including the United States Geological Survey and the Ordnance Survey of Great Britain. Altitude matrices may be generated automatically

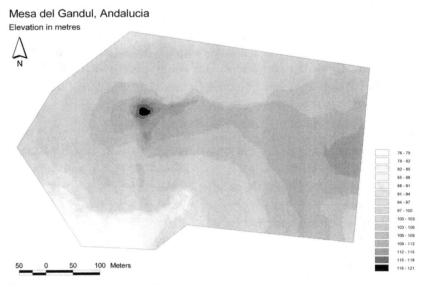

Mesa del Gandul, Andalucia
Elevation in metres

N

50   0   50   100 Meters

76 - 79
79 - 82
82 - 85
85 - 88
88 - 91
91 - 94
94 - 97
97 - 100
100 - 103
103 - 106
106 - 109
109 - 112
112 - 115
115 - 118
118 - 121

Figure 11.2. An altitude matrix: although they are not clearly visible, this map uses a raster representation of elevation in which the individual samples are each allocated their height values. The key on the right shows the heights in meters.

from point data or from digitized contours—a process that is a specific case of *spatial interpolation*. Altitude matrices are the most widely used form of elevation model for the generation of slope maps, aspect maps, analytic hill shading, and for the analysis of visibility, but there are some inherent problems with this type of model, notably that the sampling interval of an altitude matrix is the same for areas of high variability as for very flat areas, usually resulting in considerable data redundancy. This can lead to very large data files and consequently to very slow processing of data. The choice of *resolution* is critical when using elevation data: if the cell size is too small, then the file will be very large, with massive redundancy; conversely, if the cell size is too large, small-scale variations that may be significant will be obscured. With a few notable exceptions (e.g., Hageman and Bennett 2000; Kvamme 1990b), very little attention has been directed in the archaeological literature to the use and derivation of altitude matrices.

An alternative to the altitude matrix is the vector-based triangulated irregular network (TIN) model of elevation (Peucker et al. 1978). This was devised as a flexible and robust method of representing elevation that is more efficient than regular matrices while allowing for the calculation of valuable derivative maps such as slope and aspect. A TIN consists of a sheet of connected triangular faces, usually produced from a Delaunay triangulation of irregularly spaced observation points. TINs can easily be built up from irregular x, y, z point observations, such as those generated by survey work (Figures 11.3, 11.4, 11.5). Unlike regular matrices, this allows TIN models to include higher densities of observations in areas where this is most important—areas of high variability—while using fewer observations for relatively flat areas. Nodes of the TIN can also be arranged so that the model specifically follows ridges or valleys and respects flat areas such as lakes.

Creating Elevation Models from Contours

Altitude matrices and TINs can be created using a variety of spatial interpolation methods (see later discussion), but the most common practice in archaeology and geography has been to

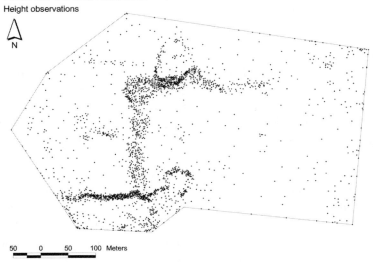

Mesa del Gandul, Andalucia
Height observations

50 0 50 100 Meters

Figure 11.3. TIN creation, step 1. This shows the distribution of observed elevation values on an archaeological site. One of the advantages of TIN modeling over altitude matrices is that the height observations need not be regularly spaced. In this case there are many more observations where the terrain changes rapidly.

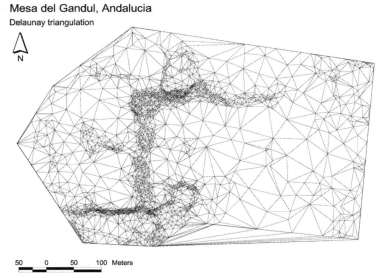

Mesa del Gandul, Andalucia
Delaunay triangulation

50 0 50 100 Meters

Figure 11.4. TIN creation, step 2. The individual observations are connected to form triangles using a Delaunay triangulation.

Mesa del Gandul, Andalucia
TIN with lateral illumination

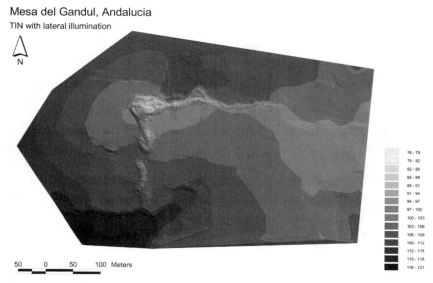

	76 - 79
	79 - 82
	82 - 85
	85 - 88
	88 - 91
	91 - 94
	94 - 97
	97 - 100
	100 - 103
	103 - 106
	106 - 109
	109 - 112
	112 - 115
	115 - 118
	118 - 121

50   0   50   100 Meters

Figure 11.5. TIN creation, step 3. Once created, a TIN can be used in much the same way as an altitude matrix. This illustration shows the model with artificial lighting from one side, showing to good effect the form of the defenses of this Iberian protohistoric and Roman town site.

generate elevation models from contour data. Despite its widespread—and usually rather uncritical—use for archaeological analysis, the generation of regularly spaced height values from contours presents particular problems. Algorithms can take a variety of forms, including very unreliable *horizontal scan* and *vertical scan* algorithms, which scan the contours from left to right or top to bottom, respectively, averaging out the values between known cells. More satisfactory are *steepest ascent* algorithms that search in either four or eight directions from the unknown cell, ensuring that the new value is based only on the contours that produce the steepest slope. Better still are *weighted average* algorithms, which use estimated unknown cells with the average elevation value of nearby locations, weighted for the distance to the source contour lines. Kvamme (1990b) has experimented with a variety of such algorithms and demonstrated the significant differences that can result from the use of the different interpolation algorithms. In many applications, such as the calculation of slope or aspect maps, these effects may produce unacceptably distorted results.

Further considerations arise when vector contours are used as the primary source of elevation data for the generation of a TIN. Although contour data are perhaps the most commonly available source of elevation information, they are also the most difficult to use in TIN creation (ESRI 1997). To create the nodes of the TIN, contour lines have to be regularly sampled to yield a set of points. Most TIN-creation algorithms enable you to specify this sample interval (through specifying *weed* and *proximal* tolerances), and in relatively uniform terrain this may cause few problems. However, when there are complex topographic features, for example, spurs or promontories, there is a good chance that none of these resample points will adequately capture the complexity of the feature and highly significant topographic points are missed. It is therefore important to ensure that any additional topographic data that may be available (for example, spot heights) is incorporated into the TIN-generation process and that, where possible, use is made of *intelligent point selection* algorithms (ESRI 1997).

Products of Elevation Models

Elevation itself can be analytically useful in many situations— we may be interested in the tree line in relation to the position of archaeological sites, or we may wish to estimate or model a hypothetical flood, for example. Alongside these uses elevation data can be used to generate a very large number of *secondary products* that can be even more useful to archaeological analysis.

Calculation of *slope* from altitude matrices is relatively straightforward. Slope can be measured either in degrees (from 0° to 90°) or in percent, in which case 0° is 0 percent and 90° becomes 100 percent. Slope is generally estimated from the geometry of the values in a local neighborhood, which may include four, eight, or more values that may also be weighted. *Aspect* can also be estimated from the geometry of a local neighborhood; it is usually calculated in degrees with either 0° or 360° representing north. It is often reclassified from degrees (or radians) into the eight main compass directions.

One familiar product of elevation models is the analytic shading map. This is closely related to slope and aspect, using both to estimate the intensity of reflected light that would be seen by an observer who was situated perpendicularly above the terrain. Results can be extremely convincing; they are particularly effective when visualized "draped" over a three-dimensional diagram of terrain. These visually attractive products can be very useful for the visual interpretation of landform, because they represent terrain in a way familiar to the eye, allowing subtle features of the terrain—and, it should be added, of artifacts introduced by the interpolation procedures!—to be rapidly picked out.

Another application of elevation models is in hydrological modeling. Modules to undertake simple simulations of hydrological processes are available in several commercial GIS and have obvious applications in archaeology. Most operate by simulating the direction and magnitude of flows in either an altitude matrix or TIN, keeping a cumulated count of the flow of water into and out of each element of the model. More-complex models allow some account to be made of the different characteristics of the terrain that will affect the movement of water across or into the ground. Obvious applications of hydrological modeling within archaeology include estimating the course of ancient rivers and stream networks or the identification of those parts of archaeological sites at risk of erosion. Gillings (1995, 1998) used a DEM as part of the Upper Tisza project simulating ancient flood events. Despite the lack of detailed historical and paleoenvironmental records regarding the precise extent and location of the floodwaters, this allowed some valuable conclusions to be drawn about the dynamic character of the Neolithic landscape and how ancient populations responded to it.

The usefulness of three-dimensional terrain representations is increased dramatically when different data themes are overlaid on the elevation data. In this way it is possible to interpret visually the associations between, for example, field-walking data and terrain form. More recently, increases in the computational power available on the desktop have allowed *interactive* visualization of terrain models. Here the calculation and rendering of the diagram is so rapid that it can be redisplayed fast enough to convince the eye that the terrain is moving; and input can be taken in the form of slider bars rather than typed numbers to complete the effect of interaction. Good examples of this are provided by the SG3D tool, which runs within the GRASS GIS and ArcView 3D analyst. These programs take advantage of the advanced graphics acceleration of some workstations and personal computers to display and animate wire-frame, solid, and even shaded renderings of elevation models in real time.

Spatial Interpolation

Spatial interpolation refers to methods that use the spatial characteristics of a variable and the observed values of that variable to guess what the value of the variable is at unobserved locations. Estimating topographic height from contours (see previous discussion) is a special case of this, but interpolation has a far wider range of applications than elevation data and encompasses a very wide range of methods.

Some procedures generate results through the observed data points—*exact interpolators*—whereas in *approximators* the result at the sampled locations may be different from the observed values of the samples. Some procedures produce smooth surfaces as a result, others produce surfaces whose derivatives are highly discontinuous; in other words, the surface is allowed to change slope abruptly. Most importantly, some procedures are *constrained*, so that the range of values that may be interpolated is restricted, whereas others are *unconstrained* and the interpolated values might theoretically take on any value.

Although archaeologists have often used interpolation methods to display point observations as density or other continuous surfaces, careful thought needs to be given as to whether this is an appropriate or meaningful thing to do: it *may* be useful to interpolate from the observations to estimate the density of similar artifacts or sites that might be expected to occur at unsurveyed locations. On the other hand, the interpolation of artifact densities within a *wholly* surveyed area into a continuous product has little merit.

With this in mind, however, the most straightforward method is to generate a grid in which the attribute of the grid cells is the density of the points that occur within them. This requires a grid resolution sufficient to ensure that many grid cells contain several points but not so large that the subtle variations in artifact densities are obscured by aggregation. Because different grid cell sizes may appear to produce rather different patterns, it is important to pay careful attention to this, ideally generating densities with a number of different cell sizes. Precisely this approach has been followed by, for example, Ebert et al. (1996) for display of densities of lithic flakes and angular debris.

Another approach is to generate a circular area of radius r centered on each point and to give it, as an attribute, the density derived from its source point. These circles can be added together to give what is sometimes referred to as a *simple density* operator. As the radius for the values increases, the density surface becomes more and more generalized; the density surface produced can be as local or as general as we wish. A related approach is the use of kernel density estimates (KDEs), which have recently been introduced to archaeology by Baxter et al. (1995) and Beardah (1999), although not specifically for spatial interpolation. KDEs operate in a similar manner to simple density estimates except that the circle centered at each point is replaced by a density function called the *kernel*. KDEs produce significantly smoother surfaces than the other methods described. Moreover, the kernel can be made asymmetrical so that point distributions that seem to cluster in a directional way can have a more appropriate form of density function. Bailey and Gatrell (1995) discuss the use of the KDE as a spatial interpolator.

One simple and widely used method for interpolating data measured at ordinal scale or higher is *trend surface analysis*, essentially a polynomial regression technique extended from two to three dimensions. In trend surface analysis, an assumption is made that there is some underlying trend that can be modeled by a polynomial mathematical function and that the observations are therefore the sum of this and a random error. As with regression analysis, different orders of polynomial equations can also be used to describe surfaces with increasing complexity. One disadvantage of trend surfaces is that the surface described is unconstrained. To satisfy the least squares criterion, it can be necessary for intervening values to be interpolated as very high or very low, sometimes orders of magnitude outside the range of the data. Higher-order polynomials, in particular, should therefore be used with extreme caution. Applications of trend surface analysis in archaeology have a fairly long pedigree. Hodder and Orton (1976) describe the technique and present studies, including trend surface analyses of the distribution of length-width indices of Bagterp spearheads in northern Europe and of percentages of Oxford pottery in southern Britain. Another example can be found in the analysis of Lowland Classic Maya sites by Bove (1981) and subsequently by Kvamme (1990c). Both identify spatial autocorrelation in the terminal dates of Maya settlement sites and then use a polynomial trend surface to aid further investigation and explanation of the trend. More recently, Neiman (1997) has also investigated the terminal dates of Classic Maya sites using a "loess" model of the same data. The model is a variation on trend surface analysis that provides a more local and robust estimation of trend (e.g., Cleveland 1993, cited in Neiman 1997). Neiman's complex interpretation compares the resulting "loess" trend surface with mean annual rainfall for the Maya Lowlands to argue that the Maya collapse was caused, ultimately, by ecological disaster rather than by drought or invasion. Interestingly, Neiman also turns to variogram methods to understand the structure of the data set (see later discussion).

Simple surfaces can be generated by creating a TIN from the data points (see previous discussion of models). When unknown values are assumed to lie on flat triangular facets, then the operation is linear, constrained, and behaves in a very predictable manner because unknown values must lie within the range of the three nearest known values (assuming that the interpolation is restricted to the convex hull of the data points). It produces a "faceted" model that is continuous, although its derivatives are likely to be noncontinuous. If small polynomial "patches" are used to produce a result with continuous derivatives, then the approach is sometimes referred to as *nonlinear contouring*. This provides a smooth, nonfaceted result; the higher the order of the patch, the higher the order of derivatives that will be continuous. However, it removes the constraint that the unknown values must lie between the three defining data points. Inappropriate choice of parameters or data points can therefore lead to strange and extreme folds in the result. As with higher-order polynomial trend surfaces, therefore, nonlinear contouring should be treated with caution.

A related alternative method is the use of *spline* curves, piecewise polynomial functions that may be fitted to small numbers of points that are joined by constraining the derivatives of the curve where the functions join. Because the function is, essentially, a local interpolator the polynomials used can be low-order equations, commonly quadratic or cubic. The resulting surface is also controlled by the severity of the constraint placed on the join. The main advantage of splines is that they can model complex surfaces with relatively low computational expense, so they can be quick and visually effective interpolators. Because they are inherently continuous, derivatives such as slope and aspect can be easily calculated.

An alternative strategy for interpolating values between known locations is to use numerical approximation procedures. These do not constrain the result to pass through the data points but instead use the points to approximate the values within both sampled and unsampled locations. The points used for the interpolation can be obtained in several ways. Commonly they can be selected by specifying that the nearest n points be used for each unknown value or, alternatively, by specifying a distance d within which all points are used. The weightings are calculated from some function that must decrease with distance from the known value. The most widely applied approach is that adopted by Shapiro (1993) within the GRASS GIS (r.surf.idw, r.surf.idw2, and s.surf.idw), referred to as *inverse distance weighting*; it is similar to procedures available within a number of other systems. In this method, the weighting for each data point is the square root of the distance to the unknown point, and these weighted values are then averaged to produce an estimate of the value at the unknown location. The effect is a simple, generally robust approximation procedure for the interpolation of surfaces from a wide variety of point data.

The main problem with the use of numerical average methods is that they provide no means for deciding what are the right number of points n or the ideal weights for any given interpolation. They also provide no indication about how reliable each of the interpolated values is, although it should be clear that the farther from the data points, the less reliable the interpolated values. The field of *geostatistics* addresses these issues (among others) using *regionalized variable theory* (Matheron 1971). Central to the success of geostatistics is the *semivariogram*, which relates the distance between each pair of points—the *lag*—to the influence that these points have upon one another. This is used to determine the underlying structural properties of the variable. *Kriging* and *optimal interpolation* are variogram-based techniques that extend weighted average methods to the optimization of the values of the weights to produce the best linear unbiased estimate (BLUE) of a variable at any given location. They can be used for the same type of data but produce better results in complex spatial variables.

Kriging methods have several advantages over numerical approximation. The semivariogram provides an estimate of the *residual noise* in the data and an optimal estimate of the weighting function. A useful by-product of the Kriging equations, the *estimation error* (Kriging variance), can also be mapped as a useful indicator of how reliable the interpolated values are at any point. Obviously the estimation error rises with distance from the observations, reflecting the fact that the estimation becomes less reliable. Mapping the Kriging variance also gives an indication of where the interpolation is most reliable. Against these, Kriging is heavily computational, and in many circumstances the results may not be substantially better than those obtained using a simpler method. Robinson and Zubrow (1999:79) investigated a range of spatial interpolators for simulated archaeological field data and concluded that "Kriging is computationally expensive and, if not fine tuned, it works poorly. Incidentally, it is very expensive in time to calculate and is not recommended unless you have special need and special justification. One justification could be concern about edge effects. Kriging is superior to other techniques in using local topography to infer the form along the edge."

Other archaeologists, however, have found geostatistical methods, including Kriging, to be useful. Ebert (1998), investigating their use in the analysis of real field data from Als, Denmark, found two key advantages. First, the methods allow archaeologists to study the *structure* of spatial variation through the variogram, and second, they provide the ability to produce interpolated maps of spatial distributions and to have confidence in those estimates.

Predictive Modeling

Predictive modeling, the most widespread application of GIS to archaeology, is also the application that has caused most controversy. Although predictive models predate GIS in archaeology (Kohler 1988; Thomas 1988), the explosion in predictive modeling that coincided with the early use of GIS in archaeology has meant that the methodology is inextricably linked with GIS technology. Predictive models have been created for a wide variety of archaeological situations (for examples see Kvamme 1983a, 1985; Carmichael 1990; Zubrow 1990a; Brandt et al. 1992; Maschner 1996a; Wheatley 1996; Dalla Bona 2000; Duncan and Beckman 2000; Kamermans 2000; Stancic and Veljanovski 2000; Warren and Asch 2000; Westcott and Kuiper 2000) and continue to be actively developed as tools for both archaeological management and research.

The goal of predictive modeling is to generate a spatial model that has predictive implications for future observations. In archaeological contexts, this means that the aim is to construct a hypothesis about the location of archaeological remains that can be used to predict the locations of sites not yet observed. As Kvamme (1990a:261) puts it, "a predictive archaeological locational model may simply be regarded as an assignment procedure, or rule, that correctly indicates an archaeological event outcome at a land parcel location with greater probability than that attributable to chance."

Although the term *predictive modeling* describes a wide range of approaches, broadly speaking, predictive models can be based on two different sources of information (Kvamme 1990a): theories about the spatial distribution of archaeological material and empirical observations of the archaeological record.

Models based on theory are referred to as *deductive*, or *theory-driven*, models, whereas models based on observations are referred to as *inductive*, or *data-driven*, models (sometimes as *correlative* models). Most archaeologists accept that it is not really possible to generate an *entirely* theory-driven or data-driven model, however. In the case of data-driven approaches we must choose what data to use as inputs; this is informed by theories. Conversely, any theories that we put forward as the basis for inductive models have been informed by observations of archaeological data.

It is also important to understand that the "unit of currency" of archaeological predictive models is the landscape location, not the archaeological site. In raster systems this means that the objects of the model are grid cells (Kuna 2000); in vector systems, polygonal areas of land. These have archaeological attributes, most usually the presence or absence of one or more classes of archaeological site, and they also have nonarchaeological attributes. The main aim of predictive modeling as currently practiced is to establish some connection between the archaeological characteristics of the landscape units (which we frequently do not know) and the nonarchaeological ones (which we probably do know). In other words, the object is to use nonarchaeological inputs to generate archaeological outputs.

Inputs and Outputs

Inputs to predictive models can include physical environment characteristics of the landscape, including elevation; landform derivatives such as slope, aspect, indices of ridge or drainage, local relief, geologic and soil data, nominal classifications of land class (such as canyon, plain, rim); and distances to resources such as water or raw-material sources. In cases where the vegetation is considered not to have changed significantly, vegetation classes may also be used. It is important to bear in mind that whatever inputs are used they are representative of the *modern* environment rather than the past environment. Frequently, economic measures such as the *productive capacity* of land are used, inferred from soil and other resources and knowledge about the suitability of different places for particular crops. These are essentially the same primary physical environment values, combined using theoretical models of past economic behavior. Because cultural features are more difficult to quantitatively measure, they are more difficult to include as inputs to formal models—even though, in many cases, the cultural features of a landscape can be of considerable use in predicting site locations. For example, it may be that sites occur in proximity to road networks, central places, or focal (significant) points in the natural landscape.

The output from the model may be simple or complex, and it may take a variety of specific forms. The most common type of output required from a predictive model is *presence or absence* of a particular site type. It is also possible to construct models that generate *site class*, in which case the model classifies landscape parcels into one of several site classes or into a special class of "no site." In situations where the resolution is large enough so that several sites or artifacts tend to occur in each location, then *density of sites or finds* can be considered as the output variable of the model. In this case the output may be of ordinal or of real-number data. Lastly, an extremely popular type of model produces as its output an indication of the *probability of a site* occurring at each location in the landscape. In these instances the output is usually a real number, either ranked between 1 and 0 or expressed as a percentage.

Modeling Methods

The simplest way to construct a predictive model is to establish a *decision rule*, an arithmetic expression that describes the conditions under which a particular location is likely to contain an undiscovered site. It can be based on one or more predictor variables, and its form can be derived from some theoretical hypothesis about the relationship between the inputs and the location of the sites. The simplest rules produce a yes or no answer for each landscape unit: yes if the rule determines that a site is likely to be present, no if it is not. More sophisticated decision rules may be able to produce a variety of outputs, representing different classes of archaeological outcome. Some GIS allow rules to be specified in some high-level language such as MapInfo (mapbasic), GRASS (r.mapcalc), ArcView Avenue, or Arc Info AML.

The principal alternative to defining the rules for a model deductively is to allow the characteristics of an existing set of data to determine the rules. The simplest way is to classify the predictors into a fixed number of classes and then observe how many sites occur in each of the predictor variables. It is then possible to calculate an *expected* number of sites for each class of each predictor (the number of sites multiplied by the proportion of the total area occupied by that class) and to compare this with the *observed* number of sites in each class. Each class of each variable can then be weighted: where sites are overrepresented they have a high weighting, whereas where they are underrepresented they are given a lower weighting. Some archaeologists have used the ratio of expected sites to observed sites directly as a weighting, others have opted to assign integer weightings, which can be positive for favorable areas and negative for unfavorable areas. At the same time, a significance test can be undertaken to ascertain whether the proposed predictor really can be held to be associated with the distribution of archaeological material. However the class weights are assigned, the individual predictors are then reclassified into site favorability maps and added together to produce an overall prediction.

Although these approaches are robust and useful, they leave a number of important questions unanswered. Notably, they provide no indication of the extent to which each predictor influences the model and no measure of how well the model fits the observed distribution of the sites. These questions are best answered by different kinds of *regression analysis*, in which the effect of one variable on another can be modeled by a mathematical equation. Several regression techniques have been used to generate predictive models, the most common being *linear multiple regression* and *logistic multiple regression*. The last of these, commonly referred to simply as *logistic regression*, has been the most widespread technique in archaeological predictive modeling. This is a method for generating a probability model—an equation whose output can be interpreted as the probability of site presence, given the values of the independent variables. Although it is a flexible and widely used method, the use of logistic regressions as archaeological predictive models is not without problems. It does not produce the same easily interpretable correlation coefficients as linear bivariate and multiple regression; as a result, it is far more difficult to judge how effective the model is in explaining the archaeological outcome.

Testing Predictive Models

Some significant issues in predictive modeling concern how to assess whether the model is good or bad—which, of course, first requires that we define what constitutes good and bad. One way is to consider how much better than chance the model performs, in other words, the extent to which it is an improvement on simply guessing which landscape units contain archaeological sites. This can be expressed as the *gain* of a model (Kvamme 1988). A model with a very good gain will accurately locate most of the sites in a small area, whereas a model with a poor gain will classify a high proportion of the landscape as potential sites, but that area will contain an only marginally higher proportion of the sites. Kvamme's (1988) gain statistic expresses this numerically.

Gain = 1 – (percentage of total area covered by model ÷ percentage of total sites within model area)

This results in an index that varies between 0, indicating a model with no gain—in other words one that behaves no better than chance—and 1 for "perfect" models that correctly classify 100 percent of sites in a tiny proportion of the area. It is important to note that this and other calculations of model performance rely on comparing the results of the predictive model with the data from which it was derived. Sometimes the original data are divided and a randomly selected subset of the data is withheld from the generation phase of the model for subsequent use in verification (jackknife sampling), but even then, this is essentially a method of testing how well the model relates to its data set. Ebert (2000) has criticized this as "a grossly inefficient way to determine if there is inhomogeneity in one's data," and it certainly is not a way to measure how good the model is if we define good as the ability of a model to locate new sites correctly. If this is our criterion, then the only reliable method to test a model is to devise a sampling strategy and then to undertake a comprehensive survey for new sites in those areas that the model predicts as both sites and nonsites.

Woodman and Woodward (2002) have usefully reviewed the use of logistic regression models and noted several other outstanding problems. Among these, they draw attention to the use of case-control studies. In these, it is quite usual to gather a sample of site locations—often from an existing inventory—and a sample of nonsite locations. Actually, the nonsite locations are frequently replaced with "unknown" locations, because it is unusual to have a good record of randomly selected locations that are known not to contain sites and, it is argued, the overwhelming majority of the unknown locations will not contain sites. Regardless of this questionable assumption, the use of a case-control approach means that no measure of the absolute density of sites per unit area is ever available and so all probability estimates must be *relative* estimates. To put this another way, it is not possible to use these studies to predict that one location has x percent chance of containing a site and another location a y percent chance, although it may be possible to state that location x is twice as likely as location y.

Theoretical Concerns

The development and application of predictive models of archaeological site locations has probably been the most controversial application of GIS to archaeology, with wide differences of opinion existing within the discipline (see, e.g., Gaffney and van Leusen 1995; Kuna 2000; Kvamme 1997; Wheatley 1998). Central to the critique of predictive models has been the accusation that the approach embodies a theory of archaeology that can be categorized as a form of *environmental determinism*. Some advocates claim that the utility of models to identify patterns can be isolated from their use as interpretative tools, that "statistics can be used to describe patterning in archaeological datasets in a rigorous manner without reference to the cause(s) of those patterns" (van Leusen in Gaffney and van Leusen 1995). Critics have argued that the description and modeling of patterns cannot be separated from the process of explanation in this way. Defenders of locational models have objected to the use of the term *environmental determinism* to describe the approach, arguing that the prevalence of environmental variables in archaeological predictive models is simply a product of their greater availability over *cultural variables*; it should not be taken as an indication of theoretical orientation. Moreover, Kvamme (1997) has objected on the grounds that the term is an inappropriate—even offensive—label that associates predictive modelers with late-nineteenth- and early-twentieth-century human geographers such as Rahtzel (1882) whose ideas were later widely discredited. The argument that inductive modeling can be separated from deductive, explanatory modeling has also been called into question, even described by Ebert as a product of "sheer indolence among those who think we can 'stop' at 'inductive predictive modeling'" (Ebert 2000).

A debate such as this is difficult to synthesize without reducing it to the level of caricature; further details can be found in Church et al. (2000); Ebert (2000); Gaffney et al. (1995); Kohler (1988); Kvamme (1997); Wheatley (1998).

Sites and Territories

Archaeologists have used a wide variety of methodological approaches to the distribution of archaeological sites, particularly settlement sites. These include gravity models (Hodder and Orton 1976); von Thunen's (von Thunen 1966) economic model of settlement structure; Christaller's Central Place theories of settlement hierarchy (Christaller 1966); site-catchment analysis (Vita-Finzi and Higgs 1970); and ecologically based resource-concentration models (Butzer 1982). A GIS provides a series of useful tools to allow these to be incorporated into—and often enhanced and extended—within the platform of the GIS.

Buffers and Proximity Products

The most basic ability of GISs, and one of its most useful, is the generation of distance products, either in the form of proximity buffers or continuous proximity surfaces. The most straightforward distance products may be termed *distance buffers*, and they comprise categorical products in which the classes represent a range of proximities to some archaeological feature or features. Classes may define regular intervals of distance from source—for example, every 100 m—although they can just as easily provide uneven ranges if these are more suitable (e.g., 0–500 m, 500 m–5 km, 5–100 km). Some raster systems also provide a mechanism to generate a continuous (or rather quantized) *proximity surface* product in which each grid cell has a measure of distance from archaeological features. Distance buffers and proximity surfaces have been widely used in archaeological analysis to construct hypothesis tests regarding the distribution of archaeological sites or find spots.

Voronoi Tessellation and Delaunay Triangulation

An alternative approach to the use of distance buffers is to use the archaeological sites to generate a *tessellation*. This divides the landscape into polygonal tiles based on the geometric properties of a point distribution. The most commonly used of these has been the Voronoi tessellation (also called Thiessen polygons), which is closely related to the Delaunay triangulation previously described. Voronoi tessellation has frequently been used in both archaeology and geography to define notional site territories; well-known examples of its application include the definition of territories for Neolithic long mounds (Renfrew 1973) or for Iron Age hill forts (Cunliffe 1971; Grant 1986) and the analysis of Romano-British settlement (Hodder 1972). The close association of this method of spatial allocation with the functionalist interpretative stance of early new archaeology led to the technique becoming far less used in archaeological analysis; the recent popularity of GISs has perpetuated its use somewhat: for example, see Ruggles and Church (1996); Savage (1990).

Cost and Time Surfaces

Distance products and geometrical tessellations are based solely on the Cartesian spatial properties of the data; this can be problematic if we wish to develop methodologies that take account of obstructions, barriers, and differences in the qualities of space that may have influenced transportation costs, movement, or perception of the landscape. One way to address these concerns is to use *cost surfaces*, modifications to proximity products that take account of the character of the terrain over which that proximity is measured. Two types of cost-surface algorithm have been used in archaeology: *isotropic* algorithms take account of the cost of movement across the surface but take no account of the direction of movement; *anisotropic* algorithms consider the direction of movement to affect its cost.

In isotropic cost-surface calculation, the analysis begins with the location of the features from which cost distance will be calculated, the *seed* locations, and a map of the cost of travel across each landscape unit, usually called a *friction surface*. The algorithm, beginning at each of the seed locations, cumulatively models the *cost* of reaching any point in the landscape from one of the seed points. Isotropic analysis extends this approach so that the actual friction at any location is a function both of the friction map and the direction of movement. This is important where the impediment to movement depends on direction. The most common example of this is slope, where a different cost is incurred in moving up, across, or down a given slope.

In either case, the creation of the friction surface requires careful consideration because this will determine the nature of the results of the model (van Leusen 1999). Various approaches to creating friction surfaces depend on whether the intended output is a measure of energy expenditure, time, or something else. Where the output is intended as a model of energy, then the friction surface must represent the energy expended in traversing a fixed distance. This may be closely related to the slope of the terrain. To generate the friction map from a slope map, therefore, a relationship must be postulated between slope and energy; this is not entirely straightforward. Backpacker's equations, such as that of Ericson and Goldstein (1980), estimate effort as a function of distance traveled, positive vertical height change, and negative vertical height change. Alternative sources of information about this relationship may include physiological experimental results (Llobera 2000) or knowledge about the energy needed to move a body of given mass a given height (Bell and Lock 2000). Where cost-surface analysis is intended as a time, rather than an energy model, then the friction component needs to represent the time taken to traverse each cell, expressed as a proportion of the base cost for traversal of a cell. Here a relationship between slope and time is needed to create a friction surface, and this can again be derived from backpacker's equations, several of which have been published.

The vast majority of archaeological applications have so far accepted the simplification that energy expended or time taken to move around in a landscape is a function of slope. Yet there are considerable differences in energy expended in moving over, for example, soft sand as opposed to paved road or through different types of vegetation; Marble (1996) has suggested the use of an equation that includes terms for ease of movement over terrain, weight of individual, weight of load carried, speed of travel, gradient, and a terrain factor.

Movement can be affected adversely by barriers—rivers, fences, or culturally forbidden zones—or positively by the availability of transport routes. Some algorithms allow a barrier to be explicitly coded into the friction surface with a value that will prevent movement across it, or extremely high values can be used with similar results. In a similar way, transport routes can be coded by including extremely low values of friction. It is far more difficult to model a feature as both a barrier *and* a transportation opportunity, as we may wish to do with rivers. In that case it may be possible to represent the river as a central corridor of very low friction, surrounded by a thin buffer of high cost to represent the cost involved in, for example, acquiring transportation or crossing the river.

Whichever assertion is chosen about the relationship between friction and slope, it is essential that it be clearly specified with the results. Cost surfaces published without stating the derivation of the friction surface must be treated with extreme skepticism, because the form of the result entirely depends on the choice of friction values. Moreover, it is advisable to "calibrate" the values if possible, as was done, for example, by Gaffney and Stancic (1991).

Methodologically, it is important to consider the effect on the analysis that errors and inaccuracy in the DEM may have. This is because gross inaccuracies will lead to erroneous generation of slope estimates and therefore of friction values. The resolution of the model is also significant. If it is not sufficient to permit the slopes and ridges of a landscape to be adequately represented, then there is a real danger that cost-surface results will bear no resemblance to values that would be obtained by practical methods. In addition, the algorithms implemented in many commercial GIS provide far-from-ideal estimates of cost surfaces. This is easily demonstrated by running them on uniform friction surfaces, where few produce the (theoretically correct) circular result; most generate—at best—many-sided polygons centered on the seed location.

Site-Catchment Analysis and GIS

Like predictive modeling, site-catchment analysis (SCA) is a technique that predates GIS. It was devised as a means of analyzing the locations of archaeological sites with respect to the economic resources that are available to them (Vita-Finzi and Higgs 1970; Vita-Finzi 1978). It assumes that the farther site resources are from the base, the greater the economic cost of exploiting them. At a point where the cost of exploitation outstrips the return, an economic boundary can be defined (see papers in Findlow and Ericson 1980). The capacity of GIS for extracting a variety of information about the environment and performing both geometric and statistical operations on it have led to its use for the application of SCA in archaeology (Gaffney and Stancic 1991; Hunt 1992). In such studies, the capabilities of GIS have been used to add considerable methodological sophistication to the delineation of catchment zones.

At its simplest, the exploitation territory, or *catchment*, of a site can be approximated as a circular area centered on the site in question. Estimates of where the boundaries of these territories should be placed, derived from ethnography, differ depending on the economic base of the communities. For example, the limit of the economic catchment of a sedentary agricultural site may be placed at a 1-hour walk whereas for a herding or hunting community it may be 2 hours (Bintliff 1977). Once the catchment has been defined, the proportions of given resources within this area can easily be obtained using a GIS and analyzed for comparison with the resources within the catchments of other sites. In this way, it is claimed, the commonalities and differences between sites may become apparent.

Using a GIS, it is possible to improve on the notional circular catchments commonly used to define the extents of exploitation zones. This is done using the cost-distance (time or energy) surfaces described above. We are usually interested in the return-to-base cost of each trip so may be justified in using an isotropic function. Time or energy models need to be generated for each site in turn and the cost-distance result reclassified to identify zones that are within 2 hours' walk of the sites. Finally, the relative proportions of the various soil types occurring in those zones can then be tabulated and compared with other source sites just as they are with conventional SCA.

Visibility Analysis

Visibility analysis also predates the widespread adoption by archaeologists of GIS. However, with one or two exceptions (e.g., Fraser 1983; Renfrew 1979), before GIS its incorporation within archaeological interpretations was largely anecdotal. More recently, there have been systematic attempts to exploit the visual properties of archaeological landscapes. GIS have been central to this effort because they provide archaeologists with a set of standard functions for calculating visibility products from digital models of surface topography and they permit the results of analyses to be expressed using the familiar medium of the map.

Calculating Visibility

The calculation of a line-of-sight map for a location, a relatively trivial computing problem, is available within the current functionality of most GIS. It requires only a DEM and a layer encoding the location from which to determine the view. The result—usually called a *viewshed* map—is conventionally coded with a 1 for visible and a 0 for not visible (Figure 11.6). Most systems allow restrictions to be imposed on the area to be included in the calculation, such as limiting the distance or the angle of view; most also allow specification of a notional height above the surface of the DEM for the viewer. A standard offset height of 1.7 m is often used for adult humans, although the height of a human eye above the ground does rather depend on the particular human. If we wish to investigate the viewshed for a struc-

Figure 11.6. The areas where the orthophotograph has been darkened represent those that are visible from the source location, in this case a huge artificial tower at the corner of the fortifications. Here we can see an apparent relationship between this area and the locations of the prehistoric, protohistoric and Roman funerary monuments to the north and west.

ture such as a watchtower, then the height of the viewing platform can be used instead. Some systems also return the *angle* of the line-of-sight locations that are visible, and it may be significant whether a viewer looks up or down at a site or monument: a site above the viewer's line of sight may have more visual impact or be more symbolically significant. Viewshed maps have found frequent application within archaeology, permitting, for example, the analysis of networks of watchtowers (Gaffney and Stancic 1991).

In situations where patterns of visibility within a group of sites are of interest, then individual viewshed maps can be combined to produce more useful products. The union of a series of viewshed themes—in which the landscape is classified into areas that can see any of the group, and areas that can see none—can be termed a *multiple viewshed* (Ruggles and Medyckyj-Scott

1996; Ruggles et al. 1993). Alternatively, the viewsheds for a group of sites can be summed to create a *cumulative viewshed* theme (Wheatley 1996) in which the landscape is classified according to how many sites have a line of sight to each location. Both of these can provide useful visual summaries of the way a group of sites can relate to other elements of the landscape, and they can also be used for more formal approaches to spatial analysis, such as spatial tests of association.

Examples of this type of work include the analysis of long mounds in southern England by Lock and Harris (1996:223–225) and also by Wheatley (1995, 1996), the examination of the local landscapes of Paleolithic and Mesolithic sites in Mergelland Oost, Netherlands (van Leusen 1993:4), and the work of Ruggles et al. on the topographical and astronomical significance of prehistoric stone rows (Ruggles et al. 1991; Ruggles et al. 1993). Maschner (1996b) has incorporated viewsheds as a cognitive variable in the examination of settlement location, whereas in a study of the pre-Roman town of Nepi in south Etruria viewsheds have been used to explore liminal tomb locations with respect to the town (Belcher et al. 1999).

One detailed exploration of the relationship between cognition, perception, and GIS-based visibility studies is the work of Gaffney et al. on rock art sites in southwestern Scotland (Gaffney et al. 1995). Cumulative viewsheds were used to identify zones in the landscape of increased monument awareness, with the density of such information seen as a direct correlate of sociosymbolic importance. A detailed study of the intervisibility of individual classes of monument locations was then undertaken with respect to this cumulative map. Central to the analysis was the claim that such an approach yields "a mappable, spatially variable index of perception" (Gaffney et al. 1995:222), study of which would lead to an understanding of the cognitive landscape within which the monuments were components.

A number of methodological issues should be considered when using this type of analysis, some of which may result in unforeseen errors. First, the effects of vegetation must be considered. Although patches of vegetation can easily be incorporated into a viewshed calculation, it is often difficult to reconstruct past vegetation regimes in sufficient detail. Second, it is also important to understand that viewshed calculations are not reciprocal wherever a viewer height is specified and is nonnegligible. Put simply, this means that a view from point A to point B does not imply a view from point B to point A (Fisher 1996b; Fraser 1983). Loots (1997) used different terms to describe viewshed products, distinguishing *projective* (views from) from *reflective* (views to) viewsheds. A third potential problem, particularly with cumulative viewshed analysis, is that of *edge effects*. Where a monument distribution continues outside the study area, then the cumulative viewshed map may considerably underestimate the number of lines of sight toward the edge of the study region because it does not include the viewsheds of those monuments outside the boundary. The accuracy and precision of the DEM are vital to the formal analysis of vision. Moreover, there is no simple relationship between the average error of an elevation model and the quality of visibility products: errors on hillcrests and errors near the source location will have a far greater impact on the viewshed product than errors in valley bottoms or near the target location. Partly because of these uncertainties, Fisher (1991) has argued that viewsheds are best considered as a probability surface, which can be implemented using Monte Carlo simulation techniques to create the probable viewshed. Fisher has undertaken important work in the examination of the falloff of visual clarity with distance, through the generation of fuzzy viewsheds, and the identification of unique terrain phenomena, such as horizons, within viewsheds (Fisher 1992, 1994, 1995, 1996a, 1996b).

GIS-based visibility analyses offer archaeologists a valuable set of analytic tools. To maximize their potential they need to be applied within a critical framework, tailored to the unique requirements of archaeology. In recent years archaeological GIS practitioners have begun to address both of these factors. In a recent review Wheatley and Gillings (2000) have highlighted a number of key critiques and issues that need to be addressed in any GIS viewshed study ranging from the impact of vegetation and effects of DEM errors to the theoretical implications of attempting to *map* aspects of perception.

Developing Areas

Object-Oriented Approaches

As previously discussed, the most commonly used spatial data models in archaeology are vector and raster, frequently connected to a relational database to deliver attribute data. An alternative to these is provided by the object-oriented (OO) approach to programming, most commonly associated with OO programming languages (such as C++ and Java) and OO databases. OO GIS claim to offer a new approach to the structuring of geographical space that seeks to view the world, not as a series of discrete features, or attributes, varying across space, but instead as a series of *objects*, *methods*, and *classes*. In the OO paradigm, a class is essentially a template that describes the structure of the objects held within it, whereas an object instance is quite literally an instance of the class. The instance uses the class template to define its specific attributes, each of which will have instance-specific values. In a recent discussion of OO GIS in archaeology, Tschan has illustrated this concept using the example of pottery finds (Tschan 1999). OO systems also break down the barriers between data objects themselves and the processes that operate on them by associating *methods*—routines that operate on data—with the data themselves. In this way the means of entering information into the GIS or the types of operations that may legitimately be performed on an object are closely interwoven with the data themselves. An OO GIS is complex, and it is far from clear that the OO model will become the successor to more conventional systems, but elements of OO systems are highly likely to influence future designs of systems. These offer exciting possibilities for the ways archaeologists can model the archaeological record and for spatial analysis (Ralston 1994). Commercial OO GIS already exist, although they are expensive, but as OO GIS become more accessible they are likely to become far more familiar to archaeologists.

Multidimensional GIS

Virtually all GIS packages in routine use by archaeologists are two-dimensional in nature (Harris and Lock 1996), recording the third dimension (usually elevation) as an attribute of two-dimensional space. In true three-dimensional systems, attributes are attached not to two-dimensional locations but to three-dimensional locations, permitting a true three-dimensional representation of space (Raper 1989; Worboys 1995). As with OO GIS, commercial three-dimensional GIS do exist but they tend to be either expensive or experimental (and hence, often, difficult to use). As a result they have not witnessed widespread application in archaeological research to date, although Harris and Lock (1996) have reviewed in detail the principal methodologies of three-dimensional GIS in the context of excavated archaeological data using a *voxel*-based approach. A voxel is best thought of as the three-dimensional equivalent of a two-dimensional pixel (Worboys 1995). It can be defined as a rectangular cube bounded by eight grid nodes. In a similar fashion to traditional raster data structures, the voxels can be held as a three-dimensional array with associated attribute data or as an array that describes the region of space occupied by a given object (Harris and Lock 1996). Although the voxel structure suffers from the same problems as two-dimensional raster GIS—cell-resolution effects, an inability to represent precise spatial boundaries, and a lack of topological information—in a feasibility application based on the three-dimensional interpolation and analysis of borehole data taken around a Romano-British settlement, it produced very encouraging results (Harris and Lock 1996).

Dealing with Time

Like the third spatial dimension, temporal information currently tends to be recorded and analyzed as attribute data and, at best, is used to generate time slices—static layers showing a given situation at a series of fixed points in time. Although a considerable amount of mainstream GIS research has been directed toward investigating the possibilities of temporal GIS (TGIS), the impact the fruits of these initiatives have had on archaeology has been limited (Daly and Lock 1999). This is odd, because archaeology is a discipline whose subject matter is thoroughly temporal, and discussions of time within the disciplines of archaeology and anthropology are not uncommon (Adam 1994; Gell 1992; Gosden 1994; Shanks and Tilley 1987; Thomas 1996).

The development of archaeological TGIS is complicated by the growing realization of the sheer complexity of social understandings of temporality. As Castleford (1992) has pointed out, clock time is only one understanding of temporality; many archaeologists are beginning to acknowledge the importance of philosophical and metaphysical concepts of time that researchers involved in TGIS have so far not been concerned with. The issue of integrating time into GIS may therefore be one where archaeologists can make a significant contribution to the wider discipline of GIS as a whole. Indeed, a number of researchers have already begun to explore the potential of existing raster GIS for identifying and quantifying temporal concepts (Johnson 1999; Lock and Daly 1999). Langran (1992) and Worboys (1995) both provide more detailed discussions of the mechanics of designing and implementing a TGIS.

Further Reading

A comprehensive introduction to GIS and their archaeological applications can be found in Wheatley and Gillings (2002). Readers who wish to pursue the subject further should consult more specialized publications, notably the collections of papers published in Aldenderfer and Maschner (1996); Allen et al. (1990); Johnson and North (1997); Judge and Sebastian (1988); Lock (2000); Lock and Stancic (1995); Maschner (1996a); and Westcott and Brandon (2000). Guidelines for the design of archaeological spatial databases can be found in the AHDS *GIS Guide to Good Practice* (Gillings and Wise 1998), particularly section 4, "Structuring, Organising and Maintaining Information." Of the many general textbooks on GIS, we recommend Burrough (1986), now substantially rewritten (Burrough and McDonnell 1998). A very comprehensive discussion of spatial data and spatial databases can be found in Worboys (1995), where many more methods of raster and vector storage are discussed.

References

Adam, B.
　　1994　Perceptions of time. In *Companion encyclopedia of anthropology*, edited by T. Ingold, pp. 503–526. Routledge, London.

Aldenderfer, M., and H. D. G. Maschner (editors)
1996 *Anthropology, space and geographic information systems.* Spatial information series. Oxford University Press, New York.

Allen, K.
1990 Modelling early historic trade in the eastern great lakes using geographic information. In *Interpreting space: GIS and archaeology,* edited by K. M. S. Allen, S. W. Green, and E. B. W. Zubrow, pp. 319–329. Taylor and Francis, London.

Allen, Kathleen M. S., Stanton W. Green, and Ezra B. W. Zubrow (editors)
1990 *Interpreting space: GIS and archaeology.* Taylor and Francis, London.

Amores, F., L. Garcia et al.
1999 Geographic information systems and archaeological resource management in Andalusia, Spain. In *New techniques for old times: Caa98 computer applications and quantitative methods in archaeology,* edited by J. A. Barcelo, I. Briz, and A. Vila, pp. 351–358. Archaeopress, Oxford.

Arroyo-Bishop, D., and M. T. Lantada Zarzosa
1995 To be or not to be: Will an object-space-time GIS/AIS become a scientific reality or end up an archaeological entity? In *Archaeology and geographical information systems: A European perspective,* edited by G. Lock and Z. Stancic, pp. 43–53. Taylor and Francis, London.

Bailey, T. C., and A. C. Gatrell
1995 *Interactive spatial data analysis.* Longman Scientific and Technical, London.

Baxter, M. J., C. C. Beardah et al.
1995 Some archaeological applications of kernel density estimates. *Journal of Archaeological Science* 24:347–354.

Beardah, C. C.
1999 Uses of multivariate kernel density estimates. In *Archaeology in the age of the internet: Computer applications and quantitative methods in archaeology 1997,* edited by L. Dingwall, S. Exon, V. Gaffney, S. Laflin, and M. Van Leusen, p. 107. CD-ROM. Archaeopress, Oxford.

Belcher, M., A. Harrison et al.
1999 Analyzing Rome's hinterland. In *Geographic information systems and landscape archaeology,* edited by M. Gillings, D. Mattingly, and J. Van Dalen, pp. 95–101. Oxbow Books, Oxford.

Bell, T., and G. Lock
2000 Topographic and cultural influences on walking the ridgeway in later prehistoric times. In *Beyond the map: Archaeology and spatial technologies,* edited by G. Lock, pp. 85–100. IOS Press, Amsterdam.

Bintliff, J. L.
1977 *Natural environment and human settlement in prehistoric Greece.* British Archaeological Reports, Oxford.

Biro, K. T., and I. S. Fejes
   1995   GIS applications at the Hungarian National Museum, Department of Information. In *Archaeology and geographical information systems: A European perspective*, edited by G. Lock and Z. Stancic, pp. 261–267. Taylor and Francis, London.

Blasco, C., J. Baena et al.
   1996   The role of GIS in the management of archaeological data: An example of application for the Spanish administration. In *Anthropology, space and geographic information systems*, edited by M. Aldenderfer and H. D. G. Maschner, pp. 189–201. Oxford University Press, New York.

Boaz, J. S., and E. Uleberg
   1993   Gardermoen project—use of a GIS system in antiquities registration and research. In *Computing the past: Computer applications and quantitative methods in archaeology—CAA 92*, edited by J. Andresen, T. Madsen, and I. Scollar, pp. 177–182. Aarhus University Press, Aarhus, Denmark.

Bove, F. J.
   1981   Trend surface analysis and the lowland Classic Maya collapse. *American Antiquity* 46(1):93–112.

Brandt, R., B. J. Groenewoudt et al.
   1992   An experiment in archaeological site location: Modeling in the Netherlands using GIS techniques. *World Archaeology* 24(2):268–282.

Burrough, P. A.
   1986   *Principles of GIS for land resources assessment*. Clarendon Press, Oxford.

Burrough, P. A., and R. A. McDonnell
   1998   *Principles of geographic information systems*. Oxford University Press, Oxford.

Butzer, K. W.
   1982   *Archaeology as human ecology*. Cambridge University Press, Cambridge.

Carmichael, D. L.
   1990   GIS predictive modelling of prehistoric site distributions in central Montana. In *Interpreting space: GIS and archaeology*, edited by K. M. S. Allen, S. W. Green, and E. B. W. Zubrow, pp. 216–225. Taylor and Francis, London.

Castleford, J.
   1992   Archaeology, GIS, and the time dimension: An overview. In *Computer applications and quantitative methods in archaeology 1991*, edited by G. Lock and J. Moffett, pp. 95–106. Tempus Reparatum, Oxford.

Christaller, W.
1966   *Central places in southern Germany*. Prentice Hall, New Jersey.

Church, T., R. J. Brandon et al.
2000   GIS applications in archaeology: Method in search of theory. In *Practical applications of GIS for archaeologists: A predictive modeling kit*, edited by K. L. Westcott and R. J. Brandon, pp. 135–155. Taylor and Francis, London.

Cleveland, W. S.
1993   *Visualising data*. AT&T Bell Laboratories, Murray Hill, New Jersey.

Cunliffe, B.
1971   Some aspects of hillforts and their regional environments. In *The iron age and its hillforts*, edited by D. Hill and M. Jesson, pp. 53–69. Southampton University Press, Southampton.

Dalla Bona, L.
2000   Protecting cultural resources through forest management planning in Ontario using archaeological predictive modeling. In *Practical applications of GIS for archaeologists: A predictive modeling kit*, edited by K. L. Westcott and R. J. Brandon, pp. 73–99. Taylor and Francis, London.

Daly, P. T., and G. R. Lock
1999   Timing is everything: Commentary on managing temporal variables in geographic information systems. In *New techniques for old times: Caa98 computer applications and quantitative methods in archaeology*, edited by J. A. Barcelo, I. Briz, and A. Vila, pp. 287–293. Archaeopress, Oxford.

Duncan, R. B., and K. A. Beckman
2000   The application of GIS predictive site location models within Pennsylvania and West Virginia. In *Practical applications of GIS for archaeologists: A predictive modeling kit*, edited by K. L. Westcott and R. J. Brandon, pp. 33–58. Taylor and Francis, London.

Ebert, D.
1998   *Expanding the selection of tools for spatial analysis: Geostatistics and the ALS fieldwalking data*. Department of Archaeology. Southampton, University of Southampton.

Ebert, J. I.
2000   The state of the art in "inductive" predictive modeling: Seven big mistakes (and lots of smaller ones). In *Practical applications of GIS for archaeologists: A predictive modeling kit*, edited by K. L. Westcott and R. J. Brandon, pp. 129–134. Taylor and Francis, London.

Ebert, J. I., E. L. Camilli et al.
1996   GIS in the analysis of distributional archaeological data. In *New methods, old problems: Geographic information systems in modern*

archaeological research, edited by H. D. G. Maschner, pp. 25–37. Center for Archaeological Investigation, Southern Illinois University, Carbondale.

Ericson, J. E., and R. Goldstein
    1980   Work space: A new approach to the analysis of energy expenditure within site catchments. In *Catchment analysis: Essays on prehistoric resource space*, edited by F. J. Findlow and J. E. Ericson, pp. 21–30. University of California at Los Angeles, Los Angeles.

ESRI
    1997   Arc/info version 7.2.1 online help. Environmental Systems Research Institute Inc., Redlands, California.

Findlow, F. J., and J. E. Ericson (editors)
    1980   *Catchment analysis: Essays on prehistoric resource space. Anthropology UCLA* 10(1–2). University of California, Los Angeles.

Fisher, P.
    1991   First experiments in viewshed uncertainty: The accuracy of the viewshed area. *Photogrammetric Engineering and Remote Sensing* 57(10):1321–1327.
    1992   First experiments in viewshed uncertainty: Simulating fuzzy viewsheds. *Photogrammetric Engineering and Remote Sensing* 58(3):345–352.
    1994   Probable and fuzzy models of the viewshed operation. In *Innovations in GIS*, edited by M. Worboys, pp. 161–175. Taylor and Francis, London.
    1995   An exploration of probable viewsheds in landscape planning. *Environment and Planning B: Planning and Design* 22:527–546.
    1996a Extending the applicability of viewsheds in landscape planning. *Photogrammetric Engineering and Remote Sensing* 62(11):527–546.
    1996b Reconsideration of the viewshed function in terrain modelling. *Geographical Systems* 3:33–58.

Fraser, D.
    1983   *Land and society in Neolithic orkney*. British Archaeological Reports, Oxford.

Gaffney, V., and Z. Stancic
    1991   *GIS approaches to regional analysis: A case study of the island of Hvar*. Filozofska fakulteta, Ljubljana, Slovenia.

Gaffney, V., Z. Stancic et al.
    1995   The impact of GIS on archaeology: A personal perspective. In *Archaeology and geographical information systems: A European perspective*, edited by G. R. Lock and Z. Stancic, pp. 211–229. Taylor and Francis, London.

Gaffney, V., and M. van Leusen
  1995 Postscript—GIS, environmental determinism and archaeology: A
        parallel text. In *Archaeology and geographical information systems: A
        European perspective*, edited by G. R. Lock and Z. Stancic, pp.
        367–382. Taylor and Francis, London.

Garcia-Sanjuan, L., and D. Wheatley
  1999 The state of the arc: Differential rates of adoption of GIS for European
        heritage management. *European Journal of Archaeology* 2(2):201–228.

Gell, A.
  1992 *The anthropology of time: Cultural constructions of temporal maps and
        images*. Berg, Oxford.

Gillings, M.
  1995 Flood dynamics and settlement in the Tisza Valley of north-east
        Hungary: GIS and the Upper Tisza project. In *Archaeology and geo-
        graphical information systems: A European perspective*, edited by
        G. Lock and Z. Stancic, pp. 67–84. Taylor and Francis, London.
  1998 Embracing uncertainty and challenging dualism in the GIS-based
        study of a palaeo-flood plain. *European Journal of Archaeology*
        1(1):117–144.

Gillings, M., and A. L. Wise
  1998 *GIS guide to good practice*. Oxbow, Oxford.

Gosden, C.
  1994 *Social being and time*. Blackwell, Oxford.

Grant, E.
  1986 Hill-forts, central places and territories. In *Central places, archaeology
        and history*, edited by E. Grant, pp. 13–26. University of Sheffield,
        Sheffield.

Guillot, D., and G. Leroy
  1995 The use of GIS for archaeological resource management in France:
        The Scala project, with a case study in Picardie. In *Archaeology and
        geographical information systems: A European perspective*, edited by
        G. R. Lock and Z. Stancic, pp. 15–26. Taylor and Francis, London.

Hageman, J. B., and D. A. Bennett
  2000 Construction of digital elevation models for archaeological applica-
        tions. In *Practical applications of GIS for archaeologists: A predictive
        modeling kit*, edited by K. L. Westcott and R. J. Brandon, pp. 113–127.
        Taylor and Francis, London.

Harris, T. M.
  1985 *GIS design for archaeological site information retrieval and predictive
        modelling*. Professional archaeology in Sussex: The next five years.
        Institute of Field Archaeologists, London.

1986   Geographic information system design for archaeological site information retrieval. In *Computer applications in archaeology 1986*, edited by S. Laflin, pp. 148–161. Computer Centre, University of Birmingham, Birmingham.

Harris, T. M., and G. R. Lock
1992   Toward a regional GIS site information retrieval system: The Oxfordshire sites and monuments record (SMR) prototype. In *Sites and monuments. National archaeological records*, edited by L. Larsen, pp. 185–199. National Museum of Denmark, Copenhagen.
1995   Toward an evaluation of GIS in European archaeology: The past, present and future of theory and applications. In *Archaeology and geographical information systems: A European perspective*, edited by G. R. Lock and Z. Stancic, pp. 349–365. Taylor and Francis, London.
1996   Multi-dimensional GIS: Exploratory approaches to spatial and temporal relationships within archaeological stratigraphy. In *Interfacing the past*, edited by H. Kammermans and K. Fennema, pp. 307–316. Leiden University Press, Leiden.

Hodder, I. R.
1972   Location models and the study of Romano-British settlement. In *Models in archaeology*, edited by D. L. Clarke, pp. 887–909. Methuen, London.

Hodder, I., and C. Orton.
1976   *Spatial analysis in archaeology.* Cambridge University Press, Cambridge.

Hunt, E. D.
1992   Upgrading site-catchment analyses with the use of GIS: Investigating the settlement patterns of horticulturalists. *World Archaeology* 24(2):283–309.

Johnson, I.
1999   Mapping the fourth dimension: The timemap project. In *Archaeology in the age of the internet: Caa97 and CD-ROM*, edited by L. Dingwall, S. Exon, V. Gaffney, S. Laflin, and M. Van Leusen, pp. 82. Archaeopress, Oxford.

Johnson, I., and M. North (editors)
1997   *Archaeological applications of GIS: Proceedings of Colloquium II, Uispp XIIIth Congress, Forli, Italy, September 1996.* Archaeological methods series. Sydney University, Sydney.

Judge, W. J., and L. Sebastian (editors)
1988   *Quantifying the present and predicting the past: Theory, method and application of archaeological predictive modeling.* Bureau of Land Management, U.S. Department of the Interior, Denver, Colorado.

Kamermans, H.
2000   Land evaluation as predictive modelling: A deductive approach. In *Beyond the map: Archaeology and spatial technologies*, edited by G. Lock, pp. 124–146. IOS Press, Amsterdam.

Kincaid, C.
1988   Predictive modeling and its relationship to cultural resource management applications. In *Quantifying the present, predicting the past*, edited by W. J. Judge and L. Sebastian, pp. 549–569. Bureau of Land Management, U.S. Department of the Interior, Denver, Colorado.

Kohler, T. A.
1988   Predictive locational modeling: History and current practice. In *Quantifying the present, predicting the past*, edited by W. J. Judge and L. Sebastian, pp. 19–59. Bureau of Land Management, U.S. Department of the Interior, Denver, Colorado.

Kuna, M.
2000   Session 3 discussion: Comments on archaeological prediction. In *Beyond the map: Archaeology and spatial technologies*, edited by G. Lock, pp. 180–186. IOS Press, Amsterdam.

Kvamme, K. L.
1983a *A manual for predictive site location models: Examples from the Grand Junction District, Colorado.* Grand Junction District, Bureau of Land Management, Colorado.
1983b Computer processing techniques for regional modeling of archaeological site locations. *Advances in Computer Archaeology* 1:26–52.
1985   Determining empirical relationships between the natural environment and prehistoric site locations: A hunter-gatherer example. In *For concordance in archaeological analysis: Bridging data structure, quantitative technique, and theory*, edited by C. Carr, pp. 208–238. Westport Publishers and Institute for Quantitative Archaeology, University of Arkansas, Kansas City.
1988   Using existing archaeological survey data for model building. In *Quantifying the present, predicting the past*, edited by W. J. Judge and L. Sebastian, pp. 301–428. Bureau of Land Management, U.S. Department of the Interior, Denver, Colorado.
1990a The fundamental principles and practice of predictive archaeological modelling. In *Mathematics and information science in archaeology: A flexible framework*, edited by A. Voorips, pp. 257–295. Holos-Verlag, Bonn.
1990b GIS algorithms and their effects on regional archaeological analyses. In *Interpreting space: GIS and archaeology*, edited by K. M. S. Allen, S. W. Green, and E. B. W. Zubrow. Taylor and Francis, London.
1990c Spatial autocorrelation and the Classic Maya collapse revisited: Refined techniques and new conclusions. *Journal of Archaeological Science* 17:197–207.

1992   Terrain form analysis of archaeological location through geographic information systems. In *Computer applications and quantitative methods in archaeology 1991*, edited by G. Lock and J. Moffett, pp. 127–136. Tempus Reparatum, Oxford.

1997   Ranters corner: Bringing the camps together: GIS and ED. *Archaeological Computing Newsletter* 47:1–5.

Langran, G.
1992   *Time in geographic information systems.* Taylor and Francis, New York.

Llobera, M.
2000   Understanding movement: A pilot model towards the sociology of movement. In *Beyond the map: Archaeology and spatial technologies*, edited by G. Lock, pp. 65–84. IOS Press, Amsterdam.

Lock, G. R. (editor)
2000   *Beyond the map: Archaeology and spatial technologies.* NATO science series a: Life sciences. IOS Press, Amsterdam.

Lock, G. R., and P. T. Daly
1999   Looking at change, continuity and time in GIS: An example from the Sangro Valley, Italy. In *New techniques for old times: Caa98 computer applications and quantitative methods in archaeology*, edited by J. A. Barcelo, I. Briz, and A. Vila, pp. 259–263. Archaeopress, Oxford.

Lock, G. R., and T. M. Harris
1991   Integrating spatial information in computerised sites and monuments records: Meeting archaeological requirements in the 1990s. In *Computer applications and quantitative methods in archaeology 1990*, edited by K. Lockyear and S. Rahtz, pp. 165–173. British Archaeological Reports, Oxford.

1996   Danebury revisited: An English Iron Age hillfort in a digital landscape. In *Anthropology, space and geographic information systems*, edited by M. Aldenderfer and H. D. G. Maschner, pp. 214–240. Oxford University Press, New York.

Lock, G. R., and Z. Stancic (editors)
1995   *Archaeology and geographical information systems: A European perspective.* Taylor and Francis, London.

Loots, L.
1997   The use of projective and reflective viewsheds in the analysis of the hellenistic defence system at Sagalassos. *Archaeological Computing Newsletter* 49:12–16.

Marble, D. F.
1990   The potential methodological impact of geographic information systems on the social sciences. In *Interpreting space: GIS and archaeology*, edited by K. M. S. Allen, S. W. Green, and E. B. W. Zubrow, pp. 9–21. Taylor and Francis, London.

1996   The human effort involved in movement over natural terrain: A working bibliography. Department of Geography, Ohio State University, Columbus, Ohio.

Maschner, H. D. G. (editor)
1996a   *New methods, old problems: Geographical information systems in modern archaeological research.* Cia occasional paper no. 23. Southern Illinois University, Carbondale, Illinois.
1996b   The politics of settlement choice on the northwest coast: Cognition, GIS, and coastal landscapes. In *Anthropology, space and geographic information systems,* edited by M. Aldenderfer and H. D. G. Maschner, pp. 175–189. Oxford University Press, New York.

Matheron, G.
1971   *The theory of regionalised variables and its applications.* Ecole Nationale Superieure des Mines de Paris, Paris.

Neiman, F. D.
1997   Conspicuous consumption as wasteful advertising: A Darwinian perspective on spatial patterns in Classic Maya terminal monuments dates. In *Rediscovering Darwin: Evolutionary theory and archaeological explanation,* edited by M. C. Barton and G. A. Clark, pp. 267–290.

Neustupny, E.
1995   Beyond GIS. In *Archaeology and geographical information systems: A European perspective,* edited by G. Lock and Z. Stancic, pp. 133–139. Taylor and Francis, London.

Peucker, T. K., R. J. Fowler et al.
1978   *The triangulated irregular network.* The ASP Digital Terrain Models (DTM) Symposium, American Society of Photogrammetry, Falls Church, Virginia.

Rahtzel, F.
1882   *Anthropogeographie, oder grundzuge der anwendung der erdlkunde auf die geschichte.* Engelhorn, Stuttgart.

Ralston, B. A.
1994   Object oriented spatial analysis. In *Spatial analysis and GIS,* edited by S. Fotheringham and P. Rogerson, pp. 165–185. Taylor and Francis, London.

Raper, J. (editor)
1989   *Three dimensional applications in geographical information systems.* Taylor and Francis, London.

Renfrew, C.
1973   Monuments, mobilization and social organization in Neolithic wessex. In *The explanation of culture change: Models in prehistory,* edited by C. Renfrew, pp. 539–558. Duckworth, London.
1979   *Investigations in orkney.* Society of Antiquaries, London.

Robinson, J. M., and E. Zubrow
1999   Between spaces: Interpolation in archaeology. In *Geographic information systems and landscape archaeology,* edited by M. Gillings,
D. Mattingly and J. Van Dalen, pp. 65–83. Oxbow Books, Oxford.

Ruggles, C., and R. L. Church
1996   Spatial allocation in archaeology: An opportunity for reevaluation.
In *New methods, old problems: Geographic information systems in modern archaeological research,* edited by H. D. G. Maschner, pp. 147–173.
Southern Illinois University, Carbondale, Illinois.

Ruggles, C., R. Martlew et al.
1991   The north mull project (2): The wider astronomical significance of
the sites. *Archaeoastronomy* 16:51–75.

Ruggles, C., and D. J. Medyckyj-Scott
1996   Site location, landscape visibility and symbolic astronomy: A Scottish
case study. In *New methods, old problems: Geographic information systems
in modern archaeological research,* edited by H. D. G. Maschner, pp.
127–146. Southern Illinois University, Carbondale, Illinois.

Ruggles, C. L. N., D. J. Medyckyj-Scot et al.
1993   Multiple viewshed analysis using GIS and its archaeological application: A case study in northern mull. In *Computing the past: Computer applications and quantitative methods in archaeology—CAA 92,*
edited by J. Andresen, T. Madsen and I. Scollar, pp. 125–132. Aarhus
University Press, Aarhus, Denmark.

Savage, S. H.
1990   Modelling the late archaic social landscape. In *Interpreting space: GIS
and archaeology,* edited by K. M. S. Allen, S. Green and E. B. W.
Zubrow, pp. 330–335. Taylor and Francis, London.

Shanks, M., and C. Tilley
1987   *Social theory and archaeology.* Polity Press, Cambridge.

Shapiro, M.
1993   Grass 4.1 man page for s.Surf.Idw., U.S. Corps of Engineers.

Stancic, Z., and T. Veljanovski
2000   Understanding roman settlement patterns through multivariate
statistics and predictive modelling. In *Beyond the map: Archaeology
and spatial technologies,* edited by G. Lock, pp. 147–156. IOS Press,
Amsterdam.

Thomas, A. V.
1988   A survey of predictive locational models: Examples from the late
1970s and early 1980s. In *Quantifying the present, predicting the past,*
edited by W. J. Judge and L. Sebastian, pp. 581–645. Bureau of Land
Management, U.S. Department of the Interior, Denver, Colorado.

Thomas, J.
1996   *Time, culture and identity*. Routledge, London.

Tschan, A. P.
1999   An introduction to object-oriented GIS in archaeology. In *New techniques for old times: Caa98 computer applications and quantitative methods in archaeology*, edited by J. A. Barcelo, I. Briz and A. Vila, pp. 303–316. Archaeopress, Oxford.

van Leusen, M.
1993   Cartographic modelling in a cell-based GIS. In *Computing the past: Computer applications and quantitative methods in archaeology—CAA 92*, edited by J. Andresen, T. Madsen and I. Scollar, pp. 105–123. Aarhus University Press, Aarhus, Denmark.
1999   Viewshed and cost surface analysis using GIS (cartographic modelling in a cell-based GIS ii). In *New techniques for old times: Caa98*, edited by J. A. Barcelo, I. Briz, and A. Vila, pp. 215–223. Archaeopress, Oxford.

Vita-Finzi, C.
1978   *Archaeological Sites in their Setting*. Thames and Hudson, London.

Vita-Finzi, C., and E. Higgs
1970   Prehistoric economy in the Mount Carmel area of Palestine: Site catchment analysis. *Proceedings of the Prehistoric Society* 36:1–37.

von Thunen, J. H.
1966   *Der isolierte staat*. Pergamon, Oxford.

Wansleeben, M.
1988   Applications of geographical information systems in archaeological research. In *Computer and quantitative methods in archaeology 1988*, edited by S. P. Q. Rahtz, pp. 435–451. British Archaeological Reports, Oxford.

Warren, R. E., and D. L. Asch
2000   A predictive model of archaeological site location in the eastern prairie peninsula. In *Practical applications of GIS for archaeologists: A predictive modeling kit*, edited by K. L. Westcott and R. J. Brandon, pp. 5–32. Taylor and Francis, London.

Westcott, K. L., and R. J. Brandon (editors)
2000   *Practical applications of GIS for archaeologists: A predictive modeling kit*. Taylor and Francis, London.

Westcott, K. L., and J. A. Kuiper
2000   Using a GIS to model prehistoric site distributions in the upper Chesapeake Bay. In *Practical applications of GIS for archaeologists: A predictive modeling kit*, edited by K. L. Westcott and R. J. Brandon, pp. 59–72. Taylor and Francis, London.

Wheatley, D.
    1993   Going over old ground: GIS, archaeological theory and the act of per-
            ception. In *Computing the past: Computer applications and quantitative
            methods in archaeology—CAA 92*, edited by J. Andresen, T. Madsen, and
            I. Scollar, pp. 133–138. Aarhus University Press, Aarhus, Denmark.
    1995   Cumulative viewshed analysis: A GIS-based method for investigat-
            ing intervisibility, and its archaeological application. In *Archaeology
            and geographic information systems: A European perspective*, edited by
            G. Lock and Z. Stancic, pp. 171–185. Taylor and Francis, London.
    1996   The use of GIS to understand regional variation in Neolithic wes-
            sex. In *New methods, old problems: Geographic information systems in
            modern archaeological research*, edited by H. D. G. Maschner, pp.
            75–103. Southern Illinois University, Carbondale, Illinois.
    1998   Ranters corner: Keeping the camp fires burning: The case for plu-
            ralism. *Archaeological Computing Newsletter* 50(Spring 1998):2–7.
    2000   Spatial technology and archaeological theory revisited. In *Caa96
            computer applications and quantitative methods in archaeology*, edited
            by K. Lockyear, T. J. T. Sly, and V. Mihailescu-Birliba, pp. 123–131.
            Archaeopress, Oxford.

Wheatley, D., and M. Gillings
    2000   Vision, perception and GIS: Developing enriched approaches to the
            study of archaeological visibility. In *Beyond the map: Archaeology and
            spatial technologies*, edited by G. R. Lock, pp. 1–27. IOS Press, Ams-
            terdam.
    2002   *Spatial technology and archaeology: A guide to the archaeological applica-
            tions of GIS*. Taylor and Francis, London.

Wise, A. L.
    2000   Building theory into GIS based landscape analysis. In *Caa96 com-
            puter applications and quantitative methods in archaeology*, edited by
            K. Lockyear, T. J. T. Sly, and V. Mihailescu-Birliba, pp. 141–147. Ar-
            chaeopress, Oxford.

Woodman, P. E., and M. Woodward
    2002   The use and abuse of statistical methods in archaeological site location
            modelling. In *Contemporary themes in archaeological computing*, edited
            by D. Wheatley, G. Earl, and S. Poppy, pp. 39–43. Oxbow, Oxford.

Worboys, M. F.
    1995   *GIS: A computing perspective*. Taylor and Francis, London.

Zubrow, E. B. W.
    1990a   Modelling and prediction with geographic information systems: A
            demographic example from prehistoric and historic New York. In
            Interpreting space: GIS and archaeology, edited by K. Allen, S. Green,
            and E. Zubro, pp. 307–318. Taylor and Francis, London.
    1990b   Contemplating space: A commentary of theory. In *Interpreting space:
            GIS and archaeology*, edited by K. M. S. Allen, S. W. Green, and E. B.
            W. Zubrow, pp. 67–72. Taylor and Francis, London.

12

Terrestrial Remote Sensing in Archaeology

Kenneth L. Kvamme

> [Archaeological remote sensing is] the recognition, description, and interpretation of traces of the past, either on the surface or detectable from the surface.
> Hesse (2000:35)

> Anthropoextensionism; astronomy in the wrong direction; the art of sight and sense; seeing what can't be seen, then convincing someone that you're right; having fun without touching; legitimized voyeurism.
>
> Alfoldi et al. (1993:611–612)

Remote sensing in archaeology is an evolving enterprise, largely owing to rapid advances in technology but also to the changing needs and goals of the discipline. As the planet's exploding human population results in massive developments and changes to the landscape, a consequent need makes itself felt for efficient and cost-effective methods to locate, map, and acquire information from sites important to our cultural heritage before they are forever lost. At the same time, traditional archaeological excavations and pedestrian surveys are becoming increasingly expensive and commonly examine only trivial areas. Archaeological remote sensing allows large regions to be rapidly investigated for archaeological features, at relatively low cost; it can detect features unseen on the surface, precisely map them, and offer interpretations based on their form, distribution, and context. In

short, archaeological remote sensing may offer the only pragmatic means to locate, map, and inventory much of the world's
archaeological resources.

The term *terrestrial remote sensing* refers to many methods
and techniques, including the ground-based methods of geophysics (e.g., magnetometry, ground-penetrating radar), aerial
surveys (e.g., photography, thermography), and satellite imaging. All have advantages and limitations. Remote sensing is
viewed here as any technique that acquires information through
indirect means; techniques like geochemistry that require analyses of soil samples are not examined. Finally, focus is placed on
methods that detect actual archaeological features—walls,
houses, pits, hearths, ditches, roads—as opposed to applications
that merely map environmental communities or geological circumstances using air or space data.

Remote-sensing techniques measure physical properties of
the surface or of near-surface deposits—usually in the uppermost
1–2 m in archaeology. Some methods record variations only at the
surface; others can penetrate below to a degree that varies with
soil properties, vegetation cover, and types of archaeological features. Active and passive technologies are employed. The former
might induce an electrical current or transmit a radar beam and
record a response; the latter measures natural properties, such as
reflected light or the strength of the Earth's magnetic field. Most
sensors respond to only a narrow range of physical properties, so
multiple methods generally offer greater insights. Buried cultural
features not revealed by one may be made visible by another or
provide complementary information; a hearth and burned elements of a buried house may be revealed by magnetometry and
its compacted floor by ground-penetrating radar or associated
surface vegetation changes by aerial photography (Clay 2001;
David 2001; Donoghue 2001).

Useful results are obtained from *contrasts* between archaeological features and the natural background. When archaeological deposits or features possess physical properties different
from those of the surrounding matrix, the distinction may be noticed. A buried stone foundation might be more magnetic, better
reflect radar energy, more slowly emit thermal energy, and stunt
overlying plant life compared with the surrounding earth. Con-

trasts are referred to as *anomalies* until they can be identified, a task that may require excavation. Frequently, anomalies illustrate a pattern sufficiently clear for direct interpretation, as when the rectangle of a house foundation is unambiguously expressed. It is a fundamental tenet of remote sensing (Avery and Berlin 1992:52) that patterned geometric shapes in the landscape—circles, ellipses, squares, rectangles, and straight lines—are generally of human origin; they occur much less frequently as products of nature. The survey and imaging of large contiguous areas increase the likelihood that whole cultural features with regular, interpretable geometries will be recognized. The imaging of large regions is, of course, easier with airborne or satellite methods, but faster instruments and better field practices now enable ground-based geophysical surveys of nearly a hectare per day (Kvamme 2001a).

Nature of Archaeological Sites

An archaeological site is a three-dimensional matrix of materials existing in the present, containing artifacts, human-generated constructions, and the deposits in which they lie (see Schiffer 1976). Our collected knowledge of this matrix suggests features that might be remotely detected and the sensor requirements to detect them (see Scollar et al. 1990:4–7).

Artifacts are material objects modified by people, both smaller portable artifacts (spear points, pots, knives) and nonportable artifacts that include such larger items as cut posts, building timbers, bricks, or shaped stones used in architectural constructions.

Constructions include the many types of structures, buildings, and other facilities, including places of occupancy (dwellings, public structures), nonoccupancy (storage pits, wells, burial mounds, fortification ditches), and transportation facilities (roads). Although many include multiple robust nonportable artifacts such as stone blocks or bricks, most are represented archaeologically by more subtle changes in deposits, as ditches, house pits, or storage pits become filled with sediments or buried wooden posts and structures decompose into soil.

Sediments and soils are the deposits within which artifacts and constructions lie. Most result from natural processes, but many are anthropogenic or are altered by human activity. In the latter group an *additive deposit* occurs where materials are accumulated, such as at places where refuse is dumped (middens containing food waste, bones, discarded portable artifacts) or where earth materials are placed to form constructions (burial mounds, platforms, prepared house floors, raised berms). *Deposit subtraction* occurs when sediments and soils are removed through construction of ditches, pits, or cellars or when incisions in the surface are caused by foot or vehicular traffic. Other deposits are *altered* by human activity. Intensive firing in a hearth, kiln, or a burned house can profoundly increase soil magnetism, and even the simple act of human occupation subtly raises the magnetic susceptibility of soils (see later discussion).

Properties of Archaeological Sites: What Can Be Remotely Sensed?

In general, large nonportable artifacts such as building foundations or pavement stones frequently can be remotely detected but small portable artifacts cannot (except metallic artifacts). Large masses of individual portable artifacts and other anthropogenic materials *might* occasionally be revealed by remote sensing as when a concentration of ceramic sherds subtly raises the local magnetic field or a large amount of bone from an animal kill changes subsurface electrical or thermal properties or surface vegetation patterns.

Human constructions receive focus in remote sensing because their larger sizes and relative masses of contrasting physical properties sufficiently increase detection probabilities and their regular geometric shapes make them more easily recognized as cultural anomalies. Additive deposits tend to be very different in character. Middens, filled with refuse, might be less compacted and contain inclusions of solids like bone and discarded artifacts, more soil nutrients, or different levels of moisture, altering their electrical, thermal, or surface vegetation patterns (Scollar et al. 1990; Weymouth 1986). Mound creation often employs topsoil, which generally exhibits greater magnetic susceptibility, raising the local magnetic field, whereas areas where topsoil was removed for mound or ditch construction tend to create local deflations in the magnetic field. Burned features profoundly increase soil magnetism (Clark 2000). Large constructions near the surface can affect patterns of surface vegetation: a buried stone wall retards growth or moist sediments filling a former ditch advance it, in either case altering the spectral properties of the plants (Scollar et al. 1990; Wilson 2000). Variations in deposit materials, their compaction, moisture retention, and other factors affect absorption and emissivity rates of solar radiation, causing thermal variations (Dabas and Tabbagh 2000). Finally, buried structural features can cause subtle terrain variations recordable on the surface (Newman 1993).

Sensor Mixes and Detection Probabilities

The likelihood of a buried archaeological feature being detected depends on a complex interaction among at least five factors: (1) matching the contrasting physical properties of the feature with sensors capable of detecting those properties, (2) the amount of contrast between the physical properties of the feature and surrounding deposits with respect to sensor sensitivity, (3) the size of the feature relative to the spatial resolution of the measurements, (4) the depth of the feature with respect to signal attenuation and levels of confounding noise, and (5) the degree of regular pattern the feature exhibits.

The spatial resolution of sensors determines the size of archaeological features that can be resolved, a rule of thumb being that the interval between measurements should be no greater than *half* the size of the smallest feature to be detected (allowing multiple measurements to delineate it; Weymouth 1986:347). This requirement explains why resolving small portable artifacts and features is usually impossible. In general, the closer a sensor is to the ground the greater the spatial resolution and detail that can be achieved, giving ground-based methods the overall highest detection probabilities, but aerial methods also offer very high spatial resolutions, well into the submeter range. Until recently, satellite remote sensing, with spatial resolutions only in the 10–30 m range, was too coarse to detect archaeological features, but new sensor systems offer spatial resolutions in the vicinity of 1 m. Detection probabilities are also affected by instrument sensitivity. A magnetometer with a precision of 0.1 nanotesla (nT) can detect smaller, deeper, and more subtle anomalies than one that measures only to the 1 nT level, for example.

Regular anomalies with geometric shapes (lines, circles, rectangles) are easier to recognize as archaeological features than are unpatterned ones that could also result from biological activity (tree throws, animal dens). Deep-buried archaeological features are more difficult to detect than shallow ones because the soils above may degrade the signal. Metallic litter, agricultural practices (plowing), modern constructions (fence and power lines, pipes), and biological phenomena (rodent burrows) all introduce noise to remote sensing data sets. Furthermore, complex archaeological deposits can make anomaly interpretation difficult; dense cultural stratigraphy or superimposed constructions can so jumble the signals that patterns are made unclear.

Environmental conditions at the time of data acquisition greatly influence results. Daylight, obviously required for many forms of air or space imaging, may be unnecessary for thermal remote sensing. Low sunlight is necessary to achieve the terrain shadowing in aerial photography necessary to detect relief changes. Vegetation at a particular stage of development is necessary for crop marking, visible from the air or space, and resistivity-conductivity methods cannot be explored in frozen ground. Too much or too little soil moisture can upset soil resistivity, conductivity, or thermal surveys, whereas too much moisture may impede transmission of radar energy. Buried pipes, electrical lines, or radio transmissions can negatively affect many ground-based instruments. In general, remote sensing is better in open fields with uniform ground cover than in heavily vegetated or wooded landscapes and urban areas where many methods of remote detection prove impossible (Bewley 2000; Clark 2000; Dabas and Tabbagh 2000; Scollar et al. 1990).

Ground-Based Remote Sensing

Ground-based remote sensing employs instruments on or near the surface. Most methods are geophysical, measuring physical and chemical properties of near-surface deposits—usually in the uppermost 1–2 m. Four methods are principally employed: magnetometry, electrical resistivity, electromagnetic (EM) conductivity, and ground-penetrating radar (GPR). All but the first are active methods. Resistivity and conductivity measure the same earth property, whereas the others generally assess different and mostly independent dimensions (Weymouth 1986:371).

Archaeogeophysical data are typically acquired in *area surveys* by grids that typically range from 20 × 20 m to 50 × 50 m. Ropes or tapes with meter marks are placed at right angles to form the grids. The instruments are moved along these guides to locate measurements accurately. Spatial resolution is controlled by the separation between transects, the number of samples taken per meter, and the sampling capabilities of the technology (see Clark 2000:158–164). High spatial resolutions, the closer relation of these methods to the archaeology, and the very different physical dimensions measured combine to give geophysical methods high detection probabilities for small and varied cultural features. Level fields with low vegetation make instrument passage easier whereas large rocks, trees, and other impediments hinder or prevent survey. EM fields from power lines, electrical storms, or cell phones may impede surveys with certain instruments, as can metallic litter and passing or parked automobiles.

In Europe, geophysical surveys form an integral part of archaeology and are routinely used or even required by law for site discovery and feature mapping (Schmidt 2001). Training and exposure to archaeogeophysics are commonly available to students; a large corpus of practitioners exists in private, university, and government sectors; and extensive libraries and national databases of results are available, many on the Internet (e.g., the English Heritage Geophysical Survey Database, http://www .eng-h.gov.uk/SDB, and the Austrian ArcheoProspections, http://www.univie.ac.at/Projekte/Idea/Prosp). In North America, on the other hand, programs of training are rare, the methods are relatively unused, and there are relatively few practitioners (Conyers and Gaffney 2000). Bevan (2000) estimates that perhaps 550 archaeological projects employed geophysical methods in North America through the twentieth century—only a small fraction of the total in England alone where many thousands of archaeogeophysical projects were undertaken just since 1990, as the English Heritage Geophysical Survey Database shows. This situation is rapidly changing, with annual increases in projects and funding, a growing practitioner base, an increasing list of conference presentations and publications, and now a national online database of results, the North American Database of Archaeological Geophysics (http://www.cast.uark.edu/nadag).

Magnetometry

Magnetometry surveys are generally the most productive of ground-based methods owing to very fast instrumentation (8–10 measurements/s) that allows coverage of large areas in short amounts of time (0.5–1 ha/day), high sampling rates (8–16/m), and the many characteristics of archaeological deposits that yield magnetic variations. Eight principal phenomena contribute to the formation of magnetic anomalies within archaeological sites (Clark 2000; Scollar et al. 1990; Weymouth 1986).

- *Firing of the soil* beyond the Curie point (about 600°C, depending on the material), whether purposeful (hearths, kilns) or accidental (a burned house), can intensify the local magnetic field owing to thermoremanent magnetism.
- *Accumulations of fired artifacts*, such as ceramics or bricks, can intensify the local magnetic field.
- *Variations in soils and sediments* can yield different magnetic susceptibilities, the ease with which a material becomes magnetized when subjected to a magnetic field such as the Earth's. Magnetic susceptibility is determined by the composition and concentration (mineralogy, size, and shape) of magnetizable materials.
- *Surface soil layers become magnetically enhanced* by several processes that include burning, weathering, and chemical reactions that change certain iron compounds to more

magnetic forms (Dearing et al. 1996) and magnetotactic and other bacteria that concentrate magnetic compounds (Fassbinder et al. 1990). Extended human occupations exacerbate this phenomenon through the introduction of organic and fired materials to the topsoil. Paleosols tend to retain this effect.

- *Removal of magnetically enriched topsoil* during the construction of ditches, house pits, or other excavations lowers the local magnetic field over these features.
- *Accumulations of topsoil*, in mound or sod constructions or when storage or other pit features become filled, increase the magnetic field locally.
- *Imported stone* employed in the construction of buildings or pavements might be more (igneous rocks) or less magnetic (certain limestones) than surrounding soils.
- *Iron-bearing artifacts* markedly alter the Earth's magnetic field, producing large *dipolar* measurements consisting of paired positive and negative extremes.

Magnetic field strength is measured in nanoteslas (10^{-9} tesla). At midlatitudes the Earth's field ranges from about 40,000 to 55,000 nT (Weymouth 1986:341). Anomalies of archaeological interest typically lie within plus or minus 5 nT and often far less— recent work by Becker (1995) shows anomalies in the picotesla (0.001 nT) range, requiring survey instrumentation to be extremely sensitive. Owing to the rapid falloff of magnetic field strength with the third power of distance, magnetic prospecting is typically confined to the upper 2 m of deposits, unless the magnetic source is large (Clark 2000:78–80). The instrument operator must be free of ferrous material; steel fences, passing automobiles, and magnetic fields generated by power lines all pose survey difficulties.

Early work utilized proton precession magnetometers that were capable of 0.1 nT resolution but slow, requiring 5–7 seconds for a measurement (Weymouth 1986). The Earth's magnetic field changes continuously through the day, typically by 40–100 nT in a diurnal variation, but considerably more during magnetic storms; this problem was usually handled by using a second instrument at a fixed locus that recorded temporal magnetic changes simultaneously with a roving field unit (Weymouth and Lessard 1986). By differencing the two data sets, measurements could be derived representing only spatial variation. Contemporary work employs fluxgate or cesium vapor magnetic gradiometers that yield 0.1 nT resolution or better, with rapid acquisition rates. As gradiometers they do not measure total magnetic field strength but the difference between two sensors vertically separated (usually by 0.5–1 m), yielding a vertical gradient measurement of the magnetic field free of diurnal variations (Kvamme 2001a).

Magnetometry surveys, the workhorse of archaeogeophysics, have successful case studies numbering in the thousands from around the globe. Owing to the high speed of instrumentation, a number of large magnetometry surveys have been conducted, including complete coverage across 78 ha of the Roman city of Wroxeter, England (Gaffney et al. 2000), and an even larger region at the Iron Age citadel of Kerkenes Dag, Turkey (Summers et al. 1996). A magnetic gradiometry survey of the Fort Clark trading post (1831–1861), an important center of the American fur trade in what is now North Dakota, illustrates large-area results (Figure 12.1a). It clearly reveals the rectangular trading post (about a half meter below the surface), with room blocks and rooms, bastions on the western and eastern corners, an entryway facing the Missouri River to the east, the interior compound, and even the locus of the centrally placed flagpole (verified by excavation). Outside, to the north, lies the circular earthlodge (an earth-covered domelike dwelling) and surrounding compound of the Arikara interpreter at the trading post. A large dumping ground lies to the west, composed of many anomalies representing individual cartloads of rubbish, debris composed of iron artifacts, and fired earth and ash. Finally, individual graves in a European American cemetery and borrow pits used for various constructions can be discerned to the south. Sources of the anomalies seen include a highly magnetic sandstone used for foundation blocks, the burning of the trading post in 1861, hearths, iron artifacts, mounded topsoil (especially about the interpreter's compound perimeter), and soil removal at the borrow pits and graves (Kvamme 2003).

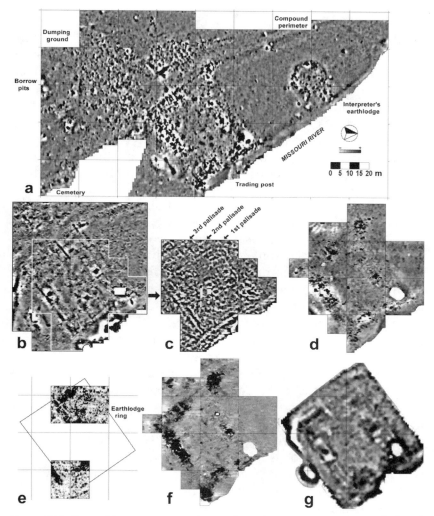

Figure 12.1. Ground-base remote-sensing results at the ca. 1831–1861 Fort Clark trading post, North Dakota: (a) magnetometry, (b) resistivity (50 cm probe separation), (c) resistivity (1.5 m probe separation), (d) EM conductivity, (e) GPR, (f) magnetic susceptibility, (g) exaggerated and enhanced surface elevation data.

Electrical Resistivity and Electromagnetic Conductivity

Resistivity and conductivity methods quantify identical aspects of deposits in very different ways. Soil resistivity to an electrical current depends on material type, moisture, dissolved ion content, density, pore space, and other factors (Weymouth 1986:319). Soil conductivity is simply the inverse of resistivity: a highly resistant material is a poor conductor. These methods are sensitive both to subsurface contrasts caused by highly resistant stone or brick (e.g., foundations or floors) and to more subtle changes in soils and sediments. Moist sediments filling a ditch might exhibit low resistivity (high conductivity), but low compaction and high porosity within a midden could yield high resistivity (low conductivity) measurements.

A resistivity survey uses a small power source and two probes to inject a current through conductive earth, which is measured. Two other probes measure voltage, and the ratio of voltage to current yields resistance, according to Ohm's law. In the traditional Wenner configuration, the four probes are separated along a line by an equal distance, with the current probes on opposite ends. In a uniform matrix, voltage varies with distance from the current probes in regular hemispheres. If voltage is measured on the surface 1 m from a current probe, it is roughly equivalent to the voltage a meter below the surface, so probe separation controls prospecting depth (Clark 2000:27–30). In practice, the subsurface may not be uniform, so the depth criterion is only an approximation; the ability to distinctly resolve buried features also decreases with depth. Because resistance partially depends on probe arrangements, it is normally converted to *resistivity*, a measure of a bulk property of soil. For the Wenner array, resistivity in ohms per meter is equal to $2\pi Rd$, where R is resistance in ohms and d is the interprobe distance in meters (Weymouth 1986:323). In current practice, large-area surveys use a twin-electrode configuration, a modified Wenner, where pairs of current and voltage probes are separated by a large distance. Only one pair, held in a rigid frame, is moved during the survey, while the other remains fixed in the ground, offering greater speed and a clearer response (Clark 2000:37–53).

Resistivity measurements taken at a single point, but with different probe separations, yield variations with depth, known as a *sounding*. A series of soundings along a transect produces a *pseudosection* (a profile of the subsurface; Aspinall and Crummett 1997); a regular collection of pseudosections yields a three-dimensional volume that allows *resistivity tomography* studies where the measurement matrix may be sliced along any axis to investigate vertical relationships, stratigraphy, or plan views at various depths—the current state of the art with specifically designed instruments (Walker 2000).

EM-induction instruments use a radio transmitter to induce an EM field in the ground. If conductive materials are present, eddy currents are generated that produce a secondary EM field, proportional to soil conductivity, which is measured by a surface receiver. Conductivity is quantified in millisiemens (mS; 10^{-3} siemens) per meter, with a theoretical relationship with resistivity equal to 1,000/ohm/m (Bevan 1983). Without probes to insert in the ground, EM instruments are very fast but typically lack the resistivity meter's ready ability to target specific depths through simple adjustments in probe separation. By changing the transmitting frequency or the separation between transmitting and receiving antennas, responses from different depths can be measured, but most instruments are manufactured with fixed settings. The most popular instrument averages soil conductivity through a depth of about 1.5 m, with peak sensitivity at 0.4 m below the instrument in a vertical dipole mode; others can prospect much more deeply. All instruments can also operate in a horizontal dipole mode simply by turning them on their side and approximately halving prospecting depth (McNeil 1980).

In very dry deposits it can be difficult or even impossible to get a current to flow in the ground with either resistivity or EM methods. This is especially true of the former, where surface dryness can produce infinitely high probe-contact resistances; in these settings EM instruments can sometimes induce currents in moister layers below (Frohlich and Lancaster 1986). Because ground moisture plays a major role, different results can be obtained depending on moisture conditions (Al Chalabi and Rees 1962). Unlike resistivity surveys, EM instruments are also sensitive to buried metals, ferrous and nonferrous, that show up as extreme values because metals are highly conductive. As in magnetic surveys, this may be an advantage or disadvantage depending on the site and research goals—whether one wants to locate metallic artifacts or avoid metallic litter. Common sampling rates for resistivity-conductivity surveys are one to two measurements per meter.

At the Fort Clark trading post, a resistivity survey at a target depth of 50 cm defines the trading post and many individual rooms as positive anomalies caused in part by foundation stones, but perhaps a quarter of them represent archaeological trenches from the 1970s, seen as high resistivity owing to lower soil compaction (Kvamme 2003; see Figure 12.1b). A second resistivity survey at a target depth of 1.5 m indicates robust negative anomalies, the loci of deep builder's trenches used to socket large outer palisade timbers in several episodes of rebuilding—likely caused by increased soil moisture within the trenches (see Figure 12.1c). An EM soil-conductivity survey emphasizes the very different results that can sometimes occur in response to the same physical properties (note the reversed response; high resistivity features seen in the resistivity data exhibit low conductivity; see Figure 12.1d).

Ground-Penetrating Radar

GPR sends rapid but distinct pulses of microwave energy into the subsurface along the length of a survey transect. These pulses reflect off such buried features as stratigraphic contacts, walls, house floors, pits, rubble, or middens. The return times or echoes from subsurface reflectors give estimates of depths, and the magnitudes of the reflected waves indicate something of the materials in the ground. Because the outcome of a series of reflected waves stacked side by side mimics a vertical section or profile along a survey transect, GPR data in their native form are ideally suited for gaining information in the vertical plane, including stratigraphic relationships (Bevan 1998:43–57; Conyers and Goodman 1997).

A complete GPR system is typically composed of a control unit, a display unit, a transducer, a number of cables, and a power source. Initial results may be viewed on a video display in real time as data are collected, making instant field interpretations possible. The transducer contains transmitting and receiving antennas in the 100–1,500 MHz range, with 300–500 MHz most popular in archaeology. As radar pulses are transmitted into the earth, their velocity changes with the electrical properties of the materials they travel through. Each velocity change returns a reflection recorded at the surface. Relative dielectric permittivity measures how easily a material polarizes when subjected to EM radiation; metals possess a nearly infinite coefficient, so they give very strong reflections. The dielectric properties of other materials vary considerably; in general, the higher the coefficient, the slower the velocity of radar waves passing through them (Conyers and Goodman 1997:32–34). The velocity of EM energy in air is about 30 cm/ns (ns = nanoseconds = 10^{-9} seconds), but much less in soils. Mussett and Khan (2000:229) report a velocity of 15 cm/nS in dry sand, 6 cm/nS in wet sand, and about 5 cm/nS in wet clay.

GPR times the microwave pulses in a two-way travel timescale that must be calibrated to estimate an approximate depth to anomalies. Knowledge of soil types and their dielectric properties offers one means. The most accurate method is to excavate to the indicated anomaly and calibrate actual depths with travel times. A third method uses the hyperbolic reflectors commonly seen in GPR profiles, which arise from the shape of a transmitted radar signal, a cone with a 60°–90° angle. This wide arc means the transducer senses echoes from a reflector before and after moving across it. The distance, and therefore time, the transmitted and reflected energy must travel is at a minimum when the transducer is vertically above the reflector and is larger before or after the approach. The consequence is a hyperbolically shaped return with a measurable width that is a function of soil velocity (Bevan 1998:50–52).

GPR signals attenuate with depth and increased soil conductivity. Penetration is less in wet soils than dry, and ion-laden deposits with high clay, salt, or organic content can limit penetration (Weymouth 1986). Signal attenuation is also a function of frequency but so is resolving power. The reflection returned by a subsurface feature depends on its size relative to wavelength or frequency. With a low-frequency antenna, subsurface features must be very large to be "seen" (Conyers and Goodman 1997), but low frequencies allow greater prospecting depths.

GPR instruments sample measurements intensively, with 20–50 scans per meter commonly sent into the earth, each digitized in 500–2,000 increments, potentially yielding tens of thousands of measurements per cubic meter! One consequence of this large data volume is a commensurate increase in the difficulty and complexity of data handling and processing, a nontrivial task. Another is that smaller areas typically are surveyed, with focus on anomalies revealed by other methods, but as computer software and hardware continue to evolve, larger surveys become increasingly feasible. New methods employ closely spaced parallel transects, 0.5 m apart or less. Software is then able to correlate and interpolate information about depth and reflector strength between the profiles, creating a three-dimensional data volume. One outcome is horizontal time slices—plan-view maps at various reflection times (a proxy for depth) below the surface that have remarkably increased the interpretability of GPR data (Goodman et al. 1995; Malagodi et al. 1996). After all, many archaeological features with regular geometric shapes, such as house floors or foundations, are easily recognized in plan view but not in cross section. Owing to its high sampling density and three-dimensional capabilities, there are high expectations for GPR, but experience shows it may or may not outperform other geophysical methods depending on conditions.

At Fort Clark, GPR was employed in two regions (see Figure 12.1e). Its greater depth sensitivity and improved spatial detail (from its higher sampling density) show anomalies not revealed by other methods (compare Figure 12.1a through d), including a circular feature 18 m in diameter, the typical signature and size of earthlodges that populate a Native American village lying a short distance away, suggesting one beneath the trading post (see Figure 12.2c for a larger view of the site showing the nearby village; Kvamme 2002).

Other Geophysical Methods

Magnetic susceptibility surveys quantify the *potential* of materials to be magnetized when subject to a magnetic field, such as the Earth's, and offer a different view of archaeological deposits than conventional magnetometry. Most are based on laboratory measurements of soil samples and are not remote sensing as defined here. Several studies have utilized the in-phase component of EM-induction instruments to measure magnetic susceptibility in the field, although only at very shallow depths, ranging from a few centimeters to perhaps 0.5 m (see Challand 1992). At Fort Clark, magnetic susceptibility measurements with an EM-induction instrument gave excellent indications of the complex of rooms thanks to the sandstone foundation blocks, with their high magnetic susceptibility (Kvamme 2002; see Figure 12.1f).

Seismic techniques, central to geological geophysics, are relatively unused in archaeology. Conceptually, they are related to GPR but record acoustic instead of microwave energy. In seismic-refraction surveys, artificial shock waves are created by a sledgehammer striking a rubber pad or through explosive detonation caps. Geophone sensors at intervals along transects record the time (in milliseconds) and amplitude of the waves as they reach each one. Variations in timing and amplitude can indicate stratigraphic layering or large anomalous features such as ditches or architectural constructions (Goulty and Hudson 1994; Tsokas et al. 1995).

Metal detectors are EM-induction instruments optimized to detect metallic objects of any kind in the near surface, usually the uppermost 0.5 m (Connor and Scott 1998). Useful for mapping concentrations of metallic debris as well as locating isolated items in recent archaeological sites, they are especially valuable on battlefields where metallic targets ranging from weapons to bullets and expended ordinance are readily located and mapped (Scott et al. 1989; Sivilich 1996).

Other methods far less explored in archaeology include induced polarization (Ovenden and Aspinall 1991), self potential (Wynn and Sherwood 1984), and gravity techniques (Linington 1966).

Surface Elevation Data

Many archaeological sites possess subtle, or even pronounced, terrain variations caused by what lies immediately beneath. In aerial archaeology, low light angles have been exploited to emphasize small altitudinal changes through shadowing, allowing poorly visible settlement and architectural details to be mapped (see also below). This can be digitally replicated with high-density surface elevations recorded across an area by on-the-ground survey teams. Vertical-relief exaggeration and analytic surface-shading algorithms (common geographic information system [GIS] methods, see later discussion on computer methods) highlight archaeological signatures in the terrain. Although time-consuming to collect, benefits include the acquisition of surface data even in heavily forested areas (difficult from the air), shadowing from virtually any light-source angle (even those impossible in nature), and exaggeration of the vertical dimension by any amount to reveal features of extreme subtlety. Most systematic work in this area has been conducted in Ireland (Doody et al. 1995; Newman 1993), and some elsewhere (e.g., Shapiro and Miller 1990). At Fort Clark nearly 4,000 elevations were recorded every meter over its surface (Kvamme 2002); computer processing removed trends in slope and analytic shading allowed visualization of internal features, including walls and individual rooms not recognizable on the surface (see Figure 12.1g). New airborne laser altimetry (see later discussion) yields high-spatial-resolution surface elevation data over large areas that will ultimately replace ground measurements.

Aerial Remote Sensing

Remote sensing from the air or space uses EM radiation reflected or emitted from the Earth's surfaces, offering a cost-efficient means for archaeological reconnaissance over wide areas (Bewley 2000:3). Aerial remote sensing uses airborne platforms; space remote sensing, orbiting satellites, the topic of a later section. Both employ similar sensors; their principal difference lies in grossly divergent distances from the Earth's surface, which until recently, has profoundly affected the spatial detail of what could be resolved from space. Aerial photography is the oldest and most-used domain of archaeological remote sensing and receives greatest focus, but other sensing devices have been placed in the air in recent decades, including passive multispectral and thermal sensors, and active radar and laser altimeter systems, making aerial remote sensing truly multidimensional.

Theory and Sensors

The EM spectrum. The sun, source of most of the electromagnetic radiation (EMR) impinging on the Earth, emits a spectrum ranging from biologically lethal gamma rays (short wavelength, high frequency) to passive radio waves (long wavelength, low frequency). For convenience, the spectrum is divided into regions possessing similar characteristics, spectral bands. In order of increasing wavelength, the bands used in remote sensing include ultraviolet (UV), visible, infrared (IR), and microwave. Although EMR travels through empty space unimpeded, the Earth's atmosphere allows certain wavelengths to pass freely (atmospheric windows, or transmission bands), whereas others are blocked (atmospheric blinds, or absorption bands), including short-wavelength gamma, X-ray, and most UV radiation. The visible band (0.4–0.7 μm) is the region most commonly used with white light composed of three segments representing the additive primary colors blue (0.4–0.5 μm), green (0.5–0.6 μm), and red (0.6–0.7 μm). The more complex IR band is commonly divided into near (NIR: 0.7–1.5 μm), middle (MIR: 1.5–5.6 μm), and far (FIR: 5.6–1,000 μm) regions but also addressed as reflected IR vs. emitted or thermal IR. On average, slightly more than half of the EMR hitting the Earth reaches the surface, the rest being reflected or absorbed by the atmosphere. A small fraction of this energy is reflected from the surface as UV, visible, NIR, or MIR radiation, detectable from air- or spacecraft. The remainder, absorbed by various surfaces, is transformed into low-temperature heat (felt as surface warming) that is reradiated continuously back into the atmosphere as long-wave thermal radiation (about 3–1,000 μm, in the MIR and FIR ranges). Finally, the longer-wavelength microwave band (1 mm to 1 m) is used in radar (from radio detection and ranging) remote sensing, some of which can pass through clouds, precipitation, tree canopies, or even dry sand (Avery and Berlin 1992:3–14; Sabins 1997:2–6).

Spectral signatures. Any surface reflects or emits EMR over a range of wavelengths in a unique manner depending on its physical composition and state. The average amount of incident radiation reflected by a surface in some wavelength interval is its spectral reflectance, or *albedo*, and emitted radiation yields information about temperature properties. This distinctive spectral-response pattern, diagnostic of particular surfaces and their states, forms a *spectral signature*, allowing surfaces to be recognized from their spectrum. Water tends to reflect blue wavelengths and almost no NIR; most healthy vegetation reflects some green light but is enormously reflective in NIR; and many distinctive properties of soils and geological deposits are discriminated in NIR and MIR bands (Avery and Berlin 1992:14–15).

Sensor types. Sensor type determines the regions of the spectrum used. Some sensors provide photographs, pictorial representations recorded directly onto photographic film; others generate an *image*, using the term in its more general meaning to refer to all pictorial representations of remotely sensed data. All photographs are images, but not all images are photographs.

Photographic cameras react to reflected radiation from a ground scene by recording variations in the intensity of light through a photochemical reaction on a frame in a roll of film. The region a camera views is determined by its angular field of view (AFOV), a geometric function of the camera's focal length relative to the edge of the film plane (format size) and platform altitude. Mapping or metric cameras are specially designed for vertical aerial photography at high resolution with minimal geometric distortion, allowing precise measurements and accurate maps to be generated. Films contain a thin emulsion of light-sensitive silver halide grains (0.1–5 µm in diameter) that undergo a photochemical reaction proportional to the number of photons hitting them during an exposure. Black-and-white (BW) films are either panchromatic (sensitive to light of all colors, from 0.25 to 0.7 µm) or IR (sensitive to 0.25–0.92 µm). Color films are normal color (sensitive to the visible spectrum, 0.4–0.7 µm) or false-color IR (sensitive to green through NIR in the 0.5–0.92 µm range), where green light is portrayed as blue, red as green, and NIR radiation as red. Filtering is generally necessary in aerial photography. Panchromatic air photos frequently use a yellow filter that absorbs UV and blue light, the principal wavelengths causing haze, making minus-blue photos. Blocking filters absorb virtually any chosen group of wavelengths, allowing red-only, green-only, or blue-only light or solely IR radiation for infrared photography (Sabins 1997:33–58; Scollar et al. 1990:77–112).

Electro-optical sensors are nonfilm detectors that convert radiation from the ground to electrical signals proportional to the amount of energy hitting them. Having much broader bandwidth than photographic systems (near UV [NUV] to FIR vs. NUV to NIR), they are sensitive to reflected and emitted EMR, the latter allowing nighttime imaging. Across-track scanners predominate. Rather than imaging an entire scene instantaneously, as does a photographic camera, they scan a series of contiguous narrow strips at right angles to the direction of platform movement via an oscillating or rotating mirror. As the platform's forward motion creates new scan lines, a two-dimensional record of EMR is built up along the flight path. The altitude of the platform coupled with the collecting mirror's AFOV determines the ground swath, or width of a scan line. The instantaneous field of view (IFOV) is a smaller angle that determines how much a scanner images at a given moment; its area represents the ground-resolution cell of a single picture element (pixel) in the imaged data. A small IFOV yields high spatial detail, but a wider one has a longer dwell time, allowing more radiation to impinge for a stronger signal and the possibility of detecting smaller variations in EMR. Multispectral scanners collect data from multiple bands simultaneously with several detectors sensitive to specific wavelengths. Hyperspectral scanners, a more recent development, do the same with a large number (e.g., 100–300) of very narrow and contiguous bands (Avery and Berlin 1992:109–134; Limp 1989:1–29; Sever 2000:29–30).

In *microwave systems*, a third class of sensors, radar sends pulses of microwave energy to the ground; depending on the physical characteristics of the surfaces and angles of incidence, varying amounts of energy are echoed or backscattered to the sensor, making it an active method employable day or night. Wavelengths vary from a few millimeters to about 1 m, a portion of the spectrum with almost no atmospheric attenuation, allowing it to perform in all weathers, passing through clouds or precipitation and even, depending on the frequencies employed, through tree canopies or dry surface deposits like sand. The microwave spectrum is itself divided into various bands, arbitrarily labeled K (0.8–2.4 cm), X (2.4–3.8 cm), C (3.8–7.5 cm), S (7.5–15 cm), L (15–30 cm), and P (30–100 cm). Each possesses different properties; in general, longer wavelengths penetrate better. Most radar systems are side looking: they acquire data at an angle off to the side of the platform, a concept pioneered by the military because it allowed safe imaging into enemy territory from friendly space. They also tend to be synthetic aperture radar systems (SARs; aperture means antenna), where the forward motion of the platform simulates an antenna much longer than the actual one carried, for much higher resolutions from greater distances. With microwave energy transmitted at an angle relative to the plane of the Earth, considerable geometric distortion and terrain foreshortening of slopes can occur. Strong echoes are represented by bright tones, weaker reflections by medium grays, and radar shadows with no return appear black. Surface properties also determine backscatter return strength and image tone. Terrain shape produces one of the largest effects, slopes perpendicular to the beam being brightest. Surface roughness relative to wavelength affects the amount of backscatter. Smooth surfaces (pavements, calm water) reflect energy away from the sensor so they appear dark, whereas rough surfaces (boulder fields, lava beds, vegetation canopies) send much of the energy back. The dielectric properties of the surface material (see previous discussion on GPR) also influence relative scene brightness. Landscapes with high soil moisture, and therefore a higher dielectric constant, produce much stronger returns than very dry deposits. In very dry sands (where the dielectric constant is extremely low), long-wave radar energy has penetrated the subsurface to depths of perhaps 4 m (see later discussion on space radar; Avery and Berlin 1992:161–192; Sabins 1997:177–210).

Digital data. A benefit of all nonphotographic systems is that analog-to-digital converters translate the electrical signals to digital numbers. Radiance values are commonly quantized into an 8-bit scale, yielding 2^8, (or 256) brightness, or gray values, per band; earlier systems used 6–7 bits, and more recent ones 10–11 bits (2^{11} = 2,048 gray values; Avery and Berlin 1992:406). High-resolution digital cameras now begin to replace film in aerial photography, and the millions of extant photographs can be readily digitized with little or no loss of detail.

Platform issues. Platforms employed for airborne imagery range from balloons and kites to aircraft of various kinds, including helicopters, small airplanes, and high-speed jets. All sensors possess a fixed AFOV, so the ground area captured in an image is solely a function of altitude: low-altitude platforms image smaller areas but provide greater spatial resolution; high-altitude or space imaging captures larger areas, commonly with less spatial detail, and problems with clouds and atmospheric haze are exacerbated. Platform velocity also affects spatial resolution. In aerial photography an aircraft's forward motion during the brief exposure can blur the image. The orientation of the sensor relative to the Earth determines whether an image is vertical or oblique: vertical when the sensor is within 3° of a perpendicular to the surface, oblique when its axis is tilted away. A high-oblique image shows the surface, the horizon, and part of the sky, whereas a low-oblique image portrays only the surface. Much air and most space remote sensing is in vertical or near-vertical formats akin to maps; and vertical images from air or space are frequently obtained systematically over a landscape with sufficient overlap to allow stereoscopy. Yet oblique aerial photography remains popular in archaeology: photos can be obtained at low cost from small airplanes with 35-mm handheld cameras, under a more flexible selection of view and lighting angles; flights can be scheduled at any time to use seasonal and lighting variations; and low altitudes allow high image detail (Bewley 2000; Wilson 2000).

All aerial imagery is topographically distorted by elevation differences within a scene, so hilltops are imaged at a larger scale than valley bottoms. With the IFOV in electro-optical and other nonphotographic sensors fixed, the size of a pixel is largely determined by height above ground, which can be variable owing to atmospheric turbulence and changes from scan to scan. These variations, plus small changes in velocity and attitude (roll, pitch, yaw), contribute to spatial or geometric distortions in scanned data beyond those seen in aerial photography (Dabas and Tabbagh 2000; Scollar et al. 1990:611–614). These effects are largely absent in satellite data, where atmospheric disturbances do not exist, and topographic, altitude, and attitude variations are trivial in relation to the sensor's altitude. Image preprocessing is required to convert geometrically distorted images into a spatially correct form in a specified map projection (see later discussion on computer methods).

Aerial Photography

Aerial photography was pioneered from balloons in the nineteenth century, with the earliest aerial photograph of an archaeological site, Stonehenge, taken in 1906. World War I (1914–1918) saw vast improvements with a move to maneuverable aircraft and trained personnel, of whom several focused on archaeological sites during the war. Outstanding aerial photographic surveys of Roman occupations were carried out in Syria during the 1920s and 1930s and in North Africa during the 1940s. O. G. S. Crawford, an observer in the British Royal Air Force, was primarily responsible for the early development and systematization of aerial archaeology. Whereas sites and features in arid lands were revealed largely by shadows cast by crumbling ruins, Crawford recognized in aerial photos taken in England prehistoric structures by crop marks, a means of detection (see below) so successful that he documented more archaeological sites in a single year than had been located by pedestrian surveys in the previous century (Bewley 2000:3–4; Wilson 2000:16–20). This methodology was perfected by the mid-1920s, and many remarkable photographs appeared in the journal *Antiquity*, founded by Crawford in 1927.

Aerial photography is now a critically important tool for archaeology, particularly in the United Kingdom, France, and Germany. Bewley (2000:4) suggests it caught on in Britain through the nature of the landscape and its archaeology, the ability of the soils to produce excellent crop marks, the availability of aircraft, relatively free airspace, and a military establishment that encouraged archaeological discoveries. In these countries aerial photography is closely integrated with other techniques as a branch of archaeological survey; there are wide areas of coverage, cost effectiveness, and a landscape perspective in the approach to sites. Extensive archives and libraries of archaeological aerial photographs have holdings numbering in the millions; the British National Association of Aerial Photographic Libraries lists more than 360 libraries (Bewley 2000:8). European aerial archaeology is highly organized, with state-sponsored agencies, funding, professional organizations, and significant archives. The systematic coverage of landscapes remains the principal goal, with resurvey and revisits to monitor changes and new conditions (Whimster 1989). Wilson (2000) argues that aerial photography is responsible for the discovery of more archaeological sites than all other methods, pedestrian or remote sensing, combined.

In North America the potential of an aerial perspective was also seen very early, with photographs of Cahokia in 1921, then Lindberg's photographs of southwestern pueblos and sites in the Yucatán peninsula in the late 1920s and early 1930s (Avery and Berlin 1992:226–227), and a Smithsonian Institution survey made more than 700 aerial photographs in the Gila Valley, Arizona, to document ancient Hohokam irrigation canals (Reeves 1936:103). Despite this, serious attention and organization of aerial archaeology have not been realized in the United States (with the possible exception of Chaco Canyon National Monument, New Mexico [Drager and Lyons 1985]), where it is rarely incorporated into regional projects, research designs, or in state-sponsored inventory programs.

Air photo interpretation. Air photo interpretation is the process of identifying objects or conditions in aerial photographs and determining their meaning and significance. It is an art and a science, with a large subjective element allied to a basis of scientific principles. Good interpretations are based on a large store of experience and knowledge of geography, geology, forestry, biology, other landscape sciences, and—in the archaeological case—familiarity with the forms and characteristics of past site and settlement types. It is important not to just recognize archaeological occurrences; other features—type of crop, ground cover, access, terrain form, aspects of the local environment—may be important. The basic question asked is, What is going on here? Positive identifications are frequent, but many are qualified as "probable" or "possible" (Lyons and Avery 1977).

In traditional air photo interpretation, certain domains or classes of phenomena are recognition elements, all of which are relevant to archaeological identifications (Avery and Berlin 1992:51–57; Lyons and Avery 1977:8–9). *Shape* refers to external form and configuration. Culturally generated objects tend to possess regular geometric shapes (see previous discussion on properties of archaeological sites) with distinct boundaries, such as a house or other buildings. Natural features tend toward irregular shapes and boundaries, although some—alluvial fans, floodplain meanders, volcanic cones—also have distinctive shapes. Relative *size* can aid identifications, because size differences occur between dwellings and public buildings, roads and trails, rivers and tributaries. Many cultural features exhibit *repetitive patterns*—trees in an orchard, ridges and furrows in prehistoric agricultural fields, or systematically placed houses within a settlement. Natural phenomena often display some degree of randomness, as with trees in a forest. *Shadows* impart depth to standing objects—buildings, bridges, trees, also ruins and mounds—and can reveal subtle variations in terrain with low-oblique illumination. *Tone or color*, a function of the film type and filter employed and of the intensity and angle of illumination, relates to surface-reflectance characteristics that help discriminate between objects and land-cover types. Closely related is *texture*, the impression of roughness or smoothness that varies between objects and surfaces. *Association* refers to a linkage, where recognition of one object tends to confirm the identity of others. In cultural landscapes individual houses combine to form settlements, fortifications go with villages, trails or roads link settlements. *Context* pertains to location in relation to environment. Villages and settlements might be confined to stream banks, farmsteads to rich agricultural lands, or defensive sites to hilltops.

In archaeological air photo interpretation, the basis for assessing all forms of aerial or satellite imagery, four general classes of phenomena that permit identification of sites and features were codified by Crawford and others (Scollar et al. 1990:33–74; Wilson 2000:38–87). Although almost solely used for archaeological identifications, each depends on a complex interplay between several of the recognition elements listed above.

Vegetation or crop-mark sites are caused by the differential response of plants growing on the surface to what lies buried beneath. It is the principal reason why archaeological sites can be seen from the air. Each plant acts as a kind of subsurface sensor, with roots penetrating to a depth roughly equal to its height above ground and sensitive to particular soil characteristics in its immediate vicinity—moisture, material composition, nutrients.

In an agricultural field of uniform crop type, literally millions of similar and uniformly placed plants are distributed over a broad area. When viewed from the air, changes in plant size and color can be readily detected that arise from two possible affects of buried archaeological features on plants. *Retarded growth* occurs when archaeological features—stone walls, floors, plaster or tile concentrations, packed earth, pavements near the surface— inhibit growth by reducing nutrients, moisture, or other factors; typical results are color differences, height variations, or density changes from yellowing, stunting, wilting, or delayed growth. *Advanced growth* typically results when plants grow over a richer, wetter soil or moisture trap that results in taller or more robust plants, color changes relative to other plants, or increased densi- ties; they usually point to archaeological features like ditches, trenches, pits, or depressions of any kind. Different crops react in various ways, and responses of mixed plant types within fields are generally less homogeneous (Wilson 2000:67–87). Changed conditions across the seasons and years cause responses to vary so that features visible at one time may not be seen in another. Figure 12.2a shows vegetation marks from two years indicating different components of the fortification system at Whistling Elk village, a fourteenth-century settlement in South Dakota.

Shadow-mark sites indicate elevation changes in the surface caused by standing ruins, structures, or mounds but also by sub- tle rises over shallowly buried architectural features and small depressions over ditches, pits, roads, or trails (see previous dis- cussion). They can become visible under low sunlight illumina- tion angles (e.g., 10°–30°). Shadows on slopes facing away from the sun immediately adjacent to bright sunward-facing slopes exaggerate whatever landscape hints might be present, many of which may not be readily visible on the surface (Bewley 2000:5). At Double Ditch village, a fifteenth-to-eighteenth-century settle- ment in North Dakota, shadows highlight circular depressions, the loci of former earthlodges, fortification ditches, and low mid- den mounds (see Figure 12.2b).

Soil-mark sites arise from variations in soil color in open fields, particularly freshly plowed ones, caused by differences in mineralogy or moisture content. Imported foreign materials (bricks, plasters, clays), introduced organics, baking of soils, or

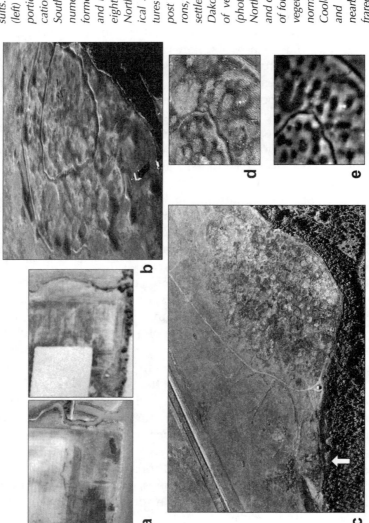

Figure 12.2. Aerial remote-sensing results. (a) Vegetation marks from 1968 (left) and 1946 (right) showing different portions of the fourteenth-century fortification system at Whistling Elk village, South Dakota. (b) Shadow marks reveal numerous circular depressions signifying former earthlodges, fortification ditches, and midden mounds at the fifteenth-to-eighteenth-century Double Ditch site, North Dakota (photo credit: State Historical Society of North Dakota). (c) Features of the 1831–1861 Fort Clark trading post (indicated by arrow) and its environs, including a nearby Mandan-Arikara settlement (ca. 1822–1861), in North Dakota, are revealed by a combination of vegetation, soil, and shadow marks (photo credit: State Historical Society of North Dakota). (d) Fortification ditches and depressions in the surface at the loci of former earthlodges are represented by vegetation differences in this enhanced normal-color view at Double Ditch. (e) Cooler temperatures occur in the ditch and house depressions compared with nearby high points in this thermal infrared view of the same region depicted in (d).

filling in of ditches or depressions can cause color, texture, or soil lightness changes. Changes in soil moisture can enhance these effects where fills within ditches or depressions might dry out more slowly, yielding an observable brightness or texture difference. Differential soil drying can also result from microrelief expressions where high points lose moisture more quickly than low (Scollar et al. 1990:37–48). A combination of soil, vegetation, and shadow marks highlight significant features in the environs of the Fort Clark trading post (see Figure 12.2c; compare the magnetometry image in Figure 12.1a).

Snow- and frost-mark sites are revealed by two circumstances. Variations in thermal energy emitted by archaeological deposits may cause differential melting (see later discussion on aerial thermography): compact deposits or buried rock pavements that better store thermal energy tend to radiate heat to the surface, causing snow or frost to melt over these features first. Microrelief also produces differential melting because snow or frost on slopes facing the sun disappears more quickly than on shadowed slopes. From the air, both can reveal archaeological patterns distributed through the landscape (Scollar et al. 1990:48–49; Wilson 2000:43–46).

Critical to all of these recognition domains are clear weather, good visibility, and the timing of flights. Sunrise or sunset flights during clear sunny days are necessary to record shadow sites; crop marks must be timed to crop development, itself dependent on plant type, growth cycle, drought, or rainfall abundance; soil marks are best seen after a fresh plowing when soil moisture remains high; a light snow or frost is required to reveal snow and frost markings—but these must be caught before the sun has melted them! Repeat visits at multiple times of the year can reveal different features, as can photographs of the same site from varied angles and lighting conditions. Some features are better seen back lit, side lit, or viewed down furrows rather than across them (Wilson 2000:80–83). For these reasons, aerial photography using small airplanes and handheld cameras remains beneficial: flights can be arranged at any time and photographs taken at any angle, whereas flight schedules for government or commercially produced vertical aerial photography are beyond the archaeologist's control.

Advances in and Sources of Aerial Photography. Recent advances in aerial photography include digital cameras more amenable to computer processing operations (see later discussion on computer methods) and in-flight aids like global positioning systems (GPSs) that help locate photographs and the sites and features within them. Walker and DeVore (1995) have introduced low-altitude large-scale reconnaissance, with cameras in remotely controlled model airplanes designed to fly at very low altitudes and slow speeds. Their results yield spatial resolutions of a few centimeters with greatly reduced image blurring.

In the United Kingdom, where aerial archaeology is most developed (see previous discussion), there are vast collections at the Cambridge University Collection of Air Photographs, and at the various royal commissions on historical monuments (Bewley 2000). Austria offers the Aerial Archive at the Institute for Prehistory and Protohistory at the University of Vienna (Doneus et al. 2001). In the United States high-quality vertical aerial photographs are available from numerous government agencies, and digital orthophoto maps are rapidly being placed on the Internet—but with spatial resolutions generally insufficient for archaeological purposes.

Aerial Multispectral Methods

Aerial multispectral scanner (MSS) methods potentially offer more than conventional aerial photography, because the photographic spectrum is only a small part of the EM spectrum; sensing more means seeing more. This was demonstrated in a pioneering study by Morain et al. (1981) that employed a Bendix 11-channel (from 0.38–12.25 μm) MSS with 1.25-m resolution over Bandelier National Monument, New Mexico. Supervised image classification methods showed a high degree of separability between several archaeological and natural land-cover classes, confirming that human disturbances could be detected through spectral analysis. Hemans et al. (1987) used a Xybion multispectral video camera (0.4–1.1 μm in 6 bands) from a tethered blimp at Corinth, Greece, gaining data particularly suited to defining the pattern of standing structures. The Heslerton Parish Project, in eastern Yorkshire, England, used Daedalus 11-channel MSS data (blue through thermal IR bands at 2-m resolution) in a region containing trackways, settlement enclosures, and barrows dating from the fifth century B.C. to the fifth century A.D. Compared with panchromatic aerial photographs during a peak crop-mark period, IR bands of the MSS data revealed new features, showing crop marks better than any other band, and the discovery of relict water courses forced a reinterpretation of the landscape history (Powlesland 2001; Donoghue 2001). An archaeological survey that combined the Daedalus system with aerial photography similarly concluded that "multispectral data . . . provides significantly more information than the monochrome aerial photographs in spite of their clarity and high level of spatial detail" (Donoghue and Shennan 1988:282). The more advanced Compact Airborne Spectrographic Imager (CASI), a hyperspectral device with 288 bands in the visible to NIR range, was successfully employed for identification of vegetation cover and bare ground using normalized vegetation indices and for change detection at archaeological sites, but only after spatial resolution was *decreased* to minimize errors (Barnes 2003).

Aerial Thermography

Radiation is emitted by all objects with spectral properties and magnitudes determined by temperature and the material's *emissivity*, its efficiency as an absorber and emitter. As temperature decreases, emitted energy shifts to longer wavelengths: the sun's surface temperature of about 6,000°C emits peak radiation at a wavelength of 0.48 μm, seen as light, whereas the Earth's ambient temperature of about 27°C yields a maximum emissivity at 9.7 μm, felt as heat. The latter wavelength conveniently falls within one of two transmission windows of thermal infrared (TIR) radiation in the lower atmosphere (Avery and Berlin 1992:120). Variations in surface temperature have been shown to cause differential melting of snow or frost, visible from the air (see previous discussion on aerial photography). In ground-based remote sensing, variations in the kinetic or contact temperature of surface deposits have been measured using sensitive thermometers placed directly in the soil (Noel and Bellerby 1990); yet the thermal emittance of an object that defines its radiant temperature can be remotely sensed by a noncontact TIR radiometer, with resolutions in the range of 0.01°–0.25°C. Such a device, on an airborne platform, is essential to applied work; surface temperatures vary so rapidly through the day that slow-to-acquire ground measurements are unsuitable if one wants to measure real spatial changes instead of diurnal ones.

Thermal energy from the sun, the atmosphere, or conductance from surrounding deposits causes the ground to heat. The amount of thermal energy in the ground depends on the balance between these different forms of gain and on loss by reradiation, evaporative cooling, air convection, and diffusivity. The diurnal cycle of warming in the day and cooling at night principally affects only a near-surface skin layer, perhaps to a depth of 15 cm. Thermal variation in this zone is also affected by aspect (slope facings relative to the sun), evaporative cooling from soil moisture, wind effects, and conduction from deeper units. Thermal energy in deeper deposits, principally transferred by conduction, tends to be affected by longer-term cycles, primarily weather changes of several days where temperature is consistently rising or falling. The depth limit of thermal prospecting is perhaps 1 m, dependent on the duration and intensity of a thermal cycle, the volume of the feature to be detected, and its thermal inertia contrast against the surrounding matrix (Dabas and Tabbagh 2000).

In archaeological sites thermal variations arise from several factors (Scollar et al. 1990:591–635). (1) *Microrelief variations* cause differential heating in the skin layer during daylight hours on clear days—slopes directly facing the sun capture more heat energy than slopes facing away from the sun; unlike low sun angle aerial photography, the thermal response lasts for many hours. (2) The *crop-mark phenomenon* creates a thermal effect because variations in evapotranspiration, the cooling mechanism of plants, occur according to their health or when some crops are in advance or behind others in a field. (3) *Variations in thermal inertia* cause dry porous materials to more quickly reach high maximum temperatures in the day and low minimum temperatures at night (low thermal inertia), whereas dense materials such as stone resist temperature change and remain relatively cool in the day and warm at night (high thermal inertia).

Perisset and Tabbagh (1981) used the 10.5–12.5 μm band of the ARIES radiometer, with about 1-m spatial resolution and a temperature sensitivity of less than 0.25°C, to find numerous ancient roads and field boundaries in France stemming from mi-

crorelief changes (see also Scollar et al. 1990:624). Dabas and Tabbagh (2000:630) demonstrate temperature differences in wheat
field crop marks as large as 1.5°C over the walls of buried prehistoric enclosures in France, also using the ARIES scanner. An
early study used thermal photography (acquired in 1966!) from
a Singer Reconofax IV scanner in the 8–14 µm band recorded on
film, at spatial and temperature resolutions of 0.3 m and 0.25°C,
respectively. It revealed subtle agricultural beds left by the
Sinagua culture (A.D. 1067–1200) in an area of black ash and cin-
der near Sunset Crater, Arizona. The dark color and loose packing of the ash caused it to efficiently absorb solar radiation; the
surrounding nonash surfaces had higher reflectances and densities that reduced their rates of solar absorption, making a thermal contrast visible from the air (Schaber and Gumerman 1969;
Berlin et al. 1977). More recently, Sever and Wagner (1991) used
the 6-channel thermal infrared multispectral scanner (TIMS), operated by NASA, with a typical ground resolution of about 5 m,
at Chaco Canyon, New Mexico, identifying surface and subsurface cultural features such as prehistoric roadways, buildings,
walls, and former agricultural fields. Thermal variations
recorded by a Raytheon Palm IR 250 in a low-level flight over the
Double Ditch earthlodge village in North Dakota (ca.
1400s–1780s) occur because the house and fortification ditch depressions in the surface are moister and more vegetated (see
Figure 12.2d), resulting in cooler temperatures than nearby high
points (see Figure 12.2e).

Airborne Radar

Aerial applications of radar became available with the Airborne Synthetic Aperture Radar (AIRSAR), built by NASA's Jet
Propulsion Laboratory as a radar test platform aboard a jet aircraft. Whereas early versions offered a nominal swath of 10 km,
an across-track resolution of about 20 m, and only the L-band (25
cm), recent flights also provide P- (67 cm) and C-band (5.7 cm)
channels and a resolution of 5–10 m. Adams et al. (1981) explored L-band (25 cm) data acquired in 1977–1980 over
Guatemala and Belize that yielded bright returns from the favorable geometry of sloping pyramid faces and indicated a canal
system of previously unrealized extent (covering 12,400 km^2),

made visible by slight differences in the elevation of vegetation. Moore and Freeman (1998) imaged a host of features at Angkor Wat, Cambodia, including temple complexes, previously undiscovered structures, mounds, dikes, roads, and reservoirs. Failmezger (2001) describes another application using 2.5-m aerial SAR data to map historical field locations and other features at the Oatlands Plantation, a large historical complex that once held numerous structures, agricultural fields, and slave quarters in early nineteenth-century Virginia.

Laser Altimetry

Previous sections have emphasized the importance of surface form, or microrelief, as a quality that gives information about subsurface archaeological conditions, quantifiable directly through surface measurements on the ground or indirectly through shadowing in aerial imagery or as temperature variations in aerial thermography. Field measurements of elevation, although promising in their potential, require heavy investments in time, labor, and costs. Recent advances in laser altimetry, the measurement of height using a laser range finder, make acquisition of high-resolution elevation data trivial. Frequently called Lidar (light detection and ranging), it is the optical equivalent of radar and consequently an active method, capable of rapidly generating accurate and dense digital models of topography as well as the vertical structure of other surfaces (buildings, trees) from the air. Lidar is a fast-evolving technology for wide-area mapping that provides remarkable surface detail, with absolute vertical accuracy currently as good as 15 cm (relative accuracy between adjacent measurements on a uniform surface is considerably higher) and horizontal sampling densities well less than a meter in conventional applications (Flood 2001).

Although relatively new and currently expensive, Lidar has already seen archaeological results (Barnes 2003; Holden et al. 2001). With considerable surface expression in many archaeological sites around the globe (e.g., Figure 12.1g), from standing ruins in the Middle East and American Southwest to abandoned medieval towns in Europe or earthlodge depressions and mound groups left by Native Americans, Lidar represents a huge breakthrough in the mapping and understanding of archaeological landscapes and quantification of topographic effects that might affect other remote-sensing data (e.g., electrical resistivity, GPR, and other methods with a terrain response).

Satellite Remote Sensing

Photographs from the first manned space flights, dating to the 1960s, revealed the potential of an Earth perspective from space. Regular coverage of the Earth is now obtained from orbiting satellites that employ conventional film or multispectral digital sensors. Until only a few years ago, available satellite imagery was of low spatial resolution, but new satellites have become available that can image archaeological sites *and features within them* from space. This capability is sure to progress as new systems are launched and technology advances.

A host of satellite programs are sponsored by government agencies and commercial enterprises; several have played a more central role in archaeology. Landsat (for *land satellite*) was the first satellite program for collecting repetitive, synoptic, multispectral imagery for monitoring and analyzing Earth resources and environment; Landsat 1 was launched in 1972, with Landsat 2–5 and 7 following in subsequent years. Several sensor systems have been deployed, including the MSS introduced in the previous section, the thematic mapper (TM), and the enhanced thematic mapper (ETM+). SPOT, a French program, is the Systéme Pour l'Observation de la Terre; five SPOT satellites have been launched since 1986, each carrying high-resolution viewers (HRVs). Both programs were important in the early development of archaeological space remote sensing and continue to be used (Limp 1989; Sever 2000). Details of these and other satellites are summarized in Table 12.1.

Early Explorations

Early studies with satellite data focused on environmental zone or land-cover mapping (e.g., Ebert 1978; Drager et al. 1982), because spatial resolutions were too coarse for archaeological sites and features. Johnson et al. (1988) used TM data to classify a northern Mississippi region into natural physiographic

Table 12.1. Satellite Systems Employed in Archaeological Remote Sensing

Satellite System	Bands*	Wavelength	Pixel Size (m)	Swath (km)	Launch Date
Landsat 1–3	Multispectral (G*, R, NIR1, NIR2)	0.5–1.1 μm	79	185 × 185	1972–1978
Landsat 4,5	Multispectral (B, G, R, NIR, MIR1, MIR2, FIR)	0.45–12.5 μm	30, FIR 120	185 × 185	1982, 1984
Landsat 7	Multispectral (B, G, R, NIR, MIR1, MIR2, FIR)	0.45–12.5 μm	30,FIR 60	185 × 185	1999
	Panchromatic	0.52–0.9 μm	15		
SPOT 1–3	Multispectral (G, R, NIR)	0.5–0.89 μm	20	60 × 60	1986–1993
	Panchromatic	0.5–0.73 μm	10		
SPOT 4–5	Multispectral (G, R, NIR, MIR)	0.5–1.75 μm	20, 10	60 × 60	1998, 2002
	Panchromatic	0.48–0.71 μm	10, 5		
Corona KH-4B	Panchromatic–film camera	0.5–0.7 μm	2–10	14 × 188	1967
KVR-1000	Panchromatic–film camera	0.51–0.76 μm	1–2	40 × 180	1987
Ikonos	Multispectral (B, G, R, NIR)	0.45–0.9 μm	4	13 × 13	1999
	Panchromatic	0.45–0.9 μm	1		
Quickbird	Multispectral (B, G, R, NIR)	0.45–0.9 μm	2.5	17 × 17	2001
	Panchromatic	0.45–0.9 μm	0.61		
SIR-C / X-SAR	Microwave (X, C, L spectrum)	3–24 cm	10–50	30–60	1994
Radarsat	Microwave (C)	5.7 cm	8–100	50–500	1995

Note: G, ;R, ; B, ; NIR, near infrared; B, ; MIR, middle infrared; FIR, far infrared.

provinces; frequencies of archaeological finds were then compared between them to define environmental markers with high probabilities of archaeological locations.

Early work actually detected archaeological sites with satellite data, despite coarse spatial resolutions of, typically, 80 m. One group focused on statistical assessments of archaeological spectral properties. Distinct spectral reflectances of immediate site areas were shown by Findlow and Confeld (1980) in New Mexico and by Custer et al. (1986) in coastal Delaware. This indicated that archaeological sites possess spectral properties different from surrounding landscapes detectable from space.

Obtaining recognizable imagery from space was initially confined to very large sites and features. Quann and Bevan (1977) identified the shadows of the pyramids at Giza, for example. Similarly, Ebert and Lyons (1980) defined nearly 80 km of Hohokam canals in the Phoenix basin, and Richards (1989) illustrated ancient rainwater-concentration structures in Egypt with early Landsat data. Showalter (1993) later employed 30-m resolution TM data in the Phoenix basin with a much-improved result in canal detection. Using 10-m resolution SPOT panchromatic data, which offered greatly improved spatial detail over previous systems, Romano and Tolba (1995) mapped portions of the Roman centuriation in the vicinity of Corinth, Greece. In general, initial use of satellite data for the direct imaging of archaeological features was disappointing, Johnson et al. (1988:130) decrying,

> Our findings corroborate those of earlier workers who have applied satellite imagery analysis. . . . Because of the general lack of detectable surface expression, extensive alteration to the landscape, and predominance of vegetation, site specific signatures are not a realistic goal . . . remote sensing may not be able to live up to some of the exaggerated claims made by earlier workers.

Not realized at the time was the inevitable increase in spatial resolution that would ultimately make remote sensing from space practical and useful.

Recent Advances: High-Resolution Satellite Programs

High-spatial-resolution satellite imagery (<4 m) sufficient to detect and map individual archaeological features is very recent; we are now at the dawn of true archaeological feature mapping from space-based platforms (Fowler 2002). High-resolution satellite data were first made publicly available in the mid-1990s in the form of Russian KVR and U.S. Corona panchromatic photographs, both from spy satellite programs (the latter acquired in the 1960s–1970s and recently decommissioned), with spatial resolutions as high as about 2 m (see Table 12.1). Fowler (1996) reports KVR-1000 photography that shows crop marks in the Stonehenge region of England. Kennedy (1998) does the same for Corona data, presenting clear imagery of prehistoric settlements in Turkey. As photography, these data are neither multispectral nor digital, and most users emphasize their similarity to aerial photography (e.g., Comfort 1997:7).

In 1999 the Ikonos satellite was launched, followed by QuickBird in 2001. These commercial satellites offer multi-spectral data at 4 m and spatial resolution at 2.4 m, respectively, with panchromatic data at 1 m and 0.6 m, respectively (see Table 12.1); more high-resolution satellites will soon join them. Archaeologists have already begun to exploit these data (Fowler 2000; Wheatley and Gillings 2002:74), although few definitive applications have yet been published. An Ikonos image of the pyramids at Giza reveals the tremendous spatial detail available (Figure 12.3a).

Space Radar

In 1981 the U.S. Space Shuttle Imaging Radar (SIR-A) captured the attention of archaeologists by revealing ancient canyons and paleochannels buried meters below the Sahara desert. The microwave energy easily penetrated the subsurface in this region of dry sands with low dielectric constant (El Baz 1997; McCauley et al. 1982). Conventional excavations later found prehistoric sites, dating as far back as the Acheulean, along these "radar rivers" (Wendorf et al. 1987),

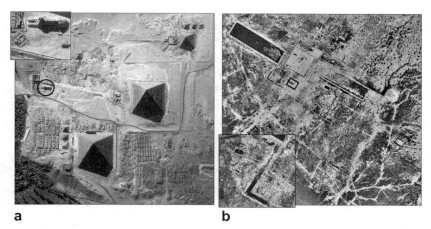

a   b

Figure 12.3. Satellite remote-sensing results. (a) Ikonos 1 m resolution panchromatic image of Giza, Egypt, featuring the Great Pyramids and the Sphinx, the latter shown in detail in the inset (credit: Space Imaging; collected November 17, 1999). (b) The 1994 SIR-C flight acquired this X-band SAR image of Angkor Wat, Cambodia, and environs (inset shows detail; credit: NASA/JPL image p-45156).

but this work did not directly detect archaeological sites. In the 1994 SIR-C flight, X-band SAR data were acquired over the ancient city of Angkor Wat, Cambodia (see Figure 12.3b), revealing temples, new structures, mounds, roads, and other features (Moore and Freeman 1998; see also previous discussion on airborne radar). Sever (2000:36) shows L- and C-band SIR-C images of the Great Wall of China, and Holcomb (1998) overviews theory, method, and additional archaeological applications, including discovery of the "lost city of Ubar" buried beneath the sands of Oman but located in SIR-A, SIR-B, and other imagery at the convergence of tracks through the desert. Radar satellites, including Canada's RadarSat, now provide regular coverage and a wide range of data (see Table 12.1; Sabins 1997:236). The Shuttle Radar Topography Mission of 2000 created detailed (30-m) digital elevation models covering 80 percent of the Earth's land surface—polar regions were omitted—by radar interferometry, a process that compares two images acquired at slightly different locations to obtain elevation information. These data are sure to affect archaeological and other mapping around the world.

Computer Methods: Image Processing and GISs

Computer manipulation and processing of data is now essential to nearly all remote sensing, an activity nearly as important as collecting the actual data because noise, defects, and distortions in raw imagery obscure important information. Various filtering and enhancement methods tease out hidden information, exposing subtle features. The computer methods used depend on the remote-sensing technology and on site-specific field conditions at the time of data acquisition. In general, correction of geometric distortions and scale changes arising from platform variations in altitude, attitude, or velocity and surface elevation changes (common to aerial data), reduction of noise (unwanted information like plow marks), removal of background trends (such as broad geological patterns), image sharpening, improvements to contrast and brightness, design of color palette schemes, and registration of the data to common map coordinate systems through rubber-sheet algorithms are minimally undertaken (Ciminale and Loddo 2001; Haigh 2000; Scollar et al. 1990:207–306). Figure 12.4a illustrates how defects in raw resistivity data, including data spikes (erroneous extreme measurements), a broad geological trend, survey grid imbalances, and a plow-zone response, are effectively removed to produce a sharp, clear, and more interpretable image of the fourteenth-century earthlodge village of Whistling Elk, South Dakota (Figure 12.4b). Frequently, general-purpose image processing, photogrammetry, or GIS software (which often includes elements of the first two) contains all necessary tools; special-purpose software is sometimes also required.

GISs are general-purpose programs for the handling, storage, manipulation, and analysis of any form of spatially referenced information. In little more than a decade they have revolutionized applications, approaches, and regional databases in archaeology (Kvamme 1999; Wheatley and Gillings 2002). Virtually all remote-sensing data occur in a raster format, as regular matrices composed of rows and columns of measurements. Raster GISs now routinely include image-processing components and procedures for georeferencing, vital for placing imagery within map coordinates. Visualization of remote-sensing

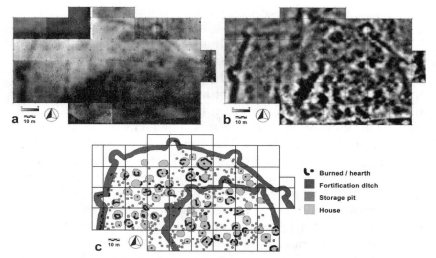

Figure 12.4. The importance of digital image processing is evident in comparing (a) *the raw resistivity image with* (b) *the final processed outcome at the fourteenth-century Whistling Elk village, South Dakota.* (c) *Interpretations of the aerial (Figure 12.2a), resistivity* (b), *magnetometry and conductivity data (not illustrated) from Whistling Elk village allow creation of a series of vector polygons transcribed onto a base map.*

data is facilitated by graphical capabilities that range from multicolored to pseudo-three-dimensional views that enhance recognition of significant features, presentation, and interpretation. Information from multiple sensors is stored as separate GIS layers so outcomes in one may easily be compared with another for the same point—important because each sensor can yield very different but complementary information and other data sets from an area (e.g., excavation data, surface collections) may easily be examined, queried, linked, and correlated. Powlesland et al. (1997) observe,

> The potential offered by the combination of a seamless mosaic of digital MSS imagery, draped onto a three-dimensional landscape model and superimposed with geophysical surveys, vector plots of plans, and databases linked to photographic images, field notes and spot find information in a Geographic Data Management System is tremendous, providing for the first time the facility for detailed landscape management and assessment on the desktop.

Benefits, Goals, Future Directions

Remote-sensing surveys provide a rapid means of data collection that can provide 100 percent coverage of large areas, with costs far less than excavation. They can guide expensive excavation and testing programs to features of potential archaeological interest. Indications can be given about the depth, areal extent, and distribution of cultural features, as well as of soil types and other subsurface conditions. The volume of excavations can be reduced, with smaller artifact collections recovered, and lowered curation costs. Traditional invasive methods generally damage or destroy the very resources they were designed to investigate; remote-sensing methods, nondestructive, leave the resource intact—an important consideration for culturally sensitive burial, sacred, or ceremonial sites.

In North America, the digging of numerous small holes, about 0.5 m in diameter, throughout a landscape is the principal method of prospecting for archaeological remains. Staggering numbers of these shovel test pits have been excavated across the continent at great cost; the vast majority have discovered no archaeological traces (Kintigh 1988; Shott 1985:457). Against the costs, time, and labor of this unproductive, slow, and primitive prospecting, remote sensing promises informed guidance to the placement of expensive excavations in places likely to yield cultural features of interest and contribute to a coherent and informed investigation.

Finally, when conditions and sensor mixes are correct, remote sensing can produce detailed maps of subsurface features over large areas, revealing arrangements of dwellings or other structures, rooms within them, internal room features, streets, lanes, trails, public spaces, dumping areas, middens, mounds, gardens, storage features, fortification systems, and other elements. This capability allows the direct study of settlement form and content through the remote-sensing analysis alone, as *primary data sets* to study site structure, content, and organization; to examine spatial patterns and relationships; and to directly confront specific questions. Because large buried cultural landscapes can be revealed, an alternative perspective on regional or landscape archaeology opens as space is viewed in terms of hectares or square kilometers rather than the square meters typical of archaeological excavations. This broader view engenders new and richer perspectives on human uses of space and past interactions with landscapes. Remote sensing therefore offers a rich adjunct to regional or landscape archaeologies beyond their utility as simple discovery tools (Bewley 2000; David 2001; Donoghue 2001; Kvamme 2003).

Despite these benefits, remote sensing is not a panacea to archaeology. It is constrained by conditions at the time and place of data acquisition—soil type, ground moisture, ground cover—potentially leading to poor or no archaeological feature contrasts; it is particularly difficult within urban or forested landscapes. Costs, frequently viewed as a drawback, must be balanced against the actual larger costs of management and planning decisions based on little knowledge of what lies beneath the ground, of badly placed excavations, and of failing to locate archaeological features, human remains, and other culturally sensitive deposits before their disturbance, resulting in expensive and complex later mitigation.

Cultural Resources Inventory: Interpreted and Transcribed Maps

The production of a final end-image that clearly portrays subsurface features of possible cultural origin through extensive data processing and enhancement is not necessarily the ultimate goal of remote sensing: the utility of results is greatly benefited by an analytic phase that interprets and transcribes features accurately onto maps. Transforming information in remotely sensed imagery into a record of the archaeology is complicated but important. It requires knowledge of the kinds of features that might occur, experience in their remote-sensing signatures, which can vary regionally, the amount of regular or geometric pattern expressed, and technical knowledge of cartography and mapping. Transcribed maps are composed of points, lines, and polygons—vectors in GIS parlance—that represent significant anomalies interpreted in the processed raster imagery of the various remote-sensing products (so interpretation can be viewed as a raster-to-vector conversion process). Interpretations are built up, and cumulate, through inspection of each remote-sensing data source for a given piece of ground. Some features may be revealed by only a single sensor, whereas others are visible in several data sets, allowing their presence to be verified, expanded, and ultimately codified and classified (Whimster 1989). GIS technology is particularly useful because recognized features may be digitized on screen directly into a map coordinate system and image manipulation tools can locally enhance or highlight features to facilitate their recognition. With transcribed vectors entered into regional GIS-driven databases, a permanent inventory of known or suspected archaeological features is developed, essential to guide management and planning decisions and future work (Bewley 2000:8; Wilson 2000:225–235). Figure 12.4c illustrates how interpretations of vegetation marks in aerial photography (see Figure 12.2a) are combined with interpretations of resistivity (see Figure 12.4b), magnetometry, and conductivity data (not illustrated) from Whistling Elk village, South Dakota, to yield vector polygons transcribed onto a base map.

Future Directions

Data fusion, the current state of the art in satellite remote sensing (Iyengar and Brooks 1997), merges digital information from multiple sensor types; it is sure to grow in importance and see application in archaeology. In some ways it is a natural outgrowth from GIS technology, where multiple layers of coregistered remotely sensed data, each from a different sensor type, are held within the same database. From a theoretical standpoint we know that a single sensor cannot detect the full range of physical contrasts exhibited by an archaeological feature. Whereas multisensor data might be displayed side by side or merged by GIS graphics through overlays or color compositing, data fusion uses theoretical, statistical, and contextual linkages within the data to yield a new information set holding the many similarities and differences in the original inputs and a richer, more interpretable view of anomalies within a region (Kvamme 2001b; Piro et al. 2000).

As remote sensing continues to grow, systematic data archiving will achieve large importance. Although remote sensing does not destroy its primary evidence, as does archaeological excavation, information can be lost unless it is properly archived, a frequently neglected task. Traditional archival preservation focuses on *objects* that contain information—on paper or as photographs—but contemporary remote-sensing data takes digital form. The goal of digital archiving is to preserve information in *any* type of medium while maintaining its content and structure so that records can be transferred from one format and medium to others that might evolve. The issues are (1) media degradation (5–10 years for magnetic; perhaps 30 for optical), (2) hardware evolution (changes in disks, tapes, compact disks (CDs), digital video disks (DVDs), and (3) changes in data storage formats. Digital archiving requires reliable backups (duplicate copies), data refreshment (copying information to new media as the original approaches its life span or to new forms as technology evolves), data migration (copying from outmoded data formats to contemporary ones supported by current software), and good documentation. The last is essential because the structure and content of the information must be fully known to migrate from one set of data structures or formats to another without information loss (see Bewley et al. 1999; Schmidt 2001). On these issues, see also chapter 31.

Satellite sensors will continue to improve, with greater spatial, spectral, and temporal resolutions, lower costs, and greater ease of access. Yet orbital constraints limit frequencies and times of data collection, cloud cover obscures many scenes, spatial resolutions are generally lower than airborne sensors, and most perspectives are vertical or near vertical; imagery from small airplanes can be acquired at any time, from any angle to optimize lighting and view, and at much higher spatial resolutions. For this reason, the old technology of oblique aerial photography taken by archaeologists will remain important. The coverage of satellite scenes offers some potential for wide-area prospecting, should automatic image classification and other detection algorithms become sufficiently developed to identify archaeological features (e.g., see Mathias-Lemmens et al. 1993).

It is only through remote sensing that archaeologists will be able to map, analyze, and interpret large archaeological regions and cultural landscapes in much of the globe. Its central role in a planetary inventory of cultural resources is obvious. With prohibitive costs, labor requirements, and ethical issues raised in excavating large regions—the only other means to realize what lies beneath the surface—only small exposures can ever be made. Remote sensing is sure to occupy a more central stage in the future of archaeological research and practice.

Acknowledgments

I am grateful to Herb Maschner for the patience shown me in this project. Chris Chippindale revealed his consummate editorial skills with an edit of a draft version that greatly improved and streamlined the presentation. Work at the Fort Clark trading post and Double Ditch was supported by grants from the PaleoCultural Research Group, Flagstaff, Arizona, and the State Historical Society of North Dakota. Stan Ahler and Fern Swenson of these respective institutions are thanked for their support. Bill Hunt of the Midwest Archeological Center, Lincoln, Nebraska, gave many insights that aided in the interpretation of the Fort Clark data. Work at Whistling Elk was supported by a grant from the National Center for Preservation Technology and Training.

References

Adams, R. E. W., W. E. Brown, Jr., and T. Patrick Culbert
1981 Radar mapping, archaeology, and ancient Maya land use. *Science* 213:1457–1463.

Al Chalabi, M. M., and A. I. Rees
1962 An experiment on the effect of rainfall on electrical resistivity anomalies in the near surface. *Bonner Jahrbücher* 162:226–271.

Alfodi, Tom, Pauline Catt, and Peter Stephens
1993 Definitions of "remote sensing." *Photogrammetric Engineering and Remote Sensing* 59:611–612.

Aspinall, A., and J. G. Crummett
1997 The electrical pseudo-section. *Archaeological Prospection* 4:37–47.

Avery, Thomas E., and Graydon L. Berlin
1992 *Fundamentals of remote sensing and airphoto interpretation.* 5th ed. Macmillan, New York.

Barnes, Ian
2003   Aerial remote-sensing techniques used in the management of ar-
        chaeological monuments on the British Army's Salisbury Plain
        training area, Wiltshire, UK. *Archaeological Prospection* 10:83–90.

Becker, H.
1995   From nanotesla to picotesla—a new window for magnetic prospect-
        ing in archaeology. *Archaeological Prospection* 2:217–228.

Berlin, G. L., J. R. Ambler, R. H. Hevly, and G. G. Schaber
1977   Identification of a Sinagua agricultural field by aerial thermogra-
        phy, soil chemistry, pollen/plant analysis, and archaeology. *Ameri-
        can Antiquity* 42:588–600.

Bevan, Bruce W.
1983   Electromagnetics for mapping earth features. *Journal of Field Archae-
        ology* 10:47–54.
1998   *Geophysical exploration for archaeology: An introduction to geophysical
        exploration.* Midwest Archeological Center Special Report 1. Na-
        tional Park Service, Lincoln, Nebraska.
2000   An early geophysical survey at Williamsburg, USA. *Archaeological
        Prospection* 7:51–58.

Bewley, Robert H.
2000   Aerial photography for archaeology. In *Archaeological method and
        theory: An encyclopedia,* edited by Linda Ellis, pp. 3–10. Garland Pub-
        lishing, New York.

Bewley, Robert, Danny Donaghue, Vince Gaffney, Martijn Van Leusen, and Ali-
    cia Wise
1999   *Archiving aerial photography and remote sensing data.* Oxbow Books,
        Oxford.

Challand, Adrian
1992   Field magnetic susceptibility measurement for prospection and ex-
        cavation. In *Geoprospection in archaeology,* edited by P. Budd,
        B. Chapman, C. Jackson, R. Janaway, and B. Ottaway, pp. 33–41.
        Oxbow Monographs 18. Oxbow Books, Oxford.

Ciminale, M., and M. Loddo
2001   Aspects of magnetic data processing. *Archaeological Prospection*
        8:239–246.

Clark, Anthony
2000   *Seeing beneath the soil: Prospection methods in archaeology.* Routledge,
        London.

Clay, R. Berle
2001   Complementary geophysical survey techniques: Why two ways are
        always better than one. *Southeastern Archaeology* 20:31–43.

Comfort, Anthony
   1997   Satellite remote sensing and archaeological survey on the Eu-
          phrates. *Archaeological Computing Newsletter* 48:1–8.

Connor, Mellisa, and Douglas D. Scott
   1998   Metal detector use in archaeology: An introduction. *Historical Ar-
          chaeology* 32:76–85.

Conyers, Lawrence B., and Christopher Gaffney
   2000   Some reflections on the Society for American Archaeology annual
          meeting. *Archaeological Prospection* 7:145–146.

Conyers, Lawrence B., and Dean Goodman
   1997   *Ground-penetrating radar: An introduction for archaeologists.* AltaMira,
          Walnut Creek, California.

Custer, Jay F., Timothy Eveleigh, Vytautas Klemas, and Ian Wells
   1986   Application of Landsat data and synoptic remote sensing to predic-
          tive models for prehistoric archaeological sites: An example from
          the Delaware coastal plain. *American Antiquity* 51:572–588.

Dabas, Michel, and Alain Tabbagh
   2000   Thermal prospecting. In *Archaeological method and theory: An ency-
          clopedia*, edited by Linda Ellis, pp. 626–630. Garland Publishing,
          New York.

David, A.
   2001   Overview—the role and practice of archaeological prospection. In
          Handbook of archaeological sciences, edited by D. R. Brothwell and
          A. M. Pollard, pp. 521–527. John Wiley, New York.

Dearing, J. A., K. L. Hay, S. M. J. Baban, A. S. Hudleston, E. M. H. Wellington,
   and P. J. Loveland
   1996   Magnetic susceptibility of soil: An evaluation of conflicting theories
          using a national data set. *Geophysical Journal International*
          127:728–734.

Doneus, Michael, Aloois Eder-Hinterleitner, and Wolfgang Neubauer
   2001   Archaeological prospection in Austria. In *Archaeological prospection,
          fourth international conference on archaeological prospection*, edited by
          Michael Doneus, Alois Eder-Hinterleitner, and Wolfgang
          Neubauer, pp. 11–32. Austrian Academy of Sciences Press, Vienna.

Donoghue, D. N. M.
   2001   Remote sensing. In *Handbook of archaeological sciences*, edited by
          D. R. Brothwell and A. M. Pollard, pp. 555–563. John Wiley, New York.

Donoghue, Daniel, and Ian Shennan
   1988   The application of remote sensing to environmental archaeology.
          Geoarchaeology 3:275–285.

Doody, Martin, Paul Synnott, Redmond Tobin, and Barry Masterson
1995 A topographic survey of the inland promontory fort at Castle Gale, Carrig Henry, Co. Limerick. In *Discovery Programme reports: 2, project results 1993*, pp. 39–44. Royal Irish Academy, Dublin.

Drager, Dwight, James Ebert, and Thomas Lyons
1982 Remote sensing and nondestructive archeology: Approaches to cultural resource management. In *The San Juan Basin tomorrow: Planning for the conservation of cultural resources in the San Juan Basin*, edited by F. Plog and W. Wait, pp. 219–244. National Park Service, Albuquerque, New Mexico.

Drager, Dwight L., and Thomas R. Lyons
1985 *Remote sensing photogrammetry in archeology: The Chaco mapping project*. National Park Service, Albuquerque, New Mexico.

Ebert, James
1978 Remote sensing and large-scale cultural resources management. In *Remote Sensing and nondestructive archeology*, edited by Thomas Lyons and James Ebert, pp. 21–34. National Park Service, Washington, D.C.

Ebert, James I., and Thomas R. Lyons
1980 Prehistoric irrigation canals identified from Skylab III and Landsat imagery in Phoenix, Arizona. In *Cultural resources remote sensing*, edited by T. R. Lyons and F. J. Mathien, pp. 209–228. National Park Service, Albuquerque, New Mexico, and University of New Mexico.

El Baz, Farouk
1997 Space age archaeology. *Scientific American* 277:40–45.

Failmezger, Victor
2001 High resolution aerial color IR, multi-spectral, hyper-spectral and SAR imagery over the Oatlands Plantation archaeological site near Leesburg, Virginia. In *Remote sensing in archaeology*, edited by Stefano Campana and Maurizio Forte, pp. 143–148. All'Insegna del Giglio, Florence.

Fassbinder, J., H. Stanjek, and H. Vali
1990 Occurrence of magnetic bacteria in soil. *Nature* 343:161–163.

Findlow, Frank J., and Linda Confeld
1980 Landsat imagery and the analysis of archaeological catchment territories: A test of the method. In *Essays on prehistoric resource space*, edited by F. Findlow and J. Erickson, *Anthropology UCLA* 10:31–52.

Flood, Martin
2001 Laser altimetry: From science to commercial Lidar mapping. *Photogrammetric Engineering and Remote Sensing* 67:1209–1217.

Fowler, Martin J. F.
1996 High-resolution satellite imagery in archaeological application: A Russian satellite photograph of the Stonehenge region. *Antiquity* 70:667–671.
2000 The Coliseum of Rome from 681 kilometres. *AARGnews* 20:47–50.
2002 Satellite remote sensing and archaeology: A comparative study of satellite imagery of the environs of Figsbury Ring, Wiltshire. *Archaeological Prospection* 9:55–69.

Frohlich, B., and W. J. Lancaster
1986 Electromagnetic surveying in current Middle East archaeology: Application and evaluation. *Geophysics* 51:1414–1425.

Gaffney, C., J. A. Gater, P. Linford, V. Gaffney, and R. White
2000 Large-scale systematic fluxgate gradiometry at the Roman city of Wroxeter. *Archaeological Prospection* 7:81–99.

Goodman, D., Y. Nishimura, and J. D. Rogers
1995 GPR time-slices in archaeological prospection. *Archaeological Prospection* 2:85–89.

Goulty, Neil R., and A. L. Hudson
1994 Completion of the seismic refraction survey to locate the vallum at Vindobala, Hadrian's Wall. *Archaeometry* 36:327–335.

Haigh, J. G. B.
2000 Developing rectification programs for small computers. *Archaeological Prospection* 7:1–16.

Hemans, F., J. W. Myers, and J. Wiseman
1987 *Remote sensing from a tethered blimp in Greece.* Center for Remote Sensing Technical Paper 2. Boston University, Boston.

Hesse, Albert
2000 Archaeological prospection. In *Archaeological method and theory: An encyclopedia*, edited by Linda Ellis, pp. 33–39. Garland Publishing, New York.

Holcomb, Derrold W.
1998 Application of imaging radar to archaeological research. In *Manual of remote sensing*, Vol. 2, edited by F. M. Henderson and A. J. Lewis, pp. 769–776. John Wiley, New York.

Holden, N., P. Horne, and R. H. Bewley
2001 High-resolution digital airborne mapping and archaeology. In *Aerial archaeology: Developing future practice*, edited by R. H. Bewley and W. Raczkowski, Vol. 337:173–180. NATO Science Series I: Life and Behavioral Sciences. Elsevier, Amsterdam.

Iyengar, Sundararaja, and Richard R. Brooks
　1997　*Multi-sensor fusion: Fundamentals and applications with software*. Prentice Hall, New York.

Johnson, Jay K., Thomas L. Sever, Scott L. H. Madry, and Harry T. Hoff
　1988　Remote sensing in large scale survey design in northern Mississippi. *Southeastern Archaeology* 7:124–131.

Kennedy, David
　1998　Declassified satellite photographs and archaeology in the Middle East: Case studies from Turkey. *Antiquity* 72:553–561.

Kintigh, Kieth W.
　1988　The effectiveness of subsurface testing: A simulation approach. *American Antiquity* 53:686–707.

Kvamme, Kenneth L.
　1999　Recent directions and developments in geographical information systems. *Journal of Archaeological Research* 7:153–201.
　2001a　Current practices in archaeogeophysics: Magnetics, resistivity, conductivity, and ground-penetrating radar. In *Earth sciences and archaeology*, edited by P. Goldberg, V. Holliday, and R. Ferring, pp. 353–384. Kluwer/Plenum, New York.
　2001b　Archaeological prospecting in fortified Great Plains village sites: New insights through data fusion, visualization and testing. In *Archaeological prospection, 4th international conference on archaeological prospection*, edited by Michael Doneus, Alois Eder-Hinterleitner, and Wolfgang Neubauer, pp. 141–143. Austrian Academy of Sciences Press, Vienna.
　2002　Final report of geophysical investigations conducted at the Fort Clark Trading Post, Fort Clark State Historic Site (32ME2), 2000–2001. Manuscript on file, State Historical Society of North Dakota, Bismarck.
　2003　Geophysical surveys as landscape archaeology. *American Antiquity* 68:435–457.

Limp, W. Fredrick
　1989　*The use of multispectral digital imagery in archeological investigations*. Research Series No. 34. Arkansas Archeological Survey, Fayetteville.

Linington, R. E.
　1966　Test use of a gravimeter on Etruscan chamber tombs at Cerveteri. *Prospezioni Archaeologiche* 1:37–41.

Lyons, Thomas R., and Thomas E. Avery
　1977　*Remote sensing: A handbook for archeologists and cultural resource managers*. National Park Service, Washington, D.C.

McCauley, J. F., G. G. Schaber, C. S. Breed, M. J. Grolier, C. V. Haynes, B. Issawi, C. Elachi, and R. Blom
1982   Subsurface valleys and geoarchaeology of the eastern Sahara revealed by Shuttle radar. *Science* 218:1004–1020.

McNeil, J. D.
1980   Electromagnetic terrain conductivity measurements at low induction numbers, technical note TN-6. Geonics Limited, Mississaugua, Ontario.

Malagodi, S., L. Orlando, S. Piro, and F. Rosso
1996   Location of archaeological structures using GPR method: Three-dimensional data acquisition. *Archaeological Prospection* 3:15–23.

Mathias-Lemmens, J. P. M., Zoran Stančič, and Ruud G. Verwaal
1993   Automated archaeological feature extraction from digital aerial photographs. In *Computing the past, computer applications and quantitative methods in archaeology, CAA92*, edited by Jens Andresen, Torsten Madsen, and Irwin Scollar, pp. 45–51. University of Aarhus Press, Aarhus, Denmark.

Moore, Elizabeth H., and Anthony Freeman
1998   Circular sites at Angkor: A radar scattering model. *Journal of the Siam Society* 86:107–119.

Morain, Stanley A., Charles Nelson, Mike E. White, and Amelia M. Komareck
1981   Remote detection of prehistoric sites in Bandelier National Monument. In *Remote sensing multispectral analysis of cultural resources: Chaco Canyon and Bandelier National Monument*, edited by Thomas R. Lyons, pp. 39–59. National Park Service, Washington, D.C.

Mussett, Alan E., and M. Aftab Khan
2000   *Looking into the Earth: An introduction to geological geophysics.* Cambridge University Press, Cambridge.

Newman, Connor
1993   The Tara survey interim report. In *Discovery Programme reports: 1, project results 1992*:70–93. Royal Irish Academy, Dublin.

Noel, M., and T. J. Bellerby
1990   A recording soil temperature probe for thermal archaeological prospection. *Archaeometry* 32:83–90.

Ovenden, S. M., and A. Aspinall
1991   Frequency mode induced polarization studies for geophysical exploration in archaeology. In *Archaeological Sciences 1989*, edited by P. Budd, B. Chapman, C. Jackson, R. Janaway, and B. Ottaway, pp. 305–315. Oxbow Monographs 9. Oxbow Books, Oxford.

Perisset, M. C., and A. Tabbagh
  1981   Interpretation of thermal prospection of bare soils. *Archaeometry* 23:169–187.

Piro, S., P. Mauriello, and F. Cammarano
  2000   Quantitative integration of geophysical methods for archaeological prospection. *Archaeological Prospection* 7:203–213.

Powlesland, Dominic
  2001   The Heslerton Parish project: An integrated multi-sensor approach to archaeological study of eastern Yorkshire, England. In *Remote sensing in archaeology*, edited by Stefano Campana and Maurizio Forte, pp. 233–255. All'Insegna del Giglio, Florence.

Powlesland, Dominic, James Lyall, and Daniel Donoghue
  1997   Enhancing the record through remote sensing: The application and integration of multi-sensor, non-invasive remote sensing techniques for the enhancement of the Sites and Monuments Record, Heslerton Parish Project, N. Yorkshire, England. *Internet Archaeology* 2. Electronic document, http://intarch.ac.uk/journal/issue2/pld_toc.html.

Quann, J., and B. Bevan
  1977   The pyramids from 900 kilometers. *MASCA Newsletter* 13:12–14.

Reeves, Dache
  1936   Aerial photography and archaeology. *American Antiquity* 2:102–107.

Richards, T. S.
  1989   Evidence of ancient rainwater concentration structures in northern Egypt as seen on Landsat MSS Imagery. *International Journal of Remote Sensing* 10:1135–1140.

Romano, David G., and Osama Tolba
  1995   Remote sensing, GIS and electronic surveying, reconstructing the city plan and landscape of Roman Corinth. In *Computer applications and quantitative methods in archaeology 1994*, edited by J. Huggett and N. Ryan, pp. 163–174. BAR International Series 600. Tempus Reparatum, Oxford.

Sabins, Floyd F.
  1997   *Remote sensing: Principles and interpretation.* 3rd ed. W.H. Freeman, New York.

Schaber, Gerald G., and George J. Gumerman
  1969   Infrared scanning images: An archeological application. *Science* 164:712–713.

Schiffer, Michael B.
  1976   *Behavioral archaeology.* Academic Press, New York.

Schmidt, Armin
2001 *Geophysical data in archaeology: A guide to good practice.* Oxbow Books, Oxford.

Scollar, I., A. Tabbagh, A. Hesse, and I. Herzog
1990 *Archaeological prospection and remote sensing.* Cambridge University Press, Cambridge.

Scott, Douglas D., Richard A. Fox, Jr., Mellissa Connor, and Dick Harmon
1989 *Archaeological perspectives on the battle of the Little Bighorn.* University of Oklahoma Press, Norman.

Sever, Thomas L.
2000 Remote sensing methods. In *Science and technology in historic preservation,* edited by R. Williamson and P. R. Nickens, pp. 21–51. Kluwer Academic/Plenum, New York.

Sever, T. L., and D. W. Wagner
1991 Analysis of prehistoric roadways in Chaco Canyon using remotely sensed digital data. In *Ancient road networks and settlement hierarchies in the New World,* edited by C. Trombold, pp. 42–52. Cambridge University Press, Cambridge.

Shapiro, Gary, and James J. Miller
1990 The seventeenth-century landscape of San Luis de Talimali: Three scales of analysis. In *Earth patterns: Essays in landscape archaeology,* edited by W. M. Kelso and R. Most, pp. 89–101. University of Virginia Press, Charlottesville.

Shott, M.
1985 Shovel-test sampling as a site discovery technique: A case study from Michigan. *Journal of Field Archaeology* 12:457–468.

Showalter, Pamela S.
1993 A Thematic Mapper analysis of the prehistoric Hohokam canal system, Phoenix, Arizona. *Journal of Field Archaeology* 20:77–90.

Sivilich, Daniel M.
1996 Analyzing musket balls to interpret a Revolutionary War site. *Historical Archaeology* 30:101–109.

Summers, G. D., M. E. F. Summers, N. Baturayoglu, Ö. Harmansah, and E. Mcintosh
1996 The Kerkenes Dag survey: An interim report. *Anatolian Studies* 46:201–234.

Tsokas, G. N., C. B. Papazachos, A. Vafidis, M. Z. Loukoyiannakis, G. Vargemezis, and K. Tzimeas
1995 The detection of monumental tombs buried in tumuli by seismic refraction. *Geophysics* 60:1735–1742.

Walker, A. R.
2000   Multiplexed resistivity survey at the Roman town of Wroxeter, *Archaeological Prospection* 7:119–132.

Walker, James W., and Steven L. De Vore
1995   *Low altitude large scale reconnaissance: A method of obtaining high resolution vertical photographs for small areas.* National Park Service, Denver.

Wendorf, F., A. E. Close, and R. Schild
1987   A survey of the Egyptian radar channels: An example of applied field archaeology. *Journal of Field Archaeology* 14:43–63.

Weymouth, John W.
1986   Geophysical methods of archaeological site surveying. In *Advances in archaeological method and theory,* Vol. 9, edited by Michael B. Schiffer, pp. 311–395. Academic Press, New York.

Weymouth, J. W., and Y. A. Lessard
1986   Simulation studies of diurnal corrections for magnetic prospection. *Prospezioni Archeologiche* 10:37–47.

Wheatley, David, and Mark Gillings
2002   *Spatial technology and archaeology: The archaeological application of GIS.* Taylor and Francis, London.

Whimster, Rowan
1989   *The emerging past: Air photography and the buried landscape.* Royal Commission on the Historic Monuments of England, London.

Wilson, D. R.
2000   *Air photo interpretation for archaeologists.* Arcadia Publishing, Charleston, South Carolina.

Wynn, Jeffrey. C., and Susan I. Sherwood
1984   The self-potential (SP) method: An inexpensive reconnaissance and archaeological mapping tool. *Journal of Field Archaeology* 11:195–204.

13

Archaeological Chemistry

Joseph B. Lambert

Chemistry is concerned with matter and its changes. All of the materials of archaeology, from stone tools to human skeletal remains, have compositions that may be analyzed by modern chemical techniques. This composition depends on the geologic source of artifactual raw materials, on chemical processing that humans may have imposed on the raw materials, on biological processes when the material had a biological source, and on changes that may have occurred during burial or its equivalent.

A wealth of information may be derived from chemical analysis of archaeological materials (Lambert 1997). Understanding differences in the chemical composition of raw materials as a function of geologic source can determine the ultimate source of artifacts and thereby define trade routes. Analysis of chemically processed artifacts, such as ceramics, glass, and metal alloys, can help re-create ancient technology and trace its development. Analysis of biological residues can provide information on ancient human diet. Chemical changes that occur over time may be transformed into chronological information by a host of dating techniques, which are discussed elsewhere in this volume. Chemical markers that are deposited in the soil by human activities can serve to locate archaeological sites or features within a site and are discussed elsewhere in this volume as well. Natural deposits over time can provide information on ancient climate from their chemical composition. Chemical methods during conservation are central to the stabilization, preservation, and restoration of archaeological materials. Climate analysis and conservation are not within the scope of this volume.

This chapter focuses on three areas: determining the source of materials used for artifacts (provenance), chemical processing of raw materials by humans (ancient technology), and chemical analysis of biological residues (human diet).

Analytical Methods

The instrumental method of choice depends on whether the material to be analyzed is inorganic or organic (for reviews, see Goffer 1980; Parkes 1986; Pollard and Heron 1996; Tite 1972). Inorganic material usually is analyzed without initial purification. The analysis thus reflects either the gross or the surface composition and normally provides some sort of listing of constituent chemical elements and their proportions. The workhorses of elemental analysis in archaeology today are instrumental neutron activation analysis (NAA), X-ray fluorescence (XRF), and inductively coupled plasma (ICP). X-ray photoelectron spectrometry (XPS) and proton or particle-induced X-ray emission (PIXE) are relatively esoteric but still useful techniques. Emission spectrometry (ES) is rarely used today, and atomic absorption (AA) much less so than in the past.

The choice of technique depends on a number of factors. (1) *Cost and availability.* XRF, ICP, and AA are quite accessible, whereas instrumentation for PIXE, XPS, or NAA is more expensive and less available. (2) *Accuracy.* Methods such as ICP and AA that analyze solutions can achieve very high accuracy. Those that analyze solids must depend on calibration of elemental proportions as a function of the matrix (the overall composition). The results can vary from poor to excellent. (3) *Sensitivity* and *sample size.* Emerging instrumentation based on synchrotron X-ray sources may revolutionize elemental analysis in terms of sample size, but that development has not yet occurred in archaeology. Excellent sensitivity, thereby minimizing sample size, already is achieved by both ICP and NAA. (4) *Sample destruction.* Methods such as ICP or AA that require dissolution destroy the sample entirely. One important early development in the use of XRF was a portable probe that allows analysis directly on the artifact, without removal of a sample. Some other techniques allow nondestructive analysis of only relatively small samples. (5) *Depth of analysis.* When the sample to be analyzed is a solid, the analytical method may interrogate elemental information at only the surface (XPS) (Lambert et al. 1999), slightly more deeply (XRF), or all the way through (NAA for the most part). Consequently, interpretation of the analytical data must be carried out with full knowledge of whether they refer to the surface or to the bulk. (6) *Elemental range.* Some methods such as XPS and ICP offer almost the entire periodic table for study, whereas others such as NAA and XRF examine a more limited range of elements. The specific composition therefore can dictate the choice of analytical method, to ensure that needed elements are available for analysis.

Many other modern analytical methods do not examine elemental composition of inorganic materials but provide related, more specialized information. X-ray diffraction (XRD) of powders yields a diffraction pattern that often can identify the specific chemical compounds or minerals present. The method is used in the analysis of pigments or clays, for example. Electron spin resonance (ESR; also called electron paramagnetic resonance, or EPR) requires that the sample contain unpaired electrons. Whereas electrons engaged in chemical bonds are paired, bond breakage can lead to unpaired electrons. Also, many metals naturally possess unpaired electrons. Thus ESR is used, on the one hand, to measure the age of materials from the accumulation of unpaired electrons from bond breakage and, on the other hand, to examine specific properties of metals. For example, metallic oxidation states sometimes may be identified from analysis of the ESR spectrum. Infrared (IR) spectrometry (and the closely related Raman spectrometry) is sensitive to the frequencies at which chemical bonds undergo vibrations. The frequencies can serve to identify particular types of bonds. The method has been found to be particularly useful in the analysis of pigments. Mössbauer spectroscopy, a relatively obscure method, provides profiles of a very limited number of elements. It has been used to examine oxidation states of iron in ceramics, for example. Methods such as Mössbauer spectroscopy, ESR, and XPS that provide oxidation state information expand upon elemental profiles by subdividing a particular element into a number of different forms. Because color is highly dependent on oxidation states of metal constituents, these techniques often are used to examine colorants in artifacts.

Organic materials require entirely different analytical approaches. In the first place, except for certain dyes, organic materials almost always are mixtures. A food residue on a piece of pottery may consist of dozens or hundreds of compounds. Organics may be analyzed in bulk as the mixture or may initially be separated into individual compounds. Separation methods usually involve chromatography, of which there are many varieties. Gas chromatography (GC) volatilizes the sample, passes it through a column to effect separation, and often yields a profile of pure compounds. Liquid chromatography (LC) gives similar information based on materials that remain in the liquid phase. The separated compounds are passed sequentially into a mass spectrometer, and mass spectrometry (MS) provides the molecular weight of the compound. From the molecular weight and other mass spectral information, it often is possible to identify many components of the original mixture. The combined methods are called GC-MS and LC-MS.

Many spectroscopic methods are used for bulk analysis of organics (for a review of these methods, see Lambert et al. 1998). Infrared spectroscopy provides a rapid, preliminary approach. Ultraviolet or visible spectroscopy (UV-vis) looks at a different range of frequencies but also provides useful information on simple organic mixtures, dyes in particular. Nuclear magnetic resonance (NMR) spectroscopy, by far the most general method for analyzing organic mixtures (Lambert et al. 2000), yields a profile of the different types of carbon atoms (or hydrogen atoms) present in the molecule. Whereas inorganic mixtures most commonly are characterized by the profile of elements present, organic mixtures are characterized by NMR according to the profile of different types of one or two elements. All of these techniques (NMR, IR, UV-vis, MS, GC, LC) are widely available in chemical laboratories.

Provenance

The chemical composition of a particular type of artifactual raw material can vary with geographic source. The procedure of determining provenance by chemical analysis requires characterization of all possible sources and comparison of the composition of the artifact with each of these sources. There are three general approaches to such an analysis: elemental profiles, isotopic profiles, and organic profiles.

Elemental Profiles

Elemental analysis of an artifact yields a listing of constituent elements and their percentages. The potential sources of the raw materials must be sought. Samples from each source are analyzed in a similar fashion and characterized statistically. Artifact compositions then are compared to those of the sources to determine possible matches. Often the artifacts themselves are used to define a set of hypothetical sources without reference to analyses of actual raw materials. A large number of artifacts are analyzed, and the resulting elemental profiles are sorted into groupings that may represent distinct sources. The usual statistical method is pattern analysis, which sorts data into groups, whose constituents have maximal similarities in composition with other members of the same group and maximal differences from members of all other groups. Because some elements correlate with each other, the process usually involves combining sets of elements into *principal components*. The result is comparisons among these components rather than among all the elements. Figure 13.1 shows a plot of the first two principal components of the elemental analysis of white glaze samples from the Song and Yuan dynasties of China (Leung et al. 2000). Three distinct sources of raw materials are suggested: Ding, Tianxizheng, and combined Guantai-Pengcheng. One Guantai sample (g-a1) does not fit into this pattern, suggesting a different source. No clay raw materials were examined in this case.

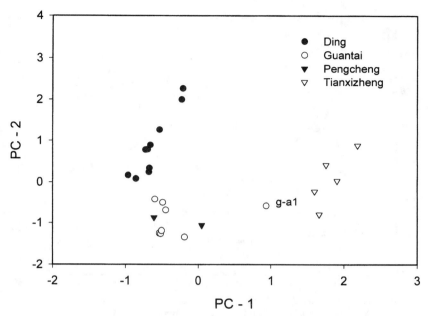

Figure 13.1. Plot of the first two principal components for the elemental analysis of white glazes from ancient Chinese porcelains. Reproduced from P. L. Leung, M. J. Stokes, C. Tiemei, and Q. Dashu, Archaeometry 42:138, 2000.

Isotopic Profiles

Instead of elemental proportions, chemists can use isotopic proportions, particularly for lead, an element present in a wide variety of artifacts, including metals, glass, glaze, pigments, inks, tiles, and piping. Lead occurs naturally as several different isotopes. Because various heavier elements (e.g., uranium, thorium) decay radioactively to form the stable lead isotopes, proportions of the isotopes (lead-207, -208, -209) vary from place to place, depending on the local radiochemical history. The approach is analogous to that used with elemental analysis, whereby the potential sources of raw materials initially are characterized. Artifacts then are analyzed and compared with the sources. Samples are sorted statistically, and plots are constructed between isotopes. Figure 13.2 shows a plot of the ratios $^{208}Pb/^{206}Pb$ vs. $^{207}Pb/^{206}Pb$, in which good separation is

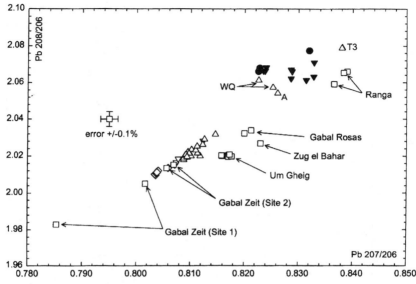

Figure 13.2. Plot of lead isotope ratios for Egyptian sources of lead ore. A. J. Short-land, P. T. Nicholson, and C. M. Jackson, Archaeometry *42:155, 2000.*

demonstrated for a number of ore sites for lead (Shortland et al. 2000).

This general procedure of fingerprinting raw materials by elemental or isotopic composition and then determining the provenance of an archaeological artifact has been applied to a large number of materials, including basalt, flint, marble, limestone, native copper, obsidian, quartzite and sandstone, soapstone, and turquoise. All these materials are stone, which was not processed chemically. Chemical transformation of raw materials by human intervention can alter the elemental profile, thus preventing direct comparison of artifacts with raw materials. Profiling and pattern analysis, of course, is still possible for processed materials such as leaded alloys, pottery, and glass, but ascertaining provenance becomes difficult. In the case of pottery, elemental analysis often is used to characterize clay sources. As described above, the sources are hypothetical, because changes that occur between raw clay and finished ceramic usually render comparisons of the two materials problematic. For this reason processed artifacts often are examined without reference to specific sources, as for the Chinese glaze in Figure 13.1. The same problems arise for glasses and metals. The mixing of metal constituents by melting also means that a metal artifact can have been produced from several ore sources. Although processing has little effect on isotopic ratios, mixing of metal sources, as when scrap metal is used, still could compromise the analysis. The lower likelihood that silica sources are mixed renders lead isotope analysis of glasses, tiles, and bricks more reliable.

Provenance studies thus suffer from four substantial limitations. (1) All ancient raw-material sources must be sampled. Whereas clay sources are legion, sources of obsidian, turquoise, and soapstone are limited. These latter materials thus have provided success stories in provenance determination (Williams-Thorpe 1995). (2) All the raw-material sources must be different. The history of marble-provenance studies began with five sources easily distinguished by oxygen and carbon isotopes (Craig and Craig 1972). Over time the number of characterized sources rose to over a hundred. The simple two-dimensional plot acquired many redundancies, some up to five deep (that is, up to five sources had the same oxygen and carbon isotopic ratios). Further distinctions could be drawn by including additional modes of analysis, for example, elements such as strontium. (3) Chemical processing must not alter the raw-material profile. The process of turning clay into a finished ceramic involves purification and mixing. Temper normally is added to minimize shrinkage and prevent cracking. The addition of sand, shells, mica, volcanic ash, and any number of other materials profoundly alters the elemental makeup. Glass production involves the mixing of several raw materials. Metals must be produced from ores often in several chemical steps, and of course metal raw materials may be mixed. All this processing can compromise any association between raw materials and the final product. This problem sometimes is sidestepped by making internal comparisons of artifacts, without specific reference to actual sources of raw materials. (4) The material should be unaltered during burial (or its equivalent). Archaeologists deal with artifacts and human residues that can be millions of years old, although the timescale more usually is in thousands of years. During this period, the materials are subject to decay, *diagenesis*. The chemical integrity of the object slowly breaks down, dependent largely on the environment experienced by the artifact (soil, aqueous). Metals are particularly subject to corrosion, but even the most robust glass or ceramic also can decay. Diagenesis can involve both the loss of original elements and the gain of others originally absent. Aqueous and oxygenated environments are particularly conducive to diagenesis. Thus the best conditions for avoiding diagenesis are the same as for overall preservation: extremely dry, cold, or anaerobic (oxygen-free) environments.

Organic Profiles

Organic materials are especially subject to decay and hence often are archaeologically rare and precious. These usually are plant or animal products such as fabrics, hide, wood, or food residues. Some organic materials, processed geologically over time, often attain stonelike properties with considerable robustness. These include amber (fossilized plant resins) and jet (coal-like materials). Although inorganic analysis of trace components of organics sometimes provides useful information on provenance, the organic portion itself may be analyzed readily. Much of the resulting information pertains to the technology of the organic material and is considered in the next section, but sources of raw materials also may be determined.

The procedure has some similarities to elemental or isotopic fingerprinting, but in the case of organics the variable is the type of organic carbon. Chemists classify organic structures according to the chemical bonding of the constituent carbon atoms. Thus when all carbons possess only single bonds (C—C), the molecules are said to be *saturated*. These are the alkanes or paraffins. When double bonds are present (C=C), the molecules are said to be *unsaturated* and are called alkenes or olefins. When oxygen is present, new compounds result: alcohols when there are OH groups; ketones, aldehydes, carboxylic acids, or esters when there are double bonds involving oxygen (C=O). Nitrogen occurs in amines (with N—H or N—

C bonds) and in amides (with NH/C and C=O bonds next to each other).

These compounds may be analyzed by various spectroscopic methods. Electronic (ultraviolet and visible) spectroscopy often is used to characterize dyes, because the cause of color is closely related to the cause of spectral changes in the ultraviolet and visible regions of the electromagnetic spectrum. IR spectroscopy is a quick and qualitative method for determining the presence of many functional groups, but it lacks precision. NMR spectroscopy can characterize the carbon compounds of almost any material. UV-vis experiments may be carried out on very small amounts of dyes (extracted, for example, from fabric), but IR and particularly NMR spectroscopy require rather large amounts of material and usually are destructive.

Both IR and NMR spectrometries have been used for determining provenance of ancient resins. Amber is an easily worked, attractive material highly valued for millennia. It was traded from the Baltic region throughout ancient Mediterranean cultures, but it is found worldwide. The NMR or IR spectrum is related to sources of raw materials by distinguishing the various peaks (Lambert and Poinar 2002). Amber is mined just like inorganic ores, and the mining sites may be characterized spectroscopically, just as inorganic materials are characterized by elemental or isotopic profiles. Fossilized resins enjoy a methodological advantage similar to those of obsidian or soapstone, in that the number of sources is relatively limited. Thus, NMR and IR have been used successfully to determine provenance, particularly in the characterization of European resins.

Technology

Human beings became chemists when they began to transform matter purposefully from one chemical form to another (in contrast to the many chemical processes that are determined genetically in the plant and animal worlds). Controlled burning of fuels (grass, wood) was almost certainly the first chemical activity of humans. Fires convert natural organic materials into carbon dioxide and water, with the heat of reaction supplying the desired result. Cooking of food probably was the second chemical activity, whereby high temperatures provided by fires converted raw food to longer-lasting and safer comestibles. Thus the earliest forms of chemical technology resulted in energy and food production. Technology also led to processed objects such as stone axes and pottery. We shall draw a distinction, however, between chemical and nonchemical processing. Manipulation of stone rarely involved anything more than the physical process of carving or chipping (although fire sometimes played a role). Agriculture may involve some chemistry but is primarily a manipulation of the biological environment. The conversion of fibers to textiles may include some chemical cleaning but is basically a series of physical manipulations. Even with elimination of the vast technological expanses of stoneworking, agriculture, and textiles, chemistry nonetheless played a major role in many other cultural activities. Modern chemical analysis often can unravel the details of ancient technologies associated with ceramics, glass, metals, dyes and pigments, plaster, and many organic materials.

Ceramics

For the most part, pottery and other ceramics (bricks, tiles) are made up of three components: the appropriate clay, the right proportion of water to create plasticity, and a temper or filler to control evaporation of water and to avoid shrinkage and cracking (Rice 1987). Depending on the type of clay and the temperature of firing, the product can be classified as terra-cotta, earthenware, stoneware, or porcelain. The process of firing transforms the aluminosilicate matrix of the clay irreversibly into an entirely new chemical substance. When covered with a vitreous glaze, the material can become majolica, faience, or porcelain. Pigments may be added to the surface for coloring.

Chemistry can assist in understanding and replicating these manufacturing processes. Elemental analysis and powder X-ray diffraction often can identify the specific type of clay mineral. Pattern analysis of the elemental composition can suggest sources of the clay raw materials or can sort ceramics according to compositional categories. The composition of the glaze may be analyzed and the cause of color elucidated. The temperature at which the clay was fired may be determined and the atmosphere characterized as either oxidizing or reducing. In this fashion, for example, chemists have learned that both the reds and the blacks of classical Greek ceramics were caused by iron in the clay. The red was from a high-oxidation-state form (hematite, Fe_2O_3) and the black from a low-oxidation-state form (FeO or Fe_3O_4).

Glass

Glass may have been a by-product of the technology of either metals or glazed pottery. The primary constituent of glass, called the *former*, consists of silica from sand or crushed siliceous stones (Brill 1963). Because the melting point of silica could not be reached by ancient pyrotechnologies, the key discovery was the need to add a modifier, or *flux*, from plant or mineral sources to lower the melting point. The flux usually contained sodium or potassium. To increase the stability of glass (sodium and potassium ions tend to dissolve in water), a third component, the *stabilizer*, was added, made up of calcium (usually from lime), magnesium, or aluminum. Thus early glasses have been called soda-lime from the two additives. Other metals were added to the mix to create opacity, a colorless appearance, or specific colors.

Chemical analysis can establish distinctions among various types of glass (Sayre and Smith 1961). Most silica sources contain sufficient natural iron impurities to give a greenish tint to the glass. The earliest glass objects (from Mesopotamia and Egypt) retained this tint. During the first millennium B.C., the use of antimony as a decolorizer was widespread in the Mediterranean world. Antimony-laced glass had a clearer, more nearly colorless appearance. Shortly before the beginning of the Christian era, manganese supplanted antimony as the decolorant in Roman glass (not a Roman discovery but probably Syro-Palestinian). Examination of the amounts of antimony and manganese thus provides chronological and geographical information.

Whereas sodium was the primary constituent of the modifier for centuries, after Roman times many European ceramics contained potassium in place of sodium, presumably reflecting availability of raw materials to inland manufacturing sites. Lead, used commonly as the modifier in glaze, also served as the modifier in some Islamic glasses and in European crystal. The earliest Chinese glass used lead as the modifier and barium (rather than calcium) as the stabilizer. This formula, retained through the Han dynasty (to A.D. 220), eventually was supplanted by the more stable soda-lime formulation of the West. Chemical analysis thus reveals a wide variety of manufacturing options.

Chemical subtleties have produced many esthetic variations in glass. Opacity was originally produced by high levels of lead or calcium antimonate. A jadelike appearance of glass was achieved in China during the Tang dynasty (A.D. 618–907) by the use of calcium fluoride (fluorite, CaF_2) for opacity. The ancient Egyptians achieved rich colors in glass by adding metal ions. Reds, greens, and blues came from copper, violet from iron, and blue from cobalt. Islamic glassmakers impregnated glass surfaces with a metal oxide and fired it in a reducing atmosphere to produce small amounts of the free metal. This process created a metallic or mirrorlike surface called *lusterware*. Controlled percentages and sizes of gold particles in the glaze produced a rich ruby color, as in the Chinese *famille rose*. All these esthetic triumphs may be understood through chemical analysis.

Metals

Determination of the alloy composition of a metal artifact is a relatively straightforward operation, allowing the chemist to distinguish important structural differences. Copper is strengthened through alloying (as bronze) with a number of other elements, including arsenic, tin, and lead. When zinc is the alloying element, the product has the golden hue characteristic of brass. Iron becomes much stronger (as steel) when mixed with small amounts of carbon or phosphorus (because these elements are not metals, the process is not alloying). Precious metals (gold, silver, and platinum) were alloyed with each other in both the Old and New Worlds and with baser metals such as copper. This rich mix of metallic constituents produced a vast array of materials available for utilitarian and esthetic purposes. Chemists are able to explain how the elemental constitution determines these properties (Wertime 1973).

Fabrication of a metal object can take place by various procedures, including casting (conversion to liquid metal, pouring into molds, and solidification), working (physical manipulation as with hammering of either cold metals or those softened on a forge), annealing (heating after working), and joining (connecting two possibly distinct metal pieces with a solder that had been developed because of its low melting and adhesive properties). Analysis of these techniques is usually done by microscopy, particularly with the electron microscope.

Chemical analysis can elucidate various procedures used to decorate metal materials, including enamel (attachment of a glassy paste to the metallic surface followed by heating to fuse them), niello (silver sulfides mixed with wax to produce, after melting out the wax, a metallic black appearance), and gilt (processes to place gold on the surface of a base metal to give it the appearance of gold).

In addition to understanding the relationship of function or appearance to constitution, the chemist can shed light on the original processes whereby metallic ores were turned into pure metals. Although gold is usually found in nature in the pure state, and copper sometimes, most metals must be produced from naturally occurring materials in which the metals are mixed with other elements, usually oxygen or sulfur. The ore typically bears no physical resemblance to the free metal. The smelting of ores to produce metallic copper, iron, and silver is often complex. Analysis of the metal products themselves, of by-products such as slag (glassy materials containing silicates and other unwanted constituents of the ore), and of physical remnants of ancient hearths or mines can assist in understanding the ancient smelting processes.

Dyes and Pigments

Technology associated with ceramics, glass, and metals usually involved high temperatures and, hence, kilns, forges, and hearths. Not all chemical reactions require the assistance of high temperatures. Chemical processes associated with achieving the purely esthetic ends of applying color to materials often were carried out at room temperature. Dyes are chemical compounds, usually organic, that may be bound directly to a substrate. They contrast with pigments, usually inorganic, which require another substance, termed a *binder*, to adhere to the substrate. *Direct dyes* require no further chemical processing to adhere. Water-insoluble *vat dyes* first are altered to a form more amenable to binding to a fabric and then are regenerated on the fabric, for example, by oxidation. *Mordant dyes* use a chemical intermediary (the mordant) for attachment to the substrate. Spectroscopic analysis of the dyes can assist in understanding these processes.

Pigments do not dissolve in most media, including water, so they require the binder to permit attachment to the substrate. Usually this is a physical process (no chemical reaction occurs), so that the pigment and the binder remain in separate phases. For conversion to a paint, the pigment is mixed with a solvent as well as a binder. The solvent keeps the mixture fluid until application is complete and then evaporates. Elemental, spectroscopic, and microscopic examination of pigments can help understand their technology.

Most ancient dyes and pigments occurred naturally as mineral ores, as plant products, or as animal residues. Thus iron oxides such as hematite produced reds and browns, and charcoal produced black. The technology of preparing royal purple from mollusks in the eastern Mediterranean or of preparing cochineal red from coccus insects in the New World was subtle and complex, but the dyes corresponded closely to the naturally occurring material (McGovern and Michael 1990). Unique substances, not occurring in nature, also were produced. By 2500 B.C. the Egyptians had combined sand, calcium carbonate, and copper ore to produce Egyptian blue, creating a reliable source of a blue pigment for wall paintings and supplanting the less available cobalt blue and lapis lazuli. Egyptian blue may represent the first pure synthetic chemical. The Maya produced an even more impressive synthesis, combining the blue organic vegetable dye indigo with a white clay to produce a blue pigment, now called Maya blue. The inorganic matrix stabilized the often-sensitive organic material.

Synthetic Stone

Plaster may have been the first processed chemical substance. Invented at least 14,000 years ago in southwest Asia, plaster was formed by heating limestone or gypsum to drive off carbon dioxide and form lime. This powdery product could be stored and transported. At the appropriate time and place, it was converted into a paste by the addition of water. The paste was applied to a surface or poured into a form, where it reabsorbed carbon dioxide from the atmosphere to set as a stony substance. In this way people could improve surfaces or produce stone of a desired shape by using forms or molds. Fillers such as sand were added to extend the amount of material. The Romans used clay as the filler to produce cement. The aluminosilicate matrix of the clay required water rather than atmospheric carbon dioxide to set. Cement can set even under water. The addition of pebbles or crushed stones produced concrete. The relative proportions of the components may be determined by elemental analysis, microscopy, or powder X-ray diffraction. Chemistry can gauge the sophistication of the technology while helping understand how the materials were developed.

Organics

Because organics comprise many types of materials, the subject is multifaceted. Processing of food (aside from cooking) certainly involves organic chemistry. The conversion of grains to beer was one of the first applications of organic chemistry to food technology. The grain, usually barley, is converted to a malt, which is boiled in water to break down the polymeric starches into sugars. Fermentation through the action of yeast converts the sugars to alcohol. The process may be 8,000 years old. The making of wine dispenses with the first step (malting), because sugars already are presence in grapes. Grape sugars then are allowed to ferment in the presence of yeast. Organics such as tartaric acid, which occur naturally in wine, are sufficiently robust to survive on the interior surface of wine containers that are several thousand years old. The detection of tartaric acid on the surface of a jar or pot is considered sufficient evidence to demonstrate that the object was involved in wine manufacture or storage. Similar analysis of certain fatty acids (such as oleic acid) is considered strong evidence that the object was involved in the manufacture or storage of olive oil. This type of analysis usually is carried out by the combined methods of extraction, component separation by GC, and compound analysis by mass spectrometry.

Processing of wood products in the ancient world led to tars and pitches, which were used as adhesives (as for repairing pottery), sealants (coatings for wood or rope), medicines, and preservatives in wine. Heating of wood, bark, or peat drives off volatiles to produce a viscous residue called pitch. IR, NMR, or GC/MS analysis of the surviving materials often can identify the source of the pitch as pine, spruce, or coal, for example.

Human Remains

The most important information that can be derived from chemical analysis of human remains concerns the diet of the individuals. Such information may be derived from residues of their unconsumed food (indirect remains) or from their skeletons and fossilized excrement (direct remains). Van der Merwe (1982) has commented that food residues reflect the menu from which humans chose, but bone and excrement specify the foods that were actually consumed.

Indirect Remains

Remains of possible comestibles may be found at an archaeological site as seeds, pollen, wood, phytoliths, animal bone or teeth, hides, and so on. These are not often subjects for chemical research. Biological analysis can provide important data on their botanical or zoological identity.

Chemical analysis has been uniquely useful in understanding the often-pyrolyzed materials found on cooking vessels. The process is analogous to that used in analyzing containers for the storage and transportation of liquids. Pottery employed in cooking often retains a dark stain from food residues. Extraction of this material with solvent, separation by GC, and analysis of the components by mass spectrometry can provide a listing of the chemical compounds present in the stain. The structures of these compounds often can be related to the types of food that had been present in the vessels. Pyrrole and toluene are markers for proteins; furan for sugars; organic acids for fats, waxes, and oils; and specific steroids for certain vegetables. Figure 13.3 illustrates a gas chromatogram from food residues on pottery. Literally dozens of compounds are present.

Food residues also may be analyzed for their isotopic composition. The ratios of the two stable isotopes of carbon (^{13}C and ^{12}C) and of the two stable isotopes of nitrogen (^{15}N and ^{14}N) vary from foodstuff to foodstuff because biochemical reactions are sensitive to isotopic identity (lighter isotopes often react more quickly). Carbon isotopes can be used as indicators of maize consumption; nitrogen isotopes, of legumes. A plot of the nitrogen isotopes vs. the carbon isotopes thus distinguishes three classes of foods: maize, legumes, and all other.

Direct Remains

Isotopic analysis of food remains carries over to the analysis of animal remains. Van der Merwe (1982) found that leaves from woody shrubs had on average 26 parts per thousand (ppt) less ^{13}C than a standard, whereas subtropical grasses had only 12 ppt less. This difference suggested a method to distinguish actual diet, provided that the ratios are translated into the tissue of the animals that consumed the plants. From the archaeological perspective, the tissue must be obtained from bone residues, originally from collagen present in bone. Using modern animals with known diets, van der Merwe found that bone from animals that consumed only leaves from woody shrubs (browsers) had 21 ppt less ^{13}C than the standard and bone from animals that consumed only grasses (grazers) had 7 ppt less. Thus the translation from plant to animal bone involves a shift of about 5 ppt, but the distinction could still be made between browsers and grazers.

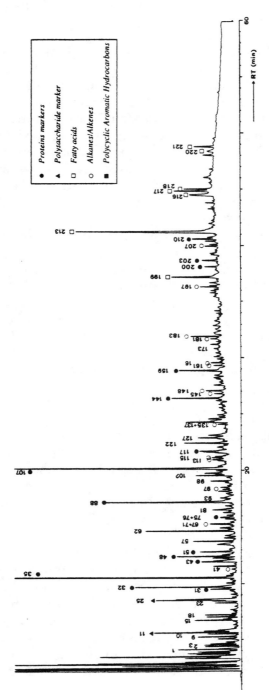

Figure 13.3. Gas chromatogram of the products from the pyrolysis of pottery residues from a Late Iron Age or Early Roman site called Uitgeist-Groot Dorregeest in the Netherlands. Reproduced from T. Oudemans and S. Boon, Journal of Analytical and Applied Pyrolysis 20:207, 1991. Reprinted with the permission of Elsevier Science-NL, Amsterdam, the Netherlands.

Humans are omnivores, but a large portion of their diets always has been plants. Van der Merwe's study of the carbon ratios of Woodland Indians from North America demonstrated dramatically when maize (a subtropical grass) was introduced. Figure 13.4 shows the ratio of carbon isotopes (expressed as the deficit of ^{13}C in ppt) as a function of time. During the Archaic period and through the Early and Middle Woodland periods (up to about A.D. 800), the ratio stayed very close to 21 ppt, characteristic of consumption of woody shrubs, as by browsers. Upon introduction of maize, the ratio changed rapidly, moving to 10 ppt by A.D. 1200 (the Mississippian period). This ratio suggests a diet of some 70 percent maize by this time. More refined dietary analysis may be achieved by including nitrogen as well as carbon isotopes. Nitrogen isotopes have been found to be useful not only in testing for legume consumption but also as a measure of marine sources of food.

Limited organic analysis has been carried out directly on human remains. Evershed and co-workers have found that cholesterol in the soil is a reliable marker of animal remains. Extracts from fossilized human excrement (coprolites) have indicated

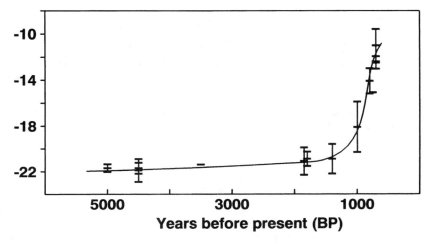

Figure 13.4. Changes in the proportion of carbon-13, expressed as parts per thousand, in human skeletal collagen from the North American Woodlands people. N. J. van der Merwe, in New Developments in Archaeological Science, *A. M. Pollard, editor, p. 255, 1992, Oxford University Press, Oxford.*

that coprostanol is a reliable marker. Evershed's analysis of samples from a suspected Roman cesspit was able to map its dimensions from the presence of coprostanol in the soil (Bethell et al. 1993).

Chemical analysis of amino acids derived from proteins was developed originally by Bada as a method of dating (Masters and Bada 1987). Amino acids in living organisms exist as a single mirror image. At death, these amino acids begin to revert to a 50:50 mixture of both mirror images by the process called racemization. Unfortunately, dates obtained by this method initially proved to be unreliable, because chemical racemization was subject to a number of variables. Amino acids in many eggshells, particularly the thick shells of ostrich, emu, and the extinct ratite, have proved to be more resistant to these variables. Use of such widely available shell fragments from African sites has yielded reliable dates. The method is of potential importance because it can be applied to organic materials whose age is beyond the range of carbon-14 dating (ca. 50,000 years).

Conclusion

Through elemental analysis of inorganics, molecular (spectroscopic) analysis of organics, and isotopic analysis of both, chemistry provides archaeology with a wide range of information about artifact provenance, ancient technology, human diet, and chronology. Because most chemical methods are destructive, analysis is usually, but not always, carried out on samples with no commercial or esthetic value.

References

Bethell, P. H., R. P. Evershed, and L. J. Goad
    1993   The investigation of lipids in organic residues by gas chromatography. In *Prehistoric Human Bone: Archaeology at the Molecular Level*, edited by Joseph B. Lambert and Gisela Grupe, pp. 229–235. Springer-Verlag, Berlin.

Brill, Robert H.
   1963   Ancient glass. *Scientific American* 209(5):120–126.

Craig, H., and V. Craig
   1972   Greek marbles: determination of provenance by isotopic analysis. *Science* 176:401-403.

Goffer, Zvi
   1980   *Archaeological chemistry.* John Wiley, New York.

Lambert, Joseph B.
   1997   *Traces of the Past: Unraveling the Secrets of Archaeology through Chemistry.* Helix Books/Perseus Books, Reading, Massachusetts.

Lambert, Joseph B., Charles D. McLaughlin, Catherine E. Shawl, and Liang Xue
   1999   X-ray photoelectron spectroscopy and archaeology. *Analytical Chemistry* 71:614A–620A.

Lambert, Joseph B., and George O. Poinar, Jr.
   2002   Amber: the organic gemstone. *Accounts of Chemical Research* 354(8):628–636.

Lambert, Joseph B., Catherine E. Shawl, and Jaime A. Stearns
   2000   Nuclear magnetic resonance in archaeology. *Chemical Society Reviews* 29:175–182.

Lambert, Joseph B., Herbert F. Shurvell, David A. Lightner, and R. Graham Cooks
   1998   *Organic structural spectroscopy.* Prentice-Hall, Upper Saddle River, New Jersey.

Leung, P. L., M. J. Stokes, C. Tiemei, and Q. Dashu
   2000   A study of ancient Chinese porcelain wares of the Song-Yuan Dynasties from Cizhou and Ding kilns with energy dispersive X-ray fluorescence. *Archaeometry* 42:129–140.

Masters, Patricia A., and Jeffrey L. Bada
   1987   Amino acid racemization dating of bone and shell. In *Archaeological Chemistry II*, edited by Giles F. Carter, pp. 117–138. American Chemical Society, Washington, D.C.

McGovern, P. E., and R. H. Michael
   1990   Royal purple dye: the chemical reconstruction of the ancient Mediterranean industry. *Accounts of Chemical Research,* 23:152–158.

Parkes, P. A.
   1986   *Current scientific techniques in archaeology.* St. Martin's Press, New York.

Pollard, A. Mark, and Carl Heron
   1996   *Archaeological chemistry.* Royal Society of Chemistry, Cambridge.

Rice, P. M.
　　1987　*Pottery Analysis: A Sourcebook.* University of Chicago Press, Chicago.

Sayre, E. V., and R. W. Smith
　　1961　Compositional categories of ancient glass. *Science* 133:1824–1826.

Shortland, A. J., P. T. Nicholson, and C. M. Jackson
　　2000　Lead isotopic analysis of Eighteenth-Dynasty Egyptian eyepaints and lead antimonate colourants. *Archaeometry* 42:153-157.

Tite, M. S.
　　1972　*Methods of physical examination in archaeology.* Seminar Press, London.

Van der Merwe, Nikolaus J.
　　1982　Carbon isotopes, photosynthesis, and archaeology. *American Scientist* 70:596–606.

Wertime, T. A.
　　1973　The beginnings of metallurgy: A new look. *Science* 182:875–887.

Williams-Thorpe, O.
　　1995　Obsidian in the Mediterranean and Middle East. *Archaeometry* 37:217-248.

14

Statistics for Archaeology

Mark Aldenderfer

Statistical analysis has become an integral part of modern archaeology. Even the briefest glance through the literature reveals a stunning diversity of methods that range from simple explorations of data structure to complex multivariate analyses. Every subfield of archaeology uses statistics to a greater or lesser extent, and a basic understanding of statistical inference and what it can (and cannot) do is a fundamental requirement for every student of archaeology. Indeed, it is almost impossible to read, but more importantly understand, an issue of *Journal of Archaeological Science*, for example, without a firm foundation in basic statistics and at least a passing awareness of multivariate or more specialized methods. Most graduate programs and many undergraduate majors require their students to take at least one course in statistics, and a number of programs in the United States and United Kingdom, such as Arizona State University or the University of Sheffield, have developed specialized tracks of study for those interested in becoming archaeological statisticians (Aldenderfer 1998b). Many programs now offer courses specifically designed to teach the fundamentals of statistical inference within an explicitly archaeological framework, a much-needed departure from the not-too-distant past, when students were encouraged to take statistics classes wherever they could find them, such as in psychology, geography, sociology, or biology. Although one could learn the basics of inference in these courses, they were poor substitutes for classes that highlighted typical archaeological problems and how to investigate them using statistical inference.

But there is more to the application of statistical methods in archeology than simply knowing when and how to calculate a confidence interval or frame a null hypothesis. Although it is relatively easy to teach the mechanics of statistics, and infinitely easier than 30 years ago to do so given the widespread availability of very powerful desktop software, the hard part, and the part that the field is still working on, is the teaching about how statistics are properly integrated into the research enterprise. It is not so much knowing the place of quantitative analysis in some sort of cycle or flowchart of doing science, but is instead a knowledge about how to use data known to be variable, uncertain, and noisy to make compelling arguments about the past. Statistics, then, is as much about theory, model building, and clear thinking as it is about data analysis per se.

It is my intention in this chapter to define basic concepts, briefly explore the historical context of the introduction of statistics to archaeology, examine key aspects of current practice, and make some assessment of where statistics in the field may be going.

Basic Definitions

Quantification, mathematics, and statistics have each played important roles in modern archaeology, but it is important to distinguish them carefully from one another. Quantitative methods are those that manipulate numbers and use measurement in the research process. Johnson (1978:46) notes that "quantification is concerned with the numerical description of empirical situations"; elsewhere, following Kaplan (1964:212–213), I have defined the notion of a quantitative idiom, which is simply a recognition that measurement and the manipulation of numbers are seen as useful ways to obtain insight into some phenomenon or process (Aldenderfer 1987a:14). A quantitative idiom involves more than simply using statistics or mathematics in research and instead is a way of *thinking* about a problem. That is, quantification is thought to be both useful and valuable as a means by which to approach a problem. The success of a quantitative idiom relies on the development of successful quantitative measurements of empirical phenomena. Measurement is closely related to quantification, because it is the assignment of numbers to some object, entity, or process according to some rule. Measurement is important, because it allows us to use mathematics, which in turn gives us the possibility of creating more precise descriptions of the things in which we are interested. Measurement, however, must take place within a meaningful context. Although we must assume we can measure anything of which we can conceive, being able to measure things per se does not make the measurement meaningful. How we derive meaningful measurements is a complex topic, but briefly, meaning first originates in theory, which provides guidance on variable selection, category meaning, and to some extent, definition of presumed interrelationships between variables (Aldenderfer 1998b:112). Unfortunately, measurement in many applied settings is strictly ad hoc and has no formal mathematical (or logical) foundation beyond simple counting and arithmetic. In many cases, what is measured is based on what can be measured, with little attention given as to *why* certain variables are selected for analysis.

Mathematics is a highly structured form of reasoning that proceeds from assumption to deduction to conclusion (Davis and Hersh 1981:6). It employs an abstract, axiomatic, formal language that is content free. That is, mathematics can be about anything or nothing depending on how it is used. The mathematical foundation of statistics is probability theory, which very simply is the mathematical modeling of chance variation or random phenomena. Statistics is a branch of mathematical reasoning that deals with the logic of inference under conditions of variability, uncertainty, and error. As Hacking (1965:1) puts it, "the foundation of statistics is to state a set of principles which entail the validity of all correct statistical inference, and which do not imply that any fallacious inference is valid." Although there are hundreds of statistical methods, there are only two fundamental approaches to statistical analysis: frequentists and Bayesians. The primary difference between the two approaches lies in their treatment of probabilities: frequentists (the large majority of statisticians) examine data in the light of some a priori model (normality, linearity, etc.), and the analysis, estimation, and testing that follow are focused solely on the parameters of that model. In contrast, Bayesians incorporate data-independent judgments (created by experts, experience, or experiments) on what the parameters of the model could resemble (the so-called prior distribution; see later discussion) and combine these with the collected data to test the model. Both approaches, however, test hypotheses (framed in statistical terminology, and which are usually not similar to the hypotheses that drive research) and, in practice, tend to overlap.

Traditionally, statistics tend to be subdivided into often crosscutting categories based on the number of variables handled by the method (univariate, bivariate, and multivariate), the strategy of their use (descriptive or exploratory vs. inferential or confirmatory), the field of application (e.g., spatial, biometrical), or statistical model employed (directional, bootstrapping, distribution free, parametric, nonparametric, etc.). Not surprisingly, there is a long history of borrowing, trading, modification, and reinvention of statistical techniques across different scientific disciplines.

Historical Overview

Over the years, there have been a number of useful historical surveys of statistical analysis in archaeology. Clark and Stafford (1982) published one of the first, in which they reviewed the introduction of quantitative methods to Americanist archaeology through a citation analysis of *American Antiquity*. Among the trends they identified was the very sharp increase in the number of papers in the journal devoted to the use or description of quantitative methods in the interval 1960–1964. The rate of growth of all applications of statistics over the preceding 30 years was essentially flat. After that interval, growth rates quickly became exponential. The reasons for this explosive growth are numerous but perhaps of greatest importance was the emergence of the so-called new archaeology, a self-designated movement that was perceived by its practitioners as an objective, scientific approach to archaeology. Among its innovations was the introduction of statistics and other quantitative methods to archaeological practice (Ammerman 1992:233–236). This process mirrored that taking place at the time in other social science disciplines such as geography, which witnessed its quantitative revolution slightly earlier (Burton 1963). Another factor that stimulated the use of statistics was the availability of quantitative data from scientific techniques such as radiocarbon dating, X-ray diffraction analysis, and chemical characterization of archaeological materials (Orton 1992:137). This rapid growth was also assisted by the appearance of powerful and more widely available computers and statistical software, which for the first time made multivariate analysis practical. There was both good and bad in this—good in that archaeologists could explore the use of these techniques and bad in that many of those uses were rife with errors in practice and interpretation that sometimes went unrecognized for years (see, for example, White and Thomas 1972).

One of the seminal (but flawed) papers of this period was the factor analysis of Mousterian lithic assemblages by Lewis and Sally Binford (1966), in which they attempted to define tool kits that were postulated to have a seasonal and functional interpretation in contrast to the prevailing model that variability in these assemblages represented culture or ethnicity (Aldenderfer 1987b:95–102). This paper had a very profound influence on archaeology, and for many, it legitimized a novel and compelling approach to the past that moved beyond what was then seen as sterile classification of artifacts in service of prehistory (Read 1989:6–7).

Indeed, various statistical methods had already been brought into service as a part of the debate on how best to create classifications of archaeological objects. Albert Spaulding (1953) argued that statistical approaches were both appropriate and necessary for the discovery of artifact types and that nominal scale methods, such as the chi-square technique, were able to discover types in collections of objects through the identification of co-occurring sets of variables that may have had cultural significance to their makers. He believed that numerical techniques were superior to then-existing methods of artifact classification, which he felt were highly subjective and arbitrary. Although laudable, his approach had numerous problems, not the least of which was his argument that artifact types were best defined as "non-random artifact clusters" and that a statistical method was the best way to discover them (Doran and Hodson 1975:168–169). His paper lent early support to a pernicious belief that statistical hypothesis testing per se was the same as testing archaeologically meaningful hypotheses, a problem that has plagued every field in which statistics are routinely employed (Sterne and Davey-Smith 2001).

Archaeologists in Great Britain explored different statistical methods for artifact classification, using cluster analysis and the theoretical underpinnings of numerical taxonomy, a radically empirical approach to biological classification (Doran and Hodson 1966; Hodson et al. 1966). In contrast to Spaulding's focus on variables, this approach created classifications based on similarities among objects. The debate between these camps and their chosen approaches—so-called item clustering vs. variable clustering—persisted well into the 1980s (Cowgill 1982, 1990; Aldenderfer 1987a; Ammerman 1992). And like Spaulding's method, clustering has its own set of serious problems, which include, for example, an ad hoc approach to variable selection, and a lack of a well-defined statistical model of clusters (Aldenderfer and Blashfield 1984).

These examples reflect another trend that developed once the new archaeology and its emphasis on science and objective analysis took hold of the archaeological community: the so-called great borrowing of the late 1960s through the 1980s (Aldenderfer 1998b:92). Various scientific fields were ransacked for statistical methods—psychology had already been raided for factor analysis, and biology had given up clustering. Now human geography provided the field with a plethora of spatial statistics and methods (Hodder and Orton 1976), ecology offered up ordination methods such as principal components and multidimensional scaling (Cowgill 1968), and statistics itself provided us with sampling (Mueller 1975) as well as many other methods, including correlation and regression, contingency table analysis, t-tests, significance testing, and more (Thomas 1976). The pace of growth was so rapid that highly critical review articles appeared almost immediately (Thomas 1978; Clark 1982; Scheps 1982). Although these reviews made it clear that the introduction of statistics to the field was desirable, they showed forcefully that the majority of archaeologists employing statistics in their research had little experience with them and that many were prone to making quite elementary mistakes in their application and interpretation. This is not surprising given that archaeologists then had little formal training in statistics. A more subtle problem, however, and one that persists today, is that in many instances, the borrowing took place within an archaeological vacuum. That is, without a well-reasoned quantitative idiom within which to use these methods, the results of their application to archaeological data were often confusing, inappropriate, or irrelevant.

But borrowing was not the sole theme of the 1980s, because a number of authors began to explore in a careful manner how statistics and archaeological research could be combined effectively. The first textbook written for archaeological applications appeared at the end of the decade (Shennan 1988), and authors like Read (1985, 1987) and Carr (1985a, 1985b, 1987) began to look closely at how to resolve the problem of discordance—that is, the lack of fit between methods chosen, the data at hand and what they are said to represent, and the overall goals of the analysis. As Read (1989:66) has put it, "[there] is growing awareness that archaeological data have complex structure that is not resolved merely through application of more complex statistical methods."

For these authors, statistics were not simply tools but instead part of a larger analytic process. Read (a mathematician and anthropologist) attempted to explain using mathematical formalisms, the nature of statistical reasoning, and how it could be successfully integrated into scientific research. His examples were always elegant, but they seemed to have little impact on the field simply because they were highly symbolic and difficult for nonmathematicians to follow. Carr (1987:220–224) likewise attempted to show how theory, problem, data, and method were linked in a recursive manner but chose to explore this line of reasoning by advocating the use of middle range theory and a variant of exploratory data analysis (EDA) he called "constrained" EDA (CEDA), by which he meant an EDA that had deductive constraints as defined by the problem. Although CEDA never took off, EDA has (see later discussion), and his point remains valid—it is necessary to explore data structure thoroughly and completely from different perspectives before undertaking a complex statistical analysis. By the end of the decade, the majority of the most commonly employed statistical methods (all univariate, many bivariate, and standard multivariate methods) had been introduced to the discipline and employed with some regularity but not necessarily with much-improved ability (Cowgill 1986; Whallon 1987).

By the advent of the 1990s, archaeologists of a quantitative mind-set were prepared to explore the details of statistical practice and archaeological interpretation. In a brief polemic, Orton (1992:137) offered his vision (or wish list, really) of the development of quantitative methods for the 1990s. His four top observations were (1) the need for methodological progress in specific, well-defined areas, including intrasite spatial analysis and multiple correspondence analysis, (2) that greater attention be paid to the quality of data via an increased use of sampling, (3) the effective integration of different data types in a quantitative analysis, and (4) more attention to education—how to train archaeologists to use existing methods properly. Although his list harkens back to earlier, still-unresolved concerns (data quality and sampling, for example), it is also quite forward looking through his focus on developing specific methods for specific situations and calling for a thorough evaluation of how students *should* be taught to use statistics and quantitative methods. Ammerman (1992:250–252), writing at the same time, was somewhat more pessimistic about the outcome of archaeology's experience with statistics and quantitative methods throughout the 1970s and 1980s. Like Orton and Read, he wrote that the discipline, in its infatuation with the new and novel, failed to properly place these methods on a solid inferential foundation and that unthinking borrowing had actually retarded the progress of these methods in the field, rather the opposite effect from what their adherents had intended. He was especially concerned with lost opportunities for the training of graduate students and noted that "we still need methods that are better tailored to archaeological problems" (1992:252). Earlier, Kintigh (1987) had also made a plea for the development of methods suitable for the oddities of archaeological data.

By decade's end, many of the predictions and desires expressed at its start had been realized or at least discussed in some detail (Aldenderfer 1998b). Some subfields of archaeology, most notably archaeometry, intrasite spatial analysis, faunal studies, and sampling (Nance 1990, 1993) had by this time begun to explore their subject matter in effective and nuanced ways. In archaeometry, for example, debate moved from the simple demonstration of novel or new methods and presentation of results to discussions of the finer points of archaeological interpretation and statistical modeling. For example, Bishop and Neff (1989:69–70) made a strong case for modeling, rather than simply summarizing, compositional data. That is, since any multivariate method will discover and often impose some sort of structure on a set of data, it behooves the investigator to think deeply about just what might account for elemental composition in the sample. They illustrate the difference between modeling and summarization with an example of ceramic analysis focused on distinguishing the effects of tempering vs. natural elemental compositions in clay sources when attempting to determine the sources of different pottery types. They show that without careful model development, it is very easy to confound their effects and make serious errors in interpretation. Arnold et al. (1991), Papageorgiou et al. (2001), and Baxter and Jackson (2001) have extended this argument. Other authors have reviewed the use of various aspects of compositional analysis with the goal of examining details of specific methods or details of analysis. Baxter (1992, 1994b) has reviewed the use of discriminant analysis in compositional studies, Harbottle (1991) has examined differences in the use of Mahalanobis and Euclidean distances in compositional studies of ceramics, Baxter (1991) and Baxter et al. (1990) have compared principal components and correspondence analysis as applied to compositional data, and Baxter and Heyworth (1991) discuss correlation matrices in the context of compositional studies. Baxter (1994a) provides a very thorough collection of references of applied analyses in compositional studies that spans more than two decades of research. Baxter (2001b) has examined the problem of how to select variables for compositional analysis through the development of models of compositions and not rely on standard assumptions that drive many statistical methods used in compositional analysis (e.g., multivariate normality mixtures). A good recent summary of statistical methods in service to archaeometry is Baxter and Buck (2000). What marks the maturing of statistical practice in archaeometry is the development of a robust quantitative idiom (see later discussion) and the intensive interaction between statisticians and archaeologists.

Intrasite analysis grew substantially during this decade and, like archaeometry, has begun to explore in-depth the connection between method and anthropological process. The early development of intrasite analysis was almost wholly empirical and ad hoc and was devoted to the borrowing or discovery of methods that could discover spatial pattern primarily in terms of anomaly and coincidence. Most of the methods borrowed were point-pattern models coming directly from plant ecology or human geography, such as nearest-neighbor analysis (Hodder and Orton 1976:30–52), or were novel inventions on the part of archaeologists, like Kintigh and Ammerman's (1982) k-means clustering procedure for spatial data or Whallon's (1984) unconstrained clustering. As a number of authors have noted, the failure to connect spatial pattern with anthropological process led to frustration and outright rejection when these methods were applied to real archaeological data, and led to a number of reviews of foundational issues and comparisons of method performance using either simulated or ethnoarchaeological data (Blankholm 1991; Kintigh 1990; Gregg, Kintigh, and Whallon 1991). Others, such as Orton (1992:138), called for new statistical approaches that seek to define edges of artifact distributions and segregate them from others. More recently, some authors, notably Levy et al. (2001) and Craig and Aldenderfer (2005), have begun to explore how to examine intrasite data using geographic information systems (GISs). What makes these approaches interesting is that instead of thinking about intrasite spatial analysis as a statistical problem, they examine the spatial distribution of artifacts at a site from a combined anthropological and information infrastructure perspective. In other words, they are concerned with building models of spatial activity at sites and are simultaneously developing the GIS-based infrastructure that will allow them, eventually, to apply certain statistical methods to the data in a coherent manner. In this way, this approach begins to re-semble what archaeometrists have done: build models with ex-plicit, but not initial, concern for the statistical or quantitative models that will ultimately be used to assess model validity.

Aspects of Current Practice

In this section, I explore topics of continued and current impor-tance in the use of statistical analysis in archaeology. It is not meant to be exhaustive, but instead focuses on ongoing issues and problems.

Exploratory Data Analysis

EDA is more of a philosophy of data analysis rather than a set of statistical models and techniques. First developed by John Tukey (1977), EDA focuses on how to examine a data set and how to interpret its structure once discovered. Indeed, EDA en-courages the analyst to make few assumptions about the data and instead to allow the data to speak for themselves. Used with caution, EDA can help an analyst to gain insight into data struc-ture, identify outliers and extreme cases, define variables that are likely to be important for further analysis or consideration, test assumptions about data structure, and transform noisy data so that they can be used with more conventional techniques.

Developed originally by Tukey (1977), EDA relies heavily on graphical techniques and data visualization. Scatterplots, bi-plots, residual plots, box-and-whisker charts, and stem-and-leaf diagrams are among the simple graphical methods employed. It also relies heavily on terms such as location (central tendency of data), shape (what the data distribution looks like), and spread (how widely scattered are the data) as interpretative devices. The creative use of plots can help to identify distributional forms, identify outliers, and assess data structure. Figure 14.1 presents a data summary generated by JMP 5.0, a statistical soft-ware program, for width measurements on two types of projec-tile points. Inspection of the histogram, box-and-whisker chart, and normal quantile plot shows that the data in Figure 14.1a are

Distributions
width

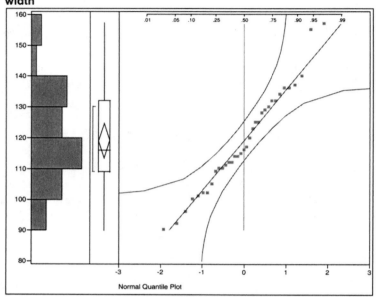

Figure 14.1a.   Type 1 width distributions.

Distributions
width

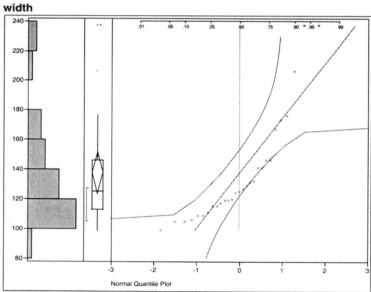

Figure 14.1b.   Type 2 width distributions

distributed normally, and thus would require no transformation or cleaning. Further, no outliers are present. In contrast, the data in Figure 14.1b show that the data are skewed to the left. This is especially apparent in the histogram, but the quantile plot shows that most data values fall within the 95 percent confidence intervals calculated for this distribution. The box-and-whisker chart reveals that three points are well separated from the bulk of the data, and in EDA terms, these are extreme outliers. Since the data are badly skewed, a logarithmic transformation could be used to center the data, although this does little to reduce the problems caused by the outliers.

Although admittedly many of the methods espoused by Tukey are somewhat obscure, his and others' emphasis on defining more data types beyond those accepted by classical methods, the use of transformations, and the ways graphical methods are integrated into the research process are enormously helpful because they give the analyst tremendous insight into archaeological data, which are by nature highly variable and noisy because they are generally affected by unknown transformative processes or have been collected with unknown biases.

Despite the obvious appeal of EDA and its utility, relatively few archaeologists have used EDA extensively (Voorrips 1990:8). Carr (1985, 1987) advocated his CEDA approach but gained few adherents. Until the publication of Drennan's (1996) introductory text on statistics for archaeologists, there had been no sustained demonstration of EDA's value to archaeology. However, because of its elegant simplicity and capacity to deal with noisy data, it has a strong role to play in the statistical analysis of archeological data.

Testing Statistical Hypotheses and Archaeological Inference

It is a commonplace to believe that the primary reason one does statistics is to test hypotheses. According to Thomas (1976:209), this is a fairly straightforward procedure of six steps: (1) state the statistical hypothesis, (2) select a level of statistical significance, (3) select an appropriate statistical model, (4) define the region of rejection, (5) perform the computations and make the statistical decision, and (6) state this decision in nonstatistical terms. This all seems very simple, but as is often the case, it is not. In fact, hypothesis testing as it is generally conceived is a controversial procedure that many practicing scientists, as well as statisticians, have advised against. In archaeology, Cowgill (1977) sounded an early alarm, but his advice has gone for the most part unheeded. Archaeologists continue to test all sorts of statistical hypotheses despite good advice to the contrary. What is it about such testing that is problematic? The mechanics of testing are not in dispute, but instead, it is all about the logical status of hypothesis testing within a research environment.

The origins of the debate reach back to the origins of modern statistics in the early twentieth century. R. A. Fisher, one of the founding figures of statistical inference, created the idea of the null hypothesis, which can be thought of as a hypothesis, tested through the calculation of a statistic for possible rejection, under the assumption that it is true. Additionally, there is the implication that observed effects (for example, the distributions of data values between two samples) are the result of chance. The null hypothesis is set against the alternative hypothesis, which is usually some statement within the larger research environment for which we are seeking empirical support. As Fisher saw it, one could calculate the p value, which he interpreted as an index measuring the strength of evidence against the null hypothesis. He advocated $p < .05$ (5 percent significance) as a standard level for concluding that there is evidence against the hypothesis tested, though not as an absolute rule. "If P is between 0.1 and 0.9 there is certainly no reason to suspect the hypothesis tested. If it is below 0.02 it is strongly indicated that the hypothesis fails to account for the whole of the facts. We shall not often be astray if we draw a conventional line at 0.05" (Fisher 1950:80 in Sterne and Davey-Smith 2001:226). But he was also careful to say that how the p value was interpreted was a matter for the researcher, who would necessarily compare the results of this test with other data. Note also what was *not* tested in his original approach: the alternative hypothesis. In other words, by rejecting the null hypothesis, one is not simultaneously or necessarily accepting the alternative. The reasons for this are numerous: multiple plausible alternatives may exist, but this formalism tests only one; there are multiple null hypotheses that can be constructed, and the results of a statistical test may vary dramatically (i.e., the null may be denied in one test, but accepted by another) *solely* because of how the null is framed; because of inadequate sample sizes, the null hypothesis may be incorrectly rejected (Fisher's Type I error). In other words, despite having a reputation of being objective, testing the null hypothesis in this manner is highly subjective.

This perception led two important statisticians of the day, Jerzy Neyman and Karl Pearson, to extend the notion of hypothesis testing to include a different sort of error (Type II) that Fisher's approach ignored: accepting the null hypothesis when it in fact is false. Among the solutions offered by Neyman and Pearson was to insist that researchers define a precise alternative hypothesis and, further, specify in advance of statistical testing acceptable levels of Type I and II errors (Goodman 1993; Lehmann 1993). Defining the alternative is critical: one must not only say that the alternative hypothesis is plausible; one must *also* say how *much* difference from the null might exist. For instance, if one wishes to determine if the mean length of a projectile point style decreases from period A to period B, one must specify *how much* of a difference should be observed. This is a much stricter criterion and is almost never accomplished in common practice. "Instead, only the easy part of Neyman and Pearson's approach—that the null hypothesis can be rejected if P < 0.05 (type I error rate 5 percent)—has been widely adopted" (Sterne and Davey-Smith 2001:227). As most of those who have a had a statistics course know, $p < .05$ is an important number. In the Neyman-Pearson approach, a value of $p = .051$ means that we cannot reject the null hypothesis, whereas if $p < .49$, we can reject it. If this seems arbitrary, it is, and what we are left with is the following: a procedure ill suited to doing what we really want to be doing—assessing empirical support for our ideas, reliance on a highly arbitrary, up-down, accept-reject approach to testing statistical hypotheses, susceptibility to temptation in the framing of null hypotheses, which are often meaningless in any case, and finally, persisting in believing, even though we should know better, that rejection of the null somehow implies acceptance of the alternative. In fact, as Cowgill (1977:353) states, even if one succeeds in framing, then testing, hypotheses in this manner, the hypotheses themselves are not explanations but merely measures of the degree to which we have evidence to support one or the other. As numerous authors have noted, the persistence in this belief is remarkable despite its real drawbacks as a tool for scientific research (Rozeboom 1960). Among the reasons cited for our continued reliance on it include ignorance of alternatives, the ease with which it can be performed in all commonly available statistical software packages, and of course, the dead hand of traditional usage.

But there are alternatives that are simple and effective. Cowgill (1977:362–366) argues that instead of running significance tests, we should be calculating standard errors of parameter estimates and confidence intervals, a call echoed by numerous statisticians across many scientific fields. Yet another approach is to forgo reliance on a strict interpretation of the p value and to instead discuss what a given value might mean in commonsense terms. Drennan (1996:163) provides an example of how this might be done by contrasting two ways of framing a question (Table 14.1). His approach is similar to Fisher's original conception of such testing. In medicine, however, the stakes are much higher, and consequently, one may chose different decision levels. Statisticians in this field tend to be highly conservative and generally begin their assessment of the evidence against the null hypothesis at the $p < .01$ level, with strong evidence

Table 14.1. Comparing Two Ways of Thinking about Significance Testing

Significance Testing to Reject the Null Hypothesis		Significance Testing so that Results Are due to Chance	
The difference observed between Formative and Classic period house floor size is nothing more than chance: true or false?		How likely is it that the observed difference in Formative and Classic period house floor size is due to nothing more than chance?	
$p = .80$	True	$p = .80$	Extremely likely
$p = .06$	True	$p = .06$	Fairly unlikely
$p = .05$	False	$p = .05$	Fairly unlikely
$p = .01$	False	$p = .01$	Very unlikely

Source: After Drennan 1996:163.

against the null hypothesis indicated by $p < .001$ (Sterne and Davey-Smith 2001:229).

Note that these examples are more than simply shifting words around; they are instead a change in the way to think about the data and probabilities, which is more accord with the goals of scientific research.

Other approaches to significance testing that have not yet appeared in the archaeological literature include graphical methods, which include plotting p values, confidence levels, power levels, and other measures (Loftus 1993), and the computation of maximum likelihood ratios (Dixon and O'Reilly 1999). A maximum likelihood ratio is a quantity that compares the likelihood of the data based on one model with the likelihood of the data based on a second, competing model. Multiple models can be tested simultaneously. Maximum likelihood ratio modeling is much closer to our goal of testing multiple alternative hypotheses and provides us with the tools to compare the relative merits of different models and how they match up against the data. Finally, the whole field of Bayesian statistical inference and reasoning offers useful and appropriate alternatives to significance testing (see later discussion).

In summary, although there may well be specific instances in which one might wish to perform significance testing in archaeological contexts, we are well advised to avoid such testing. A final piece of advice: go back and read Cowgill's (1977) paper—it was remarkably prescient for its times in archaeology, and it is still important and useful today.

Spatial Statistics

Although archaeologists have long been interested in spatial analysis, they have had less interest in, and consequently less experience with, spatial *statistics*. Kvamme (1990, 1993, 1994) has reminded us that spatial statistics are quite different, and generally more complex, from their nonspatial counterparts. Spatial analysis need not use statistical or quantitative methods and can be as simple as reading and interpreting a map. However, as we usually want to learn more from our data, spatial analysis necessarily includes a wide range of quantitative and statistical techniques. However, it is important to understand the differences between data and spatial data. A simple definition of spatial data is data that "are spatially located *and* explicit consideration is given to the possible importance of their spatial arrangement in the analysis or in the interpretation of results" (Bailey and Gatrell 1995:8; see also Wheatley and Gillings 2002:126). The key term in this definition is "explicit consideration," which means that there is some reason to believe that space (that is, the location of the observation) has an effect on its value and that statistical models and analyses for examining these data must be appropriately modified to include this. The possibility that the spatial propinquity of two observations has an effect on their values violates a basic assumption of modern statistics—independence between observations. In spatial terms, standard statistical techniques assume (or ignore because they are not explicitly modeled) two things: (1) that observations have been created by a stationary spatial process, or in other words, their statistical properties do not vary with their absolute location, and (2) that any covariance between two observations depends on their distances and not on the direction in which they are separated. In technical terms, the underlying spatial process exhibits isotropy. Because many classes of archaeological data and the research questions that generate them are inherently spatial, it is obvious that consideration of these assumptions should take place routinely. However, there are certain kinds of spatial data for which statistics can be calculated that are not concerned with these assumptions, so it is necessary to be careful about what is meant when discussing spatial data.

Spatial data include the following types: points represented simply by their location, points that have value and are distributed across space, points with or without value that have been aggregated by some decision rule, and points distributed across a space and that are assumed to represent a continuous process. Many of the most popular methods of intrasite analysis, including nearest-neighbor analysis, Hodder and Okell's A, and local density analysis are examples of techniques based on statistical models of association and the degree to which these points are clustered or randomly or evenly distributed across a space. In this case, concerns about stationarity and isotropy are not relevant. Methods that aggregate points of this kind into quadrants are likewise unconcerned with this problem (Bailey and Gatrell 1995:84). These methods, once highly popular during the great borrowing (Hodder and Orton 1976:33–38), are little used in archaeology today.

However, if we are concerned about the values a point may have in that space, then we need to consider the degree to which these points (and their values) can be said to be autocorrelated, which is "if the presence of some quantity in a county (sampling unit) makes its presence in neighbouring counties (sampling units) more or less likely, we say that the phenomenon exhibits spatial autocorrelation" (Cliff and Ord 1973). In other words, the underlying spatial process may not be stationary or isotropic or both. Kvamme (1990) provides a good discussion of this problem in the context of predictive modeling. Using site location data from east central Arizona, he examined three variables—slope, aspect, and elevation—in the locations of 30 habitation sites. The research question of interest was to determine if there was any apparent locational preference for certain values of these variables in site placement. Using a technique developed by Cliff and Ord (1973) to detect autocorrelation, he showed that slope and aspect were not spatially autocorrelated and that, therefore, standard statistical techniques could be employed in their analysis. Elevation, however, was autocorrelated, and if it had been examined using standard statistical tests, the results of the test would have been biased toward "an overstatement of significance and an increased risk of a Type I error" (Kvamme 1990:379). He recommended that standard tests for spatial autocorrelation, such as Moran's I (for ratio, interval, or ordinal-scale data) or Geary's coefficient c, be calculated whenever similar situations are encountered. Should autocorrelation be discovered, other techniques are available to filter or remove the potential effects of space, although these methods are computationally difficult (Cressie 1993).

But in many cases, what is of greater interest is the discovery that the data *are* autocorrelated and that there is some spatial process that is causal to the observed distribution of points. This is often the case when the values of points are known (or assumed) to have a continuous distribution across space. In this case, more sophisticated and complex spatial methods can be employed that create other kinds of statistical indices and interpretative aids, such as trend surface analysis and kriging (Bailey and Gatrell 1995:143–217; Chilès and Delfiner 1999; Wheatley and Gillings 2002:195–200). These are also called spatial interpolation methods, in that they calculate surfaces from the sampled points. Through careful examination of the results, patterns of residuals, or data not explained by general spatial trends in the data, can be identified and evaluated. Kriging has been used extensively in geology to discover so-called nuggets, or areas of high concentrations of minerals, but has seen useful application in archaeology as well (Schieppati 1983; Aldenderfer 1998:60–69). Although these methods are commonly labeled as *spatial analytic*, they are in fact spatial statistics used in specific contexts to solve specific problems.

One interesting area of spatial statistics that has not found its way into archaeology is the field of circular or directional statistics (Mardia 1972; Batschelet 1981; Jammalamadaka and Sengupta 2001). Many phenomena in the natural world have a directional component, which can be measured either as a cycle of time, sphere, or compass rose. Animal migrations have been modeled with these methods, as have been the movements of pollutants, cycles of body temperature, sunspot activity, and wind and wave directions at different times of year. Standard statistical methods cannot be applied to these data because they are not linear, and therefore special techniques have been developed to create statistical tests of uniform direction (no single direction is more common than another), tests for comparing two groups of directions, correlation, regression, and other methods. Although I am not aware of any direct archaeological application of these techniques, a similar approach to circular data has been realized with the ring and sector approach to intrasite spatial analysis (Boekschoten and Stapert 1993; Stapert 1992; Figures 14.2a and b). The approach is similar to local density analysis; multiple rings and sectors of varying dimensions can be examined. In Figure 14.2a, a hearth at the Hamburgian site of Oldeholtwolde is used as the center of the ring. Artifact distributions of different types are shown to fall in different sectors (Figure 14.2b). In this case, the authors note that the bulk of the tools are found in the northern sectors of the site, and to them, this suggests the presence of a drop zone. Exhausted cores, in contrast, were found in different sectors and distances from the hearth, suggesting that the distribution of cores defined a forward toss zone. Directional statistics could be used to determine whether the directions in which tool categories are tossed are significantly different. In its present form, the ring and sector method seems more appropriately described as an exploratory method, and recently, geographers have begun to develop exploratory spatial data analysis (ESDA), which is simply the extension of EDA thinking in a spatial context (Haining 2003). Spatial properties of data are considered, such as the identification of spatial outliers, assessment of spatial autocorrelation by evaluation of

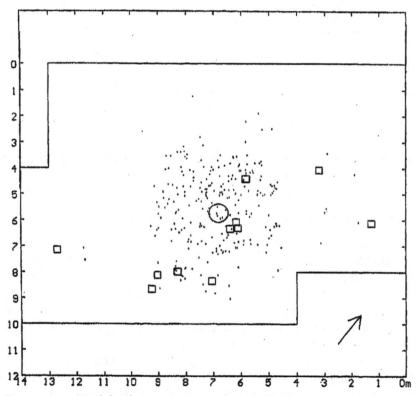

Figure 14.2a.   Tool distributions in sectors (from Boekschoten and Stapert 1993:Figure 4a).

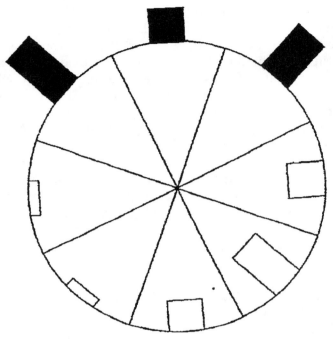

Figure 14.2b.   Hearth (circle) with artifacts (from Boekschoten and Stapert 1993:Figure 1).

changes in gradients of data distributions, and the plotting of residuals against other spatial data.

Resampling, Bootstrapping, and Jackknifing Methods

Classic frequentist models of statistical analysis require the investigator to assume that a sample of data has a particular distributional form, such as the familiar normal (or Gaussian) distribution. EDA can be used to explore data to determine just what kind of distribution the data may represent. There are situations, however, when because of very small sample sizes or other concerns, the investigator is unwilling or unable to assume the data have a particular distribution form. To resolve issues in data analysis under these circumstances, a whole series of computational approaches to statistical inference have been developed, including bootstrapping, jackknifing, and Monte Carlo simulation. Despite differences in approach, computation, sampling procedures, and interpretations, these methods can be referred to under the general rubric of resampling (Efron and Tibshirani 1993).

These methods to varying degrees involve the creation of many (often thousands) of samples of a known data set to extract as much information as is possible from it while avoiding the use of statistical formulae. Through this process, the user is able to assess the degree to which a result of an experiment is a likely or unlikely result. Because it focuses on the data at hand, it avoids making any sorts of statistical assumptions and lets the data "speak for themselves." Used properly, it is possible to estimate population parameters of the sample (such as the population mean), and also to compute confidence intervals around it. Whereas critics note that the quality of the analysis wholly depends on the adequacy of the sample of observations at hand (the primary assumption of resampling) and specific aspects of the method selected, its proponents argue that, while this is true, resampling forces the user to think more carefully about data and its variability in a creative manner instead of trying to force data into a probably ill-chosen formula selected on the basis of rote learning. In short, the resampling method emphasizes the process of reasoning and the use of intuition rather than the details of formulaic approaches (Simon 1993, 1994:290).

If sampling and the bootstrap method are so appealing, why have they not seen more use in introductory statistics classes? Simon suggests that the apathy and hostility resampling has faced are in part generational, which may dissipate as a new generation of statisticians moves into faculty positions. Professional statisticians have adopted resampling as an approach for solving particularly difficult problems in mathematical statistics, and it is also making slow inroads as a way to teach statistics to undergraduates.

Archaeologists employed a number of resampling approaches. Kintigh (1984, 1989) has used Monte Carlo sampling to generate pseudoconfidence intervals around the results of diversity analyses and k-means clusters of spatial data, and Ringrose (1992) uses the bootstrap to evaluate the results of correspondence analysis in a similar fashion. Ringrose (1993b) described an analytic approach in contrast to Monte Carlo simulation of assemblage diversity, and Kaufman (1998) used a jack-knifing approach to examine diversity analyses. Baxter (2001a), in a useful review, has evaluated the strengths and weaknesses of different resampling methods as they have been applied to the evaluation of assemblage diversity. This use of resampling will likely continue to grow in popularity in our discipline. As to resampling's potential effect on the educational process, I think it difficult to predict. I believe that given the problems we face with the interpretation of variability in our data sets and the inability of classical methods to assist us under normal circumstances (i.e., small samples, nonnormal distributions, poorly specified models, etc.), resampling can help us to think more carefully about data and its analysis.

Robust Quantitative Idioms, Statistical Inference, and Archaeological Reasoning

Read (1987:167–168) made a useful set of distinctions regarding populations and variables. A well-defined (WD) population is one in which each of its entities is the outcome of a single process. That is, any variability in the population can be attributed to a known or knowable source (also termed *process*). All other populations are by this reasoning not well-defined (NWD). In some cases, the population is the data set under consideration and is assumed to be representative of all possible examples of that population. Sometimes this assumption is reasonable, but often it is not. As Drennan (1996:261–267) argues, although we may chose to continue with an analysis when we know the sample is inadequate, at least thinking about it in population terms exposes biases in the sample and helps to identify what an adequate population (or sample) would be. WD variables are those that can be clearly tied to the process of interest in the population, preferably by theory but acceptably by hypothesis. NWD variables, then, are those that may commonly be used because of tradition or experience but may not have much to do with the process of interest. Note that these definitions are not fixed; a NWD variable (say, length of a projectile point) in one analysis might be WD in another. Everything depends on the nature and degree of the relationship of the population at hand, the variables of interest, and the problem under study.

I have taken these four categories and created a familiar 2 × 2 table to explore how they characterize archaeology (Figure 14.3). Standard statistical inferences, as with robust quantitative idioms, are found in heaven, where both variables and populations are WD. Take an example from medical research. A drug company is concerned with determining the efficacy of a new drug designed to lower blood pressure. Two groups of people with similar ages and health statuses are selected; one is given a placebo and the other the drug. The variable examined would be, for example, average blood pressure, with the hope that blood pressure in the second group will decline. Statistical tests

		Variables	
		WD	NWD
Population	WD	Heaven	Limbo
	NWD	Purgatory	Hell

Figure 14.3.   Relationships between populations and variables in archaeology.

are run on the two groups to determine if the drug (the process) led to a statistically significant decline in blood pressure in the second group. Whatever the result, the inference will be a valid measure because, insofar as possible, the population has been controlled and the drug has been directly connected by chemistry and biology to blood pressure. As should be obvious, there are few circumstances in archaeological research that can be found in heaven because we seldom have good control over the population (sample, data set, etc.) or the variables used to examine it.

We are more likely to find ourselves in purgatory, limbo, or hell. Some early statistical approaches to archaeological classification were quite hellish. The early application of cluster analysis was based on numerical taxonomy, which in its most extreme form urged analysts to include as many variables as possible to improve the chances of creating a better classification of a set of entities (Aldenderfer and Blashfield 1984:20). This kind of naive empiricism, combined with heuristic methods having little statistical justification, led to the creation of classifications that had little consistency but were nevertheless interpreted, then used in subsequent analysis. Another hellish approach is to measure what can be measured because of tradition or custom, and to seek structure within these data in hopes that pattern will emerge. This kind of data dredging has little intellectual or theoretical warrant and appears to have been used as a substitute for thinking in many archaeological applications.

The nature of many archaeological populations is also hellish. Almost every archaeological collection has one bias or another, and it is often impossible to know what the extent of the bias is and how it has affected its composition. Cowgill (1986:378–385) has written eloquently on how, even when we think we are doing a good job sampling a site, region, or collection of objects, our preconceptions and ignorance about sampling procedures can be appalling. Until Schiffer's (1976) systematic work on what he called behavioral archaeology, the field was aware of the kinds of natural and cultural processes that structure (and bias) the archaeological record, but this awareness was not sufficient to force change in practice. Middle range theory was an attempt to systematize observations about some of these processes, and as I have shown in this chapter, theoretical thinking of this kind is crucial to the development of robust quantitative idioms. Unfortunately, most archaeologists have ignored potential biases in their populations by using the justification that "we have to work with what we have," an accurate, but incomplete statement.

Read offered some advice on how to improve our situation, but his solutions were concerned more with the mechanics of data analysis rather than thinking about the larger context of the research. There are ways to earn merit and move heavenward that are more strategic in scope. In hell or limbo, it is possible to improve your variables. The most obvious way to do so is to develop much better models of process. That is, one must be clear on modeling goals—why are we doing this research?—the theoretical context of the research—what thinking guides the research?—and given both, what kinds of models, and of what composition, will allow us to achieve our ends? In other words, build better models of process! A good archaeological example comes from archaeometry, where Bishop and Neff (1989), Arnold et al. (1991), and Baxter (2001b) have sought to develop models of artifact composition based on statistics and probability (what kind of mathematical model best describes how chemical elements are distributed in artifacts?) as well as ethnoarchaeology (how do decisions by potters affect ceramic composition?). Although the resultant models can be enormously complex, it is apparent that if they are successful, they can identify variables that could be observed in the archaeological record of ceramics that could be used in the analysis of situations in which direct analogies are nonexistent. I have also emphasized the role of theory as a necessary part of this process. Some research problems have more direct connections to theory. For example, Eerkens and Bettinger (2001) have appealed to psychological theories and studies of human vision and decision making of how mechanical errors of replication or production are committed by craftsmen to model the standardization of artifact production. Using these insights, they used standard statistical concepts (such as the coefficient of variation) to measure relevant variability in different artifact categories and proposed robust statistical tests to measure how standardized an artifact class might be within this context.

It is also possible to improve one's populations if one resides in purgatory or hell. Here, the solution is obvious: pay more attention to sampling and the biases that may have been operative during data collection. This is clearly an archaeological, not statistical, problem in that, whereas statistics may be able to tell us how much confidence we should have in some inference obtained from their application, they cannot tell us directly about the sample biases (Drennan 1996:261–267). One must carefully examine the collection at hand and consider just what sort of population it may represent. In many cases, collections are both small and finite, and if they cannot be augmented, any inferences made on them must be treated with real caution. If the analyst has responsibilities in how such populations are discussed, the consumer of this information is likewise responsible for cautiously using the results of the research.

Can we characterize subfields in terms of their relative positions between heaven and hell? Not easily, because samples, populations, and models differ so widely, but archaeometry seems near to purgatory, if not already there. Chemical composition studies are especially close, because there is general agreement on the kinds of variables (elements) best used in compositional analysis (Baxter and Jackson 2001), and as I have already noted, a number of models of compositional structure built within an anthropological framework have already been developed. Some aspects of faunal studies are likewise in purgatory or near it. One obvious advantage is that animal skeletons are finite entities. That is, depending on the species, they are composed of fixed and invariant numbers of bones that are articulated in a single manner. In one sense, nature has standardized the object of study. Thus animal bones of sufficient size or possessing identifiable landmarks can be identified as to their place in the skeleton (i.e., the skull, left humerus, etc.). These invariant properties are of course contingent on the successful identification of the species, but once this is achieved, quantitative estimates of numbers of individuals can be made.

Despite inevitable disagreements, faunal analysts have come to a remarkable level of consensus on basic definitional issues and thus are in an enviable position when it comes to the development of a robust quantitative idiom. Although scientists from other fields may express shock and possibly some amusement at this statement, such agreement on foundational issues in archaeology is often rare. For example, although confusion has not been totally eliminated, faunal analysts know for the most part what it is they are counting and, perhaps more importantly, why. Lyman (1994) discusses the varied, but generally consistent, definitions of MNI (minimum number of individuals), MAU (minimum number of animal units), NISP (number of identified specimens), and MNE (minimum number of elements), for example. Most faunal analysts are now aware of the different contexts for the proper use of these different ways of counting. This, combined with numerous analyses of taphonomic processes that affect bone survivorship and studies of human-mediated modifications of faunal assemblages (hunting, butchering, trade, etc.), bodes well for the continued development of a meaningful quantitative idiom.

Intrasite analysis, despite the tremendous amount of activity that it has witnessed over the decades, remains in limbo and may often slide unwillingly and unhappily back into hell. Unfortunately, I think this is despite the volume of work that has been devoted to it. As previously noted, much of the earliest research on intrasite analysis was borrowed directly from geography, plant ecology, and geology with little consideration of whether these borrowings were appropriate. The development of purely statistical approaches to the problem has intensified over the years. As Ammerman (1992:252) puts it, "our best data (sites like Pincevent and Veberie) are currently ahead of our best methods." What he is saying is that, although we are capable of excavating sites like these with exquisite care, the methods we tend to use in their analysis are crude by comparison, and our interpretations of them suffer accordingly. Despite their seeming statistical sophistication, they can examine the distribution of only a single variable (an artifact class) across the site (via some point process method), examine covariation of two classes simultaneously (measures of spatial association), or in the aggregate (all classes via a density method, cluster analysis, or spatial interpolation). None of these methods can incorporate the analysis of site facilities, such as kitchen rocks, post molds, or other features in a meaningful manner. Orton (1992:138) echoes some of these concerns but asks for more of the same—better statistics. Interpretation of these data tends to be disjointed and ad hoc. And although considerable ethnoarchaeology has been devoted to the analysis of the determinants of site structure across a wide variety of settings (Kroll and Price 1991), these observations have generally not been tied to improvements in quantitative methods (although see Gregg, Kintigh, and Whallon 1991 for an exception). Clearly, the variables examined in intrasite analysis as well as the models that articulate them to a body of method are very poorly defined, and it seems likely that from a purely statistical standpoint our best sites, or indeed most sites, will always be ahead of our best methods. What is needed, then, are not better statistics but better linking arguments and models. The GIS-based approaches described previously are attempts to do this, and we can expect more examples of this approach to appear in the field.

Bayesian Statistics in Archaeology

A Bayesian approach to statistical inference is a clear and compelling alternative to the frequentist model, which dominates archaeology and most other areas of empirical research. Bayesian statistical thinking is not new, having been envisioned by the Reverend Thomas Bayes in the middle of the eighteenth century. Despite its potential importance, it has been only slowly adopted by scientists and statisticians. Very simply, the Bayesian approach incorporates a set of formal tools and methods that allow the investigator to include subjective, a priori information into the analytic process. Another way to phrase this is that Bayesian statistics allow us to go from an a prior probability on some proposition to a posterior probability based on this new information. As new information is acquired, new prior probabilities may be created and, consequently, new posterior probabilities calculated. Importantly, these prior beliefs are expressed as probability distributions. As Spiegelhalter et al. (1999:512) state, "There are strong philosophical reasons for using a bayesian approach, but the current literature emphasizes the practical advantages in handling complex interrelated problems and in making explicit and accountable what is usually implicit and hidden, thereby clarifying discussions and disagreements. Perhaps the most persuasive reason is that the analysis tells us what we want to know: how should this piece of evidence change what we currently believe?"

There are real differences between frequentist and Bayesian methods (Table 14.2). As can be seen, there is less emphasis on hypothesis testing, and the primary emphasis of the entire approach seems to be as a means to support making good decisions, rather than adhering to arbitrary criteria. But of greatest importance is that Bayesian methods seem to be closer to the real goals of empirical analysis, which is based on making inferences about the data, rather than making decisions about a parameter per se (like the mean, for instance).

Although Cowgill (1977:361) made an early brief mention of Bayesian analysis, the approach was not used significantly in

Table 14.2. Comparison of Frequentist and Bayesian Methods

Issue	Frequentist Methods	Bayesian Methods
Prior information other than that in the study being analyzed	Informally used in design	Used formally by specifying a prior probability distribution
Interpretation of the parameter of interest	A fixed state of nature	An unknown quantity which can have a probability distribution
Basic question	How likely is the data, given a particular value of the parameter?	How likely is a particular value of the parameter given the data?
Presentation of results	Likelihood functions, p values, confidence intervals	Plots of posterior distributions of the parameter, calculation of specific posterior probabilities of interest, and use of the posterior distribution in formal decision analysis

Source: Spiegelhalter et al. 1999.

archaeology until the late 1980s. The standard reference work and best introduction to Bayesian statistics in the field is Buck, Cavanagh, and Litton (1996). As they show, Bayesian methods have been applied to archaeological problems of stratigraphy and the construction of relative chronologies (Allum et al. 1999; Buck and Sahu 2000), field survey (Cavanagh et al. 1988), biometrical estimation of skeletal populations (Aykroyd et al. 1999), intrasite analysis (Robertson 1999), and other topics. However, Bayesian methods have become absolutely essential to the interpretation of radiocarbon dating and the calibration of dates. In fact, more than 40 percent of the published applications of Bayesian analysis in archaeology through 2001 were concerned with radiocarbon dating. What is so valuable about Bayesian approaches here is that the dates can be compared with stratigraphic information, artifact finds, and other data to evaluate which dates seem to make better sense. In other words, these other data can be used to construct reasonable prior probabilities about which dates are most likely to be correct in some context, and posterior probabilities can be then calculated on that basis. Specific applications in this arena that have been published include advice on how to select samples for dating (Buck and Christen 1998), estimating occupation span of a phase or site (Buck et al. 1994), evaluation of sequences of dates in stratigraphic order (Steier and Rom 2000), and of course the calibration of dates (Buck, Litton, and Smith 1992; Ramsey 1995; Buck, Christen, and James 1999).

What seems to have held back the growth of Bayesian approaches in archaeology in specific and other disciplines in general is that they are somewhat more challenging from a mathematical perspective than are frequentist methods, software that implements them in a practical sense has been virtually nonexistent until the 1990s, there has been no compelling case made for how Bayesian methods are superior to frequentist methods, and finally, there has always been the (unfounded) suspicion that these methods are more subjective than classical methods because of the use of prior probabilities in routine calculations. Of these, the latter two are the most problematic. As more exemplars are published that demonstrate that Bayesian methods are powerful alternatives to classical methods, this problem will diminish, but it will take time simply because there are so few widely known practitioners of Bayesian methods in archaeology. Also, better demonstrations on the order of the BCal calibration program (Buck et al. 1999) will be needed to show how these methods can be profitably used in other contexts. As for claims that Bayesian methods are subjective and therefore unscientific, it has been demonstrated repeatedly that there are also subjective elements in the classical approach (especially in the interpretation and creation of the null hypothesis). The possibly biased assignments of prior probabilities have been especially targeted in this critique, and although it is plausible, it is also true that any reasonable Bayesian approach *must* present a convincing argument for the choice of prior probabilities. Despite these concerns, I see Bayesian statistics growing substantially in importance in archeology over the next decade.

Getting Help

Statistical applications in archaeology are now getting to the point of maturity that, despite advances in training, many methods will remain beyond the grasp of most archaeologists. Certainly Bayesian methods fall into this category, as do many of the more complex spatial and multivariate statistical methods. Getting help from an expert, then, is necessary. But what are the best sources of help? Obviously, one source is to consult a statistician, and this has been done by archaeologists since the introduction of quantitative methods to the field. It is not done without risk, however. The advantage here is that the archaeologist need not become an adept in matters numerical but can instead rely on the hard-won expertise of someone else. The key, obviously, is finding a specialist with the right training and the flexibility of mind to grasp the essentials of the archeological problem simultaneously with the most appropriate quantitative measures. The debate between Trevor Ringrose, a professional statistician, and Fiona Marshall and Tom Pilgram is a good example of how difficult it is to accomplish this (Aldenderfer 1998:95–96). Ringrose (1993a) critiqued an application of multiple regression analysis in the analysis of bone counts by Marshall and Pilgram (1991). After some give-and-take, Ringrose (1995:103) admitted, "I was guilty of rushing into print thinking I knew more about bovid anatomy than I in fact did whereas Marshall and Pilgram were guilty of rushing into print thinking that they knew more about regression than they in fact did." This example shows that both parties to the collaboration have to find ways to make it clear what each needs in order to do what they do best.

This tends not to be easy: "Unfortunately, not all archaeologists regard statisticians as useful creatures, and there are, in any case, not enough interested statisticians to go around" (Baxter 1994a:219). Another drawback of collaboration is that the hired gun will, because of personal interest and training, be prone to fit particular models to archaeological situations with only a cursory understanding of the real demands of the data set and problem and despite the best efforts of the archaeologist to keep the analysis on track. Baxter (1994a:222–223) discusses this issue in regard to the application of Bayesian methods to archaeological problems. Collaboration has been and will continue to be important as cutting-edge mathematics and other quantitative approaches are imported to very specific archaeological problems. However, special caution must be employed in the use of collaborative approaches to insure that there is no repeat of indiscriminate borrowing; just because something can be done doesn't mean that it should be.

Another source of help, but one that is taking a long time to realize, is the development of true specialists in archaeological statistics and quantification. Kintigh (1987) called for the development of these specialists as a part of his plea that statistical methods become more tailored to the intricacies of archaeology and archaeological data. The obvious advantage of this is that the archaeologist, by merit of training, has a deep understanding of the structure of archaeological data within a particular subfield and is aware of his or her ultimate goals for research. Its drawback, however, is equally obvious: it can be extremely time-consuming to accomplish given the demands of becoming both a good archaeologist and a good mathematician or statistician. What seems to be critical here is that the nascent specialist devote his or her time to a subfield and not to the issue of quantification in archaeology as a whole. Although we will always need generalists in quantitative methods who are willing to provide overviews of the state of development of the field, my belief is that Kintigh's desire for robust methods will be fulfilled primarily from this pool of subfield specialists with sufficient quantitative training and archaeological expertise. Whether our field will hire them is another matter, because at least in the United States, archaeologists tend to be selected first by region, then by specialty. If current hiring trends continue, smaller departments will seek generalists over specialists, thus providing little long-term incentive for a student to become what could be considered narrowly focused on quantitative methods.

Help can be sought out in the exemplars of quantitative or statistical analysis in a subfield of interest. People tend not to listen to hectoring or polemics, often will not listen to lectures, and they will not be much interested in taking classes and such. But they will be compelled to pay attention to really good pieces of research. We need to encourage our specialists to develop these exemplars and get them published in the best journals.

No matter what route one takes to find help, one thing should be clear: all archaeologists should by now be aware that going it alone without the expert advice of a statistician or an archaeologist specially trained in quantitative methods is no longer acceptable. We've come a long way from the great borrowing and needn't repeat those mistakes.

Quantitative Methods, Statistics, and Archaeological Theory

Most archaeologists would agree that there is little consensus in the realm of archaeological theory. To some, this represents chaos, whereas to others this is a healthy, natural state of affairs that indicates the field is growing, maturing, and becoming relevant to a wider variety of intellectual communities. Many see this state of affairs continuing into the foreseeable future. Although most archaeologists currently serving in the academy, the private sector, and government received their training from the processual school, wherein quantitative methods were highly valued, the increasing importance of postprocessual approaches to the field has suggested to some that quantitative methods may be less valued as the influence of postprocessual thinking grows. There are certainly grounds for concern. Some disciplines that have taken a strongly narrative turn, such as sociology and history, have active communities of doubters. Consider this quotation from the *Dictionary of Critical Sociology*:

> Quantification: The process of transforming natural and social dynamics into number systems. There are major political problems with this practice: one loses information as one transforms behavior into word systems, more information is lost when word systems are replaced by number systems and still more when summary statistics are used to replace the original data. One could describe quantification as a process by which undesirable information is discarded. The political question is who decides what is undesirable? . . . And referring to human beings as so many numbers tends to strip them of their humanity. Quantification is the great god of American social science but should be viewed with much reservation. (Mazur 2003; emphasis mine)

Although one might agree with the sentiment, one may also be alarmed by the tone. Indeed, many fields (information science and organizational science, surprisingly) are now polarized by differences between the so-called quants and quals—respectively, those who rely on quantitative approaches and those who prefer to use qualitative methods in their research. Will this happen in archeology?

My guess is that it will not. Our great diversity of interests makes it very unlikely, because we house under our own intellectual umbrella archaeometrists, environmental archaeologists, and postmodern writers of narrative. Even one of the classics of postprocessual archaeology—*Re-Constructing Archaeology: Theory and Practice* (Shanks and Tilley 1987)—relied on the results of a factor analysis for its insights. Indeed, it depends on how we construct our quantitative idioms and how we put them into practice. Critical theorists in other fields have developed such idioms that are consistent with their theoretical and political interests (Kwan 2002).

Another way quantitative methods are likely to thrive in the future is in the so-called trading zone (Galison 1997; Aldenderfer 2003). In his study of technological change in physics, Galison (1997:803–844) defined the trading zone as the "place" where ideas, concepts, and methods may be borrowed between disparate theoretical orientations without borrowing the "whole" package of concepts and their meanings. In other words, although theories or theoretical orientations may themselves be incommensurate, it may be the case that certain methods can be traded through the zone and given meaning in a new area because of a quantitative idiom. Thought of in this way, it is easy to see how factor analysis can serve both processualists and postprocessualists *as long as* the idiom successfully gives meaning to the numbers used in the analysis in both.

Future Trends

In Tibetan Buddhism, because there is great conviction that the future can show itself through indicatory omens, there is a corresponding importance placed on the development of abilities to uncover, understand, read, and interpret these omens. Doing so requires years of meditation and training, and most of those who enter this training stop long before they master these secret arts. Making predictions about the future shape of theory in archaeology rests on similar skills in reading omens and portents, but unlike the Roman Catholic pope, I make no claims for infallibility. The following discussion is not so much a revelation of the future, but a list of desires, much like that offered by Orton (1992) in his view for the 1990s.

Tighter Integration of Spatial Statistics with GIS Software

The desire for a more complete integration of spatial statistics and GISs has long been a goal of GIS specialists (Goodchild et al. 1992). Factors that have impeded this integration are numerous and include a lack of widely held standards and significant disciplinary differences as to what sorts of statistics should be included in such an integration. What is good for the economist is not good for the geologist, nor for the archaeologist, for that matter.

Also, the increasing commercialization of GIS and statistical software, as well as the expense of maintaining it for a wide and diverse audience, has been a major problem. GIS technology is seen by its corporate creators more as a data management and integration tool to be sold to governments and corporations, and not surprisingly, the interests of academics are poorly represented when it comes to the development of feature sets and analytic tools. Although there is an open-source community in the GIS world, it has been unable to substantially influence the development of GIS software. Likewise, the commercial developers of standard statistical software packages, such as SPSS, SAS, S+, JMP, SYSTAT, and STATA, until recently did not see a large market for spatial statistics, and few such methods have been integrated into these packages. Niche markets, some of them quite large and wealthy, such as geology, were able to develop spatial analytic or statistical packages, especially for mining engineering and mineral exploration. Poorer disciplines, such as archaeology, made do with the more affordable geostatistics packages and imported data back and forth between the GIS and the statistical software.

By the end of the 1990s, things had improved substantially. ESRI, in its release of ArcGIS 8, its flagship GIS platform, included significant improvements, such as ESDA tools, spatial interpolation and analysis models, and more. This trend was strengthened with the release of ArcGIS 9 in 2004. It was clear the company had been listening to some academic GIS voices (Anselin 1998, 2000). One of the major standard statistics packages, S+, was also listening and created a seamless link between it and ESRI's ArcView, a relationship that continues (Bao et al. 2000). Another powerful spatial statistics package—SPACESTAT, first released in 1991—now has direct links to ArcView. Finally, in 2002, SAS announced the development of SAS Bridge for ESRI, which allows users to run SAS programs within the ArcGIS environment. All of these developments are good news, but the sad truth of the situation is that if you do not use one of ESRI's products, exploring this functionality is impossible.

It is unrealistic to believe that archaeology can redirect the outcomes of this increasing commercialization in either standard statistical software or GIS. However, what we can do as a field is work together and develop sharing networks of extensions and add-ons of various statistical procedures within the packages we have chosen to focus our efforts on. This will be even more important as GIS technology begins to move toward the deployment of a truly three-dimensional GIS platform, wherein not only can a three-dimensional object be visualized but also queried (Wheatley and Gillings 2002:241–242). This will enhance GIS technology tremendously for our field, and we should encourage the development of tools for statistical analyses of these three-dimensional data.

Educational Initiatives

One of Orton's (1992) desires, educational initiatives, continues to be a major topic for future development. Although a nonsystematic survey I took at the end of the decade suggested that more and more departments and programs were offering classes in archaeological statistics, it was also clear that much more work needs to be done to make statistics an integral part of the curriculum (Aldenderfer 1998:106–108). As Orton (1992:139) put it, "The challenge of the 1990s is not so much to develop new techniques as to achieve a wider and more fruitful usage of what we already have." I could not agree more wholeheartedly, and I see this as our continuing challenge. To me, this means deeper thought must be devoted to the development of our quantitative idioms, so that more and more of our research can move from hellish depths to at least limbo, if not purgatory or even heaven.

But there are things that should be taught, and one area of consistent neglect is spatial statistics. These methods are complex enough to warrant special courses of their own precisely because of the inherent spatiality of archaeological data and the coming tighter integration of GISs and spatial analysis. But again, we must not be teaching these classes as mere methods but as part and parcel of an approach—a quantitative idiom.

Students must also be introduced early to the realities of radiocarbon dating and the calibration of dates. Because dating is foundational to archaeology, it is imperative that students be well-grounded in what dates are, how they are created, how they are calibrated, what that calibration actually is, and finally, how that date is then interpreted, integrated, and compared with other data. Bayesian methods, as I previously discussed, are likely to become dominant in this arena, and because this approach to statistical inference is not commonly employed in other areas of archeological inferences, those of us who teach statistics must learn Bayesian methods and teach them effectively.

Sampling

We should as a field revisit the question of sampling in archaeology. As I have already discussed, sampling was a major preoccupation of archaeology during the great borrowing, but like much of the new archaeology, it fell out of favor, especially in regional studies, where the dominant paradigm was full-coverage survey (Fish and Kowalewski 1990). There are many reasons why full-coverage surveys are useful and important, but it must be stressed that how one surveys depends on the goals of the project and not a predetermined method. Indeed, as Banning (2002) reminds us, a well-designed sampling survey can result in excellent regional coverage and is an effective alternative to full-coverage survey in many settings. But we also need to return to a careful consideration of sampling in nonsurvey contexts. In many cases, huge amounts of data are generated by excavation and survey projects, and it becomes a monumental and near-impossible task to analyze all of the data. One of the most useful features of Drennan's (1996:237–267) text is his extensive discussion of how to sample artifact collections to make valid inferences. The statistics needed to make these calculations are very simple. Taking a sample of the right size for inference is straightforward, but the question of what inferences can be drawn from that sample is not. Here, archaeology and not statistics becomes important. Sampling often involves some sort of stratification of the collection. One must think carefully about the strata, data, and research problems to ensure that the samples taken for detailed analysis are in fact germane to the problem at hand. This is the hard part of sampling, but again, consideration of it should become routine, and not surprisingly, it should be embedded as one of our quantitative idioms of how to think about data.

What Do Statisticians Think of Their Own Future?

New methods of statistical analysis appear in the pages of archaeological journals routinely. This implies that there is something of a never-ending supply of new ideas in statistics, some of which should be borrowed and adapted by archaeologists. So it seems useful to query statisticians about the next big thing in their own, admittedly very large, field. I make no claim that this sampling is thorough, but I was amazed by the consistency of thinking on "the future of statistics" when I typed those words into the Internet search engine Google.

> I believe the future for those who deal with the analysis of data is a bright one.
> Regrettably, it is not clear to me that these people will be statisticians. (Wegman 1998)

> What is the future of statistics in the present millennium dominated by information technology encompassing the whole of communications, interactions with intelligent systems, massive databases, and complex information processing networks? The current statistical methodology based on probabilistic models developed for the analysis of small data sets appears to be inadequate to meet the needs of customers for quick online processing of data and making the information available for practical use. Some methods are being put forward in the name of data mining for such purposes. A broad review of the current state of the art in statistics, its merits and demerits, and possible future developments will be presented. (Rao 2002)

> I believe that we need to plan the future of statistics and statisticians in order to (1) stimulate a new explosion of statistical science, (2) explore analogies between probability methods (to describe the population or "infinite" data sets) and statistical methods for massive data sets, and (3) stimulate educational opportunities for applied researchers who use some statistical techniques, and for statisticians who work with non-statisticians using statistical methods. (Parzen 1997:2)

Statisticians seem certain that their future lies in the emerging field of computational statistics (Wegman 1998; Table 14.3).

Table 14.3. Traditional and Computational Statistics Compared

Traditional Statistics	Computational Statistics
Small to moderate sample size	Large to very large sample size
Homogeneous data sets	Nonhomogeneous data sets
One- or low-dimensional	High dimensional
Manually computable	Computationally intensive
Mathematically tractable	Numerically tractable
Well-focused questions	Imprecise questions
Strong unverifiable assumptions	Weak or no assumptions
Relationships (linearity, additivity)	Relationships (nonlinearity); in error
Error structures (normality)	Structures (distribution free)
Statistical inference	Structural inference
Predominantly closed-form algorithms	Iterative algorithms possible
Statistical optimality	Statistical robustness

Source: Wegman 1998:4.

Obviously, their world, and ours, will be quite different if these predictions come to pass. In this view, "traditional parametric mathematical statistics is essentially a completed theory, [and] ... the character and scale of data are profoundly changing toward larger, nonhomogeneous, high-dimensional complex data sets" (Wegman 1998:5). Although traditional statistics will of course remain important and research will continue to produce novel methods in many applied fields, it is clear that real intellectual effort, as well as resources, will be directed more and more to this emerging paradigm. I think there are real opportunities, as well as serious challenges, for archaeology as it seeks to accommodate itself to this new statistical vision. There is no question that we have massive databases. Modern field methods can generate huge quantities of digital data, ranging from artifact databases through photographs to the raw (or processed) data from geophysical surveys. Indeed, it is not hard to imagine how a systematic geophysical survey over even selected areas of the survey area could produce huge amounts of data that would require the methods of computational statistics to first process then analyze. We certainly have the right stuff to be interesting to statisticians. Our challenge, however, is not to lose sight of the reasons why we are doing the research in the first place, which is presumably to answer questions about the past. In other words, we now need to develop and articulate quantitative idioms that can make data mining in archaeology useful. We don't need to make the mistakes of the past again in the borrowing that is about to come.

Another aspect of this challenge will be to develop our own standards of comparison, nomenclature, and meaning in our large databases. One example of how this might be accomplished is David Schloen's XSTAR project (Schloen 2001a). The goal of the XSTAR project

> is to create a sophisticated Internet-based research environment for specialists in textual and archaeological studies. In particular, XSTAR is intended for archaeologists, philologists, historians, and historical geographers who work with ancient artifacts, documents, and geographical or environmental data. It will not only provide access to detailed, searchable data in each of these areas individually, but will also integrate these diverse lines of evidence as an aid to interdisciplinary research . . . [and] consists of both a database structure and related interface software that will make it possible to view and query archaeological, textual, and linguistic information in an integrated fashion via the Internet. (Schloen 2001b)

Some of the data sets to be implemented in this project are a corpus of Achaemenid royal inscriptions, a Hittite dictionary, and survey and excavation data from Near Eastern sites (http://www.oi.uchicago.edu/OI/PROJ/XSTAR/XSTAR.html). If successful, this project, and ones like it, will require the services of our computational statisticians.

One final implication of this trend is that, because statisticians of the future will move toward this new paradigm, we in archaeology had better be ready to help ourselves develop the methods we will continue to need to examine our small, homogeneous, low-dimensional data!

References

Aldenderfer, Mark
    1987a Assessing the impact of quantitative thinking on archaeological research: Historical and evolutionary insights. In *Quantitative Research*

in Archaeology: Progress and Prospects, edited by Mark Aldenderfer, pp. 9–29. Sage Publications, Newbury Park, California.

1987b On the structure of archaeological data. In *Quantitative Research in Archaeology: Progress and Prospects*, edited by Mark Aldenderfer, pp. 89–113. Sage Publications, Newbury Park, California.

1998a *Montane Foragers: Asana and the South-Central Andean Archaic.* University of Iowa Press, Iowa City.

1998b Quantitative methods in archaeology: A review of recent trends and developments. *Journal of Archaeological Research* 6:91–120.

2003 Visualizing sedentarization in the Lake Titicaca basin: Interplays of technology and theory. Paper presented at the Department of Anthropology, University of Arizona, Tucson. February.

Aldenderfer, Mark, and Roger Blashfield
1984 *Cluster Analysis.* Sage Publications, Newbury Park, California.

Allum, G. T., R. G. Aykroyd, and J. G. B. Haigh
1999 Empirical Bayes estimation for archaeological stratigraphy. *Applied Statistics* 48:1–14.

Ammerman, Albert J.
1992 Taking stock of quantitative archaeology. *Annual Review of Anthropology* 21:231–255.

Anselin, Luc
1998 Interactive techniques and exploratory spatial data analysis. In *Geographical Information Systems: Principles, Techniques, Management and Applications*, edited by Paul Longley, Michael Goodchild, David Maguire, and David W. Rhind, pp. 251–264. Wiley, New York.

2000 Computing environments for spatial data analysis. *Journal of Geographical Systems* 2:201–225.

Arnold, Dean, Hector Neff, and Ronald Bishop
1991 Compositional analysis and 'sources" of pottery: An ethnoarchaeological approach. *American Anthropologist* 93:70–90.

Aykroyd, Robert G., David Lucy, Mark Pollard, and Charlotte A. Rogers
1999 Nasty, brutish, but not necessarily short: A reconsideration of the statistical methods used to calculate age at death from adult human skeletal and dental age indicators. *American Antiquity* 64:55–70.

Bailey, Trevor C., and Anthony C. Gatrell
1995 *Interactive Spatial Data Analysis.* Longman Scientific and Technical, London.

Banning, Ted
2002 *Archaeological Survey.* Kluwer Academic Publishers, New York.

Bao, Shuming, Luc Anselin, Douglas Martin, and Dianna Stralberg
  2000 Seamless integration of spatial statistics and GIS: The S-Plus for ArcView and the S+Grassland links. *Journal of Geographical Systems* 2:287–306.

Batschelet, Edward
  1981 *Circular Statistics in Biology*. Academic Press, London.

Baxter, Michael J.
  1991 An empirical study of principal component and correspondence analysis of glass compositions. *Archaeometry* 33:29–41.
  1992 Statistical analysis of chemical compositional data and the comparison of analyses. *Archaeometry* 34:267–277.
  1994a *Exploratory Multivariate Analysis in Archaeology*. Edinburgh University Press, Edinburgh.
  1994b Stepwise discriminant analysis in archaeometry: A critique. *Journal of Archaeological Science* 21:659–666.
  2001a Methodological issues in the study of assemblage diversity. *American Antiquity* 66:715–725.
  2001b Statistical modeling of artefact composition data. *Archaeometry* 43:131–147.

Baxter, Michael J., and Caitlin Buck
  2000 Data handling and statistical analysis. In *Modern Analytical Methods in Art and Archaeology*, edited by Enrico Ciliberto and Guiseppe Spoto, pp. 681–746. Wiley, New York.

Baxter, Michael J., Hilary Cool, and Michael Heyworth
  1990 Principal component and correspondence analysis of compositional data: Some similarities. *Journal of Applied Statistics* 17:229–235.

Baxter, Michael J., and Michael Heyworth
  1991 Comparing correlation matrices; with applications in the study of artifacts and their chemical compositions. In *Archaeometry '90*, edited by Ernst Pernicka and Günther A. Wagner, pp. 355–364. Birkhauser Verlag, Basel.

Baxter, Michael J., and Catherine M. Jackson
  2001 Variable selection in artefact composition studies. *Archaeometry* 43:253–268.

Binford, Lewis, and Sally Binford
  1966 A preliminary analysis of functional variability in the Mousterian of Levallois facies. *American Anthropologist* 68:238–295.

Bishop, Ronald, and Hector Neff
  1989 Compositional data analysis in archaeology. In *Archaeological Chemistry IV*, edited by R. Allen, pp. 57–86. American Chemical Society, Washington, D.C.

Blankholm, Hans Peter
1991   *Intrasite Spatial Analysis in Theory and Practice.* Aarhus University Press, Aarhus, Denmark.

Boekschoten, G., and Dirk Stapert
1993   Rings and sectors: A computer package for spatial analysis with examples from Odeholtwolde and Gönnersdorf. *Helinium* 33:20–35.

Buck, Caitlin E., William G. Cavanagh, and Clifford D. Litton
1996   *Bayesian Approach to Interpreting Archaeological Data.* Wiley, Chichester.

Buck, Caitlin E., and J. A. Christen
1998   A novel approach to selecting samples for radiocarbon dating. *Journal of Archaeological Science* 25:303–310.

Buck, Caitlin E., J. A. Christen, and G. N. James
1999   BCal: An on-line Bayesian radiocarbon calibration tool. *Internet Archaeology* 7. Electronic document, http://intarch.ac.uk/journal/issue7/buck/.

Buck, Caitlin, J. A. Christen, J. A. Kenworthy, and C. D. Litton
1994   Estimating the duration of archaeological activity using ^{14}C determinations. *Oxford Journal of Archaeology* 13:229–240

Buck, Caitlin, C. D. Litton, and A. F. M. Smith
1992   Calibration of radiocarbon results pertaining to related archaeological events. *Journal of Archaeological Science* 19:497–512.

Buck, Caitlin, and S. K. Sahu
2000   Bayesian models for relative archaeological chronology building. *Applied Statistics* 49:423–440.

Burton, Ian
1963   The quantitative revolution and theoretical geography. *The Canadian Geographer* 7:151–162.

Carr, Christopher
1985a Getting into data: Philosophy and tactics for the analysis of complex data structures. In *For Concordance in Archaeological Analysis: Bridging Data Structure, Quantitative Technique, and Theory,* edited by Christopher Carr, pp. 18–44. Waveland Press, Prospect Heights, Illinois.
1985b Alternative models, alternative techniques: Variable approaches to Intrasite spatial analysis. In *For Concordance in Archaeological Analysis: Bridging Data Structure, Quantitative Technique, and Theory,* edited by Christopher Carr, pp. 302–473. Waveland Press, Prospect Heights, Illinois.
1987   Removing discordance from quantitative analysis. In *Quantitative Research in Archaeology: Progress and Prospects,* edited by Mark Aldenderfer, pp. 185–243. Sage Publications, Newbury Park, California.

Cavanagh, William G., S. Hirst, and Clifford D. Litton
   1988   Soil phosphate, site boundaries and change-point analysis. *Journal of Field Archaeology* 15:67–83.

Chilès Jean-Paul, and Pierre Delfiner
   1999   *Geostatistics: Modeling Spatial Uncertainty.* Wiley, London.

Clark, Geoffrey
   1982   Quantifying archaeological research. *Advances in Archaeological Method and Theory* 5:217–273.

Clark, Geoffrey, and C. Russell Stafford
   1982   Quantification in American archaeology: Historical perspectives. *World Archaeology* 14:98–119.

Cliff, Andrew D., and J. Keith Ord
   1973   *Spatial Autocorrelation.* Pion, London.

Cowgill, George L.
   1968   Archaeological applications of factor, cluster, and proximity analysis. *American Antiquity* 33:367–375.
   1977   The trouble with significance tests and what we can do about it. *American Antiquity* 42:350–368.
   1982   Clusters of objects and associations between variables: Two approaches to archaeological classification. In *Essays on Archaeological Typology*, edited by Robert Whallon and James A. Brown, pp. 30–55. Center for American Archaeology Press, Evanston, Illinois.
   1986   Archaeological applications of mathematical and formal methods In *American Archaeology: Past and Future*, edited by David Melzer, Don Fowler, and Jeremy Sabloff, pp. 369–393. Smithsonian Institution Press, Washington, D.C.
   1990   Artifact classification and archaeological purposes. In *Mathematical and Information Science in Archaeology: A Flexible Framework*, edited by Albertus Voorrips, pp. 61–98. Holos, Bonn.

Craig, Nathan C., and Mark Aldenderfer
   2005   Future directions for the recording of archaeological excavations using GIS. In *Future Directions in GIS*, edited by Scott Branting. Archaeopress, Oxford, in press.

Cressie, Noel A.
   1993   *Statistics for Spatial Data.* Wiley, London.

Davis, Phillip J., and Reuben Hersh
   1981   *The Mathematical Experience.* Houghton Mifflin, Boston.

Dixon, P., and T. O'Reilly
   1999   Scientific versus statistical inference. *Canadian Journal of Experimental Psychology* 53:133–149.

Doran, James, and Fred Hodson
    1966   A digital computer analysis of Paleolithic flint assemblages. *Nature* 210:668.
    1975   *Mathematics and Computers in Archaeology.* Harvard University Press, Cambridge.

Drennan, Robert D.
    1996   *Statistics for Archaeologists: A Commonsense Approach.* Plenum, New York.

Eeerkens, Jelmer, and Robert Bettinger
    2001   Techniques for assessing standardization in artifact assemblages: Can we scale material variability? *American Antiquity* 66:493–504.

Efron, Bradley, and Rob Tibshirani
    1993   *An Introduction to the Bootstrap.* Chapman and Hall, New York.

Fish, Suzanne, and Steven Kowalewski (editors)
    1990   *The Archaeology of Regions: A Case for Full-Coverage Survey.* Smithsonian Institution Press, Washington, D.C.

Fisher, Ronald A.
    1950   *Statistical Methods for Research Workers.* Oliver and Boyd, London.

Galison, Peter L.
    1997   *Image and Logic: A Material Culture of Microphysics.* University of Chicago Press, Chicago.

Goodchild, Michael. F., Robert Haining, and S. Wise
    1992   Integrating GIS and spatial data analysis: Problems and possibilities. *International Journal of Geographical Information Systems* 6(5):407–423.

Goodman, S.
    1993   P values, hypothesis tests, and likelihood: Implications for epidemiology of a neglected historical debate. *American Journal of Epidemiology* 137:485–496.

Gregg, Susan, Keith Kintigh, and Robert Whallon
    1991   Linking ethnoarchaeological interpretation and archaeological data The sensitivity of spatial analytic methods to post-depositional disturbance. In *The Interpretation of Archaeological Spatial Patterning,* edited by Ellen M. Kroll, and T. Douglas Price, pp. 149–196. Plenum, New York.

Hacking, Ian
    1965   *Logic of Statistical Inference.* Cambridge University Press, Cambridge.

Haining, Robert
    2003   *Spatial Data Analysis.* Cambridge University Press, Cambridge.

Harbottle, Garman
1991 The efficiencies and error rates of Euclidean and Mahalanobis searches in hypergeometries of archaeological ceramic compositions. In *Archaeometry '90*, edited by Ernst Pernicka and Günther A. Wagner, pp. 413–424. Birkhauser Verlag, Basel.

Hodder, Ian, and Clive Orton
1976 *Spatial Analysis in Archaeology*. Cambridge University Press, Cambridge.

Hodson, Fred, Peter Sneath, and James Doran
1966 Some experiments in the numerical analysis of archaeological data. *Biometrika* 53:311–324.

Jammalamadaka, S. Rao, and A. Sengupta
2001 *Topics in Circular Statistics*. World Scientific Publishing, Singapore.

Johnson, Allen W.
1978 *Quantification in Cultural Anthropology*. Stanford University Press, Stanford, California.

Kaplan, Abraham
1964 *The Conduct of Inquiry*. Chandler, San Francisco.

Kaufman, Daniel
1998 Measuring archaeological diversity: An application of the jackknife technique. *American Antiquity* 63:73–85.

Kintigh, Keith
1984 Measuring archaeological diversity by comparison with simulated assemblages. *American Antiquity* 49:44–54.
1987 Quantitative methods designed for archaeological problems. In *Quantitative Research in Archaeology: Progress and Prospects*, edited by Mark Aldenderfer, pp. 126–134. Sage Publications, Newbury Park, California.
1989 Sample size, significance, and measures of diversity. In *Quantifying Diversity in Archaeology*, edited by Robert D. Leonard and George T. Jones, pp. 25–36. Cambridge University Press, Cambridge.
1990 Intrasite spatial analysis in archaeology. In *Mathematics and Information Science in Archaeology: A Flexible Framework*, edited by Albertus Voorrips, pp. 165–200. Holos-Verlag, Bonn.

Kintigh, Keith, and Albert J. Ammerman
1982 Heuristic approaches to spatial analysis in archaeology. *American Antiquity* 47:31–63.

Kroll, Ellen M., and T. Douglas Price (editors)
1991 *The Interpretation of Archaeological Spatial Patterning*. Plenum Press, New York.

Kvamme, Ken
   1990   One-sample tests in regional archaeology: New possibilities through computer technology. *American Antiquity* 55:367–381.
   1993   Spatial statistics and GIS: An integrated approach. In *Computing the Past: CAA92*, edited by Jens Anderson, Torsten Madsen, and Irwin Scollar, pp. 279–285. Aarhus University Press, Aarhus, Denmark.
   1994   GIS vs. spatial statistics: How do they fit together? *Archaeological Computing Newsletter* 38:1–2.

Kwan, Meipo
   2002   Feminist visualization: Re-envisioning GIS as a method in feminist geographic research. *Annals of the American Association of Geographers* 92:645–661.

Lehmann, E. L.
   1993   The Fisher, Neyman–Pearson theories of testing hypotheses: One theory or two? *Journal of the American Statistical Association* 88:1242–1249.

Levy, Thomas E., James D. Anderson, Mark Waggoner, Neil Smith, Adolfo Muniz, and Russell B. Adams
   2001   Digital archaeology 2001: GIS-Based excavation recording in Jordan. *SAA Archaeological Record* 3:23–29.

Loftus, Geoffrey R.
   1993   A picture is worth a thousand p values: On the irrelevance of hypothesis testing in the microcomputer age. *Behavior Research Methods, Instruments and Computers* 25:250–256.

Lyman, R. Lee
   1994   Quantitative units and terminology in zooarchaeology. *American Antiquity* 59:36–71.

Mardia, Kantilal
   1972   *Statistics of Directional Data.* Academic Press, New York.

Marshall, Fiona, and Tom Pilgram
   1991   Meat versus within-bone nutrients: Another look at the meaning of body-part representation in archaeological sites. *Journal of Archaeological Science* 18:149–163.

Mazur, Robert E.
   2003   *Dictionary of Critical Sociology.* Electronic document, http://www.public.iastate.edu/~rmazur/dictionary/a.html.

Mueller, James (editor)
   1975   *Sampling in Archaeology.* University of Arizona Press, Tucson.

Nance, Jack
1990 Statistical sampling in archaeology. In *Mathematics and Information Science in Archaeology: A Flexible Framework*, edited by Albertus Voorrips, pp. 135–163. Holos, Bonn.
1993 Statistical sampling, estimation, and analytic procedures in archaeology. *Journal of Quantitative Anthropology* 4:221–248.

Orton, Clive
1992 Quantitative methods in the 1990s. *In Computer Applications and Quantitative Methods in Archaeology 1991*, pp. 137–140. BAR International Series 577. Oxford.

Papageorgiou, Ioulia, Michael J. Baxter, and M. A. Chau
2001 Model-based artefact compositional data. *Archaeometry* 43:571–588.

Parzen, Emanuel
1997 Data mining, statistical methods, and history of statistics. Electronic document, http://stat.tamu.edu/ftp/pub/eparzen/future.pdf.

Ramsey, C. Bronk
1995 Radiocarbon calibration and analysis of stratigraphy: The OxCal program. *Radiocarbon* 37:425–430.

Rao, C.
2002 Statistics: Reflections on the past and visions for the future. Electronic document, http://hobbes.lite.msu.edu/pipermail/msu-mathed/2002-November/000137.html.

Read, Dwight
1985 The substance of archaeological analysis and the mold of statistical method: Enlightenment out of discord? In *For Concordance in Archaeological Analysis: Bridging Data Structure, Quantitative Technique, and Theory*, edited by Christopher Carr, pp. 45–86. Waveland Press, Prospect Heights, Illinois.
1987 Archaeological theory and statistical methods: Discordance, resolution, and new directions. In *Quantitative Research in Archaeology: Progress and Prospects*, edited by Mark Aldenderfer, pp. 151–184. Sage Publications, Newbury Park, California.
1989 Statistical methods and reasoning in archaeological research. *Journal of Quantitative Anthropology* 1:5–78.

Ringrose, Trevor J.
1992 Boostrapping and correspondence analysis in archaeology. *Journal of Archaeological Science* 19:615–629.
1993a Bone counts and archaeology: A critique. *Journal of Archaeological Science* 20:121–157.
1993b Diversity indices and archaeology. In *Computing the Past: CAA92*, edited by Jens Anderson, Torsten Madsen, and Irwin Scollar, pp. 279–285. Aarhus University Press, Aarhus, Denmark.

1995 Response to Pilgram and Marshall, "Bone counts and statisticians: A reply to Ringrose." *Journal of Archaeological Science* 22:99–102.

Robertson, Ian G.
1999 Spatial and multivariate analysis, random sampling error, and analytical noise: Empirical Bayesian methods at Teotihuacan, Mexico. *American Antiquity* 64:137–152.

Rozeboom, William W.
1960 The fallacy of the null-hypothesis significance test. *Psychological Bulletin* 57:416–428.

Scheps, Sheldon
1982 Statistical blight. *American Antiquity* 47:836–851.

Schieppati, Frank
1983 Archaeological Spatial Interpolation at the Site Level. Unpublished PhD dissertation, Department of Anthropology, University at Buffalo.

Schiffer, Michael
1976 *Behavioral Archaeology*. Academic Press, New York.

Schloen, David
2001a Archaeological data models and web publication using XML. *Computers and the Humanities* 35:123–152.
2001b XML System for Textual and Archaeological Research (XSTAR). Electronic document, http://xml.coverpages.org/xstar.html.

Shanks, Michael, and Christopher Tilley
1987 *Re-Constructing Archaeology: Theory and Practice*. Cambridge University Press, Cambridge.

Shennan, Steven
1988 *Quantifying Archaeology*. Edinburgh University Press, Edinburgh.

Simon, J.
1993 *Resampling: The New Statistics*. Duxbury.
1994 What some puzzling problems teach about the theory of simulation and the use of resampling. *The American Statistician* 48:290–293.

Spaulding, Albert
1953 Statistical techniques for the discovery of artifact types. *American Antiquity* 18:305–313.

Spiegelhalter, David, Jonathan Meyers, David Jones, and Keith Abrams
1999 An introduction to Bayesian methods in health technology assessment. *BMJ* 319:508–512.

Stapert, Dirk
1992 Rings and Sectors: Intrasite Spatial Analysis of Stone Age Sites. Unpublished PhD dissertation, Department of Archaeology, University of Groningen.

Steier, Peter, and W. Rom
2000   The use of Bayesian statistics for ^{14}C dates of chronologically ordered samples: A critical analysis. *Radiocarbon* 42:183–198

Sterne, Jonathan, and George Davey-Smith
2001   Sifting the evidence—what's wrong with significance testing. *BMJ* 322:226–231 (see also electronic document, http://bmj.com/cgi/content/full/322/7280/226).

Thomas, David Hurst
1976   *Figuring Anthropology: First Principles of Probability and Statistics.* Holt, Rinehart, and Winston, New York.
1978   The awful truth about statistics in archaeology. *American Antiquity* 43:231–244.

Tukey, John
1977   *Exploratory Data Analysis.* Addison-Wesley. Reading, Massachusetts

Voorrips, Albertus
1990   The evolution of a flexible framework for archaeological analysis. In *Mathematics and Information Science in Archaeology: A Flexible Framework,* edited by Albertus Voorrips, pp. 1–8. Holos-Verlag, Bonn.

Wegman, Edward J.
1998   Visions: New techniques and technologies in statistics. Paper presented at NTTS98. Electronic document, http://europa.eu.int/en/comm/eurostat/research/conferences/ntts-98/and1.

Whallon, Robert
1987   Simple statistics. In *Quantitative Research in Archaeology: Progress and Prospects,* edited by Mark Aldenderfer, pp. 135–150. Sage Publications, Newbury Park, California.
1984   Unconstrained clustering for the analysis of spatial distributions in archaeology. In *Intrasite Spatial Analysis in Archaeology,* edited by Harold Hietala, pp. 241–277. Cambridge University Press, Cambridge

Wheatley, David, and Mark Gillings
2002   *Spatial Technology and Archaeology. The Archaeological Application of GIS.* Taylor and Francis, London.

White, J. Peter, and David Hurst Thomas
1972   What mean these stones? Ethno-taxonomic models and archaeological interpretations in the New Guinea Highlands. In *Models in Archaeology,* edited by David Clarke, pp. 275–308. Methuen, London.

15

Systems and Simulacra: Modeling, Simulation, and Archaeological Interpretation

James McGlade

A cybernetic wasteland or an indispensable tool for understanding complex evolutionary dynamics? Both of these contrasting epithets have been used to describe simulation modeling methods in archaeology. The truth, as usual with such polarized opinions, lies somewhere between, as well as being rather more complex. What is true, however, is that simulation studies have occupied, and continue to occupy, a somewhat curious position in the archaeological lexicon, seemingly at once being praised as innovative (methodologically), while being subjected to criticism as regressive (theoretically) and reductionist. What is certainly true is that from its initial appearance in the 1960s, simulation has been primarily perceived as an instrumental device coeval with emerging computer technologies rather than inhabiting the domain of advanced theoretical debate. Central to this preoccupation was the apparent promise of a brave new world of prediction: simulation was heralded as a new species of electronic oracle, though one not without its failings (e.g., Clarke 1968, 1972; McGlade 1987).

Perhaps it is useful to state from the outset what this chapter is *not* about. Chiefly, it is not conceived as an exhaustive study of the history of simulation in archaeology; rather it represents—given the restrictions of space—a selective overview of what I consider to be the key moments and contributions in archaeology's somewhat stuttering love affair with simulation modeling.

For this reason, examples have been selected to pinpoint the dominant trends in simulation studies and particularly their relationship to issues in theory building over the past three decades. Thus we shall attempt to shed light on the world of formal modeling, with a view to situating it within a larger historical and theoretical context. We shall begin by revisiting its origins during the heady days of the new archaeology of the 1960s and its subsequent decline to peripheral status amid the wave of growing postprocessual critique. This will be followed by a critical look at the reemergence of formal modeling procedures during the last decade under the influence of chaos and complexity theories, and the final section of the chapter will focus on a speculative assessment of current and future trends and their potential influence on archaeological theory building.

From a methodological perspective it is possible to isolate specific archaeological themes that have used simulation, for example, settlement studies, hunter-gatherer movements, trade-exchange systems, artifact dispersal, and population dynamics. However, such an approach, though eminently logical, would underplay the chronological sequence I wish to demonstrate and, more particularly, its relationship to the development of theory over the last few decades. For these reasons, the chapter will adopt a broadly chronological structure as the most effective way of demonstrating the relationship between simulation modeling and its embedment within changing theoretical and social-cultural contexts. Practically, we shall focus on the role played by a number of key texts as representative of the main ideas and changing theoretical debates spanning archaeological practice over the last 40 years. These texts are organized so as to provide a working classification and have been chosen so as to represent three broad developmental phases: phase I, an early phase dominated by systems theory and including primary texts such as David Clarke's (1968) *Analytical Archaeology* and his influential edited volume *Models in Archaeology* (1972); phase II, a mature phase represented by studies such as Ian Hodder's (1978) edited collection *Simulation Studies in Archaeology*, Renfrew and Cooke's (1979) *Transformations: Mathematical Approaches to Culture Change*, and the volume *Theory and Explanation in Archaeology* (Renfrew et al. 1982); phase III, a third wave, charting the reemergence of formal modeling studies following their dismissal as part of the postprocessual critique of the new archaeology. As I shall emphasize, much of this work has been inspired by complexity theory and new agent-based computer-modeling techniques.

This tripartite structure, a somewhat arbitrary and clearly subjective classification, is intended, not as an exhaustive bibliographic review, but rather as a pedagogic device to provide the reader with a relatively comprehensive overview of the main ideas, debates, and contexts within which simulation modeling has evolved. Rather more attention is devoted to phase III, because it is concerned with current preoccupations and possible future trends. First, however, let us examine the roots of simulation methodology by looking at the broader issues foregrounded by the nature of the model-building process itself.

Models and Meaning

Models are of course a ubiquitous feature of human perceptual and decision-making processes. It is largely through the construction of models that humans understand and impose a coherent rationale on knowledge structures, behavior, and events (McGlade 1987, 1995b). In another sense, models are synonymous with maps, because they provide us with a sense of orientation, with simplified schemata with which we can negotiate unfamiliar or alien territory—a means of coming to terms with the other. Significantly, most of these conceptual models are implicit rather than explicit. Models in the sense used here follow Waddington's (1977) definition in which they are conceived as "tools for thought." Thus we can construe modeling as a meditation on structural possibilities and potential qualitative—as opposed to quantitative—relationships at work in human systems. As a result, we may be in a position to uncover some of the more fugitive and recondite patterns and processes, otherwise imperceptible by conventional statistical analytic methods. Models are inevitably the key to such a problem because they are capable of providing an intermediate bridge between the complexities of observational description and theoretical formulation. The importance of modeling strategies in the development of archaeological theory, and particularly its relationship to social process, was one of the lynchpins of David Clarke's vision of a new archaeology (Clarke 1968, 1972). What is of critical importance is that, whereas models act as descriptive analogues of real-world phenomena, these must not—nor should they ever—be confused with explanations of these. Rather, we should consider mathematical description as a domain whose abstract symbolic logic *informs our perception of real-world processes*, while having no necessary isomorphic relationship with them.

The crux of this argument centers on the possibility of arriving at various reduced descriptions, i.e., *proximate* solutions, which avoid the pitfalls of reductionist explanation. The epistemological problem that this poses rests on the belief that explanations are arbitrary descriptions of *a continuous learning process*, in contradistinction to explanation as a *nomothetic* goal. Checkland captures the sense of this when he argues for the replacement of a paradigm of optimizing with a paradigm of learning. As he correctly stresses, "the notion of a 'solution,' whether it optimizes or satisfices, is inappropriate in a methodology which orchestrates a process of learning which, as a process, is never ending" (1981:279).

Simulation Models

Simulation models can properly be seen as a subset of general numerical modeling methods (Lake 2001b), themselves long an integral part of archaeological analysis (e.g., Hodder and Orton 1976). Broadly speaking, simulation is the act of subjecting hypothetical models to experimental testing so as to evaluate possible behavioral outcomes. It is also the case, as we have noted previously, that models are artificial or virtual constructs; thus rather than attempting to build a real model of archaeological or social processes, the intention is to construct an artificial object based on a set of theoretical assumptions whose interactions and evolutionary behavior can be examined on the computer screen (Hanneman and Patrick 1997). As Gilbert (1997) has pointed out, simulation itself implies no particular theoretical stance on the part of the researcher: "simulations may illuminate phenomenological as well as systems thinking, realist and relativist epistemologies."

More explicitly, simulation can be seen as a species of model capable of investigating complex, multifaceted systems and, most importantly, as a means of constructing experimental scenarios that could never normally be observed. Central to computer simulation is, of course, the critical issue of change or transformation over time and the creation of an appropriate algorithm to track and analyze this change. Significantly, it enables the production of new data that can then be used to test the validity of the original model, or alternatively, as a means of erecting new hypotheses. Over the last decade, the increased sophistication of computer technology has made complex, and previously intractable, studies feasible and importantly provides archaeologists with a new type of experimental laboratory to investigate both quantitative and qualitative data as well as theory building.

With respect to our current interests, no attempt will be made here to deal with the methodological aspects of simulation. Within archaeology, comprehensive descriptions of simulation methodology have been provided by Clarke (1972), Doran and Hodson (1975), and Aldenderfer (1981a) and more recently have been summarized by Lake (2001b) in an excellent general review of numerical modeling. In addition, Cooke (1979) provides archaeologists with an invaluable (though little cited) account of the pitfalls involved in the construction and validation of simulation models.

Simulation Modeling and Archaeology

From its beginnings with the Three Age System and the onset of taxonomic ordering and seriation methods, archaeology has relied heavily on models as a prelude to the erection of hypotheses. However, most model building in archaeology has historically been informal, rather than formal. Archaeological attitudes to formal modeling processes have in many ways been influenced by Clarke's (1968, 1972) and Doran's (1970) important contributions advocating the utility of explicit modeling procedures and most importantly their emphasis on the *heuristic* nature of such enterprises. As we shall see, the impetus provided by these authors spawned a great deal of model building and simulation throughout the 1970s and early 1980s (e.g., Hodder 1978; Renfrew and Cooke 1979; Sabloff 1981; Renfrew et al. 1982). Additionally, the last three decades has witnessed an explosion in the application of computer-based statistical models to interpret phenomena such as artifact assemblages, the movement of trade-exchange materials, the diffusion of agriculture, population dynamics, the collapse of civilizations, and a variety of locational issues related to settlement patterning. Notwithstanding the inherent limitations of archaeological data—often seen as a barrier to sophisticated modeling—as Mithen (1997:213) reminds us, far from being discouraging, it is precisely *because* of the limited and fuzzy nature of archaeological data that we need to embrace simulation.

More recently, with the burgeoning of geographic information system (GIS) applications, there has been an increasing emphasis on predictive modeling of settlement location (e.g., Judge and Sebastian 1988; Kvamme 1990; Westcott and Brandon 2000). Although it may be true that predictive modeling constitutes a central concern in archaeological modeling, these properly are dealt with in chapter 11, which deals explicitly with GIS issues. In what follows, we will focus largely on non-GIS applications and attempt to provide a general overview of simulation applications, emphasizing a historical, evolutionary dimension.

Phase I: Cybernetic Worlds and Mathematical Reasoning

In a survey such as this, it is not enough to enumerate the sequence of personalities and events that conspired to produce a divergent array of archaeological models. Such activities did not occur in a theoretical vacuum nor were they simply the outgrowth of purely academic debates; rather, the history of modeling and simulation studies must be seen within the context of the sociopolitical conditions of a post–World War II situation. An important characteristic of this period was a growing belief in the benefits that technological change and progress would bring to society and to the global order generally. In both Europe and the

United States, the lion's share of research funding was focused on defense, and in many ways it was the Cold War space race that was to provide the catalyst for much fundamental research into the simulation of large interdependent systems. A critical aspect of this work was the growth of computer modeling as a predictive tool, and there was a sense that this technology would provide the keys to a brave new world of control and rational organization. Norbert Weiner, who coined the term *cybernetics* to refer to the relationship between control systems and information, was unwittingly to lay the foundations for a great deal of ensuing research in biology, engineering, and computer science.

It was this cybernetic emphasis and its systems language that dominated the early archaeological forays into simulation, represented by primary texts such as David Clarke's (1968) *Analytical Archaeology*, Jim Doran's (1970) seminal paper on systems theory and simulation, Clarke's (1972) hugely influential *Models in Archaeology*, Doran and Hodson's (1975) *Mathematics and Computers in Archaeology*, the study by Hosler et al. (1977) on the Classic Maya collapse, and finally by Jeremy Sabloff's (1981) edited volume *Simulations in Archaeology*.

It should be remembered that systems thinking was to prove the most pervasive methodology or ideology throughout the 1960s and 1970s, sweeping across both the natural and social sciences. For archaeology and anthropology, it seemed to promise, through its rational logic and subsystemic organization, the possibility of unambiguous and clear-headed solutions to previously intractable social problems. A key process in the functioning of systems, as originally presented by Von Bertalanffy (1968), involves the role of feedback, where the output of a process in turn affects the input. These are classified as negative when an event or process acts to maintain system equilibrium or positive when self-amplification occurs leading to system collapse or transformation. A number of early archaeological examples were designed to demonstrate the role of feedback mechanisms (e.g., Zubrow 1971; Thomas 1972; Ammerman and Cavalli-Sforza 1973; Chadwick 1978).

Implicit in von Bertalanffy's *General Systems Theory* is the notion that societal systems can usefully be disaggregated into a number of subsystems (e.g., economic, social, ideological) so that their interdependent causal chains might be more effectively studied. This model of society as a sequence of coupled subsystems was championed by Kent Flannery, who declared, "Culture change comes about through minor variations in one or more systems, which grow, displace or reinforce others and reach equilibrium on a different plane" (Flannery 1968:120). In applying these ideas to the Classic Maya collapse, Flannery, invoking recent work on network theory (e.g., Gardner and Ashby 1970), used the term *hyper-coherence* to suggest that increasing connectivity in a complex societal system increases the probability of collapse (Flannery 1972:421).

Similarly, such ideas formed a conceptual thread running through Clarke's (1968) hugely influential *Analytical Archaeology*. There is no doubt that *Analytical Archaeology*—despite criticisms of its abstruse language—tapped into what might be described as the prevailing systemic zeitgeist. Moreover, its confident assertions that an archaeology of the future would be more rigorous, quantifiable, and preeminently scientific were viewed by some as an exciting prospect, in view of its avowed aim of producing a rational approach to knowledge construction: i.e., the replacement of a world of culture-historical description with a Popperian hypothetico-deductive framework geared toward *explanation*.

Clarke's exhortations for a fundamental restructuring of archaeological method and theory were given substantive support by Doran (1970), who reinforced the importance of a systemic perspective by suggesting that archaeology should embrace simulation modeling as an important experimental and explanatory tool. But perhaps the most influential text of all during this first wave of computer experimentation into simulation modeling was the collection of papers edited by David Clarke (1972), *Models in Archaeology*. Here for the first time was laid out the case for explicit model building through a series of archaeological case studies. Among the most influential in demonstrating both the power and promise of simulation was Thomas's (1972) study of hunter-gatherer subsistence dynamics, where he demonstrated the feasibility of translating the seasonal round of hunter-gatherer activity patterns into an iterative computer algorithm.

The volume is also remarkable in that it includes one of the first archaeological settlement simulations. Clarke employed a random-walk model to simulate the spread of Neolithic (Band-keramik) settlement on loess soils and argued that the likelihood of settlement movement to nearest-neighbor loess locations helps to explain both the homogeneity and uniformity of material culture. This deterministic model can be seen as a typical example of the deductive methods in use at the time (see Hodder 1977 for a more sophisticated example). A related study by Ammerman and Cavalli-Sforza (1973) also examined the spread of Neolithic settlement, though in a somewhat more complex way. A random-walk procedure for settlement movement was coupled with a logistic model of population growth, so as to produce a wave-of-advance scenario that produced a linear growth pattern of ca. 1 km per year. The simplicity of the assumptions underpinning the model—particularly with respect to population growth and migration rates and the relatively coarse level of analysis—makes it an easy object of criticism. However, on the other hand, it succeeded in demonstrating a number of possible directions for future research, particularly at the local level. Similarly, in the United States, Linda Cordell's (1972) researches into Anasazi settlement showcased the utility of simulation for understanding settlement pattern dynamics, and Levison et al. (1973) presented an influential model designed to replicate the settlement of Polynesia.

However, despite these innovative attempts to demonstrate the utility of simulation methods, they continued to occupy a relatively marginal position in the archaeological mainstream. Indeed, though a much-needed boost to formal modeling methods was to be given by the publication of Doran and Hodson's (1975) *Mathematics and Computers in Archaeology*, the authors display a great deal of skepticism on simulation, commenting that despite the widespread appeal of simulation methods in a variety of disciplines—especially geography—there was yet little evidence to recommend its use in archaeology. Notwithstanding this pessimism, two notable demonstrations of the efficacy of simulation were to be seen in Wobst's (1974) study of Paleolithic social structure and Zubrow's (1975) work in the Hay Hollow Valley of Arizona. Wobst attempted to simulate the evolution of hunter-gatherer bands with a view to uncovering the "mean equilibrium size" (1974:157). This stochastic simulation was run for

400-year cycles, with the population being disaggregated so that each individual was accounted for by name, age, sex, residence, and marital status. What is important about this work is not that it can readily be mapped against specific archaeological data but that it provided a vehicle for *experimentation* rather than any precise form of prediction.

Zubrow's highly influential study employing insights from systems theory such as feedback and equilibrium was directed at understanding population-environment dynamics and provided an innovative perspective on the relations between population-carrying capacity with respect to environmental conditions and settlement size and location. The model was based on four primary components: a population-growth function, a function for checking population size against available resources, a settlement locator, and a function that controlled settlement longevity. Model output was intended to ascertain which parameters, for example, with respect to birth and death rates, could best fit the archaeological record. Although the study suggested the need to understand the effects of changes in a variety of parameter combinations, crucially, from an analytic perspective, its results were based on as few as eight simulation runs.

Summary

With hindsight, what is notable about this first wave of simulation studies is that it is wholly consistent with computer experiments being carried out across the social sciences in pursuit of more rigorous interpretations of social phenomena. Thus following exemplars from disciplines such as geography, many of these studies were less concerned with experimental, heuristic methods but rather were preoccupied with the goal of *prediction* and the possibility of simulating real-world event sequences. More problematically, these early forays tended to pay slavish allegiance to a Popperian natural sciences paradigm, focusing on issues such as refutation and verification. Significantly, a fundamental tenet of such work involved the largely implicit acceptance of a Newtonian worldview—a world articulated by ontological and epistemological certainty, grounded in deduction. Following the physical sciences, the scientific rigor associated with such a view was regarded as an eminently achievable goal to which archaeology should aspire (e.g., Fritz and Plog 1970; Watson et al. 1971); in short, the goal of explicit hypothesis *testing* seemed to take precedence over hypothesis *generation* (Wobst 1997:430).

It is somewhat ironic that archaeology's love affair with deductive nomological models and its desire to pursue a more rigorous scientific philosophy was occurring at a time when the natural sciences were increasingly finding this paradigm wanting; thus while the natural sciences were busy grappling with postpositivist, relativistic, and probabilistic models ushered in by the breakthroughs of a post-Einsteinian universe—a universe defined by its *uncertainty*—archaeology was expending an enormous amount of energy searching for theoretical structures that would enshrine models of scientific inquiry as laws, whose hallmark was the aspiration to objective *certainty*.

Phase II: System Dynamics and Morphogenesis

Our second phase might be described as a mature phase with respect to formal modeling and encompasses a period defined by a growing confidence in simulation methodologies and belief in their power to simulate whole societal systems. In many ways, it can be thought of as representing a confident world of academic self-confidence, before the onset of postprocessual doubt. Chronologically, and somewhat arbitrarily, this period encompasses influential studies such as the Classic Maya collapse by Hosler et al. (1977), Ian Hodder's (1978) edited collection *Simulation Studies in Archaeology*, Renfrew and Cooke's (1979) *Transformations: Mathematical Approaches to Culture Change*, and Sabloff's *Simulations in Archaeology* (1981) and arguably comes to a close with the publication of *Theory and Explanation in Archaeology* (Renfrew et al. 1982). In what follows, we shall focus attention on these texts, which though not exhaustive, nevertheless provide a useful set of reference points from which to construct a coherent overview of the period.

For example, Hosler et al. (1977) produced a notable contribution, demonstrating the feasibility of tackling a complex subject such as the Classic Maya collapse, by employing the systems dynamics approach popularized by Forrester (1968) and previously applied to subjects such as the growth of urbanism and the evolution of the global economy. The model structure chosen by Hosler et al. was based on a verbal model suggested by Willey and Shimkin (1973), and this was translated into a series of interacting causal loops to account for growing elite demands, increasing competition between ceremonial centers, and health problems associated with increasing population density. The model of collapse that ensues centers on an apparently fatal positive feedback linking agricultural productivity and monument building; thus declining food production leads to a decrease in food per capita and, to propitiate the gods, ceremonialism is increased, drawing labor from the agricultural sector, hence further reducing food production. As Lowe (1985:98) puts it, "In terms of control by simple feedback, the elite regulatory apparatus acted to amplify error within the system, rather than to diminish it."

Contrary to much critical opinion at the time, the model was not designed to generate exact predictions but rather, following the systems dynamics paradigm, to isolate the overall dynamic behavior, e.g., stability, thresholds, overshoot, and collapse. As the authors themselves admit, the explanation of collapse may well have been resident in factors not taken into account by the model (Hosler et al. 1977:580).[1] Although the existing archaeological data presented a problem for the resultant interpretation of this simulation, perhaps the model's weakest aspect is its failure to take account of the spatial dimension (Doran 1994:2).

It was not, however, until 1978, with the publication of Ian Hodder's edited volume *Simulation Studies in Archaeology*, that we begin to see a marked growth in the penetration of simulation studies into the archaeological mainstream. Here we have for the first time a self-confident group of studies proclaiming the arrival of formal modeling as an indispensable part of archaeological explanation. These collected papers, spanning the simulation of settlement processes (e.g., Zimmerman, O'Shea, Chadwick), exchange systems (Elliott, Ellman and Hodder), and population dynamics (Black) and methodological issues such as sampling (e.g., Donnelly, Hodder and Okell, Zubrow and

Harbaugh, Ammerman et al.), are remarkable for their focus on methodological rather than heuristic aspects of simulation. O'Shea's study of Pawnee settlement, in company with many early simulation experiments, was geared toward hypothesis testing. In line with the currency of systems thinking, it sought to model the elements of settlement location strategy. Such investigations, however, were inevitably hampered by lack of data and hence, despite their intrinsic experimental utility, tended to produce dubious, if not spurious results. Arguably more successful modeling efforts have been those directed at the interpretation of trade-exchange systems. These have figured prominently in early simulation studies (e.g., Wright and Zeder 1977) and are represented in *Simulation Studies in Archaeology* by Elliot et al., who construct a simulation of Neolithic ax dispersal using a random-walk procedure to model the movement from source to destination.

The momentum set in motion by Hodder's edited volume was further accelerated by a more ambitious undertaking represented by the publication of Renfrew and Cooke's (1979) *Transformations: Mathematical Approaches to Culture Change*, which set out to demonstrate in a rigorous fashion the role of explicitly mathematical approaches to fundamental aspects of archaeological explanation. This sophisticated agenda was to be concerned, in Renfrew's words, with "replacing anecdote by analysis." These intentions are apparent from the outset, in the preface by the eminent French mathematician and inventor of catastrophe theory, René Thom, whose work either explicitly or implicitly underpins a number of contributions. The book was also important for bringing together researchers from outside archaeology, for example, prominent mathematical biologists such as Robert Rosen with a long history of research into morphogenetic change. Moreover, it set out a self-consciously innovative and experimental agenda, much of which is crystallized in Colin Renfrew's erudite and wide-ranging introductory chapter.

Following previous trends, the core of the volume deals with models investigating the nature of sociospatial hierarchy, settlement dynamics, and system collapse. A typical example is Ian Hodder's study to understand the possible processes underlying rank-size relationships, using a wide variety of known hierarchical data sets (Iron Age hill forts, Romano-British walled towns, early Dynastic sites from Iraq, and late Helladic settlements). These data were compared with stochastically created data to achieve best-fit results. The relationship between hierarchy and political organization is another central theme explored by Renfrew and Level with their XTENT model. Effectively a more sophisticated version of central place theory, here simulation was used as a means of predicting the territorial extent of polities from archaeological data. The model was further tested using the cities of Europe as a data set, though ignoring national boundaries. Results suggested that although this type of model is not dynamic, i.e., time dependent, nonetheless it provides a useful tool for archaeologists trying to assess general principles underlying the spatial structuring of sociopolitical organizations.

Such issues that are central to settlement archaeology are also key aspects of the succeeding chapter by Alden on political interaction in the Valley of Mexico, and Chadwick's simulation of settlement patterns in Bronze Age Messenia, Greece. This latter study, although based on a set of simple rules, nevertheless was able to provide a model of settlement growth that demonstrated reasonable affinity with the known trajectory of archaeological settlement pattern over time. All of these approaches demonstrate not only the debt to geography but, more important, the utility of simulation in generating hypotheses from numerical models of interaction and distance.

Building on previous research by Renfrew (1972), Cooke and Renfrew present an innovative and perhaps ultimately overambitious modeling perspective on the evolution of culture change in the Aegean. Their espousal of a systems approach with its identification of discrete subsystemic components (population, subsistence, technology, society, trade, crafts, ideology) is one of the classic examples of early archaeological experiments in the simulation of whole societal systems. This systems study with its desire to uncover the equilibrium-seeking functions and feedback mechanisms at the heart of complex societal systems, though instructive, was later destined to become the paradigmatic example of all that was deemed to be wrong with modeling and explanation in processual archaeology (e.g., Hodder 1986; Shanks and Tilley 1987a, 1987b).[2]

But perhaps the most controversial and contentious approach among the collection of papers in *Transformations* involves Renfrew's espousal of catastrophe theory (1978; Renfrew and Poston 1979). René Thom's (1975) work on the mathematics of structural stability focused on the capacity of systems of continuous variables to generate discontinuous states through bifurcation and provoked much interest (and critique) within the social sciences during the late 1970s. Following Thom, Renfrew's previous studies had sought to use the methods of catastrophe theory to create a theoretical foundation from which a general theory of societal collapse might be constructed. Here, Renfrew and Poston tackle the familiar issue of settlement discontinuity and attempt to provide a new topological framework as the basis of interpretation. Essentially a theory of qualitative dynamics, these catastrophe models are ultimately difficult to verify but may be useful in clarifying relationships between variables so as to render them more explicit.

Significantly, *Transformations*, with its uncompromising espousal of formal modeling methods, was by the early 1980s to become the butt of postprocessual ire. With hindsight, it seemed to provide a compendium of all that was deemed to be unacceptable in the new archaeology—most especially its love affair with the natural sciences and a supposed belief in simulation as explanation: simulation as a *simulacrum* of the real world. This, despite the fact that Renfrew had made it clear that "simulation is not explanation" and that, rather, it should be viewed as a technique for examining the implications of a model (1979:202). Viewed from the present, the opprobrium heaped on the book has been somewhat overdramatized, because although there is a sometimes strident and naive championing of all things mathematical, the book boasts a number of elegant demonstrations of the power of mathematical reasoning as an *aid* to interpretation rather than any supposed substitution. Not surprisingly, Renfrew's injunction that such models should never be confused with *explanations* of phenomena was excised from subsequent straw man arguments, aimed at devaluing the pursuit of general theory.

The next milestone in the growing development of simulation studies was to come, not surprisingly, from the United

States, where a vigorous interest in simulation modeling was emerging. The fruits of this trend can be seen in Jeremy Sabloff's edited volume *Simulations in Archaeology* (1981), a compilation of presentations at an influential School of American Research Seminar held in 1978. It seemed to crystallize much of the excitement that was drawing archaeologists toward simulation studies. The clarity of thought and possibility of a rigorous approach to previously intractable archaeological problems—sentiments first expressed by Clarke and Doran—was now wedded to systems dynamics approaches pioneered by Jay Forrester (1968), with their ambitions to model whole economic and societal systems. In many ways this was a landmark volume in that it provided the first rigorous treatment of simulation method and theory from both the philosophical and practical ends of the spectrum.

Aldenderfer's contribution is significant in that it provided the first comprehensive survey of simulation studies in archaeology and at the same time presented a practical and accessible simulation primer. In a subsequent chapter he also demonstrates how simulation modeling can be used to create hypothetical artifact assemblages that can then be compared to those produced by known hunter-gatherer groups. Notable also is Zubrow's espousal of systems dynamics in his study of the growth of ancient Rome, which thus shares a number of similarities with the Mayan study by Hosler et al. (1977), previously described. The main intention was to seek an understanding of those parameters that showed the greatest sensitivity and hence the most dramatic effect on key systemic issues such as growth and decline. Interestingly, Zubrow's simulations produced a three-phase, oscillating pattern of growth and decline over a 200-year period, and the study was able to show that simulation methods can be used effectively as a laboratory within which multiple experiments can be undertaken as an adjunct to hypothesis creation. In this latter respect, this second wave of studies separates itself from the overtly deductive methods of the previous period.

This phase of unbridled faith in simulation arguably reached its high-water mark with the publication of *Theory and Explanation in Archaeology* (Renfrew et al. 1982), the proceedings of a Theoretical Archaeology Group (TAG) meeting in 1980. This volume boasts a theoretical agenda designed to tackle fundamental issues, such as the nature of explanation and morphogenetic change in societal systems, and is noteworthy for its introduction of concepts such as self-organization and the importance of emergent phenomena as a consequence of far-from-equilibrium states. These ideas emanating from studies of nonlinear dynamics in the physical sciences, and particularly the work of Ilya Prigogine and colleagues in the "Brussels school," are discussed by van der Leeuw, who examines their philosophical implications for archaeology and are given elegant expression in Peter Allen's study of urban evolution as a self-organizing process.

Theory and Explanation in Archaeology stands at the pivotal point of a rapidly changing theoretical paradigm, sitting on the cusp of a new postprocessual future. From a historical perspective, it is coeval with the onset of a new contextual discourse, represented by Ian Hodder's *Symbols in Action* (1982a) and *Symbolic and Structural Archaeology* (1982b), both of whose orientations imply an explicit rejection of simulation methodologies and, indeed, all formal modeling approaches. Amid this changing climate, it is not surprising that *Theory and Explanation in Archaeology* was to be viewed as the last bastion of an overinflated processualism. Although simulation studies were still evident, particularly in Americanist research (e.g., a study of the Classic Maya collapse by Lowe 1985), elsewhere the 1982 volume by Renfrew et al. appears to mark the swan song of the second wave of simulation modeling in archaeology—at least as an important and influential theoretical focus.

Notwithstanding archaeology's shift to embrace the uncertainties of a postmodern worldview, formal modeling contributions continued to appear in more pragmatic contexts such as artifact sampling and include van der Velde's (1987) study of the patterning of archaeological distributions. But perhaps of more importance in demonstrating the continuing relevance of simulation was Mithen's (1990) influential study of hunter-gatherer decision making. This work, demonstrably moving against the theoretical grain with its simulation of faunal assemblages (cf. Aldenderfer 1981b) and explicit modeling of decision-making criteria, was to become the subject of a well-documented debate between Mithen and Thomas (see Mithen 1991) contesting the validity of simulation method and theory and, more fundamentally, the very nature of scientific explanation itself.

Summary

An air of confidence and not a little hubris can be said to characterize this second phase of simulation studies. The important point here is that the forays into the mathematics of discontinuity and morphogenesis, although innovative, tended to operate at a high level of abstraction and were, in consequence, destined to be stillborn; archaeology was unwilling or, perhaps more accurately, not yet ready to embrace the potential evolutionary implications of a new nonlinear discourse. More attractive to the leading edge of archaeological theory was the rising postmodern tide with its swingeing critique of what was perceived as the scientism underpinning processual approaches to archaeological explanation. The shifting focus toward symbolic, structural, and contextual phenomena (e.g., Hodder 1982, 1986; Shanks and Tilley 1987a, 1987b) with its stress on individual agency was to lead theoretical archaeology along an entirely new path, generating unprecedented self-criticism along with a growing sense of unease about the ethical and moral universe within which archaeological practice was situated. It seemed as though simulation studies had little to offer this reflexive theoretical turn.

With hindsight, it is easy to see that this narrowing of the theoretical compass effectively retarded discussion on important issues of causality, structure, contingency, and discontinuous evolution—central issues foregrounded by previous morphogenetic approaches. In fact, almost a decade was to pass before attention was to focus on research into nonlinear dynamics, self-organization, and chaos.

Hiatus and Postmodern Sermons

Taking its cue from the antiscience polemic sweeping through the social and political sciences in the late 1970s, archaeology (taking its lead from geography), sought to distance itself from any vestige of the natural sciences paradigm. But there were costs: in dismissing the utility of models drawn from the natural and physical sciences, archaeological theory cast itself in a reduced intellectual milieu; paradoxically, the important theoretical gains established by a vigorous postprocessual debate were to some extent compromised by a narrowing of the intellectual terms of engagement within which archaeological theory and practice could proceed. For example, there is a strident dogmatism in many contributions during the 1980s, such as *Social Theory and Archaeology* (Shanks and Tilley (1987a), which ends with a series of quasi-biblical aphorisms on what is considered permissible archaeological practice.

The effects of this seismic shift in theoretical and methodological priorities were predictably profound with respect to the world of computation and modeling. Thus it was that throughout the 1980s and at least part of the 1990s simulation studies and formal modeling of any kind were regarded as somewhat passé, the outworn remnants of a bankrupt positivist discourse. In view of the burgeoning fashion for symbolic, structural, and Marxist methods, mathematical approaches to knowledge construction were implicitly deemed illegitimate and reeked of scientism. Commonly, they were caricatured as belonging to a world populated by lab-coated elites, enmeshed in a world of abstruse numerical jargon.

The growing preoccupation with social theory meant that there was no room in the new postmodern pantheon for ideas supported by mathematical or rule-based logic. Essentially, the avowed rationality of these techniques, and particularly their purported neglect of the knowing subject, was seen as incompatible with more subjectivist approaches focused on human agency. It was thus that, in a very short time, we see David Clarke moving from the status of innovator and new-archaeology guru to that of pariah.[3] With hindsight, what is remarkable about this period, apart from the missionary zeal displayed by the supporters of each side, is the restricted nature of the discourse and the rules of engagement (e.g., see contributions in Bapty and Yates 1990). It seemed that the invocation of Derrida, Foucault, or other poststructuralist philosophers was enough to ward off the evil spirits of a positivist priesthood represented by David Clarke, Colin Renfrew, and not least by Lewis Binford. With hindsight, there is something pseudodramatic (not to say humorous) about the way these latter were portrayed as part of a dark underworld, hell-bent on proselytizing a regressive worldview and thus incompatible with the "true" faith inscribed in Foucauldian, Lyotardian, or other approved gospels.[4] What is frequently forgotten is that the quasi-religious zeal of these reformers, although providing an incisive critique, had an ultimately debilitating effect on archaeological theory building as a pluralistic territory. In its place we see a reinforcing of a binary universe within which materialist or idealist polarities define distinctive and discrete philosophical entities—territories identified by opposing and irreconcilable epistemological positions.

Phase III: Nonlinear Dynamics, Chaos, and Complexity Theory

This third wave charts the reemergence of formal modeling studies, following their dismissal as part of the postprocessual critique. Much of this work is inspired by the spread of nonlinear dynamics and complexity theory from the physical and natural sciences, not least because of the availability of new computer-modeling techniques. As we shall see, it includes an array of research ranging from Lansing and Kremer's (1993) simulation of Balinese temple networks to new agent-based approaches (Gilbert and Doran 1994), particularly the study by Doran et al. (1994) on Upper Paleolithic culture change and other agent-based modeling of settlement systems (Kohler and Van West 1996), as well as studies of Mesolithic foraging (Lake and Mithen 1998; Lake 2000). Also under this rubric is the parallel, but related, research strain represented by McGlade's (1995) integrated proposal for modeling social-environmental dynamics and archaeological explorations of chaos and complexity foregrounded by van der Leeuw and McGlade (1997a) and Bintliff (1997, 1999).

Complexity and Complex Systems

Recent years have seen the arrival of a new interdisciplinary approach to the analysis of complex, nonlinear systems and a gradual incorporation of these ideas into fields as far apart as chemistry, physics, ecology, urban and regional geography, and the social sciences generally (see Edmonds 1996; McGlade and van der Leeuw 1997; and Byrne 1998 for useful reviews). Complex systems are those systems "whose aggregate behavior is both due to, and gives rise to, multi-scale structural and dynamical patterns which are not inferable from a system description that spans only a narrow window of resolution" (Parrott and Kok 2000).

As a new interdisciplinary field, complexity theory (Waldrop 1992; Kauffman 1995) is essentially concerned with studying the general attributes of nonlinear systems and chaotic dynamics. Beginning in the early 1990s, this perspective and its central ideas have penetrated the social sciences, and they have been viewed as having important consequences for conventional epistemologies (Hayles 1991; Reed and Harvey 1992; Gilbert and Doran 1994; Harvey and Reed 1994; Shermer 1995; Byrne 1998). In contrast to the larger social science community, archaeology as a whole has been hesitant to embrace the implications of the complexity discourse. Nevertheless, over the last decade, a number of archaeologists have pointed to the importance of such ideas, particularly their potential for generating a new understanding of causality and with it the nature of long-term change (McGlade 1990, 1995, 1999; Kohler 1993; van der Leeuw and McGlade 1997; Bintliff 1997).

Although complexity theory may be fashionable at the moment, it must be remembered that the underlying principles are far from new. For example, the central ideas underlying phenomena such as chaotic dynamics, bifurcation, phase transitions, and emergent behavior have a long history and form the core of studies in nonlinear dynamics and complex systems theory (e.g., Thom 1975; Nicolis and Prigogine 1977; Haken 1977; Allen 1982; Thompson and Stewart 1986; Ruelle 1991).

Among the most influential research has been that of Ilya Prigogine and colleagues (e.g., Nicolis and Prigogine 1977; Prigogine 1978, 1980; Prigogine and Stengers 1984) with their investigations of far-from-equilibrium phenomena and the study of system transformation in terms of order through fluctuations.[5] Indeed, it was the introduction of this work into the social sciences, largely by Peter Allen (e.g., 1982), that provided the context for the first archaeological discussions of nonlinear dynamics (e.g., van der Leeuw 1981, 1982; Allen and McGlade 1987) and led to the first explicit models exploring the nature of chaotic behavior within archaeological contexts (McGlade 1990). Further exploration of these ideas formed one of the central themes of a 1990 Cambridge conference and its resulting proceedings, *Time, Process and Structured Transformation in Archaeology* (van der Leeuw and McGlade 1997).[6] In many ways this volume, following on from the morphogenetic paradigm that underwrote many of the contributions to the Southampton conference (Renfrew et al. 1982), was designed to introduce archaeologists to a variety of modeling approaches from other disciplines—a number of which (e.g., from biology, physics, geography) had pioneered research into nonlinear systems and chaos theory. These concerns are comprehensively laid out in the introductory chapter by McGlade and van der Leeuw and the chapter by Erwin, where a strong case is made for the integration of a nonlinear perspective to the archaeology of long-term change. Particular attention is focused on the importance of rates of change (temporalities) and issues of scale, as opposed to the conventional archaeological view that reads the long-term as a sequence of additive snapshots—the accumulation of short-term events.

As with most edited volumes, it is difficult to lump all contributions under one coherent heading. Significantly, there are a number of attempts to shed new light on erstwhile archaeological problems such as the spread of disease, urbanization, megafauna extinction, and trade-exchange issues. In contrast to the older systems paradigm that focused on functionalist, adaptationist explanations and a preoccupation with prediction, several chapters (e.g., Erwin, Day, McGlade, and van der Leeuw and McGlade) point to the role of chaotic dynamics in generating wholly unpredictable outcomes. Attention is instead focused on uncovering nonlinear attractors, i.e., sets of characteristics, or signatures, that characterize the long-run behavior of the system trajectory.

Such ideas are illustrated in two studies that deal respectively with prehistoric exchange dynamics (McGlade 1997b) and urban evolution (van der Leeuw and McGlade 1997b). In both cases it is shown that nonlinear dynamics operating at the heart of complex interaction scenarios can generate unexpected structural change, and, in the former study on exchange dynamics in prestige-goods economies, this is seen to have important consequences for the maintenance of social control and the continued exercise of power.

In an important contribution, Zubrow uses a GIS to explore the spatial dynamics of the spread of disease in the New World during the sixteenth century. The study is based on a model of epidemic diffusion that is fitted to known data on the spatial location of known pre-epidemic populations, and the resulting predictions are subsequently compared to archaeological and historical data sets. Zubrow's results provide a particularly robust demonstration of the power of spatial simulation models and their ability to create interpretive scenarios that would be otherwise impossible to conceive. The ability of simulation to generate new data is also apparent in Mithen's simulation of prehistoric mammoth-population dynamics (1994), and his study provides insights into the possible formation of archaeological assemblages from Russia and North America. A variety of simulation scenarios are used to highlight the relationships between human predation and climatic fluctuations and how they may have combined to create a plausible explanation for mammoth extinction at the end of the Pleistocene.

Reynolds's (1997) contribution continues this biological-cultural theme by focusing on the relationship between genetic and cultural information systems through the construction of two automata, an experience generator (EG) and a knowledge-base integrator (KI), as representations of genetic and cultural information systems. These are employed ultimately to create a hypothetical simulation of the hierarchical nature of information storage within the human mind. Of key interest in Reynolds's study is its evolutionary content: that is, the way that the model itself is able to modify its own behavior—effectively changing the rules.

Jim Doran's work on agent-based approaches to simulation (the EOS project discussed later) is also included here as a demonstration of the increasing popularity of concepts derived from artificial intelligence (AI). Doran argues that these can provide a source of general theory relating to an improved understanding of the possible trajectories that sociocultural systems may follow. Specifically, Doran uses the architecture of distributed AI to explore the emergence of social structure and leadership from a set of unstructured rules and disparate knowledge categories. Significantly, he reminds us that although mathematical analysis provides us with "precise incontrovertible demonstration," currently it operates at too high a level of abstraction to shed light on details. Doran's perceptive comments are not so much pessimistic as realistic and are echoed in what is perhaps the volume's most erudite contribution, by the pioneering mathematical biologist Robert Rosen. Inserting a cautionary note into any unbridled enthusiasm for systems dynamics approaches, he argues with respect to social systems that they tend to be poorly represented by generalized mathematical models and that, ultimately, the power of mathematical description is likely to be effective only within highly focused and limited contexts.

The mathematical emphasis of this book—in common with previous simulation volumes—guarantees that it will not reach a general archaeological public, particularly given the general lack of numerical sophistication in the discipline. Indeed, simulation studies by their very nature are destined to remain a specialist—though nonetheless important—branch of archaeological investigation. On the other hand, although it is clear that many of the theoretical and methodological forays into the nature of complex systems represented by this book may not stand the test of time, this is not important. Rather, their explicitness and exploratory nature are designed to establish sets of alternative interpretive criteria with a view to illuminating future research trajectories (cf. Lake 2001b:730).

Complex Adaptive Systems and Emergent Phenomena

By way of contrast to much of the top-down modeling described above, more recent emphasis on bottom-up or micro-level theorizing has favored a move toward multiagent models—perhaps the dominant modeling paradigm of the 1990s. Broadly speaking, an *agent* can be seen as an autonomous goal-directed software entity able to interact with an environment or resource (Axelrod and Cohen 1999). Agents can be individuals or a variety of collective entities such as households. Groups of agents, as interacting collectives, are usually defined as multiagent systems: that is, a collection of self-contained problem-solving systems. Outside archaeology, these approaches have been used as vehicles, or test beds, for the exploration of spatiotemporal complexity and have had a substantial impact on disciplines such as physics, urban geography, ecology, and biology, from whence they have mutated to archaeology. Their universal applicability has been advocated, most forcibly by those researchers aligned with the Santa Fe group. In fact, it is the emergence of the Santa Fe Institute in 1988, under the guidance of Murray Gell-Mann and Philip Anderson, that has done most to promote the field of complexity studies—albeit within rather narrow terms of reference. Essentially, these explorations of complex adaptive systems (CASs) and emergent phenomena dubbed "artificial life" (Langton 1989, 1992) build on research into autopoetic, or self-replicating, systems (Varela et al. 1974). This work on the evolutionary behavior of self-replicating systems (Kauffman 1993), coupled with genetic algorithm research (Holland 1975), has led to the pronouncement of a general hypothesis that all complex systems emerge and preferentially maintain themselves at the "edge of chaos" (Langton 1990).

Self-Organization and Scale Invariance

One of the key insights claimed for CAS structures is their ability to self-organize (e.g., Holland 1992; Kauffman 1993). Despite the implication from Americanist literature that self-organized phenomena are a recent product of CAS research at Santa Fe (Gumerman and Gell-Mann 1994; Kauffman 1995), it needs to be remembered that the paradigm of self-organization has a somewhat longer history mainly because of the work of Ilya Prigogine on nonlinear dynamics and dissipative structures (Nicolis and Prigogine 1977; Prigogine 1978, 1980). In fact this paradigm was first introduced to an archaeological audience a decade ago by Prigogine's colleague Peter Allen (1982a, 1982b) and to anthropology by Adams (1988).

Social systems as self-organized systems are best defined as multiscalar entities, such that they can be represented as a nested set of semiautonomous levels (McGlade 1995). The fractal, or self-similar, nature of these dynamical structures has yet to be fully integrated into archaeological research designs—though from a geomorphological perspective there is much that can be done (see, e.g., Turcotte 1997). In fact, study of the fractal nature of archaeological data is only in its infancy, in part because cultural data are notoriously difficult to quantify. However, in an important contribution, Olivier (1995, 1999) has invoked fractal concepts to provide a radically different reading of Iron Age funerary assemblages. Olivier shows how the particular observational scale adopted ultimately constrains and radically affects our reading of temporal and spatial dynamics. More fundamentally, this innovative research reveals the scale invariance or fractal nature latent in the data. As Olivier argues, such findings strike at the heart of conventional readings of the nature of archaeological assemblages and have important epistemological consequences for archaeological interpretation. The potential of such perspectives has also been advocated by Bintliff (1997, 1999) as providing new insights into structural change and recently by Bentley and Maschner (2001) in terms of artifact life spans and stylistic change. These authors follow Bak and colleagues (Bak et al. 1988; Bak and Chen 1991) whose work in physical systems has identified "self-organized criticality" as a key aspect in understanding scalar growth. In this evolutionary model, periods of stasis alternate with avalanches of change that generate chain reactions between agents. Self-organized critical systems are said to evolve to a critical state, that is, one poised between order and chaos (Kauffman 1994; Bak 1996). Whether the universalist claims of those such as Gell-Mann (1994), Kauffman (1995), and Bentley and Maschner (2001, 2003) for the ubiquity of self-organized critical processes at the heart of society and culture will be borne out remains to be seen.

Power-Law Distributions

One of the properties claimed for complex systems of all types—biological, social, economic—is that they display power-law structures; that is, change occurs at all scales—incrementally and as catastrophic avalanches (Bentley and Maschner 2001). Ever since Vilfredo Pareto (1896) showed that the distribution of income in households obeys a power-law distribution, social scientists and particularly economists have devoted a great deal of research to the topic. Scientists have also noted that the fossil record exhibits power-law distributions with respect to the magnitude of extinction events and species lifetimes (Newman 1996, 1997).

Generally speaking, it has been observed that real, large systems with many autonomous but interacting components are characterized by power-law distributions. The power-law distribution is, in effect, an observed statistical signature of large systems of autonomous, interacting entities such as software agents. Power-law structures, thus, have become a central aspect of agent-based research. A convincing argument for their ubiquity is the finding by Adamic and Huberman (1999) that the distribution of visits to World Wide Web sites is also a power-law distribution. Currently, the paucity of archaeological examples of fractal structures and self-organized critical phenomenon would suggest that it is not viewed as a fruitful research area; however, as Bentley and Maschner (2001) have demonstrated, the future for archaeological studies of stylistic variation may yet lie in this direction.

Agent-Based Models in Archaeology

Two separate strands can be detected in the development of agent-based approaches in Anglo-American archaeology: the first emanating from Europe and inspired by developments in artificial intelligence and the second, largely Americanist, deriving from interdisciplinary research on the origins of life at the Santa Fe Institute.

Of the former research focus, the first important contributions were made by Jim Doran (e.g., 1982) who, as we have noted above, began adapting the methods of distributed artificial intelligence (DAI) to create new computational architectures for the exploration of classic archaeological problems such as the Maya collapse and the behavior of societal systems in general. DAI methods were applied to hunter-gatherer studies (Doran et al. 1994, 1995) and specifically to the emergence of social complexity in the Paleolithic of southwestern France.

The second Americanist strain, flying under the rubric of CASs (e.g., Lewin 1992; Kauffman 1991, 1993; Holland 1992; Gell-Mann 1992) and largely based on the use of SWARM, a general purpose simulation platform (Minar et al. 1996; Swarm Development Group 1999), has perhaps been the most influential. The individualist emphasis of these models and their focus on the emergence of collective (global) behavior from individual (local) agent interactions, and particularly their ability to display self-organizing dynamics, have generated a great deal of interest. Indeed it has been argued that these approaches may provide archaeologists with a suite of powerful tools that promise new means of testing hypotheses about human behavior and decision making in prehistory as well as providing alternative perspectives on classic archaeological problems such as the diffusion of agriculture in Europe (e.g., Bogucki 2000).

Among the most prominent advocates of the CAS approach have been Tim Kohler and colleagues, who in a series of innovative contributions (Kohler 1993; Kohler and Carr 1997; Kohler and Van West 1996; Kohler et al. 2000; Van West and Kohler 1995) have demonstrated the value of using SWARM agent simulation methods to understand settlement dynamics in the Anasazi region of the American Southwest. For example, using the household as the primary observational unit (or agent), Kohler and Van West (1996) have investigated the relative payoffs to households of food sharing vs. hoarding under a variety of production regimes. This research formed the basis for more elaborate multiagent modeling exploring the relationships between climate, settlement, production, consumption, and interhousehold exchange. As the authors have pointed out, although the agents respond to environmental criteria, the model does not include sociocultural aspects; clearly, social, political, and ideological factors could have formed an important aspect of settlement abandonment, and the incorporation of these criteria with respect to decision making is currently under investigation.

A recent showcase for agent-based approaches was a Santa Fe meeting held in 1998 and published as *Dynamics in Human and Primate Societies: Agent-Based Modelling of Social and Spatial*

Processes (Kohler and Gumerman 2000). Significantly, archaeological problems provide some of the most substantive and innovative contributions; for example, Lake's modeling of foraging decisions is located within the specific context of the Mesolithic Islay, and an agent-based approach is used to examine the role of hazelnut gathering in determining land-use exploitation. But perhaps the real importance of Lake's study is in its provision of a generic modeling platform for the exploration of spatially referenced agent-based behaviors. Aspects of human-environment interaction also form the basis of the contributions by Kohler et al. and Dean et al., both of which tackle issues of settlement growth and abandonment from a bottom-up perspective.

Noteworthy also for its rigorous approach to modeling is the contribution by Reynolds (1986), who explores the utility of decision-tree methods for investigating state formation processes in the Oaxaca valley and particularly their ability to generate predictive models that incorporate the role of conflict and warfare in sociopolitical change.

Building on previous simulation work in Bali (Lansing 1991; Lansing and Kremer 1993), Stephen Lansing provides a particularly instructive example of CASs in his exploration of the spatial dynamics of Balinese temple networks. These are modeled as a coevolutionary network driven by various cooperative and noncooperative strategies. Simulation results demonstrate that this self-organizing system is sensitive to small changes in local payoffs, which trigger cascades of change. This appears to have an adaptive function, increasing the capacity of the system to adapt to situations such as technological innovation in irrigation or, for example, a new rice pest or other crop pathologies (Lansin and Kremer 1993 :221).

Although this study is exploratory in nature, what is noteworthy is its self-confident assertion that the future of simulation is agent based. Whereas this may to a large extent be true for the study of ecological and physical systems—unencumbered by the vagaries of values, intentionality, and self-reflection—human systems enmeshed in webs of nonlinear causalities cannot be easily corralled to fit the constraints of multiagent architectures. For example, it is not clear to what extent human systems can be adequately described by rule-based methods. Thus as archaeologists move increasingly toward CAS methodologies, it is important to remember Doran's earlier injunction on the need to address some of the fundamental ontological problems with an artificial-societies approach or, more pointedly, in the words of O'Sullivan and Haklay (2000), "is the world agent-based?"

Darwinian Archaeologies

Related to the previously noted agent-based developments is the growth of a parallel research area in simulation studies as a consequence of recent developments in Darwinian archaeologies (e.g., Maschner 1996; Barton and Clarke 1997). This research is involved in exploring potential analogies between genetic and cultural transmission as an aid to understanding the mechanisms of culture change. Notable examples include Neiman's (1995) simulation of artifact style frequency distributions by analogy with cultural drift and mutation, Bentley and Maschner's (2001) evolutionary approach to stylistic change, and Shennan's (2001) work on cultural transmission theory. Related studies invoking biological exemplars (e.g., Steele et al. 1998; Zubrow 1990), and particularly population biology, are in many ways a continuation of a long tradition of interest in behavioral ecology and testify to the vigorous interest in evolutionary approaches within archaeology. For example, Shennan and Wilkinson (2001) have applied an explicitly evolutionary approach to the study of change in pottery decoration from early Neolithic central Europe, and Shennan (2002) has sought to explore the relationships between genetic and cultural traits as the basis for a new evolutionary framework. The increasing popularity of these neo-Darwinian approaches promises a likely increase in the number of simulation studies over the next few years.

Alternative Readings of Complexity

Challenges to the epistemological foundations within which the dominant scientific paradigm is situated have emerged in recent years (e.g., Berdoulay 1989; Hodder 1992, 2000; Shanks and Tilley 1987b), and this has led to specific critiques of the state of modeling in archaeology (e.g., Yoffee 1994; McGlade 1995, 1997a,

1999, 2002). Significantly, the largely instrumentalist nature of archaeological modeling has been questioned by McGlade (1997a, 2002), particularly with respect to the ability of current modeling paradigms to deal with (1) the coevolution of socionatural systems, (2) social inequalities and power relations, and (3) the representation of cultural knowledge. These issues are centered on the need to approach the modeling problematic from a pluralistic perspective—one that recognizes the need to create an alternative reading of the construction of archaeological knowledge and consequently its modelization (McGlade 1995a, 1995b, 1997a, 1999). Conceptually, this approach to complexity is the opposite of the hardwired artificial-societies philosophy promoted by the Santa Fe researchers. From a methodological perspective, it argues not for the ontological certainty of a genetic algorithm but rather for an integrated multiscalar modeling architecture, one that privileges neither top-down nor bottom-up methods. It is suggested that the limitations of such approaches can be obviated through a hybrid methodology, one that is more attuned to the manner societal systems can oscillate between hierarchical (top-down) and heterarchical (bottom-up) organizational structures.

What this means is that explanation (such as it can ever exist) is a domain characterized by multiple perspectives, a species of thick description wherein multiple representations (maps) can coexist. Importantly, this is not simply a descent into a type of relativist free-for-all but rather a more rigorous investigation of the structural, functional, and conceptual diversity that characterizes all complex systems. The conceptual pluralism implied by this latter point stresses the need for multiple lines of converging evidence for any understanding of complex, human-modified ecosystems (cf. Holling 1995).

A fundamental aspect of this approach, according to McGlade (1995), is that it opposes the conventionally held definition of models as abstract representations of some real-world phenomena and replaces this with the notion of models as a dialogic resource—the carrier of multiple possible arguments and formalizations—a sketchbook of experimental scenarios. Within this schema four basic knowledge domains are identified as forming the basis of any model of complexity: *conceptual, de-*

scriptive, instrumental, and dialogic, and these are correlated with specific model representations (McGlade 2002).

Summary

In general, the meeting of complexity theory and archaeology has produced a new, fertile terrain for simulation research, and the current popularity of agent-based approaches (despite a number of limiting assumptions) suggests they will come to play an increasingly influential role over the next decade. More specifically, the embeddedness of agent-based models within GIS platforms, now de rigueur in fields such as biology, ecology, and environmental management, can also be expected to experience growth within archaeology. However welcome these developments are, and mindful of archaeology's previous history with new "toys," they must be treated with some caution. For this reason, the underlying assumptions of these models, both conceptual and methodological, must be clearly understood. For example, the structure of many agent-based models assumes a one-way causation, i.e., from the individual to an emergent collective (e.g., Epstein and Axtell 1996); thus the social can emerge from the individual but not the other way round. Additionally, the notion underlying these models is that the structure and changes within societal groups can readily be reduced to the decisions and actions of individuals—clearly a contentious issue, though one that has received little discussion in the literature. As O'Sullivan and Haklay (2000) have pointed out, these methodological individualist underpinnings are in fact common to the reductive ontology of many models flying under the banner of CASs. One obvious problem with such models of artificial societies is that they are situated in a *computational* world and care must be taken to avoid the real danger in assuming a homologous relationship between computational complexity and the nature of complexity exhibited by sociocultural systems (Yoffee 1994; McGlade 2002).

On the other hand, it is clear that the discrete nature of multiagent models renders them eminently useful for investigations into a variety of complex structural (morphogenetic) issues, particularly those related to emergent phenomena. However, from an archaeological or anthropological perspective, such model solutions will have meaning only insofar as they are harnessed to more sophisticated readings of social-natural interaction, especially agency—paradoxically, perhaps the most weakly defined aspect of these models.

The Future: Some Epistemological Issues

Although the future for simulation modeling in archaeology appears perhaps brighter than it has done for a number of years, a number of issues and problems require attention in the next phase of simulation research.

Instrumentalist Concerns

From a general perspective, there is a sense that current simulation research is consistent with the historical nature of computer-based modeling in archaeology; that is, it is largely methodologically driven, and this essentially instrumentalist position has meant that too little attention has been focused on theory building. In particular, attention needs to be devoted to issues of social interaction and organization and the way that communicative action is inevitably bound up with issues of power and legitimation. An understanding of the preeminence of social power as a prerequisite to understanding human societal systems is curiously absent from multiagent and DAI approaches (Castelfranchi 1990). Additionally, as Wright (2000:382) has pointed out, the representation of cultural knowledge is weakly developed in models purporting to represent social and cultural change.

Temporalities

Clearly, more research must be devoted to one of the central aspects of simulation methodology, *time*; typically, simulation models in archaeology display a naive conception of long-term change. At their root, there is an inadequate understanding of temporalities and the way they interact in social-natural contexts to produce coevolutionary dynamics (McGlade 1995a, 1995b, 1999). Despite some archaeologists' continuing assertions to the contrary, the long term is not simply the cumulative product of a series of discrete events. In effect, more attention needs to be devoted to representing the multitemporalities that constitute ecological and social event structures and whose interpenetration creates particular societal signatures at differing spatiotemporal scales.

Ontological Reduction

Equally, there is a need for a rapprochement between complex causality, temporality, and the new evolutionary synthesis that is the outcome, not of any reductionist epistemology, but of a revised view of complexity theory, one that must critically examine its epistemological and ontological foundations. For example, the dominant epistemology underwriting current simulation studies is reductionist and, as I have earlier noted, displays a disconcerting mapping of the biological onto the social.

Although it is abundantly clear that the nature of social interaction and organization, with all their attendant irregularities and idiosyncrasies, precludes any exact homology with the processes that operate in the natural sciences, nevertheless I shall argue here that the symbolic logic underpinning simulation models—particularly those concerned with nonlinear phase transitions and structural transformations—has a fundamental contribution to make to the elucidation of societal structuring. As I have intimated, to emphasize the possibility of a mathematical description of a particular social phenomenon does not mean that the phenomenon under investigation is *equivalent* to its mathematical description. Societal phenomena are, after all, irreducible on account of (1) the intrinsic complexity of social systems and (2) their existence as dynamic, open systems, subject to matter, energy, and information exchange and hence evolution. Rather, what it does stress is the possibility of constructing formal analogs, or indeed metaphors, that, as with their linguistic counterparts, serve both to heighten our awareness or understanding of a particular entity or process and to pre-sent a creative solution in a lateral, descriptive alternative.

Methodological Individualism

Contemporary society is characterized by an individualist rather than a collectivist philosophy. In fact this is consistent with much of our late-twentieth-century preoccupations in the liberal industrial West. These ideas are manifest in an aversion for top-down, macroscale perspectives and an avid espousal of methodological individualist approaches. Archaeology in consequence has become interested in recovering the individual in prehistory as the basic unit of analysis, and the diffusion of agent-based modeling can be seen as a direct consequence of this trend, focusing attention on the capacity of individual events and microscale behavior to generate global structure. Caution needs to be exerted, however, because as I have pointed out, intrinsic structural problems exhibited by agent architectures, i.e., the fact that collective structure can emerge from the individual but not the other way around, have potentially debilitating ramifications for any modeling of societal systems. It needs to be remembered that prehistoric societies were frequently defined by group- and community-based identities, where individual agency, for example, was normally constrained by specific cultural contexts.

Master Narratives: Universalist Explanation

The real problem is that by pursuing an evolutionary master narrative based on adaptive evolution and the universalist assumptions of edge-of-chaos phenomena, we are in danger of undermining the real lessons of nonlinear dynamics and indeed, the intrinsic nature of complexity itself. It needs to be remembered that a focus on chaos and complexity is not simply the addition of another set of analytic tools: it is something far more radical. Rather, it undermines our treasured, reassuring ideas of order and hierarchical structuring—the logical systems that have underpinned Western science since Aristotle. More radically still, it irreversibly alters our comfortable notions of causality, demonstrating how structure can be the outcome of a sequence of contingent events that collectively can generate unpredictable evolutions (Gould 1991). It follows that any analysis of societal systems thus must take into account the possibility that such trajectory discontinuity and developmental cul-de-sacs may lie behind the *longue durée* of sociocultural evolution. Recent interest in searching for the laws of complexity may ultimately find them illusory. Rather, diversity and its propensity to create novelty is the leitmotif of all evolutionary processes, whether biological or social, and it is perhaps to the investigation of such phenomena that future simulation studies in archaeology must turn.

Conclusion

Contrary to the aspirations of some archaeologists, there is no mathematics of culture change waiting to be uncovered; clearly the pursuit of such an idea, apart from its inherent reductionism, is a chimera. Culture, being more than the sum of its myriad and complex parts, is irreducible and yields only partial and incomplete explanations to the interrogative methods of symbolic logic and other algebraic formulations. On the other hand, the tools of mathematical inquiry can be used to gain insight into specific sets of relationships occurring between selected variables. This more focused use of simulation is consistent with Rosen's (1997) comments when he argues that simulation modeling, of necessity, occupies a restricted domain in archaeological inquiry. It is thus concomitant upon archaeologists to use simulation methods to explore this territory as rigorously as possible.

C. H. Waddington—one of the great pioneers of mathematical biology—was correct in identifying models as tools for thought—nothing more, nothing less. To reify them or to accord them more status than this is as much a fallacy as it is an intellectual conceit. On the other hand, the power of formal modeling techniques must not be ignored or disregarded as the pastime of computer buffs. Their utility lies in their ability to contribute both creative and diverse interpretations of a given problem; they provide an important means of access from what is known to what is unknown. Thus explanatory phenomena in archaeology—at all scales of investigation, from interactions at the individual or household level to the interpretation of events as long-term history—can be greatly enhanced by a rigorous and problem-oriented application of simulation modeling procedures. Whether as quantitative or qualitative experiments, metaphors, direct analogues, or similes, they operate as indispensable heuristic devices.

In the final analysis, simulation is clearly not a species of magic perpetrated by a computer-obsessed elite nor is it the panacea oft claimed by proponents of the new archaeology or more recent neoprocessualists; its powers of prognostication are decidedly limited. Rather, the real utility of simulation studies as we move into the new millennium lies in the provision of an experimental, creative arena within which archaeologists can conduct a variety of theoretical and methodological inquiries, remaining mindful of the age-old modeler's proviso: garbage in, garbage out.

Notes

1. In fact more recent work has cast doubt on the notion of a Mayan collapse, focusing instead on a shift in dominance from one region (the southern lowlands of Yucatán) to another (the northern lowlands).

2. It is, however, worth noting Renfrew's (p. 346) disclaimer (conveniently omitted by critics) that "the model proposed cannot be regarded as simulating in any meaningful sense, the early development of Aegean civilization."

3. This rejection of computer-aided modeling was of course not particular to archaeology and was being played out across the social sciences generally; indeed, geographers had trodden this path before and were engaged in a type of internecine warfare in which all debates were framed in a reductive polarity as each side searched for the intellectual high ground represented by epistemological purity.

4. It needs to be remembered that this was essentially a Eurocentric debate, because postprocessual debates were largely absent from Americanist theory; in fact, the empiricist and pragmatic nature of archaeology in the United States was largely hostile to structuralist and poststructuralist thought.

5. It is something of a curiosity that the contribution of this seminal research within the history of chaos theory has been seriously downplayed by Americanist authors.

6. From the chronological perspective adopted here, this volume, as the proceedings of a 1990 Cambridge conference, is problematic because a number of its research concerns fit neatly into our second-wave classification, whereas on the other hand, the focus on chaos and complexity aligns it with more recent theoretical developments.

References

Adamic, L. A., and B. A. Huberman
1999 The Nature of Markets in the World Wide Web. Xerox Palo Alto Research Center, Palo Alto, California.

Adams, R. N.
1988 *The Eighth Day: Social Evolution and the Self-Organization of Energy.* University of Texas Press, Austin.

Aldenderfer, M. S.
1981a Simulation for archaeology: An introductory essay. In *Simulations in Archaeology*, edited by J. A. Sabloff, pp. 11–49. University of New Mexico Press, Albuquerque.
1981b Creating assemblages by computer simulation: The development and use of ABSIM. In *Simulations in Archaeology*, edited by J. A. Sabloff, pp. 67–118. University of New Mexico Press, Albuquerque.

Allen, P. M.
1982a Self-organization in the Urban System. In *Self-organization and Dissipative Structures: Applications in the Physical and Social Sciences*, edited by W. C. Shieve and P. M. Allen, pp. 132–158. University of Texas Press, Austin.
1982b The genesis of structure in social systems: The paradigm of self-organization. In *Theory and Explanation in Archaeology*, edited by A. C. Renfrew, M. J. Rowlands, and B. A. Segraves, pp. 347–374. Academic Press, London.

Allen, P. M., and J. M. McGlade
1987 Evolutionary Drive: The effects of microscopic diversity, error-making and noise. *Foundations of Physics* 17(7):723–738.

Ammerman, A. J., and L. L. Cavalli-Sforza
1973 A population model for the diffusion of early farming in Europe. In *The Explanation of Culture Change*, edited by A. C. Renfrew, pp. 342–357. Duckworth, London.

Axelrod, R., and M. D. Cohen
1999 *Harnessing Complexity: Organizational Implications of a Scientific Frontier.* The Free Press, New York.

Bak, P.
1996 *How Nature Works: The Science of Self-Organized Criticality.* Springer-Verlag, New York.

Bak, P., and K. Chen
1991 Self-Organized Criticality. *Scientific American* 264(1): 46–53.

Bak, P., C. Tang, and K. Weisenfeld
1988 Self-Organized Criticality. *Physical Review A* 38: 364–374.

Bapty, I., and T. Yates
    1990   *Archaeology after Structuralism: Post Structuralism and the Practice of Archaeology.* Cambridge University Press, Cambridge.

Barton, C. M., and G. A. Clarke (editors)
    1997   *Rediscovering Darwin: Evolutionary Theory and Archaeological Explanation.* Archaeological Papers of the American Anthropological Association No. 7. American Anthropological Association, Washington, D.C.

Bentley, R. A., and H. D. G. Maschner
    2001   Stylistic change as a self-organized critical phenomenon: An archaeoloigcal study incomplexity. *Journal of Archaeological Method and Theory* 8(1).
    2003   *Complex Systems and Archaeology.* University of Utah Press.

Berdoulay, V.
    1989   Place, meaning and discourse in French language geography. In *The Power of Place,* edited by J. Agnew and J. Duncan, pp. 124–139. Unwin Hyman, London.

Bintliff, J. L.
    1997   Catastrophe, Chaos and Complexity: The Death, Decay and Rebirth of Towns from Antiquity to Today. *Journal of European Archaeology* 52:67–90
    1999   Structure, contingency, narrative and timelessness. In *Structure and Contingency: Evolutionary Processes in Life and Human Society,* edited by J. Bintliff, pp. 132–148. Leicester University Press, Leicester.

Bogucki, P.
    2000   How agriculture came to north-central Europe. In *Europe's First Farmers,* edited by T. D. Price, pp. 197–218. Cambridge University Press, Cambridge.

Byrne, D.
    1998   *Complexity Theory and the Social Sciences.* Routledge, London.

Castelfranchi, C.
    1990   Social power: A point missed in multi-agent DAI and HCL. In *Decentralised AI,* edited by V. Demazeau and J. P. Mueller, pp. 49–63. Elsevier, Amsterdam.

Chadwick, A. J.
    1978   A computer simulation of Mycenean settlement. In *Simulation Studies in Archaeology,* edited by I. Hodder, pp. 47–57. Cambridge University Press, Cambridge.

Checkland, P.
    1981   *Systems Thinking, Systems Practice.* John Wiley, Chichester.

Clarke, D. L.
1968   *Analytical Archaeology.* Methuen, London.
1972   *Models in Archaeology.* Methuen, London.

Cooke, Kenneth L.
1979   Mathematical approaches to culture change. In *Transformations: Mathematical Approaches to Culture Change,* edited by C. Renfrew and K. L. Cooke, pp. 45–81. Academic Press, London.

Cordell, L. S.
1972   Settlement Pattern Changes at Wetherill Mesa, Colorado: A Test Case for Computer Simulation in Archaeology. Unpublished. PhD dissertation, University of California, Santa Barbara.

Dean, J. S., G. J. Gumerman, J. M. Epstein, R. L. Axtell, A. C. Swedlund, M. T. Parker, and S. McCarroll
2000   Understanding Anasazi culture change through agent-based modelling. In *Dynamics in Human and Primate Societies,* edited by T. A. Kohler and G. J. Gumerman, pp. 179–205. Santa Fe Institute Studies in the Sciences of Complexity, Oxford University Press, Oxford.

Doran, J. E.
1970   Systems theory, computer simulations, and archaeology. *World Archaeology* 1:289–298.
1982   A computational model of socio-cultural systems and their dynamics. In *Theory and Explanation in Archaeology: The Southampton Conference,* edited by A. C. Renfrew, M. J. Rowlands, and B. A. Segraves, pp. 375–388. Academic Press, New York.

Doran, J. E., and F. R. Hodson
1975   *Mathematics and Computers in Archaeology.* Edinburgh University Press, Edinburgh.

Doran, J. E., M. Palmer, N. Gilbert, and P. Mellars
1994   The EOS project: Modelling Upper Palaeolithic Social Change. In *Simulating Societies: The Computer Simulation of Social Phenomena,* edited by N. Gilbert and J. Doran, pp. 195–222. UCL Press, London.

Edmonds, B.
1996   What is Complexity? In *The Evolution of Complexity,* edited by F. Heylighen and D. Aerts. Kluwer, Dordrecht.

Epstein, J. M., and R. Axtell
1996   *Growing Artificial Societies: Social science from the bottom up.* Brookings Press and MIT Press, Boston.

Flannery, K. V.
1968   The Olmec and the Valley of Oaxaca: A model of inter-regional interaction on Formative times. In *Proceedings of the Dumbarton Oaks Conference on the Olmec,* edited by E. P. Benson, pp. 119–130. Dumbarton Oaks, Washington, D.C.

1972   Cultural Evolution of Civilizations. *Annual Review of Ecology and Systematics* 3:399–426.

Forrester, J.
1968   *Principles of Systems.* Wright-Allen Press, Cambridge, Massachusetts.
1973   *World Dynamics.* Wright-Allen Press, Cambridge, Massachusetts.

Fritz, J., and F. Plog
1970   The nature of archaeological explanation. *American Antiquity* 35:405–412.

Gardner, M. R., and W. R. Ashby
1970   Connectance of large dynamical (cybernetic) systems: Critical values for stability. *Nature* 228:784.

Gell-Mann, M.
1992   Complexity and Complex Adaptive Systems. In *The Evolution of Human Languages,* edited by J. A. Hawkins and M. Gell-Mann, pp. 1–18. Santa Fe Institute Studies in the Sciences of Complexity, Proceedings Vol. XI. Addison-Wesley, Redwood City, California.

Gilbert, N.
1997   A Simulation of the Structure of Academic Science. *Sociological Research Online.* 2(2). Electronic document, http://www.socresonline.org.uk/socresonline/2/2/3.html.

Gilbert, N., and J. Doran (editors)
1994   *Simulating Societies: The Computer Simulation of Social Phenomena.* UCL Press, London.

Gould, S. J.
1991   *Wonderful Life: The Burgess Shale and the Nature of History.* Penguin, Harmondsworth.

Gumerman, G. J., and M. Gell-Mann (editors)
1994   *Understanding Complexity in the Prehistoric Southwest.* Santa Fe Institute Studies in the Sciences of Complexity. Proceedings Vol. XVI. Addison–Wesley, Reading, Massachusetts.

Haken, H.
1977   *Synergetics.* Springer-Verlag, Berlin.

Hanneman, R., and S. Patrick
1997   On the uses of computer-assisted simulation modelling in the social sciences. *Sociological Research Online* 2(2):1–7. Electronic document, http://www.socresonline.org.uk/socresonline/2/2/5.html.

Harvey, D. L., and M. H. Reed
1994   The evolution of dissipative social systems. *Journal of Social and Evolutionary Systems* 17(4):371–411.

Hayles, N. K.
    1991   *Chaos and Order.* University of Chicago Press, Chicago.

Hodder, Ian
    1977   Some new directions in spatial analysis in archaeology. In *Spatial Analysis in Archaeology*, edited by D. L. Clarke. Academic Press, London.
    1978   (editor) *Simulation Studies in Archaeology.* Cambridge University Press, Cambridge.
    1982a   *Symbols in action: Ethnoarchaeological studies of material culture.* Cambridge University Press, Cambridge.
    1982b   (editor) *Symbolic and Structural Archaeology.* Cambridge University Press, Cambridge.
    1986   *Reading the Past.* Cambridge University Press, Cambridge
    1992   *Theory and Practice in Archaeology.* London, Routledge.
    2000   *Towards Reflexive Method in Archaeology: The example of Çatalhoyuk.* British Institute of Archaeology at Ankara, and McDonald Institute for Archaeological Research.

Hodder, I., and C. Orton
    1976   *Spatial Analysis in Archaeology.* Cambridge University Press, Cambridge.

Holland, J. H.
    1975   *Adaptation in natural and artificial systems: An introductory analysis with applications to biology, control and artificial intelligence.* University of Michigan Press, Ann Arbor.
    1992   *Adaptation in Natural and Artificial Systems: An Introductory Analysis with Applications to Biology, Control and Artificial Intelligence.* MIT Press, Cambridge, Massachusetts.

Holling, C. S.
    1995   What Barriers? What Bridges? In *Barriers and Bridges to the Renewal of Ecosystems and Institutions*, edited by L. H. Gunderson, C. S. Holling and S. S. Light, pp. 3–34. Columbia University Press, New York.

Hosler, D., J. A. Sabloff, and D. Runge
    1977   Simulation Model Development: A Case Study of the Classic Maya Collapse. In *Social Processes in Maya Prehistory*, edited by N. Hammond, pp. 552–590. Academic Press, London.

Judge, W. J., and Sebastian, L. (editors)
    1988   *Quantifying the Present and predicting the Past: Theory, Method and Application of Archaeological Predictive Modeling*, pp. 1–18. Bureau of Land Management, Denver, Colorado.

Kauffman, S. A.
    1991   Coevolution to the edge of chaos: coupled fitness landscapes, poised states, and coevolutionary avalanches. *Journal of Theoretical Biology* 149:467–505.

1993   *The Origins of Order: Self-organization and Selection in Evolution.* Oxford University Press, Oxford.

1994   Whispers from Carnot: The Origins of Order and Principles of Adaptation in Complex Nonequilibrium Systems. In *Complexity: Metaphors, Models and Reality,* edited by G. A. Cowan, D. Pines, and D. Meltzer, Vol. XIX, pp. 83–136, Santa Fe Institute Studies in the Sciences of Complexity. Addison-Wesley, Reading, Massachusetts.

1995   *At Home in the Universe: The Search for Laws of Self-Organization and Complexity.* Oxford University Press, Oxford.

Kohler, T. A.
1993   News from the North American Southwest: Prehistory on the Edge of Chaos. *Journal of Archaeological Research* 1:267–321.

Kohler, T. A., and E. Carr
1997   Swarm Based Modelling of Settlement Systems in Southwestern North America. In *Archaeological Applications of GIS,* edited by I. Johnson and M. North. Archaeological Methods Series 5. Sydney University, Sydney.

Kohler, Timothy A., and George J. Gumerman (editors)
2000   *Dynamics of Human and Primate Societies: Agent-based Modeling of Social and Spatial Processes.* Oxford University Press, Oxford.

Kohler, T. A., and C. R. Van West
1996   The calculus of self interest in the development of cooperation: Sociopolitical development and risk among the northern Anasazi. In *Evolving Complexity and Environment: Risk in the Prehistoric Southwest,* edited by Joseph A. and Bonnie B. Tainter, pp. 169–196. Santa Fe Institute Studies in the Sciences of Complexity. Proceedings Vol. XXIV. Addison-Wesley, Reading, Massachusetts.

Kohler et al.
2000   Be There Then: A Modelling Approach to Settlement Determinants and Spatial Efficiency Among Late Ancestral Pueblo Populations of the Mesa Verde Region, U.S. Southwest. In *Dynamics of Human and Primate Societies: Agent-based Modeling of Social and Spatial Processes,* edited by Timothy A. Kohler and George J. Gumerman, pp. 145–178. Oxford University Press, Oxford.

Kvamme, K. L.
1989   Geographic Information Systems in regional archaeological research and data management. In *Archaeological Method and Theory,* Vol. 1, edited by Michael Shiffer, pp. 139–203. University of Arizona Press, Tucson.

Lake, M. W.
2000   MAGICAL, computer simulation of Mesolithic foraging. In *Dynamics in Human and Primate Societies: Agent-based modelling of Social and*

Spatial Processes, edited by T. A. Kohler and G. A. Gumerman, pp. 107–143. Oxford University Press, Oxford.

2001a The use of pedestrian modelling in archaeology, with an example from the study of cultural learning. *Environment and Planning B: Planning and Design* 28:385–403.

2001b Numerical modelling in archaeology. In *Handbook of Archaeological Sciences*, edited by D. R. Brothwell and A. M. Pollard, pp. 723–732. John Wiley, Chichester.

Lake, M. W., and S. J. Mithen
  1998 The MAGICAL Project: Integrating simulation modelling and GIS analysis in archaeology with an application to Mesolithic Scotland. Manuscript on file.

Langton, C. G.
  1989 Artificial Life. In *Artificial Life,* edited by C. G. Langton, pp. 1–47. Addison-Wesley, Redwood City, California.

  1990 Computation at the edge of chaos: Phase transitions and emergent computation. *Physica D* 42:12–37.

  1992 Life on the edge of chaos. In *Artificial Life II,* pp. 41–91. Addison-Wesley, New York.

Lansing, J. S.
  1991 *Priests and Programmers: Technologies of Power in the Engineered Landscape of Bali.* Princeton University Press, Princeton, New Jersey.

Lansing J. Stephen and James N. Kremer
  1993 Emergent Properties of Balinese Water Temple Networks: Coadaptation on a Rugged Fitness Landscape. *American Anthropologist* 95(1):97–114.

Levison, Michael, R. Gerard Ward, and John W. Webb
  1973 *The Settlement of Polynesia: A Computer Simulation.* University of Minnesota Press, Minneapolis.

Lewin, R.
  1992 *Complexity: Life on the Edge of Chaos.* Macmillan, New York.

Lowe, J. W. G.
  1985 *The Dynamics of the Apocalypse.* University of New Mexico Press, Albuquerque.

McGlade, J.
  1987 Chronos and the Oracle: Some thoughts on Time, Time-Scales and Simulation. *Archaeolgical Review from Cambridge* 6(1):21–31.

  1990 The Emergence of Structure: Modelling Socio-Cultural Change in the Later Prehistory of Wessex. Unpublished PhD dissertation, University of Cambridge.

  1995a Archaeology and the ecodynamics of human-modified landscapes. *Antiquity* 69:113–132.

1995b An integrative multiscalar framework for human Ecodynamic research in the Vera basin, south-east Spain. In *L'homme et la dégredation de l'environnement*. XVe Rencontres Internationales d'Archéologie et d'histoire d'Antibes. Éditions APDCA, Juan-Les-Pins.

1997a GIS and integrated archaeological knowledge systems. In *Archaeological Applications of GIS: Proceedings of Colloquium II, UISPP XIIIth Congress, Forli, Italy, September 1996*, edited by L. Johnson and M. North. Sydney University Archaeological Methods Series 5. Archaeological Computing Laboratory, Sydney. CD-ROM.

1997b The Limits of Social Control: Coherence and Chaos in a Prestige-Goods Economy. In *Archaeology: Time and structured transformation*, edited by S. E. van der Leeuw and J. McGlade, pp. 298–330, Routledge, London.

1999 The times of History: Archaeology, narrative and nonlinear causality. In *Archaeological Approaches to Time*, edited by T. Murray, pp. 139–163. Routledge, London.

2002 In *Complex Systems and Archaeological Research: Empirical and Theoretical Applications*, edited by A. Bentley and H. D. G. Maschner. University of Utah Press, Salt Lake City.

McGlade, J., and S. E. van der Leeuw
1997 Introduction: Archaeology and nonlinear dynamics—new approaches to long-term change. In *Time, process and structured Transformation in Archaeology*, edited by S. E. van der Leeuw and J. McGlade, pp. 1–32. Routledge, London.

Maschner, H. D. G. (editor)
1996 *Darwinian Archaeologies*. Plenum, New York.

Minar, N., R. Burkhart, Langton, C., and M. Askenazi
1996 The Swarm Simulation system: A tool-kit for building multi-agent simulations. Electronic document, http://www.santafe.edu/projects/swarm/. June 21, 1996, Santa Fe Institute, Santa Fe.

Mithen, S. J.
1990 *Thoughtful Foragers: A study of prehistoric decision making*. Cambridge University Press, Cambridge.

1991 A cybernetic wasteland? Rationality, emotion and Mesolithic foraging. *Proceedings of the Prehistoric Society* 57(2):9–14.

1994 Simulating prehistoric hunter-gatherer societies. In *Simulating Societies: The computer simulation of social phenomena*, edited by N. Gilbert and J. Doran, pp. 165–193. UCL Press, London.

Neiman, F. D.
1995 Stylistic variation in evolutionary perspective: Inferences from decorative diversity and interassemblage distance in Illinois Woodland ceramic assemblages. *American Antiquity* 60:7–36.

Newman, M. E. J.
  1996 Self-Organized Criticality, Evolution and the Fossil Extinction Record. *Proceedings of the Royal Society London B* 263:1605–1610.
  1997 Evidence for Self-Organized Criticality in Evolution. *Physica D* 107:293–296.

Nicolis, G., and I. Prigogine
  1977 *Self-Organization in Non-Equilibrium Systems*. Wiley International, New York.

O'Sullivan, D., and M. Haklay
  2000 Agent-based models and individualism: Is the world agent-based? *Environment and Planning A* 32(8):1409–1425.

Olivier, L.
  1995 The Shapes of Time: An archaeology of funerary assemblages in the West Halstatt province. Unpublished PhD dissertation, University of Cambridge.
  1999 The Hochdorf 'princely' grave and the question of the nature of archaeological funerary assemblages. In *Time and Archaeology*, edited by T. Murray, pp. 109–138. Routledge, London.

Pareto, V.
  1896 *Cours d'economie politique*. Lausanne.

Parrott, L., and Kok, R.
  2000 Incorporating complexity in ecosystem modelling. *Complexity International* 7:1–19. Electronic document, http://www.csu.edu.au/ci/.

Prigogine, I.
  1978 Time, Structure and Fluctuations. *Science* 201:777–785.
  1980 *From Being to Becoming: Time and Complexity in the Physical Sciences*. W. H. Freeman and Company, New York.

Prigogine, I., and I. Stengers
  1984 *Order out of Chaos: Man's New Dialogue with Nature*. Bantam, New York.

Reed, M. H. and Harvey, D. L.
  1992 The new science and the old: Complexity and realism in the social sciences. *Journal for the Theory of Social behaviour* 22:356–379.

Renfrew, A.C.
  1972 *The Emergence of Civilisation*. London.
  1978 Trajectory discontinuity and morphogenesis, the implications of catastrophe theory for archaeology. *American Antiquity* 43:203–244.
  1979 System collapse as social transformation. In *Transformations: Mathematical approaches to culture change*, edited by A. C. Renfrew and K. L. Cooke, pp. 481–506. Academic Press, London.

Renfrew, Colin M., J. Rowlands, and B.A. Segraves (editors)
  1982 *Theory and Explanation in Archaeology*. Academic Press, New York.

Renfrew, Colin, and Kenneth L. Cooke
   1979   *Transformations: Mathematical Approaches to Culture Change.* Academic Press, New York.

Renfrew, A. C., and T. Poston
   1979   Discontinuities in the endogenous change of settlement pattern. In *Transformations: Mathematical approaches to culture change,* edited by A. C. Renfrew and K. L. Cooke, pp. 425–436. Academic Press, London.

Reynolds, R. G.
   1986   An adaptive computer model for the evolution of plant collecting and early agriculture in the eastern valley of Oaxaca. In *Guila Naquitz: Archaic foraging and early agriculture in Oaxaca, Mexico,* edited by K. V. Flannery, pp. 439–507. Academic Press, London.
   1997   Why does cultural evolution proceed at a faster rate than biological evolution? In *Time, Process and Structured Transformation in Archaeology,* edited by S. E. van der Leeuw and J. McGlade, pp. 269–282. Routledge, London.

Rosen, Robert
   1997   Are our modelling paradigms non-generic? In *Time, Process and Structured Transformation in Archaeology,* edited by S. van der Leeuw and J. McGlade, pp. 383–395. Routledge, New York.

Ruelle, D.
   1991   *Chance and Chaos.* Princeton University Press, Princeton, New Jersey.

Sabloff, Jeremy
   1981   *Simulations in Archaeology.* School of American Research advanced seminar series. University of New Mexico Press, Albuquerque.

Shanks, M., and C. Tilley
   1987a *Social Theory and Archaeology.* Polity Press, Cambridge.
   1987b *Re-Constructing Archaeology: Theory and Practice.* New Studies in Archaeology. Cambridge University Press, Cambridge.

Shennan, S. J.
   2001   Demography and cultural innovation: A model and its implications for the development of Modern Human culture. *Cambridge Archaeological Journal* 11:5–16.
   2002   *Genes, Memes and Human History.* Thames and Hudson, London.

Shennan, S. J., and J. R. Wilkinson
   2001   Ceramic style change and neutral evolution: A case study from Neolithic Europe. *American Antiquity* 66(4):577–593.

Shermer, M.
   1995   Exorcising Laplace's demon: Chaos and antichaos, history and metahistory. *History and Theory* 34:59–81.

Steele, J., J. Adams, and T. Sluckin
1998 Modelling palaeoindian dispersals. *World Archaeology* 30:286–305.

Swarm Development Group
1999 The Swarm Simulation System. Electronic document, http://www.swarm.org.

Thom, R.
1975 *Structural Stability and Morphogenesis.* Benjamin, Reading.

Thomas, D. H.
1972 A computer model of Great Basin Shoshonean subsistence and settlement patterns In *Models in Archaeology,* edited by D. L. Clarke. Methuen, London.

Thompson, J. M. T., and H. B. Stewart
1986 *Nonlinear Dynamics and Chaos.* John Wiley, Chichester.

Turcotte, D. L.
1997 *Fractals and Chaos in Geology and Geophysics.* Cambridge University Press, Cambridge.

Van der Leeuw, S. E.
1982 How objective can we become? Some reflections on the nature of the relationship between the archaeologist, his data and his interpretations. In *Theory and Explanation in Archaeology,* edited by C. Renfrew, M. Rowlands, and B. A. Segraves, pp. 431–458. Academic Press, London.

Van der Leeuw, S. E., and J. McGlade
1997a *Time, Process and Structured Transformation in Archaeology.* Routledge, London.
1997b Structural change and bifurcation in urban evolution: A nonlinear dynamical perspective. In *Archaeology: Time and structured transformation,* edited by S. E. van der Leeuw and J. McGlade, pp. 331–372. Routledge, London.

Van der Velde, P.
1987 Post-depositional decay: A simulation. *Analecta Praehistorica Leidensia* 20:168–175.

Van West, C. R., and T. A. Kohler
1995 A Time to Rend, A Time to Sew: New Perspectives on Northern Anasazi Sociopolitical Development in Later Prehistory. In M. Aldenderfer and H. D. G. Maschner (eds). *Anthropology, Space, and Geographic Information Systems.* Oxford University Press, Oxford, pp. 112–139.

Varela, F., H. Maturano, and R. Uribe
1974 Autopoiesis: The organization of living systems, its characterisation and a model. *Biosystems* 5:187–196.

Von Bertalanffy, L.
1968 *General Systems Theory.* George Braziller, New York.

Waddington, C.
   1977   *Evolution and consciousness.* Addison-Wesley, Reading, Massachusetts.

Waldrop, M.
   1992   *Complexity: The emerging science at the edge of order and chaos.* Simon and Schuster, New York.

Watson, P. J., C. Redman, and S. Leblanc
   1971   *Explanation in Archaeology: An explicitly scientific approach.* Academic Press, New York.

Westcott, K. L., and R. J. Brandon
   2000   *Practical Applications of GIS for Archaeologists: A Predictive Modeling Toolkit.* Taylor and Francis, London.

Willey, G. R., and D. B. Shimkin
   1973   The Mayan collapse: A summary view. In *The Classic Maya Collapse,* edited by T. P. Culbert, pp. 457–501. University of New Mexico Press, Albuquerque.

Wobst, H. M.
   1974   Boundary conditions for Palaeolithic social systems: A simulation approach. *American Antiquity* 39:147–178.
   1997   Modern hominids' unfolding sociality. *Antiquity* 71(272):475–485.

Wright, H. T.
   2000   Agent-based modelling of small scale societies: State of the art and future prospects. In *Dynamics of Human and Primate Societies: Agent-Based Modelling of Social and Spatial Processes,* edited by T. A. Kohler and G. J. Gumerman, pp. 373–385. Oxford University Press, Oxford.

Wright, H. T., and M. Zeder
   1977   The simulation of linear exchange systems under equilibrium conditions. In *Exchange Systems in Prehistory,* edited by T. Earle and J. Ericson, pp. 233–253. Academic Press, New York.

Yoffee, N.
   1994   Memorandum to Murray Gell-Mann concerning: The complications of Complexity in the prehistoric southwest. In *Understanding Complexity in the Prehistoric Southwest,* edited by G. J. Gumerman and M. Gell-Man, pp. 341–358. Santa Fe Institute Studies in the Science of Complexity. Proceedings Vol XVI, Reading, Massachusetts.

Zubrow, E. B. W.
   1971   Carrying capacity and dynamic equilibrium in the prehistoric Southwest. *American Antiquity* 36:127–138.
   1975   *Prehistoric carrying Capacity: A model.* Cummings, Menlo Park, California.
   1990   The depopulation of native America. *Antiquity* 64:754–765

16

Experimental Archaeology

Izumi Shimada

Experimental archaeology is a method of testing our ideas about and discovering the past through experiments. It has a long history and has been employed widely throughout the world in solving or shedding light on many archaeological issues. Introductory archaeology textbooks commonly speak of informative experiments or field testing of archaeological reconstruction. The rubric of experimental archaeology has subsumed everything from garbology (the systematic study of modern culture from its garbage and disposal behavior, e.g., Rathje and Murphy 1992) through the design and excavation of artificial, scale models of archaeological sites (e.g., Chilcott and Deetz 1964; Jewell 1963; Ashbee and Jewell 1998) to the raising of monumental structures (e.g., Mayan pyramids [Erasmus 1965], Easter Island *moai* statues [Van Tilbug and Ralston 1999], Stonehenge [Stone 1924; Richards and Whitby 1997]), to comparative, energy input-output studies of different agricultural techniques and tools (e.g., Mathieu and Meyer 1997; Saraydar and Shimada 1973), and to the trans-Pacific *Kon-Tiki* expedition (Heyerdahl 1950). Replication and related studies of ancient flintknapping techniques alone number in the hundreds (e.g., Graham et al. 1972; Johnson 1978; Schick and Toth 1993; Whittaker 1994). A journal specializing in experimental archaeology, *The Bulletin of Experimental Archaeology* (ISSN 0262-4176), was published between

1980 and 1990 by the University of Southampton. Conferences focused on this subject have been relatively common in the United States and Europe (e.g., Andrieux 1988).

The previous listing, far from exhaustive, amply illustrates the versatility of the methodology. Binford (1981:25, 29, 32) viewed experimental archaeology and complementary ethnoarchaeology as the two primary means by which to establish the middle range theories or "'Rosetta stones' that would permit accurate conversion from observations on statics [material remains] to statements about dynamics [the past culture]." It is a widely held impression that experimental archaeology has contributed greatly to the advancement of method and theory in archaeology. However, a critical evaluation of experimental designs, results, and their interpretations reveals the equivocal nature of this assessment.

The purpose of this chapter is to define the growth, logical structure, and limitations of experimental archaeology. It will also chart directions and how it can contribute more productively to the advancement of archaeology. The historical section is not intended to be a comprehensive review of the relevant literature (see Ascher 1961; Coles 1973, 1979; Graham et al. 1972; and Hester and Heizer 1973 for descriptions or critiques of experiments up to the late 1970s); instead, it is meant to highlight major developments in the growth of this approach and to provide background for later discussion of the essential features of the experiments and recommended procedures. The last section discusses persistent problems facing experimental archaeology and possible solutions using an illustrative case.

Growth of Experimental Archaeology: A Brief Review

Informal and short-term experiments using archaeological artifacts to determine their fabrication and functions are documented in Europe by the late seventeenth century. Trigger (1989:61–62) credits the Royal Society of London (founded in 1660), with its emphasis on observation, classification, and experimentation, with popularizing such experiments during the early eighteenth century. By the mid-nineteenth century, Scandinavian scholars had became a major force in archaeological experimentation. They had developed not only a sophisticated and holistic vision of prehistoric lifeways but also a correspondingly comprehensive methodology, including interdisciplinary investigation and experimental testing for a detailed technological and functional understanding of ancient implements (Coles 1973:160, 164; 1979:13). For example, J. J. Worsaae conducted experiments on archaeological formation processes, determining how animal remains entered the archaeological record by feeding diverse animal bones to dogs (Trigger 1989:7, 82). His contemporary Sven Nilsson, a Swedish zoologist, advocated the functional study of tools through systematic comparison of ethnographic data and experimentally produced use wear (Trigger 1989:80, 86, 98).

In American archaeology, the development of early functionalism during the late nineteenth and early twentieth centuries was closely interwoven with experimental studies to elucidate the function, usage, and manufacture of ancient tools (Trigger 1989:270–271). Coles (1979:26) observes that, by the end of the nineteenth century, "experiments with ancient sites, materials, objects and techniques were well-established as a legitimate exercise" in archaeological reconstruction. Ascher (1961a:793–794) sees these nineteenth- and early-twentieth-century "imitative" experiments as presaging modern (post–World War II) archaeological experiments. The nineteenth-century popularity of imitative experiments stemmed in large measure from the persistence of indigenous technologies and lifestyles in many parts of the world, which provided readily accessible analogue models (Coles 1979:3, 26–27). The decline in their popularity from about 1910 to 1945, on the other hand, was related to rapid global westernization and the shift of ethnographic studies away from technical aspects of material culture to political and social organization. The period spanning the two world wars was generally characterized by an "unending series of single isolated experiments" on technical issues, with a few exceptional studies (e.g., Pope 1923) that were larger in scale, thorough, and longer in duration (Coles 1979:27, 30; also see Ascher 1961a).

The post–World War II era saw a blossoming of experimental archaeology as a manifestation of the renewed functionalist emphasis in archaeology and the greater appreciation of scientific or objective methods of analysis brought about by the influx of innovations such as radiocarbon dating and elemental characterization. As alluded to earlier, Scandinavian archaeologists played a key role in the establishment of modern experimental archaeology. They emphasized rigorous comparative studies, long-term investigations built on multiple stages of interrelated experiments, and broadening the scope of investigation to include behavior related to the usage or manufacture of artifacts. One exemplary program was started by Hans-Ole Hansen (1962), who constructed full-scale replicas of prehistoric Danish houses by carefully utilizing archaeologically documented materials and techniques. His work was characterized by an imaginative approach and provided a model for subsequent house-building and destruction experiments that have been widely conducted in "living museums" throughout western Europe and the United States (Coles 1979:32; 152–153). Further, Hansen's study "played a vital role in interesting both archaeologists and the public in the value of full-sized replicas as well as in the auxiliary work that can be conducted within and around these structures" (Coles 1979:32).

The daring attempt by another Scandinavian, Thor Heyerdahl (1950, 1952), to cross the Pacific from Peru on a balsa raft, the *Kon-Tiki*, was well publicized and helped to put the experimental approach on the map, at least in the minds of the public, though skeptics pointed to the inconclusiveness of such imitative experiment. In general, Coles (1979:32) sees the shared theme of post–World War II experiments as a total commitment to appropriate materials and technology and search for "objective and observable truth."

Though Coles's assessment of the experiments of this era is generally positive, leading archeologists had mixed opinions regarding the potential of the experimental approach. Grahame Clark (1953:353), for example, observed that replicative flint-knapping experiments "have not . . . done more than demonstrate possible ways in which various forms could have been produced, and it is noteworthy that different experimenters have arrived at much the same result by different means." The inconclusive nature of experimental results and the principle of multiple solutions will be discussed later. Clark (1953:353), at the same time, recognized that experiments can be a cost-effective means of providing valuable insights and new perspectives on technological processes. H. L. Movius Jr. saw replicative experiments as a promising way out of the typological stalemate by focusing attention on the manufacturing process instead of the form of finished tools. At the same time, he recognized that "one should be familiar with the techniques themselves in order to detect them and assess their significance" (Movius 1953:165). A similar concern with the "amateur nature of the experiments" and attendant skepticism over their results was voiced by Semenov (1964:2), the Russian pioneer of use-wear studies. Problems of competence and practice effects (i.e., practice makes perfect) in enacting a given ancient activity persist to this day; they are considered later.

The Avdat and Shivta experimental farms in the Negev desert and the Experimental Earthwork on Overtown Down in Wiltshire, England, that were constructed, respectively, in 1958–1960 (Evenari et al. 1971) and 1960 (e.g., Ashbee and Jewell 1998; Jewell and Dimbleby 1966; also Bell et al. 1996) deserve special note here for their large-scale, long-term commitment, controlled character, and cautious documentation (including quantification of processes involved) and interpretation. The former were constructed as an integral part of an interdisciplinary investigation into the desert agriculture of the Iron Age (ca. first millennium B.C.) based on careful collection and management of runoff from occasional rains that typically amount to less than 100 mm per year (Evenari et al. 1971:2–3). A wide variety of fruit trees and shrubs as well as field (e.g., cereals, legumes, and vegetables) and pasture plants have been cultivated in reconstructed terraces at these farms (2.6 and 0.7 hectares, respectively). Critical variables such as the ratio of runoff to rainfall, crop yields, tree-growth rates, labor expenditures, soil moisture and nutrient levels, and evapotranspiration rate have been carefully monitored since the inception of the experiment, which continues today (Evenari et al. 1971:179–228).

At Overtown Down, for systematic assessment of natural factors and processes and their effects in transformation, the earthwork is being excavated at intervals of 2, 4, 8, 16, 32, 64 and

128 years. Though this project serves as a model for many archaeological site formation experiments, most of the recent studies of this genre (e.g., the effects of trampling on surface artifacts) simply do not measure up in most aspects of the experimental design.

By the beginning of the 1960s, there was a clear recognition of not only the potential but, more importantly, the limitations and challenges that faced experimental archaeology. In one of the few publications to appear to date on the basic epistemological and operational issues of experimental archaeology, Ascher (1961a:794) laments the stagnant and unsystematized nature of this field:

> [Its] potential has never been realized. The imitative experiment has failed to receive general acceptance because the evaluation of the procedures and results of such experiments are ambiguous. This ambiguity can be traced in part to the fact that the locus of the imitative experiment, and the theory and logic involved in executing imitative experiments, are unclear.

An even harsher criticism was voiced a generation later. Tringham (1978:171) argued that "experiments in archaeology have for the most part been justifiably ignored because of (1) their lack of a strong theoretical base and a resulting lack of general applicability in testing archaeological hypotheses . . . and (2) their lack of rigor and attention to scientific experimental procedure in design, execution, recording, and analysis." Regrettably, these criticisms are still largely applicable today.

To Ascher (1961a:793), imitative experiments "entail[ed] operations in which matter is shaped, or matter is shaped and used, in a manner simulative of the past" and were aimed at "testing beliefs about past human behavior." To fulfill the potential of experimental archaeology, Ascher (1961a) sought to add much more rigor to the derivation, formulation, and testing of specific inferences regarding past cultural behavior and application of the results of such testing. He (1961a:803, 807–808) emphasized the importance of assessing multiple working (i.e., plausible) hypotheses in this inferential process. His paper "Experimental Archaeology" (1961a) should be viewed as an integral part of his broader effort to clarify the basic processes and means involved in archaeological interpretation. Long preceding observations and studies by Binford (e.g.,

1981), Schiffer (e.g., 1976, 1987), and others (e.g., Grayson 1986:77–78; Trigger 1989:362–363), Ascher conducted ingeniously conceived archaeological experiments and ethnoarchaeological and archaeological formation studies toward this goal (e.g., Ascher 1961b, 1962, 1968).

In addition to his discussion of the essential components and logical structure underlying experiments in archaeology, Ascher (1961a:809–810) presented three basic guidelines that "both limit and direct an experiment."

1. The subject to be investigated in the proposed experiment (i.e., "objective material") "must be known to have been available, or could have been available, in the aboriginal setting."
2. The "effective material" or "material which is used to produce a change in the objective material or is changed through the use of the objective material . . . must be, or simulate, a means available to aboriginal people, or be in accord with a material which is known to have been or could have been available in an aboriginal setting." In a flintknapping experiment, for example, the objective materials are commonly chert or flint nodules; the effective materials, soft or hard hammer.
3. The experiment must be conducted within the potential and limitations of the "physical characteristics" (e.g., hardness of lithics) of the objective and effective materials.

These guidelines and the accompanying five-part experimental procedures are in essence a formalized version of what many Scandinavian experimenters were implicitly practicing in the immediate post–World War II era. Later, Coles (1973:15–16; 1977; 1979:46–48) and others (e.g., Reynolds 1978; Schiffer and Skibo 1987; Tringham 1978) elaborated on Ascher's guidelines and procedures, which will be detailed later. Suffice it to state here that his procedural outlines not only remain valid but continue to challenge us.

The 1970s saw a number of important developments in experimental archaeology that relate to the challenges and limitations identified earlier. One was a greater effort to combine ethnoarchaeology and the experimental approach as advocated by Nilsson more than 100 years earlier. Coles (1979:39; also 1973:17) declared that "ethnography is one of the most neglected fields of experimental archaeology." Skibo (1992:18) pointed out that ethnoarchaeology and experimental archaeology have the same focus on "the interface between material culture, on the one hand, and human behavior, organization, meaning, and environment, on the other" and the objective of "understanding the past by addressing questions with modern-day material culture." In hybrid "ethnographic experiments, the operators carry out activities in their own social context in patterns familiar to them or to their immediate ancestors" (Tringham 1978:171; e.g., Childs and Schmidt 1986; David and Kramer 2001, particularly chapters 6 and 11; Erickson 1988; White and Thomas 1972; Yellen 1977). These experiments differ from ethnoarchaeological observations in that the behaviors or actions under study are manipulated (e.g., isolated, repeated, or revived; Tringham 1978:171). For example, I (Shimada 1978) combined observation and interview of modern Navajo masons with analysis of the limestone and sandstone they worked and their time-motion and energy input-output (via indirect calorimetry) in a controlled setting to gain an understanding of the labor requirements and organization involved in prehistoric Chacoan masonry. More recently, Skibo (1992) conducted a comprehensive study of use-related alterations of ceramics in a Kalinga village in the Philippines by meticulously tracking a preselected sample of ceramics (limited to two basic vessel forms) through their entire "life histories."

Though ethnographic experiments offer a number of advantages (see later discussion), as with ethnographic analogies, evaluation and application of their results to prehistoric settings require the utmost caution, including careful consideration of comparative contexts and the level at which behavioral patterns and material correlates are defined. My work suffered from the small-scale and inadequate contextualization of my study. Skibo's study, on the other hand, remains difficult to apply to archaeological situations where vessel form ranges are much wider, complete vessels are far rarer, and their life histories could have encompassed multiple functions.

Another noteworthy development was an increasing effort to integrate archaeometry and quantify archaeological experiments and archaeology in general (e.g., Bronitsky 1986, 1989; De Atley and Bishop 1991; Erickson 1985; Jones 2002; Kingery 1987, 1996; Mathieu and Meyer 1997; Rollefson 1991; Tringham et al. 1974; cf. Killick and Young 1997; Plog and Upham 1989). This trend has received a boost from the recent interest in the technology and organization of craft production and reexamination of the culture-technology interface. By archaeometry, we mean the application of analytic methods from the biological, chemical, and physical sciences for archaeological purposes. In fact, most of the archaeometric methods available today are capable of producing precise, reliable, quantitative measurements. Thus their integration in archaeological experiments allows an effective objective assessment and comparison of experimental outcomes. At the same time, we must temper our thirst for precision and quantification by reminding ourselves that we are typically studying human behavior before the emergence of scientific knowledge and precise recipes for productive activities (see Ingold 2000; Smith 1965, 1970).

Though there are increasing numbers of experiments with prior and subsequent analyses of materials involved (e.g., Bronitsky 1986; 1989), they are predominantly focused on "techno-functions" of archaeological ceramics and metals. The resultant publications are found primarily in more specialized outlets such as *Archaeometry* and *Journal of Archaeological Sciences.*

We need not only consider greater integration of archaeometry but also greater emphasis on elucidation of processes and the interface between human behavior and material culture (Schiffer and Skibo 1987; Tringham 1978), as Clark (1953:353) and Movius (1953:165) called for more than 50 years ago. In this regard Tringham's (1978) advocacy of "behavioral experimentation" as opposed to "experimentation on the by-products of human behavior" needs to be considered. The latter aims at reconstruction of the human and natural agents responsible for a wide variety of modifications of materials before, during, and after deposition in the archaeological record, and determination of the potential and limitations of the intrinsic qualities of materials for human use (Tringham 1978:182). In contrast, the former is built on the results of the latter and is "designed to test (1) the relationship of human operators to material, in such terms as the efficiency of energy input-production output ratios, and (2) the factors of social organization that contribute to variability in the materials" (Tringham 1978:183, 184–197). In other words, behavioral experiments are intended to test behavioral regularities in time and space. This is a commendable but lofty aim.

Saraydar and Shimada (1973; also Saraydar 1976) attempted just such an experiment by comparing slash-and-burn and semi-modern cultivation techniques as measured by energetic input and output. The ultimate aim was cross-cultural comparison of different agricultural systems through quantification of key variables such as human behavior and agricultural yields (also see Erickson 1985, 1996; Reynolds 1979, 1999). In reality, behavioral experiments in the sense of Tringham have not been conducted often because of procedural and interpretive difficulties. These challenges include control of numerous variables and defining the justifiable parameters of the activity under study, effects of different human operators, and behavioral significance of quantitative data. In addition, given that ethnoarchaeology plays a key role in the testing of hypotheses in Tringham's conception, those ancient activities for which there are no historical or modern analogues pose a serious problem.

Though Binford's call for middle range theory building is said to have inspired many experiments in the 1980s (Trigger 1989:363), as seen in the previous discussion, other concurrent or earlier contributing developments should be kept in mind. One aspect of recent experimental archaeology that deserves our attention is its educational role. In western Europe (to a lesser extent in the United States; see Jameson 1997) where open-air, or living, museums are widely found, the experiential and public educational aspects of experimental archaeology are emphasized as much as scholarly concern with testing of hypotheses about the past (e.g., Reynolds 1978, 1979, 1999; Stone and Molyneaux 1994; Stone and Planel 1999). This thrust, which can be traced back to the late 1950s, has gained greater impetus in recent decades with increasing calls on both sides of the Atlantic for archaeologists to play an active, if not proactive, role in guiding public conception, use, protection, and understanding of the past and its remains (e.g., Pyburn and Wilk 1995; Sabloff 1998; Shanks and Tilley 1987). These museums (e.g., West Stow in Suffolk, Britain, and the Historical-Archaeological Research Center at Lejre, Denmark) embrace a philosophy that contrasts with that of traditional museums in regard to the roles that archaeology and the public play in the understanding and dissemination of knowledge about the past. Fundamentally, these "museums" are full-scale, dynamic, long-term re-creations of past living, working, and environmental conditions that are faithfully based on available archaeological evidence—settlements, farms, or workshops set in their original or approximate landscapes. Butser Ancient Farm, established in Hampshire, southern England, by Peter Reynolds (1979, 1999) in 1972, for example, is a functioning version ("long-term working interpretation") of an Iron Age (ca. 300 B.C.) farmstead occupying 6 ha of land where prehistoric varieties of wheat and other crops are cultivated. Though this farm has an active program of student education and public visitation (which is an important source of financial support), it has always remained an "open air research laboratory" and not been driven by specific educational requirements (Reynolds 1979, 1999). A North American example of a hybrid research-educational reconstruction site is Colonial Williamsburg in Virginia (Hume 1999).

Many aspects of these re-created settlements are open for the visitors to touch and participate in. In other words, experience is seen as the most effective didactic means and visitors are encouraged to be active participants in their own education about the past. Archaeological research is directly linked to public education. In this regard, experimental archaeology is a means by which available archaeological knowledge and understanding are translated into a careful reconstruction of the past, during the process of which our ideas (those of both the public and the archaeologist) are tested and refined.

In sum, over the past 150 years or so, numerous archaeological experiments in the broad sense of the term have been conducted.[1] It is fair to say that over this time span archaeological experiments generally have improved, and they are seen today as an important component of archaeological methodology.

Increasingly, experiments are planned that start with explicitly stated questions, hypotheses, and aims. However, despite efforts to identify and control all independent variables, serious limitations and problems persist. We turn our attention to these problems in a later section. First we examine the question of what is meant by and entailed in experiments.

Recommended Procedures

Studies subsumed under the rubric experimental archaeology vary considerably in scale, scope, duration, rigor of control over variables, and aims. Scientific testing and discovery, on the one hand, and public education through experience, on the other, are two poles of the stated aims of experimental archaeology. At the scientific end of the spectrum, the experiment may empirically test our hypothesis by replicating particular artifacts or material effects or, conversely, attempt to define the operational principles of a given technological process. Duration may vary from brief one-off events to sustained research lasting decades.

Given the observed variability among archaeological experiments, it is not surprising that there are divergent definitions of experimental archaeology. Ascher (1961a:793) equated it with imitative experiments that aim to test beliefs about past cultural behavior. Coles (1973:18; cf. 1979:33, 36–39) considered it "a tool by which some of the basic economic activities of ancient man, those concerned primarily with subsistence and technology, can be assessed for their development and their competence." Ingersoll and MacDonald (1977:xii) adopted the much more inclusive definition that it is an approach that "seeks to test, evaluate, and explicate method, technique, assumptions, hypotheses, and theories at any and all levels of archaeological research" through definition and control of as many variables as possible. More recently, Skibo (1992:18) defined it as the "fabrication of materials, behaviors, or both, in order to observe one or more of the processes involved in the production, use, discard, deterioration, or recovery of material culture." For Schiffer et al. (1994:198) it is a method of studying process through the control of relevant variables within an artificial system.

In spite of varied definitions, it is safe to state that contemporary experimental archaeology is built around the experiment as a means of discovery and answering a specific question by empirical trial or testing a specific hypothesis. Accordingly, the definition of experimental archaeology used here is that it is a structured method for empirically testing our beliefs about and discovering the past material world and human activities through experiments.

The term experiment is used quite loosely in archaeology and anthropology in general to speak of trials or testing of methods or techniques to determine their efficacy or worthiness (e.g., Lewis 1953; Nadel 1951; chapters in parts II and IV of Ingersoll and MacDonald 1977). As Lewis (1953:463) observed, such trials should be referred to as "experimental methods" and should be clearly differentiated from experiments. Skibo (1992:18) defines "experiments in archaeology" in the same way that "experimental methods" are defined above. His usage is not followed here because of the contrary precedence and because the experiment denotes a specific method as defined later here.

Experiment is both underutilized in archaeology and not well understood by many of its practitioners, perhaps because they have had little or no training in experimentation. The same can be said about the attendant formulation and testing of explicit, testable, multiple, working hypotheses. Graduate training in archaeology today invariably includes at least one course each of statistics and quantitative analysis and research design. Although students may gain a good appreciation of the importance of selecting appropriate statistical methods and writing good research proposals, designing good experiments has not been a priority.

An experiment is certainly not a prerogative of or confined to any specific field. As described later, it is simple in conception. It is a systematized empirical method of inquiry that involves first the delineation of all known variables that have been shown to affect a particular empirical phenomenon or entity in question and then the controlled manipulation of the independent variables to determine their effects on the dependent variable. The independent variables are the ones the researcher can or attempts to control, whereas the dependent variables are those that are being tested in relation to the changing state of the independent variables. An experiment, then, entails a systematic effort not only to identify but also to control as many relevant variables as possible. The more variables are defined and controlled, the clearer and more dependable are the results. As discussed later, different types of archaeological experiments have been defined in accordance with the degree of variable control.

Commonly, the plan of an experiment has three major components, outlined in the following (Cochran and Cox 1992:10–14; also Beveridge 1961; Kempthorne 1952; Kirk 1995; inter alia). Bernard (2002:106–108) offers a five-step procedure for experiments in social science that is fundamentally an elaboration of this three-step procedure.

1. A lucid and specific statement of the experimental objectives that explains why a particular experiment is being conducted and the extent to which generalizations are to be made from the experimental results (i.e., the nature of inferences)
2. A description of the planned experiment that outlines such matters as experimental treatments, the nature, duration, scale, and size of the experiment and the experimental subjects and materials
3. An outline of the methods to be employed in analyzing and assessing the results (e.g., statistical tests)

The first statement commonly takes the form of the questions to be answered, the hypotheses to be tested, or the effects to be determined. The most common problems here are vagueness (e.g., identity of relevant variables or the nature of their relationships) and excessive ambition (e.g., the number of experiments required to achieve the stated aims). The immediate goals of each experiment should be distinguished from the long-term objectives of the whole experimental program. The extent of generalization to be made from the experimental results also should be specified.

Experimental treatment refers to the different procedures whose effects are to be observed, measured, and compared. In other words, the manner in which independent variables are manipulated (e.g., the manner in which a force is applied on a given lithic) in producing the effects under study (e.g., the size of resultant flakes) must be made clear. At the same time, the conditions under which the treatments are to be compared need to be defined. Are we dealing with artificial laboratory conditions or with more realistic clinical or field situations? Clearly, the conditions are determined by the research objectives and the use that is to be made of the experimental results.

Improving Experimental Archaeology

Recommended procedures for experiments in archaeology (Ascher 1961a:810–11; Coles 1973:15–17; 1977; 1979:36–48; Reynolds 1977, 1978, 1979, 1999; Tringham 1978:178–180) are basically an elaboration of the preceding tripartite plan for experiments in general. A synthesis of their works together with my comments follows.

Specification of the guiding research questions and attendant explicit, multiple, testable hypotheses. Clearly conceived, worthwhile questions are the fundamental determinant of any experiment. Commonly, questions and hypotheses emerge from a careful examination of available data that elucidate what merits our attention. In addition, any pertinent premises and theoretical base as well as all other major aspects of the experimental design should be specified and justified. Van Fraassen (1980:77) concludes that "on the one hand, theory is a factor in experimental design; on the other, experimentation is a factor in theory construction."

Selection of the appropriate experimental materials (both objective and effective materials) that are known to have been available, or could have been available, in the aboriginal setting. Thorough background research is critical in this selection process. Documentation with appropriate archaeometric analyses as well as camcorders and other recording devices should begin at this stage and continue throughout the experiments.

Performance of a set of related experiments to test competing hypotheses. Here, the experience, skill, capabilities, and knowledge of the experimenter and operators (actors), as well as the quality of experimental design, all play an important role. Use of scale or partial models must be clearly stated because it also affects the assessment of experimental results. The axiom that the whole is more than the sum of its parts should be kept in mind.

Observation of the experimental results. Continuous, careful observation of multiple variables is difficult and should be augmented by the means described in step 2. Though an experiment is basically an observational study, the actors' perspective on the behavioral experiment should be elicited for comparison with observational data for a better understanding of the decision making that guides behavior. It is crucial that operation of any experiments be faithful to their design and be conducted in a consistent manner for the entire span. However, long-lasting field experiments or those involving many variables are more likely to produce unexpected problems during the operation of the experiment. If and when any improvisation is made, it should be carefully recorded and its effects honestly assessed.

Interpretation of the experimental results as inference. This point relates to the oft-heard remark that experimental results are not conclusive. Thomas (1999:181) declares, "Replicative experiments do not 'demonstrate the reality' of anything; experiments demonstrate only that a given technique could have been used in the past—that it was *not impossible.*" The inconclusive nature of experimental results must be accepted as inevitable because we cannot prove something that happened in the past through modern observation and experience. What can be achieved with greater confidence is refutation of at least some of the competing plausible hypotheses or models. Issues related to determination of the plausibility and reliability of experimental results are considered in depth later.

Search for corroborative evidence for assessment of plausibility. The relative merits of results of the experiment that tests a competing hypothesis must be determined by comparing them with the available archaeological data (upon which the hypotheses were based), results from testing of other competing hypotheses, and as many lines of independent evidence as possible.

In general, Coles's (1973:18; also 1979:47–48) advice regarding assessment of the archaeological experiment still holds. "[It] should be assessed in terms of its reliability, that it asked the right questions of the material, that the procedure adopted was appropriately conceived and honestly applied, and that the results were observed and assessed fairly. Errors in the experiment, in selection of materials, in process, in observations, should be openly stated." The need for caution, honesty, and modesty in assessing and generalizing results cannot be overstated. Equally important is publication of a detailed and honest description of the entire experiment. Only with such documentation can the experiment be replicated and repeated by not only the original researcher but also independent researchers.

Planning of a new round of experiments. Pursuant to the self-corrective process vital to any research, completion of the prior steps should lead to repetitions of the same experiment to increase confidence in its results or, conversely, reformulation of hypotheses and attendant planning of a new experiment.

Challenge and Solutions

The preceding historical review and recommended procedures highlight major challenges facing experimental archaeology. These challenges are discussed in the following together with strategies for dealing with them.

Asking Worthwhile Questions

Experimental archaeology has evolved to the point that "experiments" driven by simple questions such as What will happen? or Does it work? are rarely seen today. There is today much more concern with processes of material transformations and associated behavior or the interface between material culture and human behavior than with producing seemingly identical, final material effects. This concern subsumes Reynolds's (1999:128) second category of experiment focused on "process and function" and what Tringham (1978) called "experimentation on the by-products of human behavior," as well as Coles's (1979:38–39) second and third levels of experiment that test "for the processes and production methods" and artifact functions, respectively.

The focus on process is inevitable because of the inconclusiveness of experimental results (discussed later) and the principles of multiple solutions and functional equivalence. The principle of multiple solutions states that there is usually more than one way of solving a given problem; functional equivalence implies that more than one alternative method or pattern can fill the same function or have the same consequence (e.g., Cancian 1968:33). These two principles imply that observed, seemingly identical, final material effects can be produced by different behaviors or processes. In other words, not only do we need to compare the initial and final material features but also to study the intervening transformation and associated behaviors. Such an effort calls for numerous related experiments. A good example of this genre is the long-term laboratory experiment program on the effects of different pastes and surface treatments on pottery conducted by M. B. Schiffer and his students (e.g., Schiffer and Skibo 1987; Schiffer et al. 1994; Skibo et al. 1989; Young and Stone 1990).

For some archaeologists the above focus on low-level principles may not be ambitious enough. Nonetheless, "behavioral experimentation" aimed at testing cross-cultural behavioral regularities faces major difficulties and must be built on the productive results of "experimentation on the by-products of human behavior." Likewise, Coles's (1979:43) fourth-level (highest) experiment that examines the "broader implications of technology and function to the society itself" is not only "beyond the limits of clearly observable actions" but yields results that are tenuous and difficult to assess. What is being advocated here is a continuing refinement of experiments focused on processes in the manner described in the section below. This goal is attainable and can form a sound foundation for implementation of productive behavioral experimentation.

Related to the previously noted concern with the nature of the research questions being posed is the manner in which these questions are experimentally tested. The first step of the previously discussed experimental procedure called for formulation of multiple plausible hypotheses. The method of multiple working hypotheses has long been established in the sciences and guards against narrowing our perspective and self-fulfilling experimental results. This method is preached but not effectively practiced in archaeology (see Kelley and Hanen 1988:317–338).

In dealing with cultural behavior, given the principles of multiple solutions and functional equivalence, the experimenter must strive to generate as many plausible hypotheses as possible for testing. As with the ability to recognize potentially significant relationships between variables, this task largely depends on the experimenter's systematic observation, intellectual acumen and knowledge of both objective and effective materials as well as related processes.

Sustained, Multistage, and Multilineal Experimentation

One of the most persistent problems we face is the seemingly widespread misconception of what can be expected and is entailed in experimental testing. Expectations of quick but meaningful outcomes still seem relatively common. Many experiments are conducted on a short-term basis and concluded after one or two sessions or as soon as the expected or seemingly successful results are obtained. Admittedly many experiments are conducted by students for learning purposes and are short in funds, duration, and expertise. However, if experimental archaeology is to contribute to advances in archaeology, this limited vision and attitude must be replaced with clear recognition that the quality of experiments and reliability of their results hinge largely on the amount of time, thinking, and generally, effort invested in preparing and conducting experiments. Field experiments or those that involve human subjects require lengthy preparation and repeated trials. In general, the experiment as a method of inquiry is simple in conception, but its implementation requires discipline and perseverance as much as creativity and originality.

Perseverance and long-term commitment are needed for a number of reasons. To eliminate the possibility of spurious results, the experiment must be repeated to see if the same results can be obtained; seemingly successful results from a single experiment should never be considered reliable. Reynolds (1999:127), for example, considers "a minimum of five 'replicates'" needed to constitute an "adequate replication." An important implication of such a requirement is the need to secure adequate funding to keep the investigative team and facilities together for sufficient time.

For those experiments involving human operators, assessment of experimental results requires the utmost caution (e.g., Tringham 1978:183). An observed performance may not reflect the operator's capability (i.e., competence) because he or she may not have been healthy or motivated (Shimada 1978:222–223). In fact, performance can be readily affected if the actors are privy to the experimenter's expectations of the experimental outcomes. This is a strong argument against the experimenter (i.e., the investigating archaeologist) serving as the actor, who should be carefully selected in accordance with the nature of activities and the hypothesis under examination and should not be aware of the experimenter's expectations. The ethnographic experiment (see later description) involving local experts and informants as the actors circumvents this problem.

Internal consistency in the results obtained in multiple runs of the same experiment performed by multiple actors strengthens the reliability of the results. It should be noted that it may require numerous runs before a consistent pattern emerges. Other means for increasing the reliability of experimental results are readily available in many publications dealing with experimental design and analysis (Beveridge 1961; Cochran and Cox 1992; Kempthorne 1952; Kirk 1995; inter alia). However, given the principles of multiple solutions and functional equivalence, repetition of the experiment does not resolve the question of plausibility of the given reconstruction or hypothesis. This question led to the preceding recommendations to search for independent corroborative evidence, including that derived from different experiments, and the planning of new experiments. Implementation of these two final steps further necessitates a long-term commitment on the part of the experimenter.

In regard to the difficulty of assessing the plausibility of a given hypothesis or replication, the following measures are suggested: (1) integration of archaeometry and quantification, (2) realization of complementary laboratory and field experiments, (3) comparison of observers' and actors' views for those experiments involving human enactments, and (4) proper placement of experiments within the broader context of archaeological research.

Integration of Archaeometry and Quantification

Archaeometry and quantification allow objective assessment and comparison of experimental results. In addition, archaeometry adds an important dimension to the observer's perspective. Though we have seen their integration in experiments concerned with ancient ceramic or metallurgical technology, there should be better integration at preoperational, operational, and postoperational stages of archaeometry and quantification in all experiments. With short-term or small-scale experiments still quite common, the number of samples is often too small for meaningful statistical analysis, and preexperiment and postexperiment materials analysis is limited or simply not considered.

A variety of physical methods of chemical analysis such as neutron activation analysis, electron probe microanalysis, and X-ray diffraction analysis can provide information on chemical composition, chemical compounds, and mineral phases that corroborates or refutes conventional observations on visible attributes. What seems similar or even identical on the exterior or to the naked eye may prove to be significantly different in material structure or microscopic properties (e.g., electrochemical deposition vs. surface depletion gilding), thereby allowing us to effectively compare products of different plausible reconstruction to aboriginal objects. Some techniques such as Mössbauer spectroscopy or metallographic microscopy can in fact provide valuable information on the *processes* of ceramic firing (e.g., Wagner et al. 1998, 2000) or metalworking (e.g., Smith 1960, 1973; van der Voort 1984), respectively. In other words, the judicious selection and integrated use of archaeometry can result in an effective assessment of experiments in terms of not only their material results but also their transformational processes (Shimada and Wagner 2001). Both experimental archaeology and archaeometry are essential to defining what some scholars refer to as a *biography of objects* (e.g., Jones 2002; Lamberg-Karlovsky 1993).

Only a handful of archaeologists are competent in a wide variety of archaeometric analyses (Lechtman and Steinberg 1979:141). Active collaboration of appropriate archaeometrists in all or even a few stages of archaeological experiments is urged (cf. Tringham 1978:176) to maximize archaeometric information potential and minimize use of questionable equipment, techniques, or samples. For example, even the seemingly simple task of measuring the firing temperature in a pottery kiln requires careful planning to determine the duration and interval of measurements and the appropriate placement of multiple thermocouples and attachment of clay balls (buffers) to the thermocouple tips to even out the effects of spurious, momentary fluctuations in the temperature of the combustion gases (e.g., Wagner et al. 1994, 1998, 1999; see also Kingery 1982:42). At the same time, one cannot expect the active participation of archaeometrists, often from chemistry, materials science, geology, or biology, without research issues of some significance beyond time-space specifics to both archaeologists and specialists. Close coordination is critical, particularly in regard to the manner in which the variables are to be measured and the results to be assessed. Long-term planning in archaeometric studies is essential because it often takes many years before a consistent or comprehensive picture of the material properties of the sampled objects emerges. Much the same can be said about field experiments (e.g., those dealing with site formation processes; Ashbee and Jewell 1998).

The fact that these archaeometric techniques produce quantitative results adds to their attraction. Quantification is generally better suited and easier for experiments concerned with material effects. Ascher (1961a:807) conceived experiments in archaeology to be distinct from those in the natural sciences because the former deals with cultural behavior that is shaped by many unknown variables and not readily amenable or possible to quantify. Though quantification of human behavior should not be blindly pursued, some activities are quantifiable, and some research questions warrant quantification (Saraydar 1976; Saraydar and Shimada 1973:344–345; Shimada 1978:211; Tringham 1978:179). For example, two distinct methods of accomplishing an identical task or two different stages of the same evolving technology can be compared (e.g., work-hour ratio and energy expended in felling trees with a stone vs. a steel ax [e.g., Mathieu and Meyer 1997] or energy expended and harvest yield of ancient vs. modern cultivation techniques or crops [e.g., Erickson 1985, 1996; Evenari et al. 1971; Reynolds 1979, 1999]).

Complementary Laboratory and Field Experiments

In any experiment, the ideal is that all relevant variables are well-defined and controlled. The more variables defined and controlled, the clearer and more dependable the results. In terms of degree of variable control, different types of archaeological experiments have been defined. What Skibo (1992: 21–22; also Tringham 1978:171) calls "laboratory experiments" are those that are most rigorous, artificial, and easy to replicate. In a controlled laboratory environment, it is relatively easy for the experimenter to isolate and focus on the independent and dependent variables under study. Greater control over these variables can be achieved by minimizing human involvement, for example, by employing a mechanical device that allows precise control over the angle and force involved in flintknapping (e.g., Speth 1974; Tringham et al. 1974) or an electric kiln with precise temperature control to fire pottery (e.g., Bronitsky and Hamer 1986; Schiffer and Skibo 1987; Wagner et al. 1994, 1998). For the sake of examining in depth the effects of a specific independent variable on a dependent variable, modern materials or tools may substitute for those that are known to have been available, or could have been available, in the aboriginal setting. In general, laboratory experiments that utilize (presumably justifiable) modern substitutes (e.g., Schiffer et al. 1994) are called "simulation experiments" (Coles 1979:36; cf. Reynolds 1999:128 for a different usage of the term), whereas those that faithfully replicate abundant material remains or use aboriginal materials are known as "reconstruction experiments" (Merkel 1990:79). Reynolds (1999:128) suggests the designation "construct experiments" for those that are based on little or no aboriginal material remains (e.g., construction of ancient buildings based on postholes) to avoid semantic confusion with "reconstruction experiments."

However, the artificiality of the condition created raises the serious question of the relevance of the results of laboratory experiments to any question that involves human behavior. What do the results of laboratory experiments mean in real-life terms? For example, discrete "performance characteristics" such as the rate of thermal conduction in pottery (Schiffer and Skibo 1987) are etic (imposed by the observer) attributes, and their significance to prehistoric potters and users begs for an answer. Indeed, many real-life activities do take into account environmental factors, are continuous, and require rapid or simultaneous assessment of multiple variables, rather than being discrete or segmented and guided by orderly decision making on one variable at a time, which many laboratory experiments impose or assume for the sake of variable control and feasibility.

Laboratory and field experiments may be viewed as two ends of a continuum in the rigor of experimental control. Field experiments are conducted in physical or social settings that presumably approximate archaeological situations. In ethnographic experiments, a variant of field experiments, local individuals (actors) conduct activities in familiar settings in patterns familiar to them or to their immediate ancestors (Tringham 1978:171), thereby thwarting questions regarding competence (see later discussion). If archaeologists are sufficiently competent with the activity under study, they may serve as the actors. The behavior or actions under study are usually manipulated (e.g., isolated, repeated, or revived; Tringham 1978:171). In essence, ethnographic experiments are the archaeological version of the clinical trials routinely conducted in psychology and medicine and are seen as an effective countermeasure to the previously noted skepticism over the behavioral relevance of laboratory experiments.

With extraneous and relevant variables that are difficult or impossible to control or even to identify (e.g., winds and ambient temperature), determination of the relationship between independent and dependent variables in field experiments is thought to be harder to achieve (Skibo 1992:22). Yet the difficulty of gaining control over variables is more a matter of degree than kind. As with experiments in any discipline, devising an effective design for a field experiment requires patience, trial runs, and creative thinking more than simply following a recipe. As Tringham (1978:171) notes, the value of experiments for archaeological interpretation does not necessarily decrease with the change from laboratory to field conditions.

Though it is easy to dwell on the contrast between field and laboratory experiments, they are complementary and should be conducted in tandem for comprehensive testing and discovery. For example, Skibo (1992:23) recommends, "ideally, addressing a particular archaeological problem should proceed first through the controlled laboratory stage, to investigate the processes involved, and then to the field stage." Both should be integral parts of any design for an archaeological experiment. Archaeometry and quantification provide the means for effective comparison of respective results. Only by conducting both and comparing their results can we effectively resolve the issues of the clarity, reliability, and behavioral significance of experimental results.

A number of archaeological experiments have productively combined these two types of experiments, but not enough. One good example of the kind of integration being urged here is J. F. Merkel's (1983, 1990) experimental study of Bronze Age copper smelting at Timna, the Negev desert, Israel. Over a span of 4 years, he conducted 32 full-scale smelting and remelting-refining experiments that were organized in three stages. The first two stages consisted of laboratory simulation and reconstruction experiments; the last stage was a realistic reconstruction experiment conducted in the field at Timna. Systematic archaeometric comparisons between excavated remains and experimental products provided the basis for formulation of multiple plausible models and the design of experiments to test them. It should be emphasized that Merkel's study was part of a long-term, multidisciplinary investigation of regional mining and smelting activities (Rothenberg 1990). The experiment benefited from mutual feedback with different facets of the investigation. Integration of experimental study in a comprehensive and long-term archaeological investigation is a key to experimeental success.

Actor, Observer, and Archaeometric Perspectives

We have already seen that involvement of human actors in any experiment introduces a variety of difficulties. This is where archaeometry, quantification, and ethnographic experiments become relevant. As noted earlier, archaeometric data provide an independent line of evidence to corroborate or refute the experimenter's observations. Involvement of local experts in ethnographic experiments often minimizes the question of competence. At the same time, their technical competence and knowledge should not be taken for granted. Schiffer and Skibo (1987:596, 598; also see Ingold 2000; Smith 1965, 1970) warn against assuming that "all technological knowledge is explicit and can be elicited from any practitioner of the technology" and that "technological knowledge is composed entirely of science-like understanding." Their competence and knowledge can be gauged by examining their material products in terms of measurable indices of skill (albeit not without problems; e.g., Carr 1995; Costin and Hagstrum 1995; Schiffer and Skibo 1987) and whether their products are socially accepted.

Many experiments, however, focus on exactly those behaviors that have no modern or historical analogues, for example, pre-Hispanic smelting of arsenic bronze using small bowl furnaces and blowtubes (e.g., Shimada and Merkel 1991). This is where what is known as the "practice effect" in educational psychology becomes a major concern. Clearly, learning new behavior (including new motor skills) takes time and the more one practices, the better one gets in its execution. Not only does the experimenter need to be honest in recognizing the practice effect but the actors should be allowed sufficient practice runs. Archaeometry and quantification can assist in assessment of practice effects.

It is also urged that the actors' perception of their behavior (not their presumed technological knowledge) be elicited and compared with that of the observer (i.e., the experimenter). Such comparison is particularly important in assessing practice and improvisation effects as well as garnering their personal insights on the processes of decision making and material transformation, which in turn, may lead to formulation of new questions and hypotheses. Aboriginal technologies involve a good deal of nonverbal thinking that is not readily recorded in writing or drawing (Ferguson 1977; Gordon 1993). As noted earlier, in field experiments involving a complex activity, the identification, observation, and control of relevant variables can be quite challenging. But these are exactly the sort of experiments that need to be attempted. In this regard the actors' vision of the variables affecting their behavior can be quite helpful. Though human subjects are known to adjust their perceptions as they see fit and so to subvert reality, a careful comparison of their views against archaeometric and observational data can offer a valuable opportunity to gain a holistic understanding of human behavior and its material effects. In sum, it is suggested that assessment and interpretation of results of behavioral experiments be based on data and insights from the three complementary perspectives of the observer, the actor, and archaeometry (Shimada 1978, 1999).

Illustrative Case

The preceding recommendations and their interrelationships are graphically presented in Figure 16.1. It illustrates the place and role experimental testing has played over the past decade in the Sicán Archaeological Project's effort to gain a holistic understanding of ceramic production spanning ca. 1000 B.C. to A.D. 1100 in the Lambayeque region on the Peruvian north coast (e.g., Shimada et al. 1998; Shimada and Wagner 2001; Wagner et al. 1994, 1998).

Our program of experiments is nested within long-term, regional, and interdisciplinary investigation. A premium has been placed on locating and excavating ceramic production sites as well as a variety of use contexts to gain a balanced picture of products as well as their distribution, usage, and production. Such integration ensures the comprehensive background information essential for planning experiments and assessing their results. Experiments on the Formative ceramic firing process were conducted in multiple stages starting with a simulation experiment in the United States that used a two-thirds-scale model kiln built with commercially available clays. The second stage was a series of reconstruction field experiments with a full-scale replica kiln the same general size and shape of the excavated kilns. The replica kiln was built using local materials identified by prior archaeometric analyses and situated very close to the excavated kilns. With a special permit from the National Institute of Culture of Peru, we constructed the third stage to employ an excavated, 2,700-year-old kiln that was partially reconstructed to test the same set of hypotheses regarding the duration, effective maximum temperature, and atmospheric conditions of firing, as well as the source of carbon for black pottery. Each

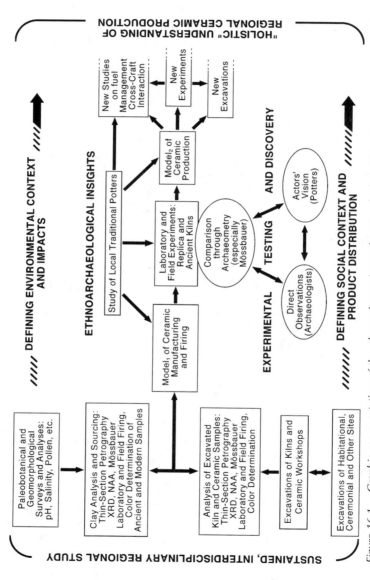

Figure 16.1. Graphic representation of the place of experimental testing (both field and laboratory experiments) and its role in the Sicán Archaeological Project's effort to gain a holistic understanding of pre-Hispanic ceramic production on the Peruvian north coast.

stage involved multiple experiments for practice and testing of competing hypotheses. Professional potters familiar with pre-Hispanic pottery techniques and firing collaborated in the latter two stages to minimize the competence problem. One of them had been the focus of earlier ethnoarchaeological study of mine. They made replica vessels with the techniques and local materials defined by prior archaeometric analyses and managed the firing. They also provided helpful actors' perceptions of the firing. Critical to the success of this long-term experimental study is the close collaboration of archaeometric specialists in designing and implementing experiments as well as interpreting and publishing results. They also conducted laboratory experiments for independent testing. Archaeometry and quantification played a crucial role in comparison and assessment of experimental results. Finally, with the recent excavation of a 1,000-year-old ceramic workshop that used kilns essentially the same size and shape as their Formative counterparts, our experimental study of ceramic technology continues to this day (e.g., Shimada and Wagner 2001). Growing out of earlier rounds of experiments are new experiments that explore the possibilities of technological fertilization between metalworking and pottery making and their competition for quality fuels (Wagner et al. 2001).

Conclusion

The impressive diversity of research topics covered and number of published cases give a false sense of the ease with which archaeological experiments can be conducted and the contribution they have made to advances in archaeological method and theory. Experimentation has much to offer archaeology. There is no doubt that participation in experiments inside and outside open-air museums provides a personal understanding that is difficult to gain in any other way for both the archaeologist and the public, a process of self-enlightenment. Similarly, experiments can yield information unobtainable by traditional research methods on technological processes. They also provide a basis for assigning the archaeological record directly or indirectly to behavior, an inferential process critical to middle range theory building.

At the same time, experimental archaeology still suffers from serious weaknesses. The cost effectiveness and ease of experimental testing have been overstated or misunderstood, so that short-term, small-scale experiments still abound detached from any long-term and comprehensive archaeological research. Experimentation is a long-term, self-correcting process involving repeated cycles of discovery and testing; it should not be conceived as one-time events or simple tasks. Also, compliance with established procedures has been inadequate. Increasingly, the guiding research questions and hypotheses to be tested and variables to be controlled and observed have been described, but the recording, assessment, and interpretation of results leave much to be desired.

To produce convincing results and contribute to advancement in archaeology, we need (1) long-term multistage programs of experiments that focus more on the interface of behavior and material culture and processes and (2) greater efforts to follow the recommended experimental procedure with emphasis on better integration of archaeometry and quantification, realization of complementary laboratory and field experiments, and comparison of observers' and actors' views (the latter for those experiments involving human enactments). Experiments are most productive when they are planned as an integral part of the multifaceted methodology of a sustained, problem-oriented archaeological investigation. Such integration ensures continuing refinement of the experimental design and that its results will be interpreted in appropriate contexts. There are no shortcuts in fulfilling the potential of experimental archaeology; productive experiments in any discipline require careful and thorough background research and planning, long-term commitment, creativity, and flexibility as well as discipline and perseverance.

Acknowledgments

I am indebted to Gordon Bronitsky, Clark Erickson, Melody Shimada, D. Ann Trieu, and Ursel Wagner for their valuable editorial and substantive comments on earlier drafts of this manuscript. I am, however, solely responsible for any errors or misrepresentations that may remain.

Note

1. Today, a Web site managed by Roeland Paardekooper in Leiden, the Netherlands, http://www.exarc.net/extern/literature.htm, offers an exhaustive bibliography (more than 4,000 entries, though many are regional European publications difficult to access) of experimental archaeology, its role in public education, and other broadly related topics. A forum for exploring and exchanging information on the productive use of experimental archaeology and how it can be used to improve our interpretation of the past is provided by another Web site, http://network54.com/Hide/Forum/62401, which has both message and chat facilities.

References

Andrieux, Philippe
    1988 Réflexions sur l'expérimentation et application: Les métaux. Technologie Préhistorique —Ouvrage collectif sous la direction de J. Tixier. *Collection Notes et Monographies Techniques* 25:73–96. CNRS, Paris.

Ascher, Robert A.
    1961a Experimental archaeology. *American Anthropologist* 63:793–816.
    1961b Analogy in archaeological interpretation. *Southwestern Journal of Anthropology* 17:317–25.
    1962 Ethnography for archaeology: A case from the Seri Indians. *Ethnology* 1:360–69.
    1968 Time's arrow and the archaeology of a contemporary community. In *Settlement archaeology*, edited by K. C. Chang, pp. 43–52. National Press Books, Palo Alto, California.

Ashbee, Paul, and Peter Jewell
    1998 The experimental earthworks revisited. *Antiquity* 72:485–504.

Bell, M., P. J. Fowler, and S. M. Hillson (editors)
    1996 *The experimental earthwork project 1960–1992*. Research Report 100. Council for British Archaeology, York.

Bernard, H. Russell
    2002 *Research methods in anthropology: Qualitative and quantitative approaches*. AltaMira, Walnut Creek, California.

Beveridge, W. I. B.
    1961 *The art of scientific investigation*. Mercury, London.

Binford, Lewis R.
    1981   *Bones: Ancient men and modern myths.* Academic Press, New York.

Bronitsky, Gordon
    1986   The use of materials science techniques in the study of pottery con-
            struction and use. In *Advances in Archaeological Method and Theory,*
            pp. 209–273. Academic Press, New York.
    1989   (editor) *Pottery technology: Ideas and approaches.* Westview Press,
            Boulder, Colorado.

Bronitsky, Gordon, and R. Hamer
    1986   Experiments in ceramic technology: The effects of various temper-
            ing materials on impact and thermal shock resistance. *American An-
            tiquity* 51:89–101.

Cancian, F.
    1968   Varieties of functional analysis. In *International encyclopedia of the so-
            cial sciences,* Vol. 6 edited by D. Sills, pp. 29–43. Macmillan and the
            Free Press, New York.

Carr, Christopher
    1995   A unified middle-range theory of artifact design. In *Style, society, and
            person: Archaeological and ethnological perspectives,* edited by Christo-
            pher Carr and Jill E. Nitzel, pp. 171–258. Plenum Press, New York.

Chilcott, John H., and James Deetz
    1964   The construction and uses of a laboratory archaeological site. *Amer-
            ican Antiquity* 29:328–337.

Childs, S. T., and P. R. Schmidt
    1986   Experimental iron smelting: The genesis of a hypothesis with im-
            plications for African prehistory and history. In *African iron work-
            ing—ancient and traditional,* edited by Randi Haaland and Peter
            Shinnie, pp. 121–141. Norwegian University Press, Oslo.

Clark, J. Grahame
    1953   Archeological theories and interpretation: Old World. In *Anthropol-
            ogy today: An encyclopedic inventory,* edited by Alfred L. Kroeber, pp.
            343–360. University of Chicago Press, Chicago.

Cochran, William G., and Gertrude M. Cox
    1992   *Experimental designs.* 2nd ed. John Wiley, New York.

Coles, John M.
    1973   *Archaeology by experiment.* Hutchinson, London.
    1977   Experimental archaeology—theory and principles. In *Sources and
            techniques in boat archaeology,* edited by S. McGrail, pp. 233–244. In-
            ternational Series S 29. British Archaeological Reports, Oxford.
    1979   *Experimental archaeology.* Academic Press, London.

Costin, Cathy L., and Melissa Hagstrum
   1995   Standardization, labor investment, skill, and the organization of ceramic production in late prehispanic highland Peru. *American Antiquity* 60:619–641.

David, Nicholas, and Carol Kramer
   2001   *Ethnoarchaeology in action.* Cambridge University Press, Cambridge.

De Atley, Susan P., and Ronald L. Bishop
   1991   Toward an integrated interface for archaeology and archaeometry. In *The ceramic legacy of Anna O. Shepard*, edited by R. L. Bishop and F. W. Lange, pp. 358–380. University of Colorado Press, Niwot, Colorado.

Erasmus, C.
   1965   Monument building: Some field experiments. *Southwestern Journal of Anthropology* 21:277–301.

Erickson, Clark L.
   1985   Applications of prehistoric Andean technology: Experiments in raised field agriculture, Huatta, Lake Titicaca, Peru, 1981–1983. In *Prehistoric intensive agriculture in the tropics*, edited by Ian Farrington, pp. 209–232. International Series 232. British Archaeological Reports, Oxford.
   1988   An archaeological investigation of a raised field agriculture in the Lake Titicaca basin of Peru. Unpublished Ph.D. dissertation, University of Illinois, Urbana-Champaign.
   1996   *Investigación arqueológica del sistema agrícola de los camellones en la cuenca del lago Titicaca del Perú.* Programa Interinstitucional de Waru Waru and Centro para Información para el Desarrollo, La Paz, Bolivia.

Evenari, Michael, Leslie Shanan, and Naphtali Tadmor
   1971   *The Negev: The challenge of a desert.* Harvard University, Cambridge Press.

Ferguson, Eugene S.
   1977   The mind's eye: Nonverbal thought in technology. *Science* 197:827–836.

Gordon, Robert B.
   1993   The interpretation of artifacts in the history of technology. In *History from things: Essays on material culture*, edited by Steven Lubar and W. David Kingery, pp. 74–93. Smithsonian Institution Press, Washington, D.C.

Graham, John, Robert F. Heizer, and Thomas Hester
   1972   *Bibliography of replicative experiments in archaeology.* Department of Anthropology, Archaeological Research Facility, University of California, Berkeley.

Grayson, Donald K.
  1986   Eoliths, archaeological ambiguity, and the generation of "middle-range" research. In *American archaeology past and future: A celebration of the Society for American Archaeology 1935–1985*, edited by D. Meltzer, Dan Fowler, and Jeremy A. Sabloff, pp. 77–133. Smithsonian Institution Press, Washington, D.C.

Hansen, Hans-Ole
  1962   *I built a Stone Age house.* Phoenix, London.

Hester, Thomas R., and Robert F. Heizer
  1973   *Bibliography of archaeology I: Experiments, lithic technology, and petrography.* Module in Anthropology 29. Addison-Wesley, Reading, Massachusetts.

Heyerdahl, Thor
  1950   *The Kon-Tiki expedition: By raft across the South Seas.* Allen and Unwin, London.
  1952   *American Indians in the Pacific.* Allen and Unwin, London.

Hume, Ivor N.
  1999   Resurrection and deification at Colonial Williamsburg, USA. In *The constructed past: Experimental archaeology, education and the public*, edited by Peter Stone and Ph. G. Planel, pp. 90–103. Routledge, London.

Ingersoll, David, and William MacDonald
  1977   Introduction. In *Experimental archaeology*, edited by Daniel Ingersoll, John E. Yellen, and William Macdonald, pp. ii–xviii. Columbia University Press, New York.

Ingold, Tim
  2000   *The perception of the environment: Essays on livelihood, dwelling and skill.* Routledge, London

Jameson, J. H. (editor)
  1997   *Presenting archaeology to the public.* AltaMira, Walnut Creek, California.

Jewell, Peter A.
  1963   *The experimental earthwork on Overtown Down, Wiltshire: 1960.* British Association for Advancement of Science, London.

Jewell, P. A., and G. W. Dimbleby
  1966   The experimental earthwork on Overtown Down, Wiltshire, England: The first four years. *Proceedings of the Prehistoric Society* 32(11):313–342.

Johnson, L. Lewis
  1978   A history of flint-knapping experimentation, 1838–1976. *Current Anthropology* 19:337–372.

Jones, Andrew
  2002 *Archaeological theory and scientific practice.* Cambridge University
        Press, Cambridge.

Kelley, Jane H., and Marsha P. Hanen
  1988 *Archaeology and the methodology of science.* University of New Mex-
        ico, Albuquerque.

Kempthorne, O.
  1952 *The design and analysis of experiments.* John Wiley, New York.

Killick, David, and Suzanne Young
  1997 Archaeology and archaeometry: From casual dating to a meaning-
        ful relationship? *Antiquity* 71:518–524.

Kingery, W. David
  1982 Plausible inferences from ceramic artifacts. In *Archaeological ceram-
        ics,* edited by J. S. Olin and A. D. Franklin, pp. 37–45. Smithsonian
        Institution Press, Washington, D.C.
  1987 Microstructure analysis as part of a holistic interpretation of ce-
        ramic art and archaeological artifacts. *Archaeomaterials* 1:91–99.
  1996 A role for material sciences. In *Learning from things: Method and the-
        ory of material culture studies,* edited by W. David Kingery, pp.
        175–180. Smithsonian Institution Press, Washington, D.C.

Kirk, Roger E.
  1995 *Experimental design: Procedures for the behavioral sciences.* 3rd ed.
        Brooks and Cole, Pacific Grove, California.

Lamberg-Karlovsky, Carl C.
  1993 The biography of an object: The intercultural style vessels of the
        third millennium B.C. In *History from things: Essays on material cul-
        ture,* edited by Steven Lubar and W. David Kingery, pp. 270–292.
        Smithsonian Institution Press, Washington, D.C.

Lechtman, Heather N., and Steinberg
  1979 The history of technology: An anthropological point of view. In *The
        history and philosophy of technology,* edited by G. Bugliarello and
        D. B. Doner, pp. 135–160. University of Illinois Press, Urbana.

Lewis, Oscar
  1953 Controls and experiments in field work. In *Anthropology today: An
        encyclopedic inventory,* edited by Alfred L. Kroeber, pp. 452–475.
        University of Chicago Press, Chicago.

Mathieu, J. R., and D. A. Meyer
  1997 Comparing axe heads of stone, bronze, and steel: Studies in exper-
        imental archaeology. *Journal of Field Archaeology* 24:333–350.

Merkel, John F.
    1983   A reconstruction of Bronze Age copper smelting, experiments based on archaeological evidence from Timna, Israel. Unpublished Ph.D dissertation, University College London.
    1990   Experimental reconstruction of Bronze Age copper smelting based on archaeological evidence from Timna. In *The ancient metallurgy of copper*, edited by Beno Rothenberg, pp. 78–122. Institute for Archaeo-Metallurgical Studies, Institute of Archaeology, University College London, London.

Movius, Hallam L., Jr.
    1953   Old World prehistory: Paleolithic. In *Anthropology today: An encyclopedic inventory*, edited by Alfred L. Kroeber, pp. 163–192. University of Chicago Press, Chicago.

Nadel, S. F.
    1951   *The foundations of social anthropology*. Free Press, Glencoe, Illinois.

Plog, Fred, and Steadman Upham
    1989   Productive specialization, archaeometry, and interpretation. In *Pottery technology: Ideas and approaches*, edited by Gordon Bronitsky, pp. 207–216. Westview Press, Boulder, Colorado.

Pope, Saxon T.
    1923   A study of bows and arrow. *University of California Publications in American Archaeology and Ethnology* 13(9):329–414.

Pyburn, Anne, and Richard Wilk
    1995   Responsible archaeology is applied anthropology. In *Ethics in American archaeology: Challenges for the 1990s*, edited by Mark J. Lynott and Alison Wylie, pp. 71–76. Society for American Archaeology, Washington, D.C.

Rathje, William L., and Cullen Murphy
    1992   *Rubbish! The archaeology of garbage*. HarperCollins, New York.

Reynolds, Peter J.
    1977   Experimental archaeology and the Butser Ancient Farm Research Project. In *The Iron Age in Britain—review*, edited by John Collis, pp. 32–40. University of Sheffield, Sheffield.
    1978   Archaeology by experiment: A research tool for tomorrow. In *New approaches to our past: An archaeological forum*, edited by Timothy C. Darvill, Mike Parker Pearson, R. W. Smith, and R. M. Thomas, pp. 139–155. University of Southampton Press, Southampton.
    1979   *Iron Age farm—the Butser experiment*. British Museum, London.
    1999   Butser Ancient Farm, Hampshire, UK. In *The constructed past: Experimental archaeology, education and the public*, edited by Peter Stone and Ph. G. Planel, pp. 124–135. Routledge, London.

Richards, Julian C., and Mark Whitby
   1997   The engineering of Stonehenge. In *Science and Stonehenge*, edited by Barry Cunliffe and Colin Renfrew, pp. 231–256. Proceedings of the British Academy 92. Oxford University Press, Oxford.

Rollefson, G. O.
   1991   The critical role of technological analysis for prehistoric anthropological inference. In *Materials issues in art and archaeology II*, edited by Pamela B. Vandiver, J. Druzik, and G. S. Wheeler, pp. 365–374. Materials Research Society, Pittsburgh, Pennsylvania.

Rothenberg, Beno (editor)
   1990   *The ancient metallurgy of copper: Archaeology-experiment-theory*. Institute for Archaeo-Metallurgical Studies, Institute of Archaeology, University College London, London.

Sabloff, Jeremy A.
   1998   Distinguished lecture in archaeology: Communication and the future of American archaeology. *American Anthropologist* 100(4):869–875.

Saraydar, Stephen
   1976   Quantitative experiments in archaeology: New approaches to the study of prehistoric human adaptations. Unpublished Ph.D dissertation, Cornell University.

Saraydar, Stephen, and Izumi Shimada
   1973   Experimental archaeology: A new outlook. *American Antiquity* 38:344–350.

Schick, Kathy D., and Nicholas Toth
   1993   *Making silent stones speak: Human evolution and the dawn of technology*. Simon and Schuster, New York.

Schiffer, Michael B.
   1976   *Behavioral archeology*. Academic, New York.
   1987   *Formation processes of the archaeological record*. University of New Mexico Press, Albuquerque.

Schiffer, Michael B., and James M. Skibo
   1987   Theory and experiment in the study of technological change. *Current Anthropology* 28:595–622.

Schiffer, Michael B., James M. Skibo, T. C. Boelke, M. A. Neupert, and M. Aronson
   1994   New perspectives on experimental archaeology: Surface treatments and thermal response of the clay cooking pot. *American Antiquity* 2:197–217.

Semenov, S. A.
   1964   *Prehistoric technology*. Cory, Adams and Mackay, London.

Shanks, Michael, and Christopher Tilley
  1987 *Reconstructing archaeology: Theory and practice.* Cambridge University Press, Cambridge.

Shimada, Izumi
  1978 Behavioral variability and organization in ancient constructions: An experimental approach. In *Papers on the economy and architecture of the ancient Maya*, edited by Raymond Sidrys, pp. 209–235. Institute of Archaeology, UCLA, Los Angeles, California.
  1999 Archaeometry, experimental archaeology, and ethnoarchaeology: A three-fold approach to behavioral insights. Paper presented at the 16th Annual Visiting Scholar Conference of the Center for Archaeological Investigations, "Archaeometry as Anthropology: Material Culture and Technology." Carbondale, Illinois.

Shimada, Izumi, Victor Chang, David Killick, Hector Neff, Michael Glascock, Ursel Wagner, and Rupert Gebhard
  1998 Formative ceramic kilns and production in Batán Grande, north coast of Peru. In *Andean ceramics: Technology, organization and approaches*, edited by Izumi Shimada, pp. 23–61. MASCA, The University Museum, University of Pennsylvania, Philadelphia.

Shimada, Izumi, and John F. Merkel
  1991 Copper alloy metallurgy in ancient Peru. *Scientific American* 265:80–86.

Shimada, Izumi, and Ursel Wagner
  2001 Peruvian black pottery production and metal working: A Middle Sicán craft workshop at Huaca Sialupe. *Materials Research Society Bulletin* 26:25–30.

Skibo, James M.
  1992 *Pottery function: A use-alteration perspective.* Plenum, New York.

Skibo, James M., Michael B. Schiffer, and Kenneth C. Reid
  1989 Organic-tempered pottery: An experimental study. *American Antiquity* 54:122–146

Smith, C. Stanley
  1960 *A history of metallography.* University of Chicago Press, Chicago.
  1965 Materials and the development of civilization and science. *Science* 148:908–917.
  1970 Art, technology and science: Notes of their historical interaction. *Technology and Culture* 11:493–549.
  1973 The interpretation of microstructures of metallic artifacts. In *Application of science in examination of works of art*, edited by W. J. Young, pp. 13–53. Museum of Fine Arts, Boston, Massachusetts.

Speth, John D.
  1974 Experimental investigations of hard-hammer percussion flaking. *Tebiwa* 17:7–36.

Stone, E. H.
1924 *The stones of Stonehenge.* Scott, London.

Stone, Peter G., and Brian L. Molyneaux (editors)
1994 *The presented past: Heritage museums and education.* Unwin Hyman, London.

Stone, Peter G., and Ph. G. Planel
1999 *The constructed past: Experimental archaeology, education and the public.* Routledge, London.

Thomas, David H.
1999 *Archaeology: Down to earth.* Harcourt Brace College Publishers, New York.

Trigger, Bruce G.
1989 *A history of archaeological thought.* Cambridge University Press, Cambridge.

Tringham, Ruth
1978 Experimentation, ethnoarchaeology, and the leapfrogs in archaeological methodology. In *Explorations in ethnoarchaeology,* edited by Richard A. Gould, pp. 169–199. University of New Mexico Press, Albuquerque.

Tringham, Ruth, Glenn Cooper, George Odell, Barbara Voytek, and Anne Whitman
1974 Experimentation in the formation of edge damage: A new approach to lithic analysis. *Journal of Field Archaeology* 1:186–196.

Van der Voort, G. F.
1984 *Metallography: Principles and practice.* McGraw-Hill, New York.

Van Fraassen, B. C.
1980 *The scientific image.* Clarendon Press, Oxford.

Van Tilbug, Jo Anne, and Ted Ralston
1999 Engineers of Easter Island. *Archaeology* 52(6):40–45.

Wagner, U., R. Gebhard, E. Murad, J. Riederer, I. Shimada, and F. E. Wagner
1994 Kiln firing at Batán Grande: Today and in Formative times. In *Archaeometry of pre-Columbian sites and artifacts,* edited by D. A. Scott and P. Meyers, pp. 67–84. Getty Conservation Institute, Marina del Rey, California.
1998 Production of Formative ceramics: Assessment by physical methods. In *Andean ceramics: Technology, organization and approaches,* edited by I. Shimada, pp. 173–197. MASCA, University of Pennsylvania, Philadelphia.

Wagner, U., R. Gebhard, W. Häuser, T. Hutzelmann, J. Riederer, I. Shimada, J. Sosa, and F. E. Wagner
1999 Reducing firing of an early pottery making kiln at Batán Grande, Peru: A Mössbauer study. *Hyperfine Interaction* 122:163–170.

Wagner, U., I. Shimada, D. Goldstein, and W. Häusler
    2001   Sicán kilns and furnaces: Field firings and archaeometric studies. *Hyperfine Interaction* C: 1–4.

Wagner, U., F. E. Wagner, W. Häusler, and I. Shimada
    2000   The use of Mössbauer spectroscopy in studies of archaeological ceramics. In *Radiation in art and archaeometry*, edited by D. C. Creagh and D. A. Bradley, pp. 417–443. Elsevier. Science Publishers, Amstardam.

White, J. P., and D. H. Thomas
    1972   What mean these stones? Ethno-taxonomic models and archaeological interpretations in the New Guinea Highlands. In *Models in archaeology*, edited by David L. Clarke, pp. 275–308. Methuen & Co., London.

Whittaker, J. C.
    1994   *Flintknapping: Making and understanding stone tools.* University of Texas Press, Austin.

Yellen, John
    1977   *Archaeological approaches to the present.* Academic Press, New York.

Young, Lisa C., and Tammy Stone
    1990   The thermal properties of textured ceramics: An experimental study. *Journal of Field Archaeology* 17:195–203.

17

Reflexive Methods

Ian Hodder

Is the glass half full or half empty?
It depends on whether you are drinking or pouring.

—Bill Cosby 2001

There is increasing debate today about what might be called reflexive field methods in archaeology. We have become used to thinking reflexively and critically about interpreting and writing about the past (Tilley 1991; Joyce 1994). But reflection and critique have also begun to be applied to archaeological work in the field (e.g., Carver 1989; Chadwick 1998; Bender et al, 1997; Shanks and McGuire 1996; Tilley 1989; Lucas 2000; Andrews et al. 2000). These reflexive methods in archaeological field method have sometimes been influenced by new approaches to ethnography (e.g., Clifford and Marcus 1986; Gupta and Ferguson 1997). But because archaeology is closely allied to the natural sciences, there have also been influences from critical studies of laboratory science (e.g., Latour and Woolgar 1986). In archaeology this is an emerging area of debate of which I cannot claim to give a synthetic account. Rather, I will provide some general discussion illustrated largely from my own experiences at Çatalhöyük (Hodder 2000).

The Problem

It is important to start with what reflexive archaeologists are reacting against. What is the problem that we feel needs resolving? There are several areas of concern, ranging from the practical and professional to the ethical.

First, archaeological fieldwork has become increasingly codified, distanced, and neutral. The filling in of forms and the following of routines have become common (Figure 17.1). The reasons for this are several. Perhaps most important is the increasing professionalism of field archaeology from the 1960s onward in the United States and Britain, associated with rescue and cultural resource management (CRM) archaeology. Compliance with regulations and regulatory bodies meant the need to develop systematic and comparable procedures. In Britain there was also the desire to make the excavation team less hierarchical—the provision of standardized procedures meant that all team members could participate equally.

Figure 17.1. Excavation and documentation in the South area at Çatalhöyük in 1999.

Another influence on excavation method in the period after the 1960s was the espousal by processual archaeology of an objectivist stance. Within this framework of hypothesis testing, codification and standardization allowed the whole excavation process to be seen as efficient and scientific. The process was supposed to be neutral and objective in that any two archaeologists, if properly trained, would make the same observations as they dug. They might later disagree about the interpretation, but at least the basic descriptions would be fixed. The hypotheses could be tested against rigorously collected and sampled data.

Several problems have emerged with this conception of archaeological field method as standardized, repeatable, and codified. Practicing field archaeologists often came to be seen just as technicians—those that collected and recorded the data. The interpretation or explanation was seen as a separate step, coming later, and carried out by other people, often in other institutions such as universities. Indeed, one of the major splits that have emerged in many countries is between a technical field discipline and a research-based academic discipline. Many field archaeologists have come to resent and reject the evaluation of their craft as technique and have sought ways of introducing the interpretive process into their work.

Most practicing field archaeologists know that digging is not just a matter of recording and describing hard data. As archaeologists dig there is a lot of doubt and uncertainty about whether this pit cuts into that (or the other way around), about whether this dark layer is a shallow pit or a hearth, and so on. They know that digging is all about interpretation, and that different people will make different interpretations—they will see different things in the soil as they dig. The basic descriptions are not fixed at all—they can be changed as new data are collected.

Other splits were induced by the objectivist stance. Artifacts are taken out of their contexts and distributed among specialists who write their own reports. An object thus is treated as if its meaning were separate from the context in which it is found. The basic description seems fixed and unrelated to the objects it is found with. But we know that the same object (e.g., a pointed piece of bone) might be described as a needle or as an awl or as a point—or as a mere splinter—depending on whether it is found in male or female graves, etc. At Çatalhöyük clay balls were interpreted as slingshots until it was realized that they were found near ovens and therefore could be shown to be used in cooking (as pot boilers).

A second suite of problems to which reflexive archaeology responds deal with ethical issues. For example, the idea that archaeology should be seen as a natural science had a major influence on the way archaeologists dealt with their overall project. Lucas (2000) has provided a fascinating account of the ways field method is linked to theoretical stance. But beyond this linkage, theory and method also had an impact on the way archaeologists dealt with the communities within which they did fieldwork. Trigger (1984) has argued that processual or objectivist archaeology showed little interest in the lives of specific Native American groups. Such groups were seen as examples of cross-cultural generalizations rather than as peoples with specific histories. In the same way, the objectivist stance toward fieldwork was that the aim was to do archaeology—which meant excavating and doing survey to answer questions of universal scientific value. Little emphasis was placed by funding institutions on the wider engagement of archaeologists with local communities. If ethnographers abroad had to spend time learning local languages and participating in social life over a year or more, archaeologists' efforts with local groups tended to be confined to practical considerations.

Archaeologists talk of themselves going into "the field." *Field* is a bounded concept. And archaeologists often talk of digging "my site," or they ask about "your site." The field boundedness is associated with a sense of academic ownership. And yet, increasingly today, this notion of a separated field (both disciplinary and spatial) is untenable. Increasingly, archaeologists work closely with local communities and indigenous peoples (see chapter 34 of this volume). Interpretive centers, visitor centers, site tours, and tourist facilities are provided. Collaborative projects are developed. The challenge is not simply to work with indigenous people but in doing so to find a way of full engagement in the setting of priorities, in the choice of agendas, and in the interpretation of the record. Increasingly, archaeologists do much more than just dig. They have become enmeshed in a complex social process that may involve conflicting claims to land or identity, that involves working with clients, contractors, sponsors, government agencies, diverse local and global communities, and so on. Archaeology is often better described, not as the excavation of the past, but as the insertion of excavation into the relationship between people and their pasts. Thus it cannot be distant and unconcerned; it has to engage with the social process within which it is embedded. It becomes unethical to set agendas and methods that do not resonate with the concerns of all stakeholders in a site excavation or in a cultural heritage project.

Another ethical issue concerns the (mis)use of public resources. At the height of the expansion of rescue and CRM archaeology in the 1960s and 1970s, standardized and codified methods were used to produce site archives, few of which were transformed into full published accounts. The massive data archives that were produced often proved very difficult to use later on. It became clear that analysis and interpretation of the archives from this period were hindered by the extreme codification—to the point that it was difficult to understand a site from its finds and data records.

This last set of ethical issues in fact takes us back to some epistemological problems about the nature of archaeological inquiry. Archaeology is by definition a destructive method, abolishing the very relationships it seeks to study. As archaeologists we seek to observe stratigraphical and contextual relationships. But to observe them we have to dig them up and destroy them. Thus archaeology cannot be an experimental science. An experiment cannot be repeated on what has been destroyed, even if it can be repeated on other deposits, sites, or in experimental contexts. But because these deposits, sites, and contexts are indeed "other," there can be no strict experimentation because it is not possible to hold variables absolutely constant. It follows that a close mimicking of the methods of the experimental sciences is not helpful.

Archaeologists have a dual role—as destroyers and as preservers of the cultural heritage. They thus have a particular social responsibility to record what is destroyed so that it can be useful to the cultural heritage. The archives that are produced must be full, accessible, and well documented so that later generations can return and reconsider the data that have been destroyed. The archive must allow further consideration of the data, and it must be able to withstand critical evaluation. It must therefore be surrounded in documentation about its own construction. Because later generations cannot return to the data, they must be able to return to an archive that has recorded as fully as possible its own construction in the process of destroying the data.

What Is Reflexive Archaeology?

Reflexive archaeology tries to accept this inescapable reality and to respond to the problems just identified. It tries to help archaeologists *reflect*, to think about what they are doing and have done, and it tries to help nonarchaeologists reflect on what archaeologists are doing and have done. I have suggested that there are four strands to a reflexive field archaeology (e.g., Hodder 1999).

The first is *reflexivity* itself. By this I mean the examination of the effects of archaeological assumptions and actions on the various communities involved in an archaeological process, including other archaeologists and nonarchaeological communities.

The second is *relationality* or *contextuality*. The central point here is that an artifact or feature excavated has meaning partly in relation to other finds from the same or related contexts. But the artifact or feature also has meaning partly in relation to the specific context of knowledge production. This is partly the hermeneutic point that everything depends on everything else within an interpretive whole. Arguments in archaeology proceed, in my view, not from testing theory against data, but from fitting bits of evidence together so that they make sense within a whole (a whole made up of past and present). To achieve a full relationality, the archaeological process needs to be highly integrated and interdisciplinary. Relationality also implies flexibility in the research process. If everything depends on everything else, then as one variable is changed in an analysis so there are knock-on effects on all other variables. Databases and conclusions need to be seen as momentary and always subject to change.

The third is *interactivity*. The aim is to provide mechanisms for people to question and criticize archaeological interpretations that are being made, as they are being made and as they are committed to the archive. One way to achieve this goal is to encourage dialogue between the varied different specialists and communities that fragment the archaeological domain. Increasingly, new technologies allow such dialogue and interaction. The World Wide Web and Internet allow global debate and engagement. Data can be handled quickly in digital form so that they can be immediately available for scrutiny. Visual images and video can be manipulated and explored in ways that open up the data to wider and more immediate examination.

The fourth strand of a reflexive archaeology concerns *multivocality*. Because a wide range of conflicting interests are often involved in the archaeological process, mechanisms need to be provided so that different discourses can take place. This may involve archaeologists from different backgrounds, with traditions of different methods. Or the different groups may be the different stakeholders and interest groups.

One theme that lies behind all these strands of a reflexive approach is *nondichotomous* thinking. This takes the argument back to the initial point about a reflexive approach—that it involves reflecting on assumptions and taken-for-granteds. It involves thinking about the social implications of the archaeological scientific procedures. Much theoretical discussion in archaeology, from the work of Gardin (1980) to Schiffer (1976), has long been concerned with definitions of types of entity. Whether the discussion is of types of ceramic or lithic tool, of types of depositional process, or of types of unit, unit recording sheet, and unit composition, the aim has been to categorize and to define. More generally, archaeologists have built clear boundaries around the discipline and its subdivisions; in recent decades these boundaries have been carefully policed, especially in contrast to all forms of "fringe" archaeology.

The professionalization of the discipline has underpinned these boundary-maintaining and dichotomizing processes. There should be one right way to define categories and to excavate; codification allowed repeatability and definable standards. The internal specialization of the discipline led to the definition of ever more fragmented groupings and subgroupings (ceramic specialists, Iron Age ceramic specialists, Wessex Iron Age ceramic specialists, and so on). Each of these subdisciplines developed its own discourse and methods (how to work as a phytolith or micromorphology specialist, etc). The increasing specialization seen within archaeology is a necessary part of professionalization, and it is also a necessary component of the growth and development of archaeological and scientific techniques.

But in my view a mature and responsible discipline benefits also from the blurring of boundaries and the mixing of genres. It has to be able to be open to critique and compromise, as many people have realized in the dispute about the reburial of Native American remains. Internally, there have to be mechanisms for the data to be "put back together again." Archaeological science suffers if the definition of terms becomes the main focus, or if subdisciplinarity specialization gets in the way of dialogue. It is only by putting the data back together again that the layer, pit, house, site, region can be understood as a whole. Dichotomous thinking impedes better-quality archaeological investigation. It also impedes the relationship between archaeologists and the wider world in which they work.

The Mechanisms

In practice, what does reflexive archaeology involve? What difference does it make in the field? And does it produce better or just different archaeology? In this chapter I attempt to answer these questions, but one immediate point should be made. In my own experience, reflexive approaches do not so much replace existing approaches as add to them. In reflexive archaeology many of the advances in field method made over the last century are retained. The systematic working through, layer by layer, and the scientific recording of the deposits and finds are necessary. Codification is necessary so that a coherent archive can be produced and layers, contexts, and sites compared. There has to be some confidence that a systematic approach has been followed. All the arsenal of techniques available to the archaeologist, from soil descriptions to Harris matrices to sieving (screening), residue analysis, and the recovery of phytoliths, remain at the core of a reflexive approach. Sampling has to be carefully designed and systematically pursued.

While doing all this, the reflexive archaeologist has to do more, because the data recovery process has to be embedded in reflection and documentation. The data discovery and description have to be set within an envelope of reflexivity. It is this envelope that allows scrutiny and critique and reevaluation. It is this envelope that allows greater awareness of assumptions and taken-for-granteds. It is this envelope that allows participation, interactivity, and dialogue. The moment of excavation itself is changed by enveloping it in information and reflection so that it becomes a different experience. The excavator still works scientifically and systematically, filling in forms and taking samples and grid coordinates. But in addition the reflexive excavator is also doing other things—talking to specialists and community members, writing diaries, making videos, recording his or her phenomenological experience, and so on. In the next section I describe some of these extra mechanisms that add to the tasks of a reflexive field excavator.

Interpretation at the Trowel's Edge

One important move is to get away from the idea that excavation is just a technique and a describing of data. As the trowel moves over the ground, following the interface between two layers, for example, judgments are being made all the time about where the layers go, which layer is above which, how many layers intersect at this point, whether the layer is defined by color or by a change in texture, whether one should follow a vein of small pebbles, and so on. As the excavator works, she is thinking of stories or interpretations: *this* layer is above *that* because it *abuts* wall A, which is *over* wall B, and so on. If the excavation process is seen as just a technique, it might be assumed that the excavator does not need to interpret as she digs. But in fact, excavators need to be encouraged to interpret and tell stories as they dig (Andrews et al. 2000; Tringham and Stevanovic 2000). In this way they are less likely to make mistakes (resulting from inconsistencies in the account) and more likely to think of alternative hypotheses during the excavation.

As the trowel moves over the ground it responds to changes in texture and color, but always in a way informed by a particular perspective. The knowledge of the archaeologist influences the way the site is dug. There are many famous examples of this, such as the inability of archaeologists trained in northern Europe to "see" mud-brick walling in the Near East. But more generally, if excavators have limited knowledge of what they are excavating (is this a human or animal bone? is this fourth- or third-century pottery?), they will be less able to excavate and interpret correctly. If they do not know that a yellow-green deposit they have come across is actually dung, they may misinterpret a stable as a house, or not see a slight foundation trench for a wall used to pen animals.

So one aim of a reflexive approach is to get the archaeologists as they dig to have as much information as they can so that they can have good judgment about what it is they are digging. From this viewpoint, digging is not just a technique; it is a highly skilled and difficult balancing of lots of different types of information. But how is it possible to empower the excavator with all the information that is needed? Nowadays, in many countries, excavators may be relatively unskilled. And the specialization of archaeological skills and knowledge has led to a separation of field from laboratory and from university. Thus excavators often work in a relative vacuum, distant from the faunal specialists, soil scientists, and archaeobotanists who could help them make sense of what they are digging.

One solution, used at Çatalhöyük (Hodder 1999, 2000), is to bring many different scientific specialists to the site so that they can examine material as it comes out of the ground. The project has invested in on-site laboratories and in-the-field techniques (e.g., in-the-field phytolith or soil chemical analysis) so that a wide range of data specialists can work at the site. There is frequent movement between laboratory and trench as people seek each other's advice and try to enhance interpretation through increased information. This interaction is formalized at Çatalhöyük by "priority tours," which every day or two bring specialists in a wide range of different types of data to the trench itself so that a dialogue can take place between excavator and data specialist (Figure 17.2). The aim of these tours is twofold.

Figure 17.2.   A wide range of specialists discuss data and interpretation with an excavator at Çatalhöyük during a priority tour.

Their first function is to decide collectively on which units (bounded soil units) should be prioritized for intensive study and sampling. The decision is made on a wide range of criteria—how many of a particular type of unit have been excavated so far, the importance of the unit for making sense of an area of the site, and so on—the criteria themselves being subject to negotiation. The material from priority units is fast-tracked through the system so that laboratory specialists can look at the material quickly and feed back that information to the excavators. So the second function of the priority tours is to inform the excavator of what has been found in recently or currently excavated units. Specialists may pass on information about types of phytolith found, types of animal bone, fragmentation indices of bone and pottery, carbonized plant remains, densities of lithic debitage, and so on. In this way the excavator is empowered to make a more informed interpretation, and excavation strategy can be directed more efficiently. Digging in this way is all about listening, collaborating, discussing, and then making judgments as close to the trowel's edge as possible.

Collaborative and Integrated Interpretation

The same point can be extended to all stages in the interpretive process; an artifact or feature excavated by an archaeologist has a meaning, which depends on its relation to other objects and features. Thus, to take some very simple examples, a clay ball may be thought to be a pot boiler if found with ovens and cooking pots but a slingshot if found with defensive walls and weapons; a coin may be thought residual if found with pottery of much later date. Excavation reports too often consist of a description of the excavated features followed by an account of each artifact type. Each artifact category is described, studied, analyzed, and interpreted separately. Often little attempt is made to put the data back together again so that integrated accounts can be achieved.

Computerized data handling facilitates changes in this situation. Separate databases can be networked so that information can be shared and passed around. As one component changes so do all others, in an iterative process. Far-flung laboratories can connect data through the Internet and on the Web. Maps, plans, drawings, data points can be digitized and distributed through information networks. Archaeological contexts—buildings, pits, landscapes—can be reassembled so that the interaction between different types of data can be explored.

At Çatalhöyük, those working on the microdebitage found on plaster floors in houses changed their interpretation of the lithic material when the phytolith evidence showed that finely woven mats had been placed over the floors. Indeed, this example shows that it is not only the *interpretation* but the *data* themselves that change as a result of integrated collaboration. It had been thought that the small lithic material found in floor deposits must be from the surfaces of the floors or perhaps trampled into the floors. The evidence of the mats contributed to a changed view in which the lithic material was seen as part of the makeup of the floor.

To capitalize on these interactions, the postexcavation process at Çatalhöyük involved bringing excavation and data-specialist staff together to work through the material from the site context by context (Figure 17.3). For each context (unit, fea-

Figure 17.3. Postexcavation collaborative discussion at Çatalhöyük involving specialists in figurines, beads, and burial; wood; excavation; data analysis; fauna; micromorphology; and archaeobotany.

ture, space, building), the evidence was "put back" together again. The data might involve histograms of lithic debitage, pie charts of charred plant remains, actual sherds recovered, chemical residue results, micromorphology slides, stone-axe fragments, and so on. Interpretations were reached through intensive dialogue that aimed at consensus or at least at a range of possible interpretations.

Multiple Community Engagement

Another aspect of reflexive archaeology is that it recognizes that different people, from different backgrounds, will be interested in the past in different ways and will see different things in the soil as they dig. In practical terms at Çatalhöyük, this means that we have different teams that dig different parts of the site.

These teams come from Poland, Greece, the United States, and Britain. As they dig, each team finds that it approaches the site differently and comes up with rather different results (see Tringham and Stevanovic 2000).

But a reflexive archaeology also involves listening to and learning from other communities. At Çatalhöyük, as we analyze and interpret the finds, we have been working with a group from the local village (Figure 17.4). It might be thought that the distance in archaeological education between a Turkish farmer and an archaeological chemist would be too large for useful dialogue about specific interpretations of a 9,000-year-old site. Part of the effort of the discussion was thus to inform. Once a sufficient level of knowledge had been obtained, the local community group contributed significantly to a wide range of topics, from how ovens were used and why ovens were placed where they are in the houses to questions of abandonment, memory,

Figure 17.4.   Postexcavation discussion between data specialists and local community members at Çatalhöyük, facilitated by a social anthropologist, dealing with the interpretation of finds.

and social strategy. No assumptions were made in this process of any direct link between past and present communities. Rather, the dialogue occurred because the local community knew about the archaeological site through working on it, and because they understood better than the archaeological teams some of the physical characteristics of living in that environment. Most of all, however, they participated as an interested stakeholder in this particular past.

Examples of a new openness to alternative perspectives are provided by the now numerous cases of archaeologists and Native American groups working together in the United States and Canada. As one such instance, in 1994 the Arizona Archaeological Council held a workshop to bring together diverse groups of archaeologists and Native Americans so that they could share in a dialogue dealing with the links between archaeology and oral traditions. It was noted that cultural anthropologists and archaeologists had long discounted the historical value of Native American historical traditions (Anyon et al. 1996). Yet recently there has been a renewed interest in linking Native American oral traditions and archaeological evidence.

This type of collaboration, when occurring at the archaeological site itself, may involve changes of method and a blurring of genres. In excavations in the Andes, foreign archaeologists are often obliged to hold rituals to ensure the success of the project or to placate the spirits or gods on the recovery of a human or llama burial. In recent Caltrans (California Department of Transportation) archaeological projects in California, Native Americans and archaeologists have worked side by side in developing ways of interacting with Native American pasts (Dowdall and Parrish, personal communication). The non–Native American archaeologists have agreed to follow the rules specified by tribal rules and taboos. For example, women and partners of women who are menstruating do not participate in the excavations or laboratory analysis.

In an increasingly globalized economy, many of the communities with whom archaeologists engage are far-flung. Diaspora communities may wish to be engaged in the archaeology of their homelands. Widely dispersed New Age spiritual groups may feel attached to particular ritual sites. All forms of "tourist" can gain extended involvement with sites through the Internet (Edmonds and McElearney 1999). Today many archaeological projects place information on the World Wide Web (Aldenderfer 1999), and there have been various attempts to place raw data on the Web so that a diversity of widely dispersed groups can engage not only with the site but also with its analysis and interpretation. Here the notion of collaborative and integrative archaeology extends to global communities.

Setting the Research Design

One of the most important struts of processual archaeology's attempt to introduce science and positivism in archaeology was the planning of field research. The emphasis on hypothesis testing was, and still is, interpreted by many as requiring that clear expectations should be set. This was positive in that some question, and some idea about how to get an answer to that question, is required before a site or a region can be approached. It is not possible to "just dig." One has to start somewhere, with a certain set of tools. And the hypotheses direct the questions and the methods. The hypothesis-testing stance of processual archaeology forced archaeologists to be explicit about their goals and methods.

But problems of various kinds emerge if this strategy is followed too closely. Especially if the project occurs abroad or in land claimed as ancestral by local groups, the setting of goals needs to be sensitive to interests beyond those of the research design. The choice of questions is often in practice the result of a dialogue between multiple stakeholders. Sponsors, government agencies, contractors may all have their own purposes. The archaeologist has to embed the research design within the social world.

Another problem is that the rigid setting of hypotheses, test implications, and methodologies can lead to bad archaeology. Even with the proliferation of geophysical techniques, no archaeologist can know with certainty what is in the ground before the trench is dug. There are always surprises and new turns of events; the unexpected happens. In practice, in the field archaeologists know they are continually changing their goals, hypotheses, and methods. Indeed, they need to do so to fulfill their responsibility to the site and the communities that surround it. It would be the height of irresponsibility to ignore the evidence as it unfolds. To put an extreme case, suppose that one was testing a hypothesis about the prehistoric economy of a site and wanted to look at proportions of animal bones recovered. If art were unexpectedly found on fragile materials in the same levels, the archaeologist would have a responsibility to care for that art and to make an attempt to understand it. Hypotheses, goals, and methods need to develop in tandem with discovery.

In my view, it is wrong to expect archaeologists and students to go into the field with tight research designs that have been developed without consultation with stakeholders and are to be followed through to expected results. It is wrong in my view for archaeologists to aim at simply finding evidence to support their expectations, to verify their hypotheses. A reflexive approach involves a to-and-fro between initial hypotheses and the data. It also involves an interaction between initial hypotheses and the social world in which the data are embedded.

Different Forms and Media of Engagement

The emphases on objective science and neutral recording in archaeology have limited the types of information that are recorded. It has been assumed that the data have to be visible and quantifiable. As a result, many aspects of the experiences of excavation are left unrecorded. A number of archaeologists have begun to include a phenomenological perspective in their accounts (e.g., Bender et al. 1997). Experiments with light and sound in ancient sites have developed, and archaeologists have begun to explore the movements of bodies around sites and monuments (e.g., Barrett 1994). But it is also possible to record the bodily experiences of archaeologists as they excavate. After all, archaeologists spend more time in a building digging out its fill than any other human being is ever likely to spend in that same space, at least since the end of its use. The careful excavation of a building or a pit may involve weeks or months of intensive daily interaction with the building or pit. Some basic parameters of the functioning of that physical space may become apparent during that period. Subjective as such assessments are, they are linked to an enduring materiality and physicality. Thus the arrangement of space might mean that sound travels in a certain way, bypassing certain spaces. Intervisibility might be compromised by patterns of light and dark rooms. Movement may be difficult because of the cluttering of features in a room. These phenomenological characteristics of space are not reducible to some form of quantitative spatial analysis (e.g., Hillier and Hanson 1984). Field excavators need not only to record lengths and breadths but also to write about their experiences of working in spaces and of working in ancient places.

These experiences can be expressed in a variety of ways. Some form of writing remains the dominant mode, and this is discussed further later. But it is also the case that archaeologists are beginning to experiment with other forms of expression. Indeed, there is some evidence of a real blurring of genres between archaeology, art, and ritual. Shanks (Pearson and Shanks 2001) has explored the relationship between archaeology and theater and has been involved in performances that take place at sites. Installation art is increasingly found at sites (Hamilakis et al. 2001; Figure 17.5), adding to a longer tradition of performance of opera at amphitheaters and the like. Rituals are now common at many early monuments around the world, from Stonehenge to Machu Picchu. Such ceremonies may allow the sacred to be experienced. Such events may open the site to an alternative range of experiences that resonate with nonarchaeologists; there is also evidence that archaeologists are beginning to be interested in "staging" as a way of learning about and expressing different dimensions of the past.

Different Forms of Representation

Archaeologists recognize that there are many ways they record or represent what they find. There are unit sheets, feature sheets, and space sheets or forms that describe the primary data but there are also sketch drawings, plans, sections or profiles, photographs, and notebook entries. There may be micromorphology slides of the deposits, three-dimensional plans of buildings built using PenMap and AutoCAD. There may be plots of

Figure 17.5.   Installation art at Çatalhöyük by Adrienne Momi in 2001.

microartifact distributions, plots of inorganic and organic chemistry residues, and so on.

But these different modes of representation are not neutral. The form of representation itself influences how a deposit is excavated and described. A pit is dug in a certain way so as to allow a profile drawing. A trench may be dug and the grass clipped in a certain way so as to allow a neat photographic record or to allow an in-phase perspective of the features in a building. The blurring between reality and representation is clear when different scales of analysis are considered. To say, "there are 30 long-bone fragments in this unit," is to represent reality at a particular scale of resolution. The statement may refer only to bone recovered in the excavation process and in dry screening. But smaller fragments of long bones may have been recovered in wet screening and sorting, although at this smaller size range they may have been identified only as bone fragments (rather than long-bone fragments). High phosphate readings may suggest the disappearance through taphonomic processes of yet further bones. Thus any description or data entry is itself a representation at a particular scale of analysis.

As we excavate a building we may have to conserve the walls or plasters or wooden timbers. A decision has to be made about how that conservation should take place (Matero 2000). The data "walls" are influenced by the conservation process and the chemical and other interventions that are chosen—they are partly produced by the conservation process that represents them.

The same point is also relevant to all illustrations that seek to represent archaeological deposits and features. On-site and artifact illustration have often become highly codified in archaeology. The standardization of illustration has the benefit of providing the conventions through which comparison is possible. But codified illustration also limits the ability to understand the data from different perspectives. Or, more importantly, because the representational process is complicit in constructing the data in the first place, standardization of representation puts blinkers on our analyses. It prevents us seeing that the data change when viewed differently. Indeed, standardization is unscientific in that it produces bias and limits our ability to explore the data. If reality is multidimensional, it needs to be explored from different perspectives.

One response is to evaluate critically the production and consumption of images in archaeology (e.g., Moser 1998). But in the field numerous responses are possible. It is possible to work alongside an illustrator willing to experiment with different modes of representation and different styles of drawing and painting (Swogger 1998). It may be possible to work with an artist able to explore the site in an artistic mode in addition to the codified archaeological conventions (Leibhammer 2000). The different modes of representation might involve heavily annotated drawings that are always being added to as interpretations change. This annotation breaks down some of the mystique of the visual image, and it embeds the image within a context, facilitating later reevaluation. Close interaction between illustrator and field archaeologist allows ideas to be tried out—to be made concrete in the drawing—thus allowing evaluation and critique.

These same advantages of close interactions between archaeologist and illustrator or artist are seen in the increasing use by archaeologists of visualization software. From geographic information systems (GISs) to virtual reality, it becomes increasingly possible to experiment and play with visualizations of ideas. But the media themselves promote the idea that images, although powerful, are always constructed and changeable. The ability to tinker with digital images may help to remove some of the fixity, wonder, and awe associated with "final" drawings or photographs. The handling of and playing with images and representations may foster critique. But there is a danger that the play itself becomes the goal. So there is also the need for reflection on image making. Particularly in the context of new digital technologies, we need to ask questions: Who has access to the technologies so that they can experience new high-tech representations? Who is excluded? Who benefits from this portrayal of the past? Who has the skills to decode this image? Is mystique being created around these images? At what point does this computer model become simply another computer game?

Archaeological Writing

Archaeologists have become used to the idea that they need to write different reports of their work for different communities. This is another aspect of the process of representation. The same author, describing the same site, will produce very different reports, often using different data and even different conclusions, depending on the audience. Reports written for heritage managers, local administrators, academics, children, funding providers, and the popular market will vary widely.

Reflexive archaeology uses this relationship between audience and mode of writing to criticize forms of writing that exclude interested groups and to foster wider interaction and participation. For example, I have examined the writing styles used in archaeological site reports from the eighteenth century to the present day (Hodder 1989). A major trend has been toward distanced, neutral accounts in which the voice of the author is masked and in which the contingency, uncertainty, and nonlinearity of the research process are hidden behind a timeless, certain, and linear account. More recently, however, archaeologists have begun to experiment with writing that incorporates multiple perspectives (e.g., Tilley 1991). Especially in the gender literature there has been an increasing concern to write in ways that position people in the past and the archaeologist as author in the present (Kus 1992; Tringham 1996; Spector 1993; but see Edmonds 1999 for an example outside gender archaeology). In a particularly interesting example, Joyce (1994) uses a storyboard technique to write a nonlinear account of the life of the archaeologist Dorothy Popenoe. Such techniques can now be extended into digital media, and the development of CD-ROMs for interactive, multimedia engagement with archaeological sites is now increasingly found (e.g., Stevanovic 2000). In these ways, a supposedly singular archaeological past is diffracted by different forms of writing into a kaleidoscope of forms; potentially each reader at each moment may be able to construct a different version.

Documenting the Documentation

As already noted, codified documentation in archaeology is central to the construction of archives that can be used and compared. Codification remains an essential part of a reflexive approach. But what is also needed is an enveloping of the codified records in a reflexive context so that people can later reuse the archive by relating it to the agenda according to which it was constructed. The finds can best be reinterpreted through an understanding of that original agenda.

There are numerous ways in which the records can be embedded within an outer layer of documentation. Databases and archives can be tagged with a history that describes changes made through time. Diaries can be written that describe the thought processes of the excavators and lab analysts. At one time, much archaeological recording was done in the form of diaries. Increased codification often led archaeological teams to dispense with the diaries and to use solely codified forms. But there remains a need for diary writing, and this can easily be achieved by typing straight into a computer. Diary entries thus become part of the database and can be searched for key words.

Another way of documenting the documentation is to use digital video. This allows visual information, sound, and words to be used to provide a record of the excavation and postexcavation process in a range of information that allows the excavation process to be embedded within a greater depth and richness of context than is possible in texts and pictures and drawings alone. The excavators can be shown explaining what they are finding and discussing their interpretations as they develop them. They can point out what they have found, which on-site editing allows via insets and close-ups. The video clips can be added to the site database and, again, recovered using key words. In this way it is possible for later archaeologists to evaluate more clearly the claims that are made by the excavators. The later reinterpretation can discover relationships between what was found and what the excavators were preoccupied with at the time. The video clips may show data that were not seen at the time or that can be reinterpreted with hindsight. They may show things that were missed, and they may explain why the site came to have the meaning it did for the excavators.

Conclusion

All in all, reflexive archaeology has many components. I have been able to summarize here only some aspects that others and I have found most useful in practice. But the basic idea is that the process of digging is not just a matter of describing what is in the soil. Rather, it is a matter of discussing and debating all the possible things that the data could mean. It is about enveloping the excavation and analysis processes in dialogue, critical reflection, and documentation. Reflexive archaeology embeds the archaeological process within the social process.

I have left one question unanswered: is reflexive archaeology better archaeology or is it just different? In my view it is a better archaeology, for two sets of reasons. First, it is better science. It does not make false claims about finding what one expects to find or about imposing standardized methods. Rather it responds to what is found and tries to use a wide range of techniques to make sense of what is found. It tries to surround the excavator in greater knowledge. It is more rigorous because starting assumptions and taken-for-granteds are always being reevaluated and open to critique, especially as different partners in the process bring their different perspectives. It records more data, including the phenomenological. The emphasis on the integration of different types of data allows a site or region to be more fully explored and for more variables to be brought into consideration simultaneously.

Second, it is better because it is more socially responsible and so more sustainable over the long run. It accepts the need for collaboration with diverse stakeholders and interest groups. It supports the need for site-management plans and for long-term conservation and protection strategies as central components of the archaeological process. It seeks to provide archives that are usable and open to reevaluation and critique. It is concerned to develop multiple ways of engaging with the site. As I have argued elsewhere (Hodder 1999), this emphasis on social engagement with a diversity of groups is appropriate in a globalized world—by which I mean a world in which a major tension is between the local and the global. On the one hand, the archaeological site is increasingly embedded within local rights and identities. On the other hand, sites are increasingly of importance to diasporic groups, international agencies, and corporate interests. They are increasingly available in globalized media such as the Web. In this other, present-day context it becomes important for the archaeologist to look beyond the narrow confines of the discipline and accept a broader engagement.

References

Aldenderfer, M.
  1999 Data, digital ephemera, and dead media: Digital publishing and archaeological practice. *Internet Archaeology* (online journal) 6. Electronic document, http://intarch.ac.uk/journal/issue6/.

Andrews, G., J. Barrett, and J. Lewis
  2000 Interpretation not record: The practice of archaeology. *Antiquity* 74:525–530.

Anyon, R., T. J. Ferguson, L. Jackson, and L. Lane
  1996 Native American oral traditions and archaeology. *Society for American Archaeology Bulletin* 14:2:14–16.

Barrett, J.
1994   *Fragments from antiquity.* Blackwell, Oxford.

Bender, B., S. Hamilton, and C. Tilley
1997   Leskernick: Stone worlds; alternative narratives; nested landscapes. *Proceedings of the Prehistoric Society* 63:147–178.

Carver, M.
1989   Digging for ideas. *Antiquity* 63:666–674.

Chadwick, A.
1998   Archaeology at the edge of chaos: Further toward reflexive excavation methodologies. *Assemblage* (online journal) 3. Electronic document, http://www.shef.acuk/~assem/3/3chad.htm.

Clifford, J, and G. Marcus
1986   *Writing culture: The poetics and politics of ethnography.* University of California Press, Berkeley.

Edmonds, M.
1999   *Ancestral geographies of the Neolithic.* Routledge, London.

Edmonds, M., and G. McElearney
1999   Inhabitation and access: Landscape and the internet at Gardom's Edge. *Internet Archaeology* (online journal) 6. Electronic document, http://intarch.ac.uk/journal/issue6/.

Gardin, J.-C.
1980   *Archaeological constructs.* Cambridge University Press, Cambridge.

Gupta, A., and J. Ferguson
1997   *Anthropological locations.* University of California Press, Berkeley.

Hamilakis, Y., M. Pluciennik, and S. Tarlow
2001   Academic performances, artistic presentations. *Assemblage* (online journal) 6. Electronic document, http://www.shef.ac.uk/~assem/issue6.

Hillier, B., and J. Hanson
1984   *The social logic of space.* Cambridge University Press.

Hodder, I.
1989   Writing archaeology: Site reports in context. *Antiquity* 63:268–274.
1999   *The archaeological process.* Blackwell, Oxford.
2000   (editor) *Towards Reflexive Method in Archaeology: The example of Çatalhoyuk.* British Institute of Archaeology at Ankara, and McDonald Institute for Archaeological Research.

Joyce, R.
1994   Dorothy Hughes Popenoe: Eve in an archaeological garden. In *Women in archaeology,* edited by C. Claasen. University of Pennsylvania Press, Philadelphia.

Kus, S.
   1992   Toward an archaeology of the body and soul. In *Representations in archaeology*, edited by J.-C. Gardin and C. S. Peebles, pp. 168–177. Indiana University Press, Bloomington.

Latour, B., and S. Woolgar
   1986   *Laboratory life: The construction of scientific facts.* Princeton University Press, Princeton, New Jersey.

Leibhammer, N.
   2000   Rendering realities. In *Towards reflexive method in archaeology: The example at Çatalhöyük*, edited by I. Hodder, pp. 129–142. McDonald Institute Monograph and British Institute of Archaeology at Ankara Monograph 28.

Lucas, G.
   2000   *Critical approaches to fieldwork: Contemporary and historical fieldwork.* Routledge, London.

Matero, F.
   2000   The conservation of an excavated past. In *Towards reflexive method in archaeology: The example at Çatalhöyük*, edited by I. Hodder, pp. 71–89. McDonald Institute Monograph and British Institute of Archaeology at Ankara Monograph 28.

Moser, S.
   1998   *Ancestral images: The iconography of human origins.* Cornell University Press, Ithaca.

Pearson, M., and M. Shanks
   2001   *Theatre/archaeology. Disciplinary dialogues.* Routledge, London.

Schiffer, M.
   1976   *Behavioral archaeology.* Academic Press, New York.

Shanks, M, and McGuire, R.
   1996   The craft of archaeology. *American Antiquity* 61:75–88.

Spector, J.
   1993   *What this awl means.* Minnesota Historical Society, St. Paul.

Stevanovic, M.
   2000   Visualizing and vocalizing archaeological *archival* record: Narrative vs image. In *Towards reflexive method in archaeology: The example at Çatalhöyük*, edited by I. Hodder, pp. 235–238. McDonald Institute Monograph and British Institute of Archaeology at Ankara Monograph 28.

Swogger, J.
   1998   Image and interpretation: The tyranny of representation? In *Towards reflexive method in archaeology: The example at Çatalhöyük*, edited by I.

Hodder, pp. 143–152. McDonald Institute Monograph and British Institute of Archaeology at Ankara Monograph 28.

Tilley, C.
1989   Archaeology as theatre. *Antiquity* 63:275–280
1991   *The art of ambiguity: Material culture and text.* Routledge, London.

Trigger, B.
1984   Alternative archaeologies: Nationalist, colonialist, imperialist. *Man* 19:355–370.

Tringham, R.
1996   Endangered places in prehistory. *Gender, Place, and Culture* 1(2): 169–204.

Tringham, R., and M. Stevanavic
2000   Different excavation styles create different windows into Çatal-höyük. In *Towards reflexive method in archaeology: The example at Çatalhöyük,* edited by I. Hodder, pp. 111–118. McDonald Institute Monograph and British Institute of Archaeology at Ankara Monograph 28.